Practical C

Giulio Zambon

Practical C

Giulio Zambon
Harrison, Aust Capital Terr
Australia

ISBN-13 (pbk): 978-1-4842-1768-9   ISBN-13 (electronic): 978-1-4842-1769-6
DOI 10.1007/978-1-4842-1769-6

Library of Congress Control Number: 2016959617

Managing Director: Welmoed Spahr
Lead Editor: Steve Anglin
Technical Reviewer: Rohan Walia
Editorial Board: Steve Anglin, Pramila Balan, Laura Berendson, Aaron Black, Louise Corrigan, Jonathan Gennick, Robert Hutchinson, Celestin Suresh John, Nikhil Karkal, James Markham, Susan McDermott, Matthew Moodie, Natalie Pao, Gwenan Spearing
Coordinating Editor: Mark Powers
Copy Editor: Kezia Endsley
Compositor: SPi Global
Indexer: SPi Global
Artist: SPi Global

Distributed to the book trade worldwide by Springer Science+Business Media New York, 233 Spring Street, 6th Floor, New York, NY 10013. Phone 1-800-SPRINGER, fax (201) 348-4505, e-mail orders-ny@springer-sbm.com, or visit www.springeronline.com. Apress Media, LLC is a California LLC and the sole member (owner) is Springer Science + Business Media Finance Inc (SSBM Finance Inc). SSBM Finance Inc is a Delaware corporation.

For information on translations, please e-mail rights@apress.com, or visit www.apress.com.

Apress and friends of ED books may be purchased in bulk for academic, corporate, or promotional use. eBook versions and licenses are also available for most titles. For more information, reference our Special Bulk Sales–eBook Licensing web page at www.apress.com/bulk-sales.

Any source code or other supplementary materials referenced by the author in this text are available to readers at www.apress.com/9781484217689. For detailed information about how to locate your book's source code, go to www.apress.com/source-code/. Readers can also access source code at SpringerLink in the Supplementary Material section for each chapter.

Printed on acid-free paper

Contents at a Glance

Contents

About the Author

Giulio Zambon's first love was physics, but he decided to dedicate himself to software development more than 30 years ago, back when computers were still made of transistors and core memories, programs were punched on cards, and FORTRAN only had arithmetic IFs. Over the years, he learned a dozen computer languages and worked with all sorts of operating systems. His specific interests were in telecom and real-time systems, and he managed several projects to their successful completion.

Zambon's career took him to eight cities in five different countries, where he worked as a software developer, systems consultant, process improvement manager, project manager, and chief operating officer. Since early 2008, he has lived in a peaceful suburb a few kilometers north of Canberra, Australia, where he can dedicate himself to his many interests and in particular to writing software to generate and solve numeric puzzles. Visit his web site, `http://zambon.com.au/`, to see the full list of the papers and books he has authored.

About the Technical Reviewer

Rohan Walia is a senior software consultant with extensive experience in client/server, web-based, and enterprise application development. He is an Oracle Certified ADF Implementation Specialist and a Sun Certified Java Programmer. Walia is responsible for designing and developing end-to-end applications consisting of various cutting-edge frameworks and utilities. His areas of expertise are Oracle ADF, Oracle WebCenter, Fusion, Spring, Hibernate, and Java/J2EE. When he's not working, Walia loves to play tennis, hike, and travel. Walia would like to thank his wife, Deepika Walia, for using all her experience and expertise when reviewing this book.

CHAPTER 1

Introduction

Because this is a book of recipes, you will not find a description of C, although to ensure that we are all on the same page (pun entirely intended!), I sometimes include brief explanations of individual features of the language. Chapter 2 also covers some aspects of C that are often sources of mistakes.

For an introduction to C, you can refer to the classical K&R (Kernighan's and Ritchie's *The C Programming Language*), Apress's own *Beginning C*, by Ivor Horton, and a number of other books specifically on the subject.

I have developed all the recipes described in this book using the GNU Compiler Collection (gcc) version 4.8.4 within the Eclipse development environment (release 4.5.0, Mars) running under Linux-GNU Ubuntu 14.04 LTS on a 64-bit laptop.

The current version of the C standard is ISO/IEC 9899:2011, usually referred to as C11, which extends the previous version of the standard (ISO/IEC 9899:1999, nicknamed C99). The gcc C compiler supports C99 and C11. For a complete list of gcc options concerning versions of C, you can refer to gcc.gnu.org/onlinedocs/gcc/C-Dialect-Options.html.

You need to compile most of the code you will find in this book with the -std=c99 option because I use the Java-like format of for loops, with the control-variable definition included in the for statement. For example:

```
for (int k = 0; k < N; k++)
```

Previous versions of C require you to define the control variable outside the for statement, as such:

```
int k;
for (k = 0; k < N; k++)
```

Coding Style

There are several aspects that constitute a coding style. By understanding my coding style, which I have obviously used in all examples in this book, you will find it easier to follow my code.

Indentation

Looking at the source code attached to this book, you will notice that all closed braces that end block statements are indented, as shown in Listing 1-1.

Electronic supplementary material The online version of this chapter (doi:10.1007/978-1-4842-1769-6_1) contains supplementary material, which is available to authorized users.

Listing 1-1. The Author's Coding Style

```
1. void dar_list(Dar *stk) {
2.   if (stk == NULL) {
3.     printf("Nothing to list\n");
4.     }
5.   while (stk != NULL) {
6.     printf("%p %zu %zu\n", stk, stk->size, stk->n);
7.     stk = stk->down;
8.     }
9.   }
```

The open braces in lines 1, 2, and 5 are appended to the previous line, while the closed braces in lines 4, 8, and 9 are indented. This style must be unusual because Eclipse and other development environments do not foresee it, while the two widely used styles shown in Listings 1-2 and 1-3 are fully supported.

Listing 1-2. Spread-Out Coding Style

```
1. void dar_list(Dar *stk)
2. {
3.   if (stk == NULL)
4.   {
5.     printf("Nothing to list\n");
6.   }
7.   while (stk != NULL)
8.   {
9.     printf("%p %zu %zu\n", stk, stk->size, stk->n);
10.    stk = stk->down;
11.  }
12. }
```

The spread-out style of Listing 1-2 is... well... spread out. Besides requiring more effort to follow the flow of a source, it also creates the impression that block statements are independent of the conditional or iterative statements that precede them. For example, you need to notice that the if in line 3 is not followed by a simple statement and a semicolon in order to realize that the block statement is executed only when the if condition is true. It also has a conceptual problem that you will find described in the comments about Listing 1-3. Obviously, if you need to achieve targets based on number of written lines of code, you might like to adopt this style!

Listing 1-3. Compact Not-Indented Coding Style

```
1. void dar_list(Dar *stk) {
2.   if (stk == NULL) {
3.     printf("Nothing to list\n");
4.   }
5.   while (stk != NULL) {
6.     printf("%p %zu %zu\n", stk, stk->size, stk->n);
7.     stk = stk->down;
8.   }
9. }
```

The style shown in Listing 1-3 is probably the most widely used. The K&R uses it (with the exception of writing the open brace that begins a function body on a new line). It is good but, IMO, it has two problems: one conceptual and one practical.

The conceptual problem is that both braces delimiting a block statement belong to the block statement itself, which is indented. Then, why shouldn't the closing brace (and, in the case of the spread-out style, the opening brace too) be indented as well? For example, the closing brace in line 8 of Listing 1-3 belongs to the block statement that begins in line 5 and contains the printf() and the assignment to stk. Then, it should be placed below the s of stk, rather than below the w of while.

The practical problem is that by not indenting the closed braces, you compromise the visual clarity of what I call "the flagging effect." To illustrate what the flagging effect is, I took a screenshot of Listing 1-1 and produced Figure 1-1 by adding some shading.

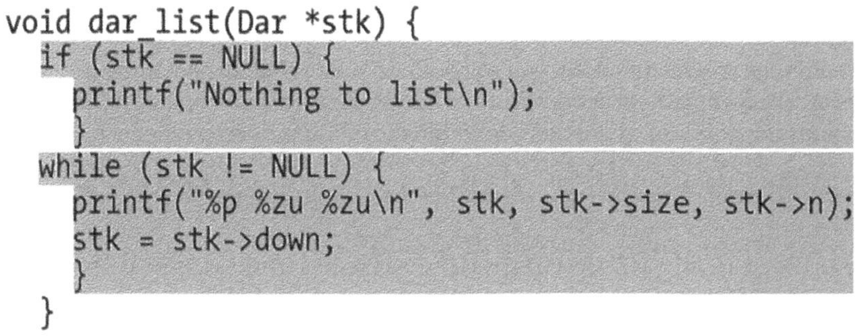

```
void dar_list(Dar *stk) {
    if (stk == NULL) {
        printf("Nothing to list\n");
    }
    while (stk != NULL) {
        printf("%p %zu %zu\n", stk, stk->size, stk->n);
        stk = stk->down;
    }
}
```

Figure 1-1. *The flagging effect of my coding style*

As you can see, everything that depends on the if-condition "hangs" from the if statement, and everything contained in the while-loop hangs from the while statement. This definitely makes reading the source code easier.

One more word concerning ifs and elses.

I often see chains of ifs and elses written like this:

```
if (condition 1) {
  ...
} else if (condition 2) {
  ...
} else {
  ...
}
```

This might be graphically pleasing and very compact, but it doesn't reflect the fact that the ifs and the elses are not shown to be at the same level (which they are). Here is how I would write such a piece of code:

```
if (condition 1) {
  ...
  }
else if (condition 2) {
  ...
  }
else {
  ...
  }
```

Naming and Other Conventions

This book includes several libraries of functions, each one consisting of a C file and the corresponding header file (e.g., `string.c` and `string.h`). Each library is characterized by a small number of identifying letters that prefix the names of all exported macros, variables, and functions (e.g., `str`). Macro constants (i.e., macros without parameters) are in capital letters (e.g., `STR_LOG`), while with names of function-like macros only the prefix is capitalized (e.g., `STR_crash()`). In names of exported variables and functions, the prefix is in lowercase (e.g., `str_stack` and `str_list()`).

The names of most integer variables begin with a letter in the range `i` to `n`, especially if they are very short. This is a legacy of my initial experience with computers: the first computer language I learned (more than 40 years ago!) was FORTRAN, which automatically identified variables with names beginning with one of those letters to be of type `INTEGER`. I have to admit I am not perfectly consistent in following this rule when naming integer variables, but you will never find in my code a non-integer variable that starts with one of the "integer" letters. I simply couldn't!

If you look at modules containing several functions, you will perhaps notice that the functions are in alphabetical order, so that you always find them at once without having to search for them. To be able to refer to non-exported functions regardless of where they are within the module, I declare them at the beginning of the C file.

Also for convenience, I write a line of comment immediately before each function, with the name of the function on the far right:

```
//------------------------------------------------------------- str_clean_up
```

I also use a similar convention when interrupting the flow of the code, such as:

```
if (str == NULL) return;                                        //-->
```

By marking individual functions and exits on the right margin, I make them easily identifiable.

This brings to mind another convention: never exceed 80 characters in each line of code. It is another legacy of my early programming experience, when I typed my FORTRAN programs on punch cards, which had 80 columns. Although, to be accurate, only the columns between 6 and 72 could be used for executable code (in case you are curious, the first column was used to identify comments, columns 2 to 4 to label statements, column 5 to identify continuation lines, and columns 73 to 80 to number the cards). Eighty columns seems a reasonable length to keep the code well readable.

In any case, the important thing in programming is not what conventions you adopt but the fact that you stick to them maniacally. By being disciplined and consistent, you will make your code easier to understand and more maintainable.

I consider consistency and discipline essential qualities of a good programmer. When training new programmers, I even checked that spacing within statements was the same throughout the module, that there were no spaces appended at the end of any line, and that no tabs were used. Nowadays, development environments strip trailing spaces automatically, but the rule of no-tabs is still useful, for example, for pasting portions of your code into a document.

The Use of goto

When I learned programming, there were no block statements. Therefore, the only way of implementing them was with gotos. For example, a construct like this:

```
if (condition) {

  // condition satisfied
  ...
  }
else {

  // condition not satisfied
  ...
  }

// whatever
...
```

was implemented in FORTRAN with something like this (in the early 1970s, FORTRAN was strictly all-caps, and remember that lines that start in the first column are comments):

```
      IF (condition) GOTO 1

C CONDITION NOT SATISFIED
      ...
      GOTO 2

C CONDITION SATISFIED
    1 ...

C WHATEVER
    2 ...
```

The C equivalent would be:

```
if (condition) goto yes;

// Condition not satisfied.
...
goto done;

// Condition satisfied.
yes: ...

// whatever
done: ...
```

Nobody would use C in this way, but the taboo that surrounds the use of gotos in structured languages is not justified (perhaps taboos never are, but let's not digress). Consider for example the following piece of code:

```
if (condition_1) {

  // Satisfied: 1.
  ...
  if (condition_2) {

    // Satisfied: 1 and 2.
    ...
    if (condition_3) {

      // satisfied: 1, 2, and 3.
      ...
      if (condition_4) {

        // satisfied: 1, 2, 3, and 4.
        ...
        // Here a big chunk of code happens to follow
        } // condition_4
      } // condition_3
    } // condition_2
  } // condition_1
```

How far do you go? Every additional if would push the big chunk of code farther to the right. Would you handle ten conditions in this way? I wouldn't. Here is an alternative using gotos:

```
if (!condition_1) goto checks_done;                           //-->

// Satisfied: 1
...
if (!condition_2) goto checks_done;                           //-->

// Satisfied: 1 and 2
...
if (!condition_3) goto checks_done;                           //-->

// Satisfied: 1, 2, and 3
...
if (!condition_4) goto checks_done;                           //-->

// Satisfied: 1, 2, 3, and 4
...

checks_done:                                                  //<--
...
// Here a big chunk of code happens to follow
```

This is just an example of a situation where you might consider the use of gotos. Then, perhaps, decide that they are inappropriate. I am only arguing that refusing to use a valid construct on an emotional, rather than rational and practical, basis would be wrong.

How to Read This Book

Whenever a chapter relies on information presented earlier in the book, you will find a clear reference to the previous relevant chapter. Therefore, you can safely skip the chapters that you don't find immediately helpful. In other words, you might like to concentrate on the chapters you find more useful for the code you are developing right now rather than read the book sequentially.

Chapter 2, "Tricky Bits," talks about aspects of C that are often misunderstood and can cause the introduction of puzzling bugs.

Chapter 3, "Iteration, Recursion, and Binary Trees," introduces you to recursion techniques and binary trees.

Chapter 4, "Lists, Queues, and Stacks," helps you choose between the possible ways of representing collections of items.

Chapter 5, "Exception Handling," tells you how to trap problems that occur at runtime instead of simply letting the program crash.

Chapter 6, "String Utilities," describes a way of allocating strings dynamically, rather than statically at compile time.

Chapter 7, "Dynamic Arrays," adapts to generic arrays some of the functions described in Chapter 6 for strings (which are nothing else than null-terminated arrays of characters).

Chapter 8, "Searching," describes linear and binary searches and how you can use binary search trees.

Chapter 9, "Sorting," explains techniques to bring order to sets of unordered items.

Chapter 10, "Numerical Integration," describes numerical methods to calculate areas under a plot line and volumes under a surface.

Chapter 11, "Embedded Software," talks about special issues you have to take into account when writing real-time software that operates close to the hardware.

Chapter 12, "Databases," explains how to interact with SQL databases in C.

Chapter 13, "Web Server Using Mongoose," describes how to embed a web server in your program.

Chapter 14, "Game App: "MathSearch"," tells you how to develop a program that generates a numeric puzzle.

Appendix A lists all abbreviations and acronyms used in the book.

Appendix B summarizes SQL commands that control databases.

## CHAPTER 2

Tricky Bits

C includes features that are often misunderstood and can therefore cause problems and unexpected results. This chapter talks about those tricky bits (pun intended!).

The Scope and Life of Variables

The *scope* of a variable defines *where* the variable can be used, while the *life* of a variable defines *when* it can be used. The two are not independent. They rather represent different ways of defining where a variable maintains its validity.

Broadly speaking, C supports two types of variables: local and global.

Local Variables

Local variables are defined within a function or a block statement. You can use them from the line where they are defined to the closing brace of the function or block. Consider for example the small function shown in Listing 2-1 (it is not very smart, but it will do).

Listing 2-1. A Small Function

```
1. int multi_sum(int n1, int n2, int do_mult) {
2.    int retval = n1;
3.    if (do_mult) retval *= n2);
4.    else retval += n2;
5.    return retval;
6.  }
```

The variables n1, n2, do_mult, and retval are all local, but while the three formal parameters are valid anywhere within the function (i.e., from line 2 to line 5), retval is only valid from line 3.

The memory needed to store the values of such dynamic variables is allocated on the program stack when the function is called. Then, when the function returns, the stack pointer is moved back to where it was before the function call, and the variables *go out of scope*. That is, for all practical purposes, they cease to exist.

When the function is called, one variable for each parameter is allocated on the program stack and the values of the corresponding arguments are copied into them.

For example, if you call the function as follows:

```
int n1 = 3;
int result = multi-sum(n1, 5, 1);
```

© Giulio Zambon 2016
G. Zambon, *Practical C*, DOI 10.1007/978-1-4842-1769-6_2

The n1 local to the function will contain 3, n2 will contain 5, and do_mult will contain 1.

The fact that the same name n1 is used outside and inside the function does *not* mean that there is a single variable with that name: the two 3s are stored in different locations.

This means that you can rewrite the function as follows:

```
int multi_sum(int n1, int n2, int do_mult) {
  if (do_mult) n1 *= n2);
  else n1 += n2;
  return n1;
  }
```

All without affecting the value held by n1 outside the function.

If a function returns a pointer to a local variable, this can lead to serious problems. The compiler checks whether you do something like that, but only issues a warning. For example, if you compile a function like this:

```
int *ptr(int n) { return &n; }
```

The compiler issues the following warning:

```
warning: function returns address of local variable [-Wreturn-local-addr]
```

But you might ignore the warning (although you should never ignore warnings!). In any case, you could easily write code to which the compiler wouldn't react at all:

```
int *ptr(int n) {
  int *p = &n;
  return p;
  }
```

If you invoke the nasty little function ptr() with something like this:

```
int main(void) {
  int *nn = ptr(7);
  printf("%d\n", *nn);
  }
```

The program will duly print on the console 7, as expected. But define a trivial, do-nothing function like this:

```
void nothing(int n1) { int n2 = n1; }
```

And sneak it in between the execution of ptr() and the printing of nn, as shown in Listing 2-2, and you will have a surprise. The program will print out 10 instead of 7, although you haven't touched nn.

Listing 2-2. A Small Program

```
int main(void) {
  int *nn = ptr(7);
  nothing(10);
  printf("%d\n", *nn);
  }
```

This is because the execution of the do-nothing function re-uses the dynamic address pointed by nn, thereby changing its content.

Obviously, you have the same problem if you return the address of any variable local to the function, whether it is an input parameter as in the previous example or not. For example, this will not work either:

```
int *ptr(int n) {
  int val = n;
  return &val;
  }
```

But if you make the local variable val static, as in:

```
int *ptr(int n) {
  static int val;
  val = n;
  return &val;
  }
```

the program of Listing 2-2 will print 7. This is because the storage class static applied to a local variable causes the compiler to allocate space for it in the data segment of the program *at compile time*. Such a variable lives as long as the program, and that's why it maintains its value. The presence of a static variable makes the function non re-entrant (more about this issue in a later chapter, when talking about concurrency), but it allows you to extend its scope by returning its address.

Although such use of a local static variable doesn't cause immediate problems, it is bound to make your code more difficult to understand and to maintain. It is not something I would recommend. Worse of all, it would allow you to modify the value of a local variable from outside the function.

Static local variables are normally used to keep a value unchanged between subsequent executions of a function or, to describe it from a different point of view, to pass a value from one execution of a function to its next execution.

An important point to keep in mind is that, while the compiler does not initialize local dynamic variables, it does clear local variables when they are static by setting numeric types to 0, char to '\0', and pointers to NULL.

That said, it is a good practice to initialize all your variables in any case. You can easily initialize any variable to zero with the universal initializer {0} as in the following examples:

```
anytype simple_var = {0};
anytype array[SIZE] = {0};
anytype multi_dim_array[SIZE1][SIZE2][SIZE3] = {0};
```

To summarize, local variables by default are only valid within the block where they are defined and they live as long as the block lives. If they are defined to be static, they live for the duration of the program and they can be accessed outside the block in which they are defined, although the practice is discouraged.

Limiting the Scope of Local Variables

All programmers make mistakes. They are only human (still!). And the sooner a bug is detected, the easier it is usually to fix it. At best, you should try to identify as many problems as possible at compile time, even before the program runs. One of the ways you can do so is to limit the scope of local variables to the minimum.

This is because when you use a variable for several purposes within a big chunk of code, it becomes more likely that you forget to re-initialize it when you should.

The fact that you use different variables for different purposes also lets you name each one of them more appropriately, thereby improving the readability and maintainability of your code.

Furthermore, if you define large arrays locally, they will pile up on the program stack and might—despite the ever-increasing amount of memory available to programs that execute on desktop or laptop computers—"hit the ceiling" (so to speak) and cause a crash.

To limit the scope of a variable, all you need to do is enclose its definition and the code that uses it in a brace-delimited block statement:

```
...
{ // here the block begins
  double d_array[N];
  ...
  } // here the block ends and the stack space used up by d_array is recovered
```

The practice of enclosing chunks of code in block statements also encourages you to keep the code as close as possible to at least some of the variables it operates on.

From C99 on, you can define the control variable of for loops within the for statement:

```
for (int k = 0; k < 5; k++) {
  ...
  }
```

You need to compile all this code with the option -std=c99 because I almost always take advantage of this feature. You can limit the scope of for loop control variables with any version of C by enclosing the loop inside a block statement, as in the following example:

```
{
  int k;
  for (k = 0; k < 5; k++) {
    ...
    }
  }
```

It won't slow down your code.

gcc supports several versions of the C standard (check out gcc.gnu.org/onlinedocs/gcc/C-Dialect-Options.html for the full list) and you can select them with the -std option. By default, gcc expects C to conform to the 1990 release of the ISO 9899 standard (which actually makes the option -std=c90 unnecessary). The most recent supported version of the ISO C standard (although, at the time of writing, not 100%) is 2011, and you can select it with the compiler's option -std=c11. New releases of the standard not only add features to the compiler, but they often also make obsolete some features of previous, older releases.

Global Variables

Global variables are those defined outside functions. As they are exported by default, they are global in the sense that they can be accessed anywhere from within the program. And they remain valid throughout the life of the program.

The use of the keyword extern is often source of confusion. To understand it, you need to understand the difference between a *definition* and a *declaration* of a variable.

A definition is where you direct the compiler to allocate memory for the variable, while a declaration is where you tell the compiler that you are going to use a variable that has already been defined somewhere else.

For example,

```
int ijk[5] = {0};
```

tells the compiler to allocate memory for an array of five integers and assign to its first location the name ijk. If ijk is defined outside any function, it is statically allocated and made available to the whole program.

If the program consists of several modules and one of them (other than the module where ijk is defined) needs to access ijk, you need to declare ijk in that module:

```
extern int ijk[5];
```

Note that you are only allowed to initialize a variable where you define it. Although you can write the declarations directly inside the module where you need to access the variable, the recommended practice is that you write it in a header file named like the C file where the variable is defined. For example, if ijk is defined in whatever.c, you write the declaration in whatever.h. Then, all you need to do is #include "whatever.h" in the module where you need to use ijk.

All global variables are statically allocated and made available to the whole program by default. This enables you to assign a different meaning to the storage class static: you can prevent other modules from referring to a variable. That is, if you define a variable outside all functions with the storage class static, you will not be able to refer to it with extern.

Given the importance of this distinction, I will express it in yet another way, which should make it completely clear: while static added to a definition within a function potentially increases the scope of that variable to the whole program, when you add it to a global variable, it limits its scope to the module where you have defined the variable.

Functions

In C all functions are global because you cannot define a function within another function. Most of what I said about global variables in the previous section applies to functions. In particular, the scope of static functions is restricted to the module where they are defined.

The only apparent difference is that many programmers (including me) omit the keyword extern when declaring functions but not when declaring global variables. In fact, you can also omit the extern keyword when declaring variables, as long as you initialize each variable only in one module (otherwise, the compiler reports the error that there are multiple definitions of the same variable).

In other words, the compiler considers the definition to be where the variable is initialized while all the others are declarations. But what if the variable is not initialized anywhere? In that case, the compiler decides on its own which one is the definition. As the compiler allocates memory for global variables in the data segment, strictly speaking, it doesn't really matter where the variable is defined and where it is declared, as long as definition and declaration match. But I find this situation somewhat "unpleasant" (for lack of a better word). Perhaps it has to do with the fact that I have programmed quite a bit with Java. Anyhow, although the distinction is somewhat illusory, you will find that in my code all global variables appear with the keyword extern in the header file that corresponds to the source where they are defined. And, although it is often redundant, they are all initialized.

Call by Value

C passes arguments to functions with a mechanism called "by value." This is because when you use a variable as a function argument, C, instead of passing to the function the address of the variable, it passes its value. Although it's not always clear to new programmers what the implications of this mechanism are, few bother to read about it. Eager to start coding, some new developers look at a few examples and move on. At the very least, that attitude results in puzzled reactions when the program behaves erratically or the compiler complains.

The formal parameters of functions are placeholders. For example, the function

```
int funct(int kk, int jj) {
```

13

```
  int retval = 0;
  ...
  return retval;
  }
```

has two int parameters and returns an int value. When you invoke the function with a statement like

```
int result = funct(3, 7);
```

the program allocates space for two int local variables on the stack, copies into it the values 3 and 7, and begins execution of funct() (this is not all it does, because, at the very least, it also needs to remember where within the program the function was invoked, so that execution can continue from there when the function returns, but let's not digress).

When the function returns, the program copies to result the value stored in retval.

What we are interested in is the fact that the values 3 and 7 are *copied* to variables local to the function. This means that everything you do to kk and jj within the function has no effect outside.

So, for example, if you invoke funct() as follows:

```
int kk = 3;
int jj = 7;
int result = funct(kk, jj);
```

the two variables kk and jj of the calling program remain unchanged no matter what you do with kk and jj within the function. The fact that they have the same name is irrelevant, because the two pairs of variables have disjoint scopes.

Now consider the following modified version of funct(), in which kk and jj are pointers:

```
int functp(int *kk_p, int *jj_p) {
  int reval = 0;
  ...
  jj_p++;
  (*kk_p)++;
  ...
  return retval;
  }
```

You could invoke it as follows:

```
int kk = 3;
int jj = 7;
int result = funct(&kk, &jj);
```

When the function is invoked, the program copies the *address* of kk to the local variable kk_p and the *address* of jj to the local variable jj_p. Incidentally, note that you could have kept the local names kk and jj, but it is better to change them to reflect the fact that they are pointers. This will also make the description of what happens easier to understand.

After jj_p is incremented, it points to the memory location that follows the address of jj as defined in the calling program, which is a dangerous thing to do. Nevertheless, although I cannot imagine what you might be trying to achieve with such an operation, in itself the increment has no consequences.

The situation is different when you increment (*kk_p) because, by doing so, you change the value of the variable kk in the calling program from 3 to 4. As you can imagine, such side effects can have catastrophic results and should only be used when strictly necessary and when you know what you're doing. That said, any programming instructor or teacher would most likely mark down an assignment containing such a statement.

Let's see an example involving a string:

```
void string_to_upper_lower(char *s, int (*f)(int));
```

The purpose of the function is to convert a whole string to upper- or lower-case. It has two parameters: s is the string to be converted and f is a pointer to a function that accepts a single parameter of type int and returns a value also of type int.

Here is what the function could look like:

```
void string_to_upper_lower(char *s, int (*f)(int)) {
  if (s != NULL) {
    while (*s != '\0') {
      *s = (*f)(*s);
      s++;
      }
    }
  }
```

You can invoke it as in the following example:

```
#define <ctype.h>
char test_s[] = "abcDEF";
printf("toupper: \"%s\" -> \"%s\"\n", string_to_upper_lower(test_s, &toupper));
printf("tolower: \"%s\" -> \"%s\"\n", string_to_upper_lower(test_s, &tolower));
```

And here is what the little test program prints out:

```
toupper: "abcDEF" -> "ABCDEF"
tolower: "abcDEF" -> "abcdef"
```

Notice that string_to_upper_lower() increments the address of the string (i.e., of the array of characters) but that has no effect on the value of s in the calling program because the s local to the function is the copy of the variable s local to the calling program. But this doesn't prevent you from modifying the content of the string because there is only one string, and you have its address.

Before moving on, just for fun, here is a more compact (and somewhat fancy) implementation of string_to_upper_lower():

```
void string_to_upper_lower(char *s, int (*f)(int)) {
  if (s != NULL && *s != '\0') do *s = (*f)(*s); while (*++s != '\0');
  }
```

You can omit the second part of the if-condition if you don't mind invoking toupper() or tolower() once when the input string is empty (which would have no effect).

If you want a function to be able to change the address of an array instead of only its elements, you need to pass to the function the address of the array's address. For example, here is how you could implement a function that swaps two pointers:

```
void swap(void **a, void **b) {
  void *temp = *a;
  *a = *b;
  *b = temp;
  }
```

If you execute swap() as follows:

```
char *a = "abcdEFG";
char *b = "hijKLM";
swap(&a, &b);
printf("\"%s\"  \"%s\"\n", a, b);
```

you get:

```
"hijKLM"  "abcdEFG"
```

One last point before moving on. When you pass to a function an array as argument, you have seen that the compiler copies the array address to a variable local to the function. But structures, although they can contain lots of components, are handled like simple data types. The compiler makes a local copy of the structure, rather than of its address. You can test it very simply by running the following short program:

```
typedef struct a_t { int an_int; } a_t;
void a_fun(a_t x) { x.an_int = 5; }
void main(void) {
  a_t a_struct = { 7 };
  a_fun(a_struct);
  printf("%d\n", a_struct.an_int);
  }
```

You will see that, although you have set an_int to 5 within the function, the value printed out is the initialization value 7.

Preprocessor Macros

Macros are an extremely powerful tool, but also something that easily leads to confusion. The two key points you need to pay attention to when developing macros are:

- When expanded, macros can result in statements different from what you had in mind.

- The arguments of a macro are calculated every time they appear in the expansion, and this can cause unwanted side effects.

To understand the first issue, consider the following classical example:

```
#define SQR(x) x*x
printf("%d\n", SQR(3+2));
```

You expect the result of SQR(3+2) to be 5 squared = 25, but what you get is 11 because the macro expansion results in the following printf():

```
printf("%d\n", 3+2*3+2);
```

What you need to do is enclose the xs in parentheses as in:

```
#define SQR(x) (x)*(x)
```

But, although that would fix the problem you had with the SQR() macro, in general, you need to do more if you want to be completely safe. Consider the following example:

```
#define DIFF(a, b) (a)-(b)
printf("%d\n", 5 - DIFF(3, 2));
```

You might expect to have 4 as a result, as 3 - 2 = 1 and 5 - 1 = 4. But you are going to get zero instead, because the macro expansion results in the following printf():

```
printf("%d\n", 5 - (3)-(2));
```

To be safe, you have to ensure that the macro never results in uncalculated expressions:

```
#define SQR(x) ((x)*(x))
#define DIFF(a, b) ((a)-(b))
```

Concerning the second issue (i.e., macros that cause side effects), consider the following example:

```
#define SQR(x) ((x)*(x))
int x = 5;
printf("%d;%d\n", SQR(x++), x);
```

You might expect 25;6 as a result, but you get 30;7. This is because, with the macro expanded, the printf() becomes as follows:

```
printf("%d;%d\n", ((x++)(x++)), x);
```

x is incremented twice because it is calculated twice within the macro. To avoid this type of problem, each macro parameter should only appear once within the macro expansion. Here is a safer version of the same macro:

```
#define SQR(x) ({  \
  int _x = x;      \
  _x * _x;         \
  })
```

When the macro is expanded, x is only calculated once and its value is assigned to _x. It is then _x rather than x that appears twice within the macro expansion. The macro is so simple that you could even write it in a single line:

```
#define SQR(x) ({ int _x = x; _x * _x; })
```

The value returned by the macro is the result of the expression that appears in the last line of the compound statement. Note that when the macro returns a value, you need to enclose the compound statement in round brackets.

Booleans

In C, zero in its different manifestations (e.g., 0, '\0', or NULL) is considered to be false; everything else is considered to be true.

With the following definitions

```
float real = 1.0;
int array[] = { 6, 0, 25, 40};
char *string = "This is a string";
```

all the following conditions are true:

```
real
array[0]
array[3] - array[2]
strchr(string, 0x20)
strstr(string, string)
array
```

and

```
365
75 / 2 * 2
-11
```

are also true, while the following ones are false:

```
0.0
50 - 25 << 1
array[1]
strchr(string, 'u')
strstr(string + 6, "is")
array != &array[0]
```

In Java, variables of type boolean can only have two values: true and false, but there is no equivalent data type in C.

Many C programmers define a new data type as follows:

```
typedef enum { false, true } bool;
```

The C99 standard also supports a similar definition, to be found in stdbool.h:

```
#define bool    _Bool
#define true     1
#define false    0
```

Personally, I'm not so fond of these definitions because they a provide a false sense of security: they make you think that a variable of type bool can only have two values. In a sense this is true, but nothing prevents you from assigning to it any value. It seems a contradiction, doesn't it? Consider the following example:

```
#include <stdbool.h>
```

```
bool choice = false;
choice = -335;
printf("%d\n", choice);
```

You will be surprise to find out that the value printed on the console is 1. Neat. But try to simulate the corruption of memory by doing something like this:

```
#include <stdbool.h>
bool choice = false;
int *naughty = &choice;
*naughty = -335;
printf("%d\n", choice);
```

The value printed on the console will be 177! Where did that come from? To find out, you need to know that negative numbers are stored as two-complements. You will learn what that means later on in this chapter. To understand how a -335 becomes a 177, you only need to know that -335 is kept in the 32 bits of memory allocated to an int variable as 0xFFFFFEB1. If you are not familiar with hex notation, each hexadecimal digit represents the value stored in four bits, with A meaning 10, B meaning 11, and so on until F, which means 15. Now, variables of type bool are only allocated eight bits of space. Therefore, when you display choice, you will only see the byte that contains 0xB1, which in decimal is 11 * 16 + 1 = 177. You might wonder why the "right-most" eight bits are seen in choice instead of the left-most ones, but, again, to understand that, you have to read Chapter 11.

It's quite bad, isn't it? But it gets worse. To see how, modify the dirty little program (playing with pointers can get dirty) as follows:

```
bool choice[4] = {0};
int *naughty = &choice;
*naughty = -335;
for (int k = 0; k < 4; k++) printf(" %2x", choice[k]);
printf("\n");
```

Now choice is an array of four Booleans. They are initialized to 0 (i.e., false), but when the array is printed out, here is what you get:

```
0xb1 0xfe 0xff 0xff
```

You know that the first byte is the 177 you already saw when choice was a simple variable. But now you see that the whole -335 is there (forget the order of bytes for the time being). It makes sense: you tell the compiler that naughty points to an int (which is a 32-bit long) and then store in that location the number -335. It is not surprising that the whole number is copied, thereby corrupting the three following bytes.

This examples shows how the misuse of pointers can lead to a mess. But it also shows that the type bool is not as safe as you might have felt.

When I want to implement Booleans, I usually do it his way:

```
#define FALSE 0
#define TRUE  1
```

And then, I assign them to int variables but prefer to check those variables for FALSE. Perhaps it is equally possible for memory corruption to change a variable from TRUE to FALSE as it is to change it from FALSE to TRUE. An interesting problem for a mathematician. But I am no mathematician, and my feeling (well possibly wrong) is that there are more ways in which a variable could be set by mistake to a non-zero value than to zero. That's why I tend to check for FALSE. If you are a mathematician and demonstrate that my feeling is misplaced, please let me know!

Obviously, you could be overcautious and write super-defensive code like this:

```
if (a_flag == FALSE) {
  ...
  }
else if (a_flag == TRUE) {
  ...
  }
else {
  // this should never happen  ->  abort the program
  }
```

Then, you would be sure that only 1 is interpreted as TRUE. Many years ago, I wrote a short paper about this issue and I titled it *The Third Boolean Alternative*. But it was more for fun than for any other reason. What matters is that being aware of this issue might help you discover why your code behaves erratically. In some cases, you might find it more convenient to check for corruption as shown here rather than single-stepping through the code with a debugger.

Structure Packing

C structures let you create complex data types by assigning an identifier to a collection of components of different types. What many don't know is that the C compiler doesn't necessarily pack the components tightly together within the structure. This is because, to speed up memory access, the compiler pads with dummy bytes the components that occupy less than an integral number of words (usually consisting of 32 bits = 4 bytes).

For example, consider the structure:

```
typedef struct z_t {
  char c;
  int  i;
  } z_t;
```

Assuming that a character occupies one byte and an integer four (you can easily check this by printing out sizeof(char) and sizeof(int)), the structure should occupy five bytes, right? One for the char and four for the int. Wrong! You only need to print out sizeof(z_t) to see that the structure requires eight bytes.

This is because the compiler has automatically added padding bytes after the character to align the following integer to a word boundary. It is as if you had defined your structure as follows:

```
typedef struct z_t {
  char c; char padding[3];
  int  i;
  } z_t;
```

Unfortunately, it doesn't help to swap the two components around. That is, if you define the character after the integer, the size of the structure remains eight.

But consider that in a complex structure you might have several components consisting of a single character. Then, it would pay to define them one after the other. For example, the structure:

```
typedef struct z_t {
  char  c;
  int   i;
  char  ccc[3];
  } z_t;
```

occupies 12 bytes, while:

```
typedef struct z_t {
  char   c;
  char   ccc[3];
  int    i;
  } z_t;
```

only occupies eight, because no padding is used after c. Effectively, the compiler saw the initial structure as follows:

```
typedef struct z_t {
  char   c; char pad1[3];
  int    i;
  char   ccc[3]; char pad2;
  } z_t;
```

Incidentally, note that ccc can fit together with c in a single word because it occupies exactly three bytes. If you are thinking of a char array as a null-terminated C string and therefore requiring an additional character, think again: it is true that you implement a C string as an array of characters, but an array of characters is not necessarily a C string. You can use the ccc component to store three characters or a C string with two characters plus the terminating null, but if you define the length to be three, that's the space you get. Don't get confused by the fact that functions like sprintf() automatically write a null: you still need to explicitly allocate space for that null.

Saving a byte here and there might not seem much. And even if you needed to define large arrays z_t structures, nowadays when you measure memory in Giga- or Terabytes, you might think that wasting some Kilo- or even Megabytes is a non-issue. But where is your pride as a C programmer? I would find it somewhat disturbing to think that there are "holes" in my data!

In any case, you should be aware of the issue and, as you will see in the chapter about embedded software, there are cases where you cannot ignore the presence of gaps within structures.

As an aside, while C compilers are free to insert padding into structures in order to achieve word alignment of the components, the C99 standard requires compilers to generate arrays without gaps. That is, no padding is allowed between elements that do not occupy full words. So, for example, an array of characters defined as

```
char cx[5][3];
```

is guaranteed to occupy exactly 15 bytes. If array elements were padded to 32-bit words, cx would occupy 5 x 4 = 20 bytes.

Characters and Locales

Characters are represented in computers like everything else: with a string of bits. In the 1950s and 1960s, when programs were entered into computers on punch cards, characters were encoded in six bits. UNIVAC computers used Fieldata encoding, while IBM chose BCD. By the early 1970s, with the advent of minicomputers, the 7-bit ASCII encoding became a de-facto standard. Today, for back compatibility, the first 128 characters of the UTF-8 encoding are identical to those defined in ASCII.

Although seven bits are sufficient to represent common Latin/English characters, to represent accents, diacritical signs, and non-Latin alphabets, you need more than one byte. For example, the two hex bytes c2 and a2 (i.e., 194 and 162 in decimal) represent in UTF-8 the cent character ¢.

I found the following couple of sentences on the website of the Freie Universität Berlin (`www.chemie.fu-berlin.de/chemnet/use/info/libc/libc_19.html`). I'm sure they will not mind that I reproduce them here:

Different countries and cultures have varying conventions for how to communicate. These conventions range from very simple ones, such as the format for representing dates and times, to very complex ones, such as the language spoken.

Internationalization of software means programming it to be able to adapt to the user's favorite conventions. In ANSI C, internationalization works by means of locales. Each locale specifies a collection of conventions, one convention for each purpose. The user chooses a set of conventions by specifying a locale.

If you are running GNU/Linux on your computer and type the command `locale`, you get a list like that shown in Listing 2-3 (empty lines removed).

Listing 2-3. Default Locale

```
LANG=en_AU.UTF-8
LANGUAGE=en_AU:en
LC_CTYPE="en_AU.UTF-8"
LC_NUMERIC="en_AU.UTF-8"
LC_TIME="en_AU.UTF-8"
LC_COLLATE="en_AU.UTF-8"
LC_MONETARY="en_AU.UTF-8"
LC_MESSAGES="en_AU.UTF-8"
LC_PAPER="en_AU.UTF-8"
LC_NAME="en_AU.UTF-8"
LC_ADDRESS="en_AU.UTF-8"
LC_TELEPHONE="en_AU.UTF-8"
LC_MEASUREMENT="en_AU.UTF-8"
LC_IDENTIFICATION="en_AU.UTF-8"
LC_ALL=
```

In the United States, you will probably get that the locales associated to the different items are all "`en_US.UTF-8`".

In Germany, they could be "`de_DE.UTF-8`". And so on.

In general, a tag that identifies a locale consists of a language code (e.g., en) and a capitalized country code (e.g., AU), usually followed by the encoding (e.g., UTF-8).

Useless to say that Microsoft uses its own proprietary locale identifiers based on numbers that identify language and territory. But the concepts I describe here for GNU/Linux remain valid in general terms.

Notice that there exist different environment variables associated with locales that affect different items. For example, the setting of `LC_MONETARY` only affects how currency values are written, `LC_TIME` affects dates and times, etc.

To find out which locales are available on your GNU/Linux system, you can type the command `locale -a`. You will get a list similar to that shown in Listing 2-4 (empty lines removed).

Listing 2-4. Available Locales

```
C
C.UTF-8
en_AG
en_AG.utf8
en_AU.utf8
en_BW.utf8
en_CA.utf8
en_DK.utf8
```

```
en_GB.utf8
en_HK.utf8
en_IE.utf8
en_IN
en_IN.utf8
en_NG
en_NG.utf8
en_NZ.utf8
en_PH.utf8
en_SG.utf8
en_US.utf8
en_ZA.utf8
en_ZM
en_ZM.utf8
en_ZW.utf8
POSIX
```

Not all locales available on your system are compiled and accessible by default. This is done to save space, but you can easily compile additional locales. For example in GNU/Linux, you can type the command

```
sudo locale-gen de_DE.UTF-8
```

to compile the German locale, as you can easily verify by typing locale -a.

The simple program in Listing 2-5 shows how you can use setlocale() to switch between locales.

Listing 2-5. Setting Locales

```
#include <stdio.h>
#include <stdlib.h>
#include <locale.h>

int main(int argc, char *argv[]) {
  struct lconv *lc;

  char *where = "en_US.UTF-8";
  setlocale(LC_MONETARY, where);
  lc = localeconv();
  printf ("%s: %s %s\n", where, lc->currency_symbol, lc->int_curr_symbol);

  where = "en_AU.UTF-8";
  setlocale(LC_MONETARY, where);
  lc = localeconv();
  printf ("%s: %s %s\n", where, lc->currency_symbol, lc->int_curr_symbol);

  where = "de_DE.UTF-8";
  setlocale(LC_MONETARY, where);
  lc = localeconv();
  printf ("%s: %s %s\n", where, lc->currency_symbol, lc->int_curr_symbol);

  return EXIT_SUCCESS;
  }
```

And here is its output:

```
en_US.UTF-8: $ USD
en_AU.UTF-8: $ AUD
de_DE.UTF-8: € EUR
```

To find out more about the names of locales, you can refer to www.gnu.org/software/libc/manual/html_node/Locale-Names.html.

Normal and Wide Characters

As already said, in UTF-8 the first 127 characters (i.e., those that only need seven bits) are identical to ASCII. But all other codes require two to four bytes. You can distinguish them easily because the bytes have the most significant bit (MSB) set. For example, the no-break space is encoded with the two bytes c2 a0 (i.e., 11000010 10100000).

You can store UTF-8 characters in normal C strings, and functions like printf() have no problems in printing them correctly. For example, if you execute:

```
char *s = "€ © 𒋫 ♥";
printf("%zu \"%s\"\n", strlen(s), s);
for (int k = 0; k < strlen(s); k++) printf("%02x ", (unsigned char)s[k]);
printf("\n");
```

you get

```
15 "€ © 𒋫 ♥"
e2 82 ac 20 c2 a9 20 f0 90 8e ab 20 e2 99 a5
```

The normal C string s, which stores four special characters separated by spaces, is 15 bytes long. The for loop prints the string one character at a time in hexadecimal format and, knowing that 0x20 is a space, you can easily see how UTF-8 encodes the special characters with a variable number of bytes:

€	e2 82 ac
©	c2 a9
𒋫	f0 90 8e ab
♥	e2 99 a5

In case you are curious, the cuneiform character is an old Persian sign TA. Nice, isn't it? A good place to see all UTF-8 codes is www.utf8-chartable.de.

C can deal with multibyte characters in normal C strings, but it has also introduced wchar_t, a type specifically designed for *wide characters*. That is, for characters that require more than one byte to be encoded. Not surprisingly, different systems use different encodings. For example, GNU/Linux uses wchar_t to represent 32-bit characters encoded in UCS-4/UTF-32 (although some ports of GNU/Linux to particular computers might not do so), while Microsoft uses the same wchar_t type to represent 16-bit characters encoded in UTF-16.

To handle wide characters and strings, you need to set a locale and then use dedicated functions, as in the following simple example:

```
setlocale(LC_CTYPE, "");
```

```
wchar_t wc = L'€';
wprintf(L"A wide character: %lc\n", wc);
```

which produces the following output:

```
A wide character: €
```

Notice the L before the character used to initialize wc and before the format string of wprintf(), to indicate that they are wide. Also notice the l in the %lc formatting code, to indicate that the character is wide.

Setting the locale to the empty string directs the program to adopt the system's default locale. If you are thinking that instead of setting the default locale you should be able to omit the statement altogether, think again. If you do so, the output will be:

```
A wide character: EUR
```

Smart! But not necessarily what you need.

There is one delicate issue when printing wide characters, though: printf() and wprintf() write to the same character stream stdout, but they cannot share it. This is because stdout has an *orientation*: it can output either normal or wide characters, but not both at the same time. When the program starts, stdout has no orientation, but as soon as you use it to print normal characters, stdout becomes oriented and suppresses all output of wide characters. Similarly, if you start a program by printing wide characters, stdout can no longer print normal ones.

stdout loses its orientation after it is closed (and re-opened), but I am somewhat reluctant to potentially have to close and re-open stdout several times, which is in any case a tricky thing to do. If you need to print both normal and wide characters, I suggest that you *clone* stdout, so that you can use the original stdout for printing normal characters and the cloned stdout for printing wide characters or vice-versa.

The program in Listing 2-6 shows you how to do this.

Listing 2-6. Cloning stdout

```
#include <stdio.h>
#include <stdlib.h>
#include <locale.h>
#include <wchar.h>
#include <string.h>
#include <unistd.h>

int main(int argc, char *argv[]) {

  // Printing UTF-8 characters in normal C-strings...
  char *s = "€ © ♫ ♥";
  printf("%zu \"%s\"\n", strlen(s), s);
  for (int k = 0; k < strlen(s); k++) printf("%02x ", (unsigned char)s[k]);
  printf("\n");

  // ... and as wide characters after cloning stdout.
  int stdout_fd = dup(1);
  FILE *stdout2 = fdopen(stdout_fd, "w"); // compile with -gnu99
  //
  setlocale(LC_CTYPE, "");
  wchar_t wc = L'€';
  fwprintf(stdout2, L"A wide character: %lc\n", wc);
```

```
//
fclose(stdout2);
close(stdout_fd);

return EXIT_SUCCESS;
}
```

You need to include `unistd.h` to avoid getting the "`implicit declaration of function 'dup'`" and of function `'close'` warnings. Additionally, you should add the option `-std=gnu99` when you compile the program with gcc. This will remove the "`implicit declaration of function 'fdopen'`" warning.

To check and set a stream orientation, you can use the function `fwide()`:

```
int orientation = fwide(stdout, 0);
```

With 0 as the second argument, `fwide()` returns the current orientation: `-1` indicates normal characters and `1` indicates wide characters. So, for example,

```
wprintf(L"Stream orientation: %d\n", fwide(stdout, 0));
wprintf(L"Stream orientation: %d\n", fwide(stdout, 0));
```

prints

```
Stream orientation: 0
Stream orientation: 1
```

while

```
printf("Stream orientation: %d\n", fwide(stdout, 0));
printf("Stream orientation: %d\n", fwide(stdout, 0));
```

prints

```
Stream orientation: 0
Stream orientation: -1
```

This is because the orientation, initially 0, is set to either wide or normal after the first `wprintf()`/`printf()`. You can also use `fwide()` to set the orientation (a positive value for wide and a negative value for normal). For example:

```
wprintf(L"Stream orientation: %d\n", fwide(stdout, 3));
wprintf(L"Stream orientation: %d\n", fwide(stdout, 0));
```

prints

```
Stream orientation: 1
Stream orientation: 1
```

To conclude this section on normal and wide characters, we need to look at how we can convert from one to the other. First of all, let's see how you can convert single multibyte characters to wide characters. The code in Listing 2-7 shows you how to convert a string to a wide string one character at a time.

Listing 2-7. String to Wide String One Character a Time

```
char *s = "€ © ⴼⵜⵔ ♥";
setlocale(LC_CTYPE, "");
wprintf(L"Normal string: %2d \"%s\"\nConversion\n", strlen(s), s);
wchar_t ws[100] = {};
size_t conv_size = 0;
int next = 0;
wchar_t wc;
int k = 0;
do {
  conv_size = mbtowc(&wc, &s[next], strlen(s) - next);
  if (conv_size) {
    wprintf(L"%4d: %d -> %zu '%lc'\n", next, (int)conv_size, sizeof(wc), wc);
    next += (int)conv_size;
    ws[k++] = wc;
    }
  } while (conv_size > 0);
wprintf(L"Wide string: %zu \"%ls\"\n", wcslen(ws), ws);
```

Here is the output the code in Listing 2-7 produces:

```
Normal string: 15 "€ © ⴼⵜⵔ ♥"
Conversion
   0: 3 -> 4 '€'
   3: 1 -> 4 ' '
   4: 2 -> 4 '©'
   6: 1 -> 4 ' '
   7: 4 -> 4 'ⴼⵜⵔ'
  11: 1 -> 4 ' '
  12: 3 -> 4 '♥'
Wide string: 7 "€ © ⴼⵜⵔ ♥"
```

Notice how all wide characters occupy four bytes.

The code in Listing 2-7 is a nice exercise, but (not surprisingly) you can convert a whole string with the single function call:

```
size_t n = mbstowcs(ws, s, 100);
```

It sounds good, but how are the characters actually encoded in a wchar_t? You can find out by appending the following lines of code to the piece shown in Listing 2-7:

```
wprintf(L"\n");
for (int k = 0; k < 7; k++) {
  for (int j = 0; j < 4; j++) {
    wprintf(L"%02x ", ((unsigned char *)ws)[k*4 + j]);
    }
  wprintf(L" '%lc'\n", ws[k]);
  }
```

Note that the code only works with compilers and systems that, like gcc on GNU/Linux, define wchar_t to be 32-bit wide. This is what you get:

```
ac 20 00 00    '€'
20 00 00 00    ' '
a9 00 00 00    '©'
20 00 00 00    ' '
ab 03 01 00    'ༀ'
20 00 00 00    ' '
65 26 00 00    '♥'
```

Wow! What code is that? Okay, I'll tell you: it is UTF-32 with the most significant byte stored last. So, now you know that in a normal string the Euro sign is encoded with UTF-8 with the most significant byte first (e2 82 ac), while in wide characters the encoding is UTF-32 with the most significant byte last (ac 20 00 00).

At least, this is how it works with Ubuntu, which is a release of GNU/Linux. The general concepts are identical on other systems, although the number of bytes in each wchar_t and the encoding will change. In Microsoft systems, for example, wchar_t is 16-bits wide and wide characters are encoded with UTF-16. But in Windows the locale names are different, as they use 16-bit numbers. You can find their list at msdn. microsoft.com/en-au/goglobal/bb964664.aspx.

The bottom line, to reiterate a point I already made, is that wide characters and strings can easily make your code unportable, unless you use conditional compilation.

Now, to convert a wide character to multibyte, you can use wctomb() as shown in the following example:

```
char airplane[5];
size_t n_c = wctomb(airplane, L'✈');
airplane[n_c] = '\0';
wprintf(L"\nWide to multibyte char %zu: %lc -> %s\n", n_c, L'✈', airplane);
```

The string airplane is long enough to contain the maximum number of characters in multibytes (i.e., four) plus the terminating null. Also, you need to write in the output a terminating null after the last character of the multibyte.

The output is:

```
Wide to multibyte char 3:✈ -> ✈
```

To convert wide strings to multibyte, you can use wcstombs():

```
char ss[100];
n_c = wcstombs(ss, L"♦♦", 100);
wprintf(L"\nWide to multibyte string %zu: %ls -> %s\n", n_c, L"♦♦", ss);
```

With strings you don't need to append a terminating null because the input string is terminated with a wide null that will be converted to the normal one. The output is:

```
Wide to multibyte string 6: ♦♦ -> ♦♦
```

Dealing with Numbers

Sooner or later, you will need to know how numbers are stored in a C variable. You might think the matter straightforward and never give it a thought, but I believe that any serious programmer should know things like what *two's complement* means or when to use double instead of float.

Integers

On my Ubuntu system, I can use the types char, short, int, and long to store integer numbers into 1, 2, 4, and 8 bytes, respectively.

Table 2-1 shows the minimum number of bits that the C99 standard requires and the actual number of bits provided by Ubuntu and Windows.

Table 2-1. *Integer Sizes*

Type	C99	Ubuntu	Windows
char	8	8	8
short	16	16	16
int	16	32	32
long	32	64	32
long long	64	64	64
pointer	Implementation dependent	64	64

The major difference between Ubuntu (and other GNU/Linux systems, including Macs) and Windows is that the latter uses 32 bits for longs (yes, also with 64-bit processors). For portability, you can include the standard header stdint.h and use the types int8_t, uint8_t, int16_t, uint16_t, int32_t, uint32_t, int64_t, and uint64_t. I could have written the examples and the code for this book using these standard integer types, but I didn't because I find them somewhat distracting. Perhaps it is because you actually need to read the numbers 8 to 64 in order to understand what type you are dealing with, while you can identify the traditional types at a glance. And for a book like this, clarity and easy-reading are very important.

If you include in your variable definition the additional type specifier unsigned, the minimum value of all the resulting types is 0, while the maximum corresponds to all bits set to 1, which is given by: $2^{\#bits} - 1$. This is because, when all the bits 0 to #bits (where 0 is the LSB) are set to 1, you only need to add one to have (in binary) a number consisting of a 1 followed by #bits zeros. For example, the maximum unsigned short is $2^{16} - 1 = 65535$.

The maximum values are defined in the standard header limits.h. So, if you execute

```
printf("%u %u %u %lu\n", UCHAR_MAX, USHRT_MAX, UINT_MAX, ULONG_MAX);
```

you obtain:

```
255 65535 4294967295 18446744073709551615
```

Things become slightly more complicated when you need signed numbers (which is the default, although, if you fancy it, you can add the type specifier signed). The trick is to use the MSB as a sign bit: the number is positive when the MSB is 0, and negative when it is 1.

If you left it at that, short could hold numbers between -32767 (all 16 bits set to 1) and +32767 (the MSB set to 0 and the remaining 15 set to 1). But then, you would have two signed zeroes: +0 would be a number with all 16 bits set to 0, and -0 would be a number with the MSB set to 1 and all the others to 0. This would pose problems to programmers and chip designers.

To resolve this issue, the following strategy has been universally adopted: to store an N-bit negative number, you subtract its absolute value from 2^N. To understand how it works in practice, let's see how you store -127 into a signed char. In binary, 127 is 0b01111111 (i.e., $1 + 2 + 4 + 8 + 16 + 32 + 64$). The 2^N for one byte is 0b100000000 (i.e., 2^8 = 256). As you subtract binary numbers exactly like you subtract decimal numbers, the result is 0b10000001. As another example, lets see how -1 looks. In binary, 1 is 0b00000001, and when you subtract it from 0b100000000, you obtain 0b11111111.

This strategy removes the double-zero, because now 0b10000000, which used to be -0, represents -128.

Instead of making the subtractions, you can easily determine the representation of negative numbers by flipping all their bits and adding 1. For example, if you flip 127 (i.e., 0b01111111), you get 0b10000000, and when you add 1, you obtain the correct representation (i.e., 0b10000001). The number you obtain by flipping the bits is called the one's complement because if you add it to the original one you obtain all 1s. What you store in memory to represent a negative number is called the two's complement because you can obtain it by adding 1 to the one's complement.

After this explanation, it should be obvious to you that if you execute:

```
printf("%d %d %d %ld\n", CHAR_MIN, SHRT_MIN, INT_MIN, LONG_MIN);
printf(" %d  %d  %d  %ld\n", CHAR_MAX, SHRT_MAX, INT_MAX, LONG_MAX);
```

you obtain:

```
-128 -32768 -2147483648 -9223372036854775808
 127  32767  2147483647  9223372036854775807
```

One more thing before moving on—the convention for writing numbers is that the least significant digit is on the right. For example, you write one hundred and twenty three as 123. You do the same when you write numbers in any base, including binary (where the digits can only be 0 and 1) and hexadecimal (where each digit is anything between 0 and F). So, for example, the number 0x12345678 means that 8 corresponds to 16^0, 7 to 16^1, etc.

But when a number is stored in computer memory, the order of bits and bytes is not always the same. For example, if you store the number 0x12345678 into a 32-bit integer, what goes into the byte with the lowest memory address?

On my Ubuntu system, I wrote the following three lines of code:

```
int ii = 0x12345678;
unsigned char *pip = (unsigned char *)&ii;
for (int i = 0; i < sizeof(ii); i++) printf("%02x", pip[i]);
```

and it printed out 78563412.

As each pair of hexes is a byte, it means that the gcc in Ubuntu writes the least significant byte first (i.e., in the lowest memory address). In *computerese*, this choice is called *little endianness*.

Floating-Point Numbers

To state the (almost) obvious: floating-point numbers are numbers with a decimal point.

Significant Digits, Truncation, and Rounding

To understand how you represent floating-point numbers in computers, you need to know the scientific notation of numbers. Here are some examples of how you can write the number 123.456 with the scientific notation:

```
123.456 * 10⁰
```
$$123.456 * 10^0$$
$$1234.56 * 10^{-1}$$
$$12345.6 * 10^{-2}$$
$$123456 * 10^{-3}$$

```
1234560 * 10⁻⁴
12.3456 * 10¹
1.23456 * 10²
0.123456 * 10³
0.0123456 * 10⁴
```

The first part is called *coefficient*, 10 is the *base*, and the power of 10 is the *exponent*. Every time you move the decimal point of the coefficient to the left, you obtain a number that is 10 times smaller. Therefore, if you want to keep the value of the original number, you need to increase by one the exponent. And, obviously, if you move the decimal point to the right, you need to decrease the exponent accordingly. 10^0 is equal to 1 and is therefore normally omitted, which makes the familiar way of representing decimal numbers without the power of 10 a particular case of the scientific notation.

The accepted convention is to write numbers in scientific notation with a single digit on the left of the decimal point. In the example, `1.23456 * 10²`.

In any case, the numbers listed above are not completely equivalent. To convince yourself that this is the case, consider the result of dividing 20 by 3. It is *approximately* 6.66. If you play with the scientific notation of 6.66 as you did with that of `123.456`, you have:

```
6.66 * 10⁰
66.6 * 10⁻¹
666 * 10⁻²
6660 * 10⁻³
66600 * 10⁻⁴
0.666 * 10¹
0.0666 * 10²
0.00666 * 10³
0.000666 * 10⁴
```

Everything seemed reasonable with `123.456` because we didn't know how the number had been calculated, but we know that 6.66 is the result of 20/3, and that makes some of its representations look odd. To understand why, write

```
20/3 = 6660 * 10⁻³
```

and then multiply both sides of the expression by 1000. The result is:

```
20000/3 = 6660
```

Now, that is wrong!

The problem is that we are used to considering zeros as nothing. But that is not always true. The 0 of 6660 is *significant*. When you write 20/3 = 6.66, you specify three significant digits, but 6660 has got four significant digits. On which basis did you decide that the three sixes were to be followed by a zero?

And what about the following two representations?

```
0.666000 * 10¹
0.066600 * 10²
```

They are also wrong because they add respectively three and two significant zeros (those on the right of the three sixes). The following two rules tell you what is significant:

- All non-zero digits are significant.

- All zeroes that are on the right of non-zero digits are significant.

The second rule also means that zeroes between non-zero digits are significant.

When you calculate 20/3 by hand and obtain 6.66, you first get 6 with the rest of 2, then 0.6 with the rest of 0.2, and then 0.06 with the rest 0.02, at which point you stop. This way of approximating a calculation is called *truncation* (from the Latin verb *truncare* that means to mutilate entirely).

Well, you know that if you refine the calculation of 20/3 you keep getting sixes. Therefore, if you decide to apply *rounding* instead of truncation while keeping three significant digits, you can say that 20/3 is approximately 6.67. When you state that 20/6 is 6.67, you are rounding up, while when you state that 10/3 is 3.33, you are rounding down.

One thing you need to keep in mind: you can only round numbers if you can calculate/estimate more than the digits that constitute your result. If you want to show all the digits you can calculate, you can only truncate. In most practical situations this will have no effect, but not in all cases.

These considerations are important because the number of significant digits in any computer operation is less than infinite. More about this in the next section.

It is customary to simplify the scientific notation by replacing the power of 10 with the letter e followed by the exponent, like in the following example: $1.23 * 10^{-5} = 1.23e-5$.

Representing Floating-Point Numbers

Computer calculations dealing with fractional results are approximate. For example, I just executed on my computer the following three lines

```
printf("%2zu %10.8f\n", sizeof(float), (float)10/3);
printf("%2zu %19.17f\n", sizeof(double), (double)10/3);
printf("%2zu %22.20Lf\n", sizeof(long double), (long double)10/3);
```

and the result was:

```
 4 3.33333325
 8 3.33333333333333348
16 3.33333333333333333326
```

As you can see, the higher the number of bytes used to represent the number, the larger the number of significant digits.

All floating-point numbers are stored in scientific notation, with the block of memory that holds the number divided into three parts: the sign bit, the exponent, and the *mantissa*. Mantissa, the name used in Mathematics to refer to the part of a logarithm after the decimal point, is how the coefficient of the scientific notation is called in computing.

The IEEE 754-2008 standard specifies how you encode floating-point numbers in computers and has been universally accepted, although some parts have not yet been implemented at the moment of writing. The University of Baltimore makes it available at www.csee.umbc.edu/~tsimo1/CMSC455/IEEE-754-2008.pdf.

In agreement with the standard, the float data type available in C encodes a floating-point number in 32 bits as follows (bit 0, the LSB, is on the right):

```
meaning: seeeeeeeemmmmmmmmmmmmmmmmmmmmmmm
bits:    <---8--><--------23----------->
```

where s is the sign bit, the 8 bits marked e are the exponent, and the 23 bits marked m are the mantissa.

Similarly to what you saw for decimal numbers in the previous section, you can represent the same number in many different ways by shifting the significant digits of the mantissa left or right and accordingly increase or decrease the value of the exponent. But with computer representation of floating-point numbers, the possibility of representing the same number in different ways is unacceptable because comparison between numbers would become complicated and time consuming.

The convention adopted in the IEEE 754 standard is similar to that adopted in the scientific notation for decimal numbers: you shift the number left or right until a single non-zero digit (i.e., a 1, because there are only 0s and 1s in a binary number) remains on the left of the decimal (oops! of the binary or fractional) point, and adjust the exponent accordingly (just that now the exponent indicates a power of 2 rather than a power of 10).

The sign bit refers to the whole number, but the exponent must have its own sign to represent numbers with absolute value between 0 and 1. To accommodate this, the standard specifies that the exponent is to be stored shift-127 encoded. That is, to obtain the actual exponent of a number you subtract 127 (i.e., 0x7f) from the number encoded in the eight eeeeeeee bits. For example, an exponent of 0 is stored in the eight bits as 127, 1 as 128, -1 as 126, etc.

So far so good. But the standard adds a twist to the encoding and asks: why should we memorize the 1 on the left of the point? It is always there and we know that it is a 1 (with decimal numbers expressed in scientific notation any digit between 1 and 9 can be on the left of the point, but with binary numbers it can only be a 1). We might as well drop it and avoid wasting a bit space!

"Wait a minute!" you might say. "When I represent the number 1 as a floating-point number and drop its only non-zero digit, how do I distinguish it from the representation of 0?" The solution adopted by the standard is to arbitrarily (but conveniently and pleasingly) use the all-zero binary encoding to represent the number 0. Then, 0 is represented with 0x00000000 and 1 with 0x3f800000. Note that the 23 LSBs (i.e., the mantissa) of 1 are 0 because, once you move the only non-zero digit to the left of the fractional point, the number 1 entirely consists of zeroes (I repeat it here just in case you didn't completely get it the first time!). Also note that the sign bit of 1 is 0 and the 8-bit exponent is 0b01111111, which is 127. Indeed, when you subtract 127 from the exponent and reinstate the 1 that was removed from the left of the fractional point, you obtain 1 * 2^0, which is 1.0, as it should be!

To make another example, the encoding of -1 in a float is 0xbf800000. The only difference from the encoding of 1 is that the most significant bit of the whole representation is 1 instead of 0 because the most significant hex is set to 0xb, or 0b1011, instead of 0x3, or 0b011. But that is the sign bit! It makes entirely sense.

One last example: 0.5 is encoded with 0x3f000000: like in the representation of 1, the sign bit and the mantissa are 0, but the exponent is 0x3f00, or 0b01111110, which is 126. When you subtract from the exponent 127 and reinstate the removed 1, you obtain 1 * 2^{-1}, which is, surprise surprise, 0.5.

By deciding to represent 0 with the all-zero encoding, the standard makes it impossible to store the number 2^{-127} because, after the shift-127 of the exponent, it would become indistinguishable from 0. But "losing" such a small number in order to have a convenient representation of 0 is a small price to pay. The standard introduces further limitations by defining additional arbitrary encodings

```
0x7f800000: +infinity
0xff800000: -infinity
0x7fc00000 and 0x7ff00000: +Not-a-Number (NaN)
```

All in all, you calculate a floating-point number in decimal from its IEEE 754 binary representation as follows (a funny syntax, but it should be clear what it means):

```
decimal number = (1 - sign bit * 2) * 2^(exponent bits - 127)  * 1.mantissa bits
```

If you like it better, you can replace (1 - sign bit * 2) with the C-like equivalent (sign bits ? -1 : 1).

Everything said about float applies to double and long double although, obviously, different numbers of bits are used for exponent and mantissa. The IEEE 754 standard specifies double and long double to have respectively 11 and 15 bits for the exponent, and 52 and 112 for the mantissa, plus, obviously, the sign bit.

But your system might implement floating-point numbers differently. Table 2-2 shows the results of executing the following statements on Ubuntu (the macros are defined in the standard header float.h):

```
printf("Property\tfloat\tdouble\tlong double\n");
printf("mantissa:\t%d\t%d\t%d\n", FLT_MANT_DIG, DBL_MANT_DIG, LDBL_MANT_DIG);
printf("# dec. digits:\t%d\t%d\t%d\n", FLT_DIG, DBL_DIG, LDBL_DIG);
```

```
printf("max:\t%9.5e\t%18.14e\t%22.17Le\n", FLT_MAX, DBL_MAX, LDBL_MAX);
printf("min:\t%9.5e\t%18.14e\t%22.17Le\n", FLT_MIN, DBL_MIN, LDBL_MIN);
```

Table 2-2. *Floating-Point Encoding in Ubuntu*

Property	float	double	long double
mantissa+sign bits:	24	53	64
# decimal digits:	6	15	18
max:	3.40282e+38	1.79769313486232e+308	1.18973149535723177e+4932
min:	1.17549e-38	2.22507385850720e-308	3.36210314311209351e-4932

The number of bits reserved for the mantissa of the float type is 24 instead of 23 as previously stated because the *_MANT_DIG macros defined in float.h include the sign bit in their count. The length of the mantissa of the double type also matches the standard. But LDBL_MANT_DIG does not conform to the standard because it is 64, while the standard specifies 113.

The standard also specifies the number of exponent bits: 8 for float, 11 for double, and 15 for long double. Indeed, if you add the number of mantissa+sign bits to the exponent bits, you obtain 24+8 = 32 (i.e., four bytes) for float, 53+11 = 64 (i.e., eight bytes) for double, and 113+15 = 128 (i.e., 16 bytes) for long double.

Assuming that the gcc running on Ubuntu conforms to the standard of 15 exponent bits for long double numbers, as the mantissa of the long double type only uses 64 bits instead of the specified 113, what happens to the 49 bits that are unaccounted for?

To shed some light on this issue, look at the standard header ieee754.h, and in particular at the definitions associated with little endianness. For convenience, I reproduce it as Listing 2-8 after removing some of the (for us) inessential code and applying some reformatting. The definition of long double refers to IEEE 854 instead of IEEE 754 because IEEE 854 was only incorporated into IEEE 754 in the 2008 release and nobody has updated in ieee.754.h. But it doesn't matter.

Listing 2-8. ieee754.h (Partial)

```
// Single-precision format.
union ieee754_float {
  float f;
  struct {
    unsigned int mantissa:23;
    unsigned int exponent:8;
    unsigned int negative:1;
    } ieee;
};

// Double-precision format.
union ieee754_double {
  double d;
  struct {
    unsigned int mantissa1:32;
    unsigned int mantissa0:20;
    unsigned int exponent:11;
    unsigned int negative:1;
    } ieee;
};
```

```
// Double-extended-precision format.
union ieee854_long_double {
  long double d;
  struct {
    unsigned int mantissa1:32;
    unsigned int mantissa0:32;
    unsigned int exponent:15;
    unsigned int negative:1;
    unsigned int empty:16;
    } ieee;
};
```

In the definitions of Listing 2-8 you find for float and double the bit sizes of mantissa and exponent shown in Table 2-2. Because of the little endianness, which applies to floating-point as well as to integer types, the mantissa appears first, and is therefore stored in memory locations that have lower addresses than the rest.

But, when you look at the definition of long double, you find that there is an additional 16-bit field named empty and that mantissa and sign add up to 65 bits, not 64 as defined in float.h by LDBL_MANT_DIG and shown in Table 2-2. So, the missing bits are in fact 48, rather than 49 as calculated in the assumption that LDBL_MANT_DIG included the sign bit. And yet, the bit field named empty only accounts for 16 of the 48 missing bits and 32 remain undefined and unaccounted for.

This is a practical book. Therefore, to solve this riddle, we take a practical approach. The following code defines floating-point numbers of all three types, sets them to 1, and prints their contents in hexadecimal:

```
float f = 1;
unsigned char *c = (unsigned char *)&f;
for (int i = 0; i < sizeof(f); i++) printf("%02x", c[i]);
printf("\n");
//
double d = 1;
c = (unsigned char *)&d;
for (int i = 0; i < sizeof(d); i++) printf("%02x", c[i]);
printf("\n");
//
long double ld = 1;
c = (unsigned char *)&ld;
for (int i = 0; i < sizeof(ld); i++) printf("%02x", c[i]);
printf("\n");
```

The output on Ubuntu is:

```
0000803f
000000000000f03f
0000000000000080ff3f000000000000
```

Because of the little endianness of the numbers, you need to reverse the byte ordering if you want to have numbers like you are used to seeing them, with the least significant bytes on the right (i.e., big-endian):

```
float: 3f800000
double: 3ff0000000000000
long double: 0000000000003fff8000000000000000
```

As the variables of all three types store the value 1, the sign bit (i.e., the MSB) is 0.

You have already seen that 0x3f800000 is how 1 is stored in a float. The eight exponent bits are set to 127 (i.e., 0b01111111) and the rest (i.e., the 23 bits of mantissa) are 0. Nothing new to learn from that.

Concerning the double, the 11 bits of the exponent are encoded with a shift that has the same function of the mentioned shift-127 used for the float type. As the shift of the float type, which has eight exponent bits, is 2^7-1, the shift of the double type, with 11 exponent bits, is $2^{10}-1$, or, in binary, 0b01111111111. You only need to shift it one position to the right to make space for the number's sign bit and you have 0x3ff, which matches the expansion of the double encoding of 1. With this exercise you have also learned that double exponents are encoded with a shift-1023.

Concerning the long double, an exponent of 15 bits means that it is encoded with a shift of $2^{14}-1$, which in decimal is 16383 and in binary 0b011111111111111. When you shift it to the right one bit to make space for the sign bit, you obtain 0x3fff. But if you look at the big-endian encoding shown above, you see that there is a set bit immediately following the 15 bits of the exponent (i.e., 0x3fff is followed by an 0x8). That bit is the MSB of the mantissa, and its presence means that gcc implements the long double type *without* dropping the 1 before the fractional point! That is, one of the 64 bits of mantissa doesn't contain any information because it is always set.

Notice that the 0x3fff of sign and exponent are preceded by 6 bytes all 0. These are the 48 missing bits. They occupy the most significant end of the 16 bytes of long double numbers.

Just for fun, I set them all to 1 and checked what the compiler would do. Here is the code I added:

```
for (int i = 1; i <= 6; i++) c[sizeof(ld) - i] = 0xff;
printf("%Lf\n", ld);
for (int i = 0; i < sizeof(ld); i++) printf("%02x", c[i]);
printf("\n");
```

And here is the output:

```
1.000000
0000000000000080ff3fffffffffffffff
```

The compiler ignores the 48 set bits and still prints 1.0! As a further test, I added another piece of code to check what happened to those bits when I copied a long double to another. Listing 2-9 shows the whole test.

Listing 2-9. Checking the Unused Bits in Long Double

```
 1. long double ld = 1;
 2. unsigned char *c = (unsigned char *)&ld;
 3. for (int i = 1; i <= 6; i++) c[sizeof(ld) - i] = 0xff;
 4. printf("%Lf\n", ld);
 5. for (int i = 0; i < sizeof(ld); i++) printf("%02x", c[i]);
 6. printf("\n");
 7. long double ld2;
 8. c = (unsigned char *)&ld2;
 9. for (int i = 1; i < sizeof(ld2); i++) c[i] = i;
10. ld2 = ld;
11. printf("%Lf\n", ld2);
12. for (int i = 0; i < sizeof(ld2); i++) printf("%02x", c[i]);
13. printf("\n");
```

The output:

```
1.000000
0000000000000080ff3fffffffffffffff
```

```
1.000000
0000000000000080ff3fffff0c0d0e0f
```

In other words, the compiler copies to the new long double two of the six bytes set to 0xff in ld. Those are the 16 bits defined as empty in ieee754.h. The remaining 32 bits of ld2, which are undefined in ieee754.h, are left unchanged. The initial code of the test did not include line 9. As a result, those 32 bits where left to the rubbish value they happened to contain when ld2 was defined.

Now that you know how the compiler handles the 48 unused bits (the 16 defined in ieee754.h are copied across and the other 32 are ignored), you could hide messages in tables of long doubles, and the people using the tables would remain unaware of them! I leave it up to you to speculate on how many spies have actually used this method to hide information...

You could be tempted to append an unsigned int empty1:32; to ieee854_long_double.ieee and see whether also the currently ignored 32 bits are copied across, but it would certainly not happen unless you recompiled gcc. I haven't tried it but, in any case, you shouldn't fiddle with the system unless you really know what you are doing.

Checking for Equality of Floating-Point Numbers

As you have seen, floating-point numbers have a limited precision. That is, you can only depend on a given number of digits. Table 2-2 tells you that for float variables that number is 6 and for double is 15.

But those simple numbers don't tell you the whole story. Approximations (rounding or truncation) occur every time you manipulate floating-point variables. For example, execute the following two lines of code (cos() is a function returning a double):

```
double d = cos(M_PI/2);
printf("%18.15: it is%s zero.\n", d, (d == 0.0) ? "": " not");
```

and you will get:

```
0.000000000000000: it is not zero.
```

Trigonometric and other functions in the C library are calculated with polynomial approximations. It is therefore unreasonable to expect all 64 bits of cos(M_PI/2) to be zero.

We know that the mantissa of double (without counting the sign bit) occupies 52 bits. Therefore, the precision of a number stored as a double cannot be better than $\pm2^{-52}$. You don't need to calculate it. If you include the standard header float.h and print DBL_EPSILON, you will get 2.22045e-16. That's nice: the e-16 explains why with double you can only rely on 15 decimal digits.

Let's explore the matter further with another simple program:

```
double d = cos(M_PI/2);
for (int k = -9; k <= 9; k++) {
  double dx = d + DBL_EPSILON * k;
  printf("%2d %18.15f: it is%s zero.\n", k, dx, (dx == 0.0) ? "": " not");
  }
```

You subtract 7*DBL_EPSILON from the calculated value of the cosine, add one DBL_EPSILON at the time, and compare each value against zero. Here is what you get:

```
-7 -0.000000000000001: it is not zero.
-6 -0.000000000000001: it is not zero.
-5 -0.000000000000001: it is not zero.
```

37

```
-4 -0.000000000000001: it is not zero.
-3 -0.000000000000001: it is not zero.
-2 -0.000000000000000: it is not zero.
-1 -0.000000000000000: it is not zero.
 0  0.000000000000000: it is not zero.
 1  0.000000000000000: it is not zero.
 2  0.000000000000001: it is not zero.
 3  0.000000000000001: it is not zero.
 4  0.000000000000001: it is not zero.
 5  0.000000000000001: it is not zero.
 6  0.000000000000001: it is not zero.
 7  0.000000000000002: it is not zero.
```

Neat! Because of rounding, all values between -2*DBL_EPSILON and +DBL_EPSILON give you a result correct to 15 decimal digits. But in no case the result equals 0.

If you print the cosine after changing the formatting of the floating-point number from %18.15f to %20.17f, you display the next two decimal digits:

```
0.00000000000000006: it is not zero.
```

Now you can see that, although the difference between the calculated value and zero is less than a third of DBL_EPSILON, it isn't zero.

Instead of checking for equality two floating-point numbers, you could decide that they are equal if they differ by less than the corresponding EPSILON (FLT_EPSILON for float, DBL_EPSILON for double, and LDBL_EPSILON for long double).

Although it sounds reasonable, it is in fact a bad test because it is only applicable to numbers that are much larger than EPSILON. For example, consider the two double numbers 1.24e-14 and 1.22e-14. The type double can store 15 significant digits and the two numbers already differ in their third one. Therefore, they are clearly different. And yet, when you calculate their difference, you obtain 2e-16, which is less than DBL_EPSILON, which is approximately 2.2e-16.

In other words, a test of equality only based on checking whether the difference of two numbers (obviously, in absolute value) is less than EPSILON is not good enough. The two numbers of the example are two orders of magnitude larger than DBL_EPSILON, but the same problem occurs with much larger numbers. Moreover, all numbers smaller in absolute value than EPSILON would be considered to be equal!

The problem occurs because you cannot use EPSILON in absolute terms, as EPSILON only tells you how many decimal digits you can store in a floating-point variable.

EPSILON only represents a lower limit of the difference below which you can consider two numbers to be equal. In a real-life case, you will probably be satisfied with a much less stringent condition. For example, if the values you are comparing are the result of measurements, it doesn't make sense to compare more significant digits than your measuring process and devices can provide.

The matter is tricky, because our minds work well with absolute numbers but tend to ignore significant digits, and this can lead to invalid results. If you are not convinced, consider this: modern measuring devices have digital displays, but not all displayed digits are always meaningful. For example, if you are using a voltmeter with an accuracy of ±0.01V to measure a voltage of approximately 100V, you can correctly write the result of your measurement as 100.00 ±0.01V. But if you have the same accuracy when you measure 1 Volt, you only have three significant digits and should write 1.00 ±0.01 despite the fact that the instrument might display the measured value as 1.0000V.

The same issue applies to floating-point numbers stored in computers.

To properly check two floating-point numbers for equality, first of all, you need to check whether their sign bits are the same. If they are not, the numbers are certainly different.

The next step is to compare the exponents. Remember that when the compiler stores a floating-point number in memory, it calculates the exponent in such a way that the most significant non-zero bit is on the left of the fractional point (and can therefore be dropped). This means that, if the two exponents are different, the numbers must be different.

Once you have checked that the signs and the exponents are the same, you could check that enough digits of the mantissa are identical to satisfy your requirement of equality. That is, if you consider two numbers to be equal when their first N decimal digits are identical (up to the number of decimal digits listed in Table 2-2), you would need to check N/log(2) bits, or N*3.322. For example, if you are dealing with numbers considered to be equal when they have the same 4 most significant digits, you could compare the first 4*3.322 = 13.29 bits (i.e., 14) bits of the mantissa.

But this is not going to work in a reliable way because the number of bits you would need to compare is not the same for all numbers. You just saw that for four decimal digits you should compare 13.29 bits of the mantissa. For some numbers, 13 bits will be sufficient, for others, you will need 14 bits. The only consistent way to compare numbers is to decide how many bits of the mantissa you want to have equal.

This is not a comfortable way of checking for equality, but we are going to pursue it anyway because it will be a good exercise.

Listing 2-10 shows the function num_fltcmp(), which, instead of simply checking for equality, also determines which number is larger.

Listing 2-10. num_fltcmp()

```
 1. //----------------------------------------------------------------- num_fltcmp
 2. int num_fltcmp(float a, float b, unsigned int n_bits) {
 3.   if (n_bits > FLT_MANT_DIG - 1) n_bits = FLT_MANT_DIG - 1;
 4.   if (a == b) return 0;                                        //-->
 5.   union ieee754_float *aa = (union ieee754_float *)&a;
 6.   union ieee754_float *bb = (union ieee754_float *)&b;
 7.
 8.   // Compare the signs.
 9.   char a_sign = (char)aa->ieee.negative;
10.   char b_sign = (char)bb->ieee.negative;
11.   if (a_sign != b_sign) return b_sign - a_sign;               //-->
12.   if (a == 0) return ((b_sign) ? 1 : -1);                     //-->
13.   if (b == 0) return ((a_sign) ? -1 : 1);                     //-->
14.
15.   // Compare the exponents.
16.   char a_exp = (char)aa->ieee.exponent - 127;
17.   char b_exp = (char)bb->ieee.exponent - 127;
18.   if (a_exp != b_exp) {
19.     int ret = (a_exp > b_exp) ? 1 : -1;
20.     return (a_sign) ? -ret : ret;                             //-->
21.   }
22.
23.   // Compare the mantissas.
24.   int n_shift = (int)sizeof(unsigned int) * 8 - FLT_MANT_DIG + 1;
25.   unsigned int a_mant = (unsigned int)aa->ieee.mantissa << n_shift;
26.   unsigned int b_mant = (unsigned int)bb->ieee.mantissa << n_shift;
27. # define MASK 0x80000000 // 2^31
28.   for (int k = 0; k < n_bits; k++) {
29.     if ((a_mant & MASK) != (b_mant & MASK)) {
30.       int ret = (a_mant & MASK) ? 1 : -1;
```

```
31.         return (a_sign) ? -ret : ret;                                    //-->
32.         }
33.     a_mant <<= 1;
34.     b_mant <<= 1;
35.     }
36. # undef MASK
37.   return 0;
38.   } // num_fltcmp
```

To make it work, you need to include the standard headers float.h, ieee754.h, and math.h. Note that the gcc linker requires you to explicitly link the GNU math library, which is not included by default. To do this on GNU/Linux, you need to specify the options -lm and -L/usr/lib/x86_64-linux-gnu/.

Also note that first you check whether the numbers are identical (line 4). It could be, and if that is the case, you can immediately return 0. It could also be that both numbers are zero.

If one number is negative, it is certainly less than the other. Therefore, if the sign bits are different, you can return their difference (line 11). Note that which number you subtract from which détermines when you return -1 and when you return 1. The convention used in num_fltcmp() is the same used in the standard library functions strcmp() and memcmp(): it returns -1 when the first number is less than the second.

Now, if the two signs are the same, you need to consider the possibility that one of the two numbers is the special case in which all bits are zero. Note that they cannot be both zero because you have already checked for that possibility in line 4.

If the first number is zero (line 12), it is less than the second number when the second number is positive. Similarly, in line 13, if the second number is zero, you return 1 when the first number is positive.

Having taken care of the signs and of the possibility that one or both of the numbers are zero, you can compare the exponents.

We know that the exponent of a float occupies eight bits. Therefore, in lines 16 and 17 we can use a char to store them. If you execute the code

```
float f1;
union ieee754_float *ff1 = (union ieee754_float *)&f1;
f1 = 1e-38;
char exp = (char)ff1->ieee.exponent - 127;
printf("%d\n", exp);
f1 = 1;
exp = (char)ff1->ieee.exponent - 127;
printf("%d\n", exp);
f1 = 3e+38;
exp = (char)ff1->ieee.exponent - 127;
printf("%d\n", exp);
```

you get:

```
-127
0
127
```

Going back to the code of num_fltcmp(), if the exponents are different, in line 20 you return 1 if a_exp is greater than b_exp, but only when the numbers are positives. When they are negative, the smallest mantissa corresponds to the largest number.

You will remember that FLT_MANT_DIG includes the sign bit in the count. Therefore, the number n_shift as calculated in line 24 is the number of bits you need to shift the mantissa (without sign bit) to obtain the most significant bit of an unsigned int variable.

Then the MSBs of a_mant and b_mant (see lines 25 and 26) are also the MSBs of the corresponding mantissas. To have the mantissa, so to speak, "left-justified" lets you easily check its bits one by one: by repeatedly shifting the number one bit to the left, all bits occupy the most-significant position one after the other. This is the function of the for loop that starts in line 28 and the shifting left of the two mantissas takes place in lines 33 and 34. The advantage of using this algorithm is that you can check all the bits without having a different mask for each one of them.

The loop continues for n_bits, but it is aborted with a return if two corresponding bits are different. The comparison of the bits of the two mantissas is done in line 29. Once determined that the two bits are different, if the bit of the first mantissa is 1, it means the corresponding bit of the second mantissa is 0, and a is greater than b. But this is only true if the two numbers are positive (we know that they have the same sign, otherwise we would have returned in line 11). If they are negative (i.e., if the sign bit of either number is 1), a is less than b.

Before moving on, we are going to confirm that deciding how many bits of the mantissa need to be equal is not going to deliver pairs of numbers that have the same number of identical decimal digits. To do so, we execute the code in Listing 2-11.

Listing 2-11. Testing num_fltcmp()

```
1.  int N = 3;
2.  srand(123456789);
3.  float max_x = 10.0;
4.  float d[] = {
5.      -0.1, -0.01, -0.001, -0.0001, -0.00001, -0.000001, 0,
6.       0.000001,  0.00001,  0.0001,  0.001,  0.01,  0.1
7.      };
8.  int nd = sizeof(d) / sizeof(float);
9.  for (int k = 0; k < N; k++) {
10.    float x = (float)rand() / RAND_MAX * max_x;
11.    printf("\n%9.7f  ", x);
12.    for (int i = 1; i < FLT_MANT_DIG; i++) printf("%2d", i % 10);
13.    printf("\n");
14.    for (int j = 0; j < nd; j++) {
15.      printf("%10f:", d[j]);
16.      for (unsigned int i = 1; i < FLT_MANT_DIG; i++) {
17.        int res = num_fltcmp(x, x + d[j], i);
18.        if (res) printf(" %c", (res > 0) ? '+' : '-');
19.        else printf("  ");
20.      }
21.      printf("\n");
22.    }
23.  }
```

You select N random float numbers (lines 2 and 10) and compare each one of them (for loop starting in line 9) with another number obtained by adding to the random number the variations stored in the array d (lines 4 to 7). When you do the comparisons for each combination of random number and variation, you specify between 1 and the maximum of 23 bits of mantissa.

Listing 2-12 shows the result for the first three numbers (the choice of the pseudo-random seed is purely arbitrary).

Listing 2-12. Testing num_fltcmp() - output

```
1. 9.1507225   1 2 3 4 5 6 7 8 9 0 1 2 3 4 5 6 7 8 9 0 1 2 3
2.  -0.100000:           + + + + + + + + + + + + + + + + + +
```

```
 3.   -0.010000:                     + + + + + + + + + + + +
 4.   -0.001000:                       + + + + + + + + + + +
 5.   -0.000100:                           + + + + + + + + +
 6.   -0.000010:                                   + + + +
 7.   -0.000001:                                     + + +
 8.    0.000000:
 9.    0.000001:                                          -
10.    0.000010:                                - - - - -
11.    0.000100:                            - - - - - - -
12.    0.001000:                          - - - - - - - -
13.    0.010000:                  - - - - - - - - - - -
14.    0.100000:              - - - - - - - - - - - - -
15.
16.  7.6355686    1 2 3 4 5 6 7 8 9 0 1 2 3 4 5 6 7 8 9 0 1 2 3
17.   -0.100000:                 + + + + + + + + + + + + + + + + + +
18.   -0.010000:                   + + + + + + + + + + + + + + + +
19.   -0.001000:                     + + + + + + + + + + + + + +
20.   -0.000100:                       + + + + + + + + + + + +
21.   -0.000010:                         + + + + + + + +
22.   -0.000001:                                 + + +
23.    0.000000:
24.    0.000001:                               - -
25.    0.000010:                           - - - - -
26.    0.000100:                       - - - - - - - -
27.    0.001000:                   - - - - - - - - - -
28.    0.010000:             - - - - - - - - - - - - - -
29.    0.100000:           - - - - - - - - - - - - - - -
30.
31.  3.2907567    1 2 3 4 5 6 7 8 9 0 1 2 3 4 5 6 7 8 9 0 1 2 3
32.   -0.100000:               + + + + + + + + + + + + + + + + + + + +
33.   -0.010000:                 + + + + + + + + + + + + + + + + + +
34.   -0.001000:                     + + + + + + + + + + + + + +
35.   -0.000100:                         + + + + + + + + + +
36.   -0.000010:                           + + + + + +
37.   -0.000001:                           + + + + + +
38.    0.000000:
39.    0.000001:                             - - -
40.    0.000010:                           - - - - -
41.    0.000100:                       - - - - - - - -
42.    0.001000:                 - - - - - - - - - - -
43.    0.010000:             - - - - - - - - - - - - -
44.    0.100000:           - - - - - - - - - - - - - - - -
```

The first row of each number's result shows the number itself and provides a heading with the number of mantissa bits considered to determine equality. Each one of the following rows shows an increment applied to the random number to obtain the second one and results for all choices of number of bits. A plus-sign means that num_fltcmp() identifies the first number to be greater than the second one, while spaces indicate equality.

The results show that the behavior of the function depends on the sign of the variation. For example, when you subtract 0.000001 from the first number (line 7), the function recognizes the two numbers to be different when at least 21 bits of the mantissa are considered. But when the same quantity is added to the number (line 9), you need all 23 available bits to recognize that the numbers are different.

When you compare the results for different numbers, you see that the same variation requires different numbers of bits to be recognized. For example, and very dramatically, a variation of -0.1 applied to the third number (line 31) is already recognized with three bits of mantissa, while the same variation requires five bits with the second number and six with the first one. And notice that in none of three cases, the variation causes a borrowing, thereby causing a change in the preceding decimal digit.

Remember that one decimal place corresponds to approximately 3.3 bits (not surprising when considering that a factor of 8 is exactly three bits). Therefore, you can easily find differences of several bits due to conversion and rounding.

In the source code attached to this chapter, you will also find the function num_fltequ(). It is a simplified version of num_fltcmp() that returns 1 when it finds that the numbers are equal (within the given tolerance) and 0 when they are not. The update is simple and I will not bother you with a listing. But be aware that the issue of variability for num_fltcmp() also applies to num_fltequ().

Listing 2-13 shows the double-equivalent of num_fltcmp().

Listing 2-13. num_dblmp()

```
1. //-------------------------------------------------------------- num_dblcmp
2. int num_dblcmp(double a, double b, unsigned int n_bits) {
3.    if (n_bits > DBL_MANT_DIG - 1) n_bits = DBL_MANT_DIG - 1; //#
4.    if (a == b) return 0;                                         //-->
5.    union ieee754_double *aa = (union ieee754_double *)&a; //#
6.    union ieee754_double *bb = (union ieee754_double *)&b; //#
7.
8.    // Compare the signs.
9.    char a_sign = (char)aa->ieee.negative;
10.   char b_sign = (char)bb->ieee.negative;
11.   if (a_sign != b_sign) return b_sign - a_sign;              //-->
12.   if (a == 0) return ((b_sign) ? 1 : -1);                    //-->
13.   if (b == 0) return ((a_sign) ? -1 : 1);                    //-->
14.
15.   // Compare the exponents.
16.   int a_exp = (char)aa->ieee.exponent - 1023; //#
17.   int b_exp = (char)bb->ieee.exponent - 1023; //#
18.   if (a_exp != b_exp) {
19.     int ret = (a_exp > b_exp) ? 1 : -1;
20.     return (a_sign) ? -ret : ret;                            //-->
21.     }
22.
23.   // Compare the mantissas.
24.   unsigned long a_mant = (unsigned int)aa->ieee.mantissa1
25.                        | (unsigned long)aa->ieee.mantissa0 << 32 ·
26.                        ; //#
27.   unsigned long b_mant = (unsigned int)bb->ieee.mantissa1
28.                        | (unsigned long)bb->ieee.mantissa0 << 32
29.                        ; //#
30.   int n_shift = (int)sizeof(unsigned int) * 8 - DBL_MANT_DIG + 32 + 1; //#
31.   a_mant <<= n_shift;
32.   b_mant <<= n_shift;
33. # define MASK 0x8000000000000000 //# 2^63
34.   for (int k = 0; k < n_bits; k++) {
35.     if ((a_mant & MASK) != (b_mant & MASK)) {
36.       int ret = (a_mant & MASK) ? 1 : -1;
```

```
37.        return (a_sign) ? -ret : ret;                              //-->
38.        }
39.     a_mant <<= 1;
40.     b_mant <<= 1;
41.     }
42. # undef MASK
43.    return 0;
44.    } // num_dblcmp
```

The function is functionally identical to num_fltcomp(). But there are some differences and, to make your life easier, I have marked all the updated/new lines with the comment //#. The updates that resulted in lines 3, 5, 6, 16, 17, and 33 of Listing 2-13 are pretty clear, but lines 24 to 32 (which replace lines 24 to 26 of num_fltcomp() shown in Listing 2-10) require some explanation.

The mantissa of float is a field of 23 bits (ieee754_float.ieee.mantissa in ieee754.h). As such, it can be stored in a single variable of type unsigned int. But the mantissa of double consists of 52 bits and is defined in two separate bit fields (ieee754_double.ieee.mantissa1 and ieee754_float.ieee.mantissa0). Therefore, you need to stick the two pieces together in a variable of type unsigned long, paying attention that the 64 - 52 = 12 unused bits within the unsigned long are least significant. Only if you shift the mantissa as far as possible to the left can you test all the bits with a single mask. You could shift it to the right and use 1 as a mask for all precisions, but then, you would test the bits starting from the LSB, while you want to test them beginning with the MSB.

As ieee754_double.ieee.mantissa1 is first, it means that it is the least significant part (little endianness, remember?). Therefore, you only need to assign it to the unsigned long (lines 24 and 27). But to copy the most significant 32 bits of the mantissa (i.e., ieee754_double.ieee.mantissa0), you need to typecast it to an unsigned long and shift it to the left 32 bits before oring it into place.

This can be confusing. Perhaps a little diagram will help. mantissa1 (the field that contains the least significant 32 bits of the mantissa) is stored in memory as

```
AAAAAAAA BBBBBBBB CCCCCCCC DDDDDDDD
    ^                   ^
   LSB                 MSB
```

where AAAAAAAA indicates the least significant byte and CCCCCCCC the most significant one. When in line 24 of Listing 2-13 you copy the field mantissa1 of the first number to a_mant, a_mant becomes

```
AAAAAAAA BBBBBBBB CCCCCCCC DDDDDDDD 00000000 00000000 00000000 00000000
    ^                                                      ^
   LSB                                                    MSB
```

mantissa0 is stored in memory as

```
EEEEEEEE FFFFFFFF 0000GGGG 00000000
    ^                   ^
   LSB                 MSB
```

because only the 20 least significant bits are defined in the bit-field mantissa0. When you typecast mantissa0 to unsigned long in line 25, it becomes:

```
EEEEEEEE FFFFFFFF 0000GGGG 00000000 00000000 00000000 00000000 00000000
    ^                                                      ^
   LSB                                                    MSB
```

Then, when you shift to the left 32 bits, you shift the four lower bytes to higher memory positions (again, because the least significant bytes are stored first). That is, you drop the most significant four bytes and replace them with the first four bytes, which include the 20 most significant bits of the mantissa. The resulting unsigned long is:

```
00000000 00000000 00000000 00000000 EEEEEEEE FFFFFFFF 0000GGGG 00000000
         ^                                                ^
         LSB                                              MSB
```

When you bitwise OR the converted mantissa0 to a_mant, you obtain

```
AAAAAAAA BBBBBBBB CCCCCCCC DDDDDDDD EEEEEEEE FFFFFFFF 0000GGGG 00000000
         ^                                                ^
         LSB                                              MSB
```

To bring the MSB of the mantissa to be the MSB of a_mant, you now need to shift a_mant 12 bits left, which you do in line 30. The result is:

```
00000000 AAAA0000 BBBBAAAA CCCCBBBB DDDDCCCC EEEEDDDD FFFFEEEE GGGGFFFF
         ^                                                ^
         LSB                                              MSB
```

If the representation in memory were big endian, with the most significant bytes in the lowest memory location, a_mant would be stored like this (obtained by swapping the first byte with the last, the second with the second last, etc.):

```
GGGGFFFF FFFFEEEE EEEEDDDD DDDDCCCC CCCCBBBB BBBBAAAA AAAA0000 00000000
^                                                            ^
MSB                                                          LSB
```

With this representation, it is clear, isn't it?

The function num_ldblmp() is almost identical to num_dblmp(). You will find it in the source code attached to this chapter together with the code to test all comparing functions.

But in the line

```
if (n_bits > LDBL_MANT_DIG - 1) n_bits = LDBL_MANT_DIG - 1; //#
```

the -1 has a different reason to be there than the -1 in line 3 of num_dblmp(). In num_ldblmp() you subtract 1 because the most significant bit of the mantissa has not been dropped, while in num_dblmp() you subtract a 1 because DBL_MANT_DIG includes the sign bit (while, as already discussed, LDBL_MANT_DIG doesn't).

This difference is reflected in lines 30 to 32, which in num_ldblmp() become:

```
a_mant <<= 1;
b_mant <<= 1;
```

Concerning the functions equivalent to num_fltequ() for double and long double, I leave them up to you as an exercise.

Listings 2-14 to 2-16 show three small utility functions that you might find useful: num_to_big_endian() swaps the bytes around, num_binprt() prints a given number of bytes in binary, and num_binfmt() formats a number of bytes into a string with one character per bit.

Listing 2-14. num_to_big_endian()

```
//-------------------------------------------------------------- num_to_big_endian
void num_to_big_endian(void *in, void *out, int n_bytes) {
  unsigned char *from = in;
  unsigned char *to = out + n_bytes - 1;
  for (int k = 0; k < n_bytes; k++) *to-- = *from++;
  } // num_to_big_endian
```

Listing 2-15. num_binprt()

```
//-------------------------------------------------------------------- num_binprt
void num_binprt(void *p, int n, int space, int line) {
  unsigned char c;
  while (n > 0) {
    c = *((unsigned char *)p++);
    for (int nb = 0; nb < 8 && n > 0; nb++) {
      printf("%c", (c & 128) ? '1' : '0');
      c <<= 1;
      n--;
      }
    if (space) printf(" ");
    }
  if (line) printf("\n");
  } // num_binprt
```

Listing 2-16. num_binfmt()

```
//-------------------------------------------------------------------- num_binfmt
void num_binfmt(void *p, int n, char *s, int space) {
  unsigned char c;
  while (n > 0) {
    c = *((unsigned char *)p++);
    for (int nb = 0; nb < 8 && n > 0; nb++) {
      *s++ = (c & 128) ? '1' : '0';
      c <<= 1;
      n--;
      }
    if (space) *s++ = ' ';
    }
  *s = '\0';
  } // num_binfmt
```

You will find a description of num_binfmt() in Chapter 11, when I talk about embedded software.

Summary

In this chapter, you have familiarized yourself with some aspects of C that often cause problems. More specifically, you learned the difference between local and global variables, the implications of the call-by-value mechanism used to pass arguments to functions, why the use of Boolean variables can be misleading, how to use locales, how to work with wide characters and strings, how to floating-point numbers are stored in memory, and how to deal with them.

CHAPTER 3

Iteration, Recursion, and Binary Trees

Iteration and recursion are strategies to solve complex problems by repeatedly performing simpler operations. But while iteration involves repeating the same operation in a loop, recursion means partially solving increasingly simpler cases of the problem until you reach base cases for which you already have a solution.

In this chapter you will first learn the difference between iteration, which means repeating the same sequence of steps, and recursion, in which each steps contains further instances of themselves like Matryoshka dolls. This will give you the tools to understand binary trees, from their generation to their display.

Iteration

In practical terms, iteration means repeating a piece of code in a loop. C supports iterations in three formats: for loops, while loops, and do-while loops.

fors and whiles are functionally identical. For example, you can replace

```
for (int k = 0; k < 42; k++) {
  ...
  }
```

with

```
{
  int k = 0;
  while (k < 42) {
    ...
    k++;
    }
  }
```

where the braces that surround the while loop have the sole purpose of limiting the scope of the control variable k. In general, you can always convert a for into a while and vice versa as follows:

```
for (definition; condition; change) {
  ...
  }
```

is equivalent to

© Giulio Zambon 2016
G. Zambon, *Practical C*, DOI 10.1007/978-1-4842-1769-6_3

```
{
  definition;
  while (condition) {
    ...
    change;
    }
}
```

The difference between for/while to do-while is that with do-while the condition is checked at the end of the loop instead of at the beginning. As a result, with do-whiles, you always execute the code inside the loop at least once.

Obviously, you can always replace a do-while with a while. All you need to do is bypass the while condition for the first iteration and perhaps adjust the value of the control variable. In some cases, the conversion is immediate or trivial. For example, you can replace the following do-while:

```
char *string = NULL;
do {
  ...
  string = a_function(parameters);
  ...
  } while (string);
```

with:

```
int k1 = 1;
char *string = NULL;
while (string || k1) {
  k1 = 0;
  ...
  string = a_function(parameters);
  ...
  }
```

The condition k1 ensures that the first iteration is executed. Note that by placing the k1 condition after the existing one, you ensure that it is only checked twice: when the while loop is entered and when it is exited. If you had placed it before the string condition, it would have been checked at the beginning of each iteration.

In any case, when you encounter a problem that "naturally" lends itself to be solved with a do-while loop, you should use it.

As you can always convert one type of loop into another, the choice is more a matter of taste than anything else. That said, it makes sense to use a for loop when you need a control variable as a counter or as an array index. Some programmers use one type of loop for everything, to the point of writing inelegant code. For example, why would you write for (;;) to implement an endless loop instead of using while (1)?

Recursion

In practice, you use recursion when you define functions that invoke themselves within their own definitions.

A Simple Example

If you search the Web, you will find that everybody who writes about recursion starts by showing the calculation of factorials as an example, and who am I to change such an established practice? Listing 3-1 shows a small function to calculate a factorial recursively, while Listing 3-2 shows the equivalent function based on an iteration.

Listing 3-1. fact_r()

```
unsigned long fact_r(int n) {
  unsigned long fact = 1;
  if (n > 1) fact = fact_r(n - 1) * n;
  return fact;
  }
```

The statement

```
fact = fact_r(n - 1) * n;
```

is where fact_r() invokes itself recursively.

Listing 3-2. fact_i()

```
unsigned long fact_r(int n) {
  unsigned long fact = 1;
  while (n >= 2) fact *= n--;
  return fact;
  }
```

The only difference between the two functions is that in fact_i() you replace the recursive call of fact_r() with the loop

```
while (n >= 2) fact *= n--;
```

Calculating a factorial is a very simple problem that can be easily solved with a loop. Therefore, it doesn't make much sense to implement a recursive function. But every recursion step requires the overhead of executing a function call, and I was curious to see how much slower fact_r() would be of fact_i(). To compare the execution times, I wrote the small program, shown in Listing 3-3.

Listing 3-3. factorial.c

```
#include <stdlib.h>
#include <stdio.h>
#include <time.h>

unsigned long fact_r(int n) {
  unsigned long fact = 1;
  if (n > 1) fact = fact_r(n - 1) * n;
  return fact;
  }
```

```
unsigned long fact_i(int n) {
  unsigned long fact = 1;
  while (n >= 2) fact *= n--;
  return fact;
  }

double how_long(int n, int n_meas, unsigned long (*f)(int)) {
  unsigned long fact;
  unsigned long t = (unsigned long)clock();
  for (int k = 0; k < n_meas; k++) fact = (*f)(n);
  t = (unsigned int)clock() - t;
  double td = (double)t / n_meas;
  printf("%s: %lu\n", (f == &fact_r) ? "Recursion" : "Iteration", fact);
  return td;
  }

//---------------------------------------------------------------------- main
int main(void) {
  double t_r = how_long(20, 10000000, &fact_r);
  double t_i = how_long(20, 10000000, &fact_i);
  printf("r=%f i=%f r/i=%f\n", t_r, t_i, t_r / t_i);
  return EXIT_SUCCESS;
  }
```

It prints out on the console small reports like the following one:

```
Recursion: 2432902008176640000
```

```
Iteration: 2432902008176640000
```

```
r=0.097437 i=0.047077 r/i=2.069734
```

where the times are measured in microseconds. To be precise, the times are measured in *ticks*, and there are CLOCKS_PER_SEC ticks in a second. If you look at the standard header file time.h, you will find that it includes another file, bits/time.h, where CLOCKS_PER_SEC is defined to be one million. Therefore, one tick is one microsecond.

The program in Listing 3-3 shows that using recursion to calculate a factorial takes more than twice the time you need if you use an iteration. In case you are curious, I calculated 20! because ULONG_MAX (defined in the standard header limits.h) is 18,446,744,073,709,551,615, which is only about 7.6 times the factorial of 20. I would have not been able to calculate factorials of numbers greater than 20 with those simple functions.

Incidentally, if you need to deal with very large numbers, instead of reinventing the wheel, you should use the GNU Multiple Precision Arithmetic Library, which you can find at gmplib.org.

Binary Trees

A binary tree is a tree data structure in which each node has at most two children. Listing 3-4 shows a representation of a 25-node binary tree in which most nodes have two children.

Listing 3-4. A 25-Node Binary Tree Over Six Levels

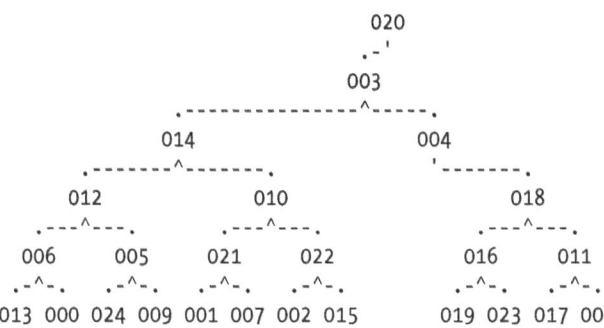

Listing 3-5 shows an example of a more sparse binary tree in which the 25 nodes extend over nine levels.

Listing 3-5. A 25-Node Binary Tree Over Nine Levels

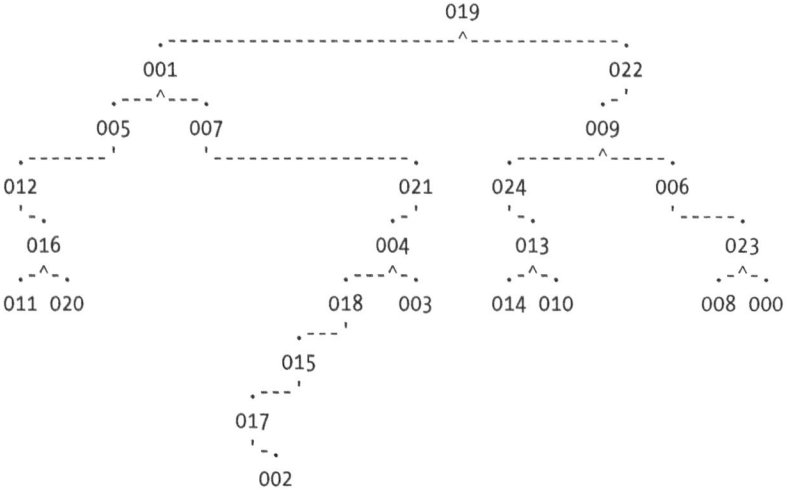

Note that the node identifiers of single children are never immediately below their parents. You do this to preserve the information of whether you are looking at a *left* or at a *right* child. As each node has its own identifier, you might think as irrelevant to identify on which side of its parent a child is located. In many cases, you would be right. But this is not the case when the ordering of the nodes is significant. Then, following the direction in which European languages are written, you consider the left child to come first and the right child to come last. It will become clear when we will talk about traversing trees and ordered trees.

I decided to introduce binary trees in this chapter because they are useful to illustrate recursion. But binary trees are much more useful than just examples to illustrate a technique, as you can use binary trees to model any problem that involves series of yes/no decisions. Perhaps the most obvious application of binary trees is in searches, in which each node corresponds to an item and you can find any particular item by navigating down the search tree. Chapter 8 dedicates a section to this subject.

In fact, the range of applications that rely on binary trees is too large to go through here. For example, almost every 3D video game uses *binary space partition* trees to identify the objects it needs to render. And compilers use *syntax* trees to parse statements.

The bottom line is that, sooner or later, you will find it useful to be familiar with binary trees. And I think it is impossible to fully grasp them without *seeing* them represented in graphical form. That's why, as soon as I thought of introducing binary trees, I knew I needed to be able to represent them on a page. I then decided pretty quickly that my best option was to use "ASCII art" to represent the trees because dealing with graphics packages is extremely time consuming (if you want to have nice images, that is). What I didn't realize was that presenting trees graphically was not trivial. It took me more days than I cared to count. And then, once I had done it, I couldn't have possibly given you the code without explaining it. This resulted in a very large section dedicated to displaying binary trees, which is only marginally relevant to the subject of this chapter. If you want to skip it, please feel free to do so, but I had fun writing the code and you would probably find it interesting to go through it at least once.

You can define a node in a minimalist way as follows:

```
typedef struct btr_node btr_node;
struct btr_node {
  int id;
  int value;
  btr_node *child[2];
};
```

As you can see, it only includes an integer to identify the node (i.e., a *key*), an integer value, and an array that points to the two children. You will find this definition in the file btree.h, which is the header file of btree.c, where all the functions dealing with binary trees are kept.

The simplest way of keeping a tree is as an array of nodes. For example, you could store the tree shown in Listing 3-4 in the following array:

```
btr_node nodes[25] = {0};
```

The tree of Listing 3-4 was built by linking the nodes to one another, as shown in Listing 3-6.

Listing 3-6. List of Nodes for a 25-Node Tree

#	id	val	idL	idR	Address	Left	Right
0:	0	1	-1	-1	0x1459010:	(nil)	(nil)
1:	1	1	-1	-1	0x1459028:	(nil)	(nil)
2:	2	1	-1	-1	0x1459040:	(nil)	(nil)
3:	3	5	14	4	0x1459058:	0x1459160	0x1459070
4:	4	4	-1	18	0x1459070:	(nil)	0x14591c0
5:	5	2	24	9	0x1459088:	0x1459250	0x14590e8
6:	6	2	13	0	0x14590a0:	0x1459148	0x1459010
7:	7	1	-1	-1	0x14590b8:	(nil)	(nil)
8:	8	1	-1	-1	0x14590d0:	(nil)	(nil)
9:	9	1	-1	-1	0x14590e8:	(nil)	(nil)
10:	10	3	21	22	0x1459100:	0x1459208	0x1459220
11:	11	2	17	8	0x1459118:	0x14591a8	0x14590d0
12:	12	3	6	5	0x1459130:	0x14590a0	0x1459088
13:	13	1	-1	-1	0x1459148:	(nil)	(nil)
14:	14	4	12	10	0x1459160:	0x1459130	0x1459100
15:	15	1	-1	-1	0x1459178:	(nil)	(nil)
16:	16	2	19	23	0x1459190:	0x14591d8	0x1459238
17:	17	1	-1	-1	0x14591a8:	(nil)	(nil)
18:	18	3	16	11	0x14591c0:	0x1459190	0x1459118

```
19:  19   1  -1  -1   0x14591d8:         (nil)         (nil)
20:  20   6   3  -1   0x14591f0:   0x1459058         (nil)
21:  21   2   1   7   0x1459208:   0x1459028   0x14590b8
22:  22   2   2  15   0x1459220:   0x1459040   0x1459178
23:  23   1  -1  -1   0x1459238:         (nil)         (nil)
24:  24   1  -1  -1   0x1459250:         (nil)         (nil)
```

The columns id, idL, and idR identify each node and its left and right children, while the columns Address, Left, and Right show the corresponding addresses in memory. The column number shows the position of the node within the array where the nodes are stored. id and # are identical because the nodes were initialized that way. As you can easily verify, node 20, being the root of the tree, is the only one that never appears in either L or R. Note that missing children have a null address and are indicated with an id of -1.

To produce a node list like the one in Listing 3-6, you can use the function btr_list_nodes(), shown in Listing 3-7.

Listing 3-7. btr_list_nodes()

```
//----------------------------------------------------------- btr_list_nodes
void btr_list_nodes(int with_addresses) {
  printf("  #   id val idL idR     Address         Left       Right\n");
  for (int k = 0; k < n_nodes; k++) {
    btr_node *node = &nodes[k];
    printf("%3d:%4d%4d%4d%4d", k, node->id, node->value,
        (node->child[0]) ? node->child[0]->id : -1,
        (node->child[1]) ? node->child[1]->id : -1
        );
    if (with_addresses) {
      printf("%12p:%12p%12p", node, node->child[0], node->child[1]);
      }
    puts("");
    }
  } // btr_list_nodes
```

Pretty straightforward. If you need to obtain the position within the array of nodes of a node of which you know the address, you can use the simple function btr_get_node_index(), shown in Listing 3-8. Listing 3-9 shows the opposite function, which gives you the address of a node in a given position within the array of nodes.

Listing 3-8. btr_get_node_index()

```
//--------------------------------------------------------- btr_get_node_index
int btr_get_node_index(btr_node *node) {
  int k_node = 0;
  while (&nodes[k_node] != node) k_node++;
  return k_node;
  } // btr_get_node_index
```

Listing 3-9. btr_get_node_address()

```
//------------------------------------------------------------ btr_get_node_address
btr_node *btr_get_node_address(int k_node) {
  return &nodes[k_node];
  } // btr_get_node_address
```

Trivial functions like btr_get_node_address() are necessary because the array nodes is statically defined in btree.c, and therefore invisible to the rest of the program. It makes sense to keep nodes private, so that, if you wanted, you could ensure that you access it correctly. For example, you could modify btr_get_node_address() as follows:

```
btr_node *btr_get_node_address(int k_node) {
#if BTR_DEBUGGING
  if (k_nodes < 0 || k_nodes >= n_nodes) {
    fprintf(stderr,
        "btr_get_node_address: index %d < 0 or >= %d\n", k_node, n_nodes);
    fflush(stderr);
    abort();                                                  // -->
    }
#endif
  return &nodes[k_node];
  } // btr_get_node_address
```

By setting the flag BTR_DEBUG to 1 in btree.h, you could switch on the checking of k_node while testing your code. Later, you could set BTR_DEBUG to 0 to avoid the overhead.

Similarly, you could decide to use functions like btr_get_node_value() and btr_set_node_value(), shown in Listings 3-10 and 3-11, or similar functions to get/set the id and the children addresses.

Listing 3-10. btr_get_node_value()

```
//------------------------------------------------------------ btr_get_node_value
int btr_get_node_value(int k_node) {
  return nodes[k_node].value;
  } // btr_get_node_value
```

Listing 3-11. btr_set_node_value()

```
//------------------------------------------------------------ btr_set_node_value
void btr_set_node_value(int k_node, int value) {
  nodes[k_node].value = value;
  } // btr_set_node_value
```

Before looking at how to display trees as shown in Listings 3-4 and 3-5, you need to look at Listings 3-12 and 3-13, which show how you calculate the depth of a tree (i.e., its number of levels). Listing 3-12 shows an iterative calculation and Listing 3-13 a recursive one.

Listing 3-12. btr_calc_tree_max_depth_i()

```
1.  //-------------------------------------------------- btr_calc_tree_max_depth_i
2.  int btr_calc_tree_max_depth_i(btr_node *root) {
3.    for (int k = 0; k < n_nodes; k++) nodes[k].value = 0;
4.    int n_mod = 0;
5.    do {
6.      n_mod = 0;
7.      for (int k = 0; k < n_nodes; k++) {
8.        btr_node  *node = &nodes[k];
9.        int val_max = 0;
10.       for (int j = 0; j < 2; j++) {
11.         btr_node *child = node->child[j];
12.         if (child != NULL && child->value > val_max) val_max = child->value;
13.       }
14.       if (node->value < val_max + 1) {
15.         node->value = val_max + 1;
16.         n_mod++;
17.       }
18.     }
19.   } while (n_mod > 0);
20.
21.   return root->value - 1;
22. } // btr_calc_tree_max_depth_i
```

It works if the values of all nodes are initially zero. The for loop between line 7 and line 18 goes through all nodes in sequence, as they appear in the array nodes. It then assigns to the current node the highest value found among its children incremented by 1. After that, it repeats the whole operation with the do loop as long as at least one node value is modified.

To see how it works, consider for example the following four-node tree:

```
001
 '-.
  003
.-^-.
002 000
```

Node 0 has no children. Therefore, the for loop in lines 10 to 13 has no effect, val_max remains set to 0, and, in line 15, the value of node 0 is set to 1.

The next node checked within the for loop in lines 7 to 18 is node 1. It has a right child (node 3), but the value of node 3 is 0, because it has not been modified (yet). Therefore, again, val_max remains 0 and the value of node 1 is set to 1.

Node 2 has no children. Therefore, once more, its value is set to 1.

But when the code processes node 3, it finds that it has two children (2 and 0) and both have a value of 1. As the for loop in lines 10 to 13 picks the maximum value of the children, val_max is set to 1. As a result, line 14 sets the value of node 3 to 2.

Line 16 increments n_mod only when the value of the current node is updated. As during the first iteration of the do loop, all four nodes have had their value set (0, 1, and 2 to 1, and 3 to 2), n_mod reaches the value of 4, and the do loop makes a second iteration.

During the second iteration, the values of nodes 0, 2, and 3 remain unchanged, but the value of 1 is changed from 1 to 3, because this time the value of its only child (node 3) is 2. So, n_mod is incremented to 1 and the do loop goes through a third iteration.

This time around, though, nothing changes. n_mod remains set to 0, and the while condition fails, causing the do loop to exit.

The function returns a max_depth of 2, which is correct if the root has a level (i.e., a depth) of 0. For trees of any depth, eventually, the value assigned to the root node will count the number of nodes along the longest branch.

Note that you cannot use this function if you need to preserve the node values. This side effect is only acceptable because the value field of btr_node is only there as a workarea. Also, it uses the array nodes, which is not necessarily available in a real-life case.

And now let's look at how you can calculate the depth of a tree recursively, without modifying the value of nodes and without relying on the array of nodes.

Listing 3-13. btr_calc_tree_max_depth_r()

```
//----------------------------------------------------- btr_calc_tree_max_depth_r
int btr_calc_tree_max_depth_r(btr_node *root) {
  return calc_depth_r(root, 0);
  } // btr_calc_tree_max_depth_r
```

All the function btr_calc_tree_max_depth_r() does is call the local function calc_depth_r(), which is the recursive function where the whole work is done (see Listing 3-14).

Listing 3-14. calc_depth_r()

```
1. //----------------------------------------------------------------- calc_depth_r
2. int calc_depth_r(btr_node *node, int level) {
3.    int depth[2] = {0};
4.    for (int k = 0; k < 2; k++) {
5.       btr_node *child = node->child[k];
6.       depth[k] = (child) ? calc_depth_r(child, level + 1) : level;
7.       }
8.    return (depth[0] >= depth[1]) ? depth[0] : depth[1];
9.    } // calc_depth_r
```

Only 8 lines instead of 20. The recursive implementation is much more elegant. In line 6, the function executes itself using a child as the root of a subtree. In this way, it keeps traveling deeper and deeper within the tree as long as it finds children. When it doesn't, it returns the current depth. When a child exists, it returns the depth returned by the child and, when both children exist, it returns the depth returned by the child that sits on top of the deepest subtree.

Recursive solutions often appear more "natural" and are easier to understand. But they tend to be slower and use more memory, as each recursion includes the overhead of a function call and the instantiation on the stack of an additional set of local variables.

What is essential in recursive algorithms is that you identify a clear termination condition. Failure to do so will result in deeper and deeper recursive calls until the program crashes for lack of stack space. In the case of calc_depth_r(), the termination condition is the absence of children. Eventually, regardless of how deep the tree is, you know that the recursion will end once it will reach the leaves of the tree (i.e., the nodes without children).

Displaying a Tree Graphically

In a graphic representation of a tree, you need to resolve two general issues: where to position each node and how to connect the nodes with one another. Consider again the four-node tree you have already seen:

```
001
 '-.
   003
 .-^-.
002 000
```

By using leading zeros, you ensure that any node identifier occupies the same number of characters, thereby making it easier to position them on the page. Now look at the same tree with two axes of coordinates:

```
  column: 0    5    10
          +----+----+--->
level 0 + 001
        |   '-.
level 1 +    003
        |   .-^-.
level 2 + 002 000
        |
        V
```

The X-axis is the column position of the node identifiers, while the Y-axis is the depth level. For example, node 0 has coordinates (4,2) and node 1 has coordinates (2,1). Listing 3-15 shows a full tree of max_depth 4 (i.e., with 2(4+1) - 1 = 31 nodes).

Listing 3-15. A Full Binary Tree of max_depth 4

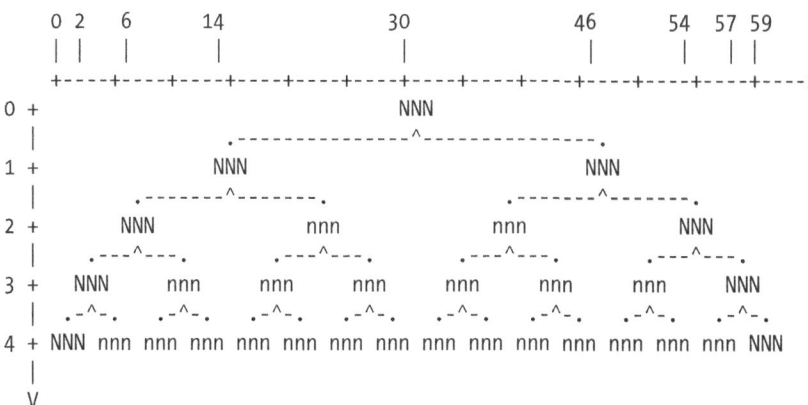

The column positions shown above the tree are those of the nodes marked with capital Ns. To ensure that the node identifiers of the deepest level have one space between them, the children of the root node are 16 characters on the left and 16 on the right of their parent. In general, you can calculate the distance of each root's child from the root node as 2max_depth. For a generic level of a parent (where the root node is the particular case for level = 0), each child is 2(max_depth - level) columns away. For example, with max_depth 4 as in the example of Listing 3-15, the nodes of the deepest level are 2(4 - 3) = 2 columns on the left and on the right of their parent.

These considerations let you outline the algorithm to represent a tree graphically:

- Calculate the coordinates of each node on the page and store them in the node structure. For example, by calculating the value field as value = column * 100 + level.

- Allocate arrays of characters to represent the levels and use sprintf() to write in them the node identifiers in their calculated positions.

- Use a similar mechanism to store the connections from parent nodes to their children.

- Print out the levels one by one.

But this cannot be the full algorithm. You will need to optimize the tree in some way because most trees you will work with will not be full. If you are not convinced, look at Listing 3-16, which shows the tree of Listing 3-15 after removing several nodes.

Listing 3-16. A Partial Binary Tree of max_depth 4

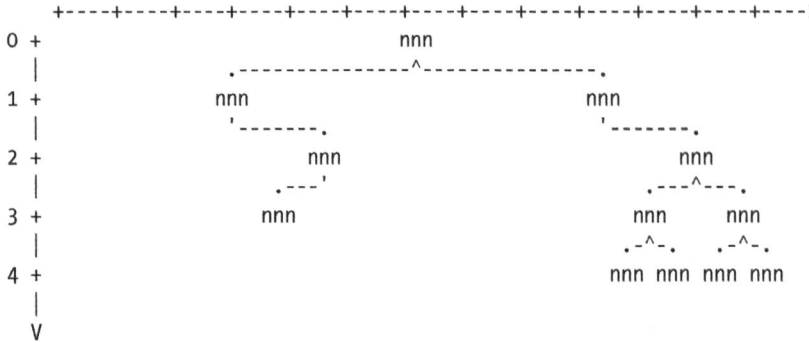

You certainly want to remove at least some of the unnecessary space, as shown in Listing 3-17.

Listing 3-17. An Optimized Representation of a Binary Tree

```
0 +         nnn
  |   .------^---.
1 + nnn       nnn
  |   '-.       '-------.
2 +   nnn           nnn
  |   .-'       .---^---.
3 + nnn       nnn     nnn
  |           .-^-.   .-^-.
4 +         nnn nnn nnn nnn
  |
  V
```

Such an optimization becomes absolutely necessary when you deal with larger trees. Consider, for example, that for a tree that has a max_depth of 20, the distance between the root node and one of its children is 220 = 1,048,576 columns!

But let's take one step at a time.

Initializing the Tree Display

To display a tree, you need first of all to determine how much space it will occupy when displayed. That is, its maximum depth, which tells you how many lines you will need to print, and its maximum width, which tells you how many characters will be in each line. With that information, you can then allocate and initialize the characters arrays in which you will compose the tree for printing.

Listing 3-18 shows the first part of the function btr_list_tree().

Listing 3-18. btr_list_tree(), Part 1, Initialization

```
1.  //------------------------------------------------------------- btr_list_tree
2.  void btr_list_tree(btr_node *root) {
3.  #define DEPTH_LIMIT 20
4.
5.    // Calculate the maximum depth of the tree
6.    max_depth = btr_calc_tree_max_depth_i(root);
7.    if (max_depth > DEPTH_LIMIT) {
8.      fprintf(stderr,
9.          "btr_list_tree: max_depth=%d exceeds the limit of %d\n",
10.         max_depth, DEPTH_LIMIT);
11.     fflush(stderr);
12.     abort();                                                    // -->
13.     }
14.
15.   // Set the value of each node to the node's coordinates expressed as
16.   // column * 100 + depth.
17.   int min_col = set_node_coords(root, 1 << (max_depth + 1), 0);
18.
19.   // Calculate the maximum number of characters needed to display the
20.   // the bottom level of the tree: 1 << max_depth nodes and
21.   // 3 digits + 1 space for each node.
22.   int bottom_w = 1 << (max_depth + 2);
23.
24.   // Allocate the strings to compose the tree for printing.
25.   int len = bottom_w - min_col + 1;
26.   char (*lines)[len + 1] = malloc((len + 1) * 2 * (max_depth + 1));
27.   if (lines == NULL) {
28.     fprintf(stderr,
29.         "btr_list_tree: failed to allocate %d characters\n",
30.         (len + 1) * 2 * (max_depth + 1));
31.     fflush(stderr);
32.     abort();                                                    // -->
33.     }
34.   for (int level = 0; level <= max_depth; level++) {
35.     char *line = lines[level * 2];
36.     char *sep = lines[level * 2 + 1];
37.     for (int i = 0; i < len; i++) line[i] = sep[i] = ' ';
38.     line[len] = sep[len] = '\0';
39.     }
40.
```

I set the maximum depth of a tree to 20 because I discovered that the program is sometimes unable to cope with larger trees. Your computer might be able to cope with larger trees than the laptop I'm using. In any case, you can always break down a large tree into smaller subtrees and print them separately. You would only need to identify the appropriate nodes and invoke btr_list_tree() with them instead of with the actual root node.

To calculate and save the coordinates of each node, in line 17, you invoke the recursive function set_node_coords(). You will find a description of set_node_coords() after Listing 3-19. For now, you only need to know that it accepts as arguments the address of a btr_node structure, the column where the node identifier is to be printed, and the level (i.e., depth) of the node. The column to write the number of the root node is calculated as 1 << (max_depth + 1). For example, the position of the root node in the full tree of Listing 3-15, with max_depth 4, was 30. The position that btr_list_tree() passes to set_node_coords() is 1 << 5 = 31, but the difference is irrelevant. It would be a problem if the position were shifted to the left rather than to the right because it would push the leftmost leaf at level max_depth to a negative column.

Note that, as for btr_calc_tree_max_depth_i(), you are free to use the value field of btr_node to store the node coordinates only because the value field was introduced precisely for the purpose of saving temporary information. Without this possibility, you would have to temporarily allocate an array to save the coordinates.

set_node_coords() returns the minimum non-blank column. For example, it would return 14 for the tree of Listing 3-16.

Line 22 of Listing 3-18 calculates the maximum number of characters that you need in order to display the bottom (i.e., deepest) level of the tree. Actually, it adds to it one character because to display x node identifiers in a line of text, you only need $x - 1$ spaces between them. But I like to keep a tiny little bit of safety margin!

Line 26 allocates space to display the whole tree. As the leftmost character used is in column min_col, the number of characters needed are bottom_w - min_col + 1. Don't get confused and think that the +1 in line 22 is for the terminating '\0'. That is taken care of in line 26. Note that in line 26 you allocate two lines of text per level, one for the node identifiers and one for the links between nodes. Also note that the number of levels is max_depth+1 because the root level is 0, rather than 1. To be precise, you don't need 2*(max_depth+1)-1 lines to represent the tree. One less would do because the bottom level only contains leaves, which don't have children. Therefore, the line of links below the bottom level of nodes is always going to be blank. But, as you will see, you will put to a good use the spare row when optimizing the tree.

The for loop with the control variable that begins in line 34 clears all the lines of text and adds to the line terminations.

As promised, before proceeding with further parts of btr_list_tree(), let's now look at set_node_coords() (see Listing 3-19).

Listing 3-19. set_node_coords()

```
1.  //------------------------------------------------------------- set_node_coords
2.  int set_node_coords(btr_node *node, int offs, int depth) {
3.    static int min_col = INT_MAX;
4.    if (offs < min_col) min_col = offs;
5.
6.    // The offset of a child with respect to the parent is given by
7.    // (1 << (max_depth - depth)), negative for child[0] and positive for
8.    // child[1] (where depth is the depth of the parent).
9.    node->value = offs * 100 + depth;
10.   int delta = 1 << (max_depth - depth);
11.   int child_offs[2];
12.   child_offs[0] = offs - delta;
13.   child_offs[1] = offs + delta;
```

```
14.   for (int k = 0; k < 2; k++) {
15.     btr_node *child = node->child[k];
16.     if (child != NULL) set_node_coords(child, child_offs[k], depth + 1);
17.   }
18.   return min_col;
19.   } // set_node_coords
```

Lines 3 and 4 is where you calculate the leftmost column you need in order to display the tree. Notice that min_col is static. Therefore, it keeps its value in subsequent executions. As set_node_coords() calls itself recursively from parent to child node (in line 16), line 4 checks all nodes in the tree. Once set_node_coords() reaches a leaf, it returns the current value of min_col and keeps doing so until it returns to line 16 of btr_list_tree() (Listing 3-18).

Notice how the column of each child is calculated in lines 12 and 13 as the column of the parent +/- the distance from it.

Composing the Tree

This is where you format the tree display by filling in the character arrays you have allocated and initialized. It is only going to be a first cut because most trees will include empty space that you will need to remove.

Back to analyzing btr_list_tree(), Listing 3-20 shows its second part, in which you write the tree into the allocated lines of text.

Listing 3-20. btr_list_tree(), Part 2, Compose the Tree

```
41.   // Compose the tree.
42.   for (int k = 0; k < n_nodes; k++) {
43.     btr_node *node = &nodes[k];
44.     int level = node->value % 100;
45.     char *line = lines[level * 2];
46.     char *sep = lines[level * 2 + 1];
47.
48.     // First print the node identifier.
49.     char num[4] = "";
50.     sprintf(num, "%03d", node->id);
51.     int col = node->value / 100 - min_col;
52.     char *where = line + col;
53.     for (int i = 0; i < 3; i++) where[i] = num[i];
54.
55.     // Then, if appropriate, print the separation line below it.
56.     col++;
57.     where = sep + col;
58.     if (node->child[0] && node->child[1]) *where = '^';
59.     else if (node->child[0] || node->child[1]) *where = '\'';
60.     //
61.     int n_dash = (1 << (max_depth - level)) - 1;
62.     if (node->child[0]) {
63.       where = sep + col - n_dash;
64.       for (int i = 0; i < n_dash; i++) *where++ = '-';
65.       where = sep + col - n_dash - 1;
66.       *where = '.';
67.     }
```

```
68.     if (node->child[1]) {
69.       where = sep + col + 1;
70.       for (int i = 0; i < n_dash; i++) *where++ = '-';
71.       where = sep + col + n_dash + 1;
72.       *where = '.';
73.       }
74.     } // for (int k..
75.
76.    // "Hide" the trailing spaces.
77.    for (int level = 0; level <= max_depth * 2; level++) {
78.      int i = len - 1;
79.      while (lines[level][i] == ' ') lines[level][i--] = '\0';
80.      }
81.
```

The big for loop with control variable k that begins in line 42 goes through all the nodes, assigns for convenience the node address to the variable node, and extracts from the node value the level of the node. It then defines in lines 45 and 46 the variables line and sep to point to two allocated lines of text, one for the node identifiers and one for the node links below the node identifiers.

You use the array of characters num defined in line 49 to hold the node identifier. Note that you need four characters because sprintf() also writes a terminating null.

Instead of using num to store the node identifier and then copy the number to its appropriate place within line, you might have liked to write the number directly into line and overwrite with a space the '\0' appended to the umber by sprintf(). If you had done so, the current lines 49 to 53 would have been replaced by something like this:

```
int col = node->value / 100 - min_col;
char *where = line + col;
sprintf(where, "%03d", k);
*(where + 3) = ' ';
```

But you would have created a problem: the rightmost node identifier is at the end of a line. This means that, after writing that node identifier, you would have replaced the line-terminating null with a space. Now, you could have checked for the presence of a null before writing the number with sprintf(), so as to avoid overwriting it with a space, but the use of num seems a cleaner solution.

The incrementing of col in line 56 is necessary because col is where you copied the leftmost digit of the three-digit node identifier. As the children of a node are spaced symmetrically on the two sides of it, it makes sense to start from the central digit of the node identifier when linking a node to its children.

In line 57, you set where to point to the character of the separation line immediately below the central digit of the node identifier. Then, in lines 58 and 59 you write the appropriate character for two or single children.

All you are left to do is write the dots above the middle digit of each child and connect them with dashes to the characters below the parent.

To calculate the distance of the children from the parent, you can use the formula 2(max_depth - level) that you first encountered in the comments about Listing 3-15. This is what line 61 of Listing 3-20 does. The -1 takes into account the presence of the dot above the children, which reduces the number of dashes by one.

The loop in lines 77 to 80 scans each line beginning from its end and replaces all spaces with nulls, so that the trailing spaces are not printed.

At this point, the allocated lines contain the tree, but not optimized in any way. It makes sense to improve the look of the tree, especially because without improvements, large trees would be practically unprintable.

Removing the Loops

The first step to optimize the tree display is to remove what I call loops. Look for example at the partial tree shown in Listing 3-21.

Listing 3-21. A Partial Tree with Loops

Node 009 can be moved 12 columns to the left and node 012 can be moved 6 columns to the right. Such movements are certainly possible when a right child only has a single child on its left (nodes 009 and 010) or a left child only has a single child on its right (nodes 012 and 000). More complicated cases involving more than one level exist, but one has to set a limit to what is worth doing.

It is best to remove loops from the root down because the higher the node, the longer the branches. Listing 3-22 shows the part of btr_list_tree() that implements this function.

Listing 3-22. btr_list_tree(), Part 3, Remove the Loops

```
82.    //******* Optimize the output by removing empty space.
83.    //------- Removing "loops".
84.    for (int level = 0; level < max_depth - 1; level++) {
85.      for (int k = 0; k < n_nodes; k++) {
86.        btr_node *parent = &nodes[k];
87.        if (parent->value % 100 == level) {
88.          for (int k_dir = 0; k_dir < 2; k_dir ++) {
89.            btr_node *node = parent->child[k_dir];
90.            if (node) {
91.              btr_node *child = node->child[1 - k_dir];
92.              if (child && !node->child[k_dir]) {
93.                int incr = - k_dir * 2 + 1; // 'incr' calculated for the node
94.                int new_col = parent->value / 100 - min_col - incr * 2;
95.                int new_col_c = child->value / 100 - min_col - incr * 2;
96.                if (new_col_c * incr < new_col * incr) new_col = new_col_c;
97.                char *line_u = lines[level * 2 + 1];
98.                char *line = lines[level * 2 + 2];
99.                char *line_d = lines[level * 2 + 3];
100.               int col = node->value / 100 - min_col;
101.               if (col != new_col) {
102.                 char num[3];
103.                 for (int i = 0; i < 3; i++) {
104.                   num[i] = line[col + i];
105.                   line[col + i] = ' ';
106.                 }
107.
```

```
108.                    if (incr > 0) { // moving to the right
109.                        int i = col + 1;
110.                        while (i < new_col) {
111.                            line_u[i] = ' ';
112.                            line[i] = ' ';
113.                            line_d[i++] = ' ';
114.                        }
115.                        line[i] = num[0];
116.                        line_u[i] = ' ';
117.                        line_d[i] = ' ';
118.                        line[++i] = num[1];
119.                        line_u[i] = '.';
120.                        line_d[i] = '\'';
121.                        line[++i] = num[2];
122.                    }
123.                    else { // moving to the left
124.                        int i = new_col;
125.                        line[i] = num[0];
126.                        line[++i] = num[1];
127.                        line_u[i] = '.';
128.                        line_d[i] = '\'';
129.                        line[++i] = num[2];
130.                        if (line[col + 3] == '\0') {
131.                            line_u[i] = '\0';
132.                            line_d[i++] = '\0';
133.                            line[i] = '\0';
134.                        }
135.                        else {
136.                            while (i <= col + 1) {
137.                                line_u[i] = ' ';
138.                                line_d[i++] = ' ';
139.                            }
140.                        }
141.                    }
142.
143.                    node->value = (new_col + min_col) * 100 + level + 1;
144.                    } // if (col..
145.                    } // if (child..
146.                } // if (node..
147.                } // for (k_dir..
148.
149.            } // if (parent->value..
150.        } // for (int k..
151.    } // for (int level..
152.
```

For each level beginning from the root (for loop in lines 84 to 151 with control variable level), you go through all nodes (for loop in lines 85 to 150 with control variable k) and only process those that belong to the current level (if in lines 87 to 149). The selected node is the parent of the node that you will try to move.

The purpose of the for loop in lines 88 to 147 is to let you check both children of the selected parent. The loop control variable k_dir determines whether you are checking the left or the right child.

After executing line 89, parent contains the address of the kth node and node contains the address of parent's child in the k_dir direction. Further, you know that parent is at level level and that node is not null.

In line 91, you determine the address of the node's child that, from the point of view of node, is in the direction of parent. This is because you select the child of node in direction 1 - k_dir. Therefore, when node is the left child of parent (with k_dir 0), child is the right child of node (with position 1). And when node is the right child of parent (with k_dir 1), child is the left child of node (with position 0).

With the if statement in line 92, you ensure that the child selected in line 91 is node's only child. This is necessary because you cannot move node if, besides the child in direction parent, it also has a child in the opposite direction.

In line 93 you set the variable incr to -1 when you need to move node to the left and +1 when you need to move it to the right. As a result, line 94 calculates the new position of node as the position of parent +/- 2 when node is on the right/left of parent. Lines 95 and 96 ensure that, by moving node as close as possible to parent, you don't move it across child. For example, the 0 of parent 018 in Listing 3-21 is in column 14. Therefore, the value of new_col for node 012 calculated in line 94 is 12. But if you were to move node 012 to column 12, you would have the following result (shown before adjusting the connections between nodes):

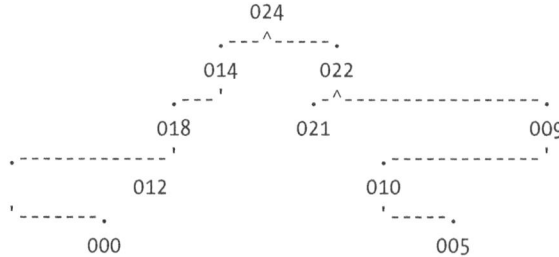

In line 95, you calculate the value of new_col_c to be 6, which is less than the 12. As a result, in line 96, you set new_col to 6. Note that by multiplying new_col_c and new_col by incr before comparing them, you ensure that the comparison is valid for both directions.

Lines 97 to 99 identify the line of text containing node (line) and those immediately above (line_u) and below (line_d), which contain the connections, respectively, to parent and child.

After calculating in line 100 the current position of node, you have all the information you need in order to move it. But you still need to check that there actually is a move to be made (line 101). It could be that, although there is a loop, the node cannot be moved because the initial and final positions coincide. If you are not convinced, see how the partial tree of Listing 3-21 looks after moving node 009.

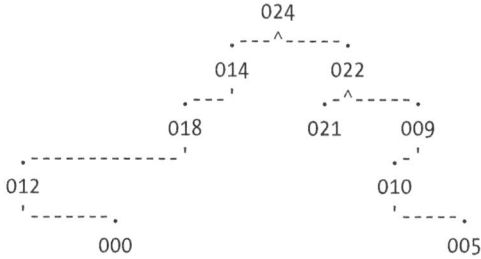

Remember that you move the nodes in order (001, 002, etc.) but from top to bottom, level by level. Therefore, the first node moved is 009 (to the left), followed by 010 (to the right) and 012 (also to the right). But, as you can see, after you have moved 009, 010 has nowhere to go and remains where it is. That is, col and new_col for node 010 are identical and the if condition in line 101 fails.

The for loop in lines 103 to 106 saves the node identifier in num and removes it from its original position. Then, all you need to do is adjust the connections to parent and child and do some cleanup.

It should be possible to handle both directions with a single piece of code, but the code in lines 108 to 141 is confusing enough as it is. That's why you are better off keeping the two directions separate.

You have to consider that when you move to the right the rightmost node of a level, you likely need to replace nulls with spaces. This is because all the characters of a line past the rightmost node in that line are nulls. For example, if you remove the right major branch from the tree of Listing 3-21, you would have the following lopsided tree:

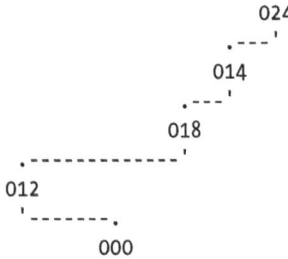

After moving node 012 six columns to the right, you would obtain the following tree:

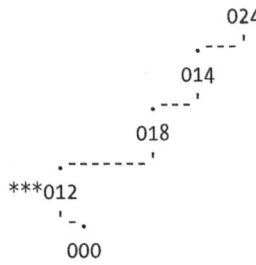

with three nulls immediately preceding 012 (shown as asterisks). Line 112 ensures that this never happens. Obviously, line 112 is redundant when the node moved to the right is not the rightmost node of its level. But if you always write spaces, you don't need to check when a node is the last one on the right.

The opposite issue exists when you move a level's rightmost node to the left because in that case you need to overwrite spaces with nulls. This is done in lines 130 to 134. To decide whether the node you are moving is the rightmost one, you only need to check whether the node identifier in its original position is followed by a null (line 130).

Finally, when you have moved the node, you update its value to reflect its new position (line 143). This makes it possible to clean up the tree further.

Repositioning the Root Node

If you look at the lopsided tree shown at the end of the previous section, you will notice that, if it were a complete tree rather than a partial one, the root (node 024) could be moved two columns to the left. Such a move is always possible when the root has a single child, because it has no parent that could get in the way. Listing 3-23 shows the code to implement such a move.

Listing 3-23. btr_list_tree(), Part 4, Move the Root

```
153.    //------- If the root has only one child, you can move the root's number to
154.    // above its only child.
155.    if (!root->child[0] || !root->child[1]) {
156.      char *line = lines[0];
157.      int col_p = root->value / 100 - min_col;
158.      int child_right = (root->child[0]) ? 0 : 1;
159.      btr_node *child = root->child[child_right];
160.      int col = child->value / 100 - min_col;
161.
162.      // Move the root's node identifier.
163.      char num[3];
164.      for (int i = 0; i < 3; i++) {
165.        num[i] = line[col_p + i];
166.        line[col_p + i] = ' ';
167.      }
168.      char *line0 = lines[1];
169.      if (child_right) {
170.
171.        // If the child is on the right side, the root number is followed by
172.        // '\0's, which have to be replaced with spaces. Otherwise, the root
173.        // number will not be seen.
174.        for (int i = 3; i < col; i++) line[i] = ' ';
175.
176.        int i = col_p + 1;
177.        while (i < col - 2) line0[i++] = ' ';
178.        line[i] = num[0];
179.        line0[i] = ' ';
180.        line[++i] = num[1];
181.        line0[i] = '\'';
182.        line[++i] = num[2];
183.      }
184.      else {
185.        int i = col + 2;
186.        line[i] = num[0];
187.        line[++i] = num[1];
188.        line0[i] = '\'';
189.        line[++i] = num[2];
190.        line0[i] = '\0';
191.        line[++i] = '\0';
192.      }
193.    }
194.
```

As you can see, the code is very similar to that used to remove a loop. It is simpler because you don't need to worry about a connector to a node above, which doesn't exist.

After removing its loops, the tree of Listing 3-21 becomes the tree shown in Listing 3-24.

Listing 3-24. A Partial Tree with Loops Removed

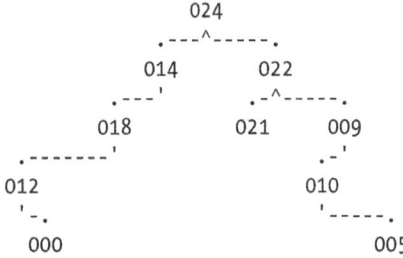

```
                 024
              .---^-----.
           014           022
         .---'         .-^-----.
      018           021        009
  .--------'                  .-'
012                        010
  '-.                        '-----.
   000                            005
```

   Actually, it would have six empty columns on its left. But we will take care of them with a cleanup operation that you will see later.

Repositioning the Leaves

The tree shown in Listing 3-24 includes three leaf-nodes. Notice that, while 000 and 021 are as close to their respective parents as possible, 005 could be moved four columns to the left. As it will become obvious if you think about it for a moment, *all* leaf-nodes can be moved as close as possible to their parents without causing any problem. This is because they have no children (possibly with further levels below them) that can get in the way. Listing 3-25 shows you how you do it.

Listing 3-25. btr_list_tree(), Part 5, Move the Leaves

```
195.   //------- Regardless of the depth, you can move all leaves to be close to
196.   // their parents.  The order in which you find them doesn't matter.
197.   // Remember that at this point, column and level are stored in value.
198.   for (int k = 0; k < n_nodes; k++) {
199.     btr_node *node = &nodes[k];
200.     if (!node->child[0] && !node->child[1]) {
201.
202.       // A childless node.  Find the parent.
203.       btr_node *parent = NULL;
204.       for (int j = 0; j < n_nodes && parent == NULL; j++) {
205.         btr_node *p = &nodes[j];
206.         if (p->child[0] == node || p->child[1] == node) parent = p;
207.       }
208.       int level = node->value % 100;
209.       int col = node->value / 100 - min_col;
210.       int col_p = parent->value / 100 - min_col;
211.       int distance = col_p - col;
212.
213.       // Move the node identifier, but only if it needs moving.
214.       if (distance < -2 || distance > 2) {
215.         int incr = (distance > 0) ? 1 : -1;
216.         char *line = lines[level * 2];
217.         char *line0 = lines[level * 2 - 1];
218.         char num[3];
219.         for (int i = 0; i < 3; i++) {
220.           num[i] = line[col + i];
221.           line[col + i] = ' ';
222.         }
223.
```

```
224.              // Write the node identifier in its new position.
225.              if (incr > 0) {
226.
227.                  // If the node is the last of the line and it is a left child,
228.                  // you need to replace the '\0's that follow its original
229.                  // position with spaces.  Otherwise it will not be seen.
230.                  if (line[col + 3] == '\0') {
231.                    for (int i = col + 3; i < col_p - 1; i++) line[i] = ' ';
232.                    }
233.                  int i = col + 1;
234.                  while (i < col_p - 2) line0[i++] = ' ';
235.                  line[i] = num[0];
236.                  line0[i] = ' ';
237.                  line[++i] = num[1];
238.                  line0[i] = '.';
239.                  line[++i] = num[2];
240.                  }
241.              else {
242.                  int i = col_p + 2;
243.                  line[i] = num[0];
244.                  line[++i] = num[1];
245.                  line0[i] = '.';
246.                  line[++i] = num[2];
247.                  if (line[col + 3] != '\0') {
248.                    while (i <= col + 1) line0[i++] = ' ';
249.                    }
250.                  else {
251.
252.                      // If a right child is at the end of a line, you have to
253.                      // hide the trailing spaces.
254.                      line0[i] = '\0';
255.                      line[++i] = '\0';
256.                      }
257.                  }
258.              } // if (distance..
259.            } // if (!node->child[0]..
260.          } // for (int k..
```

The algorithm is practically identical to the one you use to move the root (see Listing 3-23). After the move, the tree of Listing 3-24 would look as follows, with node 005 "tucked in" close to its parent:

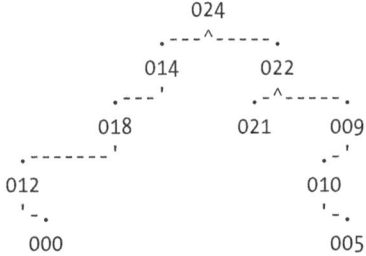

Bringing the Nodes Closer to Each Other

The links connecting the nodes could be pretty long. Even the small tree we have been working with has several links that could be shortened. It could be compacted as follows (done by hand):

```
        024
       .-^-.
      014 022
     .-'  .-^-.
    018 021 009
   .-'       .-'
  012       010
  '-.       '-.
   000       005
```

But determining which links can be shortened and then moving entire subtrees would require quite a bit of work. As a reasonable and easy-to-implement compromise, you can shorten the links as long as the node identifiers remain apart, regardless of the level they are in: imagine flattening the whole tree vertically, so that all node identifiers are in a single line. You can then proceed to move the nodes closer to each other until a single space remains between them. This will ensure that the node identifiers will remain separate within the "unflattened" tree as well. Listing 3-26 shows how you can do it.

Listing 3-26. btr_list_tree(), Part 6, Bring the Nodes Closer

```
262.  //------- Build a line with the 'or' of all lines containing numbers. The
263.  // groups of columns with empty spaces can certainly be reduced to single
264.  // columns.
265.
266.  char *l = lines[max_depth * 2 + 1];  // not used
267.  for (int j = 0; j < len; j++) l[j] = '.';
268.  int llen = 0;
269.  for (int k = 0; k <= max_depth; k++) {
270.    char *line = lines[k * 2];
271.    for (int j = 0; line[j] != '\0'; j++) {
272.      if (line[j] != ' ') {
273.        l[j] = line[j];
274.        if (j > llen) llen = j;
275.      }
276.    }
277.  }
278.  llen++;
279.  l[llen] = '\0';
280.  int count = 0;
281.  for (int j = llen - 3; j > 1; j--) {
282.    if (l[j] == '.') {
283.      count++;
284.    }
285.    else if (count < 2) { // ignore single dots
286.      count = 0;
287.    }
288.    else {
289.
```

```
290.        // j + 1 is the leftmost dot; j + count is the rightmost dot.
291.        // Overwrite in all lines the characters from j + 2 to j + count.
292.        for (int k = 0; k <= max_depth * 2 + 1; k++) {
293.          for (int i = j + 2; i <= strlen(lines[k]); i++) {
294.            lines[k][i] = lines[k][i + count - 1];
295.            }
296.          }
297.        count = 0;
298.        }
299.      }
```

The first step, from lines 266 to 279, is to overlap all lines containing nodes. That is, all lines that do not contain links. These are the even-numbered lines (i.e., with indices k * 2), one for each level of the tree. For this purpose, you can use the line immediately below the lowest level (i.e., with index max_depth * 2 + 1) because the line below a level contains the links to children of nodes that belong to that level, and the lowest level only contains leaves, which don't have children.

Line 266 defines the line l, where you overlap the levels and in line 267 you fill it up with dots. In the for loop from lines 269 to 277 you scan the levels one at the time and copy to l node identifiers. While you do so, you increase llen accordingly. After completing the loop, you increase llen by one and write to l the string-terminating null.

For example, with the following tree:

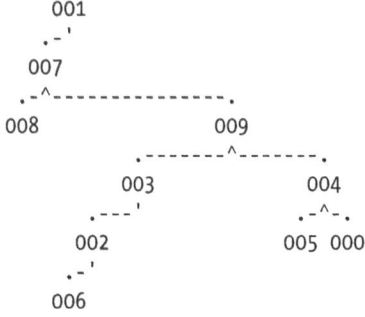

you obtains the following l:

008000602.003.....009...0050000

By looking at the tree, it is clear that you could remove all the columns with dots without bringing any pair of node identifiers in contact with each other. You could actually squeeze the tree closer together. But what is obvious for a human being can be quite complicated for a computer program. Instead of implementing a complex algorithm to check, for example, that 003 and 009 are in different levels and you can, therefore, remove all five columns with dots between those two nodes, you can play it safe and only replace sequences of dots with single dots, like this:

008000602.003.009.0050000

This is what lines 280 to 299 do. The loop with control variable j scans l. If l[j] is a dot, it increases the dot count (variable count, line 283). Otherwise, as the character is not a dot, it means that count corresponds to the number of dots in the sequence that has just ended. If the sequence has a length of 1, all you do is restart the dot counter (line 286). But if the sequence of dots is longer than 1, it means that you can remove

71

the preceding count - 1 columns *from all the lines*. This is what happens in lines 292 to 296. Obviously, before proceeding with the scanning of l. Notice that for this algorithm to work, you scan l in reverse (see line 281) and, when you overwrite a dot sequence by "pulling back" the rest of the line, you include the terminating null (see line 293).

After this operation, the 10-node tree of the example becomes:

```
    001
    .-'
   007
.-^----------.
008              009
            .---^-----.
          003         004
       .---'        .-^-.
      002          005  000
      .-'
     006
```

As you can see, 009 is now just one column away from 003 and from 005. This is not the maximum-achievable compression, but the tree looks reasonably good and I think we can leave with it.

Wrapping it all up, I have to tell you that, for the sake of clarity, I have not been completely truthful with you: the two dotted lines of the original and of the compressed tree are not those I showed you in the previous section. They are instead:

```
..............008000602.003.....009...0050000
..............008000602.003.009.0050000
```

The 14 dots in the original tree are due to the fact that 008 was initially placed 16 columns on the left of 007. Then, the algorithm that moves the leaves close to their parents (see Listing 3-25) shifted 008 to its current position, 14 columns to the right. Hence the 14 dots. And those dots remain after the compression because the algorithm shown in Listing 3-26 identifies sequences of dots by the two nodes that delimit them, and the first sequence of 14 dots starts at column zero (actually, *ends* at column zero, because you scan l from right to left).

Instead of fiddling with the compression algorithm, I have added a bit of code that removes the empty columns on the left of the tree. This is shown in Listing 3-27 together with the code that (finally!) prints the tree.

Listing 3-27. btr_list_tree(), Part 7 (and Last), Cleanup and Print

```
301.   //------- We still have to check whether there are spaces beginning from
302.   // column zero. If yes, we have to remove them.
303.   int i_space = 0;
304.   while (l[i_space] == '.') i_space++;
305.   for (int k = 0; k <= max_depth * 2 + 1; k++) {
306.     int limit = strlen(lines[k]) - i_space;
307.     for (int i = 0; i <= limit; i++) {
308.       lines[k][i] = lines[k][i + i_space];
309.       }
310.     }
311.
312.   //******* Print the tree.
313.   for (int k = 0; k < max_depth; k++) {
```

```
314.       printf("%s\n%s\n", lines[k * 2], lines[k * 2 + 1]);
315.       }
316.    printf("%s\n", lines[max_depth * 2]);
317.
318.    free(lines);
319.    } // btr_list_tree
```

Generating a Random Tree

Being able to display binary trees graphically was essential for the study of binary trees, but how do you test a function like btr_list_tree()? The only practical possibility I thought of was to write a function that could generate random trees. And once I had it, I obviously had to include it in this book!

Listing 3-28 shows a function that can generate random binary trees with a given number of nodes.

Listing 3-28. btr_random_allocate()

```
1. //-------------------------------------------------------- btr_random_allocate
2. btr_node *btr_random_allocate(int seed, int n) {
3.    n_nodes = n;
4.    if (n_nodes < 2 || n_nodes > 99) {
5.      fprintf(stderr, "More than 99 or less than 2 nodes\n");
6.      fflush(stderr);
7.      abort();                                              // -->
8.      }
9.
10.    // Allocate the arrays
11.    nodes = malloc(n * sizeof(btr_node));
12.    if (nodes == NULL) {
13.      fprintf(stderr, "btr_random_allocate 1: failed to allocate %d-tree\n", n);
14.      fflush(stderr);
15.      abort();                                              // -->
16.      }
17.    size_t avail_size = n * sizeof(btr_node *);
18.    avail = malloc(avail_size + n * sizeof(int));
19.    if (avail == NULL) {
20.      fprintf(stderr, "btr_random_allocate 2: failed to allocate %d-tree\n", n);
21.      fflush(stderr);
22.      abort();                                              // -->
23.      }
24.    int *widths = (int *)(avail + avail_size);
25.    for (int k = 0; k < n; k++) widths[k] = 0;
26.
27.    // Initialize the lists.
28.    widths[0] = 1;
29.    int depth = 1;
30.    n_avail = n;
31.    for (int k = 0, max_w = 1, left = n - 1; k < n; k++) {
32.      nodes[k].id = k;
33.      nodes[k].value = 0;
34.      nodes[k].child[0] = nodes[k].child[1] = NULL;
35.      avail[k] = &nodes[k];
```

73

```
36.      if (k > 0 && left > 0) {
37.        max_w = widths[k - 1] * 2;
38.        widths[k] = rand() % ((max_w < left) ? max_w : left) + 1;
39.        left -= widths[k];
40.        depth = k;
41.        }
42.      }
43.
44.    // Pick the root node and save it at the end of avail[].
45.    btr_node *tree = pick_avail();
46.    int k_pos_up = n_avail;
47.    avail[k_pos_up] = tree;
48.
49.    // Fill the "lower" levels of nodes one by one.
50.    for (int k = 1, k_pos = k_pos_up; k <= depth; k++) {
51.      for (int j = 0; j < widths[k]; j++) {
52.        btr_node *a_node = pick_avail();
53.        avail[--k_pos] = a_node;
54.
55.        // Choose one of the available child pointers of a node one level above.
56.        btr_node **child_p = NULL;
57.        do {
58.          int k_parent = k_pos_up + rand() % widths[k - 1];
59.          btr_node *parent = avail[k_parent];
60.          child_p = &parent->child[rand() % 2];
61.          } while (*child_p != NULL);
62.        *child_p = a_node;
63.        }
64.      k_pos_up = k_pos;
65.      }
66.
67.    free(avail);
68.    return tree;
69.    } // btr_random_allocate
```

I limited the maximum number of nodes to 99 because it seemed a large enough number to do all the testing you might like to do. You are welcome to increase the limit but, if you do so, you might hit some memory boundary.

To store the generated tree, btr_random_allocate() allocates memory from the heap (lines 11 to 16). This means that, when you are done with the generated tree, you must call btr_free() (see Listing 3-29). Otherwise, you will cause a significant memory leak.

Listing 3-29. btr_free()

```
//-------------------------------------------------------------------- btr_free
void btr_free(void) {
  if (nodes) {
    free(nodes);
    nodes = NULL;
    }
  } // btr_free
```

The array nodes, where btr_random_allocate() stores the generated tree, is defined statically in btree.c, which means that you will not be able to access it directly from your program.

btr_random_allocate() also allocates memory for two arrays: avail and widths (lines 17 to 24). The first array is used to keep a list of nodes you haven't yet linked to the tree, while the second one counts the number of nodes that belong to each level of the tree. As neither array is needed outside the function, you release them both in line 68, before returning.

The first step to form the binary tree is deciding how many nodes belong to each level. Level 0, the root of the tree, obviously consists of a single node. Accordingly, in line 28, you set widths[0] to 1.

The for loop that starts in line 31 goes through all the n nodes one by one. The first part of the loop, from lines 32 to 35, clears the nodes and copies to avail the node addresses.

You initialize the two variables max_w and left together with the loop's control variable, so that they are only valid within the loop. They represent respectively the maximum width of level 0 (which is 1 because level 0 only includes the root node) and the number of nodes that remain available after considering the root (i.e., n - 1).

You execute the second part of the loop (from line 37 to line 40) after the first iteration (i.e., for k > 0) but only if at least one node is still available (i.e., left > 0). As a result, the first iteration of the loop, for k = 0, only initializes nodes[0] and copies its address to the beginning of avail.

Line 37 calculates the maximum number of nodes that can fit in level k of the tree. As it is a binary tree, this is given by $2k$, where k is the level. Initially, for levels close to the root (i.e., for low enough ks), there will be more nodes available than the number that can fit in the current level. But after enough iterations, depending on how many nodes you require, max_w will exceed left. That's why, when you decide at random how many nodes you assign to a level, you need to do it like in line 38:

```
widths[k] = rand() % ((max_w < left) ? max_w : left) + 1;
```

The +1 is needed because you want to have at least one node per level; otherwise, you would end up with separate (smaller) trees.

In line 39 you subtract from the number of available nodes those that you have assigned to the current level, and in line 39 you remember that you have reached the current level by saving k to the variable named depth.

Don't be confused by the fact that k means two things: the position of the current node within nodes (and therefore within avail) and the current level of the tree, used to assign to it a number of nodes. I could have indeed used two separate loops, as shown in Listing 3-30.

Listing 3-30. Two Loops

```
for (int k = 0; k < n; k++) {
  nodes[k].value = 0;
  nodes[k].child[0] = NULL;
  nodes[k].child[1] = NULL;
  avail[k] = &nodes[k];
  }
for (int k = 1, max_w = 1, left = n - 1; left > 0 && k < n; k++) {
  max_w = widths[k - 1] * 2;
  widths[k] = rand() % ((max_w < left) ? max_w : left) + 1;
  left -= widths[k];
  depth = k;
  }
```

You will find this alternate formulation commented out in btree.c. Switch it on if you like it better.

In any case, at this point, you have all nodes cleared, the list of nodes saved in avail with n_avail set to n, and the number of nodes in each level stored in widths from element 0 to element depth (included).

The first thing you do to is pick the root node in line 45. Listing 3-31 shows the function pick_avail(). Although it is a short piece of code, it is appropriate to make a separate function out of it because you need it again when you pick the other nodes.

Listing 3-31. pick_node()

```
1. //-------------------------------------------------------------- pick_avail
2. // Warning: avail[] is allocated and released in btr_random_allocate().
3. btr_node *pick_avail(void) {
4.   int k_picked = rand() % n_avail;
5.   btr_node *node = avail[k_picked];
6.   n_avail--;
7.   for (int j = k_picked; j < n_avail; j++) avail[j] = avail[j + 1];
8.   return node;
9. } // pick_avail
```

It is pretty straightforward: in line 4 you pick one of the available nodes at random; in line 5 you save its address so that you can return it to btr_random_allocate(); in line 6 you decrement the number of available nodes; and in line 7 you remove the picked node from avail, the list of available nodes.

Back to btr_random_allocate() (Listing 3-28), in lines 46 and 47 you do two operations that at first sight seem useless: in line 46 you copy the number of remaining nodes (which, at this point, coincides with n - 1 because you have just picked the root node) to k_pos_up, and in line 47 you save the address of the root node at the end of avail, in the position freed when pick_avail() compacted avail to fill the place originally containing the root node (line 7 of Listing 3-31). In essence, the combined result of the invocation of pick_avail() in line 45 and the assignment in line 47 is to move the address of the root node from its original position within avail to its end.

The for loop that begins in line 50 goes top-down through the tree levels, beginning with the level immediately below the root. The for statement, besides initializing the control variable k, also defines k_pos and sets it to k_pos_up. After defining a pointer to a node address (child_p), it starts the for loop with control variable j (note that j is only used to count the iterations and is never used in the algorithm), which iterates as many times as the number of nodes assigned to the current level k. Lines 52 and 53 do for each node of the current level what lines 45 and 47 did for the root node: they move its address from its original position within avail to the position of avail freed by pick_avail() when compacting the array.

Note that line 53 decrements k_pos *before* using it to index avail. So, when processing the first node of level 1 (remember that each level has at least one node because of the +1 in line 38), k_pos, which was set to n - 1 in line 50, is decremented to n - 2 before the address of the first node assigned to level 1 is stored in avail, thereby ensuring that the address of the root node, which was saved in position n - 1 of avail, is not overwritten. These operations are repeated widths[k] times. That is, as many times as the number of nodes assigned to the current level. So, when processing of a level completes, width[j] positions of avail from k_pos on contain the addresses of the nodes belonging to that level.

The do loop from lines 57 to 61 keeps looking for a free child in one of the nodes of the level immediately above until it finds one. For example, suppose that widths[1] is 2 (which is the maximum for level 1 because the root node is the only one in level 0). Then, when processing level 1, the loop that starts in line 51 iterates twice. As we have already seen, k_pos_up during the processing of level 1 is n - 1, and the address stored in avail[k_pos_up] is the address of the root node. As widths[0] is 1, line 58 sets k_parent to n - 1 in both iterations, which results in line 59 assigning the address of the root node to parent (not a big surprise when considering that the root node is the only one in level 0!).

Once a node of the level above the current one has been chosen, line 60 selects one of its two children at random. Assuming that two nodes were assigned to level 1 (in line 38 for k equal to 1), the do loop succeeds immediately the first time it is executed (because both children of the root node are free). But during the second iteration, the do loop has a 50% chance of selecting the same child of root, in which case the while condition in line 61 fails. The do loop then tries again, and it keeps trying until it hits by chance the free child of root. Forget that according to the statisticians the do loop might be running forever. It will not, at the very least because rand() is not perfectly random!

When starting level 2, there are one or two node addresses stored in avail from position k_pos_up, and the whole process continues for deeper and deeper levels until k reaches depth. After that, all nodes are linked to each other to produce a random tree.

Traversing a Tree

Traversing a (binary) tree means visiting all nodes of a tree once. The function btr_traverse_tree() of Listing 3-32 shows a way of traversing a tree.

Listing 3-32. btr_traverse_tree()

```
//----------------------------------------------------------- btr_traverse_tree
void btr_traverse_tree(btr_node *node) {
  if (node != NULL) {
    btr_traverse_tree(node->child[0]);
    printf("%03d\n", node->id);
    btr_traverse_tree(node->child[1]);
    }
  } // btr_traverse_tree
```

It traverses the left subtree by calling itself recursively, lists the current node, and then traverses the right subtree. When applied to the tree of Listing 3-4, it produces the following output:

```
013
006
000
012
024
005
009
014
001
021
007
010
002
022
015
003
004
019
016
023
018
017
011
008
020
```

If you had checked for NULL before each recursive call, you could have achieved the same result with one less iteration, but it is more a matter of choice than anything else. Listing 3-33 shows an edited version of Listing 3-4 in which the sequence generated with btr_traverse_tree() is marked with letters.

Listing 3-33. A Marked-Up Tree

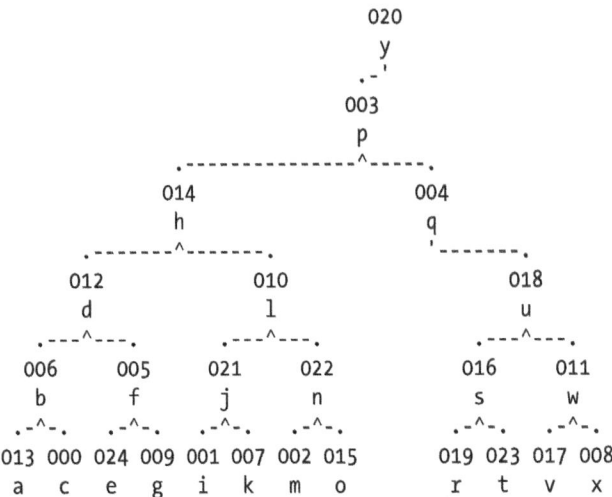

A binary tree in which the list produced by btr_traverse_tree() shows the identifiers in sequence (i.e., 000, 001, etc.) is said to be *ordered* or *sorted*. It happens when *each* node of the tree follows all its left descendants and precedes all its right descendants. The function btr_set_ordered_ids() (see Listing 3-34) is a modified version of btr_traverse_tree() that, as the name says, changes the identifier of each node to make the tree ordered.

Listing 3-34. btr_set_ordered_ids()

```
//------------------------------------------------------------ btr_set_ordered_ids
void btr_set_ordered_ids(btr_node *node) {
  static int k_node = 0;
  if (node != NULL) {
    btr_set_ordered_ids(node->child[0]);
    node->id = k_node++;
    btr_set_ordered_ids(node->child[1]);
    }
} // btr_set_ordered_ids
```

After executing btr_set_ordered_ids(), the tree in Listings 3-4 and 3-33 becomes ordered:

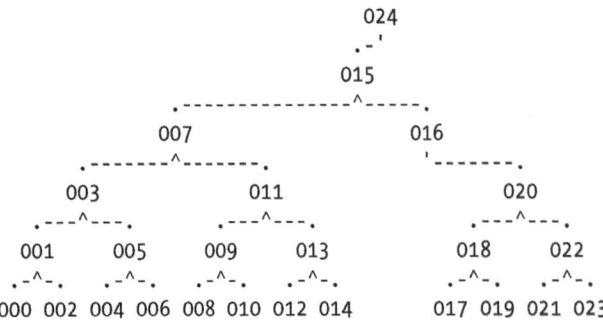

You need to traverse a tree when you search for particular values or other characteristics of nodes (e.g., number of children or values associated with additional node-structure fields). A search based on the algorithm used in btr_traverse_tree() is called *in-order*, but there are other ways of searching a tree. For example, you could look at the current node before searching deeper, or search both children subtrees before looking at the current node. All you need to do to implement those searches is change the order of the three statements inside the if of btr_traverse_tree().

You can also search a tree *breadth-first*. That is, checking the nodes level by level, from the root down. Such a search is a bit more complicated because there are no links within each level, as all parent-child links are (by definition) across levels. A practical way to do it is to add to each node such links and then link the rightmost node of each level to the leftmost node of the lower level.

For this purpose, I have added the node pointer next to btr_node and a call to the function btr_make_inlevel_links() (see Listing 3-35) at the end of btr_random_allocate(). But is also necessary to extend the initialization of the nodes in btr_random_allocate() to include the next field. You can easily do it by modifying line 34 (see Listing 3-28) as follows:

```
nodes[k].child[0] = nodes[k].child[1] = nodes[k].next = NULL;
```

I also added next to the values that btr_list_nodes() prints.

Listing 3-35. make_inlevel_links()

```
1. //-------------------------------------------------------- btr_make_inlevel_links
2. void btr_make_inlevel_links(btr_node *root) {
3.
4.   // Write the level in each node.
5.   write_level_in_nodes(root, 0);
6.
7.   // Allocate and initialize the lists to store the addresses of the
8.   // first and last nodes in each level.
9.   int depth = calc_depth_r(root, 0);
10.   btr_node **first = malloc((depth + 1) * sizeof(btr_node *) * 2);
11.   if (first == NULL) {
12.     fprintf(stderr, "btr_make_inlevel_links: failed to allocate depth lists\n");
13.     fflush(stderr);
14.     abort();                                                    // -->
15.   }
16.   btr_node **last = &first[depth + 1];
17.   for (int i = 0; i <= depth; i++) first[i] = NULL;
18.
19.   // Write the pointers within each level.
20.   for (int k = 0; k < n_nodes; k++) {
21.     btr_node *node = &nodes[k];
22.     int level = node->value;
23.     if (first[level] == NULL) first[level] = node;
24.     else last[level]->next = node;
25.     last[level] = node;
26.   }
27.
```

```
28.    // Chain the levels.
29.    for (int i = 0; i < depth; i++) last[i]->next = first[i + 1];
30.
31.    // Free the lists.
32.    free(first);
33.
34.    } // btr_make_inlevel_links
```

You can traverse the tree by level with a piece of code like this:

```
btr_node *node = root;
do {
  printf(" %03d", node->id);
  node = node->next;
  } while (node);
printf("\n");
```

to obtain the following list (still for the tree of Listing 3-4):

```
020 003 004 014 010 012 018 005 006 011 016 021 022 000 001 002 007 008 009 \
013 015 017 019 023 024
```

But wait a minute! It should list node 014 before 004. Also other nodes are not in the correct order. If you insert this code after line 25 of Listing 3-35

```
for (int i = 0; i <= depth; i++) {
  printf("%d:", i);
  btr_node *node = first[i];
  do {
    printf(" %03d", node->id);
    node = node->next;
    } while (node);
  printf("\n");
  }
```

it will print the node identifiers level by level:

```
0: 020
1: 003
2: 004 014
3: 010 012 018
4: 005 006 011 016 021 022
5: 000 001 002 007 008 009 013 015 017 019 023 024
```

In each level, the nodes are listed in the order in which they appear within nodes, rather than in the order in which they appear within the tree. But of course, the for statement in line 20 scans the array of nodes.

Such a simple breadth-first search could be sufficient in some cases, but if you want to traverse the tree from top to bottom and left to right, simply scanning the array of nodes will not do. You will need to traverse the node like you do in btr_set_ordered_ids() (Listing 3-34). To do so, you need to replace the nodes-scanning loop in lines 20 to 26 with the following single line:

```
write_level_pointers(root, 0, first, last);
```

The new function is shown in Listing 3-36.

Listing 3-36. write_level_pointers()

```
//--------------------------------------------------------- write_level_pointers
void write_level_pointers(btr_node *node, int level,
    btr_node **first, btr_node **last) {
  if (node != NULL) {
    write_level_pointers(node->child[0], level + 1, first, last);

    if (first[level] == NULL) first[level] = node;
    else last[level]->next = node;
    last[level] = node;

    write_level_pointers(node->child[1], level + 1, first, last);
    }
  } // write_level_pointers
```

Now, if you traverse the tree of Listing 3-4, you get:

```
020 003 014 004 012 010 018 006 005 021 022 016 011 013 000 024 009 001 007 \
002 015 019 023 017 008
```

with the nodes of each level listed from left to right. By using write_level_pointers(), you also make the writing of levels in the node values unnecessary. Therefore, you can remove the line

```
write_level_in_nodes(root, 0);
```

from the beginning of btr_make_inlevel_links().

More Binary Trees

To work with binary trees, you need some additional utilities. The first one is btr_blank_allocate(), which you will find in Listing 3-37.

Listing 3-37. btr_blank_allocate()

```
//------------------------------------------------------------ btr_blank_allocate
btr_node *btr_blank_allocate(int n) {
  n_nodes = n;
  if (n_nodes < 2 || n_nodes > 99) {
    fprintf(stderr, "More than 99 or less than 2 nodes\n");
    fflush(stderr);
    abort();                                                        // -->
    }
```

```
// Allocate the array of nodes
nodes = malloc(n * sizeof(btr_node));
if (nodes == NULL) {
  fprintf(stderr, "btr_blank_allocate 1: failed to allocate %d-tree\n", n);
  fflush(stderr);
  abort();                                                       // -->
  }

// Initialize the list.
for (int k = 0; k < n; k++) {
  nodes[k].id = k;
  nodes[k].value = 0;
  nodes[k].child[0] = nodes[k].child[1] = nodes[k].next = NULL;
  }
return &nodes[0];
} // btr_blank_allocate
```

btr_blank_allocate() is a subset of btr_random_allocate(). Nothing new there. To avoid duplications of code, you could use btr_blank_allocate() in btr_random_allocate(). To do so, insert the line

```
(void)btr_blank_allocate(n);
```

after the comment in line 10 of btr_random_allocate() (shown in Listing 3-27). Then, remove all the lines of btr_random_allocate() that appear in btr_blank_allocate(). They are 4 to 8, 11 to 16, and 32 to 34.

A function that you might find useful is btr_full_allocate() (see Listing 3-38), which allocates a full tree of a given depth.

Listing 3-38. btr_full_allocate()

```
1.  //------------------------------------------------------------ btr_full_allocate
2.  btr_node *btr_full_allocate(int max_depth) {
3.  #define MAX_MAX_DEPTH 20
4.    if (max_depth < 1 || max_depth > MAX_MAX_DEPTH) {
5.      fprintf(stderr,
6.          "btr_full_allocate: max_depth=%d is outside the range 1..%d\n",
7.          max_depth, MAX_MAX_DEPTH);
8.      fflush(stderr);
9.      abort();                                                 // -->
10.     }
11.
12.   // Allocate the nodes.
13.   n_nodes = (1 << (max_depth + 1)) - 1;
14.   (void)btr_blank_allocate(n_nodes);
15.
16.   // Link the nodes to their children, level by level.
17.   int next_free = 1;
18.   for (int level = 0; level < max_depth; level++) {
19.     int nn = 1 << level;
20.     int k_first = next_free - nn;
21.     for (int k = 0; k < nn; k++) {
22.       btr_node *parent = &nodes[k_first + k];
23.       parent->child[0] = &nodes[next_free++];
```

```
24.        parent->child[1] = &nodes[next_free++];
25.        }
26.    }
27.
28.    // Chain the nodes like in make_inlevel_links().
29.    // It is easier to do it here than when setting the children links.
30.    btr_node *node1 = &nodes[0];
31.    for (int k = 1; k < n_nodes; k++) {
32.      btr_node *node2 = &nodes[k];
33.      node1->next = node2;
34.      node1 = node2;
35.      }
36.
37.    return &nodes[0];
38.    } // btr_full_allocate
```

The code is pretty self-explanatory: allocate a blank tree (line 14), make the parent-child links (lines 17 to 26), and make the links within each level support breath-first searches. Here is a full tree with a maximum depth of 4:

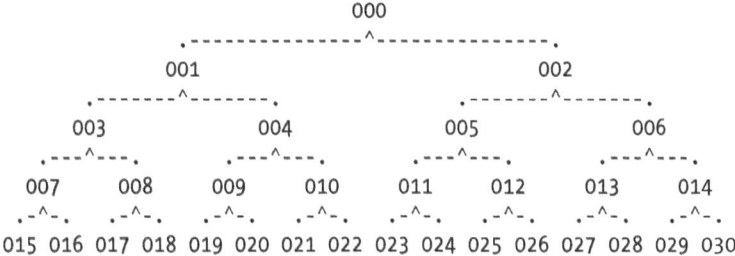

And here is the same tree after executing btr_set_ordered_ids():

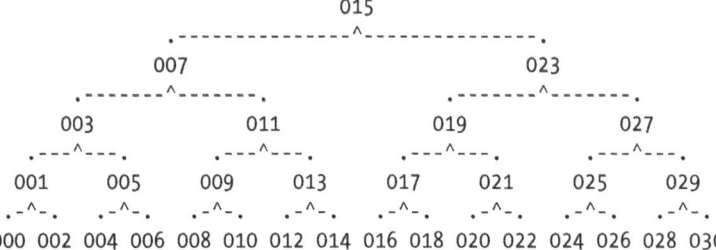

Note than you can only generate a full tree with a maximum depth of 5, because any bigger tree would include more than 99 nodes. Unfortunately, a tree with a maximum depth of 5 doesn't fit in the page, as the bottom level includes 32 nodes.

Summary

In this chapter you have learned the difference between iteration and recursion, and seen several examples of the two techniques applied to binary trees. You also learned how to represent binary trees, how to display them, and how to traverse them. And you can now generate random and full trees.

CHAPTER 4

■ ■ ■

Lists, Stacks, and Queues

We are all familiar with lists: in very generic terms, a *list* is an ordered collection of items, and in the context of programming languages, the items are simple or structured data types. Individual lists can contain items of mixed types, but in this chapter you will only see homogeneous lists, in which all items are values of a single data type.

Although C is not an object-oriented language, it makes sense to begin dealing with lists by looking at which operations you need to be able to perform on them in order to accomplish any meaningful task:

- Create an empty list (in CS's terminology, you need a *constructor*)

- Add items to a list (because dealing exclusively with empty lists is not very useful)

- Know what is in a list

- Remove items from a list

- Delete a list when you are done with it (i.e., you need a *destructor*)

Pretty obvious. But if you consider the operations in more detail, you immediately recognize that you need to define them in more detail. For example, where do you add an item to a list? At the end, at the beginning or somewhere in the middle? And, actually, how do you define beginnings and end of lists? Same story when you remove items from a list.

There are also additional operations that sooner or later you will need to perform on a list. For example, the generic expression "ordered collection" used in the first paragraph of this chapter only means that in a list each item is either before or after every other item, but you might like to reorder a list according to a particular criterion (i.e., *sort* it). And what about searching a list for a particular item?

But we are getting ahead of ourselves.

There Are Lists and Lists

Figure 4-1 shows a generic list.

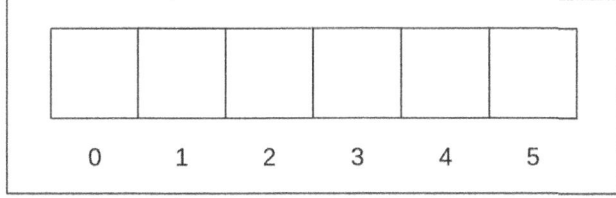

Figure 4-1. A generic list

© Giulio Zambon 2016
G. Zambon, *Practical C*, DOI 10.1007/978-1-4842-1769-6_4

The numbers from 0 to 5 provide the ordering of the items. You can imagine to have built the list by adding to an empty list first 0, then 1, etc.

The interesting bit is when you consider how to remove items from a list. There are two basic mechanisms, which result in *stacks* and *queues*. Figure 4-2 shows how you remove items from a stack.

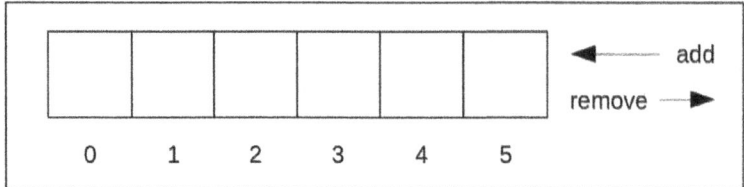

Figure 4-2. *A stack*

If you imagine Figure 4-2 rotated counterclockwise by 90 degrees, it becomes apparent why stack is the appropriate name for such a data structure. A stack data structure behaves exactly like a handgun clip (or a rifle magazine): you pop bullets from the top in the reverse order in which you pushed them in. Indeed, *push* and *pop* is how the operations of adding and removing data items onto/from a stack are called. My apologies if the reference to firearms disturbs you, but I couldn't find a better example. You see, you can remove a book from the middle of a stack of books, but you cannot remove a bullet from the middle of a clip.

A stack follows the LIFO (Last-In-First-Out) principle. Now, the expression First-In-Last-Out would have been equally valid to describe a stack, but everybody uses LIFO.

Figure 4-3 shows how you remove items from a queue.

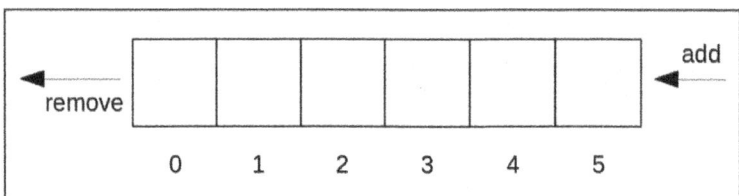

Figure 4-3. *A queue*

In a queue, you *enqueue* an item by inserting it at the *rear* and you *dequeue* it by removing it from the *front*. That is, the first item in is also the first one out (FIFO). A queue data structure behaves like a line of people waiting to enter a theater. Indeed, outside the United States, people don't "line up," they "queue up". And the rule of joining a queue at the rear and exiting it at the front applies, as nobody is allowed to "jump the queue"!

Stacks

When applied to stacks, the operations you can perform on lists become:

- Create and delete a stack

- Push and pop an item onto/from a stack

- Know what is in a stack

This section explains how to implement stacks in two different ways: as arrays and as linked lists.

Array-Based Stacks

The simplest way of implementing a list is an array, and stacks are lists.

Create and Delete a Stack

Listing 4-1 shows lst_new_stack_a(). All functions and macros associated with array-based lists end with the suffix _a.

Listing 4-1. lst_new_stack_a()

```
1.  //------------------------------------------------------------ lst_new_stack_a
2.  void lst_new_stack_a(void ***stack_ptr, int n) {
3.    if (n <= 0) {
4.      fprintf(stderr, "lst_new_stack_a: %d elements?\n", n);
5.      fflush(stderr);
6.      abort();                                                  // -->
7.      }
8.    int *ptr = malloc(n * sizeof(void *) + 2 * sizeof(int));
9.    if (ptr == NULL) {
10.     fprintf(stderr, "lst_new_stack_a: failed to allocate %d-stack\n", n);
11.     fflush(stderr);
12.     abort();                                                  // -->
13.     }
14.   int *capacity = ptr++;
15.   *capacity = n;
16.   int *size = ptr++;
17.   *size = 0;
18.   void **stack = (void **)ptr;
19.   for (int k = 0; k < n; k++) stack[k] = NULL;
20.   *stack_ptr = stack;
21.   } // lst_new_stack_a
```

The first parameter stack_ptr is the address of where lst_new_stack_a() is going to store the address of the new stack. The second parameter n defines the maximum number of items you want to be able to store in the new stack.

Don't be confused by the triple asterisk: the rightmost asterisk is present because each item is stored in a stack as a pointer to void; the middle asterisk is needed because a stack is an array of items (i.e., of type void **); the leftmost asterisk means that the parameter is a pointer to an array of pointers, needed so that you can set the stack address in the calling program from within the function.

Although the address of an item is stored in a stack as a pointer to void, you can make stacks of any data type. Most likely, you will define an item as a structure, like in the following simple example:

```
typedef struct item_t { int value; } item_t;
```

Then, a stack is an array of items:

```
item_t **stack_a = NULL;
```

To allocate a new stack of, say, five items, you can call lst_new_stack_a() like this:

```
lst_new_stack_a(5, &stack_a);
```

But, if you do so, the compiler will issue a warning because `lst_new_stack_a()` expects its second parameter to be of type `void ***` while `&stack_a` is of type `item ***`. Warnings don't cause the compilation to be aborted, but you should try to eliminate as many warnings as possible because they encourage you to be complacent and, before you know it, you overlook a warning that you shouldn't ignore. The solution is to define the following macro:

```
#define LST_new_stack_a(stack, n) lst_new_stack_a((void ***)&(stack), n)
```

which lets you invoke `lst_new_stack_a()` without causing warning and more simply:

```
LST_new_stack_a(stack_a, 5);
```

The first thing you do within `lst_new_stack_a()` is allocate a block of memory to store the stack itself and two integers. You need the two integers to remember how many items you can push onto the stack and how many you have actually pushed at any given time. What you want to do is save those two values at the very beginning of the allocated block of memory, and lines 9 to 12 show you how to do it. Notice that you can simply write `ptr++` to move forward the address because you defined `ptr` to be a pointer to int. Therefore, the `++` operator moves `ptr` ahead the number of bytes necessary to store an `int`.

After clearing the stack in lines 13 and 14, you store the stack address into the location pointed by `stack_ptr` and you are done.

Once you finish using the stack, you must free the block of memory allocated in `lst_new_stack_a()`. To do so in a clean and safe way, you can use the macro `LST_free_stack_a()` shown in Listing 4-2.

Listing 4-2. LST_free_stack_a()

```
#define LST_free_stack_a(ptr) {        \
    int **_ptr = (int **)&(ptr);       \
    if (*_ptr != NULL) {               \
      free(*_ptr - 2);                 \
      *_ptr = NULL;                    \
      }                                \
    }
```

The definition of `_ptr` serves two purposes: first, it lets you use the value of `ptr` in three different places with only one reference to `ptr`, and second, it lets you easily calculate the address of the memory block to be freed.

The first reason is due to the fact that the preprocessor replaces macros textually. Therefore, referring to a parameter only once within the macro protects you from causing problems when the parameter has side effects. For example, if you invoke `A_macro(p)` with `a_var++` as a parameter and `A_macro()` refers to p twice, the macro increments the value of `a_var` by 2, rather than by 1.

The second reason is that by typecasting the stack pointer to be a pointer to `int`, you only need to subtract 2 from it to obtain the address of the block of memory to be freed.

Push, Pop, and Info

Listing 4-3 shows the function `lst_push_a()`.

Listing 4-3. lst_push_a()

```
1. //---------------------------------------------------------------- lst_push_a
2. int lst_push_a(void **stack, void *item) {
3.   if (stack == NULL) {
4.     fprintf(stderr, "lst_push_a: stack pointer is NULL\n");
```

```
5.     fflush(stderr);
6.     abort();                                               // -->
7.     }
8.   int capacity = LST_get_capacity_a(stack);
9.   int size = LST_get_size_a(stack);
10.  int done = 0;
11.  if (size < capacity) {
12.    stack[size++] = item;
13.    Set_size(stack, size);
14.    done = 1;
15.    }
16.  return done;
17.  } // lst_push_a
```

After checking that the stack pointer is not null and that the stack is not full, you just add the new item to the free available place in the array and return. The function returns 1 when successful. Simple.

The two macros

```
#define LST_get_capacity_a(st) (*((int *)(st) - 2))
#define LST_get_size_a(st) (*((int *)(st) - 1))
```

let you easily retrieve the maximum size of the stack and its current size, while

```
#define Set_size(st, val) {*((int *)(st) - 1) = val;}
```

lets you set the stack size. The name of Set_size() doesn't include the lst_ suffix because the macro is local to the lists library.

As usual, to avoid compiler warnings and for consistency, you should invoke lst_push_a() through the macro:

```
#define LST_push_a(stack, item) lst_push_a((void **)(stack), (void *)&(item))
```

Listing 4-4 shows the function lst_top_a(), which has the dual function of retrieving and popping the stack's top item.

Listing 4-4. lst_top_a()

```
1. //------------------------------------------------------------------ lst_top_a
2. void *lst_top_a(void **stack, int remove) {
3.   if (stack == NULL) {
4.     fprintf(stderr, "lst_pop_a: stack pointer is NULL\n");
5.     fflush(stderr);
6.     abort();                                               // -->
7.     }
8.   int size = LST_get_size_a(stack);
9.   void *item = NULL;
10.  if (size > 0) {
11.    size--;
12.    item = stack[size];
13.    if (remove) {
14.      stack[size] = NULL;
15.      Set_size(stack, size);
```

```
16.     }
17.   }
18.   return item;
19. } // lst_top_a
```

If the stack is empty, lst_top_a() returns a null. If the remove parameter is true, you clear the pointer to the popped item in the stack array and update the stack size (lines 14 and 15).

The two macros

```
#define LST_pop_a(stack) lst_top_a((void **)(stack), 1)
#define LST_top_a(stack) lst_top_a((void **)(stack), 0)
```

let you execute lst_top_a() to pop or just look at the top item of the stack.

For convenience, I defined two macros to check whether the stack is empty or full:

```
#define LST_is_empty_a(st) (LST_get_size_a(st) == 0)
#define LST_is_full_a(st) ({                              \
    int *_st = (int *)st;                                 \
    LST_get_capacity_a(_st) == LST_get_size_a(_st);   \
    })
```

The two macros could check that the parameter is not NULL, but I will leave that to you.

Listing 4-5 shows the function lst_list_a(), which lists the stack content.

Listing 4-5. lst_list_a()

```
1. //--------------------------------------------------------------- lst_list_a
2. void lst_list_a(void **ptr) {
3.   if (ptr == NULL) {
4.     fprintf(stderr, "lst_list_a: stack pointer is NULL\n");
5.     fflush(stderr);
6.     abort();                                            // -->
7.   }
8.   int capacity = LST_get_capacity_a(ptr);
9.   int size = LST_get_size_a(ptr);
10.   printf("capacity=%d size=%d\n", capacity, size);
11.   for (int k = 0; k < capacity; k++) {
12.     printf("%d: %p", k, &ptr[k]);
13.     if (k < size) printf(" %p\n", ptr[k]);
14.     printf("\n");
15.   }
16. } // lst_list_a
```

Pretty straightforward. For example, if you execute the code in Listing 4-6, you get the following listing:

```
capacity=5 size=2
0: 0x1026018 0x7ffe8834bee0
1: 0x1026020 0x7ffe8834bef0
2: 0x1026028
3: 0x1026030
4: 0x1026038
```

Listing 4-6. Listing the Content of a Stack

```
typedef struct item_t { int value; } item_t;
item_t **stack_a = NULL;
LST_new_stack_a(stack_a, 5);
item_t fi = { 111 };
LST_push_a(stack_a, fi);
item_t second = { 222 };
LST_push_a(stack_a, second);
LST_list_a(stack_a);
```

Just to see the addresses is not very useful, but a generic function like lst_list_a() cannot do more than that because it has no knowledge of the items' structure. To improve on the basic function, you can add as a parameter a pointer to a callback function that knows how to handle the items.

First of all, you write a function specifically designed to handle the items on your stack. As a function to display an item only needs to know the address of the item and doesn't need to return any value, it can have the simple prototype void fun(void *). Then, you add to lst_list_a() the parameter void (*fun)(void *), which defines a pointer to the function you have just written. All you need to do to invoke your callback function from within lst_list_a() is execute fun(item_p), where item_p is the address of the item you want to display. Listing 4-7 shows an improved version of lst_list_a() that can handle a callback function.

Listing 4-7. An improved lst_list_a()

```
1. //----------------------------------------------------------------- lst_list_a
2. void lst_list_a(void **ptr, void (*fun)(void *)) {
3.   if (ptr == NULL) {
4.     fprintf(stderr, "lst_list_a: stack pointer is NULL\n");
5.     fflush(stderr);
6.     abort();                                               // -->
7.   }
8.   int capacity = LST_get_capacity_a(ptr);
9.   int size = LST_get_size_a(ptr);
10.  printf("capacity=%d size=%d\n", capacity, size);
11.  for (int k = 0; k < capacity; k++) {
12.    printf("%d: %p", k, &ptr[k]);
13.    if (k < size) {
14.      printf(" %p", ptr[k]);
15.      if (fun) (*fun)(ptr[k]);
16.    }
17.    printf("\n");
18.  }
19. } // lst_list_a
```

As you can see, all you need to do is replace line 13 of Listing 4-5 with lines 13 to 16 of Listing 4-7. The only addition is in fact line 15. The check that the function pointer is not NULL lets you use the same listing function without callback by passing NULL as last argument. The two following macros let you use lst_list_a() comfortably:

```
#define LST_list_a(st) lst_list_a((void **)(st), NULL)
#define LST_list_a_plus(st, fun) lst_list_a((void **)(st), fun)
```

If you replace

```
LST_list_a(stack_a);
```

with

```
LST_list_a_plus(stack_a, print_value);
```

in the code of Listing 4-6, here is what you get:

```
capacity=5 size=2
0: 0x1bbd018 0x7ffc02e4e370  111
1: 0x1bbd020 0x7ffc02e4e380  222
2: 0x1bbd028
3: 0x1bbd030
4: 0x1bbd038
```

The function print_value() is trivial:

```
void print_value(void *item) {
  printf("%5d", ((item_t *)item)->value);
  }
```

More on Array-Based Stacks

Array-based stacks are easy to implement, but they have a drawback: you need to decide in advance how many items your stack is going to hold. Or do you? Listing 4-8 shows the function lst_set_capacity_a(), which lets you change the capacity of a stack.

Listing 4-8. lst_set_capacity_a()

```
1.  //------------------------------------------------------- lst_set_capacity_a
2.  int lst_set_capacity_a(void ***stack_ptr, int n) {
3.    int possible = 0;
4.    if (n > 0) {
5.      void **stack = *stack_ptr;
6.      if (stack == NULL) {
7.        fprintf(stderr, "lst_set_capacity: stack pointer is NULL\n");
8.        fflush(stderr);
9.        abort();                                              // -->
10.       }
11.     int size = LST_get_size_a(stack);
12.     possible = size <= n;
13.     if (possible) {
14.       void **new_stack = NULL;
15.       lst_new_stack_a(&new_stack, n);
16.       Set_size(new_stack, size);
17.       if (size > 0) {
18.         for (int k = 0; k < size && stack[k]; k++) new_stack[k] = stack[k];
19.         }
20.       free((int *)*stack_ptr - 2);
```

```
21.        *stack_ptr = new_stack;
22.        }
23.     }
24.  return possible;
25.  } // lst_set_capacity_a
```

The algorithm is simple: allocate a new stack of the requested capacity, copy the items from the current stack to the new one, release the old stack, and replace the stack pointer in the calling program with the address of the new stack. The function returns true if the requested stack size is large enough to hold all the items that are in the current stack.

And here is the macro that you can use to invoke lst_set_capacity_a() in a simple and consistent way:

```
#define LST_set_capacity_a(stack, n) lst_set_capacity_a((void ***)&(stack), n)
```

As a further mechanism associated with stack capacity, you might decide to implement an automatic extension of the stack when it fills up. All you would need to do is modify lst_push_a() in a couple of places (refer to Listing 4-3).

First of all, you have to replace the first parameter void **stack with void ***stack_ptr. This will make it possible to change the stack address in the calling program, and you need to be able to do so in order to replace the current stack array with a larger one.

Then, immediately below line 10, you have to add the following few lines of code:

```
if (size >= capacity) {
  int new_capacity = (int)(capacity * 1.1) + 1;
  if (lst_set_capacity(stack_ptr, new_capacity)) {
    capacity = new_capacity;
    }
  }
```

Obviously, size couldn't possibly exceed capacity, as it only increases by 1 every time you invoke lst_push_a(). Therefore, it always equals capacity before exceeding it. But being defensive is a good practice to adopt.

Finally, insert the definition of stack below line 2:

```
void **stack = *stack_ptr;
```

The 1 added to new_capacity caters to the case in which the initial stack capacity is less than 10. Notice that, if the stack extension fails, capacity remains unchanged and the function returns without pushing the new item onto the stack.

I haven't tested these changes, but they should work. Please let me know if you find any bugs! It is amazing how easy it is to make mistakes even in a handful of statements...

As a further refinement, instead of hard-coding a 10% capacity increase, you could use 10% (or any other fraction) as a default and provide an additional parameter in lst_new_stack_a() to set its actual value. But then, of course, as every stack would have its own increment, you would be forced to store its value in the stack itself, beside the values of capacity and size.

Listing 4-9 shows examples of array-based stack functions, and Listing 4-10 shows the resulting output.

Listing 4-9. Usage Examples of Array-Based Stacks

```
//---------- Array-based stacks.
printf("=== Array-based stacks\n");
```

```c
// Allocate the stack
item_t **stack_a = NULL;
LST_new_stack_a(stack_a, 7);
LST_list_a(stack_a);

printf("\n=== Reducing stack capacity to 3\n");
LST_set_capacity_a(stack_a, 3);
LST_list_a(stack_a);

// Push two items onto the stack.
item_t fi = { NULL, 111 };
printf("pushed %d: %s\n", fi.value,
    (LST_push_a(stack_a, fi)) ? "ok": "stack full");
item_t second = { NULL, 222 };
printf("pushed %d: %s\n", second.value,
    (LST_push_a(stack_a, second)) ? "ok": "stack full");
LST_list_a(stack_a);

printf("\n=== Listing the stack with a call-back function\n");
LST_list_a_plus(stack_a, print_value);
printf("The stack is%s empty!\n", ((LST_is_empty_a(stack_a)) ? "" : " not"));
printf("The stack is%s full!\n", ((LST_is_full_a(stack_a)) ? "" : " not"));

// Pop them.
item_t *it = NULL;
do {
  it = LST_pop_a(stack_a);
  printf("popped %p", it);
  if (it) printf(": %d\n", it->value);
  else printf("\n");
  } while (it);
printf("The stack is%s empty!\n", ((LST_is_empty_a(stack_a)) ? "" : " not"));

// Fill up the stack to capacity.
printf("\n=== Filling up the stack to capacity\n");
for (int j = 0; j < LST_get_capacity_a(stack_a) + 1; j++) {
  printf("pushed %d: %s\n", fi.value,
      (LST_push_a(stack_a, fi)) ? "ok": "stack full");
  }
printf("The stack is%s full!\n", ((LST_is_full_a(stack_a)) ? "" : " not"));
LST_list_a(stack_a);

// Change the stack maximum size.
printf("\n=== Attempting to resize the stack with too small capacity\n");
printf("Setting capacity to 2 %s\n",
    (LST_set_capacity_a(stack_a, 2)) ? "succeeded" : "failed");
printf("Setting capacity to 4 %s\n",
    (LST_set_capacity_a(stack_a, 4)) ? "succeeded" : "failed");

// Create a second stack.
printf("\n=== Create a second stack\n");
item_t **stack_b = NULL;
```

```
LST_new_stack_a(stack_b, 2);
printf("pushed %d to the second stack: %s\n", second.value,
    (LST_push_a(stack_b, second)) ? "ok": "stack full");
printf("pushed %d to the second stack: %s\n", second.value,
    (LST_push_a(stack_b, second)) ? "ok": "stack full");

// List both stacks.
printf("stack_a: ");
LST_list_a_plus(stack_a, print_value);
printf("stack_b: ");
LST_list_a_plus(stack_b, print_value);

// Release the stacks.
LST_free_stack_a(stack_a);
LST_free_stack_a(stack_b);
```

Listing 4-10. Usage Examples of Array-Based Stacks—Output

```
capacity=7 size=0
0: 0x1841018
1: 0x1841020
2: 0x1841028
3: 0x1841030
4: 0x1841038
5: 0x1841040
6: 0x1841048

=== Reducing stack capacity to 3
capacity=3 size=0
0: 0x1841068
1: 0x1841070
2: 0x1841078
pushed 111: ok
pushed 222: ok
capacity=3 size=2
0: 0x1841068 0x7fff648ced70
1: 0x1841070 0x7fff648ced80
2: 0x1841078

=== Listing the stack with a call-back function
capacity=3 size=2
0: 0x1841068 0x7fff648ced70   111
1: 0x1841070 0x7fff648ced80   222
2: 0x1841078
The stack is not empty!
The stack is not full!
popped 0x7fff648ced80: 222
popped 0x7fff648ced70: 111
popped (nil)
The stack is empty!
```

```
=== Filling up the stack to capacity
pushed 111: ok
pushed 111: ok
pushed 111: ok
pushed 111: stack full
The stack is full!
capacity=3 size=3
0: 0x1841068 0x7fff648ced70
1: 0x1841070 0x7fff648ced70
2: 0x1841078 0x7fff648ced70

=== Attempting to resize the stack with too small capacity
Setting capacity to 2 failed
Setting capacity to 4 succeeded

=== Create a second stack
pushed 222 to the second stack: ok
pushed 222 to the second stack: ok
stack_a: capacity=4 size=3
0: 0x1841098 0x7fff648ced70   111
1: 0x18410a0 0x7fff648ced70   111
2: 0x18410a8 0x7fff648ced70   111
3: 0x18410b0
stack_b: capacity=2 size=2
0: 0x18410c8 0x7fff648ced80   222
1: 0x18410d0 0x7fff648ced80   222
```

Linked-List Stacks

If you add a pointer to the item structure, you can easily implement a stack without needing to allocate memory. Here is how the new item_t looks:

```
typedef struct item_t item_t;
struct item_t {
  item_t *next;
  int    value;
  };
```

As there is no need to allocate memory, all you need to do to start a stack is define a pointer to an item and initialize it to NULL:

```
item_t *stack = NULL;
```

Instead of adding a pointer to item_t, you could define a stack-item structure to encapsulate each item "behind the scenes":

```
typedef struct lst_item_t lst_item_t;
struct lst_item_t {
  lst_item_t *next;
  void       *item_p; // this points to the item you are actually pushing
  };
```

But then, you would need to have one of such structures available for each new item, which would cause an allocation of a small memory block. I don't know about you, but I would find such fragmentation of the heap quite unsavory. Instead of adopting such a laborious (and delicate) solution, you might as well use an array-based stack as described earlier in this chapter.

Be aware that, while with an array-based stack you can push the same item onto the same stack multiple times, you cannot do the same with linked-list stacks because each successive push would corrupt the stack. To be precise, it would make the items below the first instance of the duplicated item unreachable, and transform the stack into a loop, with catastrophic consequences.

The obvious solution to protect from duplications of items would be to scan the stack and verify that the address of the item is not yet in it. But that would be quite inefficient. An alternative could be to add a flag component like int stacked to the item structure, which you would initialize to 0 and only set it to 1 when you add the item to the stack. It would work for both array- and linked-list- based stacks, but would cause problems if the same item needed to be added to more than one stack.

Listing 4-11 shows the macros that let you perform push, pop, and info operations on linked-list stacks.

Listing 4-11. Macros to Handle Linked-List Stacks

```
1.  #define LST_list_stack(st) LST_list_stack_plus(st, lst_do_nothing)
2.  #define LST_list_stack_plus(st, fun) {     \
3.      item_t *_next = st;                    \
4.      int k = 0;                             \
5.      if (_next) {                           \
6.        while (_next) {                      \
7.          printf("%3d: %p", k++, _next);     \
8.          fun(_next);                        \
9.          printf("\n");                      \
10.         _next = _next->next;               \
11.         }                                  \
12.       }                                    \
13.     else {                                 \
14.       printf("Stack empty\n");             \
15.       }                                    \
16.     }
17. #define LST_pop(st) ({                         \
18.     item_t **_stack_p = &(st);                 \
19.     item_t *_item_p = *_stack_p;               \
20.     if (_item_p) *_stack_p = _item_p->next;    \
21.     _item_p;                                   \
22.     })
23. #define LST_push(st, it) {                       \
24.     item_t **_stack_p = &(st);                   \
25.     item_t *_item_p = &(it);                     \
26.     if (*_stack_p) _item_p->next = *_stack_p;    \
27.     else _item_p->next = NULL;                   \
28.     *_stack_p = _item_p;                         \
29.     }
30. #define LST_stack_size(st) ({  \
31.     item_t *_item_p = st;      \
32.     int _k = 0;                \
33.     while (_item_p) {          \
34.       _k++;                    \
35.       _item_p = _item_p->next; \
36.       }                        \
```

```
37.      _k;                              \
38.      })
39. #define LST_top(st) (st)
40. #define LST_is_empty(sta) (LST_stack_size(sta) == 0)
```

LST_push() (lines 23 to 29), like its counterpart for array-based stacks, accepts two parameters: a stack and an item. The purpose of lines 24 and 25 is to avoid referencing each input parameter more than once. After that, as you can see, all the macro does is chain the new item in front of the item currently on top of the stack (if any).

LST_pop() (lines 17 to 22) is even simpler, as all it needs to do is unchain the item on top of the stack (if any).

LST_stack_size() is more complicated than its array-based counterpart (LST_get_size_a()) because linked-list stacks do not maintain the stack size in a variable. Therefore, LST_stack_size() needs to measure the length of the chain of next components from the top down until it reaches the first item pushed onto the stack, which has next set to NULL.

With array-based sacks, LST_list_a_plus() passed on to the function lst_list_a() the callback function print_value(), while the address-only listing macro LST_list_a() invoked lst_list_a() with the callback parameter set to NULL.

If you attempt to do the same with the linked-list stacks, the compiler rejects the resulting NULL(_next) in line 9. And the compiler still reports an error if you only execute fun(_next) when fun is not NULL. A simple solution is to use a dummy function as callback to print an address-only list. This is the purpose of the function lst_do_nothing(), which has an empty body.

Note that the macros for linked-list stacks in general "know" the type item_t. If you compile your code with the gcc compiler, you have the possibility of using the typeof() function. Then, you can replace the following lines of Listing 4-11.

```
 3. item_t * _stack = st;   \
18. item_t ** _stack_p = &(st);  \
19. item_t * _item_p = * _stack_p;  \
24. item_t ** _stack_p = &(st);  \
25. item_t * _item_p = &(it);  \
31. item_t * _item_p = st;  \
```

with

```
typeof(st) _next = st;  \
typeof(st) * _stack_p = &(st);  \
typeof(st) _item_p = * _stack_p;  \
typeof(it) ** _stack_p = &(st);  \
typeof(it)  * _item_p = &(it);  \
typeof(st) _item_p = st;  \
```

thereby allowing the macros to work without "knowing" of the existence of item_t. To use typeof(), you need to replace the compiler option -std=c99 with -std=gnu99.

Unfortunately, I haven't found any "nice" way of making the macros work without "knowing" that the next component of item_t is named next.

I did find a "naughty" way of removing the knowledge of next from the macros. I will describe it to you so that you have another programming trick up your sleeve, but I discourage you from using it because it makes the code more difficult to maintain.

The crucial issue is that it only works if next is the first component of item_t. The idea is that if you define a structure (e.g., lst_item_t) with a pointer as first element (e.g., named nxt) and typecast item_t to it, you can use the component name of the new structure (i.e., nxt) to refer to the pointer without knowing how it is called in item_t. Very sneaky!

Here it is how it would work in practice. First of all, define in `lists.h` the following type:

```
typedef struct lst_item_t lst_item_t;
struct lst_item_t {
  lst_item_t *nxt;
  };
```

Then, as an example, Listing 4-12 shows how you need to modify `LST_pop()` (the line numbers match those of the original shown in Listing 4-11).

Listing 4-12. A Naughty Version of LST_pop()

```
17. #define LST_pop(st) ({                              \
18.     lst_item_t ** _stack_p = (lst_item_t **)&(st);  \
19.     lst_item_t * _item_p = * _stack_p;              \
20.     if (_item_p) * _stack_p = _item_p->nxt;         \
21.     (typeof(st))_item_p;                            \
22.     })
```

As you can see, you need `typeof(item_t *)` to typecast the result.

Listing 4-13 shows some examples of how to use linked-list stack macros, and Listing 4-14 shows their output.

Listing 4-13. Usage Examples of Linked-List Stacks

```
//---------- Linked-list stacks.
printf("=== Linked-list stacks\n");
item_t *stack = NULL;
item_t item_1 = { NULL, 100 };
LST_push(stack, item_1);
item_t item_2 = { NULL, 200 };
LST_push(stack, item_2);
printf("Pushed two items\n");
LST_list_stack(stack);

printf("\nList stack with call-back\n");
LST_list_stack_plus(stack, print_value);
item_t *item = LST_top(stack);
if (item) printf("Top of the stack: %d\n", LST_top(stack)->value);
else printf("The stack is empty\n");
printf("Stack size: %d\n", LST_stack_size(stack));

printf("\nPopping %d\n", LST_pop(stack)->value);
printf("Stack size: %d\n", LST_stack_size(stack));
LST_list_stack_plus(stack, print_value);

printf("\nPopping %d\n", LST_pop(stack)->value);
printf("Stack size: %d\n", LST_stack_size(stack));
LST_list_stack_plus(stack, print_value);
item = LST_top(stack);
if (item) printf("Top of the stack: %d\n", LST_top(stack)->value);
else printf("Top of the stack: stack empty\n");
```

Listing 4-14. Usage Examples of Linked-List Stacks—Output

```
=== Linked-list stacks
Pushed two items
  0: 0x7ffdb6552ec0
  1: 0x7ffdb6552eb0

List stack with call-back
  0: 0x7ffdb6552ec0  200
  1: 0x7ffdb6552eb0  100
Top of the stack: 200
Stack size: 2

Popping 200
Stack size: 1
  0: 0x7ffdb6552eb0  100

Popping 100
Stack size: 0
Stack empty
Top of the stack: stack empty
```

Queues

When applied to queues, the list operations become:

- Create and delete a queue

- Enqueue and dequeue an item

- Know what is in a queue

As we did for stacks, we will look at queues implemented as arrays and as linked lists.

Array-Based Queues

As you will see, the implementation of queues as arrays is similar to the implementation of stacks, but not quite the same.

Create and Delete a Queue

You only need one pointer when adding/removing items to/from a stack, but you need two pointers when dealing with queues. This is because you add items to an end of a queue and remove them from the other end, as shown in Figure 4-3.

So, for example, if you have a queue that has a capacity of five items, after adding four items and removing two (and assuming that removals were always performed when the queue did contain items to be removed), the pointers will be like shown in Figure 4-4.

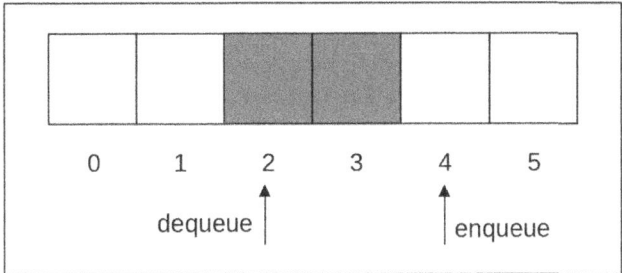

Figure 4-4. *Enqueued 4, dequeued 2*

When queue was created empty, and both enqueuing and dequeuing indices pointed to the 0th element. Then, each enqueuing and dequeuing operation moved the corresponding index to the right. If you dequeue the two items shown in gray in Figure 4-4, the indices will coincide, which is always the case when the queue is empty, regardless to what element of the array the indices point to.

If you add one more item, the enqueuing index points to element 5, which is the last element of the array. Then if you add another item, the enqueuing index *wraps around* and points to element 0. The dequeuing index behaves in the same way. In other words, the dequeuing index chases the enqueuing index and only catches up with it when the queue becomes empty.

Listing 4-15 shows lst_new_queue_a(). It corresponds to lst_new_stack_a(), as shown in Listing 4-1.

Listing 4-15. lst_new_queue_a()

```
1.  //------------------------------------------------------------- lst_new_queue_a
2.  void lst_new_queue_a(void ***queue_ptr, int n) {
3.    if (n <= 0) {
4.      fprintf(stderr, "lst_new_queue_a: %d elements?\n", n);
5.      fflush(stderr);
6.      abort();                                                  // -->
7.      }
8.    int *ptr = malloc((n + 1) * sizeof(void *) + 3 * sizeof(int));
9.    if (ptr == NULL) {
10.     fprintf(stderr, "lst_new_queue_a: failed to allocate %d-queue\n", n);
11.     fflush(stderr);
12.     abort();                                                  // -->
13.     }
14.   int *i_enq_p = ptr++;
15.   *i_enq_p = 0;
16.   int *capacity_p = ptr++;
17.   *capacity_p = n;
18.   int *i_deq_p = ptr++;
19.   *i_deq_p = 0;
20.   void **queue = (void **)ptr;
21.   for (int k = 0; k <= n; k++) queue[k] = NULL; // <=, not <
22.   *queue_ptr = queue;
23.   } // lst_new_queue_a
```

If you compare the two lines that allocate memory in lst_new_queue_a() and lst_new_stack_a(), you see two differences.

First, you allocate for a queue one extra element by adding 1 to n. This means that one element of the array remains empty after you add *N* items to a queue of capacity *N*. The purpose of the additional element is to avoid that the two indices coincide when the queue is completely full. It would still be possible to distinguish the two conditions queue-empty and queue-full, but only by saving the queue size or at least a flag indicating the queue status. Introducing a buffer element is neater and makes the algorithms simpler.

Secondly, while a stack required two parameters (capacity and size), a queue requires three parameters: enqueuing index, capacity, and dequeuing index.

It is so because in a stack the last item added (i.e., *pushed*) is also the first one removed (i.e., *popped*), which means that you perform both operation in the same place (i.e., at the top of the stack). With a queue, you add and remove items in two different places, so that you can operate on them separately: you add items at the end of the queue and remove them from the front. It will become completely clear if you think of a physical queue, like that formed by people standing in line to, say, enter a ride in an amusement park. It must be clear at any time who's first and who's last! And when you "enqueue" yourself at the end of the line, you have to wait that all those before you have moved on before the ride's assistant can "dequeue" you.

The rest of lst_new_queue_a() should be clear. Just one point requires perhaps a clarification. While for stacks in line 19 of Listing 4-1 you reset n elements (0 <= k < n), for queues (see line 21 of Listing 4-15), you reset n+1 elements (0 <= k <= n). This because of the additional element allocated for queues.

Like with stacks, you invoke the queue-allocation function with a macro:

```
#define LST_new_queue_a(queue, n) lst_new_queue_a((void ***)&(queue), n)
```

And, like with stacks (see Listing 4-2), you free queues with a macro (see Listing 4-16).

Listing 4-16. LST_free_queue_a()

```
#define LST_free_queue_a(ptr) {     \
    int **_ptr = (int **)&(ptr);   \
    if (*_ptr != NULL) {            \
      free(*_ptr - 3);             \
      *_ptr = NULL;                \
      }                            \
    }
```

Notice that the only difference between LST_free_stack_a() and LST_free_queue_a() is the number of parameters (respectively two and three). If you wanted to be more of a minimalist than I am, you could define

```
#define LST_free_a(ptr, n) {        \
    int **_ptr = (int **)&(ptr);   \
    if (*_ptr != NULL) {            \
      free(*_ptr - (n));           \
      *_ptr = NULL;                \
      }                            \
    }
```

and then

```
#define LST_free_stack_a(ptr) LST_free_a(ptr, 2)
#define LST_free_queue_a(ptr) LST_free_a(ptr, 3)
```

Enqueue, Dequeue, and Info

The wraparound of queue indices means that the queue items usually are not neatly packed in the array from its first element and without gaps like those of stacks. You can have several configurations, as illustrated by the examples shown in Figure 4-5.

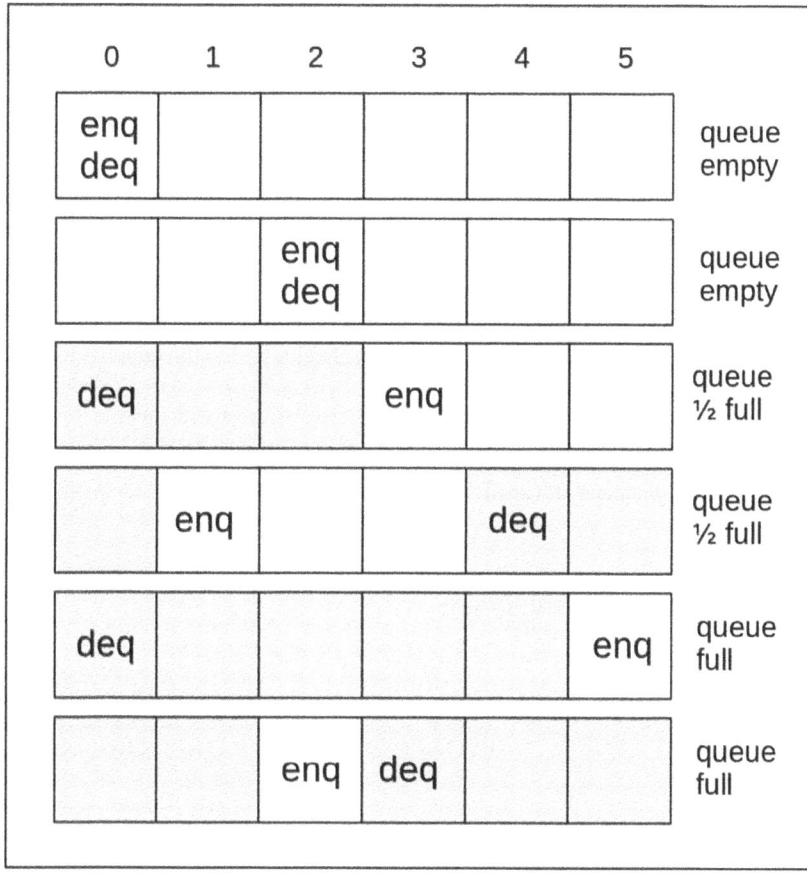

Figure 4-5. *Some possible queue configurations*

All enqueuing, dequeuing, and display functions must cope with them.

Listing 4-17 shows the function `lst_enqueue_a()`. It is the queue-equivalent of the function `lst_push_a()` for stacks shown in Listing 4-3.

Listing 4-17. lst_enqueue_a()

```
1. //------------------------------------------------------------- lst_enqueue_a
2. int lst_enqueue_a(void **queue, void *item) {
3.   if (queue == NULL) {
4.     fprintf(stderr, "lst_enqueue_a: queue pointer is NULL\n");
5.     fflush(stderr);
6.     abort();                                                  // -->
```

```
7.      }
8.    int done = 0;
9.    if (!LST_q_is_full_a(queue)) {
10.      int *i_enq_p = (int *)queue - 3;
11.      int i_enq = *i_enq_p;
12.      queue[i_enq++] = item;
13.      if (i_enq > LST_get_q_capacity_a(queue)) i_enq = 0; // >, not >=
14.      *i_enq_p = i_enq;
15.      done = 1;
16.      }
17.    return done;
18.  } // lst_enqueue_a
```

lst_enqeue_a() uses the macro LST_q_is_full() because the calculation of a queue size is not as immediate as obtaining a stack size. It then uses the enqueuing index to add the item to the queue (line 12 of Listing 4-17). Something that was not needed with stacks is the wrapping around of the enqueuing index when it reaches the end of the array (line 13). Notice that you use a strict greater-than comparison because the array has one element more than the queue capacity.

Listing 4-18 shows the macro to invoke lst_enqueue_a(), a macro to check whether the queue is full, and some additional utility macros.

Listing 4-18. Some Macros for Array-Based Queues

```
#define LST_enqueue_a(qq, item) lst_enqueue_a((void **)(qq), (void *)&(item))

#define LST_q_is_full_a(q) ({                                \
    int *_qq = (int *)q;                                     \
    LST_get_q_size_a(_qq) >= LST_get_q_capacity_a(_qq);      \
    })

#define LST_get_q_size_a(q) ({                    \
    int *_q = (int *)(q);                         \
    int _i_deq = 0;                               \
    int _i_enq = 0;                               \
    if (_q) {                                     \
      _i_deq = (*--_q);                           \
      int _i_cap = (*--_q);                       \
      _i_enq = (*--_q);                           \
      if (_i_enq < _i_deq) _i_enq += _i_cap + 1;  \
      }                                           \
    _i_enq - _i_deq;                              \
    })

#define LST_get_q_capacity_a(q) (*((int *)(q) - 2))

#define LST_q_is_empty_a(q) ({  \
    int *_q = (int *)(q);       \
    *(_q - 3) == *(_q - 1);     \
    })
```

As usual, the macros define local variables whenever they need to refer more than once to parameters. Also note that, as `LST_q_is_full()` uses `LST_get_q_size_a()` and `LST_get_q_capacity_a()`, you keep the names of parameters and local variables distinct to avoid mishaps when the program executes the expanded code.

`LST_get_q_size()` includes more statements than you might have expected because it needs to cope with the wrapping around of both indices. Notice that if you attempt to calculate the size of an uninitialized queue, the macro returns 0 instead of aborting the program.

`LST_q_is_empty()` is simpler than `LST_q_is_full()` because it only needs to check whether the enqueuing and dequeuing indices are identical. If they are, the queue is empty. Obviously, you could have also defined the macro as follows:

```
#define LST_q_is_empty_a(q) (LST_get_q_size_a(q) == 0)
```

but it seems neater and simpler to check for empty queues by comparing the indices.

The function for queues equivalent to `lst_top_a()` for stacks (see Listing 4-4) is `LST_first_a()`, shown in Listing 4-19.

Listing 4-19. lst_first_a()

```
1.  //------------------------------------------------------------------ lst_first_a
2.  void *lst_first_a(void **queue, int remove) {
3.    if (queue == NULL) {
4.      fprintf(stderr, "lst_first_a: queue pointer is NULL\n");
5.      fflush(stderr);
6.      abort();                                              // -->
7.    }
8.    void *item = NULL;
9.    if (!LST_q_is_empty_a(queue)) {
10.     int *i_deq_p = (int *)queue - 1;
11.     int i_deq = *i_deq_p;
12.     item = queue[i_deq];
13.     if (remove) {
14.       queue[i_deq++] = NULL;
15.       if (i_deq > LST_get_q_capacity_a(queue)) i_deq = 0;
16.       *i_deq_p = i_deq;
17.     }
18.   }
19.   return item;
20.  } // lst_first_a
```

The changes applied to `lst_top_a()` to obtain `lst_first_a()` are analogous to those applied to `lst_push_a()` to obtain `lst_enqueue_a()`. Again, a check on the stack size becomes an invocation of a macro (in this case, `LST_q_is_empty()`, in line 9), and an additional statement is needed to wrap around the relevant queue index (line 15).

To control the `remove` parameter in a convenient way, you can use the following two macros:

```
#define LST_dequeue_a(qq) lst_first_a((void **)(qq), 1)
#define LST_first_a(qq) lst_first_a((void **)(qq), 0)
```

Listing a queue is, not surprisingly, very similar to listing a stack, as shown in Listing 4-20.

Listing 4-20. lst_list_qa()

```
1.  //----------------------------------------------------------------- lst_list_qa
2.  void lst_list_qa(void **q, void (*fun)(void *)) {
3.    if (q == NULL) {
4.      fprintf(stderr, "lst_list_qa: queue pointer is NULL\n");
5.      fflush(stderr);
6.      abort();                                           // -->
7.    }
8.    int *i_p = (int *)q;
9.    int i_deq = *--i_p;
10.   int capacity = *--i_p;
11.   int i_enq = *--i_p;
12.   int size = i_enq - i_deq;
13.   if (size < 0) size += capacity + 1;
14.   printf("capacity=%d size=%d\n", capacity, size);
15.   for (int k = 0; k < capacity + 1; k++) {
16.     printf("%d: %p", k, &q[k]);
17.     if (q[k]) {
18.       printf(" %p", q[k]);
19.       if (fun) (*fun)(q[k]);
20.     }
21.     printf("\n");
22.   }
23. } // lst_list_qa
```

When you compare lst_list_qa() with its stack counterpart lst_list_a() shown in Listing 4-7, you see the by now familiar addition of a statement that takes care of wrapping the indices around (line 13). The main difference between listing queues and listing stacks is due to the fact that stack items are neatly packed in the array from its first element and without gaps, while queue items are not. As a result, while with stacks you can check for k < size to identify the array elements that point to items (line 13 of Listing 4-7), with queues you must check whether each element is not NULL.

This is not a big deal, and you could have done the same with stacks, but it makes it a requirement to clear the array element when you dequeue an item (line 14 of Listing 4-19); otherwise, "left-behind" pointers would give the impression that the item is still in the queue.

Actually, now that I think about it, the handling of stacks would not require any check. You would only need to replace the loop in lines 11 to 18 of Listing 4-7 (which I reproduce here for convenience):

```
11.   for (int k = 0; k < capacity; k++) {
12.     printf("%d: %p", k, &ptr[k]);
13.     if (k < size) {
14.       printf(" %p", ptr[k]);
15.       if (fun) (*fun)(ptr[k]);
16.     }
17.     printf("\n");
18.   }
```

with the following two loops:

```
for (int k = 0; k < size; k++) {
  printf("%d: %p %p", k, &ptr[k], ptr[k]);
  if (fun) (*fun)(ptr[k]);
```

```
  printf("\n");
  }
for (int k = size; k < capacity; k++) printf("%d: %p\n", k, &ptr[k]);
```

But I leave it up to you implement the change (for the record, I haven't tested it). In any case, you can use the following macros to list a queue with and without the callback.

```
#define LST_list_qa(qq) lst_list_qa((void **)(qq), NULL)
#define LST_list_qa_plus(qq, fun) lst_list_qa((void **)(qq), fun)
```

More on Array-Based Queues

You can change the capacity of a queue with the function lst_set_q_capacity_a() shown in Listing 4-21. The corresponding function for stacks was lst_set_capacity_a() (see Listing 4-8).

Listing 4-21. lst_set_q_capacity_a()

```
1.  //-------------------------------------------------------- lst_set_q_capacity_a
2.  int lst_set_q_capacity_a(void ***q_ptr, int n) {
3.    int possible = 0;
4.    if (n > 0) {
5.      void **q = *q_ptr;
6.      if (q == NULL) {
7.        fprintf(stderr, "lst_set_q_capacity: queue pointer is NULL\n");
8.        fflush(stderr);
9.        abort();                                              // -->
10.       }
11.     int *i_p = (int *)q;
12.     int *i_deq_p = --i_p;
13.     int capacity = *--i_p;
14.     int *i_enq_p = --i_p;
15.     int size = *i_enq_p - *i_deq_p;
16.     if (size < 0) size += capacity + 1;
17.     possible = size <= n;
18.     if (possible) {
19.       void **new_q = NULL;
20.       lst_new_queue_a(&new_q, n);
21.       if (size) {
22.         for (int k = 0, k_orig = *i_deq_p; k < size; k++) {
23.           new_q[k] = q[k_orig++];
24.           if (k_orig > capacity) k_orig = 0;
25.           }
26.         i_p = (int *)new_q;
27.         *(i_p - 3) = size;
28.         *(i_p - 1) = 0;
29.         }
30.       free((int *)*q_ptr - 3);
31.       *q_ptr = new_q;
32.       }
33.     }
34.   return possible;
35.   } // lst_set_q_capacity_a
```

When I started developing lst_set_q_capacity_a(), I got bogged down by the plethora of possibilities of which Figure 4-5 shows some examples. It was very tricky to decide what was the smallest capacity of the new queue that would allow you to duplicate the original queue into the new one. I was set on copying one queue into the other without changing the indices. But I then realized that the only thing that mattered what the queue size. That is, how many elements of the original array were occupied.

The current function follows the dequeuing index of the original queue (including its possible wraparound) to copy each item to the *beginning* of the new queue. This provided the unexpected bonus of making the new queue fully packed. It means that if you want to *pack* a queue you only need to invoke lst_set_q_capacity_a() with the new capacity identical to the current one. Line 24 is where you wrap around the dequeuing index.

You invoke lst_set_q_capacity_a() with the macro:

```
#define LST_set_q_capacity_a(qq, n) lst_set_q_capacity_a((void ***)&(qq), n)
```

Listing 4-22 shows examples of array-based queue functions, and Listing 4-23 shows the resulting output. I included several examples to show you how the queue changes with subsequent enqueuings and dequeuings.

Listing 4-22. Usage Examples of Array-Based Queues

```
//---------- Array-based queues.
printf("\n\n=== Array-based queues\n");

// Allocate the queue
item_t **q_a = NULL;
LST_new_queue_a(q_a, 3);
printf("capacity: %d\n", LST_get_q_capacity_a(q_a));
printf("size: %d\n", LST_get_q_size_a(q_a));
printf("queue is%s empty\n", LST_q_is_empty_a(q_a) ? "" : " not");

item_t it1 = { NULL, 1 };
printf("\nenqueuing it1 %sdone\n", (LST_enqueue_a(q_a, it1)) ? "" : "not ");
printf("size: %d\n", LST_get_q_size_a(q_a));
printf("queue is%s full\n", LST_q_is_full_a(q_a) ? "" : " not");

item_t it2 = { NULL, 2 };
printf("\nenqueuing it2 %sdone\n", (LST_enqueue_a(q_a, it2)) ? "" : "not ");
printf("size: %d\n", LST_get_q_size_a(q_a));
printf("queue is%s full\n", LST_q_is_full_a(q_a) ? "" : " not");

item_t it3 = { NULL, 3 };
printf("\nenqueuing it3 %sdone\n", (LST_enqueue_a(q_a, it3)) ? "" : "not ");
printf("size: %d\n", LST_get_q_size_a(q_a));
printf("queue is%s full\n", LST_q_is_full_a(q_a) ? "" : " not");

item_t it4 = { NULL, 4 };
printf("\nenqueuing it4 %sdone\n", (LST_enqueue_a(q_a, it4)) ? "" : "not ");

printf("\nLST_list_qa_plus: ");
LST_list_qa_plus(q_a, print_value);
```

```
item_t *it_p = LST_dequeue_a(q_a);
printf("\ndequeued item %p %d\n", it_p, (it_p) ? it_p->value : -1);
LST_list_qa_plus(q_a, print_value);

printf("\nenqueuing it4 %sdone\n", (LST_enqueue_a(q_a, it4)) ? "" : "not ");
LST_list_qa_plus(q_a, print_value);

it_p = LST_dequeue_a(q_a);
printf("\ndequeued item %p %d\n", it_p, (it_p) ? it_p->value : -1);
LST_list_qa_plus(q_a, print_value);

item_t it5 = { NULL, 5 };
printf("\nenqueuing it5 %sdone\n", (LST_enqueue_a(q_a, it5)) ? "" : "not ");
LST_list_qa_plus(q_a, print_value);

it_p = LST_dequeue_a(q_a);
printf("\ndequeued item %p %d\n", it_p, (it_p) ? it_p->value : -1);
LST_list_qa_plus(q_a, print_value);

printf("\nenqueuing it1 %sdone\n", (LST_enqueue_a(q_a, it1)) ? "" : "not ");
LST_list_qa_plus(q_a, print_value);

it_p = LST_dequeue_a(q_a);
printf("\ndequeued item %p %d\n", it_p, (it_p) ? it_p->value : -1);
LST_list_qa_plus(q_a, print_value);

printf("\nenqueuing it2 %sdone\n", (LST_enqueue_a(q_a, it2)) ? "" : "not ");
LST_list_qa_plus(q_a, print_value);

it_p = LST_dequeue_a(q_a);
printf("\ndequeued item %p %d\n", it_p, (it_p) ? it_p->value : -1);
LST_list_qa_plus(q_a, print_value);

printf("\nenqueuing it3 %sdone\n", (LST_enqueue_a(q_a, it3)) ? "" : "not ");
LST_list_qa_plus(q_a, print_value);

printf("\nmaking a new queue of a larger size %s\n",
    (LST_set_q_capacity_a(q_a, 4)) ? "succeeded" : "failed");
LST_list_qa_plus(q_a, print_value);
//
printf("\nmaking a new queue of the original size %s\n",
    (LST_set_q_capacity_a(q_a, 3)) ? "succeeded" : "failed");
LST_list_qa_plus(q_a, print_value);
//
printf("\nmaking a new queue of a smaller size %s\n",
    (LST_set_q_capacity_a(q_a, 2)) ? "succeeded" : "failed");
LST_list_qa_plus(q_a, print_value);

it_p = LST_dequeue_a(q_a);
printf("\ndequeued item %p %d\n", it_p, (it_p) ? it_p->value : -1);
LST_list_qa_plus(q_a, print_value);
```

```
it_p = LST_dequeue_a(q_a);
printf("\ndequeued item %p %d\n", it_p, (it_p) ? it_p->value : -1);
LST_list_qa_plus(q_a, print_value);

it_p = LST_first_a(q_a);
printf("first item %p %d\n", it_p, (it_p) ? it_p->value : -1);

printf("\nmaking a new queue of a size 1 %s\n",
    (LST_set_q_capacity_a(q_a, 1)) ? "succeeded" : "failed");
LST_list_qa_plus(q_a, print_value);
//
printf("\nmaking a new queue of size 0 %s\n",
    (LST_set_q_capacity_a(q_a, 0)) ? "succeeded" : "failed");
LST_list_qa_plus(q_a, print_value);

it_p = LST_dequeue_a(q_a);
printf("\ndequeued item %p %d\n", it_p, (it_p) ? it_p->value : -1);
LST_list_qa_plus(q_a, print_value);

it_p = LST_dequeue_a(q_a);
printf("\ndequeued item %p %d\n", it_p, (it_p) ? it_p->value : -1);

// Free the queue.
LST_free_queue_a(q_a);
```

Listing 4-23. Usage Examples of Array-Based Queues—Output

```
=== Array-based queues
capacity: 3
size: 0
queue is empty

enqueuing it1 done
size: 1
queue is not full

enqueuing it2 done
size: 2
queue is not full

enqueuing it3 done
size: 3
queue is full

enqueuing it4 not done

LST_list_qa_plus: capacity=3 size=3
0: 0x177801c 0x7ffdde294040    1
1: 0x1778024 0x7ffdde294050    2
2: 0x177802c 0x7ffdde294060    3
3: 0x1778034
```

```
dequeued item 0x7ffdde294040 1
capacity=3 size=2
0: 0x177801c
1: 0x1778024 0x7ffdde294050    2
2: 0x177802c 0x7ffdde294060    3
3: 0x1778034

enqueuing it4 done
capacity=3 size=3
0: 0x177801c
1: 0x1778024 0x7ffdde294050    2
2: 0x177802c 0x7ffdde294060    3
3: 0x1778034 0x7ffdde294070    4

dequeued item 0x7ffdde294050 2
capacity=3 size=2
0: 0x177801c
1: 0x1778024
2: 0x177802c 0x7ffdde294060    3
3: 0x1778034 0x7ffdde294070    4

enqueuing it5 done
capacity=3 size=3
0: 0x177801c 0x7ffdde294080    5
1: 0x1778024
2: 0x177802c 0x7ffdde294060    3
3: 0x1778034 0x7ffdde294070    4

dequeued item 0x7ffdde294060 3
capacity=3 size=2
0: 0x177801c 0x7ffdde294080    5
1: 0x1778024
2: 0x177802c
3: 0x1778034 0x7ffdde294070    4

enqueuing it1 done
capacity=3 size=3
0: 0x177801c 0x7ffdde294080    5
1: 0x1778024 0x7ffdde294040    1
2: 0x177802c
3: 0x1778034 0x7ffdde294070    4

dequeued item 0x7ffdde294070 4
capacity=3 size=2
0: 0x177801c 0x7ffdde294080    5
1: 0x1778024 0x7ffdde294040    1
2: 0x177802c
3: 0x1778034

enqueuing it2 done
capacity=3 size=3
```

111

```
0: 0x177801c 0x7ffdde294080    5
1: 0x1778024 0x7ffdde294040    1
2: 0x177802c 0x7ffdde294050    2
3: 0x1778034

dequeued item 0x7ffdde294080 5
capacity=3 size=2
0: 0x177801c
1: 0x1778024 0x7ffdde294040    1
2: 0x177802c 0x7ffdde294050    2
3: 0x1778034

enqueuing it3 done
capacity=3 size=3
0: 0x177801c
1: 0x1778024 0x7ffdde294040    1
2: 0x177802c 0x7ffdde294050    2
3: 0x1778034 0x7ffdde294060    3

making a new queue of a larger size succeeded
capacity=4 size=3
0: 0x177805c 0x7ffdde294040    1
1: 0x1778064 0x7ffdde294050    2
2: 0x177806c 0x7ffdde294060    3
3: 0x1778074
4: 0x177807c

making a new queue of the original size succeeded
capacity=3 size=3
0: 0x177801c 0x7ffdde294040    1
1: 0x1778024 0x7ffdde294050    2
2: 0x177802c 0x7ffdde294060    3
3: 0x1778034

making a new queue of a smaller size failed
capacity=3 size=3
0: 0x177801c 0x7ffdde294040    1
1: 0x1778024 0x7ffdde294050    2
2: 0x177802c 0x7ffdde294060    3
3: 0x1778034

dequeued item 0x7ffdde294040 1
capacity=3 size=2
0: 0x177801c
1: 0x1778024 0x7ffdde294050    2
2: 0x177802c 0x7ffdde294060    3
3: 0x1778034

dequeued item 0x7ffdde294050 2
capacity=3 size=1
0: 0x177801c
```

```
1: 0x1778024
2: 0x177802c 0x7ffdde294060    3
3: 0x1778034

first item 0x7ffdde294060 3

making a new queue of a size 1 succeeded
capacity=1 size=1
0: 0x177809c 0x7ffdde294060    3
1: 0x17780a4

making a new queue of size 0 failed
capacity=1 size=1
0: 0x177809c 0x7ffdde294060    3
1: 0x17780a4

dequeued item 0x7ffdde294060 3
capacity=1 size=0
0: 0x177809c
1: 0x17780a4

dequeued item (nil) -1
```

Linked-List Queues

Like with linked-list stacks, you can implement linked-list queues purely with macros. But there is a problem. When you duplicated the functionality of array-based stacks to a stack implementation based on linked lists, all you needed to represent a stack was a pointer to its top item. When you go through a similar process for queues, you need two pointers: one to the first item and one to the last. Without the former you can't dequeue, and without the latter you can't enqueue.

To solve this issue, you define the following structure type in lists.h:

```
typedef struct lst_queue_t {
  void *first;
  void *last;
  } lst_queue_t;
```

This makes possible for you to define a new queue as follows:

```
lst_queue_t queue = {};
```

You can then handle linked-list queues with the macros shown in Listing 4-24.

Listing 4-24. Macros to Handle Linked-List Queues

```
1. #define LST_dequeue(q) ({                       \
2.     lst_queue_t *_q_p = &(q);                    \
3.     item_t *_it_p = _q_p->first;                 \
4.     if (_it_p) {                                 \
5.       _q_p->first = _it_p->next;                 \
6.       if (_it_p->next) _it_p->next = NULL;       \
```

```
7.          else _q_p->last = NULL;                    \
8.          }                                          \
9.          _it_p;                                     \
10.         })
11.  #define LST_enqueue(q, it) {                              \
12.          lst_queue_t * _q_p = &(q);                        \
13.          item_t * _it_p = &(it);                           \
14.          if (_q_p->last) ((item_t *)_q_p->last)->next = _it_p;  \
15.          else _q_p->first = _it_p;                         \
16.          _q_p->last = _it_p;                               \
17.          _it_p->next = NULL;                               \
18.          }
19.  #define LST_first(q) (q.first)
20.  #define LST_list_queue(q) LST_list_queue_plus(q, lst_do_nothing)
21.  #define LST_list_queue_plus(q, fun) {    \
22.          item_t * _next = (q).first;      \
23.          int k = 0;                       \
24.          if (_next) {                     \
25.            while (_next) {                \
26.              printf("%3d: %p", k++, _next);  \
27.              fun(_next);                  \
28.              printf("\n");                \
29.              _next = _next->next;         \
30.            }                              \
31.          }                                \
32.          else {                           \
33.            printf("Queue empty\n");       \
34.          }                                \
35.          }
36.  #define LST_queue_size(q) ({    \
37.          item_t * _it_p = (q).first;  \
38.          int _k = 0;              \
39.          while (_it_p) {          \
40.            _k++;                  \
41.            _it_p = _it_p->next;   \
42.          }                        \
43.          _k;                      \
44.          })
45.  #define LST_q_is_empty(q) (LST_queue_size(q) == 0)
```

Nothing completely new when compared to the macros for linked-list stacks shown in Listing 4-11. But it is worth paying attention to a couple of points.

First of all, you must initialize new queues so that both first and last pointers are null. Failure to do so will almost certainly result in a crash. Pretty obvious, isn't it?

In LST_dequeue(), you save the pointer to the first item _it_p (line 3) and only proceed to the actual dequeuing if the pointer is not NULL. Line 5 is pretty straightforward: you set the beginning of the queue to the next item. But that is not enough: if there is no item after the one you have just dequeued, it means that the next pointer is NULL. But that means that in line 5 you have set the first pointer of the queue to NULL. You then you must set to NULL also the last pointer of the queue (in line 7). In other words, if you remove from a queue its last item, you must leave behind a properly formed empty queue.

Line 6 is, strictly speaking, unnecessary. All it does is ensure that the next pointer of the dequeued item is NULL. Although you don't need to reset it, it is neater (and safer) to completely dequeue the item.

The only difference between LST_queue_size() and LST_stack_size() is the way in which the first/top item is accessed: (q).first for queues (line 37 of Listing 4-24) and simply st for stacks (line 31 of Listing 4-11). If you wanted, you could define a macro called LST_size() that accepted the first item to be invoked by two one-line macros like the following ones:

```
LST_queue_size(q)  LST_size((q).first)
LST_stack_size(st) LST_size(st)
```

but it doesn't seem really necessary. Similarly, you could merge the the listing macros:

```
LST_list_queue_plus(q, fun)  LST_list((q).first, fun, "Queue")
LST_list_stack_plus(st, fun) LST_list(st, fun, "Stack")
```

Then, all you need to do is replace line 14 of Listing 4-11 and line 33 of Listing 4-24 with:

```
printf("%s empty\n", what); \
```

where what is the name of the third parameter of LST_list().

I leave these changes up to you. I'm happy either way because, for debugging purposes, you might like to add a printf() to stacks but not to queues or vice versa.

Concerning LST_q_is_empty(), you cannot simply compare the first and last pointers of the queue structure because, while in array-based queues the second index points to a free array element, in linked-list queues the second pointer points to an enqueued item. As a result, the two pointers is the queue structure of linked-list queues are also identical when the queue contains a single element.

As with stacks, keep in mind that you can enqueue the same item more than once to an array-based queue, but not to a linked-list queue. This is because, like with stacks, you would corrupt the chain of pointers with catastrophic consequences.

Listing 4-25 shows some examples of macro usage for linked-list queues, and Listing 4-26 shows the corresponding output.

Listing 4-25. Usage Examples of Linked-List Queues

```
//---------- Linked-list queues.
printf("\n\n=== Linked-list queues\n");
lst_queue_t queue = {};

item_t first = { NULL, 101 };
item_t second = { NULL, 202 };
item_t third = { NULL, 303 };
printf("\nenqueuing first item\n");
LST_enqueue(queue, first);
printf("enqueuing second item\n");
LST_enqueue(queue, second);
printf("enqueuing third item\n");
LST_enqueue(queue, third);
LST_list_queue_plus(queue, print_value);
printf("queue size: %d\n", LST_queue_size(queue));

item_t *it_ptr = LST_dequeue(queue);
printf("\ndequeued item %p %d\n", it_ptr, (it_ptr) ? it_ptr->value : -1);
```

```
it_ptr = LST_dequeue(queue);
printf("\ndequeued item %p %d\n", it_ptr, (it_ptr) ? it_ptr->value : -1);
item_t fourth = { NULL, 404 };
printf("enqueuing fourth item\n");
LST_enqueue(queue, fourth);
LST_list_queue_plus(queue, print_value);

it_ptr = LST_dequeue(queue);
printf("\ndequeued item %p %d\n", it_ptr, (it_ptr) ? it_ptr->value : -1);
it_ptr = LST_first(queue);
printf("first item: %p %d\n", it_ptr, it_ptr->value);

it_ptr = LST_dequeue(queue);
printf("\ndequeued item %p %d\n", it_ptr, (it_ptr) ? it_ptr->value : -1);
it_ptr = LST_dequeue(queue);
printf("\ndequeued item %p %d\n", it_ptr, (it_ptr) ? it_ptr->value : -1);
printf("queue size: %d\n", LST_queue_size(queue));
LST_list_queue_plus(queue, print_value);
```

Listing 4-26. Usage Examples of Linked-List Queues—Output

```
=== Linked-list queues

enqueuing first item
enqueuing second item
enqueuing third item
  0: 0x7ffd58604250  101
  1: 0x7ffd58604260  202
  2: 0x7ffd58604270  303
queue size: 3

dequeued item 0x7ffd58604250 101

dequeued item 0x7ffd58604260 202
enqueuing fourth item
  0: 0x7ffd58604270  303
  1: 0x7ffd58604280  404

dequeued item 0x7ffd58604270 303
first item: 0x7ffd58604280 404

dequeued item 0x7ffd58604280 404

dequeued item (nil) -1
queue size: 0
Queue empty
```

Summary

In this chapter, you saw the differences between stacks and queues and learned how to implement them as arrays and linked lists. In particular, you learned how to implement the macros summarized in Table 4-1.

Table 4-1. *Macros for Stacks And Queues*

Purpose	Stacks		Queues	
	Array-Based	Linked List	Array-Based	Linked List
Create New	LST_new_stack_a		LST_new_queue_a	
Free	LST_free_stack_a		LST_free_queue_a	
Get Capacity	LST_get_capacity_a		LST_get_q_ capacity_a	
Get Size	LST_get_size_a	LST_stack_size	LST_get_q_size_a	LST_queue_size
Test for Empty	LST_is_empty_a	LST_is_empty	LST_q_is_empty_a	LST_q_is_empty
Test for Full	LST_is_full_a		LST_q_is_full_a	
List	LST_list_a LST_ list_a_plus	LST_list_stack LST_list_stack_ plus	LST_list_qa LST_ list_qa_plus	LST_list_queue LST_list_ queue_plus
Get First Item	LST_top_a	LST_top	LST_first_a	LST_first
Add Item	LST_push_a	LST_push	LST_enqueue_a	LST_enqueue
Remove Item	LST_pop_a	LST_pop	LST_dequeue_a	LST_dequeue
Set Capacity	LST_set_capacity_a		LST_set_q_ capacity_a	

Notice that in linked-list stacks and queues, there is no need to create, free, get, or set capacity, or test for full.

Table 4-2 summarizes the functions for array-based lists. The only function needed for linked-list implementations is the dummy function lst_do_nothing().

Table 4-2. *Functions for Array-Based Stacks and Queues*

Purpose	Stacks	Queues
Create New	lst_new_stack_a	lst_new_queue_a
List	lst_list_a	lst_list_qa
Get or Remove First Item	lst_top_a	lst_first_a
Add Item	lst_push_a	lst_enqueue_a
Set Capacity	lst_set_capacity_a	lst_set_q_capacity_a

CHAPTER 5

Exception Handling

When talking about why computer programs fail, many people distinguish between user errors and developer/programmer errors (i.e., bugs). But such a distinction is, in my opinion, ill defined. For example, suppose that a program requires the users to type a date into an input field, somebody enters a negative number as day of the month, and the program crashes. It is true that the user made a mistake, but the program should have been able to recognize and cope with such input error. Where do you draw the line?

Clearly, it is not possible for a developer to write code that can cope with every possible occurrence. For one thing, it is even impossible to foresee everything that could happen. Furthermore, to deal with very unlikely events would in all probability slow down the program to unacceptable levels.

All in all, every developer must compromise between robustness and performance. A good strategy is to focus on robustness, simplicity, clarity, etc., profile the program execution (i.e., measure where the program spends execution time), and optimize the most critical parts. In general, as we humans (assuming that you are one of us!) are in many respects slower than computers, you can afford to check human inputs lavishly.

That said, if you are careful, you can also spend CPU time dealing with situations that you expect to occur seldom or never. For example, doing something meaningful with the `default` clause of a `switch` statement instead of writing the comment `/* this should never happen */` never affects program performance and can save you long hours spent chasing difficult bugs.

A distinction between types of errors more useful than user versus programmer is recoverable versus unrecoverable, whereby unrecoverable in fact includes, besides truly unrecoverable errors, errors for which you consider the effort and/or added complication necessary to recover from them to be excessive. In any case, the errors occurring at runtime that occupy the gray zone between user errors and bugs are called *exceptions*. These are errors that are not expected to occur often (or not at all). Good examples of exceptions are write errors when accessing a file or failed allocations of memory (both likely to be unrecoverable), but also a failure to open a file or a division by zero (both possibly recoverable).

In Java, exceptions are objects and their handling has been directly built into the language. In C, as you will see, you can use the `assert` mechanism to build your own exception handling. This is what this chapter is all about.

Let's start by looking at the basic operations associated with exceptions:

- You can *throw* them. That is, you can cause them to occur or, better said, you can invoke a handling function that you have associated with the exception. This might simply mean providing some information to the user and terminating the program gracefully.

- You can *catch* them. If you think that some operation or function might result in a particular exception, you can decide to trap the exception and deal with it explicitly, rather than ignore it and let it take its course. To do so, you identify one or more statements that you want to try.

© Giulio Zambon 2016
G. Zambon, *Practical C*, DOI 10.1007/978-1-4842-1769-6_5

- You can *try* them. That is, execute them without letting the operating system deal with the exception (if the exception were to occur). For example, if you think that a disk access might fail, you can *try* it, *catch* the exception, and deal with the situation instead of simply letting the operation fail.

There are other operations, but *throw*, *try*, and *catch* are the most important. In the rest of this chapter you will learn how to implement them in C.

Long Jumps

If you know how the standard C functions setjmp() and longjmp() work, feel free to skip this short section. I describe them here because many programmers might not be familiar with them.

The book *The C Programming Language* by Kernigan and Ritchie states:

> *"The declarations in <setjmp.h> provide a way to avoid the normal function call and return sequence, typically to permit an immediate return from a deeply nested function call".*

The mechanism works this way: somewhere in your code you do the following:

```
jmp_buf env;
int retval = setjmp(env)
```

Both the function and the jmp_buf type are defined in setjmp.h.

The funny thing, and what is a source of confusion, is that setjump() returns in two different ways! The first time when it is invoked directly as shown above, and the second time when you execute:

```
int val = a_non_zero_number;
longjmp(env, val);
```

Yes, you understood correctly: you invoke longjmp() and the program resumes execution after the original invocation of setjmp(). But while when invoked directly setjmp() always returns 0, when it returns as a result of you executing longjmp() with the same env, it returns the value of val. This lets you neatly distinguish between the two returns:

```
imp_buf env;
if (setjmp(env) == 0) {
  // The first time setjmp() returns here
  }
else if (setjmp(env) == 1) {
  // setjump() returns here if you execute longjmp(env, 1)
  }
else {
  // setjump() returns here if you execute longjmp(env, n) with n greater than 1
  }
```

Obviously, besides executing longjmp() in different places with different values, you can also set more than one jump environment.

You will see later in this chapter how to use the setjmp()/longjmp() mechanism to catch exceptions.

Throw

Let's start with a simple example of throwing an exception. Listing 5-1 shows a small program that does just that.

Listing 5-1. A Program That Throws an Exception

```
 1. /* Try_catch: main.c
 2.  *
 3.  * Copyright (c) 2016 by Giulio Zambon.  All rights reserved.
 4.  *
 5.  */
 6. #include <stdio.h>
 7. #include <stdlib.h>
 8. #include "exception.h"
 9.
10. int main(void) {
11.   for (int k = 0; k < 20; k++) {
12.     switch(k) {
13.       case 0:
14.       case 1 … 9:
15.         printf(" %d", k);
16.         break;
17.       default:
18.         THROW("Invalid number");
19.         break;
20.       }
21.     }
22.   printf("\n");
23.   return EXIT_SUCCESS;
24.   }
```

As you can see, the program consists of a loop containing a switch statement. The control variable of the loop, k, goes from 0 to 19, but the switch only processes 0 to 9. When k hits 10, the default case of the switch throws an exception.

The program is not particularly meaningful, but it serves the purpose of showing how you can throw an exception. The output of the program looks as follows:

Uncaught exception "Invalid number" thrown from ../src/main.c:18 0 1 2 3 4 5 6 7 8 9

The text of the exception precedes the list of numbers because it was sent to stderr, which takes precedence over stdout. THROW is a macro defined in exception.h as follows:

#define THROW(e) exception_throw(e, __FILE__, __LINE__)

The function exception_throw() prints the exception on stderr and aborts the program. That said, as you will see in a moment, it can do more than that.

Try and Catch

The error message produced by an uncaught exception is the type of message that users don't like. Although it doesn't include hexadecimal numbers and is in plain English, it has two problems: first, it is not very informative, and second, it aborts the program, which might not be necessary. That is, throwing an exception is only suitable for unrecoverable errors.

Let's catch the exception and report the problem more gracefully. To do so, you need to modify the program as shown in Listing 5-2.

Listing 5-2. A Program That Catches an Exception

```
1. /* Try_catch: main.c
2.  *
3.  * Copyright (c) 2016 by Giulio Zambon.  All rights reserved.
4.  *
5.  */
6. #include <stdio.h>
7. #include <stdlib.h>
8. #include "exception.h"
9.
10. int main(void) {
11.    char *default_exception = "Invalid number";
12.    for (int k = 0; k < 20; k++) {
13.      TRY
14.        switch(k) {
15.          case 0:
16.          case 1 ... 9:
17.            printf(" %d", k);
18.            break;
19.          default:
20.            THROW(default_exception);
21.            break;
22.        }
23.      CATCH(default_exception);
24.        fprintf(stderr, "%s: switched on %d while 0 to 9 are foreseen\n",
25.            default_exception,k);
26.      TRY_DONE;
27.    }
28.    printf("\n");
29.    return EXIT_SUCCESS;
30. }
```

The only changes are highlighted in bold. Line 11 stores the text of the exception into a variable. This lets you refer to it in the THROW (line 20), in the CATCH (line 23), and when displaying the error message (lines 24 and 25) without having to retype the text of the exception. Lines 13, 23, and 26 are three macros defined in exception.h that let you handle the default exception without causing the program to abort. This time, the output of the program is longer because execution is not aborted. Therefore, the for loop completes:

```
0 1 2 3 4 5 6 7 8 9
Invalid number: switched on 10 while only 0 to 9 are foreseen
Invalid number: switched on 11 while only 0 to 9 are foreseen
Invalid number: switched on 12 while only 0 to 9 are foreseen
```

```
Invalid number: switched on 13 while only 0 to 9 are foreseen
Invalid number: switched on 14 while only 0 to 9 are foreseen
Invalid number: switched on 15 while only 0 to 9 are foreseen
Invalid number: switched on 16 while only 0 to 9 are foreseen
Invalid number: switched on 17 while only 0 to 9 are foreseen
Invalid number: switched on 18 while only 0 to 9 are foreseen
Invalid number: switched on 19 while only 0 to 9 are foreseen
```

Listing 5-3 shows you exception.h.

Listing 5-3. exception.h

```
 1. /* exception.h
 2.  *
 3.  * Copyright (c) 2016 by Giulio Zambon.  All rights reserved.
 4.  */
 5. #ifndef EXCEPTION
 6. #define EXCEPTION
 7. #include <setjmp.h>
 8.
 9. #define EXCEPTION_STATUS_INITIAL  0
10. #define EXCEPTION_STATUS_THROWN   1
11. #define EXCEPTION_STATUS_HANDLED  2
12.
13. typedef struct Exception Exception;
14. struct Exception {
15.   char      *name;
16.   jmp_buf    env;
17.   char      *file;
18.   int        line;
19.   Exception *prev;
20.   };
21.
22. #define THROW(e) exception_throw(e, __FILE__, __LINE__)
23.
24. #define TRY {                                                 \
25.     volatile int exception_status;                            \
26.     Exception exception;                                      \
27.     exception.prev = exception_stack;                         \
28.     exception_stack = &exception;                             \
29.     exception_status = setjmp(exception.env);                 \
30.     if (exception_status == EXCEPTION_STATUS_INITIAL) {
31.
32. #define CATCH(e)                                              \
33.     if (exception_status == EXCEPTION_STATUS_INITIAL)         \
34.         exception_stack = exception_stack->prev;              \
35.     }                                                         \
36.     else if (exception.name == (e)) {                         \
37.       exception_status = EXCEPTION_STATUS_HANDLED;
38.
39. #define TRY_DONE                                              \
40.     if (exception_status == EXCEPTION_STATUS_INITIAL)         \
```

```
41.            exception_stack = exception_stack->prev;                    \
42.       }                                                                 \
43.    if (exception_status == EXCEPTION_STATUS_THROWN)                     \
44.          exception_throw(exception.name, exception.file, exception.line); \
45.    }
46.
47. extern Exception *exception_stack;
48.
49. void exception_throw(char *e, char *file, int line);
50.
51. #endif
```

It looks quite complicated (well, actually, it is!), but it will become clear as you go through this chapter.

An exception is represented with an Exception structure (lines 15 to 19). The component name is where you keep the text of an exception (e.g., "Invalid number"); you use env to set up and execute a long jump implementing the throwing of an exception; file and line store the source name and the line number where an exception is thrown; and prev links to an exception thrown before the current one.

When you execute the macro TRY, you define the variable exception_status to keep track of what happens concerning the exception (line 25 of Listing 5-3). It is automatically initialized to 0, which corresponds to EXCEPTION_STATUS_INITIAL (line 9). The exception status changes to EXCEPTION_STATUS_HANDLED when you CATCH() it (lines 36 and 37). Finally, the status EXCEPTION_STATUS_THROWN indicates that the exception has occurred and ensures that when you CATCH() it, you execute the else in line 36 of Listing 5-3.

Listing 5-4 shows exception.c.

Listing 5-4. exception.c

```
1. /* exception.c
2.  *
3.  * Copyright (c) 2016 by Giulio Zambon.  All rights reserved.
4.  */
5. #include <stdlib.h>
6. #include <stdio.h>
7. #include "exception.h"
8.
9. Exception *exception_stack = NULL;
10.
11. void exception_throw(char *e_name, char *file, int line) {
12.    Exception *p = exception_stack;
13.    if (p == NULL) { // no stack -> no TRY -> exception not caught
14.      fprintf(stderr, "Uncaught exception ");
15.      if (e_name) fprintf(stderr, "\"%s\"", e_name);
16.      else fprintf(stderr, "%p", e_name);
17.      if (file) {
18.        fprintf(stderr, " thrown from %s", file);
19.        if (line) fprintf(stderr, ":%d", line);
20.        }
21.      fflush(stderr);
22.      abort();
23.      }
24.    p->name = e_name; // stack is there -> jump to catch exception
```

```
25.    p->file = file;
26.    p->line = line;
27.    exception_stack = exception_stack->prev;
28.    longjmp(p->env, EXCEPTION_STATUS_THROWN);
29.    }
```

To follow what happens, look at Listing 5-5, which shows the program of Listing 5-2 but with the macros expanded. With the following command, you can use the compiler to list a C source after it has gone through the preprocessor:

```
gcc -E -nostdinc main.c > main_after_pp.txt
```

But I edited the output file to adjust the indentations according to the macro expansions. To make it easier, I have also re-typed the macros in their original positions, added the line numbers matching those of Listing 5-2, and labeled the lines of the macro expansions with letters.

Listing 5-5. A Program that Catches an Exception (with the Macros Expanded)

```
10. int main(void) {
11.    char *default_exception = "Invalid number";
12.    for (int k = 0; k < 20; k++) {
13.      TRY
 a       {
 b         volatile int exception_status;
 c         Exception exception;
 d         exception.prev = exception_stack;
 e         exception_stack = &exception;
 f         exception_status = setjmp(exception.env);
 g         if (exception_status == 0) {
14.          switch(k) {
15.            case 0:
16.            case 1 … 9:
17.              printf(" %d", k);
18.              break;
19.            default:
20.              THROW(default_exception)
 a             exception_throw(default_exception, "main.c", 20);
21.              break;
22.            }
23.    CATCH(default_exception);
 a         if (exception_status == 0) exception_stack = exception_stack->prev;
 b         }
 c         else if (exception.name == default_exception) {
 d           exception_status = 2;;
24.            fprintf(stderr, "%s: switched on %d while only 0 to 9 are foreseen\n",
25.                default_exception, k);
26.    TRY_DONE;
 a         if (exception_status == 0) exception_stack = exception_stack->prev;
 b         }
 c         if (exception_status == 1) exception_throw(exception.name,
 d             exception.file, exception.line);
 e       };
```

```
27.    }
28.    printf("\n");
29.    return EXIT_SUCCESS;
30.  }
```

To limit the scope of all variables defined within the exception.h macros, TRY begins with an open curly bracket (line 13a) and TRY_DONE ends with the corresponding closed one (line 26e).

As an aside, the semicolon at the end of line 26e is due to the fact that line 26 is terminated with an unnecessary semicolon. But to have lines of C code not terminated with a semicolon looks odd, and the redundant semicolon has no negative effect. The same consideration applies to the second semicolon that appears in line 23d. You could remove the semicolon from line 37 of exception.h (Listing 5-3), but that line would look odd.

The first operation within TRY is to define the variable exception_status (line 13b). It needs to be volatile because the switching of context caused by long jumps could/would have the result of losing changes made to a non-volatile variable.

The second operation within TRY is to define the variable exception of type Exception (line 13c).

The global variable exception_stack is defined and initialized to NULL in exception() (line 9 of exception.c) and exported in line 47 of exception.h. It is a pointer to a variable of type Exception. Lines 13d and 13e of the expanded main implement a *push* of the new exception (i.e., that defined in line 13d) onto exception_stack. That is, the value of exception_stack is saved in the prev component of the new exception before setting exception_stack to the address of the new exception.

At this point, prev is the only non-NULL component of the new exception.

In line 13f, the env component of the new exception is set by setjmp(), while exception_status is set to the value returned by setjmp(), which is always 0 when setjmp() is invoked directly. As a result, the if statement in line 13g succeeds (because in line 30 of exception.h, exception_status is compared with EXCEPTION_STATUS_INITIAL, which is set to 0 in line 9 of exception.h), and the switch statement that begins in line 14 is executed.

As the for loop in line 12 starts with k set to 0, the switch finds a matching case and doesn't go through its default. As a result, the THROW() in line 20 is not executed, the if in line 23a succeeds, and the new exception is *popped* off the exception stack with

```
exception_stack = exception_stack->prev;
```

In the example, this means that exception_stack is returned to its original value of NULL.

Notice that the closed brace in line 23b closes the block statement that began in line 13g. As the if in line 13g succeeded, what follows the else at the beginning of line 23c is skipped and execution continues with line 23c.

The if in line 23c fails because, as you have seen, exception_status has remained set to its initial value of 0. This means that the first iteration of the for loop completes with line 27 and execution resumes at line 13 with k set to 1.

What happened with k = 0 is repeated for all following values of k up to and including 9. When k becomes 10, the switch executes its default and invokes exception_throw() in line 20a with "Invalid number" (the string pointed by default_exception) as its first argument.

At this point, exception_stack, like in the first nine iterations of the loop, points to the new exception created in line 13c within the TRY macro. Of the exception structure, only two components have been set: prev (to NULL, in line 13d) and env (by setjmp() in line 13f).

If you look at Listing 5-4, you will see that the if in line 13 fails because p (identical to exception_stack) is not NULL, as it points to the new exception. Therefore, all exception_throw() does before returning is:

```
24.    p->name = e_name;
25.    p->file = file;
26.    p->line = line;
```

```
27.    exception_stack = exception_stack->prev;
28.    longjmp(p->env, EXCEPTION_STATUS_THROWN);
```

In line 24, it saves the address of the exception name (i.e., the same value stored in default_exception in line 11 of the main and passed down to exception_throw() as its first argument) to the exception structure (which, as you know, is on top of the exception stack). In lines 25 and 26, it saves the filename and line number where the exception was thrown.

In line 27, it removes the exception off the top of the stack. This is necessary to avoid handling the same exception more than once.

Finally, in line 28, exception_throw() executes longjmp() for the jmp_buf environment stored in the exception (notice that, although the exception is no longer on the stack, p still points to it). As second argument, it passes to longjmp() the value EXCEPTION_STATUS_THROWN, which is defined in line 10 of exception.h to be 1.

So, when exception_throw() finds an exception on the top of the stack, it never returns. Instead, by executing the long jump, it forces the system to restore the context of the main at the point where setjmp() was executed and "returns" from setjmp() with 1. In other words, execution resumes at line 13g of Listing 5-5 with exception_status set to 1.

This second time, the if in line 13g fails. But the if in line 23c succeeds, because exception.name is indeed identical to default_exception. Note that the if condition compares the string addresses, not the strings. This is one of those rare cases where you don't care about the string content and want to check that two strings are the same string, rather than they contain identical text. Obviously, you could use strcmp(), but it would have two disadvantages: first, it would prevent you from defining different exceptions with the same text, and second, it would take longer to execute. Not that it would make much of a difference, but comparing the string addresses is definitely better.

Lines 24 and 25 display the message for the user, while line 23 sets the exception status to 2 (i.e., EXCEPTION_STATUS_HANDLED). Any value would do except for 0 and 1. In fact, the only requirement for the values you assign to EXCEPTION_STATUS_INITIAL, EXCEPTION_STATUS_THROWN, and EXCEPTION_STATUS_HANDLED defined in lines 9 to 11 of exception.h is that they are different from one another.

Both if statements within the TRY_DONE macro (in lines 26a and 26c) fail because exception_status is 2. Indeed, this is the only reason for defining EXCEPTION_STATUS_HANDLED.

You might wonder what the purpose of line 26a is. After all, exception_status is set to 2 in line 23d and remains unchanged after that. So, exception_status will never be 0 in line 26a, would it?

Suppose that, for testing purposes, you commented out the CATCH and the associated fprintf() in lines 23 to 25. Then, main.c after going through the C preprocessor would look as shown in Listing 5-6.

Listing 5-6. A Program That Catches an Exception (with CATCH Commented Out)

```
10. int main(void) {
11.   char *default_exception = "Invalid number";
12.   for (int k = 0; k < 20; k++) {
13.     TRY
 a        {
 b          volatile int exception_status;
 c          Exception exception;
 d          exception.prev = exception_stack;
 e          exception_stack = &exception;
 f          exception_status = setjmp(exception.env);
 g          if (exception_status == 0) {
14.           switch(k) {
15.             case 0:
16.             case 1 ... 9:
17.               printf(" %d", k);
```

127

```
18.              break;
19.            default:
20.              THROW(default_exception)
 a              exception_throw(default_exception, "main.c", 20);
21.              break;
22.          }
23.     CATCH(default_exception);
 a          if (exception_status == 0) exception_stack = exception_stack->prev;
 b          }
 c          else if (exception.name == default_exception) {
 d          exception_status = 2;;
24.         fprintf(stderr, "%s: switched on %d while only 0 to 9 are foreseen\n",
25.            default_exception, k);
26.     TRY_DONE;
 a          if (exception_status == 0) exception_stack = exception_stack->prev;
 b          }
 c          if (exception_status == 1) exception_throw(exception.name,
 d              exception.file, exception.line);
 e          };
27.     }
28.   printf("\n");
29.   return EXIT_SUCCESS;
30.   }
```

With CATCH, the close curly brackets in line 23b completed the block statement opened in the TRY macro (line 13g), and the close bracket in TRY_DONE (line 26b) closed the block statement opened within the CATCH (line 23c). But now, with the CATCH gone, the block statement opened in TRY (line 13g) is closed in TRY_DONE (line 26b). You need line 26a to pop an unthrown exception off the stack, as was done in line 23a when CATCH was there.

But how would the program behave without a CATCH? Simple, it would end with:

```
Uncaught exception "Invalid number" thrown from ../src/main.c:20 0 1 2 3 4 5 6 7 8 9
```

This is because CATCH is no longer there to change exception_status from 1 to 2 (in line 23d). Therefore, when control reaches TRY_DONE, lines 26c and 26d execute exception_throw() a second time with the same arguments used in line 20a.

This time, though, the exception stack is empty because exception_throw() had popped the exception off the stack (line 27 of Listing 5-4) when it was executed the first time within THROW. Therefore, exception_throw() executes lines 18 to 26 (of Listing 5-4) to display the uncaught-exception message and abort the program.

So far, you have seen how TRY, THROW, CATCH, and TRY_DONE work together to handle an exception and what happens if you throw an exception and don't catch it. But, if you don't intend to catch an exception, why should you still include in your code TRY and TRY_DONE? The simple answer is that you don't! Look again at Listing 5-6 and imagine removing both TRY and TRY_DONE. Without TRY (and you must then remove TRY_DONE otherwise the code won't compile), exception_stack remains set to NULL. Therefore, exception_throw() always displays the uncaught-exception message and aborts the program.

Multiple Catches

Listing 5-7 shows an example of a program with multiple exceptions and multiple catches.

Listing 5-7. A Program with Several Exceptions and Catches

```c
1. /* Try_catch: main.c
2.  *
3.  * Copyright (c) 2016 by Giulio Zambon.  All rights reserved.
4.  *
5.  */
6. #include <stdio.h>
7. #include <stdlib.h>
8. #include "exception.h"
9.
10. int main(void) {
11.   char *exception_1 = "Exception #1";
12.   char *exception_2 = "Exception #2";
13.
14.   TRY
15.     fprintf(stderr, "Throwing exception 1\n");
16.     THROW(exception_1);
17.     fprintf(stderr, "Throwing exception 2 for the first time\n");
18.     THROW(exception_2);
19.     fprintf(stderr, "Throwing exception 2 for the second time\n");
20.     THROW(exception_2);
21.   CATCH(exception_1)
22.     fprintf(stderr, "This is the catch of 1\n");
23.   CATCH(exception_2);
24.     fprintf(stderr, "This is the first catch of 2\n");
25.   CATCH(exception_2);
26.     fprintf(stderr, "This is the second catch of 2\n");
27.   TRY_DONE;
28.   fprintf(stderr, "Done!\n");
29.   return EXIT_SUCCESS;
30.   }
```

It defines two exceptions in lines 11 and 12. It then throws exception 1 once and exception 2 twice and catches exception 1 once and exception 2 twice. When you execute it, here is what you get:

```
Throwing exception 1
This is the catch of 1
Done!
```

When exception 1 is thrown in line 16, exception_throw() causes the program to skip the rest of the TRY (lines 17 to 20) and resume execution from the CATCH() of line 21. As a result, exception 2 is never thrown.

If you swap lines 17 and 18 with lines 15 and 16, so that exception 1 is thrown between the two throws of exception 2, you get:

```
Throwing exception 2 for the first time
This is the first catch of 2
Done!
```

If you leave the throws in their original positions and swap instead the catches by moving lines 24 and 25 to be before line 21, you get the same reporting you got before swapping the catches:

```
Throwing exception 1
This is the catch of 1
Done!
```

This makes sense because what counts is the order in which the exceptions occur, not the order in which you catch them.

It should be clear to you that lines 25 and 26 are irrelevant because within the same TRY you can only catch each exception once. Execution will never reach the second CATCH.

Multiple Tries

Listing 5-8 shows an example of a program with more than one TRY.

Listing 5-8. A Program That Doesn't Work as Expected

```
1.  /* Try_catch: main.c
2.   *
3.   * Copyright (c) 2016 by Giulio Zambon.  All rights reserved.
4.   *
5.   */
6.  #include <stdio.h>
7.  #include <stdlib.h>
8.  #include "exception.h"
9.
10. int main(void) {
11.   char *exception_1 = "Exception #1";
12.   char *exception_2 = "Exception #2";
13.
14.   TRY
15.     fprintf(stderr, "Throwing exception 1\n");
16.     THROW(exception_1);
17.   CATCH(exception_1)
18.     fprintf(stderr, "Exception 1 caught\n");
19.     fprintf(stderr, "Throwing exception 2\n");
20.     THROW(exception_2);
21.   CATCH(exception_2);
22.     fprintf(stderr, "Exception 2 caught\n");
23.   TRY_DONE;
24.   fprintf(stderr, "Done!\n");
25.   return EXIT_SUCCESS;
26.   }
```

It throws exception 1 in line 16. When it catches it in line 17, it throws exception 2 (in line 20), which it then catches in line 21. Here is its output:

```
Throwing exception 1
Exception 1 caught
Throwing exception 2
Uncaught exception "Exception #2" thrown from ../src/main.c:20
```

That is, the CATCH() in line 21 doesn't catch exception 2 and the program is aborted, as confirmed by the fact that the string "Done!\n" is not printed. Can you see why this is so?

The problem is that exception 2 is thrown within the CATCH() of exception 1 instead of within the TRY. It becomes clear when you see the code with the macros expanded (see Listing 5-9).

Listing 5-9. A Program That Doesn't Work as Expected (with the Macros Expanded)

```
10. int main(void) {
11.    char *exception_1 = "Exception #1";
12.    char *exception_2 = "Exception #2";
13.
14.      TRY
 a       {
 b         volatile int exception_status;
 c         Exception exception;
 d         exception.prev = exception_stack;
 e         exception_stack = &exception;
 f         exception_status = setjmp(exception.env);
 g         if (exception_status == 0) {
15.          fprintf(stderr, "Throwing exception 1\n");
16.          THROW(exception_1);
 a           exception_throw(exception_1, "main.c", 16);
17.      CATCH(exception_1)
 a           if (exception_status == 0) exception_stack = exception_stack->prev;
 b         }
 c         else if (exception.name == exception_1) {
 d           exception_status = 2;;
18.          fprintf(stderr, "Exception 1 caught\n");
19.          fprintf(stderr, "Throwing exception 2\n");
20.          THROW(exception_2);
 a           exception_throw(exception_2, "main.c", 20);
21.      CATCH(exception_2);
 a           if (exception_status == 0) exception_stack = exception_stack->prev;
 b         }
 c         else if (exception.name == exception_2) {
 d           exception_status = 2;;
22.          fprintf(stderr, "Exception 2 caught\n");
23.      TRY_DONE;
 a           if (exception_status == 0) exception_stack = exception_stack->prev;
 b         }
 c         if (exception_status == 1) exception_throw(exception.name,
 d             exception.file, exception.line);
 e         };
24.    printf("Done!\n");
25.    return EXIT_SUCCESS;
26.    }
```

Everything works as expected for exception 1: the function setjmp() in line 14f returns twice, once with 0, which causes the execution of lines 15 to 17a, and once with 1, which causes the if in line 14g to fail. The if in line 17c succeeds and 17d to 21a are executed.

When exception 2 is thrown in line 20, the exception stack is empty because the exception pushed onto it in line 14e (within the TRY) was popped by exception_throw() when it was executed in line 16a (see line 17 of Listing 5-4). As a result, exception_throw() executed for exception 2 (line 20a of Listing 5-9) prints the uncaught message and aborts the programs.

What you need is a TRY for exception 2 within the CATCH() for exception 1, as shown in Listing 5-10.

Listing 5-10. A Program with Nested Tries

```
1.  /* Try_catch: main.c
2.   *
3.   * Copyright (c) 2016 by Giulio Zambon.  All rights reserved.
4.   *
5.   */
6.  #include <stdio.h>
7.  #include <stdlib.h>
8.  #include "exception.h"
9.
10. int main(void) {
11.   char *exception_1 = "Exception #1";
12.   char *exception_2 = "Exception #2";
13.
14.   TRY
15.     fprintf(stderr, "Throwing exception 1\n");
16.     THROW(exception_1);
17.   CATCH(exception_1)
18.     fprintf(stderr, "Exception 1 caught\n");
19.     TRY
20.       fprintf(stderr, "Throwing exception 2\n");
21.       THROW(exception_2);
22.     CATCH(exception_2);
23.       fprintf(stderr, "Exception 2 caught\n");
24.     TRY_DONE;
25.   TRY_DONE;
26.   fprintf(stderr, "Done!\n");
27.   return EXIT_SUCCESS;
28.   }
```

This time, the program prints:

```
Throwing exception 1
Exception 1 caught
Throwing exception 2
Exception 2 caught
Done!
```

You might be concerned that there could be problems because the inner TRY redefines the variables exception_status and exception already defined in the outer TRY. But you don't need to worry because the second definitions are limited to the scope of the inner TRY. This is why the curly brackets opened at the beginning of TRY and closed at the end of TRY_DONE. If you are not entirely convinced, add

```
char *a_string = "TRY 1";
```

immediately *before* the first TRY and

```
char *a_string = "TRY 2";
fprintf(stderr, "%s\n", a_string);
```

immediately *after* the second TRY. Finally, add

```
fprintf(stderr, "%s\n", a_string);
```

immediately *after* the first TRY and between the two TRY_DONEs. The program will print out:

```
TRY 1
Throwing exception 1
Exception 1 caught
TRY 2
Throwing exception 2
Exception 2 caught
TRY 1
Done!
```

As you can see, the fact that a second a_string is defined within the scope of the inner TRY doesn't affect the first a_string, which maintains its value through the execution of the inner TRY. In any case, if there had been a problem in redefining a_string, the compiler would have complained.

Examples

To conclude this chapter on exceptions, I want to show you a couple of simple examples that you could find useful. In general, you will be able to apply the exception mechanism shown in this chapter whenever you need to handle a situation that, if ignored, would lead to program termination or to a crash. At the very least, you can use a THROW() in all those cases where careless programmers traditionally write the infamous comment, "This cannot happen"!

The first example I want to show you deals with failure to allocate a block of memory. Some programmers invoke malloc() and don't bother to check that it returns a non-NULL pointer. Partly it is because malloc() seldom fails under normal circumstances: why waste time to write code that will probably never be needed? But, as rare as a malloc() failure can be, when it happens, unless you catch it, it can lead to mysterious catastrophic failures well after the allocation. The best strategy is to write a function to catch malloc() failures and use it every time you need to allocate memory. Check out Listings 5-11 and 5-12.

Listing 5-11. allocate.h

```
/* allocate.h
 */
#ifndef ALLOCATE
#define ALLOCATE
#include "exception.h"

extern char *allocate_exception;
void *allocate(unsigned n_bytes);
#endif
```

Listing 5-12. allocate.c

```
/* allocate.c
 */
#include <stdio.h>
#include <stdlib.h>
#include "exception.h"

char *allocate_exception = "Allocation failed";

void *allocate(unsigned n_bytes) {
  void *p = (n_bytes > 0) ? malloc(n_bytes) : NULL;
  if (!p) THROW(allocate_exception);
  return p;
  }
```

The function allocate() is easy to use. Instead of writing something like this:

```
char *buf = malloc(4096);
```

you write:

```
char *buf = allocate(4096);
```

Listing 5-13 shows a program that catches the allocation exception.

Listing 5-13. How to Catch an Allocation Exception

```
#include <stdio.h>
#include <stdlib.h>
#include "exception.h"
#include "allocate.h"
int main(void) {
  char *buf;
  unsigned int n = 4096;
  TRY
    buf = allocate(n);
  CATCH(allocate_exception)
    fprintf(stderr, "couldn't allocate a buffer of %d\n", n);
    exit(EXIT_FAILURE);
  TRY_DONE;
  free(buf);
  return EXIT_SUCCESS;
  }
```

To see what happens when the allocation fails, you only need to set n to 0. You will then see on the console a message like this:

```
couldn't allocate a buffer of 0
```

Another example of exception usage is when performing file I/O. Listing 5-14 shows an extended version of the program of Listing 5-13 that uses the allocated buffer to copy a file.

Listing 5-14. How to Catch File I/O Exceptions

```
 1. #include <stdio.h>
 2. #include <stdlib.h>
 3. #include "exception.h"
 4. #include "allocate.h"
 5. int main(void) {
 6. #define BUF_SIZE 128
 7. #define CLEAN_UP() {              \
 8.     if (filin) fclose(filin);    \
 9.     if (filout) fclose(filout);  \
10.     if (buf) free(buf);          \
11.     }
12.   char *open_file_exception = "could not be opened";
13.   char *write_file_exception = "I/O error when writing file";
14.   char *filename = NULL;
15.   FILE *filin = NULL;
16.   FILE *filout = NULL;
17.   char *buf = NULL;
18.   size_t n = 0;
19.
20.   TRY
21.     filename = "in.txt";
22.     filin = fopen(filename, "r");
23.     if (!filin) THROW(open_file_exception);
24.
25.     filename = "out.txt";
26.     filout = fopen(filename, "w");
27.     if (!filout) THROW(open_file_exception);
28.
29.     buf = allocate(BUF_SIZE);
30.
31.     do {
32.       n = fread(buf, 1, BUF_SIZE, filin);
33.       if (n > 0 && fwrite(buf, 1, n, filout) != n) THROW(write_file_exception);
34.       } while (n > 0);
35.
36.   CATCH(open_file_exception)
37.     printf("File %s %s\n", filename, open_file_exception);
38.     CLEAN_UP();
39.     return EXIT_FAILURE;                                          //-->
40.   CATCH(write_file_exception)
41.     printf("File %s %s\n", write_file_exception, filename);
42.     CLEAN_UP();
43.     return EXIT_FAILURE;                                          //-->
44.   CATCH(allocate_exception)
45.     printf("couldn't allocate a buffer of %d\n", BUF_SIZE);
46.     CLEAN_UP();
47.     return EXIT_FAILURE;                                          //-->
48.   TRY_DONE;
49.   CLEAN_UP();
50.   return EXIT_SUCCESS;
51.   }
```

You open the input file in lines 21 to 23, open the output file in lines 25 to 27, allocate the buffer in line 29, and copy the content of the input file to the output file in lines 31 to 34. As you can see, the three CATCHes—to trap file opening, file writing, and buffer allocations failures—are out of the way, immediately before the TRY_DONE. Notice the use of CLEAN_UP() to ensure that no files are left open and that the buffer is released.

Summary

In this chapter you learned how to use C's long-jumps to implement a mechanism to handle exceptions.

I went through a detailed walkthrough of the code because macros, like long jumps, are delicate and confusing. It made for a difficult piece of code, but I am confident that you will find the exception mechanism useful and easy to apply.

CHAPTER 6

String Utilities

In C strings are null-terminated arrays of characters. You can manipulated them with a series of functions declared in the standard header file string.h, but there are two drawbacks:

- The only way of defining new C strings at runtime is to allocate memory from the heap, and you are responsible for freeing the allocated memory when you no longer need the string. Failure to do so results in memory leaks that, over time, consume all the available memory and cause crashes. A common mistake associated with dynamically allocated strings is freeing a block of memory before you are done with it: everything will seem to work fine until you allocate that area of memory again and try to use it for a different purpose.

- C string operations are unsafe, as C provides no runtime check that the updates you make to a string are within its boundaries. It is a common mistake to modify a string beyond its end, thereby corrupting memory and causing nasty crashes.

In this chapter, I show you how you can make strings safer. It will add some overhead, but it will be a small price to pay to ensure that you avoid memory leaks and corrupted memory. Two things make C strings safer:

- A layer of buffer management on top of the standard memory management provided by C.

- Checking updates against the string boundaries.

This chapter uses the word *string* to refer to two different entities: standard null-terminated strings and structures that encapsulate the standard strings. I refer to the standard strings as *C strings*, but only when necessary to avoid confusion between the two types.

As you will see, the functionality described in this chapter relies heavily on macros. As you learned in Chapter 2, macros are unsafe when the same parameter appears in the body of the macro more than once. The rest of this chapter describes the "unsafe" versions of the macros, as this usually makes the macros easier to understand. But both versions of the macros are included in the sources attached to this book.

String Allocation and Release

The best way to ensure that all allocated memory is released is to set up an automatic mechanism that does it for you, like in:

```
STR_setup;
...
Str *a_new_string = STR_new("whatever you like");
...
STR_dismantle;
```

© Giulio Zambon 2016
G. Zambon, *Practical C*, DOI 10.1007/978-1-4842-1769-6_6

where STR_setup is a macro that defines an empty stack of string pointers; STR_new() is a macro that allocates a new string, sets it to "whatever you like", and pushes it onto the stack; and STR_dismantle is a macro that releases all the strings on the stack.

Listing 6-1 shows you the type definition of Str and the expansion of the three macros.

Listing 6-1. A Mechanism for Dynamic Strings

```
typedef struct Str Str;
struct Str {
  char   *s;    // C string
  Str    *up;   // one level higher in the stack
  Str    *down; // one level deeper in the stack
  size_t size;  // size of allocated block
  Str    **stack_p;
  };

#define STR_setup {           \
  Str *str_stack = NULL;

#define STR_list() str_list(str_stack)

#define STR_new(s) str_new(&str_stack, 0, s, '\0')

#define STR_release(str) str_release(&(str))

#define STR_release_all() str_release_all(str_stack)

#define STR_dismantle            \
  str_release_all(str_stack);  \
  }
```

As you can see, Str is a structure that keeps together a C string, two pointers to structures of the same type, and a pointer to a pointer to another Str. The component size is only useful for debugging and you can switch it off by changing in str.h the #define of STR_LOG from 1 to 0.

STR_setup defines an empty stack after opening a curly bracket, and STR_dismantle closes the curly bracket after releasing all the allocated strings. The curly brackets are important because, besides limiting the scope of the strings and their stack, it prevents memory leaks: a piece of code with STR_setup but without STR_dismantle would not compile.

Obviously, you can always make a mess if you are determined to do it, but what matters is that you don't do it by oversight. As long as you don't fiddle with the macros, they will prevent you from making many mistakes.

In addition to those shown in Listing 6-1, str.h also defines the following macros:

```
#define STR_crash(e) str_crash(e, __FILE__, __LINE__)
#define STR_list_str(str) str_list(str)
#define STR_new_str(str, s) str_new(&(str), 0, s, '\0')
#define STR_newn(len, s, c) str_new(&str_stack, len, s, c)
#define STR_newn_str(str, len, s) str_new(&(str), len, s, c)
#define STR_release_all_str(str) str_release_all(str)
```

While STR_new() allocates a new Str with exactly as many characters as needed to store a copy of the whole existing string s, STR_newn() allocates a new C string of length len, truncates the copy of s if s is longer than len, and pads the copy of s with the character supplied as the last argument if s is shorter.

You use STR_crash() to report a catastrophic problem and abort the program.

Notice that for most macros there are two versions, one of which has _str appended to their name (the only exceptions being STR_crash(), STR_setup, STR_release(), and STR_dismantle). The versions without suffix rely on the local variable str_stack, while those with the suffix obtain the stack pointer from an Str structure passed as an argument. This is possible because the component stack_p of Str always provides the pointer to the stack.

The macros rely on the following five functions:

```
void str_crash(char *e, char *file, int line);
void str_list(Str *str);
Str *str_new(Str **str_p, size_t len, char *s, char pad);
void str_release(Str **str);
void str_release_all(Str *str);
```

str_new()

The full code of str_new() is shown in Listing 6-2.

Listing 6-2. str_new()

```
1.  //--------------------------------------------------------------------- str_new
2.  Str *str_new(Str **str_p, size_t len, char *s, char pad) {
3.  #if STR_LOG
4.    if (pad == '\0') printf("=== str_new: %p %zu \"%s\" '\\0'", *str_p, len, s);
5.    else printf("=== str_new: %p %zu \"%s\" '%c'", *str_p, len, s, pad);
6.  #endif
7.    Str **str_stack_p = str_p;
8.    if (*str_stack_p != NULL) {
9.      str_stack_p = (*str_p)->stack_p;
10.     if (str_stack_p == NULL) {
11.       STR_crash("str_new: Str->stack_p found to be NULL");
12.     }
13.   }
14.
15.   // If len > 0, add 1 for the terminating '\0'. Someone has to do it,
16.   // and the user needs a C string with space for len characters...
17.   if (len == 0  &&  s != NULL) len = strlen(s);
18.   size_t size = sizeof(Str) + ((len == 0) ? 0 : len + 1);
19.
20.   // Allocate the needed memory block.
21.   void *blk = malloc(size);
22.   if (blk == NULL) {
23.     char mess[40];
24.     sprintf(mess, "str_new: Failed to allocate %lu bytes", size);
25.     STR_crash(mess);                                            // ==>
26.   }
27.
```

```
28.    // Push the block address to the Str stack.
29.    Str *new_str = (Str *)blk;
30.    new_str->up = NULL;
31.    new_str->down = *str_stack_p;
32.    new_str->size = size;
33.    new_str->stack_p = str_stack_p;
34.    if (*str_stack_p != NULL) (*str_stack_p)->up = new_str;
35.    *str_stack_p = new_str;
36.
37.    // Process the C string.
38.    char *chars = NULL;
39.    if (len > 0) {
40.      chars = (char *)(blk + sizeof(Str));
41.      size_t n_copy = 0;
42.      if (s != NULL) {
43.        size_t s_size = strlen(s);
44.        n_copy = (s_size < len) ? s_size : len;
45.        (void)memcpy(chars, s, n_copy);
46.      }
47.      if (n_copy < len) (void)memset(&chars[n_copy], pad, len - n_copy);
48.      chars[len] = '\0';
49.    }
50.    new_str->s = chars;
51.
52. #if STR_LOG
53.    printf("-> %p\n", blk);
54. #endif
55.    return new_str;
56.    } // str_new
```

Listing 6-3 shows str_crash().

Listing 6-3. str_crash(): Reporting a Catastrophic Problem

```
//------------------------------------------------------------------ str_crash
void inline str_crash(char *e, char *file, int line) {
  fprintf(stderr, "STR error \"%s\" (file %s; line %d)\n", e, file, line);
  fflush(stderr);
  abort();
  } // str_crash
```

The behavior of str_new() is determined by the value of the last two parameters, len and s (line 2 of Listing 6-2). The first one, str_p, is hidden inside the macros STR_new() and STR_newn() and explicitly passed as an argument with the corresponding _str macros. In the first case, it is a pointer to the default stack, while in the second case, it is a pointer to an Str that belongs to the stack to which you want to add a new string.

When you allocate the very first string of a stack, you must use the forms without _str because there are no existing strings that you can pass as first argument of the _str macros. In that case, the first argument (and therefore str_stack_p defined and set in line 7) points to a variable that contains the NULL pointer. As a result, the if statement in line 8 fails.

But when you allocate a subsequent string and decide to use one of the _str macros, str_p contains the address of a variable that contains a pointer to an existing Str. As a result, the if in line 8 succeeds and in line 9 you set str_stack_p to the address of the variable that contains the stack pointer (stored in the stack_p component of the string you passed as first argument). When this is the case, str_stack_p is not allowed to be NULL because it would mean that you are using as first argument of the macro an Str structure that has already been released or that was corrupted. This is why the only thing you can do if str_stack_p is NULL is crash the program (line 11).

len determines how much space str_new() allocates for a C string.

If len is 0, the function allocates from the heap exactly enough space to copy into the s component of the newly allocated Str structure the content of the string passed as third argument. This means that you can obtain a new empty Str by invoking STR_new(NULL).

If len is greater than 0 and s is NULL, the function allocates len+1 characters from the heap together with the memory necessary to store the new Str structure, and sets the s component of the structure to point to the first character not used for the Str structure. It then initializes the new C string to spaces.

Finally, if both parameters len and s are non-zero, the function proceeds like when s is NULL but, instead of initializing the whole allocated C string to spaces, it copies s to it. When s contains more than len characters, the function only copies the first len characters of s to the newly allocated C string. When s is shorter than len characters, str_new(), after copying s to the new C string, pads it with spaces.

Note that it is not possible to create an Str with a C string of length 0. If you execute either

```
Str *str = STR_new("");
```

or

```
Str *str = STR_newn(0, "", ' ');
```

no C string is created. That is, str->s, instead of pointing to an empty C string, remains NULL. This is because in line 18 of Listing 6-2 no space for a terminating '\0' is made available when len == 0. Then, consistently with line 18, line 48 (which sets the terminating '\0') is only executed when len > 0 (checked in line 39).

I don't see why you would allocate an Str structure with an empty C string but, if you wanted to, you could probably replace line 18 with

```
size_t size = sizeof(Str) + len + 1;
```

and remove the check for len > 0 in line 39. It seems easy enough, but I might have overlooked something and, as I have not tried it out, please do not not complain if it doesn't work!

Line 18 of Listing 6-2 ensure that, if len is greater than 0, an additional character for the C string termination is added when allocating space for it. Using 0 to determine whether the whole string passed as a third argument is to be copied to the newly allocated C string means that you cannot allocate an empty C string. That is, the allocated C string will always contain at least one character (besides the '\0' at the end). If you are thinking of changing the 0 to -1, think again: len is of type size_t, which is unsigned. You cannot pass to str_new() a negative number as a second argument.

Line 18 calculates the size of the block of memory to be allocated as the size of the Str structure plus the number of characters needed for the new C string. The idea is that in Line 21 you allocate everything you need in a single go.

Line 29 is only there for convenience, so that you can write clearer code, uncluttered with type castings that can be avoided.

In lines 30 to 35, you push the newly allocated Str structure on top of the existing string stack.

To me, it makes more "programming sense" to use a stack (i.e., a LIFO) instead of a queue (i.e., a FIFO) because when you are done with the strings and deallocate everything, it is more elegant (and perhaps marginally more efficient) to return to the heap the blocks in reverse order, beginning with what you have allocated last.

Lines 38 to 50 take care of all possible cases arising from the values of len and s. If len is not 0 and s is NULL, all you need to do is:

```
memset(chars, ' ', len);
chars[len] = '\0';
```

If s is a non-NULL pointer, in lines 43 to 45 you copy the first len characters of s to chars (or the whole s if it is not longer than len characters). Then, if s is shorter than chars, you fill the rest of chars with the pad character in line 47.

str_release()

The full code of str_release() is shown in Listing 6-4.

Listing 6-4. str_release()

```
1.  //------------------------------------------------------------------ str_release
2.  void str_release(Str **str_p) {
3.    Str *str = *str_p;
4.    if (str == NULL) return;                                          //==>
5.  #if STR_LOG
6.    printf("=== str_release: %p %p \"%s\"\n", *str->stack_p, str, str->s);
7.  #endif
8.
9.    Str *up = str->up;
10.   Str *down = str->down;
11.   if (up == NULL) { // str is on top of the stack
12.     if (down == NULL) {
13.       *str->stack_p = NULL; // no other strings in the stack
14.       }
15.     else {
16.       *str->stack_p = down;
17.       down->up = NULL;
18.       }
19.     }
20.   else if (down == NULL) { // str is at the bottom of the stack
21.     up->down = NULL;
22.     }
23.   else { // str is in the middle of the stack
24.     up->down = down;
25.     down->up = up;
26.     }
27.   free(str);
28.   *str_p = NULL; // to possibly force a crash if it is used again
29.   } // str_release
```

Line 4 is a "forgiving" reaction to an attempt of double-releasing a string: it simply ignores it.

A drastic alternative could be to abort the program. To do so, you would only need to replace the return of line 4 with something like CRASH("Attempted to release a NULL pointer").

All str_release() needs to do is remove the Str structure from the stack (lines 9 to 26) and return it to the heap with free() (line 27). Figure 6-1 shows graphically how the "unhooking" of a string from the middle of the stack works.

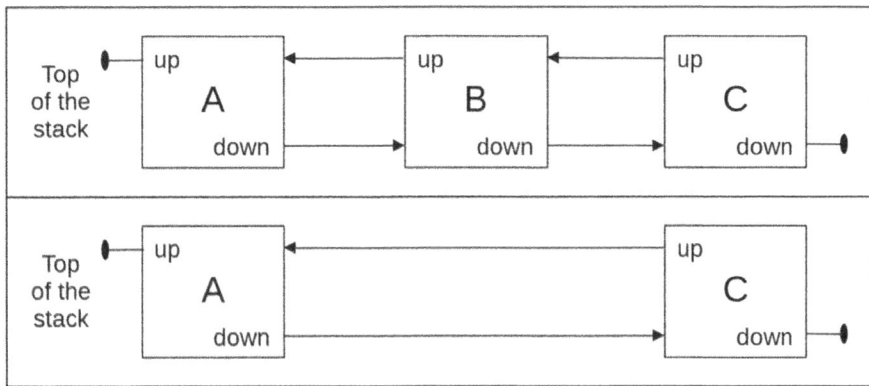

Figure 6-1. *Removing a string from the middle of the stack*

In the top part of Figure 6-1, B->up is A (line 8 of Listing 6-4) and B->down is C (line 10). To remove B, as shown in the bottom part of the figure, A->down needs to point to C (line 24), and C->up to A (line 25).

But what if you need to remove the structure at the top or at the bottom of the stack? Check out Figure 6-2.

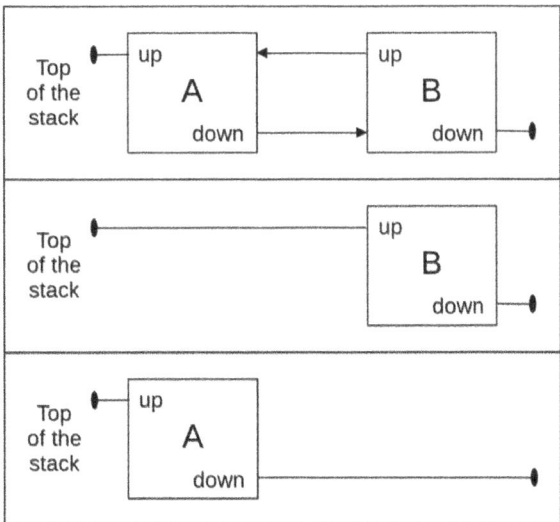

Figure 6-2. *Removing a string from the top or bottom of the stack*

To remove the top Str (A in Figure 6-2), you need to set B->up to NULL, while to remove the bottom Str (B in the figure), you need to set A->down to NULL. Programmatically, you can easily determine that A is the top because A->up is NULL. Similarly, B is clearly at the bottom of the stack because B->down = NULL.

In summary, to cover all possibilities so far examined, here is what you need to do:

```
if (str->up == NULL) { // str is at the top of the stack
  str->down->up = NULL;
  // Also set the stack address to str->down
  }
if (str->down == NULL) { // str is at the bottom of the stack
  str->up->down = NULL;
  }
if (str->down != NULL  &&  str->down != NULL) { // str is in the middle of the stack
  str->down->up = str->up;
  str->up->down = str->down;
  }
```

But there is still one case that you haven't looked at: what if you want to remove the only string present in the stack? In that case, both up and down are NULL. Here is what you need to do:

```
if (str->down == NULL  &&  str->down == NULL) { // str is in the only one in the stack
  // Set the stack address to NULL
  }
```

If you restructure the four cases to minimize the number of if statements, you have the code of Listing 6-4.

Before we move on, notice that line 4, together with line 28, prevents you from making a mess when you attempt to release twice the same string. But, obviously, if you do something like:

```
Str *str1 = str;
STR_release(str);
STR_release(str1);
```

you will crash the program, as the first execution of STR_release() will set str to NULL but leave str1 untouched.

str_release_all()

The full code of str_release_all() is shown in Listing 6-5.

Listing 6-5. str_release_all()

```
//------------------------------------------------------------ str_release_all
void str_release_all(Str *str) {
#if STR_LOG
  printf("=== str_release_all\n");
#endif
  if (str != NULL) {
    Str **stack_p = str->stack_p;
    while (*stack_p != NULL) {
      Str *p = *stack_p;
```

```
      *stack_p = (*stack_p)->down;
      p->down = NULL;
      p->s = NULL;
      p->stack_p = NULL;
      p->up = NULL;
      free(p);
      }
   }
 } // str_release_all
```

After studying str_release(), str_release_all() should be trivial. Note that you don't need to set the stack pointer to NULL when you are done because the down component of the bottom string is set to NULL. Also note that this is a case in which you cannot replace the while loop with a do; otherwise, you couldn't call str_release_all() with an empty stack without a serious risk of causing a crash.

As an additional protection against reusing strings after releasing the whole stack, all pointers within each Str found on the stack are set to NULL before releasing the structure. This follows the principle that it is better to cause a crash than use invalid pointers.

str_list()

The full code of str_list() is shown in Listing 6-6.

Listing 6-6. str_list()

```
1. //----------------------------------------------------------------- str_list
2. void str_list(Str *str) {
3.    if (str == NULL  ||  (str = *str->stack_p) == NULL) {
4.      printf("Nothing to list\n");
5.      }
6.    while (str != NULL) {
7.      char *s = (char *)((void *)str + sizeof(Str));
8.      size_t s_len = str->size - sizeof(Str);
9.      if (s_len > 0) s_len--;
10.     printf("%p %zu\n\tallocated(%zu):\t\"", str, str->size, s_len);
11.     for (int i = 0; i < s_len && s[i] != '\0'; i++) printf("%c", s[i]);
12.     printf("\"\n");
13.     if (str->s == NULL) printf("\tcurrent(0):\tnull\n");
14.     else printf("\tcurrent(%zu):\t\"%s\"\n", strlen(str->s), str->s);
15.     str = str->down;
16.     }
17.  } // str_list
```

Here is an example of a list entry:

```
0x94b100 40
    allocated(5):    "12345"
    current(5):      "12345"
```

Using the size component of Str, you can calculate the length of the allocated string (line 8) and display the string as safely as possible (lines 11 and 12), without relying on its terminating NULL.

It is very seldom that I use an assignment within the condition of an `if` statement. I did it in line 3 because I didn't like the alternative. You would have had to replace lines 3 to 5 with something like:

```
if (str == NULL) {
  printf("Nothing to list\n");
  }
else {
  str = *str->stack_p);
  if (str == NULL) printf("Nothing to list\n");
  }
```

Initially, the text `str_release_all()` displayed when it found an empty stack was "List empty". But that was before I introduced `STR_release_all_str()`. With the new macro, it became easily possible to execute the function `str_release_all()` with a `NULL` pointer as argument. The original message became then somewhat inaccurate.

Some Examples

Listing 6-7 shows a function to test allocation and release of strings.

Listing 6-7. test_allocation_release()

```
1. //---------------------------------------------------- test_allocation_release
2. void test_allocation_release(void) {
3.    STR_setup;
4.
5.    Str *str_12345 = STR_new("12345");
6.    Str *str_10_NULL = STR_newn_str(str_12345, 10, NULL, ' ');
7.    Str *str_8_abcdef = STR_newn_str(str_10_NULL, 8, "abcdef", '\0');
8.    Str *str_6_abcdefghi = STR_newn(6, "abcdefghi", ' ');
9.    STR_list_str(str_6_abcdefghi);
10.
11.    printf("-----------------------------------------------------A\n");
12.
13.    STR_release(str_6_abcdefghi);
14.    STR_list_str(str_12345);
15.    STR_release(str_10_NULL);
16.    STR_list_str(str_8_abcdef);
17.
18.    printf("-----------------------------------------------------B\n");
19.
20.    str_8_abcdef->s[2] = '{';
21.    str_8_abcdef->s[3] = '}';
22.    str_8_abcdef->s = "this is good!";
23.    STR_list();
24.
25.    printf("-----------------------------------------------------C\n");
26.
27.    str_10_NULL = STR_newn(10, NULL, '@');
28.    (void)STR_new("12345");
29.    STR_release(str_12345);
```

```
30.    STR_list();
31.    STR_release_all_str(str_10_NULL);
32.    STR_list();
33.
34.    printf("----------------------------------------------------D\n");
35.
36.    Str *str_1 = STR_new("1");
37.    STR_release(str_1);
38.    STR_list();
39.
40.    STR_dismantle;
41.
42.    } // test_allocation_release
```

After allocating some strings (lines 5 to 8), it releases in line 13 the string on the top of the stack and in line 15 a string in the middle. In lines 20 and 21, it modifies an allocated string and in line 22, it replaces an allocated string with a predefined one. In line 29, it releases the bottom of the stack (because str_12345 was the first one to be allocated). Finally, in line 37, it releases the only string from the stack.

Listing 6-8 shows the output produced by test_allocation_release().

Listing 6-8. Output of test_allocation_release()

```
1. === str_new: (nil) 0 "12345" '\0'-> 0x250d010
2. === str_new: 0x250d010 10 "(null)" ' '-> 0x250d050
3. === str_new: 0x250d050 8 "abcdef" '\0'-> 0x250d090
4. === str_new: 0x250d090 6 "abcdefghi" ' '-> 0x250d0d0
5. 0x250d0d0 47
6.    allocated(6):    "abcdef"
7.    current(6):      "abcdef"
8. 0x250d090 49
9.    allocated(8):    "abcdef"
10.   current(6):      "abcdef"
11. 0x250d050 51
12.   allocated(10):   "         "
13.   current(10):     "         "
14. 0x250d010 46
15.   allocated(5):    "12345"
16.   current(5):      "12345"
17. ---------------------------------------------------A
18. === str_release: 0x250d0d0 0x250d0d0 "abcdef"
19. 0x250d090 49
20.   allocated(8):    "abcdef"
21.   current(6):      "abcdef"
22. 0x250d050 51
23.   allocated(10):   "         "
24.   current(10):     "         "
25. 0x250d010 46
26.   allocated(5):    "12345"
27.   current(5):      "12345"
28. === str_release: 0x250d090 0x250d050 "         "
29. 0x250d090 49
30.   allocated(8):    "abcdef"
```

```
31.     current(6):      "abcdef"
32. 0x250d010 46
33.     allocated(5):    "12345"
34.     current(5):      "12345"
35. ----------------------------------------------------B
36. 0x250d090 49
37.     allocated(8):    "ab{}ef"
38.     current(13):     "this is good!"
39. 0x250d010 46
40.     allocated(5):    "12345"
41.     current(5):      "12345"
42. ----------------------------------------------------C
43. === str_new: 0x250d090 10 "(null)" '@'-> 0x250d050
44. === str_new: 0x250d050 0 "12345" '\0'-> 0x250d0d0
45. === str_release: 0x250d0d0 0x250d010 "12345"
46. 0x250d0d0 46
47.     allocated(5):    "12345"
48.     current(5):      "12345"
49. 0x250d050 51
50.     allocated(10):    "@@@@@@@@@@"
51.     current(10):      "@@@@@@@@@@"
52. 0x250d090 49
53.     allocated(8):    "ab{}ef"
54.     current(13):     "this is good!"
55. === str_release_all
56. Nothing to list
57. ----------------------------------------------------D
58. === str_new: (nil) 0 "1" '\0'-> 0x250d090
59. === str_release: 0x250d090 0x250d090 "1"
60. Nothing to list
61. === str_release_all
```

The allocation of the very first string in line 5 of test_allocation_release() (Listing 6-7) is logged by str_new() in line 1 of Listing 6-8 as:

```
=== str_new: (nil) 0 "12345" '\0'-> 0x250d010
```

The address of the stack before the operation is (nil) (i.e., NULL), and the other two arguments of str_new() are shown to be 0 for the len parameter and the predefined string "12345" for the s parameter. The address of the newly allocated string (which coincides with the address of the stack after allocation) is 0x250d010.

After that, the program allocates a string with a 10-character C string and no predefined string. It then allocates two Strs with predefines strings, respectively, shorter and longer than the allocated C string.

STR_list() displays the third string, allocated in line 7 of Listing 6-7 with

```
Str *str_8_abcdef = STR_newn_str(str_10_NULL, 8, "abcdef", '\0');
```

as follows:

```
0x250d090 49
    allocated(8):    "abcdef"
    current(6):      "abcdef"
```

Although eight characters were allocated, the trailing two are not shown because a NULL character was used for padding, and str_list() stops displaying characters when it encounters the first NULL (line 11 of Listing 6-6).

Notice that in one occasion the block of memory of a released string is allocated again: the 51 bytes allocated at address 0x250d050 in line 2 of the output (line 6 of the test function) and released in line 28 of the output (line 15 of the function) are allocated again in line 43 of the output (line 27 of the function).

The lines 20 to 22 of the function show that you can access and replace the allocated C strings normally. Lines 52 to 54 of the output show that the eight characters allocated and then modified in the C string containing "ab{}ef\0\0" are still part of the Str structure, but the s component of the structure, after executing line 22 of the function, points to the constant string "this is good!".

Although the Str structure has "forgotten" the pointer to "ab{}ef\0\0", this will not result in a memory leak because the C string was allocated as part of the block of memory that started with the Str structure. Therefore, free() will release the C string together with the Str structure.

When you no longer need the allocated C string, you might be tempted to release it back to the heap while keeping the Str structure. The easiest way to do it would be to execute:

```
my_str = (Str *)realloc((void *)my_str, sizeof(Str));
```

It would work, but only if the address pointed to by my_str remained the same. Otherwise, up to two pointers in the stack would become invalid (my_str->up->down and my_str->down->up, unless either or both my_str->up and my_str->down where NULL). Moreover, if you had assigned my_str to some other variable like in my_str1 = my_str, my_str1 would become invalid.

You cannot depend on the address of the allocated block to remain the same, even if, like it is always the case when you release the C string of an Str structure as shown above, the new block is smaller than the original one. My advice to you is not to worry about the space allocated for the C string.

Another thing: if you needed it, you could reactivate the originally allocated C string with a single line of code (yes, I have tested it):

```
if (str->size > sizeof(Str)) str->s = (char *)((void *)str + sizeof(Str));
```

where str is of type (Str *).

Multiple Stacks

You can create different stacks within the same function and operate on them simultaneously, as shown in Listing 6-9.

Listing 6-9. test_multiple_stacks()

```
1.  //-------------------------------------------------------- test_multiple_stacks
2.  void release_fun(Str *str) {
3.    STR_release(str);
4.    }
5.  void test_multiple_stacks(void) {
6.    STR_setup;
7.      printf("--------------------------------------- outer stack\n");
8.      Str *str_1 = STR_new("1");
9.      Str *str_2 = STR_new("2");
10.     Str *str_3 = STR_new("3");
11.     STR_list();
12.     STR_setup;
```

```
13.        printf("---------------------------------------- inner stack\n");
14.        Str *str_1 = STR_new("1");
15.        Str *str_2 = STR_new("2");
16.        STR_list();
17.        STR_release(str_2);
18.        Str *str_4 = STR_new_str(str_3, "4");
19.        STR_release(str_3);
20.        release_fun(str_4);
21.        printf("str_3=%p; str_4=%p\n", str_3, str_4);
22.        STR_list();
23.        STR_dismantle;
24.     printf("---------------------------------------- outer stack\n");
25.     STR_list();
26.   STR_dismantle;
27.   } // test_multiple_stacks
```

Listing 6-10 shows the output of the program.

Listing 6-10. Output of test_multiple_stacks()

```
---------------------------------------- outer stack
=== str_new: (nil) 0 "1" '\0'-> 0x1b77090
=== str_new: 0x1b77090 0 "2" '\0'-> 0x1b77050
=== str_new: 0x1b77050 0 "3" '\0'-> 0x1b770d0
0x1b770d0 42
        allocated(1):    "3"
        current(1):      "3"
0x1b77050 42
        allocated(1):    "2"
        current(1):      "2"
0x1b77090 42
        allocated(1):    "1"
        current(1):      "1"
---------------------------------------- inner stack
=== str_new: (nil) 0 "1" '\0'-> 0x1b77010
=== str_new: 0x1b77010 0 "2" '\0'-> 0x1b77110
0x1b77110 42
        allocated(1):    "2"
        current(1):      "2"
0x1b77010 42
        allocated(1):    "1"
        current(1):      "1"
=== str_release: 0x1b77110 0x1b77110 "2"
=== str_new: 0x1b770d0 0 "4" '\0'-> 0x1b77110
=== str_release: 0x1b77110 0x1b770d0 "3"
=== str_release: 0x1b77110 0x1b77110 "4"
str_3=(nil); str_4=0x1b77110
0x1b77010 42
        allocated(1):    "1"
        current(1):      "1"
=== str_release_all
```

```
---------------------------------------- outer stack
0x1b77050 42
        allocated(1):    "2"
        current(1):      "2"
0x1b77090 42
        allocated(1):    "1"
        current(1):      "1"
=== str_release_all
```

After allocating str_1 to str_3 for the outer stack, the program starts the inner stack and allocates str_1 and str_2. Those two variables "hide" str_1 and str_2 of the outer stack, so that, when str_2 is released in line 17 of the function (line 23 of the output), it is the str_2 of the inner stack that is freed. In line 18 of the function, str_4 is added to the outer stack (line 24 of the output). When str_3 is released with STR_release() in line 19 of the function (line 25 of the output) and str_4 is released in line 20 of the function (line 26 of the output) by invoking release_fun(), they are removed from the outer stack, because there are no str_3 and str_4 defined within the block statement of the inner stack.

Everything seems fine, but now look at line 27 of the output: while str_3 is NULL, str_4 still has the value it had before being released. This is because STR_release(), when invoked within release_fun(), resets str rather than str_3.

This is easy to fix. All you need to do is modify release_fun() as follows:

```
void release_fun(Str **str) {
  STR_release(*str);
  }
```

and invoke it in line 20 of the function with:

```
release_fun(&str_4);
```

But it shows how side-effecting functions can cause problems if you are not very careful.

Obviously, you can only define multiple stacks as long as the pairs of STR_setup and STR_dismantle do not cross.

String Formatting

In Australia (like in Britain), the rhetorical question "How long is a piece of string?" is used to indicate that something cannot be given a finite measurement. But the question becomes anything but rhetorical when you want to use sprintf() to format a C string.

For example, if you want to write

```
sprintf(the_string, "Invalid input: %ld\n", a_long);
```

how many characters must the_string contain? You can count the characters in the text, but how much space is a_long going to take?

The standard technique is to make the_string long enough to contain the maximum possible number of characters. Perhaps for the above example you would choose 32 (a nice power of 2, even it is irrelevant). Well, I just checked the value of LONG_MAX on my computer, and discovered that, to be completely safe, the_string needs to contain at least 35 characters (including the terminating NULL).

C provides functions to calculate the length of a printf output, but few bother to use them. The function str_printf() described in this section and the two associated macros STR_printf() and STR_printf_str() do it for you. See Listing 6-11 for an example of how to use them.

Listing 6-11. test_printf()

```
//----------------------------------------------------------------- test_printf
void test_printf(void) {
#include <limits.h>
  STR_setup;
    printf("----------------------------------------------------------\n");
    Str *str1 = STR_printf("Invalid input: %ld", LONG_MAX);
    STR_printf_str(str1, "%s%p 0x%x %1.3f", "&str1=", str1, 16, 1.2);
    STR_list();
  STR_dismantle;
  } // test_printf
```

The output of test_printf() is shown in Listing 6-12.

Listing 6-12. Output of test_printf()

```
=== str_printf: (nil) "Invalid input: %ld"
=== str_new: (nil) 34 "(null)" ' '-> 0x2173010
=== str_printf: 0x2173010 "%s%p 0x%x %1.3f"
=== str_new: 0x2173010 26 "(null)" ' '-> 0x2173070
0x2173070 67
        allocated(26):   "&str1=0x2173010 0x10 1.200"
        current(26):     "&str1=0x2173010 0x10 1.200"
0x2173010 75
        allocated(34):   "Invalid input: 9223372036854775807"
        current(34):     "Invalid input: 9223372036854775807"
=== str_release_all
```

As you can see, the allocated C string has the exact length of the formatted string. Let's look first of all at the two macros:

```
#define STR_printf(fmt, ...) str_printf(&str_stack, fmt, __VA_ARGS__)
#define STR_printf_str(str, fmt, ...) str_printf(&(str), fmt, __VA_ARGS__)
```

Nothing special in the macros (in case you are curious, VA stands for variadic); you only need to remember that the ellipsis in the macro is to be replaced with the special identifier __VA_ARGS__. Listing 6-13 shows the function str_printf().

Listing 6-13. str_printf()

```
1. //----------------------------------------------------------------- str_printf
2. Str *str_printf(Str **str_p, char *fmt, ...) {
3. #if STR_LOG
4.   printf("=== str_printf: %p \"%s\"\n", *str_p, fmt);
5. #endif
6. #include <stdarg.h>
7.   va_list va;
```

```
 8.    va_start(va, fmt);
 9.    size_t n = vsnprintf(NULL, 0, fmt, va);
10.    va_end(va);
11.    Str *str = str_new(str_p, n, NULL, ' ');
12.    va_start(va, fmt);
13.    vsprintf(str->s, fmt, va);
14.    va_end(va);
15.    return str;
16.    } // str_printf
```

va_start() accepts as arguments a variable of type va_list and the last parameter of the function preceding the ellipsis (i.e., fmt).

vsnprintf(), like snprintf(), accepts a pointer to a string into which to write the formatted output, the maximum number of characters that can be written into the output string, and a string with the formatting information. Also, like snprintf(), it returns the number of characters that could not be fitted into the output string.

But, unlike snprintf(), vsnprintf() accepts the remaining arguments in a variable of type va_list instead of as a comma-separated list.

When you invoke vsnprintf() in line 9 of Listing 6-13, you pass 0 as the maximum number of characters that can be written. As a result, vsnprintf() cannot write anything at all, and returns therefore the whole length of the string as number of characters that it couldn't write.

You can then invoke str_new() with the exact length you need to store the formatted string (line 11).

Finally, in line 13, you can use vsprintf() to write the formatted string to the C string you have just allocated.

Between the two invocations of v*printf() functions with the same argument list, you need to invoke va_end() and va_start(), because the v*printf() functions *consume* the arguments as they process them.

When doing this type of programming, it is extremely easy to overlook somewhere the NULLs that terminate strings, with results that can equate to delayed and sporadic catastrophes. Therefore, it is particularly important to check that all the terminating characters are accounted for. vsnprintf() (like snprintf()) does *not* count the terminating character in the value it returns, but it requires space for it. If, for example, the second argument is 4 and the output to be written consists of the word "stop", vsnprintf() writes "sto" to the output, appends to it the terminating NULL, and returns 1 because it couldn't write the 'p'.

So, when you tell vsnprintf() in line 9 that it can write no characters at all, the number it returns is the length of the text to be written without the terminating NULL, even if it couldn't write the NULL to the output. This is the number that you need because str_new() automatically adds 1 to store the terminating NULL (line 18 of Listing 6-2). You can then use vsprintf() (without the 'n' in its name) to write the string in line 13 of Listing 6-13 because you know that the space is available.

String Info

This section describes some macros that help you obtain information on the contents of Str structures (see Listing 6-14).

Listing 6-14. Info Macros

```
#define STR_display(str) {                                              \
    printf("%p:\n     up=%p down=%p size=%zu stack=%p\n",               \
    str, (str)->up, (str)->down, (str)->size, *(str)->stack_p);        \
    printf("     s(%lu)=\"%s\"\n", (str)->size - sizeof(Str), (str)->s); \
    }

#define STR_len(str) ((str != NULL && (str)->s != NULL) ? strlen((str)->s) : 0)
#define STR_len_allocated(str) ((str != NULL) ? ((str)->size-sizeof(Str)) : 0)
#define STR_char(str, k)                                         \
    ((str)->s != NULL && (strlen((str)->s) > k && k >= 0)        \
    ? (str)->s[k]                                                \
    : (STR_crash("STR_char: Character outside a string"), '\0'))
#define STR_string(str) ((str)->s)
```

STR_char(str, k) is equivalent to str->s[k], but it checks that str->s is not NULL and that k is within the boundaries of the string. If you need to access many characters, this could build up a significant overhead. What you could do is write your code with STR_char() but switch off the checks after testing:

```
#define STR_DEBUG 1

#if STR_DEBUG
#define STR_char(str, k)                                         \
    ((str)->s != NULL && (strlen((str)->s) > k && k >= 0)        \
    ? (str)->s[k]                                                \
    : (STR_crash("STR_char: Character outside a string"), '\0'))
#else
#define STR_char(str, k) (str)->s[k]
#endif
```

I will not mention this again, but the same consideration obviously applies to other macros.

Listing 6-15 shows a function with examples of all the macros of Listing 6-14, and Listing 6-16 shows the function's output.

Listing 6-15. test_info()

```
1.  //------------------------------------------------------------------ test_info
2.  void test_info(void) {
3.      STR_setup;
4.        printf("-------------------------------------------------info\n");
5.        Str *empty = STR_new(NULL);
6.        STR_display(empty);
7.        printf("--- \"%s\"\n", STR_string(empty));
8.        printf("--- STR_len(empty) = %zu\n", STR_len(empty));
9.
10.       printf("\n");
11.       Str *str = STR_new("0123456789ABCDEF");
12.       STR_display(str);
13.       printf("--- STR_char(\"%s\", %d) = %c\n", STR_string(str), 12,
14.           STR_char(str, 12));
```

```
15.       printf("--- Replacing the C string with \"Goofy\"\n");
16.       str->s = "Goofy";
17.       printf("--- String lengths (\"%s\"): current=%zu allocated=%zu\n",
18.           STR_string(str), STR_len(str), STR_len_allocated(str));
19.    STR_dismantle;
20.    } // test_info
```

Listing 6-16. Output of test_info()

```
 1. ------------------------------------------------info
 2. === str_new: (nil) 0 "(null)" '\0'-> 0x116b010
 3. 0x116b010:
 4.     up=(nil) down=(nil) size=40 stack=0x116b010
 5.     s(0)="(null)"
 6. --- "(null)"
 7. --- STR_len(empty) = 0
 8.
 9. === str_new: 0x116b010 0 "0123456789ABCDEF" '\0'-> 0x116b040
10. 0x116b040:
11.     up=(nil) down=0x116b010 size=57 stack=0x116b040
12.     s(17)="0123456789ABCDEF"
13. --- STR_char("0123456789ABCDEF", 12) = C
14. --- Replacing the C string with "Goofy"
15. --- String lengths ("Goofy"): current=5 allocated=17
16. === str_release_all
```

Lines 3 to 5 and 10 to 12 of Listing 6-16 show the outputs of STR_display() for an uninitialized Str and for an Str with a 16-character C string. Notice that line 12 shows a length of 17 because it calculates it as the difference between the size of the allocated block (i.e., 57) and the size of Str structures (i.e., 40). Therefore, it includes the string-terminating NULL.

String Update

In this section I describe macros and functions that set characters in strings, copy strings, convert strings to upper- or lowercase, and remove parts of strings.

You can set individual characters within a macro, without need for a function:

```
#define STR_set_char(str, k, c) {                                          \
    if((str)->s != NULL && strlen((str)->s) > k && k >= 0) (str)->s[k] = c;  \
    else STR_crash("STR_set_char: character outside a string");             \
    }
```

Obviously, you don't need a macro at all. For example, to set character 38 of a string to 'k', instead of typing STR_set_char(str, 38, 'k'), you could simply type str->s[38] = 'k'. But what if the string is, say, 30 characters long? Without the boundary checks built into the macro, you would be in trouble. As I said concerning STR_char(), you might like to modify the macro so that it only performs the checks when STR_DEBUG is set. It's entirely up to you!

But let's look at something more interesting.

String Copy

With the expression "string copy" you might mean two different operations:

- Create a new string that is identical to an existing one
- Copy the content of a string to another existing string

But the first type of operation is a duplication, rather than a copy. The term "copy" seems only appropriate when the destination string already exists. The problem with the second type of operation is that the destination string might be shorter than the source string, in which case a full copy is impossible. You could "hybridize" the two operations and allocate a new destination string but only if the existing one is too short. The problem with that solution is that the new string would be at a different location in memory, and that would cause any additional existing reference to the original destination string to become invalid.

The most reasonable solution seems to be a copy with truncation or padding when necessary. Listing 6-17 shows five examples of how to copy strings.

Listing 6-17. test_update()—String Copy

```
1. printf("\n-------------------------------------------copy_string\n");
2. str = STR_new("0123456789");
3.
4. size_t len = STR_copy_string(str, "Giulio", '$');
5. printf("--- %zu character%s copied: \"%s\"\n\n",
6.     len, (len == 1) ? "" : "s", STR_string(str));
7.
8. len = STR_copy_string(str, "Giulio", '\0');
9. printf("--- %zu character%s copied: \"%s\"\n\n",
10.     len, (len == 1) ? "" : "s", STR_string(str));
11.
12. len = STR_copy_string(str, "Giulio Zambon", '%');
13. printf("--- %zu character%s copied: \"%s\"\n\n",
14.     len, (len == 1) ? "" : "s", STR_string(str));
15.
16. len = STR_copy_string(str, "", '+');
17. printf("--- %zu character%s copied: \"%s\"\n\n",
18.     len, (len == 1) ? "" : "s", STR_string(str));
19.
20. len = STR_copy_string(str, NULL, '$');
21. printf("--- %zu character%s copied: \"%s\"\n\n",
22.     len, (len == 1) ? "" : "s", STR_string(str));
```

The first parameter of STR_copy_string() points to the destination Str; the second parameter is the source string; and the third parameter is the character to be used for padding if necessary. The output of the code in Listing 6-17 is shown in Listing 6-18.

Listing 6-18. Output of test_update()—String Copy

```
1. --------------------------------------copy_string
2. === str_new: (nil) 0 "0123456789" '\0'-> 0x1105060
3. === str_copy_string: "Giulio" '$' -> 0x1105060
4. --- 6 characters copied: "Giulio$$$$"
5.
```

```
 6. === str_copy_string: 0x1105060 "Giulio" '\0'
 7. --- 6 characters copied: "Giulio"
 8.
 9. === str_copy_string: "Giulio Zambon" '%' -> 0x1105060
10. --- 10 characters copied: "Giulio Zam"#
11.
12. === str_copy_string: "" '+' -> 0x1105060
13. --- 0 characters copied: "++++++++++"
14.
15. === str_copy_string: "(null)" '$' -> 0x1105060
16. --- 0 characters copied: "++++++++++"
```

The first example in Listing 6-17 (lines 4 to 6) replaces in str its initial value "0123456789" with "Giulio" using the $ sign for padding. Line 4 of the output (Listing 6-17) shows that STR_copy_string() doesn't count the padding in its returned value, as it only counts the 6 letters of "Giulio".

The second example in lines 8 to 10 of the code uses a NULL character for padding. This makes the destination string look exactly as the source string when you display it in line 7 of the output because the first NULL is interpreted as a terminator and the other four NULLs (the remaining three of padding plus the original terminator) are ignored. Obviously, all 10 characters of the original str (plus the terminating NULL) are still occupied by the updated string.

The third example in lines 12 to 14 of the code attempts to overwrite the 10 characters of str with the 13 characters of "Giulio Zambon". Line 10 of the output shows that the string is truncated. Obviously, no padding is needed.

The fourth example in lines 16 to 18 of the code copies an empty string to str. Its purpose is to show that, when you do so, the destination string is filled with the padding character, as shown in line 13 of the output.

Finally, the fifth example in lines 20 to 22 of the code shows what happens when you attempt to copy a NULL string. Perhaps not surprisingly, str_copy_string() leaves the destination string unchanged, as shown in line 16 of the output.

The macro STR_copy_string() is only an alias for the corresponding function:

```
#define STR_copy_string(str, st, pad) str_copy_string(str, st, pad)
```

The code of str_copy_string() is shown in Listing 6-19.

Listing 6-19. str_copy_string()

```
 1. //------------------------------------------------------------- str_copy_string
 2. size_t str_copy_string(Str *str, char *s, char pad) {
 3. #if STR_LOG
 4.    if (pad == '\0') printf("=== str_copy_string: %p \"%s\" '\\0'\n", str, s);
 5.    else printf("=== str_copy_string: \"%s\" '%c' -> %p\n", s, pad, str);
 6. #endif
 7.    if (str == NULL) {
 8.      STR_crash("str_copy_string: destination Str pointer NULL");
 9.      }
10.    else if ((str)->s == NULL) {
11.      STR_crash("str_copy_string: destination string pointer NULL");
12.      }
13.    size_t n_copy = 0;
14.    if (s != NULL) {
```

```
15.      size_t len = strlen(s);
16.      size_t space = str->size - sizeof(Str);
17.      if (space > 0) {
18.        space--;
19.        n_copy = (len > space) ? space : len;
20.        if (n_copy > 0) (void)memcpy(str->s, s, n_copy);
21.        if (n_copy < space) (void)memset(&str->s[n_copy], pad, space - n_copy);
22.        str->s[space] = '\0';
23.        }
24.      }
25.    return n_copy;
26.    } // str_copy_string
```

After checking that the destination is a proper string (lines 7 to 12), it calculates the length of the source string (line 15) and the space allocated for a C string in the destination Str (line 16). Note that, if space > 0 (condition checked in line 17), it is at least 2 because str_new() doesn't allow the allocation of empty strings. Therefore, any C string with an Str structure contains at least one character before the terminating '\0'. As a result, after the decrementing in line 18, space is at least 1, ensuring that at least one character is copied.

String Conversion

If you include <ctype.h>, you can use the two standard functions toupper() and tolower() to convert individual characters.

But we want to be able to convert entire strings. To do so in a comfortable way and without duplicating code, you can define a single function for both operations, as shown in Listing 6-20.

Listing 6-20. str_to_upper_lower()

```
1. //----------------------------------------------------------- str_to_upper_lower
2. void str_to_upper_lower(Str *str, int (*f)(int)) {
3. #if STR_LOG
4.   printf("=== str_to_upper_lower(%p)\n", str);
5. #endif
6.   if (str != NULL && str->s != NULL) {
7.     char *s = str->s;
8.     while (*s != '\0') {
9.       *s = (*f)(*s);
10.      s++;
11.      }
12.    }
13.  } // str_to_upper_lower
```

Notice that the third parameter accepts a pointer to a function that accepts an int as single parameter and returns an int, like the two standard character-conversion function.

If you define the two macros:

```
#define STR_toupper(str) str_to_upper_lower(str, &toupper)
#define STR_tolower(str) str_to_upper_lower(str, &tolower)
```

you can "hide" the choice of function behind the names of the macros.

Some not-so-experienced C programmers might be confused by the statement in line 9, but it will make sense if you consider that, if f is a function pointer (remember that you passed as argument &toupper or &tolower), *f is the function itself. Therefore, you can imagine replacing (*f)() with either toupper() or tolower(), like this:

```
*s = toupper(*s);
```

Then, it becomes obvious that line 9 simply picks the first character of the string and stores it back in the same position after conversion.

The parentheses around *f are necessary because the parentheses of a function call take precedence over the dereferencing asterisk (i.e., taking the address of the function). Therefore, if you wrote

```
*s = *f(*s);
```

you would effectively be doing the following:

```
*s = *(f(*s));
```

That is, you would be attempting to execute f (which is a pointer to a function) as if it were a function (which it's not). One good place to see the precedence of operators is en.cppreference.com/w/c/language/operator_precedence. It shows that the parentheses of a function call have precedence 1, while the dereferencing asterisk (which they call *indirection*) has precedence 2. Obviously, you could always use additional parentheses to set precedences by hand if you are not sure about the default or to remove a warning issued by an overzealous development environment, but you might like to be a minimalist in this matter, so that when you see additional parentheses, you know that they need to be there.

The logic of the function is trivial: you go through the string and convert one character at a time until you hit the terminating NULL.

String Clean Up

What I mean by string clean up is:

- Replace all non-printing characters with spaces

- Remove all leading spaces

- Remove all trailing spaces

- Replace all sequences of spaces with a single space

Consider, for example, the string " \t Giulio \t \x15 \r Zambon\t\t \x19\r". After performing the four operations listed above, it would look like this: "Giulio Zambon". Listing 6-21 shows how you do this.

Listing 6-21. str_clean_up()

```
1. //------------------------------------------------------------- str_clean_up
2. void str_clean_up(Str *str) {
3. #if STR_LOG
4.   printf("=== str_clean_up: %p\n", str);
5. #endif
6.   if (str != NULL && str->s != NULL) {
7.     char *s0 = str->s;
8.     char *s1 = s0;
```

```
9.        while (*s0 > '\0' && *s0 <= ' ') s0++; // remove leading junk
10.       if (*s0 == '\0') {
11.          *s1++ = ' ';
12.          *s1 = '\0';
13.          }
14.       else {
15.          int space_set = 0;
16.          while (*s0 != '\0') {
17.             if (*s0 > ' ') {
18.                *s1++ = *s0;
19.                space_set = 0;
20.                }
21.             else if (!space_set) {
22.                *s1++ = ' ';
23.                space_set = 1;
24.                }
25.             s0++;
26.             }
27.          if (s1 > str->s) { // we did something
28.             *s1-- = '\0';
29.             if (*s1 == ' ') *s1 = '\0'; // remove the trailing space
30.             }
31.          }
32.       }
33.    } // str_clean_up
```

After some initial checks, you define two pointers to the C string of the given Str (s0 and s1, in lines 7 and 8). You use s0 as input and s1 as output. As the cleanup operation only removes characters, if you work through the string from left to right, s1 will always coincide or be "on the left" of s0. Therefore, writing to s1 will never corrupt characters of s0 that you still have to examine.

You could have defined

```
char *s = str->s;
int k0 = 0;
int k1 = 0;
```

and replaced *s0 and *s1 respectively with s[k0] and s[k1], but using a pointer is more compact and, IMO, neater.

Line 9 is where you skip the leading spaces and non-printing characters. Notice that you cannot skip NULLs because otherwise you would go through the whole computer's memory!

The check in line 10 and the setting of s1 in lines 11 and 12 take care of the possibility that the whole input string might consist of spaces and non-input characters. In that case, you compact it into a single space.

space_set defined in line 15 is a state variable: when set to zero it indicates that the previous character of s0 you checked was a character you want to keep (i.e., neither a space nor a non-printing character). In other words, space_set is true when the last character was a space or a non-printing character.

Lines 18 and 19 are executed when the current input character (i.e., the character pointed by s0) is to be kept. Accordingly, you copy it to the position pointed by s1 and increment s1. But you also reset space_set. This means that, whenever you encounter several printing characters in sequence, you repeatedly clear space_set. You might ask: why don't we only set it when necessary? Like in:

```
if (space_set) space_set = 0;
```

But, who's to say that a check for non-zero followed by a jump is computationally more economical than a straight setting to zero? I'm not sure. The thing is, I always avoid checks if I can. And, in any case, a straight assignment is clearer.

If the `if` statement in line 17 fails, it means that the current character is either a space or a non-printing character. You only need to do something if it is the first one, because you want to reduce the sequences of spaces and non-printing characters to single spaces.

If it is the first one (i.e., if `space_set` is `false`), you write a space to the output (line 22) and remember that you have encountered a space or a non-printing character in input (line 23).

In any case, regardless of what you have encountered in input, you increment the input pointer (line 25) and move on.

After going through the whole input string, in line 27 you check that you have changed the output pointer. If that is the case, you know that the output string contains at least one character, and you close it with a `NULL` (line 28).

But wait a minute! What if there were trailing spaces and non-printing characters? Well, if there were, they will have been compacted into a single space. Therefore, you only need to check whether the last character of the string is a space. If it is, you overwrite it with a `NULL` (line 29) and you are done.

String Remove

Sometimes it is useful to remove a portion of a string. For this purpose, you can use one of the following macros:

```
#define STR_remove(str, from, before) str_remove(str, from, before)
#define STR_remove_from(str, from) str_remove(str, from, STR_len(str))
#define STR_remove_before(str, before) str_remove(str, 0, before)
```

The function `str_remove()` removes from a string the characters from position `from` (included) up to position `before` (excluded). Listing 6-22 shows five examples of how you can use it (`str` had already been defined as `Str *`) and Listing 6-23 shows the output of the code.

Listing 6-22. test_update()—Remove

```
printf("\n----------------------------------------------remove\n");
str = STR_new("0123456789ABCDEF");
printf("\n");

printf("--- Remove four characters in the middle\n");
STR_remove(str, 5, 9);
printf("--- \"%s\"\n\n", STR_string(str));

printf("--- Remove the first three characters\n");
STR_remove_before(str, 3);
printf("--- \"%s\"\n\n", STR_string(str));

printf("--- Remove the last character\n");
STR_remove_from(str, STR_len(str) - 1);
printf("--- \"%s\"\n\n", STR_string(str));

printf("--- Remove all characters except the first one\n");
STR_remove_from(str, 1);
printf("--- \"%s\"\n\n", STR_string(str));
```

```
printf("--- Remove all characters\n");
STR_remove_from(str, 0);
printf("--- \"%s\"\n\n", STR_string(str));
```

Listing 6-23. Output of test_update()—Remove

```
----------------------------------------------remove
=== str_new: 0x13ff010 0 "0123456789ABCDEF" '\0'-> 0x13ff0a0

--- Remove four characters in the middle
=== str_remove from 0x13ff0a0: from 5 before 9
--- "012349ABCDEF"

--- Remove the first three characters
=== str_remove from 0x13ff0a0: from 0 before 3
--- "349ABCDEF"

--- Remove the last character
=== str_remove from 0x13ff0a0: from 8 before 9
--- "349ABCDE"

--- Remove all characters except the first one
=== str_remove from 0x13ff0a0: from 1 before 8
--- "3"

--- Remove all characters
=== str_remove from 0x15f8010: from 0 before 1
--- ""
```

The function str_remove() is shown in Listing 6-24.

Listing 6-24. str_remove()

```
1.  //----------------------------------------------------------------- str_remove
2.  void str_remove(Str *str, size_t from, size_t before) {
3.  #if STR_LOG
4.    printf("=== str_remove from %p: from %zu before %zu\n", str, from, before);
5.  #endif
6.    if (str != NULL && str->s != NULL && *str->s != '\0') {
7.      size_t len = strlen(str->s);
8.      if (from < 0 || from >= len || before > len || before < 1
9.          || before <= from) {
10.       Str *e = STR_printf_str(str,
11.          "str_remove(%p, %zu, %zu): invalid indices (0, %zu)",
12.          str, from, before, len);
13.       STR_crash(e->s);
14.       }
15.     char *s = str->s;
16.     strcpy(s + from, s + before);
17.     }
18.   } // str_remove
```

As you can see, most of the function is devoted to checking that str is not NULL and that it includes a non-empty string (line 6), that the indices from and before are valid (line 8), and that from precedes before (line 9).

If you wanted to eliminate all the checks, you could replace the macros that invoke str_remove() with the following three:

```
#define STR_remove(str, from, before) \
    strcpy((str)->s + (from), (str)->s + (before))
#define STR_remove_from(str, from) { *((str)->s + (from)) ='\0' }
#define STR_remove_before(str, before) strcpy((str)->s, (str)->s + (before))
```

Searches

How many times do you need to find the first or last occurrence of a character or a substring within a string? In this section, you learn how find characters and substrings.

Find a Character

To be able to deal with most situations, you need four different ways of searching a string for a particular character, depending on the following two choices:

- From left to right/from right to left

- Case-sensitive/ignoring case

Additionally, when searching from left to right you should be able to start your search from a position within the string other than its beginning and, similarly, from a position other than the end when searching from right to left.

All in all, this results in the following eight macros:

```
#define STR_first_c(str, c)               str_first_c(str, c, 0, 0)
#define STR_first_c_from(str, c, from)    str_first_c(str, c, 0, from)
#define STR_first_cc(str, c)              str_first_c(str, c, 1, 0)
#define STR_first_cc_from(str, c, from)   str_first_c(str, c, 1, from)
#define STR_last_c(str, c)                str_last_c(str, c, 0, STR_len(str))
#define STR_last_c_before(str, c, before) str_last_c(str, c, 0, before)
#define STR_last_cc(str, c)               str_last_c(str, c, 1, STR_len(str))
#define STR_last_cc_before(str, c, before) str_last_c(str, c, 1, before)
```

As you can see, they rely on two functions: str_first_c() and str_last_c(). The first parameter of either function is the string to be searched; the second parameter is the character you are looking for; the third parameter determines whether the search should be done case-sensitive (value 1 and macro name with cc instead of c); and the fourth parameter specifies the position from which the search is to start.

Left to Right

Listing 6-25 shows some examples of searches from left to right, and the output of the searches is shown in Listing 6-26.

Listing 6-25. Left-to-Right Character Searches

```
printf("---------------------------------------------find character\n");
Str *str0 = STR_new("YnH 7j *^jnHN5DFgy");
char *s = STR_string(str0);
char *p = STR_first_c(str0, '-');
display_sub(s, p);
p = STR_first_c(str0, 'y');
display_sub(s, p);
p = STR_first_c(str0, 'Y');
display_sub(s, p);
p = STR_first_c(str0, 'N');
display_sub(s, p);
p = STR_first_cc_from(str0, 'N', 1);
display_sub(s, p);
p = STR_first_cc_from(str0, 'N', 2);
display_sub(s, p);
```

Listing 6-26. Output of Left-to-Right Character Searches

```
=== str_new: (nil) 0 "YnH 7j *^jnHN5DFgy" '\0'-> 0x1a7f010
=== str_first_c 0x1a7f010 '-' ignore case: false from: 0
--- "YnH 7j *^jnHN5DFgy"
    *** not found ***

=== str_first_c 0x1a7f010 'y' ignore case: false from: 0
--- "YnH 7j *^jnHN5DFgy"
 17               "y"

=== str_first_c 0x1a7f010 'Y' ignore case: false from: 0
--- "YnH 7j *^jnHN5DFgy"
  0 "YnH 7j *^jnHN5DFgy"

=== str_first_c 0x1a7f010 'N' ignore case: false from: 0
--- "YnH 7j *^jnHN5DFgy"
 12          "N5DFgy"

=== str_first_c 0x1a7f010 'N' ignore case: true from: 1
--- "YnH 7j *^jnHN5DFgy"
  1  "nH 7j *^jnHN5DFgy"

=== str_first_c 0x1a7f010 'N' ignore case: true from: 2
--- "YnH 7j *^jnHN5DFgy"
 10          "nHN5DFgy"
```

The function `display_sub()` is a simple function (see Listing 6-27) that displays the result of the search immediately below the input string, so that you can easily check what happened.

Listing 6-27. main.c: display_sub()

```
//---------------------------------------------------------------- display_sub
void display_sub(char *s, char *p) {
  printf("--- \"%s\"\n", s);
  if (p == NULL) {
    printf("      *** not found ***\n\n");
    }
  else {
    printf("%3zu ", p - s);
    int k = (int)(p - s);
    for (int i = 0; i < k; i++) printf(" ");
    printf("\"%s\"\n\n", p);
    }
  } // display_sub
```

Now that you are familiar with the macros, it is time to look at the two functions that do the work. Listing 6-28 shows str_first_c().

Listing 6-28. str_first_c()

```
1.  //---------------------------------------------------------------- str_first_c
2.  char *str_first_c(Str *str, char c, int ignore, size_t from) {
3.  #if STR_LOG
4.    printf("=== str_first_c %p \'%c\' ignore case: %s from: %zu\n",
5.        str, c, (ignore) ? "true" : "false", from);
6.  #endif
7.    char *p = NULL;
8.    if (str != NULL && str->s != NULL && *str->s != '\0') {
9.      if (from >= strlen(str->s)) {
10.       Str *e = STR_printf_str(str,
11.           "str_first: from >= length (%zu >= %zu)",
12.           from, strlen(str->s));
13.       STR_crash(e->s);
14.       }
15.     char *s = str->s + from;
16.     if (ignore) {
17.       char c_u = toupper(c);
18.       char c_l = tolower(c);
19.       while (p == NULL && *s != '\0') {
20.         if (*s == c_u || *s == c_l) p = s;
21.         else s++;
22.         }
23.       }
24.     else {
25.       p = strchr(s, c);
26.       }
27.     }
28.   return p;
29.   } // str_first_c
```

As usual, a non-negligible part of the function is devoted to checking the validity of the arguments. The search algorithm is in lines 15 to 26.

If the search is case-sensitive, `str_first_c()` uses the standard function `strchr()`. This gives you the opportunity to easily switch off the overhead due to checking by setting `STR_DEBUG` to 0. All you need to do is replace the macros `STR_first_c()` and `STR_first_c_from()` shown at the beginning of this section with the following two:

```
#define STR_first_c(str, c)          strchr((str)->s, c)
#define STR_first_c_from(str, c, from) strchr((str)->s + from, c)
```

But you cannot do the same when the search needs to be case-insensitive. Lines 17 and 18 set the two variables c_u and c_l to the upper- and lowercase versions of the character to be searched for.

To find the character you are looking for, you only need to scan the string one character at a time and stop when the current character matches either c_u or c_l.

Right to Left

Listings 6-29 and 6-30 show you respectively the code and the output of some examples of searches from right to left.

Listing 6-29. Right-to-left Character Searches

```
p = STR_last_c(str0, 'n');
display_sub(s, p);
p = STR_last_cc(str0, 'n');
display_sub(s, p);
p = STR_last_cc_before(str0, 'n', STR_last_cc(str0, 'n') - STR_string(str0));
display_sub(s, p);
p = STR_last_c(str0, 'Y');
display_sub(s, p);
p = STR_last_cc(str0, 'Y');
display_sub(s, p);
```

Listing 6-30. Output of Right-to-left Character Searches

```
=== str_last_c 0x252d010 'n' ignore case: false before: 18
--- "YnH 7j *^jnHN5DFgy"
 10            "nHN5DFgy"

=== str_last_c 0x252d010 'n' ignore case: true before: 18
--- "YnH 7j *^jnHN5DFgy"
 12              "N5DFgy"

=== str_last_c 0x252d010 'n' ignore case: true before: 18
=== str_last_c 0x252d010 'n' ignore case: true before: 12
--- "YnH 7j *^jnHN5DFgy"
 10            "nHN5DFgy"

=== str_last_c 0x252d010 'Y' ignore case: false before: 18
--- "YnH 7j *^jnHN5DFgy"
  0 "YnH 7j *^jnHN5DFgy"
```

```
=== str_last_c 0x252d010 'Y' ignore case: true before: 18
--- "YnH 7j *^jnHN5DFgy"
 17                        "y"
```

Notice that the third search uses a search to determine the position of the rightmost 'n' so that it can look for the second-to-last one.

The code of str_last_c() is shown in Listing 6-31.

Listing 6-31. str_last_c()

```
1.  //---------------------------------------------------------------- str_last_c
2.  char *str_last_c(Str *str, char c, int ignore, size_t before) {
3.  #if STR_LOG
4.    printf("=== str_last_c %p \'%c\' ignore case: %s before: %zu\n",
5.        str, c, (ignore) ? "true" : "false", before);
6.  #endif
7.    char *p = NULL;
8.    if (str != NULL && str->s != NULL && *str->s != '\0') {
9.      if (before > strlen(str->s)) {
10.       Str *e = STR_printf_str(str,
11.           "str_last_c: before > length (%zu > %zu)",
12.           before, strlen(str->s));
13.       STR_crash(e->s);
14.     }
15.     else if (before == 0) {
16.       STR_crash("str_last_c: before == 0");
17.     }
18.     char *s0 = str->s;
19.     char *s = s0 + before - 1;
20.     if (ignore) {
21.       char c_u = toupper(c);
22.       char c_l = tolower(c);
23.       while (p == NULL && s >= s0) {
24.         if (*s == c_u || *s == c_l) p = s;
25.         else s--;
26.       }
27.     }
28.     else {
29.       p = find_last_c(s0, c, before);
30.     }
31.   }
32.   return p;
33.  } // str_last_c
```

The case-insensitive search done in lines 21 to 26 is practically identical to that done in lines 17 to 22 of str_first_c() (Listing 6-28). The only difference worth mentioning is that when searching from left to right, you need to look for '\0', while when searching from right to left you need to check whether the pointer to the current character is positioned at the beginning of the string. Also, when you reach the NULL while scanning from left to right you are completely done, while when reaching the beginning of the string in the reverse search you still need to process the current character (hence the >= instead of a simple > in the condition of line 23).

As the standard C libraries don't provide a function to search for characters from right to left that's equivalent to strchr() when searching from left to right, you need to develop your own code (see Listing 6-32).

Listing 6-32. find_last_c()

```
//----------------------------------------------------------------- find_last_c
char *find_last_c(char *s0, char c, size_t before) {
  char *p = NULL;
  char *s = s0 + before - 1;
  while (p == NULL && s >= s0) {
    if (*s == c) p = s;
    else s--;
    }
  return p;
  } // find_last_c
```

As you can see, it is almost identical to lines 18 to 27 of str_last_c() (Listing 6-31). It is only convenient to write a separate function for case-sensitive reverse searches because, as you will see shortly, it is also needed when reverse-searching for substrings in str_last().

Find a Substring

The macros that search for substrings are very similar to those that search for characters, apart from the fact that substring searches are always case-sensitive:

```
#define STR_first(str, s)            str_first(str, s, 0)
#define STR_first_from(str, s, from)  str_first(str, s, from)
#define STR_last(str, s)             str_last(str, s, STR_len(str))
#define STR_last_before(str, s, before) str_last(str, s, before)
```

Therefore, I shall not bore you with further examples. You will find them in the source code attached to the book. But I will still show you the two functions str_first() and str_last().

Left to Right

Listing 6-33 shows str_first().

Listing 6-33. str_first()

```
1. //----------------------------------------------------------------- str_first
2. char *str_first(Str *str, char *s, size_t from) {
3. #if STR_LOG
4.    printf("=== str_first %p \"%s\" from: %zu\n", str, s, from);
5. #endif
6.    char *p = NULL;
7.    if (str != NULL && str->s != NULL && *str->s != '\0' &&
8.        s != NULL && *s != '\0') {
9.      if (from >= strlen(str->s)) {
10.        Str *e = STR_printf_str(str,
11.            "str_first: from >= length (%zu >= %zu)",
```

```
12.              from, strlen(str->s));
13.          STR_crash(e->s);
14.          }
15.      p = strstr(str->s + from, s);
16.      }
17.    return p;
18.    } // str_first
```

Like for the case-sensitive search in str_first_c() (line 25 of Listing 6-28), str_first() relies on a standard C function. This time, it is strstr() (line 15 of Listing 6-33).

This means that, once more, you can use STR_DEBUG to switch off the checks built into the function (although I would advise you to do this only when you have thoroughly tested your code):

```
#define STR_first(str, ss)                                              \
    (((ss) == NULL || strlen(ss) == 0) ? NULL : strstr((str)->s, ss))
#define STR_first_from(str, ss, from)                                   \
    (((ss) == NULL || strlen(ss) == 0) ? NULL : strstr((str)->s + from, ss))
```

These are more complicated than their character counterparts, which map directly to strchr(). This is due to the behavior of strstr(). When you execute something like

```
char *ss = strstr(s, "");
```

strstr() returns 0, while with

```
char *ss = strstr(s, NULL);
```

it crashes. The conditional assignment ensures that the macros return NULL in both cases, which is what str_first() does.

Right to Left

Listing 6-34 shows str_last().

Listing 6-34. str_last()

```
1. //------------------------------------------------------------------ str_last
2. char *str_last(Str *str, char *s, size_t before) {
3. #if STR_LOG
4.    printf("=== str_last %p \"%s\" before: %zu\n", str, s, before);
5. #endif
6.    char *p = NULL;
7.    if (str != NULL && str->s != NULL && *str->s != '\0' &&
8.        s != NULL && *s != '\0') {
9.      if (before > strlen(str->s)) {
10.        Str *e = STR_printf_str(str,
11.            "str_last: before > length (%zu > %zu)",
12.            before, strlen(str->s));
13.        STR_crash(e->s);
14.        }
```

```
15.      else if (before == 0) {
16.        STR_crash("str_last: before == 0");
17.        }
18.      char *s0 = str->s;
19.      size_t n = strlen(s);
20.      char *q = NULL;
21.      char c = *s;
22.      int keep_going = 1;
23.      do {
24.        q = find_last_c(s0, c, before);
25.        if (q != NULL) {
26.          if (strncmp(q, s, n)) {
27.            before = q - s0;
28.            }
29.          else {
30.            p = q;
31.            keep_going = 0;
32.            }
33.          }
34.        else {
35.          keep_going = 0;
36.          }
37.        } while (keep_going);
38.      }
39.   return p;
40.   } // str_last
```

The algorithm searches the string from right to left for the first character of the substring to be found (line 24). To do so, it uses find_last_c() (see Listing 6-32). If it doesn't find the character, it resets keep_going in line 35, thereby forcing the function to return NULL. If it finds the character, it checks whether from that position the string being searched matches the string to be found (line 26). If that is the case, the search has succeeded and the function returns the address provided by find_last_c(): line 30 saves the address and line 31 resets the keep_going flag to break out of the do loop.

But if strncmp() in line 26 returns a value other than 0, before is moved to the position of the character found by find_last_c() and the do loop goes through another iteration. This continues until keep_going becomes false, either because the substring is found or because find_last_c() in line 24 returns NULL.

Replace

Replacing in a string a single occurrence of a character or of a substring is not difficult: you search the string and manipulate it to achieve the replacement. But to replace all occurrences of a particular character or substring is a bit more delicate. This is what this section is about.

Replace a Character

Listing 6-35 shows some examples of character replacement.

Listing 6-35. Replacing a Character

```
printf("------------------------------------------replace character\n");
Str *str0 = STR_new("YnH 7j *^jnHN5DFgy");
Str *str1 = STR_newn(STR_len(str0), STR_string(str0), ' ');

STR_replace_c(str1, 'n', 'x');
printf("--- %s ->\n    %s\n", STR_string(str0), STR_string(str1));

STR_copy_string(str1, STR_string(str0), ' ');
STR_replace_cc(str1, 'n', 'x');
STR_replace_cc(str1, 'Y', 'z');
printf("--- %s ->\n    %s\n", STR_string(str0), STR_string(str1));

STR_release_all();
```

The two macros

```
#define STR_replace_c(str, old, new) str_replace_c(str, old, new, 0)
#define STR_replace_cc(str, old, new) str_replace_c(str, old, new, 1)
```

use the function

```
void str_replace_c(Str *str, char old, char new, int keep);
```

in which the fourth parameter determines whether you want to maintain the upper- or lowercase of the original character when you replace it. But when you set the fourth parameter to true, it also means that the search for characters to be replaced is case-insensitive.

Listing 6-36 shows the result of the replacements shown in Listing 6-35.

Listing 6-36. Output of Replacing a Character

```
------------------------------------------replace character
=== str_new: (nil) 0 "YnH 7j *^jnHN5DFgy" '\0'-> 0x1ae3010
=== str_new: 0x1ae3010 18 "YnH 7j *^jnHN5DFgy" ' '-> 0x1ae3060

=== str_replace_c 0x1ae3060 'n' -> 'x' keep case: false
--- YnH 7j *^jnHN5DFgy ->
    YxH 7j *^jxHN5DFgy

=== str_copy_string: "YnH 7j *^jnHN5DFgy" ' ' -> 0x1ae3060
=== str_replace_c 0x1ae3060 'n' -> 'x' keep case: true
=== str_replace_c 0x1ae3060 'Y' -> 'z' keep case: true
--- YnH 7j *^jnHN5DFgy ->
    ZxH 7j *^jxHX5DFgz

=== str_release_all
```

In the first example, you replace 'n' with 'x' but case-sensitive. As a result, the two 'n's of the string are replaced with 'x's, but the 'N' remains unchanged.

In the second example, you replace 'n' with 'x' but keeping the capitalization of the characters. And you also replace 'Y' with 'z', also case-insensitive. As a result, the two 'n's are replaced with 'x's, the 'N' is replaced with 'X', the 'Y' is replaced with 'Z', and the 'y' is replaced with 'z'.

Notice that when keep is true, it is irrelevant whether the characters are given in upper- or lowercase. Listing 6-37 shows the source code of str_replace_c().

Listing 6-37. str_replace_c()

```
1.  //-------------------------------------------------------------- str_replace_c
2.  void str_replace_c(Str *str, char old, char new, int keep) {
3.  #if STR_LOG
4.    printf("=== str_replace_c %p \'%c\' -> \'%c\' keep case: %s\n",
5.        str, old, new, (keep) ? "true" : "false");
6.  #endif
7.    if (str != NULL && str->s != NULL) {
8.      char *s = str->s;
9.      if (keep) {
10.       char old_u = toupper(old);
11.       char new_l = tolower(new);
12.       char new_u = toupper(new);
13.       while (*s != '\0') {
14.         if (toupper(*s) == old_u) {
15.           if (isupper(*s)) *s = new_u;
16.           else *s = new_l;
17.         }
18.         s++;
19.       }
20.     }
21.     else {
22.       while (*s != '\0') {
23.         if (*s == old) *s = new;
24.         s++;
25.       }
26.     }
27.   }
28. } // str_replace_c
```

When keep is false, search and replacements are trivial (lines 22 to 25 of Listing 6-37).

You do the comparison for case-insensitive replacement in uppercase (line 14), but note that you could have equally done it in lowercase. Then, when you find a match, you check the capitalization of the old character to set the new character accordingly.

Replace a Substring

Replacement of substrings is only case-sensitive, but it has the added complication that you cannot replace a substring with a longer one. Listing 6-38 shows four examples of substring replacement.

Listing 6-38. Replacing a Substring

```
printf("\n----------------------------------------replace substring\n");
str0 = STR_new("xxx.....xxxx....xxx");

str1 = STR_newn(STR_len(str0), STR_string(str0), ' ');
STR_replace(str1, "xxx", "ZZZ");
printf("--- %s ->\n    %s\n", STR_string(str0), STR_string(str1));

STR_copy_string(str1, STR_string(str0), ' ');
STR_replace(str1, "xxxx", "ZZZ");
printf("--- %s ->\n    %s\n", STR_string(str0), STR_string(str1));

STR_copy_string(str1, STR_string(str0), ' ');
STR_replace(str1, "xxxxx", "ZZZ");
printf("--- %s ->\n    %s\n", STR_string(str0), STR_string(str1));

STR_replace(str1, "xxxx", "");
printf("--- %s ->\n    %s\n", STR_string(str0), STR_string(str1));
```

In the third example, you attempt to replace a string that doesn't exist, and in the fourth and last example, you replace a string with an empty one. Listing 6-39 shows the output of the examples.

Listing 6-39. Output of Replacing a Substring

```
----------------------------------------replace substring
=== str_new: (nil) 0 "xxx.....xxxx....xxx" '\0'-> 0x1ae3010

=== str_new: 0x1ae3010 19 "xxx.....xxxx....xxx" ' '-> 0x1ae3060
=== str_replace 0x1ae3060 "xxx" -> "ZZZ"
--- xxx.....xxxx....xxx ->
    ZZZ.....ZZZx....ZZZ

=== str_copy_string: "xxx.....xxxx....xxx" ' ' -> 0x1ae3060
=== str_replace 0x1ae3060 "xxxx" -> "ZZZ"
--- xxx.....xxxx....xxx ->
    xxx.....ZZZ....xxx

=== str_copy_string: "xxx.....xxxx....xxx" ' ' -> 0x1ae3060
=== str_replace 0x1ae3060 "xxxxx" -> "ZZZ"
--- xxx.....xxxx....xxx ->
    xxx.....xxxx....xxx

=== str_replace 0x1ae3060 "xxxx" -> ""
--- xxx.....xxxx....xxx ->
    xxx.........xxx
```

You could have achieved the same result of the last example:

```
STR_replace(str1, "xxxx", "");
```

with

```
STR_remove(str1, 8, 12);
```

or

```
size_t where = STR_first(str1, "xxxx") - STR_string(str1);
STR_remove(str1, where, where + STR_len(str1));
```

or using STR_last() instead of STR_first(). But this would have only been possible because str1 includes a single instance of "xxxx".

Listing 6-40 shows the source code of str_replace().

Listing 6-40. str_replace()

```
1.  //------------------------------------------------------------------ str_replace
2.  void str_replace(Str *str, char *old, char *new) {
3.  #if STR_LOG
4.    printf("=== str_replace %p \"%s\" -> \"%s\"\n", str, old, new);
5.  #endif
6.    if (str != NULL && str->s != NULL && *str->s != '\0'
7.        && old != NULL && *old != '\0' && new != NULL) {
8.      size_t l_new = strlen(new);
9.      size_t l_old = strlen(old);
10.     if (l_new > l_old) {
11.       Str *e = STR_printf_str(str,
12.           "str_replace: new (\"%s\") longer than old (\"%s\")",
13.           new, old);
14.       STR_crash(e->s);
15.       }
16.     char *from = str->s;
17.     char *to = from;
18.     char *p = from;
19.     while (p != NULL) {
20.       p = strstr(from, old);
21.       if (p != NULL) {
22.         size_t dist = p - from;
23.         strncpy(to, from, dist);
24.         to += dist;
25.         from += dist + l_old;
26.         strncpy(to, new, l_new);
27.         to += l_new;
28.         }
29.       }
30.     strcpy(to, from);
31.     }
32.   } // str_replace
```

As the replacement is done in place, you start with three pointers to the beginning of the string: from points to the input string as the search through it progresses, to is used to build up the new version of the string after the replacements, and p is used for the searches.

You cannot use from for the searches because you need to remember where the last replaced substring ended: you search with p (line 20); if the search succeeds, you calculate how many characters of the original string need to be copied to the new (never longer) one (line 22). After copying those characters in line 23, you reposition the output pointer after them in line 24 and the input pointer after the newly found substring to be replaced. Finally, you copy to the output the replacement string in line 26 and reposition the output pointer after it.

Line 30 is needed to copy to the output string the characters that follow the last instance of the substring being replaced. Note that strcpy() also copies the terminating NULL and, with that, you are done.

Extract a Substring

It is useful to be able to extract a substring from a string. You can do this with the following three macros without needing to define a new function:

```
#define STR_sub(str, from, before)                              \
    str_new(&(str), (before) - (from), (str)->s + (from), ' ')
#define STR_sub_from(str, from)                                 \
    str_new(&(str), STR_len(str) - (from), (str)->s + (from), ' ')
#define STR_sub_before(str, before)                             \
    str_new(&(str), (before), (str)->s, ' ')
```

But if you want to add some checks to ensure that you don't exceed the string's boundaries, you might like to use the following macros instead:

```
#define STR_sub(str, from, before)  str_sub(str, from, before)
#define STR_sub_from(str, from)     str_sub(str, from, STR_len(str))
#define STR_sub_before(str, before) str_sub(str, 0, before)
```

You do the work with the function shown in Listing 6-41.

Listing 6-41. str_sub()

```
//----------------------------------------------------------------- str_sub
Str *str_sub(Str *str, size_t from, size_t before) {
#if STR_LOG
  printf("=== str_sub from %p: from %zu before %zu\n", str, from, before);
#endif
  Str *new_str = NULL;
  if (str != NULL && str->s != NULL && *str->s != '\0') {
    size_t len = strlen(str->s);
    if (from < 0 || from >= len || before > len || before < 1
        || before <= from) {
      Str *e = STR_printf_str(str,
          "str_sub(%p, %zu, %zu): invalid indices (0, %zu)",
          str, from, before, len);
      STR_crash(e->s);
      }
```

```
    new_str = str_new(&str, before - from, str->s + from, ' ');
    }
  return new_str;
  } // str_sub
```

In either case, you will be able to execute the examples shown in Listing 6-42.

Listing 6-42. Extracting a Substring

```
STR_setup;
printf("\n---------------------------------------------extract\n");
Str *str0 = STR_new("0123456789ABCDEF");
printf("\n");

printf("--- Extract four characters from the middle\n");
Str *str = STR_sub(str0, 5, 9);
printf("--- \"%s\"\n\n", STR_string(str));

printf("--- Extract the first three characters\n");
str = STR_sub_before(str0, 3);
printf("--- \"%s\"\n\n", STR_string(str));

printf("--- Extract the last character\n");
str = STR_sub_from(str0, STR_len(str0) - 1);
printf("--- \"%s\"\n\n", STR_string(str));

printf("--- Extract all characters except the first one\n");
str = STR_sub_from(str0, 1);
printf("--- \"%s\"\n\n", STR_string(str));

printf("--- Clone the string (i.e., extract all characters)\n");
str = STR_clone(str0);
printf("--- \"%s\"\n\n", STR_string(str));

STR_dismantle;
```

The last example illustrates the use of the macro STR_clone():

```
#define STR_clone(str) str_new(&str, STR_len(str), STR_string(str), ' ')
```

You could have used str_sub() as follows:

```
#define STR_clone(str) str_sub(str, 0, STR_len(str))
```

But why bother? The additional checks present in str_sub() will always succeed when you extract the whole string.

If you use the macros that invoke str_sub(), Listing 6-43 shows the output you will get when executing the code of Listing 6-42.

Listing 6-43. Output of Extracting a Substring

```
--------------------------------------------extract
=== str_new: (nil) 0 "0123456789ABCDEF" '\0'-> 0x17e6010

--- Extract four characters from the middle
=== str_sub from 0x17e6010: from 5 before 9
=== str_new: 0x17e6010 4 "56789ABCDEF" ' '-> 0x17e6060
--- "5678"

--- Extract the first three characters
=== str_sub from 0x17e6010: from 0 before 3
=== str_new: 0x17e6010 3 "0123456789ABCDEF" ' '-> 0x17e60a0
--- "012"

--- Extract the last character
=== str_sub from 0x17e6010: from 15 before 16
=== str_new: 0x17e6010 1 "F" ' '-> 0x17e60e0
--- "F"

--- Extract all characters except the first one
=== str_sub from 0x17e6010: from 1 before 16
=== str_new: 0x17e6010 15 "123456789ABCDEF" ' '-> 0x17e6120
--- "123456789ABCDEF"

--- Clone the string (i.e., extract all characters)
=== str_new: 0x17e6010 16 "0123456789ABCDEF" ' '-> 0x17e6160
--- "0123456789ABCDEF"

=== str_release_all
```

The only difference you would see when using the "reduced" macros would be the appearance of the log entries that start with "=== str_sub", as they are made from within str_sub().

But be aware that, because of the checks included in str_sub(), the macros that don't invoke it behave differently. For example, if you try to extract a substring with before <= from, str_sub() will raise an exception, but the "reduced" macros without str_sub(), obviously, will not. In particular, with before == from they will extract the whole string, and with before < from they will crash the program.

This is what it is all about: do not check the inputs at your own peril!

Concatenate Strings

You can concatenate two strings in C with strcat(), as in the following example:

```
char s0[20] = "bla bla";
char s1[10] = "Xblu blu";;
...
char *s = strcat(s0, s1);
```

The concatenation will produce the same result as if you had done:

```
char *s0 = "bla blaXblu blu";
char *s = s0;
```

In other words, strcat() writes s1 at the end of s0 assuming that there is enough space and then returns the address of s0. The other standard C function to concatenate strings, strncat(), works like strcat(), the only difference being that it lets you specify how many characters of s1 you want to append to s0.

I'm probably not telling you anything you don't already know, but I wanted to be sure that we start from the same base.

Besides the usual issue of not checking the input arguments, which is very efficient but can lead to disaster, strcat() also has the limitation that it only lets you concatenate two strings. You can do something like:

```
strcat(strcat(strcat(s0, s1), s2), s3);
```

but it would be nice if you could pass to the function any number of strings, like in:

```
super_strcat(s0, s1, s2, s3);
```

This is precisely what str_concat() lets you do:

```
Str *str_concat(Str **str0, ...);
```

str_concat() also differs from strcat() in that it creates a new Str with the combined C string instead of appending subsequent strings to the first one, a strategy that eliminates the risk of writing past the end of the first string.

Listing 6-44 shows a handful of examples and Listing 6-45 shows their outputs.

Listing 6-44. Concatenating Strings

```
STR_setup;
  printf("---------------------------------------------concat\n");
  Str *strA = STR_new("55555");
  Str *strB = STR_new("333");
  STR_setup;
    Str *strC = STR_new("4444");
    Str *strD = STR_new("22");
    printf("\n--- Concatenating \"%s\", \"%s\", \"%s\", and \"%s\"\n",
        strA->s, strB->s, strC->s, strD->s);
    Str *str = STR_concat(strA, strB, strC, strD);
    printf("--- Result: \"%s\"\n", str->s);

    printf("\n--- Concatenating \"%s\" and \"%s\"\n", strA->s, strD->s);
    str = STR_concat(strA, strD);
    printf("--- Result: \"%s\"\n", str->s);

    printf("\n--- Concatenating \"%s\" and \"%s\"\n", strB->s, strA->s);
    str = STR_concat_str(strA, strB, strA);
    printf("--- Result: \"%s\"\n", str->s);
```

```
    strB = STR_new("");
    printf("\n--- Concatenating \"%s\" with \"%s\", \"%s\", and \"%s\"\n",
        strB->s, strA->s, strB->s, strC->s);
    str = STR_concat(strB, strA, strB, strC);
    printf("--- Result: \"%s\"\n", str->s);

    STR_dismantle;

  printf("\n--- Concatenating \"%s\" on its own!\n", strA->s);
  Str *str = STR_concat(strA);
  printf("--- Result: \"%s\"\n", str->s);
  STR_dismantle;
```

While STR_concat() pushes the new string to the default stack, STR_concat_str() lets you specify the destination stack.

Listing 6-45. Output of Concatenating Strings

```
-----------------------------------------------concat
=== str_new: (nil) 0 "55555" '\0'-> 0x1539010
=== str_new: 0x1539010 0 "333" '\0'-> 0x1539050
=== str_new: (nil) 0 "4444" '\0'-> 0x1539090
=== str_new: 0x1539090 0 "22" '\0'-> 0x15390d0

--- Concatenating "55555", "333", "4444", and "22"
=== str_concat: 0x15390d0 ...
=== str_new: 0x15390d0 14 "(null)" '\0'-> 0x1539110
--- Result: "55555333444422"

--- Concatenating "55555" and "22"
=== str_concat: 0x1539110 ...
=== str_new: 0x1539110 7 "(null)" '\0'-> 0x1539150
--- Result: "5555522"

--- Concatenating "333" and "55555"
=== str_concat: 0x1539010 ...
=== str_new: 0x1539050 8 "(null)" '\0'-> 0x1539190
--- Result: "33355555"
=== str_new: 0x1539150 0 "" '\0'-> 0x15391d0

--- Concatenating "(null)" with "55555", "(null)", and "4444"
=== str_concat: 0x15391d0 ...
=== str_new: 0x15391d0 9 "(null)" '\0'-> 0x1539200
--- Result: "555554444"
=== str_release_all

--- Concatenating "55555" on its own!
=== str_concat: 0x1539190 ...
=== str_new: 0x1539190 5 "(null)" '\0'-> 0x1539090
--- Result: "55555"
=== str_release_all
```

The second-to-last example shows that you can concatenate uninitialized strings in any position.

And the last example shows that you can concatenate a single string. Not that it makes much sense, though, even if you consider it as yet another way to clone an existing string.

Also str_printf() supported a variable number of arguments (see Listing 6-13). In that case, all the function did was pass the list of parameters to vsprintf(), while str_concat() must process the arguments. The tricky aspect of it is that there is no way of knowing how many arguments are in the list!

Functions like printf() know when the to stop because the arguments that follow the formatting string must match the individual formats.

For example, in

```
printf("The length of \"%s\" is %zu\n", a_string, strlen(a_string));
```

printf() fulfills the format %s with the first argument in the variable list and %zu with the second one. After that, as there are no further formats to fulfill, printf() stops scanning for further arguments.

If you search the Internet, you will find that most examples involve telling the function how many arguments it needs to handle. That is, the standard technique is to write a function with the following prototype:

```
Str *counted_str_concat(int n_str, Str **str0, ...);
```

Then, the function "knows" through n_str how many strings to process. But that is ugly: when calling the function you would need first to count the strings you want to concatenate.

Another possibility is to write a recognizable Str after the list of strings you want to concatenate. You would invoke such a function with something like this:

```
Str *result = ended_str_concat(str0, str1, str2, str3, str_recognizable);
```

Then, the function could go through the list of argument and stop when it encounters the special Str. It's better than the "counted" function, but not entirely satisfactory: how many times would you forget to write the recognizable string at the end of your list?

To see how you do it with the help of macros, look at the following two definitions:

```
#define STR_concat(...)            str_concat(&str_stack, __VA_ARGS__, NULL)
#define STR_concat_str(str0, ...)  str_concat(&(str0), __VA_ARGS__, NULL)
```

The NULL passed to str_concat() as last argument is the recognizable string, and it removes the need of defining a terminating string. You declare the function as follows:

```
Str *str_concat(Str **str0, ...);
```

Using the macros has two advantages: the first one, shared with most other macros you have already seen in this chapter, is that you don't need to specify the default stack or remember to write an ampersand before str0; the other advantage is that you cannot forget to write a NULL as last argument of the function.

The ellipsis in the macro definitions, which matches any number of arguments, is translated into the keyword __VA_ARGS__, which in turn matches the ellipsis in the function. When you call a function, the compiler passes to it its arguments by pushing their values onto the stack starting from the last argument, so that the first argument is the first one to be popped off within the function. As a result, the arguments you pass to either macro are stacked immediately above the NULL, and &str_stack or &str0 are stacked on top. The function only sees a list of arguments, which means that it can determine the number of arguments by looking for the NULL. I confess I'm proud of this trick, which I have never seen mentioned anywhere!

Listing 6-46 shows str_concat().

Listing 6-46. str_concat()

```
1. //------------------------------------------------------------------- str_concat
2. Str *str_concat(Str **str0, ...) {
3. #if STR_LOG
4.    printf("=== str_concat: %p ...\n", *str0);
5. #endif
6.    Str **str_stack_p = str0;
7.    if (*str_stack_p != NULL) {
8.      str_stack_p = (*str0)->stack_p;
9.      if (str_stack_p == NULL) {
10.        STR_setup;
11.        Str *e = STR_printf("str_concat: Invalid reference Str (%p)", str0);
12.        STR_crash(e->s);
13.        STR_dismantle;
14.        }
15.      }
16.
17.    // First determine the number of strings and their total length.
18.    size_t tot_l = 0;
19.    va_list va;
20.    Str *str_k = NULL;
21.    va_start(va, str0);
22.    int n = 0;
23.    do {
24.      str_k = va_arg(va, Str *);
25.      if (str_k != NULL) {
26.        if (str_k->s != NULL) tot_l += strlen(str_k->s);
27.        n++;
28.        }
29.      } while (str_k != NULL);
30.    va_end(va);
31.
32.    // Then create the output string and copy into it the input strings.
33.    Str *new_str = str_new(str_stack_p, tot_l, NULL, '\0');
34.    char *s = new_str->s;
35.    va_start(va, str0);
36.    for (int k = 0; k < n; k++) {
37.      str_k = va_arg(va, Str *);
38.      if (str_k->s != NULL) {
39.        size_t len = strlen(str_k->s);
40.        (void)memcpy(s, str_k->s, len);
41.        s += len;
42.        }
43.      }
44.    va_end(va);
45.
46.    return new_str;
47.    } // str_concat
```

str_concat() goes through the list of arguments twice: the first time, in lines 23 to 29, to add up the lengths of all strings, and the second time, in lines 36 to 43, to actually do the concatenation.

The first loop keeps going until it encounters the NULL string, which always follows the strings you pass to the macro in the calling program.

Initially, there were no ifs in line 26 and line 36, but I added them because otherwise str_concat() would have not worked with uninitialized strings.

More Functionality?

It is clear that it would be possible to add more functions and macros. For example, Java provides the String methods startsWith(String) and endsWith(String). You could implement equivalent macros easily with something like:

```
#define STR_starts_with(str, ss) (!strncmp((str)->s, ss, strlen(ss)))
#define STR_ends_with(str, ss)                                        \
    (!strcmp((str)->s + strlen((str)->s) - strlen(ss), ss))
```

And then perhaps develop the corresponding functions to check the input arguments. But when do you stop?

Summary

In this chapter you learned how to build a library of functions to improve the standard handling of strings in C. Table 6-1 lists all the functions and their associated macros, while Table 6-2 lists additional macros.

Table 6-1. *List of Functions and Associated Macros*

Function Declaration	Description and Macros
void str_clean_up(Str *str);	Replaces all sequences of spaces and non-printing characters with single spaces, and removes leading and trailing spaces.
	#define STR_clean_up(str)
Str *str_concat(Str **str0, ...); WARNING: should be invoked via the macros.	Concatenates any number of Strs into a new Str.
	#define STR_concat(...) #define STR_concat_str(str0, ...)
void str_copy_string(Str *str, char *s, char pad)	Copies a string to an Str, possibly with truncation or padding. #define STR_copy_string(str, s, pad)
void str_crash(char *e, char *file, int line);	Reports a catastrophic error and aborts the program.
	#define STR_crash(e)
char *str_first(Str *str, char *s, size_t from);	Finds the first occurrence of a substring, from the beginning or not.
	#define STR_first(str, s) #define STR_first_from(str, s, from)

(continued)

Table 6-1. (*continued*)

Function Declaration	Description and Macros
char *str_first_c(Str *str, char c, int ignore, size_t from);	Finds the first occurrence of a character, either case-sensitive or not, from the beginning or not.
	#define STR_first_c(str, c) #define STR_first_c_from(str, c, from) #define STR_first_cc(str, c) #define STR_first_cc_from(str, c, from)
char *str_last(Str *str, char *s, size_t before);	Finds the last occurrence of a substring, before a given position or not.
	#define STR_last(str, s) #define STR_last_before(str, s, before)
char *str_last_c(Str *str, char c, int ignore, size_t before);	Finds the last occurrence of a character, either case-sensitive or not, before a given position or not.
	#define STR_last_c(str, c) #define STR_last_c_before(str, c, before) #define STR_last_cc(str, c) #define STR_last_cc_before(str, c, before)
void str_list(Str *str);	Lists all the strings in a stack.
	#define STR_list() #define STR_list_str(str)
Str *str_new(Str **str_p, size_t len, char *s);	Allocates a new string and adds it to a stack.
	#define STR_new(s) #define STR_new_str(str, s)
Str *str_printf(Str **str_p, char *fmt, ...);	Returns a new Str with a formatted C string.
	#define STR_printf(fmt, ...) #define STR_printf_str(str, fmt, ...)
void str_release(Str **str);	Removes a string from a stack and releases it.
	#define STR_release(str)
void str_release_all(Str *str);	Releases all the strings of a stack.
	#define STR_release_all() #define STR_release_all_str(str)
void str_remove(Str *str, size_t from, size_t before);	Removes a range of characters from a string.
	#define STR_remove(str, from, before) #define STR_remove_from(str, from) #define STR_remove_before(str, before)
void str_replace(Str *str, char *old, char *new);	Replaces all occurrences of a substring with a new one provided it is not longer than the original.
	#define STR_replace(str, old, new)

(continued)

Table 6-1. (*continued*)

Function Declaration	Description and Macros
void str_replace_c(Str *str, char old, char new, int keep);	Replaces all occurrences of a character with a new one, with the choice of maintaining upper- and lowercase.
	#define STR_replace_c(str, old, new, 0) #define STR_replace_cc(str, old, new, 1)
Str *str_sub(Str *str, size_t from, size_t before);	Extracts a substring from an Str and saves it into a new Str.
	#define STR_sub(str, from, before) #define STR_sub_from(str, from) #define STR_sub_before(str, before)
void str_to_upper_lower(Str *str, int (*f)(int));	Converts a string to upper- or lowercase.
	#define STR_tolower(str) #define STR_toupper(str)

Table 6-2. *List of Additional Macros*

Macro	Description
STR_char(str, k)	Returns the character k of an Str's C string.
STR_clone(str)	Creates a new Str identical to the given one.
STR_dismantle	Releases a stack of strings.
STR_display(str)	Prints on stdout all the components of an Str structure..
STR_len(str)	Returns the length of the C string within an Str.
STR_len_allocated(str)	Returns the size of the allocated C string within an Str.
STR_set_char(str, k, c)	Sets character k of an Str's C string to c.
STR_setup	Initializes a stack of strings.
STR_string(str)	Returns the C string of an Str.

■ ■ ■

## CHAPTER 7

Dynamic Arrays

The size of arrays in C is set at compile time. In the previous chapter, you learned a way of defining dynamically allocated C strings, which are arrays of characters. In this chapter, you will see how you can define at runtime arrays of any type. If you haven't read Chapter 6, I suggest that you quickly go through it, so that you can use it as a reference for this chapter.

That said, it doesn't mean that you can immediately convert the string functions and macros of Chapter 6 to work with any type of element because the conversion would present two immediate obstacles:

- C strings are null-terminated, while there is no equivalent end element for other types of arrays (although you could introduce one).

- The size in bytes of array elements depends on their types. Therefore, array elements can have any size.

But, with some adaptation, you can transfer the general design strategy used for strings to all arrays.

Array Allocation and Release

As with strings, you define a structure that contains all array parameters, and macros to operate on such structures (see Listing 7-1).

Listing 7-1. A Mechanism for Dynamic Arrays

```
1. typedef struct Dar Dar;
2. struct Dar {
3.   Dar    *up;    // one level higher in the stack
4.   Dar    *down;  // one level deeper in the stack
5.   size_t size;   // size of an array element
6.   size_t n;      // number of elements in the array
7.   Dar    **stack_p;
8.   };
9.
10. #define DAR_setup {         \
11.   Dar *dar_stack = NULL;
12.
13. #define DAR_get_len(ar) ({                                    \
14.   void * _ar = ar;                                            \
15.   size_t _len = 0;                                            \
16.   if (_ar) _len = ((Dar *)((void *)(_ar) - sizeof(Dar)))->n;  \
17.   _len;                                                       \
```

```
18.    })
19. #define DAR_list() dar_list(dar_stack)
20. #define DAR_new(var, ne) dar_new(&dar_stack, sizeof(var), ne)
21. #define DAR_new_a(ar, ne) dar_new(&dar_stack, sizeof(*(ar)), ne)
22. #define DAR_release(array) dar_release(&(array))
23. #define DAR_release_all() dar_release_all(&(dar_stack))
24.
25. // Macro to be executed last
26. #define DAR_dismantle                    \
27.   dar_release_all(&dar_stack);    \
28.   }
```

If you compare Listing 7-1 with Listing 6-1, which shows structure and macros for dynamically allocated strings, you will notice that there are a couple of significant differences.

Whereas the Str structure has a component that provided the size of the allocated block, Dar has two components that provide the size and number of the array elements.

Apart from the replacement of STR with DAR (which, incidentally, stands for *dynamic arrays*), the only differences between Listings 7-1 and 6-1 are in the macros that allocate new arrays. There are two reasons for that: first, you could initialize a new dynamic string with an existing string while you cannot do the same with arrays, and second, all strings were of the same type (i.e., arrays of char), which is not the case with arrays.

Allocating an Array

Listing 7-2 shows the dar_new() function.

Listing 7-2. dar_new()

```
1. //---------------------------------------------------------------------- dar_new
2. void *dar_new(Dar **dar_stack_p, size_t el_size, size_t n_el) {
3. #if DAR_LOG
4.   printf("=== dar_new: %p %zu %zu",
5.       *dar_stack_p, el_size, n_el);
6. #endif
7.
8.   // Calculate the size of the needed memory block and allocate it.
9.   size_t size = sizeof(Dar) + el_size * n_el;
10.   void *blk = calloc(size, 1);
11.   if (blk == NULL) {
12.     char mess[40];
13.     sprintf(mess, "dar_new: Failed to allocate %zu bytes", size);
14.     DAR_crash(mess);                                              // -->
15.   }
16.
17.   // Calculate the address to be returned.
18.   void *array = blk + sizeof(Dar);
19.
20.   // Push the block address to the dar stack.
21.   Dar *new_dar = (Dar *)blk;
22.   new_dar->up = NULL;
23.   new_dar->down = *dar_stack_p;
24.   new_dar->size = el_size;
```

```
25.    new_dar->n = n_el;
26.    new_dar->stack_p = dar_stack_p;
27.    if (*dar_stack_p != NULL) (*dar_stack_p)->up = new_dar;
28.    *dar_stack_p = new_dar;
29.
30. #if DAR_LOG
31.    printf(" --> %p (%p) %ul %ul\n", *dar_stack_p, array, *dar_stack_p, array);
32. #endif
33.    return array;
34.    } // dar_new
```

The use of `calloc()` instead of `malloc()` in line 10 ensures that the newly allocated array is set to zeros. Line 18 sets the address of the actual array so that it starts immediately after the space used to store the Dar structure. After initializing the Dar structure in lines 21 to 26, you push it onto the array stack in lines 27 and 28. Pretty straightforward.

To execute the function, you have the choice of two macros. The first one, DAR_new() (shown in line 20 of Listing 7-1), uses its first parameter to calculate the size of the array element, so that it can pass it on to dar_new(). Its main purpose is to "hide" to the calling program the array stack pointer. The second macro, DAR_new_a() lets you create a new array of the same type and on the same stack of an existing one.

The macro DAR_crash() invoked in line 14 is as follows:

```
#define DAR_crash(e) dar_crash(e, __FILE__, __LINE__)
```

and Listing 7-3 shows the function dar_crash(), which is practically identical to str_crash() as shown in Listing 6-3.

Listing 7-3. dar_crash(): Reporting a Catastrophic Problem

```
//------------------------------------------------------------------ dar_crash
void *dar_crash(char *e, char *file, int line) {
  fprintf(stderr, "DAR error \"%s\" (file %s; line %d)\n", e, file, line);
  fflush(stderr);
  abort();
  return NULL;
  } // dar_crash
```

Here is how you can use DAR_new() to allocate an array of four doubles:

```
double d;
double *dd = DAR_new(d, 4);
```

If you don't want to define a double variable for the sole purpose of allocating the array and don't have another double variable handy, you can also write:

```
double *dd = DAR_new((double)0, 4);
```

As already mentioned, you can also allocate a new array with the macro DAR_new_a() (shown in line 21 of Listing 7-1), which uses the address of an existing array of the type you need. For example, if dd is an array of doubles (either defined at compile time or dynamically as shown above), you can define another double array as follows:

```
double *ddd = DAR_new_a(dd, 10);
```

Note that the macro also works if the array address is NULL, because sizeof() doesn't do any memory access. This means that you could also invoke the macro as follows, although I'm not sure why you would do that, as using DAR_new() is simpler:

```
double *ddd = DAR_new_a((double *)NULL, 10);
```

Releasing an Array

Once you no longer need an array, you can free the memory it occupies by invoking the macro DAR_release(), which has the array as its only parameter:

```
#define DAR_release(array) dar_release((void **)&(array))
```

Listing 7-4 shows the dar_release() function.

Listing 7-4. dar_release()

```
1.  //---------------------------------------------------------------- dar_release
2.  void dar_release(void **array_p) {
3.    void *array = *array_p;
4.    if (array == NULL) return;                              //-->
5.    Dar *dar = (Dar *)(array - sizeof(Dar));
6.  #if DAR_LOG
7.    printf("=== dar_release: %p %p %zu %zu\n", *dar->stack_p, dar,
8.        dar->size, dar->n);
9.  #endif
10.
11.   Dar *up = dar->up;
12.   Dar *down = dar->down;
13.   if (up == NULL) { // dar is on top of the stack
14.     if (down == NULL) {
15.       *dar->stack_p = NULL; // no other arrays in the stack
16.     }
17.     else {
18.       *dar->stack_p = down;
19.       down->up = NULL;
20.     }
21.   }
22.   else if (down == NULL) { // dar is at the bottom of the stack
23.     up->down = NULL;
24.   }
25.   else { // dar is in the middle of the stack
26.     up->down = down;
27.     down->up = up;
28.   }
29.   free(dar);
30.   *array_p = NULL; // to force a crash if it is used again
31. } // dar_release
```

The only parameter of dar_release() is the address of the variable within the calling program that holds the address of the allocated array (i.e., of its first element). If the function prototype had been

```
void dar_hypothetical_release(void *array);
```

the macro would have been

```
DAR_hypothetical_release(array) dar_hypothetical_release(array)
```

The compiler would have then created the variable array within the function and copied into it the address of the allocated array, which you could have used to release the allocated memory. So, why go through the complication of passing the variable address instead of its content? The only reason is to be able to reset the variable located in the calling program from within the function. This you do in line 31 of Listing 7-4, so that the calling program "forgets" where the array was located before it was released (unless you have copied the variable somewhere else, that is).

Releasing an allocated block of memory doesn't change the data it contains. Only subsequent allocations will modify it. As a result, if you access a block of memory after you have released it, it will still contain valid (or partially valid) data for an undetermined period of time. I am not suggesting that you would do it intentionally, but it might happen as a result of a bug you have in your program. And because some of the data might still be valid, you might find it very difficult to nail down the bug, which would show up sporadically and unpredictably. By resetting the variable that used to hold the address of the allocated block, you will make such a bug more predictable, because it will cause a program crash. And more predictable bugs are easier to fix.

The check in line 5 ensures that you are not trying to release an array that you have already released or never allocated. And it only protects you from multiple releases of the same array because, as explained, you reset its address in the calling program.

The function is almost identical to str_release() (see Listing 6-4). If you haven't read Chapter 6, I suggest that at least you look at the section dedicated to str_release(). You will find it useful to fully understand how dar_release() works.

If you want to release all the dynamic arrays, instead of invoking DAR_release() for each one of them, you should use

```
#define DAR_release_all() dar_release_all(&(dar_stack))
```

Listing 7-5 shows the dar_release_all() function.

Listing 7-5. dar_release_all()

```
//----------------------------------------------------------- dar_release_all
void dar_release_all(Dar **stk_p) {
#if STR_LOG
  printf("=== dar_release_all\n");
#endif
  if (stk_p != NULL) {
    while (*stk_p != NULL) {
      Dar *p = *stk_p;
      *stk_p = (*stk_p)->down;
      memset(p, 0, sizeof(Dar) + p->size * p->n);
      free(p);
      }
    }
  } // dar_release_all
```

Notice that because the function parameter is a pointer to the stack pointer, you automatically set the stack pointer to NULL in the calling program once you are through the while loop.

Listing 7-1 also includes the macro DAR_get_len(ar) to obtain the length of an array (lines 13 to 18). To list a stack you can use the following macro:

```
#define DAR_list() dar_list(dar_stack)
```

Listing 7-6 shows the dar_list() function.

Listing 7-6. dar_list()

```
//------------------------------------------------------------------ dar_list
void dar_list(Dar *stk) {
  if (!stk) printf("Nothing to list\n");
  while (stk != NULL) {
    printf("%p %zu %zu\n", stk, stk->size, stk->n);
    stk = stk->down;
    }
  } // dar_list
```

dar_list() is much simpler than the corresponding str_list() for dynamic strings (see Listing 6-6). This is because dar_list() only prints the metadata of the arrays (the address, element size, and number of elements), while str_list() also prints the strings themselves. dar_list() cannot print the content of the arrays because it doesn't know their type. Unfortunately, C doesn't let you save and retrieve the type of variables.

Listing 7-7 shows some examples of allocation and release.

Listing 7-7. Examples of Allocation and Release

```
printf("------- Example of allocation and release\n");
DAR_setup;

int i;
printf("ii:\t");
int *ii = DAR_new(i, 20);

float f;
printf("ff:\t");
float *ff = DAR_new(f, 10);

printf("dd:\t");
double *dd = DAR_new((double)0, 4);

printf("ddd:\t");
double *ddd = DAR_new_a(dd, 10);

printf("iii:\t");
int *iii = DAR_new_a(ii, 15);

char c;
printf("cc:\t");
char *cc = DAR_new(c, 50);

printf("iiii:\t");
int **iiii = DAR_new(ii, 3);
```

```
printf("\nDAR_list:\n");
DAR_list();

printf("\ndd:\t");
DAR_release(dd);

printf("ff:\t");
DAR_release(ff);

printf("ii:\t");
DAR_release(ii);

printf("cc:\t");
DAR_release(cc);

printf("iii:\t");
DAR_release(iii);

printf("\nDAR_list:\n");
DAR_list();

printf("\niiii:\t");
DAR_release(iiii);

printf("ddd:\t");
DAR_release(ddd);

printf("iii:\t");
DAR_release(iii);

printf("\n\nDAR_list:\n");
DAR_list();

DAR_dismantle;
```

Listing 7-8 shows the output you generate when you execute the code in Listing 7-7.

Listing 7-8. Examples of Allocation and Release—Output

```
------- Example of allocation and release
ii:   === dar_new: (nil) 4 20 --> 0x789010 (0x789038)
ff:   === dar_new: 0x789010 4 10 --> 0x789090 (0x7890b8)
dd:   === dar_new: 0x789090 8 4 --> 0x7890f0 (0x789118)
ddd:  === dar_new: 0x7890f0 8 10 --> 0x789140 (0x789168)
iii:  === dar_new: 0x789140 4 15 --> 0x7891c0 (0x7891e8)
cc:   === dar_new: 0x7891c0 1 50 --> 0x789230 (0x789258)
iiii: === dar_new: 0x789230 8 3 --> 0x7892a0 (0x7892c8)

DAR_list:
0x7892a0 8 3
0x789230 1 50
0x7891c0 4 15
```

```
0x789140 8 10
0x7890f0 8 4
0x789090 4 10
0x789010 4 20

dd:    === dar_release: 0x7892a0 0x7890f0 8 4
ff:    === dar_release: 0x7892a0 0x789090 4 10
ii:    === dar_release: 0x7892a0 0x789010 4 20
cc:    === dar_release: 0x7892a0 0x789230 1 50
iii:   === dar_release: 0x7892a0 0x7891c0 4 15

DAR_list:
0x7892a0 8 3
0x789140 8 10

iiii: === dar_release: 0x7892a0 0x7892a0 8 3
ddd:  === dar_release: 0x789140 0x789140 8 10
iii:

DAR_list:
Nothing to list
```

Multiple Stacks

You can create different stacks within the same function and operate on them simultaneously, as shown in Listings 7-9 and 7-10.

Listing 7-9. Example of Multiple Array Stacks

```
 1. printf("\n------- Example of multiple stacks\n");
 2. printf("=== Set up stack 1\n");
 3. DAR_setup; // first stack
 4.
 5. printf("ii_1 (stack 1):\t");
 6. int *ii_1 = DAR_new((int)0, 10);
 7.
 8. printf("dd_1 (stack 1):\t");
 9. double *dd_1 = DAR_new((double)0, 8);
10.
11. printf("\n=== Set up stack 2\n");
12. DAR_setup; // second stack
13.
14. printf("ff_2 (stack 2):\t");
15. float *ff_2 = DAR_new((float)0, 7);
16.
17. printf("ff_1 (stack 1):\t");
18. float *ff_1 = DAR_new_dar(ii_1, (float)0, 5);
19.
20. printf("cc_2 (stack 2):\t");
21. float *cc_2 = DAR_new_dar(ff_2, (char)0, 6);
22.
```

```
23. printf("\nDAR_list_dar (stack 1):\n");
24. DAR_list_dar(dd_1);
25.
26. printf("dd_1 (stack 1):\t");
27. DAR_release(dd_1);
28.
29. printf("\nDAR_list (stack 2):\n");
30. DAR_list();
31.
32. printf("\n=== Dismantle stack 2\n");
33. DAR_dismantle; // second stack
34.
35. printf("\nDAR_list (stack 1):\n");
36. DAR_list();
37.
38. printf("\n=== Dismantle stack 1\n");
39. DAR_dismantle; // first stack
```

You set up an "outer" stack in line 3 of Listing 7-9 and an "inner" stack in line 12. Before you dismantle the inner stack in line 33, you can create and remove arrays on either stack.

Note that when you have several stacks active at the same time, each dismantling automatically applies to the last stack you set up. To make it clear, you can use indentation, as in the following example:

```
DAR_setup;                        // sets up stack 1
  ..use stack 1..
  DAR_setup;                      // sets up stack 2
    ..use stacks 1 and 2..
    DAR_setup;                    // sets up stack 3
      ..use stacks 1, 2, and 3..
      DAR_dismantle;              // dismantles stack 3
    DAR_setup;                    // sets up stack 4
      ..use stacks 1, 2, and 4..
      DAR_dismantle;              // dismantles stack 4
    ..use stacks 1 and 2..
    DAR_dismantle;                // dismantles stack 2
  ..use stack 1..
  DAR_dismantle;                  // dismantles stack 1
```

As you can see, in lines 18 and 26 of Listing 7-9, you respectively allocate and release arrays linked to stack 1 despite the fact that the innermost (i.e., default) stack is stack 2. But you can only push a new array to an outer stack when that stack is not empty. This is because you need to be able to pass to DAR_new_dar() the address of an array identifying the stack. For example, in line 18 of Listing 7-9, you use ii_1 to tell DAR_new_dar() that the new array of floating-point numbers is to be pushed onto stack 1.

Listing 7-10 shows the output of the statements of Listing 7-9.

Listing 7-10. Example of Multiple Array Stacks—Output

```
------- Example of multiple stacks
=== Set up stack 1
ii_1 (stack 1): === dar_new: (nil) 4 10 --> 0x1483090 (0x14830b8)
dd_1 (stack 1): === dar_new: 0x1483090 8 8 --> 0x14831c0 (0x14831e8)
```

```
=== Set up stack 2
ff_2 (stack 2): === dar_new: (nil) 4 7 --> 0x14832a0 (0x14832c8)
ff_1 (stack 1): === dar_new_dar: 0x14830b8 4 5
=== dar_new: 0x14831c0 4 5 --> 0x14830f0 (0x1483118)
cc_2 (stack 2): === dar_new_dar: 0x14832c8 1 6
=== dar_new: 0x14832a0 1 6 --> 0x14832f0 (0x1483318)

DAR_list_dar (stack 1):
0x14830f0 4 5
0x14831c0 8 8
0x1483090 4 10
dd_1 (stack 1): === dar_release: 0x14830f0 0x14831c0 8 8

DAR_list (stack 2):
0x14832f0 1 6
0x14832a0 4 7

=== Dismantle stack 2

DAR_list (stack 1):
0x14830f0 4 5
0x1483090 4 10

=== Dismantle stack 1
```

The two macros to extend and list a stack other than the default one are:

```
#define DAR_new_dar(ar, var, ne) dar_new_dar((void *)(ar), sizeof(var), ne)
#define DAR_list_dar(ar) dar_list_dar((void *)(ar))
```

The two functions dar_new_dar() (see Listing 7-11) and dar_list_dar() (see Listing 7-12) are fairly simple, as you only need them to invoke dar_new() and dar_list(), respectively.

Listing 7-11. dar_new_dar()

```
//--------------------------------------------------------------- dar_new_dar
void *dar_new_dar(void *ar, size_t el_size, size_t n_el) {
#if DAR_LOG
  printf("=== dar_new_dar: %p %zu %zu\n", ar, el_size, n_el);
#endif
  void *array = NULL;
  if (ar) {
    Dar *dar_p = ar - sizeof(Dar);
    array = dar_new(dar_p->stack_p, el_size, n_el);
    }
  return array;
  } // dar_new_dar
```

Listing 7-12. dar_list_dar()

```
//--------------------------------------------------------------- dar_list_dar
void dar_list_dar(void *ar) {
```

```
  if (ar) {
    Dar *dar_p = ar - sizeof(Dar);
    dar_list(*dar_p->stack_p);
    }
  else {
    printf("Nothing to list\n");
    }
  } // dar_list_dar
```

Changing the Size of an Array

Once you can dynamically allocate arrays, your first wish is probably to be able to extend them.

Unfortunately, you cannot simply add elements to an existing array. What you can do with an array allocated at runtime is make a new, larger array, copy into it the elements of the original one, and release the smaller array that you no longer need.

Obviously, you can only perform such an operation if you haven't stored in some variables the addresses of the original array and/or one or more of its elements; otherwise, you will likely cause a mess when you access memory locations that have been freed back to the heap (and possibly reallocated).

Listing 7-13 shows the dar_resize() function, which lets you move the elements of an array to an array of a different size.

Listing 7-13. dar_resize()

```
1.  //------------------------------------------------------------------ dar_resize
2.  void dar_resize(void **ar1_p, int i1, int n1, int i2, size_t n2) {
3.  #if DAR_LOG
4.    printf("=== dar_resize: %p %d %d %d %zu\n", *ar1_p, i1, n1, i2, n2);
5.  #endif
6.    if (!*ar1_p) {
7.      char mess[50];
8.      sprintf(mess, "dar_resize: input array pointer is null");
9.      DAR_crash(mess);                                             // -->
10.     }
11.   if (i2 <= 0 || i2 >= n2) {
12.     char mess[50];
13.     sprintf(mess, "dar_resize: output (%d..%zu) invalid", i2, n2);
14.     DAR_crash(mess);                                             // -->
15.     }
16.   void *ar1 = *ar1_p;
17.   Dar *dar1_p = ar1 - sizeof(Dar);
18.   if (!n1) n1 = dar1_p->n - i1;
19.   if (i1 < 0 || i1 + n1 - 1 >= dar1_p->n) {
20.     char mess[50];
21.     sprintf(mess, "dar_resize: input (%d..%d) invalid", i1, i1 + n1 - 1);
22.     DAR_crash(mess);                                             // -->
23.     }
24.   if (n1 > n2 - i2) {
25.     char mess[50];
26.     sprintf(mess, "dar_resize: from %d bytes to %zu", n1, n2 - i2);
27.     DAR_crash(mess);                                             // -->
28.     }
```

195

```
29.    size_t size = dar1_p->size;
30.    void *ar2 = dar_new(dar1_p->stack_p, size, n2);
31.    (void)memcpy(ar2 + i2 * size, ar1 + i1 * size, n1 * size);
32.    dar_release(ar1_p);
33.    *ar1_p = ar2;
34.    } // dar_resize
```

The use of the four numeric parameters is better illustrated with a diagram (see Figure 7-1).

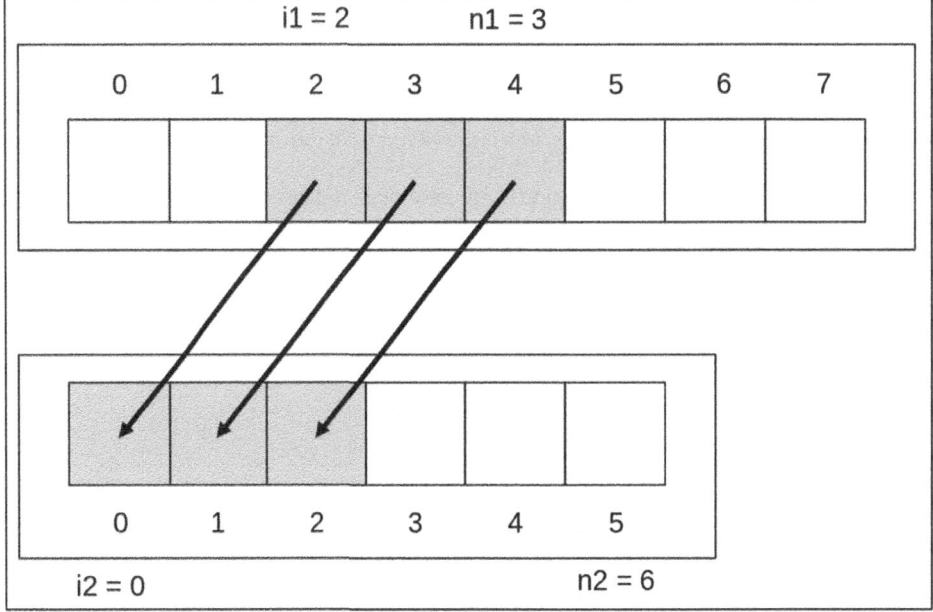

Figure 7-1. *Moving elements to a new array*

Figure 7-1 shows the result of the following call:

```
dar_resize(&array1, 2, 3, 0, 6);
```

array1 is the array of length eight shown in the upper half of Figure 7-1. dar_resize() allocates an array of length 6 (n2) and copies three elements (n1) of array1, beginning with element 2 (i1) into the new array from element 0 (i2). After that, it releases array1 and replaces it with the new array.

Most of dar_resize() is dedicated to checking the input parameters: line 6 checks that the address of the input array is not NULL; line 11 checks the output index and array size; line 19 checks the input index and number of elements, and line 24 checks that the input range fits into the output array from the specified position.

Line 18 implements a feature of the function: if you set n1 to 0, dar_resize() automatically sets it to the maximum possible, so that the range from i1 to the end of the array is copied.

Line 30 allocates the new array with elements of the same size as the original one (obtained in line 29).

In line 31, you copy all the necessary elements from the input array to the output one. By using memcpy(), you do it in the most efficient way possible. Note that you don't need to know the type of the arrays, but only how many bytes each element occupies. The first argument is the destination address, which you obtain by adding to the address of the array you have allocated in line 30 (i.e., ar2) the number of bytes occupied by each array element (i.e., size, which is calculated in line 29) times the specified destination offset (i.e., i2). The second argument of memcpy() is calculated like the first one but for the original array (i.e., ar1) with offset i1. Finally, you calculate the third argument of memcpy() by multiplying the number of elements to be moved (i.e., n1) by the size of each element (i.e., size).

This operation is guaranteed to work because the C99 standard has specified that C compilers must pack the array elements tightly together, without any padding to achieve word alignment. If there were gaps between the array elements, the amount of memory to copy would depend on the word size of your computer and perhaps even on the compiler.

Once you have built ar2 to have, beginning from position i2, n1 elements of ar1 beginning with element i1, you release ar1 in line 32. Then, in line 33, you replace in the calling program the address of ar1 (which is no longer valid) with that of ar2.

The release of the original array in line 32 must occur before replacing it with the new one in line 33. This makes sense because otherwise you would be releasing the array you have just allocated.

To use dar_resize(), you can invoke one of the following two macros:

```
#define DAR_resize(ar, i1, n1, i2, n2) \
  dar_resize((void **)&(ar), i1, n1, i2, n2)
#define DAR_extend(ar, nn) dar_resize((void **)&(ar), 0, 0, 0, nn);
```

The first one lets you set all parameters as you see fit, while the second one replaces an array with a larger one of the same type and content.

Listing 7-14 shows some examples of array resizing.

Listing 7-14. Examples of Array Resizing

```
  printf("\n------- Examples of array resizing\n");
  DAR_setup;

  int *int1 = DAR_new((int)0, 10);
  for (int k = 0; k < 10; k++) int1[k] = k + 100;
  for (int k = 0; k < 10; k++) printf("%4d", int1[k]);
  printf("\n\n");

  printf("Extend to 12\n");
  DAR_extend(int1, 12);
  for (int k = 0; k < 12; k++) printf("%4d", int1[k]);
  printf("\n\n");

  printf("Reduce to 9 and copy 5 elements from old [3] to new [4]\n");
  DAR_resize(int1, 3, 5, 4, 9);
  for (int k = 0; k < 9; k++) printf("%4d", int1[k]);
  printf("\n\n");

  printf("Reduce to 3 but keep the last element at the end\n");
  DAR_resize(int1, 8, 1, 2, 3);
  for (int k = 0; k < 3; k++) printf("%4d", int1[k]);
  printf("\n\n");

  char *c1 = DAR_new((char)0, 10);
  sprintf(c1, "abcdefghi");
  printf("%s\n\n", c1);

  printf("Reduce to 6 and copy the last 6 elements\n");
```

```
DAR_resize(c1, strlen(c1) - 5, 6, 0, 6);
printf("%s\n\n", c1);

printf("DAR_list:\n");
DAR_list();

DAR_dismantle;
```

Listing 7-15 shows the output you generate when you execute the code in Listing 7-14.

Listing 7-15. Examples of Array Resizing—Output

```
------- Examples of array resizing
=== dar_new: (nil) 4 10 --> 0xba0090 (0xba00b8)
 100 101 102 103 104 105 106 107 108 109

Extend to 12
=== dar_resize: 0xba00b8 0 0 0 12
=== dar_new: 0xba0090 4 12 --> 0xba0330 (0xba0358)
=== dar_release: 0xba0330 0xba0090 4 10
 100 101 102 103 104 105 106 107 108 109   0   0

Reduce to 9 and copy 5 elements from old [3] to new [4]
=== dar_resize: 0xba0358 3 5 4 9
=== dar_new: 0xba0330 4 9 --> 0xba0090 (0xba00b8)
=== dar_release: 0xba0090 0xba0330 4 12
   0   0   0   0 103 104 105 106 107

Reduce to 3 but keep the last element at the end
=== dar_resize: 0xba00b8 8 1 2 3
=== dar_new: 0xba0090 4 3 --> 0xba02f0 (0xba0318)
=== dar_release: 0xba02f0 0xba0090 4 9
   0   0 107

=== dar_new: 0xba02f0 1 10 --> 0xba0390 (0xba03b8)
abcdefghi

Reduce to 6 and copy the last 6 elements
=== dar_resize: 0xba03b8 4 6 0 6
=== dar_new: 0xba0390 1 6 --> 0xba03d0 (0xba03f8)
=== dar_release: 0xba03d0 0xba0390 1 10
efghi

DAR_list:
0xba03d0 1 6
0xba02f0 4 3
```

Array Copy and Duplication

This process is easy because dar_resize() already does everything you need in order to make copies of arrays.

All you need to do is add to dar_resize() a new parameter that indicates where to store the address of the new array and then make minor modifications to the function.

The new function prototype looks like this:

```
void dar_resize(void **ar1_p, int i1, int n1, void **ar2_p, int i2, size_t n2);
```

Then, replace lines 32 and 33 of Listing 7-13 with this code:

```
if (ar2_p) {
  *ar2_p = ar2;
  }
else {
  dar_release(ar1_p);  // was line #32
  *ar1_p = ar2;        // was line #33
  }
```

How simple is that?

Once you have updated dar_resize(), you need to modify the resizing macros accordingly:

```
#define DAR_extend(ar, nn) dar_resize((void **)&(ar), 0, 0, NULL, 0, nn);
#define DAR_resize(ar, i1, n1, i2, n2) \
  dar_resize((void **)&(ar), i1, n1, NULL, i2, n2)
```

And, obviously, you want to define new macros to do the copying while leaving the original array untouched:

```
#define DAR_clone(ar1, ar2) dar_resize((void **)&(ar1), 0, 0, \
  (void **)&(ar2), 0, 0);
#define DAR_copy(ar1, i1, n1, ar2, i2, n2)                    \
  dar_resize((void **)&(ar1), i1, n1, (void **)&(ar2), i2, n2)
```

Notice anything?

DAR_clone() passes 0 to dar_resize() as the last argument. This is necessary because DAR_clone() doesn't know how many elements ar1 (and hence, ar2) has. This forces you to make yet another small change to dar_resize(): in line 11 of Listing 7-13, you only crash the program if n2 < 0, not if it is <= 0; then, if n2 is zero, after line 23 you set it to the number of elements of the original array.

To avoid confusion, Listing 7-16 shows the final version of dar_resize(). The updated or new lines are marked with at signs (@).

Listing 7-16. dar_resize()—Final Version

```
. //---------------------------------------------------------------- dar_resize
@ void dar_resize(void **ar1_p, int i1, int n1,
@     void **ar2_p, int i2, size_t n2) {
. #if DAR_LOG
.   printf("=== dar_resize: %p %d %d %d %zu\n", *ar1_p, i1, n1, i2, n2);
. #endif
.   if (!*ar1_p) {
.     char mess[50];
.     sprintf(mess, "dar_resize: input array pointer is null");
.     DAR_crash(mess);                                           // -->
.     }
```

199

```
@   if (i2 < 0 || (n2 > 0 && i2 >= n2)) {
.      char mess[50];
.      sprintf(mess, "dar_resize: output (%d..%zu) invalid", i2, n2);
.      DAR_crash(mess);                                                // -->
.      }
.   void *ar1 = *ar1_p;
.   Dar *dar1_p = ar1 - sizeof(Dar);
.   if (!n1) n1 = dar1_p->n - i1;
.   if (i1 < 0 || i1 + n1 - 1 >= dar1_p->n) {
.      char mess[50];
.      sprintf(mess, "dar_resize: input (%d..%d) invalid", i1, i1 + n1 - 1);
.      DAR_crash(mess);                                                // -->
.      }
@   if (!n2) n2 = dar1_p->n;
.   if (n1 > n2 - i2) {
.      char mess[50];
.      sprintf(mess, "dar_resize: from %d bytes to %zu", n1, n2 - i2);
.      DAR_crash(mess);                                                // -->
.      }
.   size_t size = dar1_p->size;
.   void *ar2 = dar_new(dar1_p->stack_p, size, n2);
.   (void)memcpy(ar2 + i2 * size, ar1 + i1 * size, n1 * size);
@   if (ar2_p) {
@      *ar2_p = ar2;
@      }
@   else {
.      dar_release(ar1_p);
.      *ar1_p = ar2;
@      }
.   } // dar_resize
```

For the record, the parentheses around (n2 > 0 && i2 >= n2) are unnecessary because && has precedence over ||, but Eclipse annoyingly keeps suggesting we add them.

Anyhow, the change is also useful if you want to move a group of contiguous elements within an array and clear the rest:

```
dar_resize((void **)&(ar), i1, n1, NULL, i2, 0);
```

or keep a range and clear the rest:

```
dar_resize((void **)&(ar), i1, n1, NULL, i1, 0);
```

Listing 7-17 shows some examples of array copying.

Listing 7-17. Examples of Array Copying

```
//------- Examples of array copying
printf("\n------- Examples of array copying\n");
DAR_setup;

int *int1 = DAR_new((int)0, 10);
for (int k = 0; k < DAR_get_len(int1); k++) int1[k] = k + 100;
```

```
for (int k = 0; k < DAR_get_len(int1); k++) printf("%4d", int1[k]);
printf("\n\n");

printf("clone:\n");
int *int2 = NULL;
DAR_clone(int1, int2);
for (int k = 0; k < DAR_get_len(int2); k++) printf("%4d", int2[k]);
printf("\n\n");

int *int3 = NULL;
printf("Copy 5 elements from old [3] to new [4]\n");
DAR_copy(int1, 3, 5, int3, 4, 0);
for (int k = 0; k < DAR_get_len(int3); k++) printf("%4d", int3[k]);
printf("\n\n");

printf("DAR_list:\n");
DAR_list();

DAR_dismantle;
```

Listing 7-18 shows the output you generate when you execute the code in Listing 7-17.

Listing 7-18. Examples of Array Copying—Output

```
------- Examples of array copying
=== dar_new: (nil) 4 10 --> 0xac4010 (0xac4038)
 100 101 102 103 104 105 106 107 108 109

clone:
=== dar_resize: 0xac4038 0 0 0 0
=== dar_new: 0xac4010 4 10 --> 0xac4070 (0xac4098)
 100 101 102 103 104 105 106 107 108 109

Copy 5 elements from old [3] to new [4]
=== dar_resize: 0xac4038 3 5 4 0
=== dar_new: 0xac4070 4 10 --> 0xac40d0 (0xac40f8)
   0   0   0   0 103 104 105 106 107   0

DAR_list:
0xac40d0 4 10
0xac4070 4 10
0xac4010 4 10
```

Select Array Elements

Wouldn't it be useful to be able to pick out of an array all the elements that satisfy a certain criterion? For example, all the NULL elements in an array of pointers, or all the elements with a value greater than a given threshold?

I haven't seen such a function elsewhere but, whether it exists or not, we are going to implement it here.

A first, simpler, step is to count such elements. The dar_count_matches() function shown in Listing 7-19 does exactly that.

Listing 7-19. dar_count_matches()

```
//---------------------------------------------------------- dar_count_matches
int dar_count_matches(void *ar, int (*fun)(void *)) {
  int kount = 0;
  if (ar) {
    Dar *dar = (Dar *)(ar - sizeof(Dar));
    for (int k = 0; k < dar->n; k++) {
      kount += (*fun)(&ar[k * dar->size]);
      }
    }
  return kount;
  } // dar_count_matches
```

The first parameter is the array address and the second parameter is the address of a function that accepts an array element and returns 1 if the element is a match.

The function works without knowing the type of the array because it uses the element size to calculate the address of each element, which it then maps to (void *).

For example, suppose that you have an array called ar1 of structures like this:

```
typedef struct a_t {
  int value;
  } a_t;
```

and that you want to count all elements with a value greater than 3 but less than 6. The callback function would look like this:

```
int match1(void *el_p) {
  a_t *e_p = el_p;
  return (e_p->value > 3 && e_p->value < 6);
  }
```

You would call dar_count_matches() as follows:

```
int n_matches = dar_count_matches(ar1, match1);
```

Now that you know how to count the matches, saving them into an array is simple. You only need to use dar_count_matches() to know how many elements the index array must have.

Listing 7-20 shows the dar_index_matches() function.

Listing 7-20. dar_index_matches()

```
//---------------------------------------------------------- dar_index_matches
int *dar_index_matches(void *ar, int (*fun)(void *)) {
  int *ind = NULL;
  if (ar) {
    Dar *dar_p = (Dar *)(ar - sizeof(Dar));
    int n_ind = dar_count_matches(ar, fun);
    ind = dar_new(dar_p->stack_p, sizeof((int)0), n_ind);
    int i = 0;
    for (int k = 0; k < dar_p->n; k++) {
      if ((*fun)(&ar[k * dar_p->size])) ind[i++] = k;
```

```
      }
    }
  return ind;
  } // dar_index_matches
```

The compiler issues a warning for both dar_count_matches() and dar_index_matches() when you execute the callback. It says:

```
dereferencing 'void *' pointer [enabled by default]
```

It is because ar is defined to be of type (void *). Then, ar[k * dar_p->size] is of type void. You know that it isn't, but the compiler doesn't. In any case, you only need the address of the array element so that you can pass it to the callback function.

You can make the warning disappear if you insert a (char *) between the & and ar[ ], but this is an unclean solution. It only works because sizeof(char) is 1, like sizeof(void). It seems that we will have to live with this warning.

Listing 7-21 shows some examples of element selecting.

Listing 7-21. Examples of Element Selecting

```
printf("\n------- Examples of element selecting\n");
DAR_setup;

int match1(void *el_p) {
  a_t *e_p = el_p;
  return (e_p->value > 15 && e_p->value < 60);
  }
a_t *ar1 = DAR_new(el, 8);
for (int k = 0; k < DAR_get_len(ar1); k++) ar1[k].value = k * 11;
for (int k = 0; k < DAR_get_len(ar1); k++) {
  printf("%d: %d\n", k, ar1[k].value);
  }
printf("Looking for values > 15 and < 60\n");
int *ind1 = dar_index_matches(ar1, match1);
printf("#matches: %d\n", dar_count_matches(ar1, match1));
for (int i = 0; i < DAR_get_len(ind1); i++) printf("%d\n", ind1[i]);
printf("\n");

int match2(void *el_p) {
  a_t **e_p = el_p;
  return (*e_p != NULL);
  }
a_t **ar2 = DAR_new(&el, 10);
for (int k = 2; k < DAR_get_len(ar2) / 2; k++) ar2[k] = &el;
for (int k = 0; k < DAR_get_len(ar2); k++) {
  printf("%d: %p\n", k, ar2[k]);
  }
printf("Looking for non-null elements\n");
int *ind2 = dar_index_matches(ar2, match2);
printf("#matches: %d\n", dar_count_matches(ar2, match2));
for (int i = 0; i < DAR_get_len(ind2); i++) printf("%d\n", ind2[i]);
printf("\n");
```

```
printf("DAR_list:\n");
DAR_list();

DAR_dismantle;
```

Listing 7-22 shows the output you generate when you execute the code in Listing 7-21.

Listing 7-22. Examples of Element Selecting—Output

```
------- Examples of element selecting
=== dar_new: (nil) 4 8 --> 0x6f9010 (0x6f9038)
0: 0
1: 11
2: 22
3: 33
4: 44
5: 55
6: 66
7: 77
Looking for values > 15 and < 60
=== dar_new: 0x6f9010 4 4 --> 0x6f9060 (0x6f9088)
#matches: 4
2
3
4
5

=== dar_new: 0x6f9060 8 10 --> 0x6f90a0 (0x6f90c8)
0: (nil)
1: (nil)
2: 0x7ffc462b9450
3: 0x7ffc462b9450
4: 0x7ffc462b9450
5: (nil)
6: (nil)
7: (nil)
8: (nil)
9: (nil)
Looking for non-null elements
=== dar_new: 0x6f90a0 4 3 --> 0x6f9120 (0x6f9148)
#matches: 3
2
3
4

DAR_list:
0x6f9120 4 3
0x6f90a0 8 10
0x6f9060 4 4
0x6f9010 4 8
```

Summary

In this chapter, you learned how to build a library of functions to create and manipulate dynamic arrays. Table 7-1 lists all the functions and their associated macros, while Table 7-2 lists additional macros.

Table 7-1. *List of Functions and Associated Macros*

Function Declaration	Description and Macros (When Applicable)
`int dar_count_matches(void *, int (*)(void *));`	Counts the elements of an array that satisfy a defined criterion.
`void *dar_crash(char *, char *, int);`	Reports a catastrophic error and aborts the program. `#define DAR_crash(e)`
`int *dar_index_matches(void *, int (*)(void *));`	Creates an index of the elements of an array that satisfy a defined criterion.
`void dar_list(Dar *);`	Lists the array metadata in the default stack of arrays. `#define DAR_list()`
`void dar_list_dar(void *);`	Lists the array metadata in a stack of arrays. `#define DAR_list_dar(ar)`
`void *dar_new(Dar **, size_t, size_t);`	Allocates a new array and adds it to the default stack of arrays. `#define DAR_new(var, ne)`
`void *dar_new_dar(void *, size_t, size_t);`	Allocates a new array and adds it to a stack of arrays. `#define DAR_new_dar(ar, var, ne)`
`void dar_release(void **);`	Removes an array from a stack and releases it. `#define DAR_release(array)`
`void dar_release_all(Dar **);`	Removes all arrays from a stack and releases them. `#define DAR_release_all()`
`void dar_resize(void **, int, int, void **, int, size_t);`	Copies elements of an array to a new array. `#define DAR_clone(ar1, ar2)` `#define DAR_copy(ar1, i1, n1, ar2, i2, n2)` `#define DAR_extend(ar, nn)` `#define DAR_resize(ar, i1, n1, i2, n2)`

Table 7-2. *List of Additional Macros*

Macro	Description
`DAR_dismantle`	Releases a stack of arrays.
`DAR_get_len(ar)`	Returns the length of the array.
`DAR_setup`	Initializes a stack of arrays.

## CHAPTER 8

Searching

Searches work by comparing primitive or structured data types. Therefore, it makes sense to begin this chapter with a section about comparisons.

Comparisons

In general, when discussing comparisons, you need to distinguish between numbers (including pointers), null-terminated character strings and unstructured blocks of memory, and everything else.

To compare numbers, C provides the relational operators ==, !=, >, <, >=, and <=, although, as you learned in Chapter 2, dealing with floating point numbers is tricky.

For unstructured blocks of memory and null-terminated character strings, C provides several functions, which I will summarize in the next section.

For every else, which includes structs and arrays, you need to formulate algorithms specific to the type you are dealing with.

C Standard Comparison Functions

We will look first at the GNU C library functions that compare blocks of memory and then at those that compare C strings. All functions accept at least two parameters containing the addresses of the objects to be compared and return an int, with 0 indicating that the two objects are identical.

The string functions described in this section exist in two versions, one to handle normal characters (of type char) and one to handle wide characters (of type wchar_t, described in Chapter 2).

memcmp()

```
int memcmp (const void *array1, const void *array2, size_t n)
```

The function, defined in string.h, compares one by one n bytes of memory, beginning with the addresses passed as array1 and array2 and, when making the comparisons, considers the array elements to be of type unsigned char. When it finds two different bytes in the same positions of the two arrays, it subtracts the byte of array2 from the byte of array1 and returns the result typecast to int.

You should only use this function when comparing arrays of bytes. For example, comparing arrays of floating point will likely not work. You would also get unexpected results when using memcmp() to compare arrays of structures that contain *holes* (i.e., undefined bytes). This can easily happen when you include unions within the structure. For example, look at the code shown in Listing 8-1.

© Giulio Zambon 2016
G. Zambon, *Practical C*, DOI 10.1007/978-1-4842-1769-6_8

Listing 8-1. Structures with Holes

```
1. struct {
2.   char cc[2];
3.   union {
4.     int i;
5.     char c;
6.     } u;
7.   } st;
8. char *ar = (char *)&st;
9. for (int i = 0; i < sizeof(st); i++) ar[i] = -(i + 1);
10. for (int i = 0; i < sizeof(st); i++) printf("%3d", ar[i]);
11. printf("\n");
12. st.cc[0] = 1;
13. st.cc[1] = 2;
14. st.u.c = 3;
15. for (int i = 0; i < sizeof(st); i++) printf("%3d", ar[i]);
16. printf("\n");
17. st.u.i = 0x12345432;
18. st.u.c = 3;
19. for (int i = 0; i < sizeof(st); i++) printf("%3d", ar[i]);
20. printf("\n");
```

In line 8, you define a pointer to char and assign to it the address of the structure st. This lets you initialize in line 9 the memory block that contains the structure to a sequence of negative numbers, one per byte. When you print the array in line 10, you see:

```
-1 -2 -3 -4 -5 -6 -7 -8
```

You now set the components of the structure: the array cc in lines 12 and 13 and the character c within the union u in line 14. When you print the array again in lines 15 and 16, you get:

```
 1   2 -3 -4   3 -6 -7 -8
```

The output shows that your structure has two holes: one, which is two bytes long, is between cc and u, and one, which is three bytes long, is after the character c. Although you have set both fields of the structure st, five bytes have remained set to the negative initialization numbers.

The first hole (the one that contains -3 and -4) is there because the compiler aligned the union to a 32-bit word boundary. As cc is only two bytes long, the two bytes immediately preceding the union remain unchanged. They are inaccessible via the structure fields.

The three bytes after c remain unchanged because, in line 14, you set the shorter field of the union.

Now it should be clear why you shouldn't compare structures (and, obviously, arrays of structures) using memcmp(): it would flag as different two structures with different values in the holes even when their field values are identical. This is probably *not* what you want.

If you initialized all structures with the trick used in lines 8 and 9, you would be able to use memcpy(), because all holes would be initialized to the same values (any set of values would be fine, as long as all structures were identically initialized). But it would remain risky. Consider this: if you have a union, you might set its fields in different parts of the program. If you did something like you do in lines 17 and 18, you would change the second hole, as shown by the output of line 19:

```
 1   2 -3 -4   3 84 52 18
```

and end up with structures that you set to the same values (i.e., cc="12" and c=3), but that memcmp() would fail to recognize as matching.

Incidentally, unions are extremely useful if you really need them, but always somewhat tricky to use. My advice is to avoid them if you can.

wmemcmp()

```
int wmemcmp (const wchar_t *array1, const wchar_t *array2, size_t n)
```

This is a version of memcmp() that explicitly deals with wide characters, and n counts items of type wchar_t instead of bytes. The value returned is negative or positive, depending on whether the first differing wide character in array1 precedes or follows the corresponding wide character in array2.

strcmp() and wcscmp()

```
int strcmp (const char *s1, const char *s2)
int wstrcmp (const wchar_t *s1, const wchar_t *s2)
```

You are probably familiar with strcmp(), and wcscmp() is the same but for wide characters. Just a couple of points are worth making.

If s1 is an initial substring of s2, it is evaluated to be "less than" s2. This is because the terminating null is less than any other character.

Also note that these functions don't take into account the sorting conventions of the language in which the strings are written. For that, you have to use strcoll() and wcscoll().

strcoll() and wcscoll()

```
int strcoll (const char *s1, const char *s2)
int wcscoll (const wchar_t *s1, const wchar_t *s2)
```

These functions work like strcmp() and wcscmp(), but take into account the locale to decide the character ordering. To configure the locale for string comparison, you can use the setlocale() function you saw in Chapter 2 to set the system variable LC_COLLATE. For example, after executing

```
setlocale(LC_COLLATE, "de_DE");
```

the functions will follow the correct character ordering for German.

strcasecmp() and wcscasecmp()

```
int strcasecmp (const char *s1, const char *s2)
int wcscasecmp (const wchar_t *s1, const wchar_t *s2)
```

This functions are like strcmp() and wcscmp(), respectively, except that differences in case are ignored. Note that the result depends on the locale. For example, unless you set a locale associated with a language that uses diacritical marks, letters like Ä and ä will be considered to be different.

Be aware that wcscasecmp() is a GNU extension. Therefore, you can only use it when you compile with gcc and set the compiler option -std=gnu99.

strncmp(), wcsncmp(), strncasecmp(), and wcsncasecmp()

```
int strncmp (const char *s1, const char *s2, size_t n)
int wcsncmp (const wchar_t *s1, const wchar_t *s2, size_t n)
int strncasecmp (const char *s1, const char *s2, size_t n)
int wcsncasecmp (const wchar_t *s1, const wchar_t *s2, size_t n)
```

These functions are like their counterparts without an 'n' as the fourth character of their names, except that they only compare up to the first n characters.

Note that `strncasecmp()` and `wcsncasecmp()` are GNU extensions and require the gcc compiler and the `-std=gnu99` option.

Comparing Structures

It only makes sense to compare structures by comparing their components.

While you could easily decide to check for equality of two structured variables by checking that the corresponding components are equal, how do you check whether one of the variables is less than or greater than the other?

Look, for example, at the following definitions:

```
typedef struct {
  int k1;
  int k2;
  } struct_t;
struct_t a = {1, 2};
struct_t b = {2, 1};
```

Is a < b or b < a? It is your decision to make on the basis of what k1 and k2 mean. In some cases, it might be obvious. For example, if you define a structure to store the version of a program

```
typedef struct {
  unsigned int major;
  unsigned int minor;
  unsigned int build;
  } version_t;
```

it is clear that you need to compare the majors first, then the minors if the majors are identical, and finally the builds if the majors and minors both match.

All this means that you need to develop comparing algorithms specifically designed for each structure or, at least, for structures that have the key components of the same type. That said, you do have a minimum of flexibility that might make all the difference (pun intended!). You can compare variables of different structured types if the key components are identically defined and in the same order at the beginning of all structures. In that case, you can ignore the fact that the other components differ.

For example, you might need to compare structures defined as follows:

```
typedef struct {
  unsigned int number;
  unsigned int version;

  …
  } part_t;
```

If you need to modify the structure, you can still use the old comparison algorithm if you keep the key components where they are:

```
typedef struct {
  unsigned int number;
  unsigned int version;
  ...
  } part_new_t;
```

A function like the following one

```
int part_cmp(part_new_t *p1, part_new_t *p2) {
  unsigned long l1 = (((unsigned long)(*p1).number) << 32) | (*p1).version;
  unsigned long l2 = (((unsigned long)(*p2).number) << 32) | (*p2).version;
  return (l1 == l2) ? 0 : (l1 > l2) ? 1 : -1;
  }
```

will work with old, new, or a mix of structures, as long as when you compare variables of type part_t you typecast their pointers with (part_new_t *).

Comparing Arrays

Like with structures, you have to decide when two arrays are equal or when one is greater than the other (*greater*, not *larger*). This depends on the particular situation.

First of all, you need to decide when an element of the array is greater than another element. With numbers, you only need to be careful when dealing with floating point encodings. With characters, you might need to take into account their locale. And, obviously, you have to be most careful when dealing with arrays of structured variables or of pointers to structures.

Fuzziness

What does equality mean? You have already seen in Chapter 2 that equality of floating point numbers is tricky. You can resolve it, at least to a certain extent, by setting a limit to the number of digits or bits you consider. That is, by introducing *fuzziness* in your comparisons.

You can apply this concept of fuzzy comparisons to everything but, as a programmer, it's likely that sooner or later you will find it useful when dealing with strings. The developers at Google and other search engines have mastered the concept, and even incorporate into it the preferences you used in previous searches.

But here you will only learn the basics of comparing words in a fuzzy way. You have already encountered a limited fuzziness with the standard functions strcasecmp() and wscscasecmp().

Accepting Typos and Spelling Mistakes

Typos and spelling mistakes are so common that dealing with them is the most useful and widely used application of fuzziness to text.

You need to consider the following elementary kinds of typing mistakes:

- Substitution: It occurs when you replace a character with another. For example, when you type cool instead of fool. Notice that C and F are adjacent keys on the standard keyboard. It can also happen that you type Z instead of W or vice versa is you type on central and southern European keyboards, which have those two keys swapped.

- Insertion: For example, when you type soup instead of sop.

- Deletion: This is the opposite of insertion. It happens when you drop a letter from a word.

If it appeals to your sense of symmetry, you can consider an *insertion* as the substitution of a non-character with an actual character and a *deletion* as the substitution of a character with a non-character, thereby making substitution the only mechanism you need.

Anyhow, identifying the possible differences between words due to individual characters lets you define how far from each other two words are as the minimum number of elementary operations that change one word into the other. For example, *post* and *must* have a distance of two: *post -> most -> must*, or also: *post -> pust -> must*, as there is no need to go through valid words. FYI, this number is called the *Levenshtein distance*, from the name of the researcher who introduced it in 1965.

The Levenshtein distance gives you a way of defining fuzziness when comparing strings. Listing 8-2 shows how you calculate the Levenshtein distance between two strings. It is a cosmetically modified version of the function you find at en.wikibooks.org/wiki/Algorithm_Implementation/Strings/Levenshtein_distance#C.

Listing 8-2. cmpr_levenshtein_wiki()

```
1.  //------------------------------------------------------- cmpr_levenshtein_wiki
2.  int cmpr_levenshtein_wiki(char *s1, char *s2) {
3.    int l1 = strlen(s1);
4.    int l2 = strlen(s2);
5.    int mat[l2 + 1][l1 + 1];
6.    mat[0][0] = 0;
7.    for (int k = 1; k <= l2; k++) mat[k][0] = mat[k - 1][0] + 1;
8.    for (int j = 1; j <= l1; j++) mat[0][j] = mat[0][j - 1] + 1;
9.    for (int k = 1; k <= l2; k++) {
10.     for (int j = 1; j <= l1; j++) {
11.       mat[k][j] = Min3(
12.            mat[k - 1][j] + 1,
13.            mat[k][j - 1] + 1,
14.            mat[k - 1][j - 1] + ((s1[j - 1] == s2[k - 1]) ? 0 : 1)
15.            );
16.     }
17.   }
18.   return mat[l2][l1];
19.   } // cmpr_levenshtein_wiki
```

To understand how it works, we will look at what happens when you compare the two strings "post" and "must".

The lines 6 to 8 initialize a matrix with one column for each character of s1 plus 1 and a row for each character of s2 plus 1. You can see the result of the initialization in Listing 8-3, where a dot means that the element is uninitialized. The characters of the two strings are there for clarity and are not part of the matrix itself.

Listing 8-3. Initial Levenshtein Matrix

```
    p o s t
  0 1 2 3 4
m 1 . . . .
u 2 . . . .
s 3 . . . .
t 4 . . . .
```

The for loop with control variable k that starts in line 9 goes through the rows from 1 to 12, which is the length of s2. It only contains the for loop with control variable j that scans each row one character at a time.

The only statement inside the inner loop calculates three expressions and assigns the smallest value to the current cell of the matrix. The macro Min3() calculates the minimum of the three expression, as follows:

```
#define Min3(a, b, c) ({                                          \
  unsigned int aa = a;                                           \
  unsigned int bb = b;                                           \
  unsigned int cc = c;                                           \
  (aa <= bb) ? ((aa <= cc) ? aa : cc) : ((bb <= cc) ? bb : cc); \
  })
```

Of the three expressions, let's consider the third one first (line 14). The value

```
(s1[j - 1] == s2[k - 1]) ? 0 : 1
```

is traditionally called *cost*. As you can see, if the corresponding characters of the two strings are different, the cost is 1, otherwise it is 0. To complete the third expression, you add it to the value contained in the cell of the matrix, which is immediately above and to the left of the current cell. As mat[0][0] is initialized to 0 in line 6, when you make the very first comparison (between s2[0] and s1[0], which contain 'm' and 'p'), the sum simply tells you whether the two strings start with different characters. In this example, the third expression is 1, because the first characters of the two strings are different.

The second expression is the value of the cell immediately on the left of the current one incremented by 1, and the first expression is the value of the cell immediately above incremented by 1. As they are both equal to 2, the value assigned to mat[1][1] is 1. If the two initial characters had been the same, the value would have been 0.

In the second iteration of the inner loop, j becomes 2, and in line 14 you calculate the cost by comparing s2[0] with s1[1] (i.e., 'm' with 'o'). As they are different, once more, the cost is 1.

After completing the scanning of all the rows, the matrix is as follows:

```
    p o s t
  0 1 2 3 4
m 1 1 2 3 4
u 2 2 2 3 4
s 3 3 3 2 3
t 4 4 4 3 2
```

If you look at the diagonal from top-left to bottom-right, you see that the value increases every time there is a difference. This is because the cost is 1 instead of 0. Then, the very last element of the matrix (i.e., mat[12][11]) provides the distance between the two strings as the number of characters that differ.

But there is more to it.

If you compare "post" and "post"

```
    p o s t
  0 1 2 3 4
m 1 0 1 2 3
u 2 1 0 1 2
s 3 2 1 0 1
t 4 3 2 1 0
```

the matrix is symmetrical around the top-left to bottom-right diagonal, which is all 0.

Let's compare "pst" and "post" to see what happens when a character is missing. The matrix becomes:

```
    p s t
  0 1 2 3
p 1 0 1 2
o 2 1 1 2
s 3 2 1 2
t 4 3 2 1
```

The (1,1) cell is zero, because the initial letters are both 'p'. From then on though, the costs calculated as part of the third expression (line 14) for the cells of the diagonal are all 1. As a result, the major diagonal of the matrix increases with every row.

The 1 in cell (2,1) is due to the first expression (line 12), which adds 1 to the 0 immediately above.

The cells immediately below the major diagonal are the result of comparing characters of s1 one position before those in s2. In this example, their costs in rows 3 and 4 are 0 because the two characters match. As a result, the 1 in (2,1) is propagated down and right, unchanged. When you reach the bottom line, the inner loop is shorter because s1 as one character less than s2. And this means that the last of those 1s is the value you return to the calling program.

In two cells below those of the major diagonal, you compare characters that are two places apart; in three cells below the major diagonal you compare characters that are three places apart; etc. This has the effect of resynchronizing the comparisons when s1 is longer than s2.

Here is the last example:

```
    c o p b o k
  0 1 2 3 4 5 6
c 1 0 1 2 3 4 5
o 2 1 0 1 2 3 4
p 3 2 1 0 1 2 3
y 4 3 2 1 1 2 3
b 5 4 3 2 1 2 3
o 6 5 4 3 2 1 2
o 7 6 5 4 3 2 2
k 8 7 6 5 4 3 2
```

Yes, it is complicated. And when you compare strings with all three operations (substitution, insertions, and deletions), the algorithm becomes maddeningly complicated to follow. But you should have an idea of how, with insertions, the counts propagate down and to the right below the major diagonal. With deletions, the logic remains the same, only there can be more columns than rows and the cells above the major diagonal become relevant.

The algorithm as implemented in cmpr_levenshtein_wiki(), though, has a small problem: with long strings the matrix can become too large. Fortunately, once you know how to implement the algorithm, you can improve it to limit the amount of memory it requires.

The improvement takes advantage of the observation that the algorithm only uses the current row and the row immediately above it. Then, why should you keep the whole matrix in memory? All you need to do is keep the two rows you need. Also, if s1 is longer than s2, you could swap them, so that you deal with shorter rows, although you then have more of them.

The result of these considerations is shown in Listing 8-4.

Listing 8-4. cmpr_levenshtein()

```
1. //----------------------------------------------------------- cmpr_levenshtein
2. int cmpr_levenshtein(char *s1, char *s2) {
3.    if (s1 == NULL || s2 == NULL) return -1;              //-->
4.    int n1 = strlen(s1);
```

```
5.    int n2 = strlen(s2);
6.    if (n1 == 0) return n2;                              //-->
7.    if (n2 == 0) return n1;                              //-->
8.    if (n1 > n2) {
9.      char *s_tmp = s1;
10.     int n_tmp = n1;
11.     s1 = s2;
12.     n1 = n2;
13.     s2 = s_tmp;
14.     n2 = n_tmp;
15.     }
16.   int previous_row[n1 + 1];
17.   int row[n1 + 1];
18.   int *p = &previous_row[0];
19.   int *q = &row[0];
20.   for (int j = 0; j <= n1; j++) p[j] = j;
21.   for (int k = 1; k <= n2; k++) {
22.     q[0] = k;
23.     for (int j = 1; j <= n1; j++) {
24.       int cost = (s1[j - 1] == s2[k - 1]) ? 0 : 1;
25.       q[j] = Min3(q[j - 1] + 1, p[j] + 1, p[j - 1] + cost);
26.       }
27.     int *d_tmp = p;
28.     p = q;
29.     q = d_tmp;
30.     }
31.   return p[n1];
32.   } // cmpr_levenshtein
```

In lines 8 to 15, you swap the two strings when s1 is longer than s2. The function also checks that neither of the two strings is NULL (line 3).

Notice lines 6 and 7. If one of the two strings is empty, you simply return the length of the other string, because all those characters need to be inserted (or were deleted, depending on how you view it).

Line 6 also covers the case in which both strings are empty, when it correctly returns 0.

The current row is q and the row above it is p. Once you have completed a row, you swap it with the previous one in lines 27 to 29 (actually, you swap the pointers). The only element you need to initialize in q is the first one, and you do so in line 22.

You use p and q instead of the original arrays because you couldn't swap the arrays and would be forced to copy them instead.

When you compare short strings for searching, the Levenshtein distance tells you how different any string is from your search string. Besides listing the perfect matches, you might decide to display also the strings with a distance of 1 (or more).

But there is one type of typing mistake that the Levenshtein distance overestimates: the swapping of two consecutive letters, like in "Levensthein". This mistake is so common that Emacs, a text editor that first appeared in the mid 1970s and still attracts enthusiastic followers (see www.gnu.org/software/emacs/), has a command to swap the last two characters you have typed (Control+t, where t stands for transpose). The Levenshtein distance of such transposition is 2, but you might think that it should be counted as any simple typo.

If the strings are short enough (whatever that means), it's highly unlikely for more than one transposition to occur in the same string. If your intention is to find strings with a single typo or transposition, you can use cmpr_levenshtein() to filter out all strings with a distance greater than 2. Then, you can look among the strings with a distance of exactly 2 from the search string and identify those for which the distance is due to a single transposition.

Listing 8-5 shows a function that performs such a check.

Listing 8-5. cmpr_transposition()

```
1.  //----------------------------------------------------------- cmpr_transposition
2.  // Returns 1 upon finding a transposition.
3.  int cmpr_transposition(char *s1, char *s2) {
4.    if (s1 == NULL || s2 == NULL) return 0;                      //-->
5.    int n = strlen(s1);
6.    if (strlen(s2) != n) return 0;                              //-->
7.    for (int i = 1; i < n; i++) {
8.      if (s2[i] != s1[i] && s2[i] == s1[i - 1] && s2[i - 1] == s1[i]) {
9.        return 1;                                               //-->
10.       }
11.    }
12.    return 0;
13.  } // cmpr_transposition
```

The function returns 0 if either of the strings is NULL or if the two strings have different lengths. Note that in line 8, before checking for the transposition, you check that the corresponding characters in the two strings don't match. If you didn't do so, all doubles would be counted as transpositions!

Checking for typing errors and accepting as successful comparisons that result in distances greater than 0 but below a certain limit is a way of introducing fuzziness that is language independent. But every other comparison of text depends on the locale.

Searches

To search for a particular item within a set of items that are not ordered in any way, you perform what is called a *linear search:* you go through all items one by one and hope that you soon hit on what you are looking for. If the items are ordered according to any criterion, you can take advantage of that ordering to reduce the number of checks you need to make in order to find what you are looking for.

Besides searches, we are also going to talk about deletions, additions, and insertions.

Unordered Arrays of Integers

This is the simplest possible set you can work with. That's why it is a good subject to begin with.

Listing 8-6 shows the srch_lin_int() function, which applies a linear search to an array of integers.

Listing 8-6. srch_lin_int()

```
//----------------------------------------------------------- srch_lin_int
// Returns the position if found or -1 if not found.
int srch_lin_int(int num, int *ar, int n) {
  int kk = -1;
  for (int k = 0; k < n && kk < 0; k++) if (ar[k] == num) kk = k;
  return kk;
  } // srch_lin_int
```

Okay, nothing earth-shattering here. But we have to start from somewhere. You already encountered an implementation of a linear search in Chapter 7, where dar_index_matches() (see Listing 7-20) searches a dynamic array to find all elements that match defined criteria.

Concerning deletion, what does it mean to delete or remove an element from an array? It could mean that you set it to a special value agreed to in advance. This is in general a risky thing to do. But if you worked with arrays of pointers instead of integers, it would probably make sense to consider NULL as a valid empty-element value.

Another possibility is to copy the last element of the array to the position of the element to be deleted. Then, it would be sufficient to remember that the number of valid elements in the array is one less than what it was before the deletion. You cannot safely do this if somewhere in the program you save indices of some elements (because the elements can be moved), but otherwise there shouldn't be any problem. After all, the elements of the array are in no particular order; otherwise, you wouldn't use a search method that doesn't take advantage of the ordering.

But what about making an insertion? It is obviously only possible if the array includes some unused positions. Alternatively, you would have to make a copy of the existing array with some additional elements before making the insertion.

All this can be done comparatively easily if you accept the following restrictions:

- You allocate the array dynamically with malloc(). It makes it easy to extend it if necessary.

- Nowhere in the program do you save addresses or indices of array elements because you could no longer depend on them after moving elements or redefining the array.

- You allocate for all arrays two additional elements: one to store the array size and one to store the number of elements actually in use.

Listings 8-7 and 8-8 show functions to allocate and free such arrays.

Listing 8-7. srch_int_alloc()—Initial Version

```
1. //------------------------------------------------------------ srch_int_alloc
2. // Returns the address of the array or NULL if unsuccessful.
3. int *srch_int_alloc(int n) {
4.   int *buf = calloc(n + 2, sizeof(int));
5.   if (buf == NULL) return NULL;                              //-->
6.   buf[0] = n;
7.   return buf + 2;
8.   } // srch_int_alloc
```

In line 4, you allocate space for the array and for the two counters you need. You use calloc() to allocate the memory so that the whole buffer is set to zeros. In line 6, you set buf[0] to the requested number of elements. buf[1] is going to be used to store the number of elements actually used, and by leaving it set to 0, you record that the newly allocated buffer is empty. In line 7, you return to the calling program the address of buf[2], so that the programmer has n elements available, as requested. The two counters are "hidden" before the data array.

The caption of Listing 8-7 says "initial version" because, as you will see shortly, there will be a final, improved version.

Listing 8-8. srch_int_free()

```
//------------------------------------------------------------ srch_int_free
void srch_int_free(int **ar_p) {
  free(*ar_p - 2);
  *ar_p = NULL;
  } // srch_int_free
```

The function to release the array is trivial. To calculate the address of the allocated block of memory, it subtracts the space occupied by two integers from the address of the data array. Before returning, the function sets the address of the array in the calling program to NULL. If you don't care to reset the address, you can simplify the function as follows:

```
void srch_int_free(int *ar) {
  free(ar - 2);
  } // srch_int_free
```

In fact, the function is so simple that you could implement it as a macro. You would then avoid the overhead of executing a function call, but it is not likely to be of any importance, as the allocation and freeing of arrays is probably going to be an infrequent occurrence in your programs.

Listing 8-9 shows how to add elements to an array. It is more appropriate to talk about adding elements than about inserting them because the function appends new elements after the existing ones. We will talk about inserting elements when we will deal with ordered arrays.

Listing 8-9. srch_int_add()

```
1.  //-------------------------------------------------------------------- srch_int_add
2.  // Returns the number of array elements occupied after the addition
3.  // or -1 if unsuccessful.
4.  int srch_int_add(int num, int **ar_p, int incr) {
5.     int *a = *ar_p;
6.     int *buf = a - 2;
7.     int max_n = buf[0];
8.     int n = buf[1];
9.     if (n >= max_n) {
10.
11.       // The array is full.  Extend it.
12.       if (incr < 1) incr = 1;
13.       int new_max_n = max_n + incr;
14.       int *new_buf = realloc(buf, (new_max_n + 2) * sizeof(int));
15.       if (new_buf) {
16.
17.         // The extension was successful. Check whether the block has moved,
18.         // clean up the new elements, and update the array capacity.
19.         if (new_buf != buf) {
20.           buf = new_buf;
21.           a = buf + 2;
22.           *ar_p = a;
23.           }
24.         (void)memset(&a[max_n], 0, (new_max_n - max_n) * sizeof(int));
25.         buf[0] = new_max_n;
26. #if SRCH_DEBUG
27.         printf("Buffer extended from %d to %d\n", max_n, new_max_n);
28. #endif
29.         }
30.      else {
31.
32.         // The memory block couldn't be extended.
33.         // Try to allocate an expanded array from scratch.
34.         int *new_a = srch_int_alloc(new_max_n, NULL);
```

```
35.        if (new_a) {
36.
37.            // The new allocation was successful. Copy the elements across,
38.            // free the old memory block, redefine the local variables,
39.            // set the array utilization, and update the array pointer
40.            // in the calling program.
41. #if SRCH_DEBUG
42.            printf("New buffer for %d elements allocated\n", new_max_n);
43. #endif
44.            (void)memcpy(new_a, a, max_n * sizeof(int));
45.            free(buf);
46.            a = new_a;
47.            buf = a - 2;
48.            buf[1] = n; // buf[0] already set within srch_int_alloc()
49.            *ar_p = a;
50.            } // if (new_a..
51.        else {
52.
53.            // There is not enough space in the heap. No can do.
54.            return -1;                                                      //-->
55.            }
56.        } // if (new_buf.. else..
57.    } // if (n >= max_n..
58.
59.    // Let's make the addition.
60.    a[n++] = num;
61.    buf[1] = n;
62.    return n;
63.    } // srch_int_add
```

You do the actual adding of a new element in lines 60 and 61 by copying the elements to the first unused position of the array and incrementing the occupancy counter. The code in lines 9 to 57 has the sole purpose of automatically expanding the array if it has no space available to accommodate the element you want to add.

First of all, in line 14, it tries to extend the current block of memory with realloc().

If it succeeds, it could be that realloc() has moved the block. Hence the need for the code in lines 20 to 22. Otherwise, you only need to clear the newly allocated elements (line 24) and update the location that holds the size of the array (line 25). Regardless of whether the block of memory has moved or not, you don't need to copy the existing elements to a new array.

The parameter incr determines by how much you want to increase the size of the array if it happens to be full when you execute srch_ar_add(). Line 12 ensures that you always add at least one element.

It can happen that realloc() fails, although there is plenty of memory available in the system heap. This is because the locations following the array might have been allocated for some other purpose. In that case, try to allocate a fresh, larger, block, copy to it the existing array, and release the original block. This is what lines 30 to 56 are for.

Obviously, if you know that an array has enough space, nothing prevents you from adding elements to it "by hand," without using srch_int_add(). But you will have to update the "hidden" occupancy counter as well. You could write, for example:

```
int *arr = srch_int_alloc(10);
int n = 7;
for (int k = 0; k < n; k++) arr[k] = k + '0';
```

```
arr[-1] = n;
...
arr[arr[-1]++] = 123;
```

But you would have to be very careful. I don't recommend it. To let you initialize a dynamic array with data, I modified srch_int_alloc() to take an initialization array as an additional parameter, as shown in Listing 8-10.

Listing 8-10. srch_int_alloc()—Final Version

```
//---------------------------------------------------------------- srch_int_alloc
// Returns the address of the array or NULL if unsuccessful.
int *srch_int_alloc(int n, int *a) {
  int *buf = NULL;
  if (a) {
    buf = malloc((n + 2) * sizeof(int));
    if (buf == NULL) return NULL;                              //-->
    (void)memcpy(buf + 2, a, n * sizeof(int));
    buf[1] = n;
    }
  else {
    buf = calloc(n + 2, sizeof(int));
    if (buf == NULL) return NULL;                              //-->
    }
  buf[0] = n;
  return buf + 2;
  } // srch_int_alloc
```

Now that you know how to allocate, initialize, free, and add elements to an array, you only need to see how to delete elements and search for them. Listing 8-11 shows srch_int_del() and Listing 8-12 shows srch_int_find().

Listing 8-11. srch_int_del()

```
 1. //---------------------------------------------------------------- srch_int_del
 2. // Returns the number of array elements still occupied after the
 3. // deletion or -1 if unsuccessful.
 4. int srch_int_del(int k, int *ar) {
 5.    int n = ar[-1];
 6.    if (k < 0 || k >= n) return -1;                         //-->
 7.    ar[k] = ar[n - 1];
 8.    ar[-1]--;
 9.    return ar[-1];
10.    } // srch_int_del
```

srch_int_del() lets you delete an element in a given position within the array. The deletion is straightforward: it overwrites the element to be deleted with the last element of the array (line 7) and then it decrements the occupancy counter (line 8). Notice that if there is a single element in the array, line 7 copies it onto itself. You could replace lines 7 and 8 with something like this:

```
if (n == 1) {
  ar[-1] = 0;
```

```
  }
else {
  ar[-1]--;
  ar[k] = ar[n - 1];
  }
```

You are welcome to do it if you like it better.

Listing 8-12. srch_int_find()

```
//----------------------------------------------------------------- srch_int_find
// Returns the first position where the requested number is found
// or -1 if unsuccessful.
int srch_int_find(int num, int *ar) {
  int n = ar[-1];
  int kk = -1;
  for (int k = 0; k < n && kk < 0; k++) if (ar[k] == num) kk = k;
  return kk;
  } // srch_int_find
```

srch_int_find() is almost identical to srch_lin_int() shown in Listing 8-6; the only difference is that srch_int_find() retrieves the number of elements from the array buffer instead of receiving it as a parameter.

To conclude this section, Listing 8-13 shows a short program with some examples of how you can use the srch_int_*() functions.

Listing 8-13. Testing srch_int_*()

```
 1. #define Elements(ar) {                                  \
 2.     int *a = ar;                                        \
 3.     int n = a[-1];                                      \
 4.     printf("%2d:", n);                                  \
 5.     for (int k = 0; k < n; k++) printf("%3d", a[k]);    \
 6.     printf("\n");                                       \
 7.     }
 8.
 9. // Allocate an array with initialization and then release it.
10. int a_init[] = {7, -3, 0, 25, -2, 6};
11. int *arr = srch_int_alloc(sizeof(a_init) / sizeof(int), a_init);
12. Elements(arr);
13. printf("\n");
14. srch_int_free(&arr);
15.
16. // Add elements with automatic array extension.
17. int *ar = srch_int_alloc(5, NULL);
18. int n = 0;
19. for (int k = 0; k < 13; k++) {
20.   n = srch_int_add(k, &ar, k % 5);
21.   printf("%d: n=%d\n", k, n);
22.   }
23. printf("\n");
24.
25. // Search elements at random and then delete them.
```

```
26.  srand(10002);
27.  Elements(ar);
28.  int n_left = n;
29.  int n_search = 0;
30.  while (n_left > 0) {
31.    int num = (rand() % (n + 2)) - 1;
32.    n_search++;
33.    int res = srch_int_find(num, ar);
34.    if (res >= 0) {
35.      n_left = srch_int_del(res, ar);
36.      printf("%d: %d removed\n", n_search, num);
37.      Elements(ar);
38.    }
39.    else {
40. //    printf("%d: %d not found\n", n_search, num);
41.    }
42.  }
43.  srch_int_free(&ar);
44.  printf("%p\n", ar);
```

Lines 1 to 7 define a macro function that displays a small array. Lines 9 to 14 allocate a dynamic array using an existing static array to initialize it.

Lines 16 to 23 allocate an empty array of length 5 (line 17) and then add to it 13 elements one by one (for loop that starts in line 19). At the end, the array has a length of at least 13 elements initialized with their position. That is, the value of element 0 is 0, of element 1 is 1, etc. Notice that the increment is set to k % 5. This is a simple trick to have values between 0 and 4 without having to define a separate array and pick them from it.

Finally, lines 25 to 42 search elements at random with values between -1 and 13 (line 31) and every time they find the element (line 33), they delete it (line 35).

The output of the program is shown in Listing 8-14.

Listing 8-14. Testing srch_int_*()—Output

```
1.   6:  7 -3  0 25 -2  6
2.
3.  0: n=1
4.  1: n=2
5.  2: n=3
6.  3: n=4
7.  4: n=5
8.  Buffer extended from 5 to 6
9.  5: n=6
10. Buffer extended from 6 to 7
11. 6: n=7
12. Buffer extended from 7 to 9
13. 7: n=8
14. 8: n=9
15. Buffer extended from 9 to 13
16. 9: n=10
17. 10: n=11
18. 11: n=12
19. 12: n=13
20.
```

```
21. 13:  0  1  2  3  4  5  6  7  8  9 10 11 12
22. 2: 2 removed
23. 12:  0  1 12  3  4  5  6  7  8  9 10 11
24. 4: 1 removed
25. 11:  0 11 12  3  4  5  6  7  8  9 10
26. 6: 4 removed
27. 10:  0 11 12  3 10  5  6  7  8  9
28. 7: 11 removed
29.  9:  0  9 12  3 10  5  6  7  8
30. 8: 7 removed
31.  8:  0  9 12  3 10  5  6  8
32. 9: 3 removed
33.  7:  0  9 12  8 10  5  6
34. 10: 5 removed
35.  6:  0  9 12  8 10  6
36. 13: 6 removed
37.  5:  0  9 12  8 10
38. 15: 0 removed
39.  4: 10  9 12  8
40. 19: 9 removed
41.  3: 10  8 12
42. 26: 10 removed
43.  2: 12  8
44. 50: 12 removed
45.  1:  8
46. 72: 8 removed
47.  0:
48. (nil)
```

Line 1 shows that the content of the dynamic array is identical to that of the static array used for initialization.

Lines 3 to 19 show the automatic expansions that occur when you fill up the array. The lines of text that log the extensions are displayed in line 22 of srch_int_add() (Listing 8-9) because I wrote the line

```
#define SRCH_DEBUG 1
```

in search.h.

You can simulate the failure of realloc() in line 14 of srch_int_add() (Listing 8-9) by temporarily replacing that line with

```
int *buf = NULL;
```

Then, the function will always allocate a new block of memory from the heap. The only change you will see in the output is that the text printed in line 22 of Listing 8-9 will be replaced with the text printed in line 37.

Line 21 of the output (Listing 8-14) shows the initial array containing all the values from 0 to 12. When element 2 is removed, line 23 of the output shows that the array uses one element less, and that 12 has replaced 2. You can easily follow how, every time you remove an element, the last element replaces the one you have removed. This continues until, in line 46 of the output (Listing 8-14), you remove element 8, which is the last surviving element.

The number you see at the beginning of each line where deletions are logged counts the deletion *attempts*. So, the 72 you see in line 46 of the output, when you remove the last element of the array, means that the program, before removing the last element, in 72 - 13 = 59 occasions attempted to delete a value that was not in the array. To see the full output, including the failed deletions, uncomment the printf() in line 40 of the test program (Listing 8-13).

Unordered Arrays of Pointers

What you learned in the previous section about integers also applies to arrays in which the elements are pointers.

There are several reasons for using array of pointers. For example, without attempting to make an exhaustive list:

- *Flexibility*: If you design and develop code to work with pointers, and in particular with pointers to void, you can use it with any type of element. You can even built heterogeneous arrays of pointers that address different types of structures. All you need to do is insert as the first element of all structures a component that identifies the structure type, and then typecast the pointer to the structure accordingly.

- *Portability*: If the utilities you design manipulate pointers without looking at what they point to, you can use them again and again for different data structures. In fact, as you will see, you can even examine the structures contents, as long as you do it within callback functions.

- *Efficiency*: By copying and moving pointers instead of the actual data, you save CPU time and possibly memory. This is particularly useful when inserting new elements in an ordered array or when sorting an array, as both operations generally involve moving several elements.

To convert the functions

```
int srch_int_add(int num, int **ar_p, int incr); // Listing 8-9
int *srch_int_alloc(int n, int *a);               // Listing 8-10
int srch_int_del(int k, int *ar);                 // Listing 8-11
int srch_int_find(int num, int *ar);              // Listing 8-12
void srch_int_free(int **ar_p);                   // Listing 8-8
```

to handle pointers is not complicated, but there are a couple of key issues you have to pay attention to:

- Allocating space for the two counters before the address of the actual data array requires you to calculate the size of the block as 2*sizeof(int)+n*sizeof(void *) instead of simply (n+2)*sizeof(int) as you do in srch_int_alloc() (Listing 8-10).

- You need to change the types of the function parameters to reflect the fact that you are dealing with pointers to void instead of integers.

- To deal with all possible data types, you need to add to the find function a callback that does the element comparison, like you did for dar_count_matches() in Chapter 7 (Listing 7-19).

Listing 8-15 shows srch_ptr_alloc(), which is the pointer-equivalent of srch_int_alloc(), as shown in Listing 8-10.

Listing 8-15. srch_ptr_alloc()

```
1. //------------------------------------------------------------- srch_ptr_alloc
2. // Returns the address of the array or NULL if unsuccessful.
3. void **srch_ptr_alloc(int n, void *a) {
4.    int *buf = NULL;
5.    size_t n_bytes = 2 * sizeof(int) + n * sizeof(void *);
6.    buf = malloc(n_bytes);
7.    if (buf == NULL) return NULL;                              //-->
8.    if (a) {
```

```
9.      (void)memcpy(buf + 2, a, n * sizeof(void *));
10.     buf[1] = n;
11.     }
12.   else {
13.     (void)memset(buf, 0, n_bytes);
14.     }
15.   buf[0] = n;
16.   return (void **)(buf + 2);
17.   } // srch_ptr_alloc
```

Because the memory block is to contain both integers and pointers, which have different sizes, you cannot use calloc() like you did in srch_int_alloc() when dealing solely with integers. Instead, you can use malloc() and then clear the block with memset() in line 13.

srch_ptr_free(), shown in Listing 8-16, is almost identical to srch_int_free() (Listing 8-8). The only difference is that you need to typecast the array to be of type (int *). This ensures that when you subtract 2 from its address in order to obtain the address of the memory block, the compiler subtract the space needed to store two ints, rather than two pointers to void.

Listing 8-16. srch_ptr_free()

```
//---------------------------------------------------------------- srch_ptr_free
void srch_ptr_free(void ***ar_p) {
  free((int *)*ar_p - 2);
  *ar_p = NULL;
  } // srch_ptr_free
```

Listing 8-17 shows srch_ptr_add(). Its differences from srch_int_add() shown in Listing 8-9 are pretty straightforward. The lines modified in srch_int_add() to obtain srch_ptr_add() are marked with an asterisk (except when the differences are in comments).

Listing 8-17. srch_ptr_add()

```
1. //---------------------------------------------------------------- srch_ptr_add
2. // Returns the number of array elements occupied after the addition
3. // or -1 if unsuccessful.
4* int srch_ptr_add(void *obj, void ***ar_p, int incr) {
5*    void **a = *ar_p;
6*    int *buf = (int *)a - 2;
7.    int max_n = buf[0];
8.    int n = buf[1];
9.    if (n >= max_n) {
10.
11.     // The array is full.  Extend it.
12.     if (incr < 1) incr = 1;
13.     int new_max_n = max_n + incr;
14*     int *new_buf = realloc(buf, 2 * sizeof(int) + new_max_n * sizeof(void *));
15.     if (new_buf) {
16.
17.       // The extension was successful. Check whether the block has moved,
18.       // clean up the new elements, and update the array capacity.
19.       if (new_buf != buf) {
20.         buf = new_buf;
```

```
21*          a = (void **)(buf + 2);
22.          *ar_p = a;
23.          }
24*       (void)memset(*ar_p + max_n, 0, (new_max_n - max_n) * sizeof(void *));
25.       buf[0] = new_max_n;
26. #if SRCH_DEBUG
27.       printf("Buffer extended from %d to %d\n", max_n, new_max_n);
28. #endif
29.       }
30.    else {
31.
32.       // The memory block couldn't be extended.
33.       // Try to allocate an expanded array from scratch.
34*       void **new_a = srch_ptr_alloc(new_max_n, NULL);
35.       if (new_a) {
36.
37.          // The new allocation was successful. Copy the elements across,
38.          // free the old memory block, redefine the local variables,
39.          // set the array utilization, and update the array pointer
40.          // in the calling program.
41. #if SRCH_DEBUG
42.          printf("New buffer for %d elements allocated\n", new_max_n);
43. #endif
44*          (void)memcpy(new_a, a, max_n * sizeof(void *));
45.          free(buf);
46.          a = new_a;
47*          buf = (int *)a - 2;
48*          buf[1] = n; // buf[0] already set within srch_ptr_alloc()
49.          *ar_p = a;
50.          } // if (new_a..
51.       else {
52.
53.          // There is not enough space in the heap. No can do.
54.          return -1;                                          //-->
55.          }
56.       } // if (new_buf.. else..
57.    } // if (n >= max_n..
58.
59.    // Let's make the addition.
60*    a[n++] = obj;
61.    buf[1] = n;
62.    return n;
63.    } // srch_ptr_add
```

Eleven lines in all.

Listing 8-18 shows srch_ptr_del(), the pointer-equivalent of srch_int_del() shown in Listing 8-11.

Listing 8-18. srch_ptr_del()

```
//---------------------------------------------------------------- srch_ptr_del
// Returns the number of array elements still occupied after the
// deletion or -1 if unsuccessful.
```

```
int srch_ptr_del(int k, void **ar) {
  int *n_p = (int *)ar - 1;
  int n = *n_p;
  if (k < 0 || k >= n) return -1;                              //-->
  ar[k] = ar[n - 1];
  n--;
  *n_p = n;
  return n;
  } // srch_ptr_del
```

Nothing you haven't encountered before.

Finally, Listing 8-19 shows srch_ptr_find(), which corresponds to srch_int_find() shown in Listing 8-12.

Listing 8-19. srch_ptr_find()

```
1. //-------------------------------------------------------------- srch_ptr_find
2. // Returns the first position where the requested element is found
3. // or -1 if unsuccessful.
4. int srch_ptr_find(void *obj, void **ar, int (*cmp)(void *, void *)) {
5.   int *n_p = (int *)ar - 1;
6.   int kk = -1;
7.   for (int k = 0; k < *n_p && kk < 0; k++) if (!(*cmp)(ar[k], obj)) kk = k;
8.   return kk;
9.   } // srch_ptr_find
```

The most significant difference from srch_int_find() is the addition of a parameter to provide a callback function that makes the comparisons.

To show you examples of how to use the functions, I defined an array of pointers to integers. The code is shown in Listing 8-20.

Listing 8-20. Testing srch_ptr_*()

```
1. #define Elements(ar) {                                       \
2.     int **a = (int **)ar;                                    \
3.     int n = ((int *)a)[-1];                                  \
4.     printf("%2d:", n);                                       \
5.     for (int k = 0; k < n; k++) printf("%3d", *a[k]); \
6.     printf("\n");                                            \
7.     }
8.
9. int cmp_i(void *el_p, void *val_p) {
10.    int el = *(int *)el_p;
11.    int val = *(int *)val_p;
12.    return (val == el) ? 0 : (val > el) ? 1 : -1;
13.    }
14.
15. // Allocate an array with initialization and then release it.
16. {
17.    int i_init[] = {7, -3, 0, 25, -2, 6};
18.    int n_i = sizeof(i_init) / sizeof(int);
19.    void *a_init[n_i];
20.    for (int k = 0; k < n_i; k++) a_init[k] = &i_init[k];
```

```
21.    void **arr = srch_ptr_alloc(sizeof(a_init) / sizeof(void *), a_init);
22.    Elements(arr);
23.    printf("\n");
24.    srch_ptr_free(&arr);
25.    }
26.
27. // Add elements with automatic array extension.
28. int i_init[] = {0, 1, 2, 3, 4, 5, 6, 7, 8, 9, 10, 11, 12};
29. int n_i = sizeof(i_init) / sizeof(int);
30. void **ar = srch_ptr_alloc(5, NULL);
31. int n = 0;
32. for (int k = 0; k < n_i; k++) {
33.    n = srch_ptr_add(&i_init[k], &ar, k % 5);
34.    printf("%d: n=%d\n", k, n);
35.    }
36. printf("\n");
37.
38. // Search elements at random and then delete them.
39. srand(10002);
40. Elements(ar);
41. int n_left = n;
42. int n_search = 0;
43. while (n_left > 0) {
44.    int num = (rand() % (n + 2)) - 1;
45.    n_search++;
46.    int res = srch_ptr_find(&i_init[num], ar, &cmp_i);
47.    if (res >= 0) {
48.      n_left = srch_ptr_del(res, ar);
49.      printf("%d: %d removed\n", n_search, num);
50.      Elements(ar);
51.      }
52.    else {
53. //      printf("%d: %d not found\n", n_search, num);
54.      }
55.    }
56.
57. srch_ptr_free(&ar);
58. printf("%p\n", ar);
```

It is the equivalent of the code shown in Listing 8-13 to test the srch_int_*() functions. In line 33 you use the addresses of the elements of i_init to initialize the array of pointers ar. If you initialize i_init in line 28 to the same values used to test the srch_int_*() functions and also choose the same random seed (in line 39), the output of the test code is identical to that shown in Listing 8-14.

The local function cmp_i() could have been simpler and only check for equality, but returning a value that tells you whether the searched value is greater or less than an element will be useful when dealing with ordered arrays.

Ordered Arrays

The problem with linear searches is that the element you look for might be the last one you check. If the set is large, this involves making a lot of comparisons. In this section, you learn how to exploit the ordering in the set to find elements efficiently.

In the next chapter, you will see how to sort unordered arrays. For the time being, we assume that the set is already ordered and take it from there.

The most efficient way to find a particular element in an ordered array is to perform a binary search.

The concept is simple: you start by comparing the value you are looking for with the middle element of the array. If the value is, say, greater than the middle value, you know that the element you are looking for is in the second half of the array (assuming that its elements are in increasing order). When you compare the searched value with the middle element of the second half of the array, you find out whether the target element is in the fourth or in the third quarter of the array. You repeat the halving operation until either you hit the target element or you are left with a single element of the array and it is not the right one, in which case you know that the array doesn't contain the value you are looking for.

With a search on an ordered array, you don't just want to obtain the position of the element that holds a given value. You also want to know where you should insert the new element with that value if the search fails. This will allow you to search for a value and, if it is not there, know where to insert it without having to perform an additional search.

Listing 8-21 shows you how to apply the binary search to an ordered array.

Listing 8-21. srch_ptr_find_ord()

```
1. //------------------------------------------------------------ srch_ptr_find_ord
2. int srch_ptr_find_ord(void *obj, void **ar, int (*cmp)(void *, void *)) {
3.    int n = *((int *)ar - 1);
4.    if (n <= 0) return -1;                                   //-->
5.    int k0 = 0;
6.    int k1 = n - 1;
7.    int k = (k0 + k1) / 2;
8.    int cmp_res;
9.    do {
10.       cmp_res = (*cmp)(ar[k], obj);
11.       if (cmp_res) {
12.         if (cmp_res > 0) k0 = k + 1;
13.         else k1 = k - 1;
14.         k = (k0+k1) / 2;
15.       }
16.    } while (cmp_res && k1 >= k0);
17.    return (cmp_res) ? -k0 - 1 : k;
18.    } // srch_ptr_find_ord
```

After checking that the array is not empty, you set in lines 5 to 7 the variable k0 to the position of the first element (i.e., 0), k1 to the position of the last element (i.e., n - 1), and k to the position of the element in the middle of the array. Note that if the array contains an even number of elements, there is no middle element, and (k0+k1)/2 results in a truncation.

In line 10, you compare the kth element with the target value. If it is a match, you don't do anything, the do loop terminates because cmp_res is 0, and the function returns the index k of the match.

If the comparison fails, you adjust the appropriate lower or upper limit while excluding the element you have just checked (lines 12 and 13), recalculate the new position to be checked (line 14), and keep going.

If the value is not in the array, because when recalculating k0 and k1 after a failed comparison you skip the current element, eventually, either k0 will become greater than k1 or k1 will become less than k0. In either case, the do loop terminates. When that happens, you return -k0-1 (which is identical to -k1-2 because all increments are by 1).

In the calling program, if the returned value is 0 or greater, you know that the search has succeeded. If the result is negative, it means that the search has failed. Without the -1 in line 17, the search would return minus the position in which the searched value would be if present. This would not work for target values preceding all array values (i.e., less than the first one because the array is ordered): the function would return 0, which is the result returned when the searched value matches the value of the first element.

Listing 8-22 shows how you test srch_ptr_find_ord().

Listing 8-22. Testing srch_ptr_find_ord()

```
1.  int i_init[] = {1, 3, 5, 7, 9};
2.  int n_i = sizeof(i_init) / sizeof(int);
3.  void **ar = srch_ptr_alloc(n_i, NULL);
4.  for (int k = 0; k < n_i; k++) srch_ptr_add(&i_init[k], &ar, 5);
5.  Elements(ar);
6.  int k_max = i_init[n_i - 1] + 1;
7.  printf("Binary search\n");
8.  for (int k = 0; k <= k_max; k++) {
9.     int i = srch_ptr_find_ord(&k, ar, &cmp_i);
10.    if (i < 0) {
11.       i = -i - 1;
12.       if (i >= n_i) printf("%2d: %2d (past the last element)\n", k, i);
13.       else printf("%2d: %2d (currently holding %d)\n", k, i, *(int *)ar[i]);
14.       }
15.    else {
16.       printf("%2d: %2d (%d found)\n", k, i, *(int *)ar[i]);
17.       }
18.    }
19. srch_ptr_free(&ar);
```

You first define an array of integers (line 1) and use it to fill up an ordered array of pointers (line 4). Then, you search for all values from one less than the array's minimum value to one more than its maximum value (line 9). Lines 10 to 17 are only there to display the results in a clear fashion. The output of the program is shown in Listing 8-23.

Listing 8-23. Testing srch_ptr_find_ord()—Output

```
5:  1  3  5  7  9
Binary search
 0:  0 (currently holding 1)
 1:  0 (1 found)
 2:  1 (currently holding 3)
 3:  1 (3 found)
 4:  2 (currently holding 5)
 5:  2 (5 found)
 6:  3 (currently holding 7)
 7:  3 (7 found)
 8:  4 (currently holding 9)
 9:  4 (9 found)
10:  5 (past the last element)
```

Now that you know how to perform a binary search on an ordered array, you only need to see how to perform insertions and deletions.

Like with unordered arrays, we start with the deletions (because they are always easier). Listing 8-24 shows srch_ptr_del_ord().

Listing 8-24. srch_ptr_del_ord()

```
1.  //------------------------------------------------------------ srch_ptr_del_ord
2.  // Returns the number of array elements still occupied after the
3.  // deletion or -1 if unsuccessful.
4.  int srch_ptr_del_ord(int k, void **ar) {
5.    int *n_p = (int *)ar - 1;
6.    int n = *n_p;
7.    if (k < 0 || k >= n) return -1;                              //-->
8.    (void)memmove(&ar[k], &ar[k + 1], (n - k - 1)*sizeof(void *));
9.    n--;
10.   *n_p = n;
11.   return n;
12.   } // srch_ptr_del_ord
```

When you compare srch_ptr_del_ord() with srch_ptr_del() shown in Listing 8-18, you see that only line 8 is different: instead of replacing the element to be deleted with the last element of the array, you "move up" by one place all the elements that follow the one to be deleted. If you are thinking of replacing memmove() with memcpy(), don't: if you use memcpy() when source and destination overlap, it will "scramble" your array.

Note that when you need to remove the last element of the array, k is n-1. In that case, the initial value of j is n, and the for loop is not entered. Neat!

Listing 8-25 shows a piece of code that removes at random all elements of an array, and Listing 8-26 shows its output.

Listing 8-25. Testing srch_ptr_del_ord()

```
1.  int i_init[] = {0, 1, 2, 3, 4, 5, 6, 7, 8, 9, 10, 11, 12};
2.  int n_i = sizeof(i_init) / sizeof(int);
3.  void **ar = srch_ptr_alloc(n_i, NULL);
4.  for (int k = 0; k < n_i; k++) srch_ptr_add(&i_init[k], &ar, 5);
5.
6.  srand(12345);
7.  Elements(ar);
8.  int n_left = n_i;
9.  int n_search = 0;
10. while (n_left > 0) {
11.   int num = (rand() % (n_i + 2)) - 1;
12.   n_search++;
13.   int res = srch_ptr_find_ord(&i_init[num], ar, &cmp_i);
14.   if (res >= 0) {
15.     n_left = srch_ptr_del_ord(res, ar);
16.     printf("%d: %d removed\n", n_search, num);
17.     Elements(ar);
18.     }
19.   }
20.
21. srch_ptr_free(&ar);
22. printf("%p\n", ar);
```

The code is almost identical to lines 28 to 58 of the program to test the functions dealing with unordered arrays (Listing 8-20). And the output is similar too (see lines 21 to 48 of Listing 8-14).

Listing 8-26. Testing srch_ptr_del_ord()—Output

```
13:  0  1  2  3  4  5  6  7  8  9 10 11 12
1: 8 removed
12:  0  1  2  3  4  5  6  7  9 10 11 12
2: 10 removed
11:  0  1  2  3  4  5  6  7  9 11 12
3: 7 removed
10:  0  1  2  3  4  5  6  9 11 12
4: 0 removed
 9:  1  2  3  4  5  6  9 11 12
5: 5 removed
 8:  1  2  3  4  6  9 11 12
7: 1 removed
 7:  2  3  4  6  9 11 12
8: 6 removed
 6:  2  3  4  9 11 12
9: 12 removed
 5:  2  3  4  9 11
10: 2 removed
 4:  3  4  9 11
12: 11 removed
 3:  3  4  9
22: 9 removed
 2:  3  4
38: 3 removed
 1:  4
50: 4 removed
 0:
(nil)
```

But notice that, as expected, when an element is removed, the array remains ordered.
Listing 8-27 shows srch_ptr_ins_ord(), which inserts an element into an ordered array.

Listing 8-27. srch_ptr_ins_ord()

```
1. //--------------------------------------------------------------- srch_ptr_ins_ord
2. // Returns the number of array elements occupied after the insertion,
3. // -1 if the value already exists, or -2 if unsuccessful for other reasons.
4. int srch_ptr_ins_ord(void *obj, void ***ar_p, int (*cmp)(void *, void *),
5.     int incr) {
6.   int k = srch_ptr_find_ord(obj, *ar_p, cmp);
7.   if (k >= 0) return -1;                                          //-->
8.   k = -k - 1;
9.   int n = srch_ptr_add(obj, ar_p, incr);
10.  if (n <= 1) return (n == 1) ? 1 : -2;                          //-->
11.  if (k == n - 1) return n;                                      //-->
12.  void **ar = *ar_p;
13.  (void)memmove(&ar[k + 1], &ar[k], (n - k - 1)*sizeof(void *));
14.  ar[k] = obj;
15.  return n;
16.  } // srch_ptr_ins_ord
```

First of all, you ensure that the array remains free of duplicate elements by executing srch_ptr_find_ord() in line 6 and returning -1 in line 7 if the search function returns a non-negative value.

In line 8, you convert the negative value returned by srch_ptr_find_ord() to the position in which the new element is to be inserted.

To avoid duplicating the part of srch_ptr_add() (Listing 8-17) that expands the array, you invoke srch_ptr_add() from within srch_ptr_ins_ord() (line 9 of Listing 8-27) and add the new element at the end of the array.

If, after the addition, the array contains one element, it means that the new element is the first one inserted into the array. In line 10, you take care of that case and of srch_ptr_add() returning an error code.

In line 11, you check whether the new element is to be inserted at the end of the array. If that is the case, this has already been done by srch_ptr_add() and you can return immediately.

In line 13, you make space for the new element. In doing so, you overwrite the new element that srch_ptr_add() had appended to the array, but this is inconsequential, because in line 14 you store the new element in its correct position within the array.

Listing 8-28 shows a piece of code that inserts into an array elements in random order, and Listing 8-29 shows its output.

Listing 8-28. Testing srch_ptr_ins_ord()

```
1. int i_init[] = {0, 1, 2, 3, 4, 5, 6, 7, 8, 9, 10, 11, 12};
2. int n_i = sizeof(i_init) / sizeof(int);
3. void **ar = srch_ptr_alloc(5, NULL);
4.
5. srand(12345);
6. Elements(ar);
7. int n_left = n_i;
8. while (n_left > 0) {
9.   int num = rand() % n_i;
10.   int res = srch_ptr_ins_ord(&i_init[num], &ar, &cmp_i, 5);
11.   if (res >= 0) {
12.     n_left--;
13.     printf("%d inserted\n", num);
14.     Elements(ar);
15.     }
16.   }
17.
18. srch_ptr_free(&ar);
19. printf("%p\n", ar);
```

The program keeps attempting to insert into ar random elements of the array i_init until all its elements have been inserted.

Listing 8-29. Testing srch_ptr_ins_ord()—Output

```
 0:
8 inserted
 1:  8
1 inserted
 2:  1  8
9 inserted
 3:  1  8  9
7 inserted
 4:  1  7  8  9
```

```
5 inserted
 5:  1  5  7  8  9
Buffer extended from 5 to 10
11 inserted
 6:  1  5  7  8  9 11
2 inserted
 7:  1  2  5  7  8  9 11
0 inserted
 8:  0  1  2  5  7  8  9 11
4 inserted
 9:  0  1  2  4  5  7  8  9 11
10 inserted
10:  0  1  2  4  5  7  8  9 10 11
Buffer extended from 10 to 15
3 inserted
11:  0  1  2  3  4  5  7  8  9 10 11
12 inserted
12:  0  1  2  3  4  5  7  8  9 10 11 12
6 inserted
13:  0  1  2  3  4  5  6  7  8  9 10 11 12
(nil)
```

As for the deletions shown in Listing 8-26, the array remains ordered throughout.

Linked Lists and Binary Search Trees

You encountered an application of linked lists in Chapters 6 and 7, where you used the structures Str and Dar to build stacks respectively of strings and arrays, and in Chapter 3, where you use them to represent binary trees.

In this chapter, you see how to use binary trees to store and search ordered sets of values. When used in that way, all the nodes attached to the left child of a node precede that node, while all nodes attached to the right child of a node follow that node. And this is true for all nodes.

As the module btree.h/btree.c was designed to explain binary trees, rather than to use them in a practical application, you have to prune it (pun intended!) and only retain what you need.

The first step to adapt btree to what you need here is to rename the files to search_tree.h and search_tree.c and replace the prefix btr_ with srcht_ throughout.

Then, remove the functions srcht_blank_allocate(), srcht_calc_tree_max_depth_i(), srcht_free(), srcht_full_allocate(), srcht_get_node_address(), srcht_get_node_index(), srcht_get_node_value(), srcht_make_inlevel_links(), srcht_random_allocate(), srcht_set_node_value(), and srcht_set_ordered_ids(). Ensure that srcht_list_tree() invokes srcht_calc_tree_max_depth_r() instead of srcht_calc_tree_max_depth_i().

In search_tree.c, remove the local functions pick_avail(), write_level_in_nodes(), and write_level_pointers(), and the static variables nodes, n_nodes, max_depth, avail, and n_avail.

Next, define in search_tree.h the structure srcht_tree as follows:

```
typedef struct srcht_tree {
  srcht_node *root;
  int n_nodes;
  } srch_tree;
```

This is the first step to allow you to apply the five functions remaining in search_tree to any binary tree instead of a binary tree statically defined within the module.

In the srcht_node structure, rename the component next to parent.

The next step is to update srcht_list_tree() as follows:

- Replace the only parameter (i.e., srcht_node *root) with srcht_tree *tree and update the declaration in search_tree.h accordingly.

- Where you calculate max_depth, type int at the beginning of the line, so that the variable becomes local to the function (remember that it used to be a static variable).

- Remove the five lines after the comment "Find the parent" and, three lines below that, replace parent with node->parent.

- Where you execute set_node_coords(), add to it the parameter max_depth and update the function accordingly.

- Replace all occurrences of root in srcht_list_tree() with tree->root.

If you now replace next with parent also in srcht_list_nodes(), the only thing that still needs to be taken care of is the compiler errors caused by the following four pairs of lines, the first one occurring in srcht_list_nodes() and the remaining three in srcht_list_tree():

```
for (int k = 0; k < n_nodes; k++) {
  srcht_node *node = &nodes[k];
...
for (int k = 0; k < n_nodes; k++) {
  srcht_node *node = &nodes[k];
...
for (int k = 0; k < n_nodes; k++) {
  srcht_node *parent = &nodes[k];
...
for (int k = 0; k < n_nodes; k++) {
  srcht_node *node = &nodes[k];
```

The problem is clear: in Chapter 3 the nodes of the binary tree were stored in an array. It made describing the binary trees easier and both srcht_list_nodes() and srcht_list_tree() took advantage of its presence. Now, to be able to apply the functions to any tree, you need to rely purely on the tree itself, without depending on an array of structures that might not exist and to which, even if it existed, you would have no access.

The first instance of the problem is easy to solve: remove srcht_list_nodes() and extend the information provided by srcht_traverse_tree(), which currently only prints the node identifiers.

For the three instances within srcht_list_tree(), three possibilities immediately come to mind:

- Replace each for loop with a recursive mechanism,.

- Extend the node structure to include a pointer to chain the nodes.

- Build an array with the node addresses.

srcht_list_tree() is complicated enough without making it recursive. Furthermore, you would have to go through the recursive algorithm three times, once for each occurrence of the for loop. All in all, the first solution is impractical.

The idea of adding a pointer to the node structure for the sole purpose of displaying the tree is an uncomfortable thought. Fortunately, you don't need to do it, because it would result in permanently adding eight bytes (more, when CPU architectures will grow beyond 64 bits) to each node. You might as well adopt solution three and build a temporary array of pointers, which would then disappear when released back to the heap before returning from the function.

Solution three definitely seems the most efficient way, especially because you build the array once and use it three times, once for each `for` loop. The obvious disadvantage is that you need to allocate memory to store the array of pointers. Still, considering that nowadays, dynamic memory is measured in GB, even the 8MB required to store the array for one million nodes (in a 64-bit system) are affordable.

Before the comment "`Compose the tree`", you allocate and set the array as follows:

```
// Build the list of nodes.
int n_nodes = tree->n_nodes;
srcht_node **nodes = malloc(n_nodes * sizeof(srcht_node *));
build_node_array(tree->root, nodes, 1);
```

And don't forget to insert

```
free(nodes);
```

as the last statement of the function.

The function `build_node_array()`, an easy adaptation of `srch_traverse_tree()`, is shown in Listing 8-30.

Listing 8-30. build_node_array()

```
 1. //------------------------------------------------------------- build_node_array
 2. void build_node_array(srcht_node *node, srcht_node **nodes, int init_k) {
 3.    static int k = 0;
 4.    if (init_k) k = 0;
 5.    if (node != NULL) {
 6.      build_node_array(node->child[0], nodes, 0);
 7.      nodes[k++] = node;
 8.      build_node_array(node->child[1], nodes, 0);
 9.    }
10.  } // build_node_array
```

Notice the use of the parameter `init_k`: when you execute `build_node_array()` from within `srcht_list_tree()`, you set the parameter to 1, so that the static variable k is initialized to 0 (line 4 of Listing 8-30). But when you execute `build_node_array()` recursively, you set `init_k` to 0 (lines 6 and 7), so that the value kept in k is correctly incremented with each recursion (line 7). Without the initialization, the value of k would be kept until program termination, and that would prevent you from building the node array more than once, which in turn would mean that that you could only execute `srcht_list_tree()` once per program execution.

To get everything to work, you also need to remove the & from the three occurrences of `&nodes[k]` because the array of nodes used in Chapter 3 contains node structures, while the array built with `srcht_build_node_array()` contains pointers to node structures.

You will find the source code of `search_tree` in the sources for Chapter 8 attached to the book.

In order to use any of the `search_tree` functions, you need to initialize a new tree by defining a variable of type `srcht_tree`:

```
srcht_tree tree = {};
```

Inserting New Nodes

You can insert new nodes into the tree with the function `srcht_ins()` shown in Listing 8-31.

Listing 8-31. srcht_ins()

```
1.  //------------------------------------------------------------------ srcht_ins
2.  // Returns the address of the node or NULL if unsuccessful.
3.  srcht_node *srcht_ins(int id, srcht_tree *tree) {
4.    if (!tree) return NULL;                                       //-->
5.    srcht_node *node = NULL;
6.    if (srcht_find(id, tree, &node)) return NULL;                 //-->
7.    srcht_node *parent = node;
8.    node = calloc(1, sizeof(srcht_node));
9.    if (node == NULL) return NULL;                                //-->
10.   node->id = id;
11.   node->parent = parent;
12.   if (!parent) { // first node in the tree
13.     tree->root = node;
14.     tree->n_nodes = 1;
15.     return node;                                                //-->
16.   }
17.   srcht_node **child_p = &parent->child[(id < parent->id) ? 0 : 1];
18.
19.   // If the target address is already occupied, attach that node to
20.   // the new one as the appropriate child before attaching the new
21.   // node to the tree.
22.   if (!child_p) node->child[((*child_p)->id < id) ? 0 : 1] = *child_p;
23.   *child_p = node;
24.   tree->n_nodes++;
25.   return node;
26.  } // srcht_ins
```

The first interesting bit is in line 6, where you return a failure when you find in the array a node with the same identifier. You will see srcht_find() in the next pages. For the time being, all you need to know is that when the search function succeeds in finding the requested node, it saves its address in the location pointed to by the second parameter and returns 1. When the search fails, srcht_find() returns 0 after saving the address of the parent to which the node with the new ID should be attached.

When you execute line 7, you know that the search failed. Therefore, you can copy the address of the expectant parent to an appropriately named variable. This frees for other uses the variable named node and avoids confusions later on.

In line 8, you allocate a block of memory to store the node with the new identifier. If the allocation succeeds, you initialize the new node by setting its identifier and the pointer to its parent node.

In lines 12 to 16, you handle the special case when the tree is still empty, which means that the new node is going to be the tree root.

Line 17 is a bit tricky. When you reach it, you have allocated and initialized the new node and you know the address of its parent. What you don't yet know is whether the identifier of the new node is less than or greater than the parent's identifier. If it is less, you have to attach it to child[0]; otherwise, you have to attach it to child[1]. You do this check when calculating the index of the child array. Obviously, you don't need to check for equality, because if the identifier of the new node had been the same as that of the parent, the search in line 6 would have succeeded and you would have never reached line 17. Anyhow, after executing line 17, the variable child_p points to the location where you need to store the address of the new node.

You cannot immediately set child_p, though, because it might be currently holding the address of an existing node. To understand how this is possible, imagine the following situation: you have already inserted node 7 and then node 9, which means that node 9 is inserted as the right child of node 7. If you then insert node 8, you get node 7 as a parent and line 17 sets child_p to the address of the right child. But that is the same child that holds node 9.

To resolve the conflict, in line 22 you "push down" node 9 by attaching it as the right child of your new node. After saving node 9 from oblivion, you can then, in line 23, overwrite its original place as the right child.

After that, you only need to increase the counter of nodes in the tree structure and you are done.

Searching for an Identifier

Listing 8-32 shows srcht_find(), which you saw in use in line 6 of srcht_ins() (Listing 8-31).

Listing 8-32. srcht_find()

```
//---------------------------------------------------------------- srcht_find
// It returns 1 when successful, 0 when unsuccessful, and -2 when the
// search couldn't be carried out, in which case res remains unchanged.
// It sets res to the address of the requested node if its id is the
// requested id or the address of the parent node of which the node
// should have been a child if it existed. A NULL res means that there
// are no nodes in the tree.
int srcht_find(int id, srcht_tree *tree, srcht_node **res) {
  if (!tree) return -2;                                       //-->
  srcht_node *root = tree->root;
  if (root == NULL) {
    *res = NULL;
    return 0;                                                 //-->
  }
  return find(id, root, res);
} // srcht_find
```

The comment at the beginning of the function describes the function's outputs. As you can see, all it does is perform a couple of checks before executing the function find(), local to search_tree.c, where you do the actual work. You can see find() in Listing 8-33.

Listing 8-33. find()

```
1. //------------------------------------------------------------------- find
2. // Returns 1 when successful. It always sets res.
3. int find(int id, srcht_node *node, srcht_node **res) {
4.   if (node->id == id) {
5.     *res = node;
6.     return 1;                                              //-->
7.   }
8.   srcht_node *child = node->child[(id < node->id) ? 0 : 1];
9.   if (!child) {
10.    *res = node;
11.    return 0;                                              //-->
12.  }
13.  return find(id, child, res);
14. } // find
```

In lines 4 to 7, before doing anything else, you check whether you have found the node you are looking for. If yes, you save the node address in the calling program's location and return successfully.

If the current node is not the node you are searching for, in line 8 you determine whether the identifier you are trying to find is on the left or on the right of the current node, and select the corresponding child.

If the child is free, it means that the identifier you are looking for should be there but is not. As a result, you save for the calling program the address of the current node (the designated parent) and return unsuccessfully.

If a child exists, you use it to call find() recursively.

Releasing a Tree Back to the Heap

Every new node causes the allocation of a block of memory. As all the allocated blocks are linked together into the tree, you don't need to keep track of them in order to ensure that they are all released once the tree is no longer needed. Instead, you can use srcht_free_tree(), shown in Listing 8-34, to release them all with a single function call.

Listing 8-34. srcht_free_tree()

```
//---------------------------------------------------------------- srcht_free_tree
// Returns the number of nodes removed.
int srcht_free_tree(srcht_tree *tree) {
  int n = 0;
  if (tree && tree->root) {
    n = free_branch(tree->root);
    tree->root = NULL;
    tree->n_nodes -= n;
    }
  return n;
  } // srcht_free_tree
```

The function is straightforward. As you can see, like several other functions that deal with binary trees, srcht_free_tree() delegates the actual work to a local recursive function that, in this case, is free_branch() (Listing 8-35).

Listing 8-35. free_branch()

```
//---------------------------------------------------------------- free_branch
// Returns the number of nodes removed.
int free_branch(srcht_node *node) {
  int n = 0;
  if (node->child[0]) n = free_branch(node->child[0]);
  if (node->child[1]) n += free_branch(node->child[1]);
  free(node);
  return n + 1;
  } // free_branch
```

You go down the branches that start with the two children and add the number of nodes removed from them. Before returning, you remove the current node and increase the node count to take that into account.

Testing Insertion and Searches

Listing 8-36 shows a piece of code that uses all the functions you have seen so far.

Listing 8-36. testing srcht_*()

```
1.    srcht_tree tree = {};
2.    int i_init[] = {1, 3, 5, 7, 9, 11, 13, 15, 17, 19, 21, 23, 25};
3.    int n_i = sizeof(i_init) / sizeof(int);
4.    srcht_node *node = NULL;
5.    srand(1);
6.    printf("Inserting %d nodes from [ ", n_i);
7.    for (int k = 0; k < n_i; k++) printf("%d ", i_init[k]);
8.    printf("] at random.\n");
9.    for (int k = 0; k < n_i; k++) {
10.      int id = i_init[rand() % n_i];
11.      node = srcht_ins(id, &tree);
12.      if (node) {
13.        printf("Inserted node %d\n", node->id);
14. //       srcht_display_node(node);
15. //       printf("root=%p n_nodes=%d\n", tree.root, tree.n_nodes);
16.      }
17.      else {
18.        printf("=== Failed to insert node %d\n", id);
19.      }
20.    } // for (int k..
21.    printf("\n");
22.    srcht_list_tree(&tree);
23.    printf("\n");
24.    srcht_traverse_tree(tree.root, 1);
25.
26.    int n = srcht_free_tree(&tree);
27.    printf("Freed %d nodes from the tree\n", n);
```

The program inserts a number of nodes, lists them, and releases them.

The insertion of each node takes place in line 11, within the for loop that begins in line 9 and ends in line 20. The output of the program is shown in Listing 8-37.

Listing 8-37. testing srcht_*() at Random—Output

```
Inserting 13 nodes from [ 1 3 5 7 9 11 13 15 17 19 21 23 25 ] at random.
Inserted node 1
Inserted node 19
Inserted node 23
Inserted node 9
Inserted node 3
=== Failed to insert node 3
Inserted node 25
Inserted node 7
=== Failed to insert node 3
Inserted node 15
Inserted node 5
=== Failed to insert node 7
=== Failed to insert node 1
```

```
            001
             '-.
            019
      .--------^---.
     009          023
 .-----^-.         '-.
003     015         025
 '-.
  007
 .-'
005
```

```
  #   id idL idR  ..      Address       Left       Right
  0:   1  -1  19  0   0x1a2a010:     (nil)    0x1a2a040
  1:   3  -1   7  9   0x1a2a0d0:     (nil)    0x1a2a130
  2:   5  -1  -1  7   0x1a2a190:     (nil)       (nil)
  3:   7   5  -1  3   0x1a2a130:  0x1a2a190       (nil)
  4:   9   3  15 19   0x1a2a0a0:  0x1a2a0d0    0x1a2a160
  5:  15  -1  -1  9   0x1a2a160:     (nil)       (nil)
  6:  19   9  23  1   0x1a2a040:  0x1a2a0a0    0x1a2a070
  7:  23  -1  25 19   0x1a2a070:     (nil)    0x1a2a100
  8:  25  -1  -1 23   0x1a2a100:     (nil)       (nil)
Freed 9 nodes from the tree
```

The first block of lines logs the insertions. As the identifiers are chosen at random, the program fails to insert nodes when it attempts to duplicate identifiers.

After the insertion log, you see the tree produced with srcht_list_tree(), which should be familiar to you after reading Chapter 3.

Finally, the nodes of the tree are displayed by srcht_traverse_tree(). You can easily follow the links from the root node to the leaves. Notice that the identifiers are in sequence, from 1 to 25, although they are spread through the tree. It almost feels like magic, doesn't it? Sorry: I got carried away. There is obviously nothing magic about it.

Now, if you replace lines 5 to 8 of the program in Listing 8-36 with:

```
printf("Inserting the %d nodes [ ", n_i);
for (int k = 0; k < n_i; k++) printf("%d ", i_init[k]);
printf("] in sequence.\n");
```

and then line 10 with

```
int id = i_init[k];
```

you insert all identifiers in order. After shortening the array to seven elements, the output is shown in Listing 3-38.

Listing 8-38. testing srcht_*() Sequentially—Output

```
Inserting the 7 nodes [ 1 3 5 7 9 11 13 ] in sequence.
Inserted node 1
Inserted node 3
Inserted node 5
Inserted node 7
```

```
Inserted node 9
Inserted node 11
Inserted node 13
```

```
001
 '-.
  003
   '---.
      005
       '---.
          007
           '---.
              009
               '---.
                  011
                   '-.
                    013
```

#	id	idL	idR	..	Address	Left	Right
0:	1	-1	3	0	0x2415010:	(nil)	0x2415040
1:	3	-1	5	1	0x2415040:	(nil)	0x2415070
2:	5	-1	7	3	0x2415070:	(nil)	0x24150a0
3:	7	-1	9	5	0x24150a0:	(nil)	0x24150d0
4:	9	-1	11	7	0x24150d0:	(nil)	0x2415100
5:	11	-1	13	9	0x2415100:	(nil)	0x2415130
6:	13	-1	-1	11	0x2415130:	(nil)	(nil)

```
Freed 7 nodes from the tree
```

This time, all insertions succeeds, because there are no longer random repetitions. But the tree doesn't look like a tree anymore. It's obvious, if you think about it: as each insertion is for an identifier that is greater than all identifiers already inserted, it is attached to the right child of the last (i.e., rightmost) node. The result in this case is extreme, but all trees can get unbalanced because of the order in which nodes are inserted. Also the tree in Listing 8-37 shows some imbalance, in that some branches are longer than others.

You might have noticed in Listing 8-36 a commented-out line with a call to srcht_display_node(). It is a simple function to display the elements of a node in clear. You can see its code in Listing 8-39.

Listing 8-39. srcht_display_node()

```
//------------------------------------------------------------ srcht_display_node
void srcht_display_node(srcht_node *node) {
  printf("%p", node);
  if (node) {
    printf("(%d) parent=%p", node->id, node->parent);
    if (node->parent) printf("(%d)", node->parent->id);
    for (int k = 0; k < 2; k++) {
      srcht_node *child = node->child[k];
      printf(" child%d=%p", k, child);
      if (child) printf("(%d)", child->id);
    }
  }
  printf("\n");
} // srcht_display_node
```

Here is how `srcht_display_node()` displays the root node of the tree shown in Listing 8-37:

```
0x1533010(1) parent=(nil) child0=(nil) child1=0x1533040(3)
```

Deleting Nodes

Obviously, deleting nodes is the reverse of inserting them. But it is not trivial. If the node to be deleted has no children, you can just replace its address stored within the node structure of the parent (either as `child[0]` or as `child[1]`, as appropriate) with a `NULL`. But if the node you need to delete has children, the process of removing it from the tree is somewhat delicate. To understand why, have a look at Figure 8-1, which shows how you can rearrange the children of a deleted node.

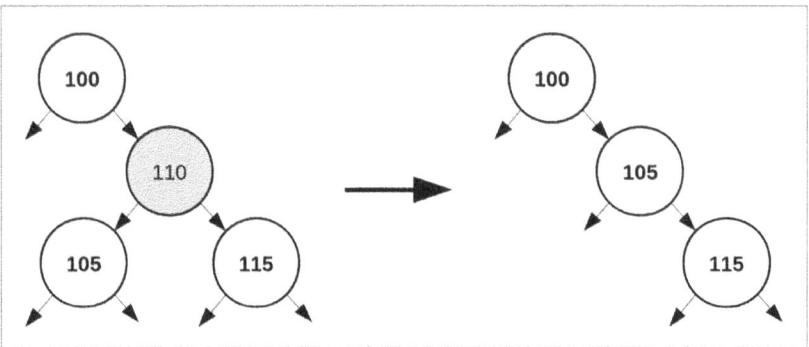

Figure 8-1. *Removing a node with children*

If node 110 of the example doesn't have a right child (i.e., if node 115 is not there), you attach node 105 to 100 and you are done. Similarly, if 105 doesn't exist, you attach 115 directly to 100.

Figure 8-2 shows an alternative way of removing node 110 that is as valid as the solution shown in Figure 8-1.

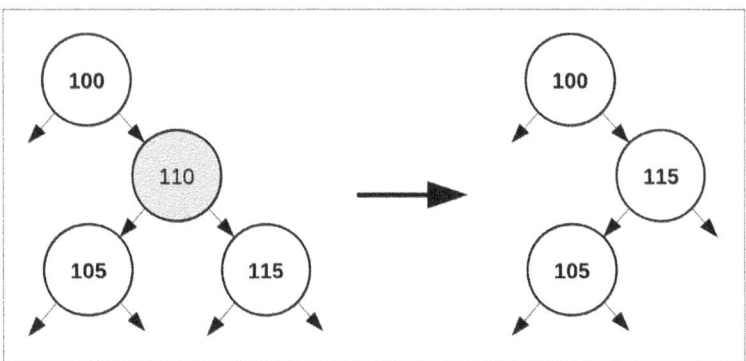

Figure 8-2. *Alternative solution for removing a node with children*

If node 105 is not there, all you need to do is attach 115 to 100, and if 115 is missing, you attach 105 directly to 100.

So far so good, but what if both nodes are present, you attempt to apply the deletion as shown in Figure 8-1, and discover that node 105 already has a right child? You could switch to making the deletion as shown in Figure 8-2, but what if node 115 already has a left child? In either one of the two scenarios, move down one of the two branches until you find a free child in the appropriate spot. To begin understanding the algorithm, refer to Figure 8-3, which shows one additional level of the tree we use as an example.

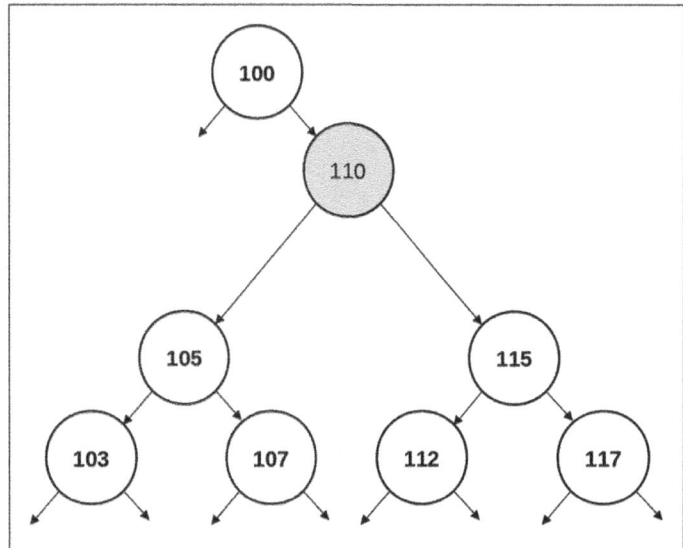

Figure 8-3. *Part of a binary ordered tree*

Because of how ordered binary trees are constructed, all nodes in the branches that start with nodes 107 and 112 have identifiers greater than 105 and less than 115. This would seem to mean that you could use any of the nodes of either branch to replace 110. But there is a catch: there is no correlation between the depth of a node and its identifier. That is, a deeper node can have an identifier lower than a higher node or vice versa. If you are not convinced, look for example at the tree shown in Listing 8-40 (FYI, I removed by hand some empty space to fit the tree within 80 columns).

Listing 8-40. A 30-Node Tree

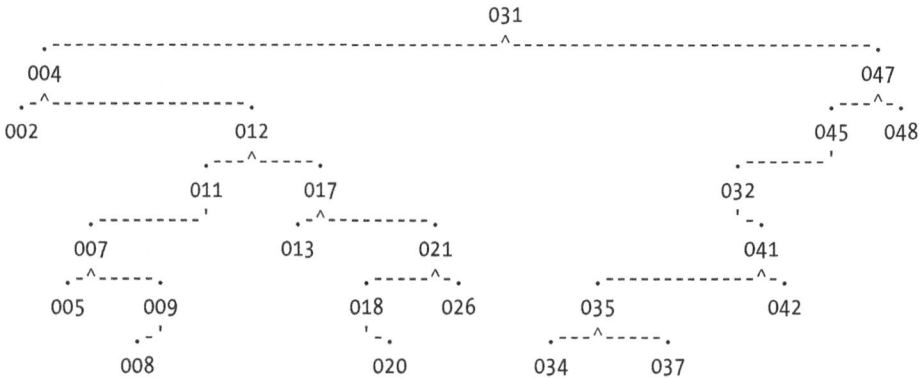

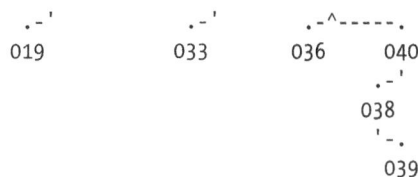

If, for example, you need to delete the root node, you know you need to replace it with one node taken out of the two branches that start with 12 (the right child of the root's left child) or 45 (the left child of the root's right child) because only those nodes are between the root's children (i.e., 4 and 47). But you cannot just pick any of those nodes. For example, 21 is between 4 and 47, but if you used it to replace 31 and move 26 up one level, you would find that node 26 would be on the left of 21, which would make the tree unordered.

The solution is to pick either the highest node in the branch that begins with 12 (26 in the example) or the lowest node in the branch that begins with 45 (i.e., 32). This is easier to do than you might think: 26 is the first node in the 12 branch that has no right child, while 32 is the first node in the 45 branch that has no left child. The function shown in Listing 8-41 adopts the strategy of going down the 45 branch, but both alternatives are equally valid.

Listing 8-41. srcht_del_node()

```
1.  //---------------------------------------------------------------- srcht_del_node
2.  // Returns 1 if successful.
3.  int srcht_del_node(srcht_node *node, srcht_tree *tree) {
4.    if (!tree || !node) return 0;                                    //-->
5.    srcht_node **hook = NULL;
6.    srcht_node *parent = node->parent;
7.    if (parent) for (int k = 0; k < 2; k++) {
8.      if (parent->child[0] == node) hook = &parent->child[0];
9.      else hook = &parent->child[1];
10.     }
11.   else { // it is the root
12.     hook = &tree->root;
13.     }
14.   srcht_node *c0 = node->child[0];
15.   srcht_node *c1 = node->child[1];
16.
17.   // Now that we have saved the pointers contained in the node structure,
18.   // we can release it.
19.   free(node);
20.   tree->n_nodes--;
21.
22.   if (!c0 && !c1) { // Simplest case: the node has no children.
23.     *hook = NULL;
24.     return 1;                                                      //-->
25.     }
26.
27.   if (!c0 || !c1) { // The node has one child.
28.     if (c0) {
29.       *hook = c0;
30.       c0->parent = parent;
31.       }
32.     else {
```

```
33.          *hook = c1;
34.          c1->parent = parent;
35.          }
36.       return 1;                                                    //-->
37.       }
38.
39.    if (!c0->child[1]) { // The node has two children. Try the simpler way.
40.       *hook = c0;
41.       c0->parent = parent;
42.       c0->child[1] = c1;
43.       c1->parent = c0;
44.       return 1;                                                    //-->
45.       }
46.    if (!c1->child[0]) {
47.       *hook = c1;
48.       c1->parent = parent;
49.       c1->child[0] = c0;
50.       c0->parent = c1;
51.       return 1;                                                    //-->
52.       }
53.
54.    // No can do. Let's follow the left branches below c1 until we hit
55.    // a NULL (i.e., until we find a node with a free left child).
56.    srcht_node *old_parent = c1;
57.    node = c1->child[0];
58.    while (node->child[0]) {
59.       old_parent = node;
60.       node = node->child[0];
61.       }
62.    old_parent->child[0] = node->child[1];
63.    if (node->child[1]) node->child[1]->parent = old_parent;
64.    *hook = node;
65.    node->parent = parent;
66.    node->child[0] = c0;
67.    c0->parent = node;
68.    node->child[1] = c1;
69.    c1->parent = node;
70.    return 1;
71.    } // srcht_del_node
```

Lines 5 to 13 set the variable hook to the address of the location where the node's address is held within the tree. In general, the location is either node->parent->child[0] or node->parent->child[1]. But, if the node to be deleted is the tree root, the parent's address is NULL and the location is tree->root.

As soon as you have saved the information contained in the node, you can release the node structure (lines 19 and 20).

If the node has no children, you don't need to do anything except reset the hook location (lines 22 to 25).

If the node has one child, you point the parent's child address (saved in hook) to the node's only child. But don't forget to set the parent address within the child to the parent address of the deleted node. This is the address saved in the variable parent, which, remember, is NULL if you are deleting the root node (lines 27 to 37).

You reach line 39 when the if condition in line 27 fails. For that to happen, neither child address of the node being deleted is NULL, which means that the node has two children.

In line 39, you check whether the right child of the node's left child (i.e., node 115 in Figure 8-1) is NULL. If it is, in the block statement that follows you rearrange the nodes as illustrated in Figure 8-1. If you fall through, in line 46 you check whether the left child of the node's right child (i.e., node 105 of Figure 8-2) is NULL and, if it is, you do what is shown in Figure 8-2.

You don't need to check whether the left child of the node's left child or the right child of the node's right child (i.e., node 103 and 107 in Figure 8-3) are available because, even if they were, you couldn't use them to rearrange the nodes of the tree while at the same time keeping the tree ordered.

In the rest of the function, you look for the first left child in the c1 branch that has no left child (i.e., the equivalent of node 32 when you deleted the root of the tree of Listing 8-40). As I already said, by going down the chain of left descendants of c1, you reach the closest identifier to the one you are deleting that is greater than that. If you had gone down the right descendants of c0 you would have reached the closest identifier that is less than what you are deleting. These are the two nodes that, when traversing the tree, are immediately after of before the node being deleted, which is why they are the replacements that cause the least change in the tree.

Listing 8-42 shows a small function that lets you delete a node given its identifier. All it does is search the tree for the node address before invoking the function srcht_del_node() that you have just seen.

Listing 8-42. srcht_del()

```
1. //----------------------------------------------------------------- srcht_del
2. // It returns 1 when successful and 0 when unsuccessful.
3. int srcht_del(int id, srcht_tree *tree) {
4.    srcht_node *node = NULL;
5.    if (srcht_find(id, tree, &node) <= 0) return 0;           //-->
6.    return srcht_del_node(node, tree);
7.    } // srcht_del
```

As you can see, the function reports a failure if it doesn't find the node (line 5). You could decide to be permissive and report as correctly deleted a node that doesn't exist in the first place. All you would need to do is replace line 5 with the following two lines:

```
int ret = srcht_find(id, tree, &node);
if (ret <= 0) return (ret) ? 0 : 1;                          //-->
```

Then, srcht_del() would report a failure only if srcht_find() failed to perform the search. When srcht_find() returned 0 to indicate that the node doesn't exist, you would return 1 to indicate a successful deletion.

I discourage you to make such a change because it might hide a logic fault in your program. Your programs should be tight and distinguish between deleting a node and find out that a node doesn't exist. And, obviously, you shouldn't ignore the return value of srcht_del()!

To test the delete functions, you can modify and extend the code shown in Listing 8-37. You can start by increasing the size of i_init from 13 to 50 elements to generate a larger (and arguably nicer) tree. To do so, you only need to replace the definition of i_init in line 2 with the two lines

```
int i_init[50];
for (int k = 0; k < 50; k++) i_init[k] = k;
```

By trial and error, I also changed the pseudo-random seed to a value that produced a reasonably balanced tree and, at the same time, one that's narrow enough to fit in the printed page. When attempting in line 9 of Listing 3-35 to insert 50 nodes picked at random, I only managed to insert 30. But that's fine. I could have replaced the for loop with a while or a do and kept going until all 50 nodes had been inserted, but the tree would have probably become too large.

To complete the changes to the code in Listing 3-37, insert the code shown in Listing 8-43 before the line where it frees the tree (line 26).

Listing 8-43. testing srcht_*()—Extension

```
1. int n_del = tree.n_nodes;
2. printf("deleting %d of %d nodes at random.\n", n_del, tree.n_nodes);
3. for (int k = 0; k < n_del; k++) {
4.    int id;
5.    int res;
6.    do {
7.      id = i_init[rand() % n_i];
8.      res = srcht_del(id, &tree);
9.    } while (res != 1);
10.   printf("%2d: Deleted %2d\n", k, id);
11.   srcht_list_tree(&tree);
12. }
13. srcht_traverse_tree(tree.root, 1);
14. printf("%p %d\n", tree.root, tree.n_nodes);
```

As you can see, it deletes all 30 nodes in random order. The do loop in lines 6 to 9 is where you invoke srcht_del(). Incidentally, if you had implemented srcht_del() to accept as deleted a nonexistent node as discussed above, the loop would have just gone through once and removed not more than one node, if at all.

Listing 8-44 shows portions of the output of the test code (updated Listing 3-37 and Listing 8-43). The initial tree is shown in Listing 8-40. The places where I removed sections of the output are indicated with ellipses.

Listing 8-44. testing srcht_*() Number Two—Partial Output

```
...
deleting 30 of 30 nodes at random.
...
                            031
     .-----------------------^-----------.
   004                                   047
 .-^---------.                         .-'
 002         012                       045
        .---^-----.                .-----'
       011       017              032
      .-'       .-^---.          '-.
      005       013   026        041
                     .-'        .-'
                     020        037
15: Deleted 31
                       032
     .-----------------------^-----------.
   004                                   047
 .-^---------.                         .-'
 002         012                       045
        .---^-----.                 .---'
       011       017               041
      .-'       .-^---.           .-'
      005       013   026         037
```

248

```
                    .-'
                020
...
   037
   .-'
004
   '-.
   013
27: Deleted  4
   037
   .-'
013
28: Deleted 37
013
29: Deleted 13
srcht_list_tree: tree empty or non-existent
   #   id idL idR ..    Address       Left       Right
(nil) 0
Freed 0 nodes from the tree
```

Balanced Trees

A balanced tree is one in which all branches have more or less the same length. That is, in which the leaves are almost equally far from the root node. The "more or less" and "almost" are necessary because you can only perfectly balance binary trees with a number of nodes equal to a power of 2 minus 1. Another way of describing a balanced tree is to say that its height (i.e., the maximum number of levels below the root) is at a minimum.

Here is a totally unbalanced tree (reproduced from Listing 8-38):

```
001
   '-.
   003
      '---.
         005
            '---.
               007
                  '---.
                     009
                        '---.
                           011
                              '-.
                              013
```

Such trees are called *degenerate* trees, because they are identical to linked lists, with no branching at all. The fact that the tree is unbalanced is because of how you insert new nodes and the order in which you insert them.

The *balancing factor* of a node is the difference between the number of nodes in its two subtrees (right minus left). For example, the root node of the above degenerate tree has a balancing factor of 6. Using the concept of balancing factor, you can define a balanced tree as a tree in which all nodes have balancing factors of -1, 0, or +1.

A balanced version (with all balancing factors equal to 0) of the tree shown above is as follows:

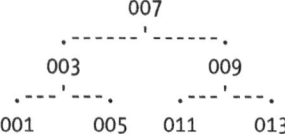

```
                007
        .------'------.
     003             009
   .---'---.       .---'---.
 001     005     011     013
```

The advantage of working with balanced trees is that all operations (i.e., searches, insertions, and deletions) are quicker because they require a lower number of comparisons. Look for example of the totally unbalanced tree shown above: to find a node in it you need to make an average of $(1 + 7) / 2 = 4$ comparisons. To find a node in the balanced tree, you only need an average of $(1 + 2 * 2 + 4 * 3) / 7 = 2.4$ comparisons.

To obtain balanced trees, you can adopt one of three possible strategies: keep the tree balanced whenever you insert or delete a node, rebalance the tree after each insertion and deletion, or balance the tree after a number of insertions and deletions, when you think that the tree has become too unbalanced to work efficiently.

The function srcht_balance_tree() (Listing 8-45) rebalances a tree based on the following idea: build an array of pointers in which the nodes are in order and construct from it a balanced tree.

Listing 8-45. srcht_balance_tree()

```
1.  //----------------------------------------------------------- srcht_balance_tree
2.  // Returns 1 if successful.
3.  int srcht_balance_tree(srcht_tree *tree) {
4.    if (!tree || !tree->root) return 0;                        //-->
5.    int n_nodes = tree->n_nodes;
6.    if (n_nodes < 3) return 1;                                 //-->
7.
8.    // Build the list of nodes.
9.    srcht_node **nodes = malloc(n_nodes * sizeof(srcht_node *));
10.   if (!nodes) return 0;                                      //-->
11.   build_node_array(tree->root, nodes, 1);
12.
13.   // Balance the tree.
14.   int k_new_root = n_nodes / 2;
15.   tree->root = nodes[k_new_root];
16.   tree->root->parent = NULL;
17.   nodes[k_new_root] = NULL;
18.   srcht_node *child = balance(0, k_new_root, nodes);
19.   tree->root->child[0] = child;
20.   if (child) child->parent = tree->root;
21.   child = balance(k_new_root + 1, n_nodes, nodes);
22.   tree->root->child[1] = child;
23.   if (child) child->parent = tree->root;
24.
25.   free(nodes);
26.   return 1;
27.   } // srcht_balance_tree
```

In lines 9 to 11, you allocate space for the array of pointers to nodes and build it using the function build_node_array() that you have already seen (Listing 8-31).

In lines 14 to 16, you pick the node in the middle of the array and connect it to the tree structure as the new root. As the nodes in the array are ordered, the new root has as many nodes preceding it as it has following it (or as close to it as possible when n_nodes is even), which is precisely what you want for a balanced tree.

250

After hooking up the new root, in line 17 you set to NULL the array element that points to that node. By doing so, you hide the node, thereby making it impossible to pick it up again.

In line 18, you invoke the local function balance() to choose nodes for the root's left branch and in line 21 you do the same for the right branch. You can see balance() in Listing 8-46.

Listing 8-46. balance()

```
1. //-------------------------------------------------------------------- balance
2. srcht_node *balance(int k1, int k2, srcht_node **nodes) {
3.    int k = (k1 + k2) / 2;
4.    srcht_node *node = nodes[k];
5.    if (node) {
6.      nodes[k] = NULL;
7.      srcht_node *child = balance(k1, k, nodes);
8.      node->child[0] = child;
9.      if (child) child->parent = node;
10.     child = balance(k, k2, nodes);
11.     node->child[1] = child;
12.     if (child) child->parent = node;
13.     }
14.    return node;
15.  } // balance
```

The two parameters k1 and k2 define the range nodes on which the function is to operate. While k1 is the index of the first element, k2 is the index of the element that follows the last node of the range. When you execute balance() in line 18 of srcht_balance_tree() (Listing 8-45), you set the range to include only the nodes that precede the new root node, while when you execute it in line 21, you set the range to include only the nodes that follow the root.

In line 3 of balance() you pick up the node in the middle of the range. If its address is non-NULL, you do in lines 6 to 12 what you do in lines 17 to 23 of srcht_balance_tree() (Listing 8-45).

balance() stops calling itself recursively when the index calculated in line 3 hits a NULL address. This happens when you reach a leaf and the range has shrunk to nothing. If you didn't set to NULL the array elements of nodes after you have picked them (line 17 of srcht_balance_tree() and line 6 of balance()) the recursive calls would continue until you filled up the system stack and crashed the program.

If you execute the code shown in Listing 8-47, you obtain the output shown in Listing 8-48.

Listing 8-47. Balancing the Tree

```
1. int n_nodes = 31;
2. srcht_tree tree = {};
3. printf("Inserting %d nodes in sequence.\n", n_nodes);
4. for (int k = 0; k < n_nodes; k++) {
5.   if (!srcht_ins(k, &tree)) printf("Failed to insert node %d\n", k);
6.   }
7. if (n_nodes <= 20) srcht_list_tree(&tree);
8. printf("Balancing %ssuccessful\n", (srcht_balance_tree(&tree)) ? "" : "un");
9. srcht_list_tree(&tree);
10. int n = srcht_free_tree(&tree);
11. printf("\nFreed %d nodes from the tree\n", n);
```

In line 7 you check that the number of nodes is within the maximum number of levels that srcht_list_tree() can handle. This is necessary because, by inserting the nodes in sequence, you create a degenerate tree, with one node per level.

251

Listing 8-48. Balancing the Tree—Output

```
Inserting 31 nodes in sequence.
Balancing successful
                                015
              .----------------^----------------.
            007                                 023
      .-------^-------.                   .-------^-------.
     003             011                 019             027
  .---^---.       .---^---.           .---^---.       .---^---.
 001     005     009     013         017     021     025     029
.-^-.   .-^-.   .-^-.   .-^-.       .-^-.   .-^-.   .-^-.   .-^-.
000 002 004 006 008 010 012 014   016 018 020 022 024 026 028 030

Freed 31 nodes from the tree
```

Perfect balancing!

Summary

In this chapter, you learned about standard comparison functions, how to compare structures and arrays, and how to use fuzzy comparisons of text to handle typos and spelling mistakes.

After learning how to do linear searches, additions, and deletions on unordered arrays of integers and pointers, you saw how to perform searches, insertions, and deletions on ordered arrays.

Finally, you learned how to use binary search trees to store, list, update, and search ordered sets of data, and how to optimize binary trees by balancing them.

CHAPTER 9

Sorting

In the previous chapter, you read about ordered arrays and binary trees. In particular, you learned how to work with ordered arrays of pointers to insert, delete, and find individual items.

In this chapter, you will learn methods to bring order to unordered arrays.

Insertion Sort

The simplest way to sort an array is to go through its elements one by one and move them to their correct positions. This is what you do when you sort the cards in your hand while playing a card game.

Listing 9-1 shows how easy it is to apply insertion sort to an array of pointers.

Listing 9-1. sort_insertion()

```
1.  //-------------------------------------------------------------- sort_insertion
2.  void sort_insertion(void **ar, int (*cmp)(void *, void *)) {
3.    int n = *((int *)ar - 1);
4.    if (n <= 1) return;                                        //-->
5.    for (int k = 1; k < n; k++) {
6.      void *el = ar[k];
7.      int j = k - 1;
8.      while (j >= 0 && (*cmp)(el, ar[j]) >= 0) j--;
9.      j++;
10.     if (j < k) {
11.       (void)memmove(&ar[j + 1], &ar[j], (k - j)*sizeof(void *));
12.       ar[j] = el;
13.     }
14.   }
15. } // sort_insertion
```

The for loop that starts in line 5 selects an array element at a time starting from the second one.

In line 6, you save the address of the selected element. Then, in line 8, you compare the selected element with the elements that precede it within the array as long as those elements have a larger key.

When you exit the while loop, j points to the first element found that has a key below that of element k. This means that you should insert element k before element j+1. When all elements preceding k have a lower key, it means that k is already where it should be. When that happens, the while loop is never entered and j remains set to k-1. That's why, after incrementing j in line 9, you only need to execute lines 11 and 12 if j < k.

In line 11, you move "right" one place the elements from j to k-1 (thereby overwriting the kth position) and, in line 12, you write the address of the kth element in the jth position.

© Giulio Zambon 2016
G. Zambon, *Practical C*, DOI 10.1007/978-1-4842-1769-6_9

The advantage of using this sorting method is that it is simple and doesn't use extra memory because it sorts the array in place. Its disadvantage is that it might have to make lots of comparisons and memory moves.

We have only considered arrays in which all keys/values are different. But if you need to sort arrays in which the same key can appear more than once, insertion sort has another feature that you might find useful: it doesn't swap around elements that have the same key. In other words, elements with identical keys remain in the order they had before sorting.

Incidentally, if you swap the two arguments of the comparison function invoked in line 8, the array is sorted in descending order.

Shell Sort

Shell sort (named after Donald Shell, who first published the algorithm) is a variant of insertion sort. The idea is that you can move into place elements more quickly if you compare them with distant elements before applying the insertion sort as shown in the previous section. That is, when comparing an element with those that precede it within the array, you make more than one pass with decreasing distances between elements.

The tricky part is deciding how big the gaps should be. In fact, the problem has not yet been completely solved.

Listing 9-2 shows a variant of sort_insertion() that lets you choose the distance between elements. Then, to implement a Shell sort, you only need to execute the function repeatedly with decreasing distances.

Listing 9-2. shell_step()

```
 1. //------------------------------------------------------------------ shell_step
 2. void shell_step(void **ar, int (*cmp)(void *, void *), int dist) {
 3.    int n = *((int *)ar - 1);
 4.    if (n <= 1) return;                                    //-->
 5.    for (int k = 1; k < n; k++) {
 6.      void *el = ar[k];
 7.      int j = k - 1;
 8.      while (j >= 0 && (*cmp)(el, ar[j]) >= 0) j -= dist;
 9.      j = (j < 0) ? 0 : j + 1;
10.      if (j < k) {
11.        (void)memmove(&ar[j + 1], &ar[j], (k - j)*sizeof(void *));
12.        ar[j] = el;
13.        }
14.      }
15.    } // shell_step
```

As you can see, shell_step() is almost identical to sort_insertion(): in line 8 you replace

j--

with

j -= dist

Then, to avoid accessing elements outside the lower array boundary when dist > 1, you change line 9 from

j++;

to

```
j = (j < 0) ? 0 : j + 1;
```

For example, you can implement sort_shell() as follows:

```
void sort_shell(void **ar, int (*cmp)(void *, void *)) {
  shell_step(ar, cmp, 7);
  shell_step(ar, cmp, 3);
  shell_step(ar, cmp, 1);
  } // sort_shell
```

Incidentally, to avoid duplications in the code, you can replace the whole body of sort_insertion(), as shown in Listing 9-1, with shell_step(ar, cmp, 1);

It is interesting to play with the distances and see how they affect the number of comparisons.
Listing 9-3 shows a small program to explore that effect.

Listing 9-3. How Distances Affect the Number of Comparisons

```
 1. #define N 100
 2. #define N_REP 100
 3.
 4. int n_comp = 0;
 5.
 6. //----------------------------------------------------------------------- main
 7. int main(int argc, char *argv[]) {
 8.   int dist[] = {2,3,4,5,6,7,8,9,10,11,12,13,14,15,16,17,18,19,20,21,22,23,24};
 9.   int n_dist = sizeof(dist) / sizeof(int);
10.   int i_a[N];
11.   for (int k = 0; k < N; k++) i_a[k] = k;
12.   void **p_a = srch_ptr_alloc(N, NULL);
13.   srand(1);
14.   for (int k_dist = -1; k_dist < n_dist; k_dist++) {
15.     printf("%2d", (k_dist >= 0) ? dist[k_dist] : 1);
16.     for (int k_rep = 0; k_rep < N_REP; k_rep++) {
17.       fill_random(p_a, i_a);
18.       n_comp = 0;
19.       if (k_dist >= 0) {
20.         sort_shell_step(p_a, &cmp_i, dist[k_dist]);
21.         }
22.       sort_shell_step(p_a, &cmp_i, 1);
23.       printf("\t%d", n_comp);
24.       }
25.     printf("\n");
26.     }
27.   srch_ptr_free(&p_a);
28.   return EXIT_SUCCESS;
29.   }
```

The array dist defined and initialized in line 8 contains the distances used for the test. I initially included a handful of distances with gaps. This is why you see an array, although the values stored in it are a continuous sequence.

255

The for loop that starts in line 14 goes through all the distances. For each one of them you generate N_REP times a random array of pointers (line 17) and execute first a sort with a distance dist[k_dist] (line 20) and then an insertion sort (line 22). Note that you set the initial k_dist to -1 and only execute the Shell sort from the second iteration on, when k_dist becomes non-negative (line 19). In this way, the first iteration over k_dist produces a straight insertion sort.

The fill_random() function that you execute in line 17 is shown in Listing 9-4.

Listing 9-4. fill_random()

```
 1. //------------------------------------------------------------- fill_random
 2. void fill_random(void **ar, int *iar) {
 3.   for (int k = 0; k < N; k++) ar[k] = NULL;
 4.   for (int k = 0; k < N; k++) {
 5.     unsigned int kk;
 6.     do {
 7.       kk = rand() % N;
 8.       } while (ar[kk]);
 9.     ar[kk] = iar + k;
10.     }
11.   *((int *)ar - 1) = N;
12.   } // fill_random
```

The for loop that starts in line 4 ensures that all elements of the integer array are used, while the do loop that starts in line 6 ensures that all elements of the pointer array are set. With the do loop, you keep selecting a random element of the pointer array until you find one that is available (i.e., that is NULL). It is a brute-force approach, but effective. With small arrays, it makes sense to look for free elements instead of designing an algorithm to keep track of the elements you have already set.

The comparison function you invoke in lines 20 and 22 of the program (Listing 9-3) is an updated version of the cmp_i() function you encountered in Chapter 8 (lines 9 to 13 of Listing 8-20). It is shown in Listing 9-5.

Listing 9-5. cmp_i()

```
//------------------------------------------------------------- cmp_i
int cmp_i(void *a_p, void *b_p) {
#if SORT_DEBUG
  n_comp++;
#endif
  int a = *(int *)a_p;
  int b = *(int *)b_p;
  return (b == a) ? 0 : (b > a) ? 1 : -1;
  } // cmp_i
```

As you can see, the only difference is that it increments the global counter n_comp (defined in line 4 of Listing 9-3) but only when the debug flag defined in sort.h is set. By resetting the counter in the main program (line 18 of Listing 9-3) before each application of the Shell sort, you can print in line 23 the total number of comparisons performed in the sort.

When you execute the program shown in Listing 9-3, you obtain a table with n_dist+1 rows and N_REP+1 columns. You can then use those rows and columns in a spreadsheet program to produce the diagram shown in Figure 9-1.

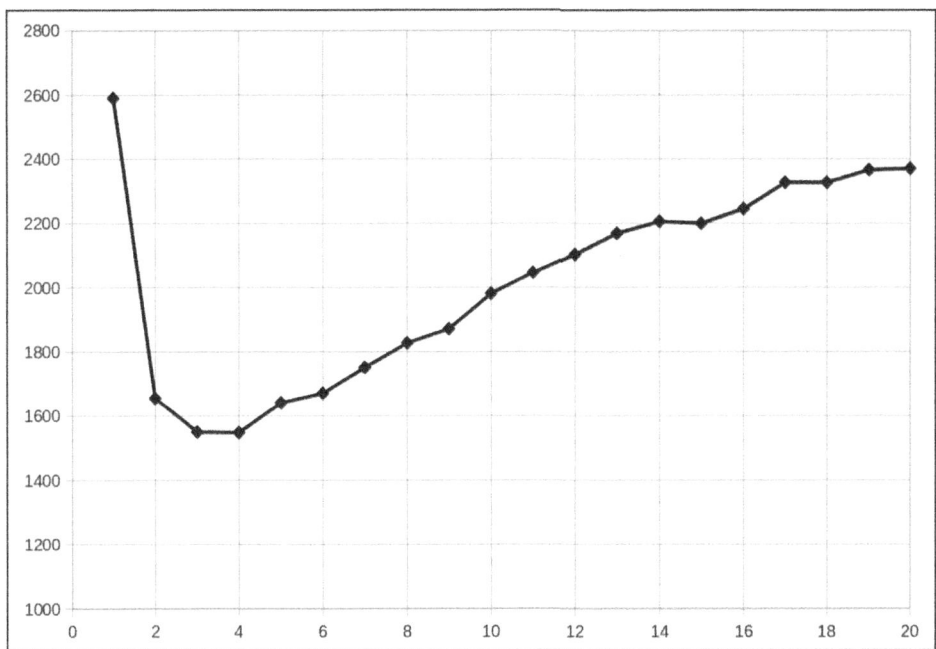

Figure 9-1. *Number of comparisons versus Shell-sort distances*

Each point is calculated by averaging the N_REP repetitions for a particular distance, to make the curve more smooth. For example, the highest point, which corresponds to the straight insertion sort, is 2590. The minimum number of comparisons of the 100 repetitions was 2177 and the maximum was 3020.

As you can see from Figure 9-1, the best result (minimum average number of comparisons) was obtained by executing a Shell-sort step with a distance of 3 or 4 before executing the insertion sort (with total counts of 1550 and 1548, respectively).

But why stop at two steps? Figure 9-2 shows what happens when you perform three steps (points marked with X) and four steps (points marked with squares).

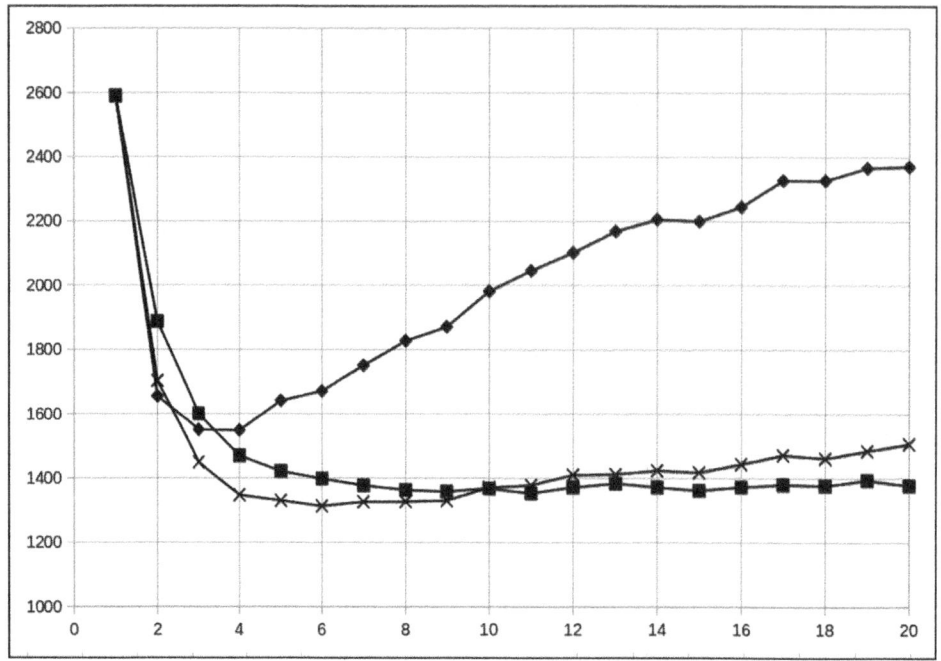

Figure 9-2. *Number of comparisons versus Shell-sort distances with more steps*

In practical terms, you produce the curve with three steps (the Xs) by inserting immediately below line 20 of Listing 9-3 the line

```
sort_shell_step(p_a, &cmp_i, 3);
```

and for four steps (the squares), you insert below line 20 of Listing 9-3 the following two lines:

```
sort_shell_step(p_a, &cmp_i, 6);
sort_shell_step(p_a, &cmp_i, 3);
```

Well, the bottom line is that, in our test, you obtain the best result by executing a total of three steps with 6, 3, and 1 distances, requiring an average of 1313 comparisons to sort the 100-element array. This is about half the number of comparisons you need with a single-step insertion sort (2590).

But how do you know how many steps and with what distances you obtain the best results with a particular set? Donald Knuth, one of the computer luminaries, recommends a method developed by Robert Sedgewick to calculate the number of steps and the distances. I couldn't resist trying it out in the case of this example, although it might be argued that it is not very practical.

The first step to apply the method is to calculate a series of numbers hs for $s = 1, 2, ...$:

$hs = 9 * 2s - 9 * 2s/2 + 1$ if s is even
$hs = 8 * 2s - 6 * 2(s+1)/2 + 1$ if s is odd

If you do the calculations, the series $h0, h1, h2, ...$ turns out to be 1, 5, 19, 41, 109, 209, ...

You stop calculating new elements when the triple of the element exceeds N, the size of the array you need to sort. In this case, N is 100. Therefore, only 1, 5, and 19 make the cut (because 3 * 41 already exceeds 100).

This means that according to Sedgewick, to sort 100 elements you should apply a distance of 19, then of 5, and finally of 1. I "patched up" the program of Listing 9-3 and made N_REP sorts with distances of 19, 5, and 1. The average number of comparisons was 1516, which is 15% higher than what I had obtained with 6, 3, and 1.

Well, it is not much higher, and the number of steps is the same...

As much as I like statistics and plots, it's time to move on!

Bubble Sort

The bubble sort derives its name from the fact that air bubbles in a liquid raise to the surface. I am somewhat sentimentally attached to bubble sort because it is the first sorting algorithm I implemented in my programming career, decades ago. After implementing it, we shall see how it compares with the Shell-sort in terms of number of comparisons.

The idea of a bubble sort is simple: you go though the array and compare all its elements in pairs; if the second one should come before the first one, you swap them. When you are through, you do it again, and keep doing it until you no longer need to swap.

Like the insertion and Shell sorts, the bubble sort is done in place.

Check it out in Listing 9-6.

Listing 9-6. sort_bubble()

```
1.  //-------------------------------------------------------------- sort_bubble
2.  void sort_bubble(void **ar, int (*cmp)(void *, void *)) {
3.    int n = *((int *)ar - 1);
4.    if (n <= 1) return;                                    //-->
5.    int swaps;
6.    do {
7.      swaps = 0;
8.      for (int k = 0; k < n - 1; k++) {
9.        void *e1 = ar[k];
10.       void *e2 = ar[k + 1];
11.       if ((*cmp)(e1, e2) < 0) {
12.         ar[k] = e2;
13.         ar[k + 1] = e1;
14.         swaps = 1;
15.       }
16.     }
17.   } while (swaps);
18. } // sort_bubble
```

Pretty simple: you compare each element with the following one (line 11) and swap them if they are in the wrong order (lines 12 and 13). When you go through all the pairs without having to make a single swap, you are done.

I tested it with the code shown in Listing 9-7.

Listing 9-7. Testing sort_bubble()

```
#define N_REP 100
  srand(1234);
  n_comp = 0;
  int i_a[N];
  for (int k = 0; k < N; k++) i_a[k] = k;
```

```
void **p_a = srch_ptr_alloc(N, NULL);
for (int k_rep = 0; k_rep < N_REP; k_rep++) {
  fill_random(p_a, i_a);
  sort_bubble(p_a, &cmp_i);
  }
printf("Bubble sort: %d\n", (int)((n_comp + 0.5) / N_REP));
srch_ptr_free(&p_a);
}
```

To my disappointment, it printed out a very high average number of comparisons: 8789. Several times higher than the best results of the Shell sort. But this result teaches us something: if you pick the first algorithm that does the job (as I did with the bubble sort long ago), you risk wasting resources. It always pays to check out a few options before settling on one.

Quicksort

Quicksort is binary and recursive: choose a *pivot* element; move the elements less than the pivot before the pivot and those greater than the pivot after the pivot; repeat the same process on the two sides of the pivot; keep going until the sides contain single elements, by which time you are done.

But it is easier said than done. First of all, how do you choose the initial pivot element and the pivots of the smaller portions of the array? And also, in most cases, you will need to accommodate more elements on one of the two sides of the pivot; what do you do then? And finally, in which order do you compare the elements with the pivot? Actually, does it matter at all?

Let's start with a simple and easy example to familiarize ourselves with the idea. Suppose that your initial, unsorted array, is like this:

```
index:  0  1  2  3  4  5  6
key:    A  E  G  D  F  B  C
```

To make it simple, let's assume that, with a stroke of luck (!), you choose the middle element as the pivot. That the middle element is also the median element (i.e., the element with equal numbers of lesser and greater elements) is unlikely, but for this first example, I want to keep things as simple as possible.

Starting from the beginning of the array, you look for an element whose key is greater than the pivot's. This is E, in position 1. Similarly, starting from the end of the array, you look for a key that is less than the pivot's. This is C, in position 6. Once you have both, you swap them, and the array becomes as follows:

```
index:  0  1  2  3  4  5  6
key:    A  C  G  D  F  B  E
```

You keep going and discover that G in position 2 is greater than the pivot, while B, in position 5 is less. You swap them and end up with the array

```
index:  0  1  2  3  4  5  6
key:    A  C  B  D  F  G  E
```

When you reach the pivot from both sides, you know that all the elements with lesser keys are on its left and all elements with greater keys are on its right. Then, you split the array in two and repeat the pivoting and swapping on the two halves:

```
index:  0  1  2  3  4  5  6
key:    A  C  B  D  F  G  E
```

Element 3, which contains D, is in bold to highlight that it is in its final position. It couldn't be otherwise because we know that its key is greater than those of the elements on its left and less than those of the elements on its right.

Looking at the first half, you choose the middle element (C, in position 1) as the pivot. This time, scanning the elements from the beginning of the array section, you reach the pivot without finding any key that exceeds C. But when you scan the array section from the right, you find that B is less than C and should be moved to the left of the pivot. Unfortunately, there is nothing to swap it with. Therefore, you shift the pivot and all following elements to the right to make space for B.

You have the same problem with the section on the right side of the initial pivot. This time, after choosing once more the middle element as the pivot (i.e., G in position 5), you find that E should go to the left of G, but there is no element preceding G that you can swap it with. To resolve the issue, you make space for E by shifting to the right the pivot and all elements on its right (in this case, none).

After doing the partitioning on the two sides of the initial pivot, you have the following array:

```
index:  0  1  2  3  4  5  6
key:    A  B  C  D  F  E  G
```

The pivots of the two sides (C and G) are highlighted in bold to indicate that they are in their final places.

You know what's going to happen next. You apply the partitioning to left and right sides of C and G. In the example, there are no elements to be partitioned on the right of either C or G.

To do the remaining partitioning, you choose A and F as pivots, discover that nothing needs to be moved around A and that E is to be moved to the left of F. Once you move E, you are done.

Listing 9-8 shows the sort_quick() function.

Listing 9-8. sort_quick()

```
//---------------------------------------------------------------- sort_quick
void sort_quick(void **ar, int (*cmp)(void *, void *)) {
  int n = *((int *)ar - 1);
  if (n <= 1) return;                                              //-->
  quick_step(ar, cmp, 0, n - 1);
  } // sort_quick
```

All sort_quick() does is check that the array contains at least two elements and invoke quick_step(), where you do the actual work (see Listing 9-9).

Listing 9-9. quick_step()

```
//---------------------------------------------------------------- quick_step
void quick_step(void **ar, int (*cmp)(void *, void *), int k1, int k2) {
  int k_pivot = partition(ar, cmp, k1, k2);
  if (k_pivot - 1 - k1 > 0) quick_step(ar, cmp, k1, k_pivot - 1);
  if (k2 - k_pivot - 1 > 0) quick_step(ar, cmp, k_pivot + 1, k2);
  } // quick_step
```

As it turns out, also quick_step() doesn't do much processing: it invokes partition() to determine a pivot elements and split the array around it. As partition() moves the elements with keys less than the pivot's to the left of the pivot and the other elements on its right, all quick_step() needs to do is call itself recursively on the two sections of the array. But note that quick_step() makes the recursive calls only for array sections that contain at least two elements.

Time to look at partition(), shown in Listing 9-10, which does the brunt of the sorting work.

Listing 9-10. partition()

```
1.  //----------------------------------------------------------------------- partition
2.  // Returns the position of the pivot.  Only works with unique keys.
3.  int partition(void **ar, int (*cmp)(void *, void *), int k1, int k2) {
4.     int k_pivot = (k1 + k2) >> 1;
5.     void *pivot = ar[k_pivot];
6.     int j1 = k1 - 1;
7.     int j2 = k2 + 1;
8.     int i1;
9.     int i2;
10.    int swaps;
11.    void *tmp;
12.    do {
13.      swaps = 0;
14.      do { i1 = (*cmp)(pivot, ar[++j1]); } while (i1 < 0);
15.      do { i2 = (*cmp)(pivot, ar[--j2]); } while (i2 > 0);
16.      if (i1 > 0) { // something before pivot?
17.        if (i2 < 0) { // something after pivot?  Do the swap.
18.          tmp = ar[j1];
19.          ar[j1] = ar[j2];
20.          ar[j2] = tmp;
21.          swaps = 1;
22.          } // if (i2 < 0..
23.        else { // nothing after the pivot? Move the pivot left.
24.          int kp = k_pivot;
25.          do {
26.            while (kp > k1 && i1 > 0) {
27.              kp--;
28.              i1 = (*cmp)(pivot, ar[kp]);
29.              if (i1 > 0) {
30.                ar[k_pivot] = ar[kp];
31.                ar[kp] = pivot;
32.                k_pivot = kp;
33.                }
34.              }
35.            if (kp > j1) {
36.              ar[k_pivot] = ar[j1];
37.              ar[j1] = ar[kp];
38.              ar[kp] = pivot;
39.              k_pivot = kp;
40.
41.              // There can still be elements between j1 and kp (both
42.              // excluded) with a key greater than that of the pivot.
43.              do { i1 = (*cmp)(pivot, ar[++j1]); } while (i1 < 0);
44.              }
45.            else {
46.              i1 = -100;
47.              }
48.            } while (kp > k1 && i1 > 0);
49.          } // if (i2 < 0.. else..
50.        } // if (i1 > 0..
```

```
51.     else { // nothing before the pivot.
52.       if (i2 < 0) { // something after pivot?  Move the pivot right.
53.         int kp = k_pivot;
54.         do {
55.           while (kp < k2 && i2 < 0) {
56.             kp++;
57.             i2 = (*cmp)(pivot, ar[kp]);
58.             if (i2 < 0) {
59.               ar[k_pivot] = ar[kp];
60.               ar[kp] = pivot;
61.               k_pivot = kp;
62.               }
63.             }
64.           if (kp < j2) {
65.             ar[k_pivot] = ar[j2];
66.             ar[j2] = ar[kp];
67.             ar[kp] = pivot;
68.             k_pivot = kp;
69.
70.             // There can still be elements between kp and j2 (both
71.             // excluded) with a key less than that of the pivot.
72.             do { i2 = (*cmp)(pivot, ar[--j2]); } while (i2 > 0);
73.             }
74.           else {
75.             i2 = 100;
76.             }
77.           } while (kp < k2 && i2 < 0);
78.         } // if (i2 < 0..
79.       } // if (i1 > 0.. else..
80.     } while (swaps);
81.   return k_pivot;
82.   } // partition
```

Yes. It's not simple. Let's go through the logic of the algorithm from the beginning.

In lines 4 to 11, you define most of the working variables you need: k_pivot is the position of the pivot in the array (the shift-right-one-bit is a fancy way to divide an integer by 2); pivot points to the actual element; j1 is the index you use to scan the array from the left (set to k1-1 because you increment it in line 14 before using it); j2 is the index you use to scan the array from the right (set to k2+1 because you decrement it in line 15 before using it); swaps is a flag to remember whether you find two elements to swap while you execute an array sweep; and tmp is a variable you use to swap array elements.

Everything happens within the big do loop that starts in line 12 and ends in line 80. You keep it going as long as you find pairs of elements that you can swap. That is, one element before the pivot with a key greater than the pivot's *and* another element after the pivot with a key less than the pivot's. To check for this condition, you scan the array from the left until j1 hits an element with a key not less than the pivot's (in line 14) and then you scan the array from the right until j2 hits an element with a key not greater than the pivot's (line 15).

In other words, when you are past the loops in lines 14 and 15, you know that the key of ar[j1] is either equal or greater than the pivot's, and the key of ar[j2] is either equal or less than the pivot's. This generates four possible cases, which you handle as follows:

A. i1 > 0 && i2 < 0: swaps ar[j1] and ar[j2]
B. i1 > 0 && i2 == 0: move the pivot left and ar[j1] to the right of it.

C. i1 == 0 && i2 < 0: move the pivot right and ar[j2] to the left of it.
D. i1 == 0 && i2 == 0: you are done => do nothing.

Case A is when both if statements in lines 16 and 17 succeed. Accordingly, in lines 18 to 20 you swap the two elements. You also set the flag swaps to true in line 21, so that the big do loop keeps looking for further swaps.

In any of the three remaining cases, you know that there cannot be any more swaps, because either you only have elements to be moved from the left of the pivot to its right (if i1 > 0) or from its right to its left (if i2 < 0), but not both. That is, you have to do the rest of the work in the current iteration of the big do loop without ever setting the variable swaps.

You handle case B in lines 24 to 48. Look at lines 24 and 26 to 34.

In line 24, you make a copy of the pivot's index and name it kp. As do loops are always executed at least once, ignore for the moment that you are entering a loop in line 25.

You know from the check in line 16 that i1 > 0 and, assuming that the pivot does not coincide with the first element of the array (which would mean that kp == k1), you enter the while loop that starts in line 26.

In line 27, you decrement kp, so that it points to the element immediately on the left of the pivot. Then, in line 28, you compare that element with the pivot. You can safely reuse the variable i1 because it has completed its job to take you to the code associated with the appropriate case (in this instance, case B).

In line 29, you check whether the element in position kp (i.e., immediately on the left of the pivot) has a key greater than the pivot's (i.e., whether i1 > 0). If that is the case, in lines 30 to 32 you swap the pivot with that element, thereby moving the pivot to the left.

The while loop in lines 26 to 34 keeps going until either you move the pivot so far left that it reaches the first position of the array (when kp == k1) or encounters an element with the key less than the pivot's (when i1 < 0). Note that i1 cannot be 0 because all keys in the array are unique.

In any case, when you reach line 35, j1 still points to the element you needed to move to the right of the pivot but couldn't because a swap was not possible, and kp points to the location on the left of the pivot, which contains an element with a key less than the pivot's (kp doesn't coincide with k_pivot because in the last iteration of the while loop, just before you exit it, the assignment made in line 32 is not executed).

In lines 36 to 38, you make a three-way swap: set the array element of the pivot to the element in j1 that needs to be moved to the right; set the j1 element to point to the element on the left of the pivot (which has a key less than the pivot's); and, finally, write the pivot's address one position to the left of where it was before the swap. And, obviously, in line 39, you update k_pivot.

So, after the three-way swap, kp and k_pivot point to the same location and j1 points to an element that is correctly located on the left of the pivot. But who's to say that among the elements between j1 and kp (both excluded), there are no additional elements that should be moved to the right of the pivot?

To handle the situation, you repeat in line 43 the statement of line 14. That is, you move j1 to the right as long as it points to nodes that have keys less than the pivot's. If, when you exit the tight loop in line 41, i1 is positive, it means that there is at least one element that should be moved to the right. As a result, the do condition in line 48 is satisfied and execution returns to line 26. Note that you don't need to go back to the beginning of the big do loop that starts in line 12 because you already know that there are no elements on the right of the pivot that could be used for a swap.

Now, it can happen that when you reach line 35, all the elements between j1 and the position the pivot was in when you executed line 26 had keys greater than the pivot's. In that case, kp equals j1 and you have already moved all those elements to the right of the pivot, including the element in j1. That is, you would have completed your partitioning. But you are not likely to exit the do loop of lines 25 to 48 because the while loop in lines 26 to 34 has left i1 set to either 0 or -1 and, at the same time, it is likely that kp > k1. Therefore, you can expect that the do condition in line 48 will still be satisfied and the loop will go through an additional iteration when you are actually done. This would have catastrophic consequences (read: a crash). The solution is to set i1 to a negative value if, when you reach line 35, kp <= j1.

Lines 53 to 77 handle case C. That is, they do for the elements on the right of the pivot what lines 24 to 48 do for the elements on the left.

To help you follow how the algorithm works its way through a real example, I sprinkled several printf() in the quicksort functions and executed the code shown in Listing 9-11.

Listing 9-11. Running Quicksort

```
#define N 10
srand(12);
n_comp = 0;
int i_a[N];
for (int k = 0; k < N; k++) i_a[k] = k;
void **p_a = srch_ptr_alloc(N, NULL);
fill_random(p_a, i_a);
Sort_list(p_a);
sort_quick(p_a, &cmp_i);
printf("Quicksort: %d\n", (int)((n_comp + 0.5) / N_REP));
srch_ptr_free(&p_a);
```

fill_random() is the local function shown in Listing 9-12 and Sort_list() is a macro defined in sort.h and shown in Listing 9-13. The output, shown in Listing 9-14, includes all types of operations—swap, move pivot to the left, move pivot to the right, and three-way swap.

Listing 9-12. fill_random()

```
//--------------------------------------------------------------- fill_random
void fill_random(void **ar, int *iar) {
  for (int k = 0; k < N; k++) ar[k] = NULL;
  for (int k = 0; k < N; k++) {
    unsigned int kk;
    do {
      kk = rand() % N;
      } while (ar[kk]);
    ar[kk] = iar + k;
    }
  *((int *)ar - 1) = N;
  } // fill_random
```

Listing 9-13. Sort_list()

```
#define Sort_list(ar) {                                      \
    int **a = (int **)ar;                                    \
    int n = ((int *)a)[-1];                                  \
    char fmt[5];                                             \
    sprintf(fmt, "%%%dd", (int)floor(log10(n - 1)) + 2);     \
    printf("%5d:", n);                                       \
    for (int k = 0; k < n; k++) printf(fmt, k);              \
    printf("\n     ");                                       \
    for (int k = 0; k < n; k++) printf(fmt, *a[k]);          \
    printf("\n");                                            \
    }
```

Notice how the string fmt is used to set the number of characters reserved for each printed number to the maximum number of digits that the number can have. That means the result is available in tabular form without using tabs and without wasting space when working with small arrays.

In order to use floor() and log10(), you need to include the standard header file math.h, but remember that the gcc linker doesn't automatically include the C mathematical library. With Linux, you will need to add to the linker m as option -l and /usr/lib/x86_64-linux-gnu/ as option -L. In Eclipse, you can do it by opening the project's properties and accessing the C/C++ Build > Settings > GCC C Linker > Libraries page.

Listing 9-14. Running Quicksort—The Output

```
1.     10: 0 1 2 3 4 5 6 7 8 9
2.         0 9 7 3 1 4 8 6 2 5
3.
4. quick_step: k1=0 k2=9
5. partition:
6.       k_pivot=4 pivot=1
7.       j1=1 (9) i1=1 j2=4 (1) i2=0
8.       move pivot (1) from 4 to 3:
9.     10: 0 1 2 3 4 5 6 7 8 9
10.        0 9 7 1 3 4 8 6 2 5
11.      move pivot (1) from 3 to 2:
12.    10: 0 1 2 3 4 5 6 7 8 9
13.        0 9 1 7 3 4 8 6 2 5
14.      move pivot (1) from 2 to 1:
15.    10: 0 1 2 3 4 5 6 7 8 9
16.        0 1 9 7 3 4 8 6 2 5
17.
18. quick_step: k1=2 k2=9
19. partition:
20.      k_pivot=5 pivot=4
21.      j1=2 (9) i1=1 j2=8 (2) i2=-1
22.      swap 2 and 8:
23.    10: 0 1 2 3 4 5 6 7 8 9
24.        0 1 2 7 3 4 8 6 9 5
25.      j1=3 (7) i1=1 j2=5 (4) i2=0
26.      three-way swap: 3 (7) to 5,4 (3) to 3, and pivot in 5 (4) to 4:
27.    10: 0 1 2 3 4 5 6 7 8 9
28.        0 1 2 3 4 7 8 6 9 5
29.
30. quick_step: k1=2 k2=3
31. partition:
32.      k_pivot=2 pivot=2
33.      j1=2 (2) i1=0 j2=2 (2) i2=0
34.
35. quick_step: k1=5 k2=9
36. partition:
37.      k_pivot=7 pivot=6
38.      j1=5 (7) i1=1 j2=9 (5) i2=-1
39.      swap 5 and 9:
40.    10: 0 1 2 3 4 5 6 7 8 9
41.        0 1 2 3 4 5 8 6 9 7
```

```
42.      j1=6 (8) i1=1 j2=7 (6) i2=0
43.      move pivot (6) from 7 to 6:
44.     10: 0 1 2 3 4 5 6 7 8 9
45.          0 1 2 3 4 5 6 8 9 7
46.
47. quick_step: k1=7 k2=9
48. partition:
49.      k_pivot=8 pivot=9
50.      j1=8 (9) i1=0 j2=9 (7) i2=-1
51.      move pivot (9) from 8 to 9:
52.     10: 0 1 2 3 4 5 6 7 8 9
53.          0 1 2 3 4 5 6 8 7 9
54.
55. quick_step: k1=7 k2=8
56. partition:
57.      k_pivot=7 pivot=8
58.      j1=7 (8) i1=0 j2=8 (7) i2=-1
59.      move pivot (8) from 7 to 8:
60.     10: 0 1 2 3 4 5 6 7 8 9
61.          0 1 2 3 4 5 6 7 8 9
62. Quicksort: 38
```

If you print `partition()` (Listing 9-10), you can follow how the algorithm works its way through the random array listed in line 2 of Listing 9-14, as it lists the updated array after every operation.

The source file `sort.c` associated with this chapter includes all `printf()`s use to produce Listing 9-14. But keep in mind that it logs the element keys by typecasting the elements to (`int *`), which works only if the array consists of pointers to `int` (as in these examples) or if, at the least, the key components of the element structures are `int`s placed at the very beginning of the structures.

It is now time to check how efficient quicksort is when compared to the best Shell-sort we came up with earlier in this chapter. To do so, you can execute the code shown in Listing 9-15.

Listing 9-15. Testing Quicksort

```
#define N 100
#define N_REP 100
srand(12);
n_comp = 0;
int i_a[N];
for (int k = 0; k < N; k++) i_a[k] = k;
void **p_a = srch_ptr_alloc(N, NULL);
for (int k_rep = 0; k_rep < N_REP; k_rep++) {
    fill_random(p_a, i_a);
    sort_quick(p_a, &cmp_i);
    }
printf("Quicksort: %d\n", (int)((n_comp + 0.5) / N_REP));
srch_ptr_free(&p_a);
```

It turns out that quicksort requires on average 795 comparisons for a 100-element array, which is a much better result than the Shell-sort, which required 1313 comparisons. It might be argued that this good result is achieved at the expense of using a more complex algorithm, with more `if`s and loops. But comparisons are expensive in terms of execution time because they involve the overhead of a callback function. Therefore, it makes some sense to count them as an indication of the algorithm's efficiency.

Incidentally, you don't need to pick as a pivot the middle element of an array. Indeed, traditionally, quicksort implementations choose as pivot the first or last elements. But choosing the middle element is likely to be a better choice. You can further improve the efficiency of the algorithm by choosing the median element of first, last, and middle array elements. To do so, you only need to insert after line 5 of partition() (Listing 9-10) the code shown in Listing 9-16.

Listing 9-16. sort_quick() Update

```
{
  if ((*cmp)(ar[k1], pivot) > 0) {
    if ((*cmp)(ar[k2], pivot) > 0) { // pivot has the largest key
      k_pivot = ((*cmp)(ar[k1], ar[k2]) > 0) ? k2 : k1;
      pivot = ar[k_pivot];
      }
    }
  else if ((*cmp)(pivot, ar[k2]) > 0) { // pivot has the smallest key
    k_pivot = ((*cmp)(ar[k1], ar[k2]) > 0) ? k1 : k2;
    pivot = ar[k_pivot];
    }
  }
```

As you execute it after the existing lines 4 and 5 of partition(), where you set the pivot to the middle element, you only need to change the pivot in four of the possible six ordering of the three values.

Incidentally, this addition was recommended by Sedgewick, whom you encountered earlier in this chapter. Anyhow, if you make this change, you increase the average number of comparisons for 100 elements from 795 to 831. But this is because the array is small, as the overhead of three additional comparisons for each invocation of partition() becomes less and less relevant when the number of elements in the array increases. Already with 1000 elements, the algorithm requires 12,461 comparisons without the added code and only 12,199 with the additional code.

Integer Arrays

Quicksort is so much better than the other algorithms, and having to sort arrays of numeric values is so common a task that I couldn't resist making a version of the three functions sort_quick(), quick_step(), and partition() for arrays of integers instead of arrays of pointers.

I could have left it for you as an exercise, but I wanted to do it anyway. Anyhow, after doing it, I asked myself: shouldn't it be possible to collapse the two cases B (i.e., move the pivot left) and C (i.e., move the pivot right) into a single piece of code? I found a way, and Listing 9-17 shows the resulting partition_int() function.

Listing 9-17. partition_int()

```
1. //--------------------------------------------------------------- partition_int
2. // Returns the position of the pivot.  Only works with unique keys.
3. int partition_int(int *a, int k1, int k2) {
4.    int k_pivot = (k1 + k2) >> 1;
5.    int pivot = a[k_pivot];
6.    int j1 = k1 - 1;
7.    int j2 = k2 + 1;
8.    int i1;
9.    int i2;
10.   int swaps;
```

```
11.    int tmp;
12.    do {
13.      swaps = 0;
14.      do { i1 = a[++j1] - pivot; } while (i1 < 0);
15.      do { i2 = a[--j2] - pivot; } while (i2 > 0);
16.      if (i1 > 0) { // something before pivot?
17.        if (i2 < 0) { // something after pivot?  Do the swap.
18.          tmp = a[j1];
19.          a[j1] = a[j2];
20.          a[j2] = tmp;
21.          swaps = 1;
22.          } // if (i2 < 0..
23.        else { // nothing after the pivot? Move the pivot left.
24.          Move_pivot_int(k1, i1, j1, -1);
25.          } // if (i2 < 0.. else..
26.        } // if (i1 > 0..
27.      else { // nothing before the pivot.
28.        if (i2 < 0) { // something after pivot?  Move the pivot right.
29.          Move_pivot_int(k2, i2, j2, 1);
30.          } // if (i2 < 0
31.        } // if (i1 > 0.. else..
32.      } while (swaps);
33.    return k_pivot;
34.    } // partition_int
```

It is much more compact than the original version shown in Listing 9-10. The two big blocks of code in lines 24 to 48 and 53 to 77 have become line 24 and line 29, respectively. Notice that the two new lines are macros, so that you don't introduce the overhead of calling functions. The Move_pivot_int() macro is shown in Listing 9-18.

Listing 9-18. Move_pivot_int()

```
1.  #define Move_pivot_int(kk, ii, jj, k_dir) {                 \
2.    int kp = k_pivot;                                         \
3.    do {                                                      \
4.      while (kp * k_dir < kk * k_dir && ii * k_dir < 0) {     \
5.        kp += k_dir;                                          \
6.        ii = a[kp] - pivot;                                   \
7.        if (ii * k_dir < 0) {                                 \
8.          a[k_pivot] = a[kp];                                 \
9.          a[kp] = pivot;                                      \
10.         k_pivot = kp;                                       \
11.         }                                                   \
12.       }                                                     \
13.     if (kp * k_dir < jj * k_dir) {                          \
14.       a[k_pivot] = a[jj];                                   \
15.       a[jj] = a[kp];                                        \
16.       a[kp] = pivot;                                        \
17.       k_pivot = kp;                                         \
18.       do {                                                  \
19.         jj -= k_dir;                                        \
20.         ii = a[jj] - pivot;                                 \
```

```
21.           } while (ii * k_dir > 0);                              \
22.        }                                                          \
23.     else {                                                        \
24.        ii = k_dir;                                                \
25.        }                                                          \
26.     } while (kp * k_dir < kk * k_dir && ii * k_dir < 0);          \
27.   }
```

As you can see, k_dir determines the direction in which you move the pivot, from left to right or from right to left, and also the "direction" of the if conditions. For example, when you are moving the pivot to the left in line 24 of the function, with jj set to j1 and k_dir set to -1, the condition in line 13 of the macro becomes:

(kp * -1 < j1 * -1)

or, removing the signs and inverting the direction of the comparison,

(kp > j1)

which is identical to the condition in line 35 of Listing 9-10 (and it well should be!).

Now, I don't know about you, but I actually prefer partition_int() (and, obviously, the original partition() shown in Listing 9-10) without the macro. It does contain duplicated code, but I find it easier to understand. Indeed, it would have been too arduous a task to write directly the partition function with the macro. I already expended quite a bit of effort without the macro not to get confused with all the indices.

In the source code for this chapter, you will find two versions of the partition function for integer: one without the macro named partition_int() and one with the macro named partition_int_macro().

To complete the handling of arrays of integers, you find sort_quick_int(), quick_step_int(), and Sort_list_int() in Listings 9-19, 9-20, and 9-21, respectively. If you compare them to the corresponding versions for arrays of pointers (Listings 9-8, 9-9, and 9-13), you will see that the differences are minimal and predictable.

Listing 9-19. sort_quick_int()

```
//-------------------------------------------------------------- sort_quick_int
void sort_quick_int(int *a) {
  int n = *(a - 1);
  if (n <= 1) return;                                      //-->
  quick_step_int(a, 0, n - 1);
  } // sort_quick_int
```

Listing 9-20. quick_step_int()

```
//-------------------------------------------------------------- quick_step_int
void quick_step_int(int *a, int k1, int k2) {
  int k_pivot = partition_int(a, k1, k2);
  if (k_pivot - 1 - k1 > 0) quick_step_int(a, k1, k_pivot - 1);
  if (k2 - k_pivot - 1 > 0) quick_step_int(a, k_pivot + 1, k2);
  } // quick_step_int
```

Listing 9-21. Sort_list_int()

```
#define Sort_list_int(a) {                              \
    int *aa = a;                                        \
    int n = ((int *)a)[-1];                             \
```

```
char fmt[5];                                           \
sprintf(fmt, "%%%dd", (int)floor(log10(n - 1)) + 2);   \
printf("%5d:", n);                                     \
for (int k = 0; k < n; k++) printf(fmt, k);            \
printf("\n      ");                                    \
for (int k = 0; k < n; k++) printf(fmt, aa[k]);        \
printf("\n");                                          \
}
```

If you really love the Move_pivot_int() macro, I leave it up to you to make a Move_pivot() for partition().

The Standard C Function

The standard C library (stdlib) includes a function that applies quicksort to an array of pointers:

```
void qsort(void *ar, size_t count, size_t size, int (*cmp)(void *, void *));
```

Does it look familiar? The only differences between qsort() and sort_quick() (Listing 9-8) are:

- qsort() has two additional parameters: the length of the array (count) and the size of the array elements (size). They are not needed in sort_quick() because you store the array length before the data in the dynamically allocated array, and all the arrays consist of pointers to void.

- The comparison function you use with qsort() returns 1 if the first argument is greater than the second, while the function used with sort_quick() does the opposite and returns 1 when the second argument is greater than the first. I should have used the same ordering of parameters to avoid any possible confusion. But it isn't really an important difference.

I still wanted to show you how quicksort works, secretly hoping that my function would perform better than the function in the standard library. This is the time to compare the two. Listing 9-22 shows the code I used in order to do it. I used sort_quick_int() (Listing 9-19) and switched off all logging by setting both SORT_DEBUG and SORT_LOG to 0 in sort.h. I could have compared qsort() with sort_quick(), which handles arrays of pointers, instead of with sort_quick_int(), which doesn't use a callback comparison function. But qsort() deals with arrays of objects like sort_quick_int(), rather than arrays of pointers to objects like sort_quick(), and only needs a callback function to be able to handle all sorts of numbers, rather than just integers.

Listing 9-22. Comparing qsort() and sort_quick_int()

```
#include <time.h>
#define USE_QSORT 0
#if USE_QSORT
#  define Sort(ar) qsort(ar, *((int *)ar - 1), sizeof(int), cmp_i_qsort)
#else
#  define Sort(ar) sort_quick_int(ar)
#  endif
#define N_REP 100000
  srand(12);
  double total = 0;
  int *a = srch_int_alloc(N, NULL);
```

```
for (int k_rep = 0; k_rep < N_REP; k_rep++) {
  fill_random_int(a);
  clock_t t0 = clock();
  Sort(a);
  clock_t t1 = clock();
  total += (double)(t1 - t0) / CLOCKS_PER_SEC * 1.E6;
  }
printf("clock: %3.0f us\n", total / N_REP);
srch_int_free(&a);
```

The plot in Figure 9-3 shows how many microseconds sort_quick_int() requires to sort arrays of increasing length versus the number of microseconds needed by qsort() to sort the same arrays. And they are exactly the same arrays, because pseudo-random sequences of numbers are reproducible. You need to execute the code in Listing 9-22 twice for each array length N: once with USE_QSORT set to 1 and once with USE_QSORT set to 0.

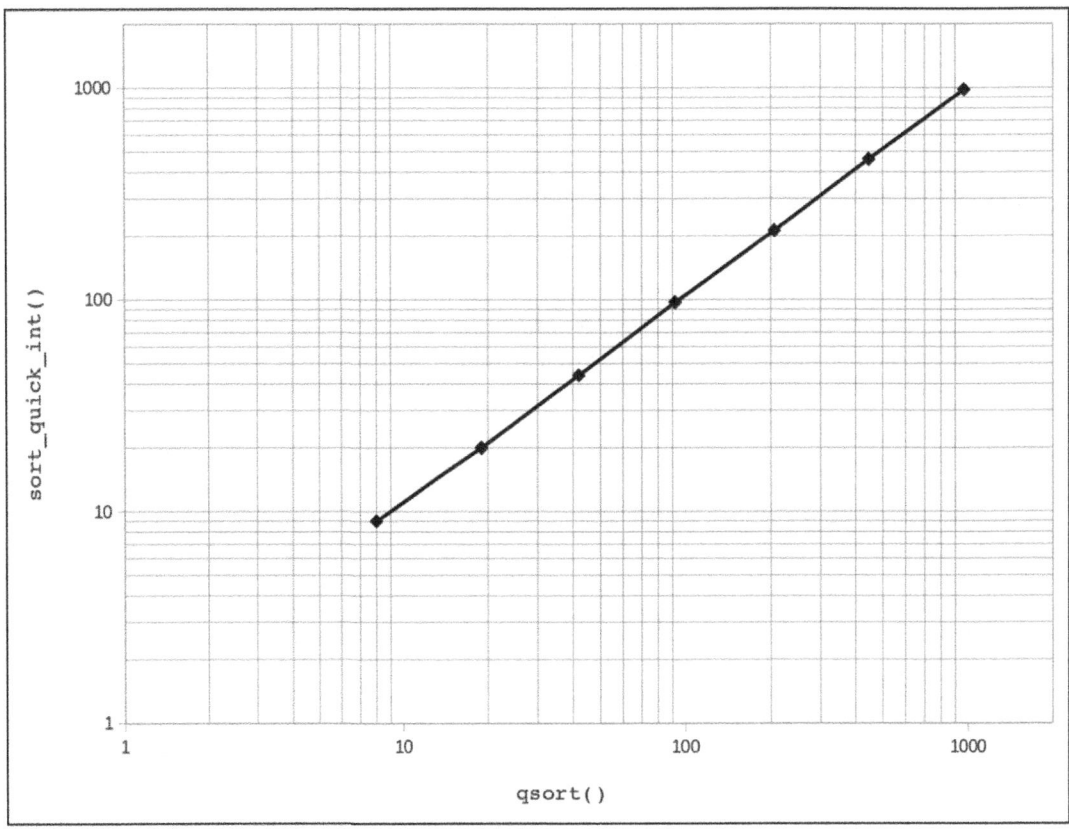

Figure 9-3. *Comparing qsort() and sort_quick_int()*

The function cmp_i_qsort() is almost identical to cmp_i(), as shown in Listing 9-5. The only difference is that the order of the parameters is reversed.

The plot is an almost perfect straight line at 45 degrees over a wide range, which means that the two functions provide almost identical results. Table 9-1 shows the actual time intervals in microseconds.

Table 9-1. *Comparing qsort() and sort_quick_int()*

N	qsort()	sort_quick_int()
100	8	9
200	19	20
400	42	44
800	92	97
1600	206	212
3200	446	460
6400	969	981

As you can see in Table 9-1, sort_quick_int() is slower than qsort(), but not by much. I am pretty satisfied with the result. To have a better idea of how the two functions compare, you can plot the difference of times in percent of the qsort() times as the array length increases. This plot is shown in Figure 9-4.

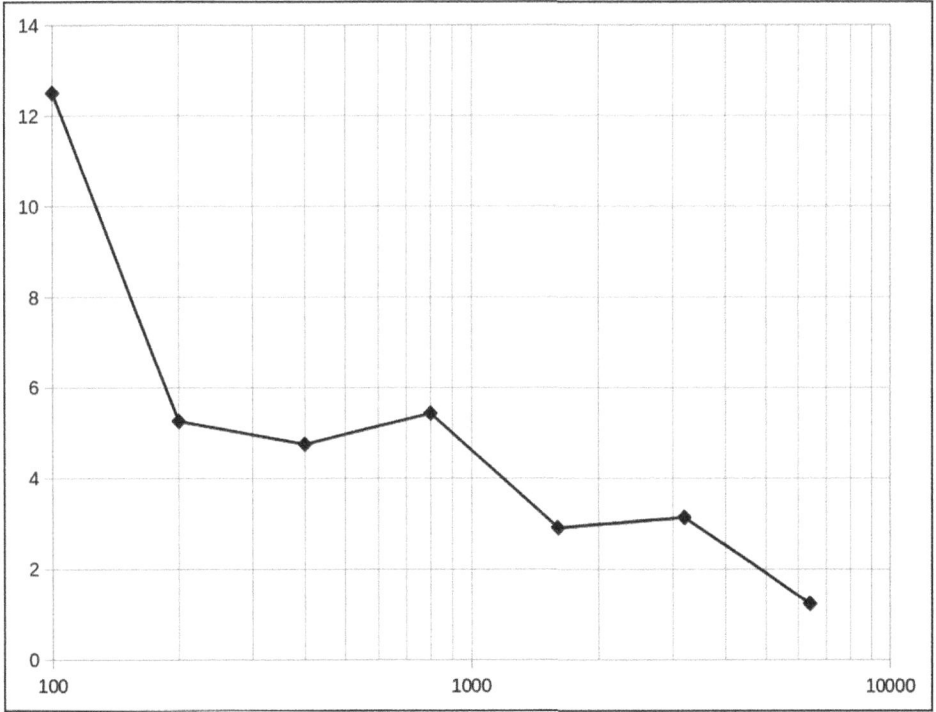

Figure 9-4. *Comparing qsort() and sort_quick_int() in terms of times differences*

273

With arrays of length 100, `sort_quick_int()` is 12.5% slower than `qsort()` but, as the number of elements increases, the percentage goes down to approximately 1.2%.

For fun, I increased the array size N to 100,000 and reduced N_REP to 2000 (to save time). It turns out that, for such big arrays, `sort_quick_int()` is 1.9% *better* than `qsort()`. We can definitely be happy with that!

Summary

In this chapter, you learned about all the common ways to sort arrays. You also saw how to measure their performance.

■ ■ ■

## CHAPTER 10

Numerical Integration

Numerical integration is the part of numerical analysis that studies how to calculate values of integrals. It is concerned with calculating definite integrals, like the example shown in Figure 10-1, rather than analytically resolve indefinite integral like that shown in Figure 10-2.

$$\int_0^1 3x^2\,dx = 1$$

Figure 10-1. *A definite integral*

$$\int 3x^2\,dx = x^3$$

Figure 10-2. *An indefinite integral*

In this chapter, you will learn how to estimate the value of definite integrals of functions in one and two independent variables. You will start with the integration of one-variable integrals with methods of increased accuracy.

Using the first part of this chapter as a basis, you will move onto integrating functions of more than one independent variable, with special attention to the two-variable cases.

Getting Started with One-Variable Functions

There are several methods to calculate integrals numerically. Some are only applicable to functions that you can calculate analytically, while others are also suitable for functions that you only have in tabular form. In general, any method for numerically approximating the value of a definite integral is called a *quadrature*.

When you have a function in analytical form, the goal of a quadrature is to attain a given level of precision in calculating its integral over the given interval while keeping the number of function evaluations as low as possible.

If you plot a function, the value of its definite integral over a given range is the size of the area below the curve. For example, Figure 10-3 shows in gray the integral of the plotted function over the interval 0-50.

© Giulio Zambon 2016
G. Zambon, *Practical C*, DOI 10.1007/978-1-4842-1769-6_10

If you imagine to cut off the hills of the curve to fill up the valleys, you can easily estimate that the area in gray is approximately half of the whole plot, which corresponds to 25. In reality, the gray area is a bit more than half: 25.78955371 ± 0.000000005.

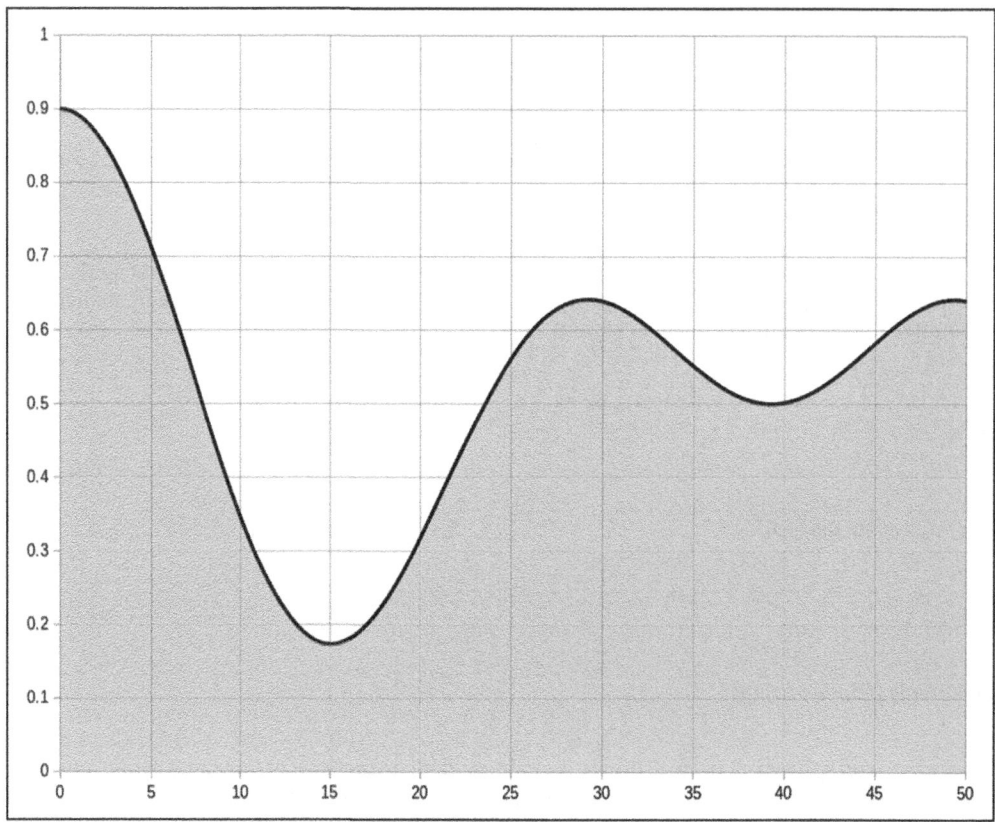

Figure 10-3. *A definite integral as the area under a curve*

When integrating functions you have in tabular form, all you have to work with is pairs of numbers, one for the variable x and one for the function $f(x)$, which you can represent in a plot as a series of points.

For example, if you have 11 values of the function shown in Figure 10-3 and assuming that they correspond to equally-spaced values of the variable, you obtain the plot of Figure 10-4.

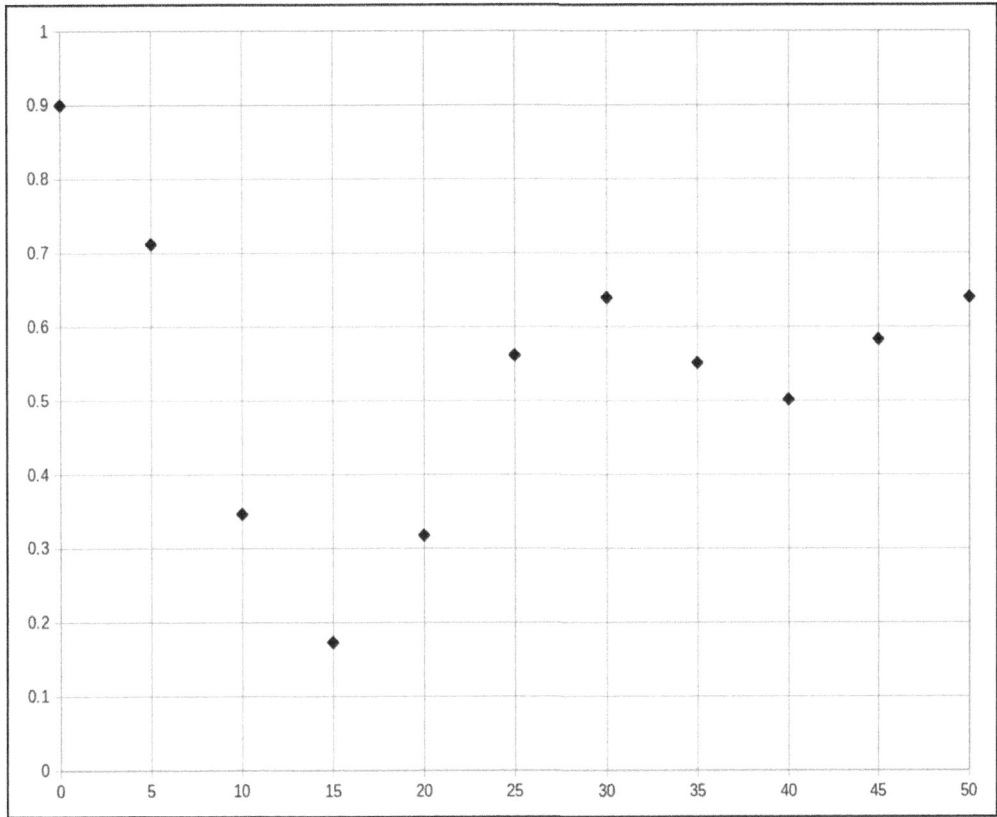

Figure 10-4. *Eleven points of a function*

You can estimate the integral of the function even *manually* by assuming that the function is a series of steps, as shown in Figure 10-5.

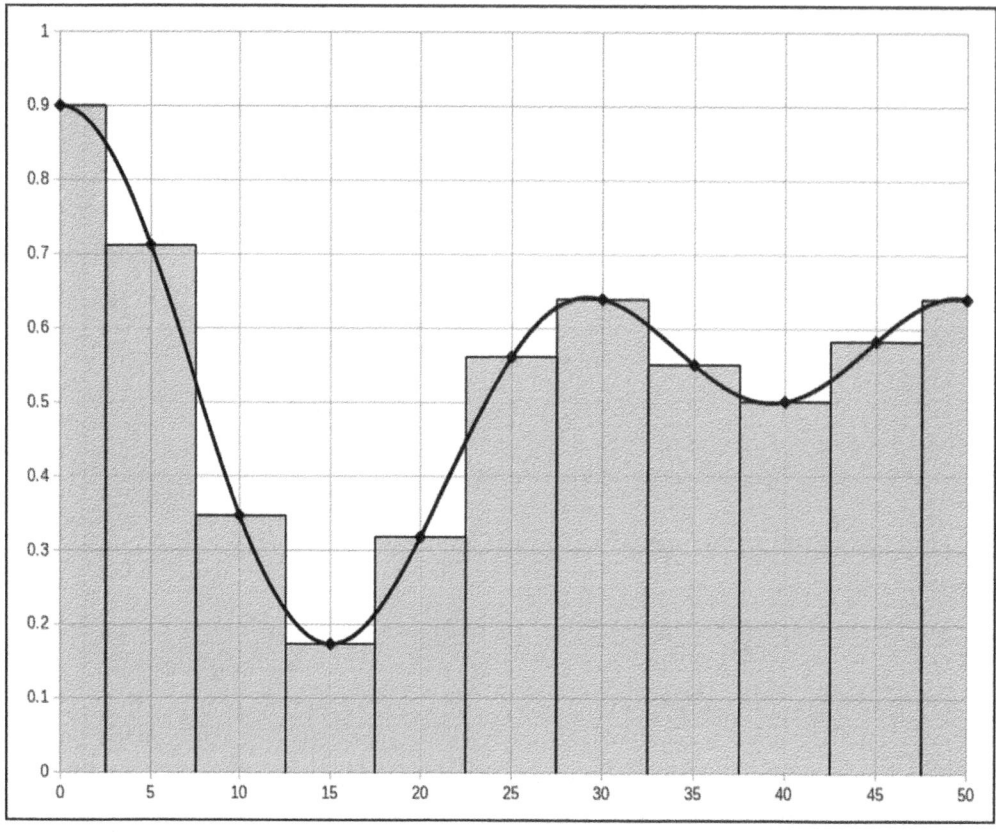

Figure 10-5. *Rectangular rule*

If you estimate the integral in this way, you obtain 25.77787292, only 0.045% below the correct value. Not bad!

The Trapezoidal Rule

The simplest quadrature rule that is actually widely used is one that replaces the rectangles with trapezoids, as shown in Figure 10-6. With this rule, you replace the horizontal segments centered on the points with straight segments that connect adjacent points.

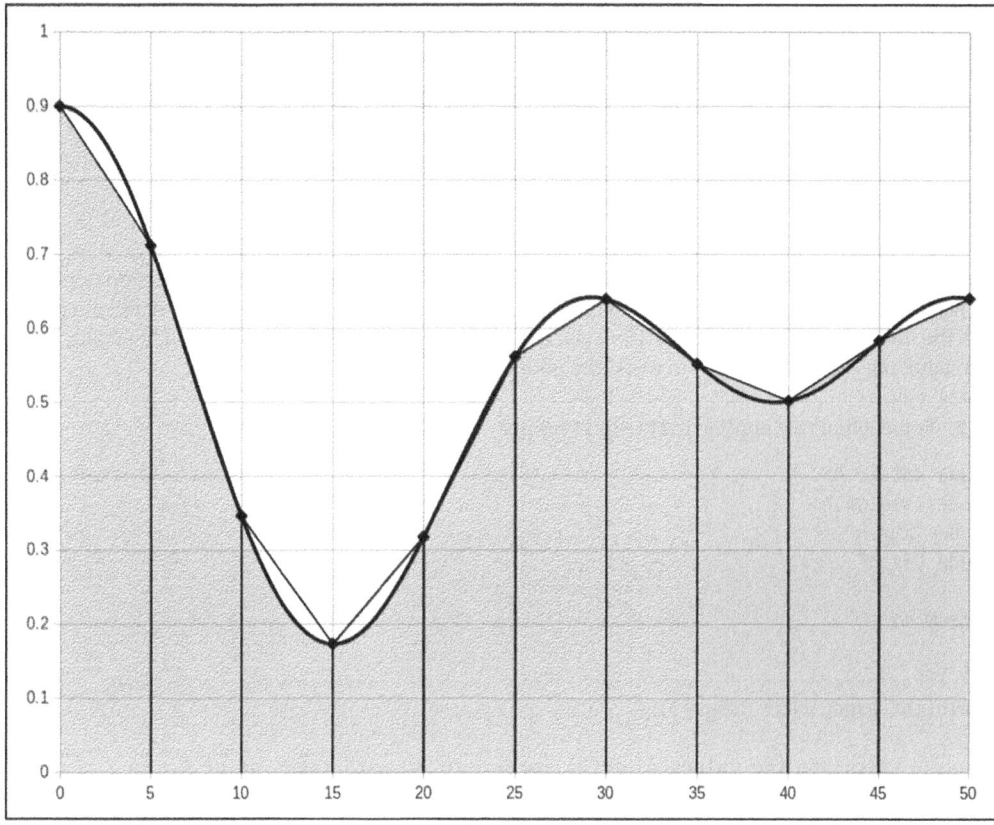

Figure 10-6. *Trapezoidal rule*

Listing 10-1 shows the itg_trapezoid_xy() function, which calculates an integral of a function in tabular form.

Listing 10-1. itg_trapezoid_xy()

```
1. //------------------------------------------------------------ itg_trapezoid_xy
2. // Returns true if successful.
3. int itg_trapezoid_xy(double *x, double *y, int n, double *res) {
4.    int ret = 0;
5.    if (!x) fprintf(stderr, "itg_trapezoid_xy: x-array address is NULL\n");
6.    else if (!y) fprintf(stderr, "itg_trapezoid_xy: y-array address is NULL\n");
7.    else if (n < 2) fprintf(stderr, "itg_trapezoid_xy: less than 2 points\n");
8.    else if (!res) fprintf(stderr, "itg_trapezoid_xy: result address is NULL\n");
9.    else {
10.     ret = 1;
```

```
11.    double val = 0;
12.    for (int k = 0; k < n - 1; k++) {
13.      val += (y[k + 1] + y[k]) * (x[k + 1] - x[k]);
14.      }
15.    *res = val * 0.5;
16.    }
17.  return ret;
18.  } // itg_trapezoid_xy
```

The arrays x and y contain the coordinates (x, f(x)) of the points that represent the function to be integrated; n is the number of points, and res_p is the address of a variable to store the value of the integral. To calculate the integral as shown in Figure 10-6, you can execute the simple program shown in Listing 10-2.

Note that for itg_trapezoid_xy() to work, the points must be in order of increasing x.

Listing 10-2. Trapezoidal rule applied to f1 with 11 points

```
1. #include <stdio.h>
2. #include <stdlib.h>
3. #include "itg.h"
4. #include "f1.h"
5.
6. #define N 11
7.
8. //------------------------------------------------------------------------ main
9. int main(int argc, char *argv[]) {
10.
11.   //------ Calculate the values of f1(x) for x = 0..50 with steps of of 5.
12.   double x[N] = {};
13.   double y[N] = {};
14.   for (int k = 0; k < N; k++) x[k] = k * 5;
15.   if (itg_fill(x, y, N, f1)) for (int k = 0; k < N; k++){
16.     printf("%4.1f %14.9f\n", x[k], y[k]);
17.     }
18.
19.   //------ Calculate the integral of f1(x) known in tabular form.
20.   double value;
21.   if (itg_trapezoid_xy(x, y, N, &value)) printf("%.8f\n", value);
22.
23.    return EXIT_SUCCESS;
24.   } // main
```

The program's output is as follows:

```
 0.0    0.900000000
 5.0    0.711812893
10.0    0.346681352
15.0    0.173169574
20.0    0.317840842
25.0    0.561305333
30.0    0.639170060
35.0    0.551255445
40.0    0.501699413
```

```
45.0    0.582804282
50.0    0.639670785
25.77787292
```

The last line of the output (printed in line 21 of the program) shows the value of the integral, which you already know from a couple of pages back.

The first 11 lines (printed in line 16 of the program) show the coordinate pairs of the points. To generate them, you use the itg_fill() function inside the if condition in line 15. See Listing 10-3 for its source.

Listing 10-3. itg_fill()

```
1.  //---------------------------------------------------------------- itg_fill
2.  // Returns true if successful.
3.  int itg_fill(Itg_coord_t *points, int n, double f(double)) {
4.    int ret = 0;
5.    if (!points) fprintf(stderr, "itg_fill: array address is NULL\n");
6.    else if (n < 2) fprintf(stderr, "itg_fill: less than 2 points\n");
7.    else if (!f) fprintf(stderr, "itg_fill: function is NULL\n");
8.    else {
9.      ret = 1;
10.     for (int k = 0; k < n; k++) {
11.       Itg_coord_t *point_p = &points[k];
12.       point_p->y = f(point_p->x);
13.       }
14.     }
15.   return ret;
16.   } // itg_fill
```

itg_fill() is a utility function that accepts an array of type Itg_coord_t with n elements and fills it with values of the given function f. As you can see in line 12 of Listing 10-3, it expects the x components of the points array to be initialized, and it uses them to calculate the corresponding ys.

The main program of Listing 10-2 initialized the xs in line 14.

The function f1, of which you calculate the integral and which is plotted in Figure 10-1, is as follows:

```
f1(x) = 0.2*cos(0.24*x) + 0.2*cos(0.16*x) + 0.5
```

In general, you will not necessarily apply the trapezoidal rule to functions of which you have the analytical form because, as you will see, you can use better rules. And f1 in particular is a function of which you can easily calculate the integral analytically, without using any numerical method. But to test the software and create good examples, it is better to use a function that you can analyze manually.

A word of warning concerning the building of the program with the gcc package. As it happens, the Math library, which you access by including math.h, is not linked to your program by default. The C compiler doesn't complain because it finds in math.h the definitions that it needs, but the linker fails with the error:

```
Failed to link with "undefined reference to 'cos'
```

The name of the Math library is libm.a. Therefore, the shell command locate libm.a will tell you where you find it. In Ubuntu 14.04, the library is in /usr/lib/x86_64-linux-gnu. To make the linker happy, you need to add the two options:

```
-lm -L/usr/lib/x86_64-linux-gnu
```

281

In Eclipse, you can add

m

to

```
C/C++ Build -> Settings -> GCC C Linker -> Libraries -> Libraries (-l)
```

and

```
/usr/lib/x_86_64-linux-gnu
```

to

```
C/C++ Build -> Settings -> GCC C Linker -> Libraries -> Library search path (-L)
```

Anyway, `itg_trapezoid_xy()` is really only suitable for functions that you know in tabular form, perhaps obtained through measurements. If you know the function analytically (as with `f1`), you should use the `itg_trapezoid()` function shown in Listing 10-4.

Listing 10-4. itg_trapezoid()

```
1.  //------------------------------------------------------------- itg_trapezoid
2.  // Returns true if successful.
3.  int itg_trapezoid(double f(double), double x0, double x1, int n, double *res) {
4.     int ret = 0;
5.     if (!f) fprintf(stderr, "itg_trapezoid: function is NULL\n");
6.     else if (x0 >= x1) fprintf(stderr, "itg_trapezoid: x-range non-positive\n");
7.     else if (n < 2) fprintf(stderr, "itg_trapezoid: less than 2 points\n");
8.     else if (!res) fprintf(stderr, "itg_trapezoid: result address is NULL\n");
9.     else {
10.       ret = 1;
11.       double h = (x1 - x0) / (n - 1);
12.       double val = 0;
13.       for (int k = 1; k < n - 1; k++) val += f(x0 + h * k);
14.       val += 0.5 * (f(x0) + f(x1));
15.       *res = val * h;
16.    }
17.    return ret;
18.  } // itg_trapezoid
```

The parameters `x0` and `x1` define the integration interval and `n` defines the number of points. Therefore, `h` is the height of the trapezoids. The area of each trapezoid can be calculated as:

```
0.5 * (fk + fk+1) * h
```

where `fk = f(x0 + h * k)`. When you add the areas of all trapezoids, you obtain:

```
0.5 * (f(x0) + 2*f1 + ... + 2*fn-2 + f(x1)) * h
```

and, by rearranging the expression as follows:

```
(f1 + ... + fn-2 + 0.5 * (f(x0) + f(x1))) * h
```

you obtain the calculation in lines 13 to 15 of Listing 10-4.

Not surprisingly, if you execute `itg_trapezoid()` with

```
itg_trapezoid(f1, 0, 50, 11, &value)
```

you obtain the same value calculated with `itg_trapezoid_xy()`.

Just for fun, here are the integrals calculated with `itg_trapezoid()` for increasing numbers of points:

```
   11  25.77787292
   20  25.78619208
   50  25.78904244
  100  25.78942827
  200  25.78952265
 1000  25.78955248
 2000  25.78955340
10000  25.78955370
15772  25.78955371
```

As the number of points increases, the value of the estimated integral approaches the value calculated analytically until, with 15,772 points, it matches the analytical value to eight decimals. Already with 100 points, the trapezoidal rule provides a result that is within 0.0005% of the analytical calculation. Figure 10-7 shows the trend in graphical form.

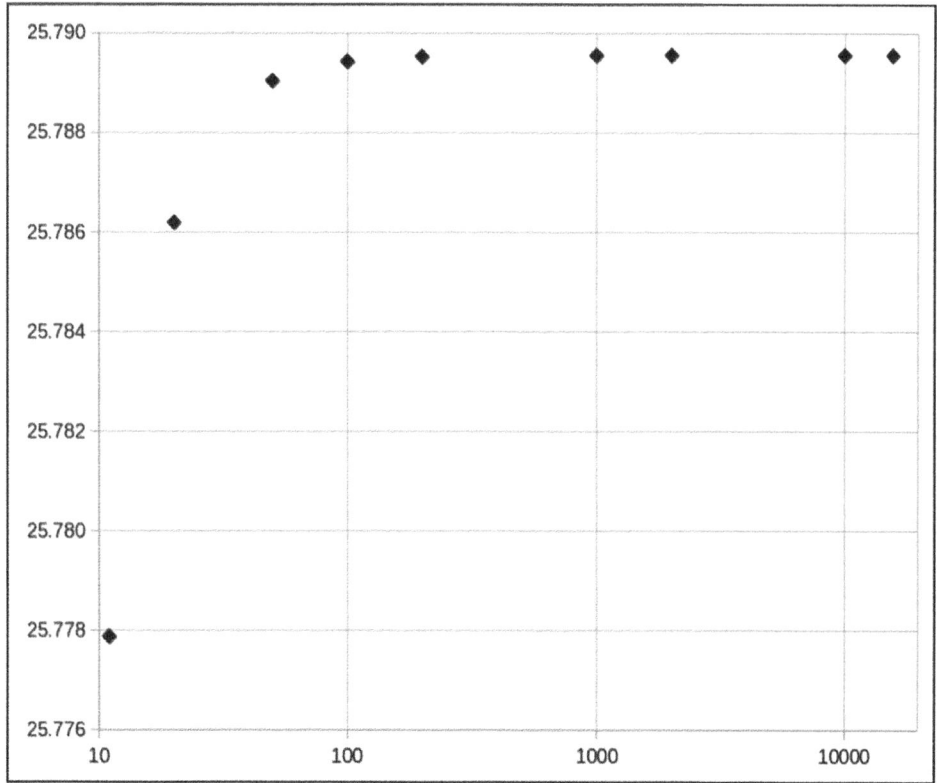

Figure 10-7. *Trapezoidal rule: accuracy versus number of points*

The Simpson's Rule

The Simpson's rule is similar to the trapezoidal rule but it replaces the straight line between two consecutive points with a parabola that passes through the two points and through the function calculated in the middle.

In more mathematically rigorous terms, with the trapezoidal rule, two consecutive points (x1, f(x1)) and (x2, f(x2)) were joined by a straight line of the type y = ax + b with equation:

y = (x - x1) * (f(x2) - f(x1)) / (x2 - x1) + f(x1)

while with the Simpson's rule, you impose the generic parabola y = a * x² + b * x + c to satisfy the following system of three linear equations in a, b, and c:

f(x1) = a * x1² + b * x1 + c
f(x2) = a * x2² + b * x2 + c
f((x1 + x2)/2) = a * ((x1 + x2)/2)² + b * (x1 + x2) / 2 + c

We are not going to go through the detailed (and tedious) transformations, but the end result is that the area between the two points x1 and x2 is estimated as:

(f(x1) + 4 * f((x1 + x2) / 2) + f(x2)) * (x2 - x1) / 6

You can then renumber the points and consider the expression to be applied to three consecutive points instead of two, with each pair of points being separated by a distance h that is half of the original (x2 - x1):

(f(x1) + 4 * f(x2) + f(x3)) * h / 3

If you add all the areas like you did for the trapezoidal rule, you find that the points that were originally the midpoints remain multiplied by four and the other intermediate points are duplicated, while the first and last points remain unchanged. All in all, with the Simpson's rule, you estimate the value of an integral over the interval x0 to xn as follows (for simplicity, I replaced f(xi) with fi):

(f0 + 4*f1 + 2*f2 + 4*f3 + … + 2*fn-2 + 4*fn-1 + fn) * h/3

But the formula is only valid for an odd number of points! That is, the maximum index n must be even (because the index starts with 0). I emphasize this issue because most implementations that you find on the Internet are wrong. They correctly state that, not considering the two endpoints, the terms with odd indices have a factor of 4 and those with even indices have a factor or 2, but they fail to impose the condition of n being even.

If you are not convinced that the condition is necessary, consider that before you renumber the terms, the Simpson's rule inserts a midpoint between each pair of existing points. Therefore, there must be one of those midpoints before the end point, which means that the second-to-last term must have a factor of 4 (because all and only the midpoints have a factor of 4). And regardless of whether the number of points N before inserting the midpoints was odd or even, when you add to it N-1 midpoints, you obtain an odd number.

That is, if you start with N points, after you insert the N-1 intermediate points, you end up with 2*N-1 points, which is odd by definition, not being divisible by 2. Therefore, the Simpson rule only applies when the total number of points is odd!

As so many web sites erroneously omit to mention that you can only apply the Simpson rule to an odd number of points, let's see a practical example. Let's use Simpson to estimate the integral of the function f(x) = x for x = 0 to 1. The function is a straight line and the exact value of the integral is 1/2.

We first use the Simpson rule with three points for x = 0, 1/2, and 1, and h = 1/2:

(f0 + 4*f1 + f2) * 1/3 = (0 + 4*1/2 + 1) * (1/2)/3 = 1/2

Not surprisingly, with such a simple function, the result is exact. But now let's apply the rule to four points (which is wrong because four is even), for x = 0, 1/3, 2/3, and 1, and h = 1/3.

```
(f0 + 4*f1 + 2*f2 + f3) * (1/3)/3 = (0 + 4*1/3 + 2*2/3 + 1) * (1/3)/3 = 11/27
```

Not good, is it? To show that the problem is due to applying the formula to an even number of points, let's also estimate the integral with five points, for x = 0, 1/4, 2/4, 3/4, and 1, and h = 1/4:

```
(f0 + 4*f1 + 2*f2 + 4*f3 +  f4) * (1/4)/3 = (0 + 4*1/4 + 2*2/4 + 4*3/4 + 1) * (1/4)/3 = 1/2
```

This confirms once more that not all apparently authoritative information you find on the Web is correct. Nothing beats a book that's been written, reviewed, and published by professionals (ahem…)!

Listing 10-5 shows the function itg_simpson(), which *correctly* implements the Simpson's rule.

Listing 10-5. itg_simpson()

```
 1. //------------------------------------------------------------- itg_simpson
 2. // Returns true if successful.
 3. int itg_simpson(double f(double), double x0, double x1, int n, double *res) {
 4.   int ret = 0;
 5.   if (!f) fprintf(stderr, "itg_simpson: function is NULL\n");
 6.   else if (x0 >= x1) fprintf(stderr, "itg_simpson: x-range non-positive\n");
 7.   else if (n < 2) fprintf(stderr, "itg_simpson: less than 2 points\n");
 8.   else if (n % 2 == 0) fprintf(stderr, "itg_simpson: n must be odd\n");
 9.   else if (!res) fprintf(stderr, "itg_simpson: result address is NULL\n");
10.   else {
11.     ret = 1;
12.     double h = (x1 - x0) / (n - 1);
13.     double val = 0;
14.     for (int k = 1; k < n - 3; k += 2) {
15.       val += (f(x0 + h * k) * 2 + f(x0 + h * (k + 1))) * 2;
16.       }
17.     val += f(x1 - h) * 4 + f(x0) + f(x1);
18.     *res = val * h / 3;
19.     }
20.   return ret;
21.   } // itg_simpson
```

When I first wrote itg_simpson(), the for loop was:

```
for (int k = 1; k < n - 1; k++) {
```

and it included a check for odd/even ks to decide whether to multiply the value of the function by 4 or by 2. But the repetition of the check n - 2 times was unsatisfactory. It seemed nicer to take the last term with an odd index (i.e., for k == n - 2) out of the loop. And then, obviously, f(x0 + h * (n - 2)) was replaced with f(x1 - h). In case you get confused with the indices, consider that f(x0 + h * (n - 1)) is another way of saying f(x1) because there are n points and you start indexing them from 0.

If you execute itg_simpson() with 11 points, the value it returns is 25.78640704, or about 0.012% below the actual value of 25.78955371 and better than with the trapezoidal rule (which was 0.045% off). This is not surprising, considering that you have "graduated" from linear to parabolic interpolation.

The Simpson's rule is better than the trapezoidal one in another respect: it matches all eight decimals of the analytically calculated result with only 265 points, while the trapezoidal rule needed 15,772 points.

The Newton-Cotes Formulas

The trapezoidal and Simpson's rules are particular cases of the Newton-Cotes quadrature formulas, which approximate with polynomials a function calculated at a sequence of regularly spaced intervals. The trapezoidal rule is called the Newton-Cotes two-point formula, while the Simpson's rule is called the three-point formula.

Here are the four formulas for 2 to 5 points:

```
2: h/2 * (f(x0) + f(x1))                                    -- trapezoidal rule
3: h/3 * (f(x0) + 4*f(x1) + f(x2))                          -- 1/3 Simpson's rule
4: h*3/8 * (f(x0) + 3*f(x1) + 3*f(x2) + f(x3))              -- 3/8 Simpson's rule
5: h*2/45 * (7*f(x0) + 32*f(x1) + 12*f(x2) + 32*f(x3) + 7*f(x4))  -- Boole's rule
```

As you saw, you can apply the two-point rule to a function calculated in any number of points.

For the three-point rule, each group contains three points, as shown in the following diagram, that list the multiplying factors of four groups and mark the group boundaries:

```
1 4 1 4 1 4 1 4 1
^   ^   ^   ^   ^
```

It means that you can only apply the 1/3 Simpson's rule to $2*g + 1$ points (where g is the number of groups), which confirms once more that you need an odd number of points.

The same diagram for Boole's rule looks like this:

```
7 32 12 32 7 32 12 32 7 32 12 32 7 32 12 32 7
^          ^          ^          ^          ^
```

It tells you that you can only apply the Boole's rule to $4*g + 1$ points. But while it is easy to remember that for the 1/3 Simpson's rule, you need an odd number of points, setting the correct number of points for the Boole's rule is a bit more annoying.

From an old IBM programmer's manual (Copyright 1967!), I got the idea of writing a function for the Boole's rule that could accept all numbers of points. The idea was simple enough: if you want to use, say, 24 points, apply the five-point rule to the first 21 and the four-point rule to the last 4. Similarly, with 23 points you apply the three-point rule to the last 3 points and with 22 points you apply the two-point rule to the last 2.

I did it, and the result is the function itg_quadr() that you see in Listing 10-6.

Listing 10-6. itg_quadr()

```
1. //---------------------------------------------------------------- itg_quadr
2. // Returns true if successful.
3. int itg_quadr(double f(double), double x0, double x1, int n, double *res) {
4.    int ret = 0;
5.    if (!f) fprintf(stderr, "itg_quadr: function is NULL\n");
6.    else if (x0 >= x1) fprintf(stderr, "itg_quadr: x-range non-positive\n");
7.    else if (n < 2) fprintf(stderr, "itg_quadr: less than 2 points\n");
8.    else if (!res) fprintf(stderr, "itg_quadr: result address is NULL\n");
9.    else {
10.      ret = 1;
11.      double h = (x1 - x0) / (n - 1);
12.      double val = 0;
13.      int n5 = (n - 1) / 4 * 4 + 1;
14.
15.      // Apply the 5-point rule.
```

```
16.        for (int k = 0; k < n5 - 1; k += 4) {
17.          val += 7 * (f(x0 + h * k)       + f(x0 + h * (k + 4)))
18.               + 32 * (f(x0 + h * (k + 1)) + f(x0 + h * (k + 3)))
19.               + 12 *  f(x0 + h * (k + 2))
20.               ;
21.          }
22.        val /= 22.5;
23.
24.        // Apply one of the simpler rules if there are further points.
25.        switch (n - n5) {
26.          case 3: // 4-point rule
27.            val += (f(x1 - 3 * h) +  3 * (f(x1 - 2 * h) + f(x1 - h)) + f(x1))
28.               * 0.375;
29.            break;
30.          case 2: // 3-point rule
31.            val += (f(x1 - 2 * h) + 4 * f(x1 - h) + f(x1)) / 3;
32.            break;
33.          case 1: // 2-point rule
34.            val += (f(x1 - h) + f(x1)) * 0.5;
35.            break;
36.          default:
37.            break; // this is the 0 case;
38.          }
39.
40.        // Complete the calculation.
41.        *res = val * h;
42.        }
43.    return ret;
44.    } // itg_quadr
```

In line 13, it calculates the number of points to which you can apply the Boole's rule. The difference n - n5 can only be 1, 2, or 3, because each additional group to which you can apply the Boole's rule requires four points.

Once you have applied the Boole's rule to the first n5 points, in line 25 you use a switch to decide which rule you can apply to the trailing points.

I was quite pleased with the function although, truth be told, I wasn't happy with always applying the "lesser" rules to the last points. It would be wrong to assume that the last points can "take" a rougher approximation.

Anyhow, you can forget itg_quadr(), because it doesn't work properly. You will find the function in the file itg.c, but I only describe it here to show how important it is to test your code thoroughly and how easy it is to take wrong turns (even IBM got it wrong!).

To understand why you shouldn't use itg_quadr(), have a look at Figure 10-8.

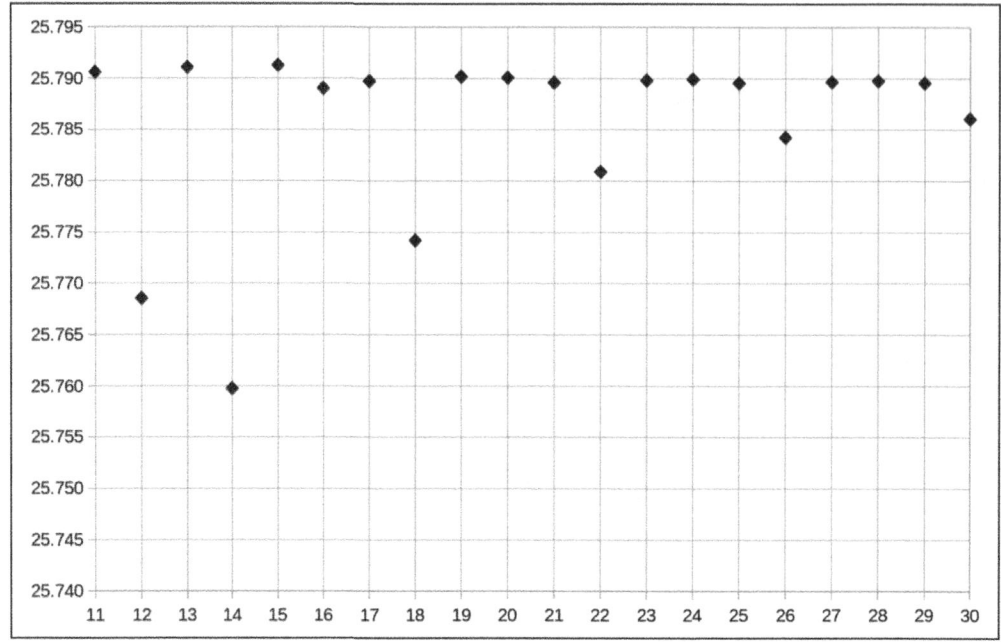

Figure 10-8. itg_quadr() *doesn't converge nicely*

It shows the value of the integral estimated with a number of points from 11 to 30. The estimates with 12, 14, 18, 22, 26, and 30 points are much worse than the others. Except for 12, they are all estimates made applying the two-point rule to the last two points. In practical terms, it means that the trapezoidal rule compromises the accuracy of the calculation.

After ditching itg_quadr(), I wrote itg_boole(), which you can see in Listing 10-7. It exclusively applies the Boole's rule and, if you set the number of points to an unsuitable value, it automatically reduces it. For example, if you set the number of points to 14, 15, or 16, it reduces it to 13.

Listing 10-7. itg_boole()

```
1.  //--------------------------------------------------------------------- itg_boole
2.  // Returns the number of points actually used if successful.
3.  int itg_boole(double f(double), double x0, double x1, int n, double *res) {
4.    int n5 = 0;
5.    if (!f) fprintf(stderr, "itg_boole: function is NULL\n");
6.    else if (x0 >= x1) fprintf(stderr, "itg_boole: x-range non-positive\n");
7.    else if (n < 5) fprintf(stderr, "itg_boole: less than 5 points\n");
8.    else if (!res) fprintf(stderr, "itg_boole: result address is NULL\n");
9.    else {
10.     n5 = (n - 1) / 4 * 4 + 1;
11.     double h = (x1 - x0) / (n5 - 1);
12.     double val = 0;
13.     double f_old = f(x0);
14.     double f_new = 0;
15.     for (int k = 0; k < n5 - 1; k += 4) {
16.       f_new = f(x0 + h * (k + 4));
17.       val += 7 * (f_old + f_new) + 12 * f(x0 + h * (k + 2))
```

```
18.              + 32 * (f(x0 + h * (k + 1)) + f(x0 + h * (k + 3)))
19.              ;
20.         f_old = f_new;
21.         }
22.       *res = val * h / 22.5;
23.       }
24.    return n5;
25.    } // itg_boole
```

The reduction takes place in line 10. Notice that the distance between two consecutive points calculated in line 11 is based on the reduced n5 rather than on the value you set via the parameter n.

The function returns the number of points actually used.

In itg_trapezoid() and itg_simpson(), you avoided double calculation of the function at the first and last points of each group by expanding the summation of the groups. In itg_boole(), you avoid the duplication by remembering in line 20 the value of the function calculated for the last point of a group in line 16, so that you can use the first function value of the following group.

The Boole's rule, by interpolating over five points, converges more rapidly than the rules you have seen in the previous sections: it matches all eight decimals of the analytically calculated result with only 89 points, while the Simpson's rule required 265 points, and the trapezoidal rule 15,772.

That notwithstanding, I have read somewhere that the Simpson's rule is the most widely used. It is simpler and, I suppose, rather than shop around for the best methods, many people simply use more points and rely on the speed of modern computers.

Deciding When to Stop

How do you know when the numerical calculation of an integral approaches the actual value well enough for your purposes?

As this is a practical book, do not expect an answer based on function variability and convergence of series. Instead, look at Listing 10-8.

Listing 10-8. itg_integr()

```
1. //----------------------------------------------------------------- itg_integr
2. // Returns the number of points used if successful.
3. int itg_integr(double f(double), double x0, double x1, double d, double *res) {
4.    int ng = 0;
5.    int n = 0;
6.    double old_res = 0;
7.    double new_res = 0;
8.    do {
9.       old_res = new_res;
10.      ng++;
11.      n = itg_boole(f, x0, x1, ng * 4 + 1, &new_res);
12.      } while (n && fabs((new_res - old_res) / new_res) > d);
13.    if (n) *res = new_res;
14.    return n;
15.    } // itg_integr
```

The only reason for keeping old_res is to compare it with new_res so that you can decide when to stop. If you execute the code shown in Listing 10-9, you obtain the output shown in Listing 10-10.

Listing 10-9. Executing itg_integr()

```
double value;
double delta = 0.1;
printf("# %-10s    n %-11s  %s\n", "req delta", "value", "err");
for (int k = 1; k < 9; k++) {
  int n5 = itg_integr(f1, 0, 50, delta, &value);
  if (n5) printf("%d%12.8f%4d%13.8f%12.8f\n", k, delta, n5, value,
      (value - 25.78955371) / 25.78955371);
  delta *= 0.1;
  }
```

Listing 10-10. Executing itg_integr()—Output

```
#  req delta    n  value        err
1  0.10000000  13  25.79106188  0.00005848
2  0.01000000  13  25.79106188  0.00005848
3  0.00100000  17  25.78974058  0.00000725
4  0.00010000  17  25.78974058  0.00000725
5  0.00001000  21  25.78959603  0.00000164
6  0.00000100  29  25.78955870  0.00000019
7  0.00000010  37  25.78955476  0.00000004
8  0.00000001  45  25.78955402  0.00000001
```

The calculation, using the Boole's rule, converges rapidly, at least with the well-behaved function f1 shown in Figure 10-3.

Initially, instead of adding one four-point group with each iteration (see line 10 of Listing 10-9), itg_integr() doubled the number of groups. The code of Listing 10-9 then produced the following output:

```
#  req delta     n  value        err
1  0.10000000   17  25.78974058  0.00000725
2  0.01000000   17  25.78974058  0.00000725
3  0.00100000   33  25.78955589  0.00000008
4  0.00010000   33  25.78955589  0.00000008
5  0.00001000   33  25.78955589  0.00000008
6  0.00000100   65  25.78955374  0.00000000
7  0.00000010   65  25.78955374  0.00000000
8  0.00000001  129  25.78955371  0.00000000
```

It seemed an overkill, and I changed the way itg_integr() increments the number of groups. But it is worth considering that to produce the bottom line of Listing 10-10 (line 8, with 45 points), itg_integr() goes through the iterations with 5, 9, 13, 17, 21, 25, 29, 33, 37, 41, and 45 points, having therefore to calculate f1 275 times. By comparison, if you double the number of groups with every iteration, you only need to calculate f1 5 (for 1 group) + 9 (2 gr.) + 17 (4 gr.) + 33 (8 gr.) + 65 (16 gr.) + 129 (32 gr.) = 258 times.

If you double the number of groups, it means that half the points of each new iteration are identical to the total number of points of the previous one. This is so because, by doubling the number of groups, you halve the distance between two adjacent points. For example, when you double the number of groups from 4 to 8, you increase the number of points from 17 to 33 and h (as we have consistently called the distance between two consecutive points along the X-axis) goes from 50/16 to 50/32.

This means that, if you find a way of remembering the values of f1 across iterations, you never need to recalculate a point, thereby reducing the 258 calculations to 129. This is easier said than done, because the values of f1 are calculated within itg_boole() (in lines 13 and 16 to 18 of Listing 10-7) and immediately used for calculating the terms of the Boole's rule.

To solve the issue without excessively penalizing the efficiency of itg_boole() you can break the problem into two parts: extracting the values of f1 from itg_boole() and feeding them back to it. Keeping the values within itg_boole() with static arrays is out of discussion, because the number of points is only known at runtime and, if possible, the function should remain re-entrant. That is, the use of static or global variables is out.

Instead, you can do it by passing to itg_boole() an array into which the function can write the values of f1 in one iteration and read them back in the next. The modified version of itg_boole() is shown in Listing 10-11 (the original version of the function is shown in Listing 10-7).

Listing 10-11. itg_boole()—Final Version

```
1.  //------------------------------------------------------------------- itg_boole
2.  // Returns the number of points actually used if successful.
3.  int itg_boole(double f(double), double x0, double x1, int n, double *res,
4.      double *fv) {
5.    int n5 = 0;
6.    if (!f) fprintf(stderr, "itg_boole: function is NULL\n");
7.    else if (x0 >= x1) fprintf(stderr, "itg_boole: x-range non-positive\n");
8.    else if (n < 5) fprintf(stderr, "itg_boole: less than 5 points\n");
9.    else if (!res) fprintf(stderr, "itg_boole: result address is NULL\n");
10.   else {
11.     n5 = (n - 1) / 4 * 4 + 1;
12.     double h = (x1 - x0) / (n5 - 1);
13.     double val = 0;
14.     double ff[5] = {};
15.     if (fv) ff[0] = fv[0];
16.     else ff[0] = f(x0);
17.     for (int k = 0; k < n5 - 1; k += 4) {
18.       ff[1] = f(x0 + h * (k + 1));
19.       ff[3] = f(x0 + h * (k + 3));
20.       if (fv) {
21.         fv[k + 1] = ff[1];
22.         fv[k + 3] = ff[3];
23.         ff[2] = fv[k + 2];
24.         ff[4] = fv[k + 4];
25.       }
26.       else {
27.         ff[2] = f(x0 + h * (k + 2));
28.         ff[4] = f(x0 + h * (k + 4));
29.       }
30.       val += 7 * (ff[0] + ff[4]) + 12 * ff[2] + 32 * (ff[1] + ff[3]);
31.       ff[0] = ff[4];
32.     }
33.     *res = val * h / 22.5;
34.   }
35.   return n5;
36. } // itg_boole
```

The new input/output array is fv (fv for function's values). The first 12 lines of the original version remain unchanged (although the lines became 13 because the addition of a new parameter caused the function definition to spill into an additional line). But f_old and f_new have been replaced with the array ff that holds all the points of a group. The element ff[0] corresponds to f_old and ff[4] to f_new, so that line 20 of Listing 10-7 (f_old = f_new) has now become ff[0] = ff[4] in line 31 of Listing 10-11.

The first time you encounter fv is in line 15, where you use its first element to set the value of the first point. Note that if fv is null itg_boole() becomes functionally identical to how it was before.

Within the loop that starts in line 17 (was line 15 in the old version), the even points (i.e., with odd indices because the index starts from 0) are always calculated (lines 18 and 19), while the odd points are retrieved from fv (lines 23 and 24), but only if fv is not null. Otherwise, they are calculated lines 27 and 28. If fv exists, the even points are saved into it (in lines 21 and 22).

The calculation of the summation term that corresponds to the current group (line 30) is more compact than the same calculation in the old version (lines 17 to 19), but it's functionally identical.

To execute itg_boole() on its own, you only need to set the new parameter to NULL. But to take advantage of the optimization, you cannot use the function itg_integr() of Listing 10-8. Use instead the new function itg_opt() shown in Listing 10-12.

Listing 10-12. itg_opt()

```
1.  //------------------------------------------------------------------ itg_opt
2.  // Returns the number of points used if successful.
3.  int itg_opt(double f(double), double x0, double x1, double d, double *res) {
4.    int n = 5;
5.    DAR_setup;
6.    int ng = 1;
7.    double old_res = 0;
8.    double new_res = 0;
9.    double *fv = DAR_new(new_res, n);
10.   double h = (x1 - x0) / (n - 1);
11.   for (int k = 0; k < n; k++) fv[k] = f(x0 + h * k);
12.   do {
13.     old_res = new_res;
14.     ng += ng;
15.     n = ng * 4 + 1;
16.     DAR_extend(fv, n);
17.     for (int k = n - 1; k > 1; k -= 2) {
18.       int k0 = k / 2;
19.       fv[k] = fv[k0];
20.       fv[k0] = 0;
21.     }
22.     n = itg_boole(f, x0, x1, n, &new_res, fv);
23.   } while (n && fabs((new_res - old_res) / new_res) > d && ng < 16384);
24.   if (n) *res = new_res;
25.   DAR_dismantle;
26.   return n;
27. } // itg_opt
```

itg_opt() uses the DAR package described in Chapter 7 to create the fv arrays. Line 11 fills in the first fv array (of length 5) to hold the initial group. Before each execution of itg_boole(), the macro DAR_extend() in line 16 doubles the length of fv, and the for loop in lines 17 to 21 spreads the values already stored in fv to occupy the whole array. Line 20 is useless, because itg_boole() only uses the odd elements of fv and ignores the content of the even elements. Feel free to remove it, but it seems neater to clean up the unused spaces of fv before entering itg_boole(). Over the years, I found that being neat, even at a cost of a minor additional overhead, often pays in the long run.

Notice that in line 23 I have introduced an upper limit of 16,384 to the number of groups. It is an arbitrary number that corresponds to 14 doublings. You could pass to `itg_opt()` as an additional parameter, but I didn't bother. Its purpose is mainly to avoid looping until you reach so many points that DAR fails to allocate the dynamic array. It happened to me when trying to integrate a divergent function (see the next section about singularities):

```
DAR error "dar_new: Failed to allocate 4294967344 bytes" (file ../src/dar.c; line 86)
```

When considering the 40 bytes needed for the DAR structure, it means that it tried to allocate space for 536,870,913 points, corresponding to 134,217,728 groups. Plenty of scope to increase the limit...

Singularities

As long as the function you integrate is sufficiently smooth, `itg_opt()` can calculate the integral of the function over a given interval as precisely as you need.

But what if you want to integrate a function that, for example, behaves like $1 / x^e$ over the interval $(0, 1)$ with $e > 0$?

For example, the integral of x^{-2} is $-1/x$. Whenever you attempt to calculate $f(0)$, you obtain INFINITY, which is a value defined in `math.h` that was introduced with C99. As a result, any integral calculated with that function over an interval that contains 0 is also INFINITY.

INFINITY indicates a singularity in the function. That is, a point (i.e., a value of the independent variable) for which the function is undefined. The name INFINITY is derived from the fact that, if you calculate the function for points closer and closer to the singularity, the value of the function becomes larger and larger. For example, if you calculate x^{-2} for $x = 1, 0.5, 0.2$, and 0.1, you obtain 1, 4, 25, and 100.

Another example of a common function that has a singularity is the tangent, for which C provides the standard Math function `tan()`. It diverges for 90 degrees, with the added complication that it is positive when you approach the singularity from the left (i.e., with increasing angles smaller than 90 degrees) and negative when you approach it from the right (i.e., with decreasing angles greater than 90 degrees).

To deal with a point of singularity like 0 for x^{-2}, you can set the value of the function to 0, as in:

```
double f2(double x) {
  double ret = 1/(x*x);
  return (ret == INFINITY) ? 0 : ret;
  }
```

That is, you replace the singularity with a 0. Unfortunately, that doesn't mean that you only need more points to calculate the integral of the "deformed" function because there is another problem: the area beneath a function that becomes infinite can also be infinite. It happens when the function close to its singularity behaves like x^{-e}, with e equal to or larger than 1. It means that, for example, if you want to calculate the integral of $x^{-0.1}$, you can. The function

```
double f2(double x) {
  double ret = exp(-0.1*log(x));
  return (ret == INFINITY) ? 0 : ret;
  }
```

when executed with

```
delta = 0.1;
printf("# %-10s       n %s\n", "req delta", "value");
```

```
for (int k = 1; k < 9; k++) {
  int n5 = itg_opt(f2, 0, 1, delta, &value);
  if (n5) printf("%d%12.8f%10d%12.8f\n", k, delta, n5, value);
  delta *= 0.1;
  }
```

produces (after commenting out the 16,384 limit on the number of groups) the following output:

```
#  req delta           n   value
1  0.10000000         17   1.07777861
2  0.01000000         65   1.10153886
3  0.00100000       1025   1.11032170
4  0.00010000       8193   1.11098963
5  0.00001000     131073   1.11110109
6  0.00000100    2097153   1.11111028
7  0.00000010   16777217   1.11111098
8  0.00000001  268435457   1.11111110
```

Maximum and Minimum

Finding a maximum and finding a minimum are identical problems, as the maximum of $-f(x)$ is the minimum of $f(x)$.

There are several methods for finding the maximum of a function in a given interval. The simplest one is the straightforward one: calculate several points of the function and pick the x with the highest value of $f(x)$. This method is obviously far from being foolproof because you might calculate the function left and right of a high peak and miss it.

But it works without any problem for reasonably well behaved functions. For example, with the function of Figure 10-3. For functions with singularities, if you use the trick of replacing INFINITY with 0 and you get 0 as either a minimum or a maximum, you have to ensure that it is not due to the "fictitious" zeros you have introduced.

In any case, Listing 10-13 shows the function itg_minmax().

Listing 10-13. itg_minmax()

```
 1. //--------------------------------------------------------------- itg_minmax
 2. // Returns the number of points used.
 3. int itg_minmax(double f(double), double x0, double x1, double d, double *min,
 4.     double *max) {
 5.   int n = 0;
 6.   if (!f) fprintf(stderr, "itg_minmax: function is NULL\n");
 7.   else if (x0 >= x1) fprintf(stderr, "itg_minmax: x-range non-positive\n");
 8.   else if (!min) fprintf(stderr, "itg_minmax: min address is NULL\n");
 9.   else if (!max) fprintf(stderr, "itg_minmax: max address is NULL\n");
10.   else {
11.     int n_incr = 50;
12.     double old_min = 0;
13.     double new_min = f((x0 + x1) * 0.5);
14.     double old_max = 0;
15.     double new_max = new_min;
16.     double interval = x1 - x0;
17.     unsigned short int rand_stat[3] = {1, 11, 111};
18.     do {
```

```
19.        old_min = new_min;
20.        old_max = new_max;
21.        n += n_incr;
22.        for (int k = 0; k < n; k++) {
23.          double val = f(interval * erand48(rand_stat) + x0);
24.          if (val > new_max) new_max = val;
25.          if (val < new_min) new_min = val;
26.          }
27.        } while (fabs((new_min - old_min) / new_min) > d ||
28.                 fabs((new_max - old_max) / new_max) > d
29.                 );
30.      *min = new_min;
31.      *max = new_max;
32.      }
33.    return n;
34.    } // itg_minmax
```

The input parameters are the function to be analyzed, the interval (x0, x1), and the accuracy d you require. The remaining two parameters provide the addresses where the function stores the estimated minimum and maximum values.

itg_minmax() starts by assigning to both min and max the value of the function in the middle of the interval (lines 13 and 15). It could have been a point chosen at random, but it is not critical.

Line 17 initializes an array used by pseudo-random generators that conform to the SVID (AT&T's UNIX System V Interface Definition) format. These generators can provide floating-point numbers with 48 significant bits and, as SVID functions are required by the XPG (X/Open Portability Guide) standard, they are available in all modern UNIX-like systems. Different values start different pseudo-random sequences, but I didn't see the need for having the possibility to change them, for example by passing additional parameters to the function.

As a comparison with SVID random generators, the mechanism based on srand()/rand() widely used in C is only required to provide 32,767 random integers (16 bits), although the GNU C library actually provides 32 bits. To see the maximum random integer generated by rand(), you can print out the value of RAND_MAX, which is defined in stdlib.h.

Note that erand48() is enabled only if you compile your program with the gcc option -std=gnu99 instead of -std=c99. You can find a description of the SVID generators at www.gnu.org/software/libc/manual/html_node/SVID-Random.html#SVID-Random.

The do loop between lines 18 and 29 iterates until two consecutive estimates of both the minimum and the maximum are within the accuracy you have requested. Every time it iterates, it adds 50 points randomly distributed within the interval (line 23).

If you execute

```
double min = 0;
double max = 0;
printf("     n     minimum     maximum\n");
int n = itg_minmax(f1, 0, 50, 0.01, &min, &max);
printf("f1: %d%12.5f%12.5f\n", n, min, max);
n = itg_minmax(f2, 0, 50, 0.01, &min, &max);
printf("f2: %d%12.5f%12.5f\n", n, min, max);
```

you obtain:

```
       n     minimum     maximum
f1: 150     0.17317     0.89989
f2: 200     0.67625     1.24259
```

Monte Carlo

The whole area of the plot of Figure 10-3 is 50, while the area in gray, which is the value of the integral, is approximately 25.79. Imagine shooting many random bullets into the plot and counting those that hit the gray area. If you cover the area of the plot with bullet holes uniformly, it must be that the number of bullets that hit the gray area n_gray are approximately n_tot * 25.79 / 50, which in turn means that n_gray * 50 / n_tot is an estimate of the integral.

This method of estimating an integral is called Monte Carlo, perhaps named after the area of the Principality of Monaco that is full of casinos, where chance plays an essential role.

As you will see, this way of calculating an integral is very inefficient because it requires calculating the function heaps of times. But for functions with points of discontinuity, the methods based on interpolating the curve (e.g., the five-point Boole's rule) work very badly because polynomials cannot really approximate steps.

Anyway, let's take one step (pun intended!) at a time and go through Listing 10-14, which shows the itg_monte() function.

Listing 10-14. itg_monte()

```
1.  //--------------------------------------------------------------- itg_monte
2.  // Returns the number of points used.
3.  int itg_monte(double f(double), double x0, double x1, double d, double *res) {
4.     int n = 13;
5.     int n_incr = 111;
6.     int n_tot = 0;
7.     if (!f) fprintf(stderr, "itg_monte: function is NULL\n");
8.     else if (x0 >= x1) fprintf(stderr, "itg_monte: x-range non-positive\n");
9.     else if (!res) fprintf(stderr, "itg_monte: result address is NULL\n");
10.    else {
11.       double min = 0;
12.       double max = 0;
13.       (void)itg_minmax(f, x0, x1, 0.01, &min, &max);
14.       min -= 0.01 * fabs(min);
15.       max += 0.01 * fabs(max);
16.       double xx = x1 - x0;
17.       double yy = max - min;
18.       double area = xx * yy;
19.       double bottom = xx * min;
20.       double old_res = 0;
21.       double new_res = bottom + area * 0.5;
22.       int n_yes = 0;
23.       unsigned short int rand_stat[3] = {1, 456, 789};
24.       do {
25.          old_res = new_res;
26.          n += n_incr;
27.          double h = xx / n;
28.          for (int k = 0; k < n; k++) {
29.             double dk = k + erand48(rand_stat) - 0.5;
30.             if (dk < 0) dk = 0;
31.             else if (dk > n - 1) dk = n - 1;
32.             double x = x0 + dk * h;
33.             double y = yy * erand48(rand_stat) + min;
34.             double val = f(x);
35.             if (y <= val) n_yes++;
```

```
36.          if (val < min) printf("%.8f < %.8f at x=%.8f\n", val, min, x);
37.          if (val > max) printf("%.8f > %.8f at x=%.8f\n", val, max, x);
38.          }
39.        n_tot += n;
40.        new_res = bottom + n_yes * area / n_tot;
41.        } while (fabs((new_res - old_res) / new_res) > d);
42.      *res = new_res;
43.      }
44.    return n_tot;
45.    } // itg_monte
```

The itg_monte() parameters are identical to those of itg_opt() shown in Listing 10-12.

itg_monte() initially "shoots" n points (defined in line 4), and then keeps shooting additional n_incr points (defined in line 5) until two consecutive estimates are close enough to each other (i.e., within d).

I took n and n_incr out of my hat (a baseball cap, actually) and played with them to see how the function would change its behavior. The value of n cannot have a big impact on the result because, even if you set it to a value close to n_incr, it quickly becomes negligible compared to the total number of points as the number of iterations increases.

Lines 11 to 15 calculate the minimum and maximum of the function to be integrated with an accuracy of 1% and then add another 1% above and below it. This ensures that the range (min, max) captures all the values of the function within the interval (x0, x1).

area, calculated in line 18, is the area to which you want to shoot your random bullets, while bottom, calculated in line 19, is the area below f's minimum.

In line 21, you calculate the first, very rough, estimate of the integral as if the curve were a horizontal line mid-way between min and max.

In line 22, you initialize n_yes to 0 and never reset it after that.

After incrementing n by n_incr in line 26, you calculate the distance along the X-axis between n equally spaced points, and shoot the n bullets with the for loop of lines 28 to 38.

In lines 29 to 32 you choose a random x. To ensure that the random points are uniformly distributed within the interval (x0, x1) while still being random, you add the result of erand48(), which is always greater than 0 and less than 1, to the control variable k and then subtract 0.5. Then, by calculating x in line 32 with dk instead of k, you ensure that your bullets always cover the whole interval (x0, x1) but remain apart from each other along the X-axis at an average distance of h.

You calculate the Y-coordinates of your bullet in line 33 and the actual value of the function in line 34.

Then, all you need to do is increment n_yes by 1 if the bullet hits the gray area below the curve.

Lines 36 and 37 are a safeguard against having defined too a narrow range along the Y-axis, but I haven't seen them printed in any of my tests.

Finally, in line 40, you calculate a new estimate of the integral.

Unfortunately, if you execute

```
delta = 0.1;
value = 0;
printf("# %-10s        n %-11s  %s\n", "req delta", "value", "err");
for (int k = 1; k < 9; k++) {
  n = itg_monte(f1, 0, 50, delta, &value);
  printf("%d%12.8f%10d%13.8f%12.8f\n", k, delta, n, value,
      (value - 25.78955371) / 25.78955371);
  delta *= 0.1;
  }
```

you get the output shown in Listing 10-15.

Listing 10-15. itg_monte()—Output

```
# req delta           n  value       err
1 0.10000000        124  26.71086788  0.03572432
2 0.01000000       1730  26.02779943  0.00923807
3 0.00100000       6235  25.74562844 -0.00170322
4 0.00010000      10270  25.83419170  0.00173086
5 0.00001000     496837  25.80034568  0.00041846
6 0.00000100    2701270  25.78366279 -0.00022842
7 0.00000010    5669587  25.78655241 -0.00011638
8 0.00000001  207292974  25.78875854 -0.00003083
```

Do you see the problem? All results after the first two differ from the analytically calculated value of the integral (i.e., 25.78955371) by more than the required amount. That is, the value in the column err is in absolute value much larger than the corresponding value in the column req delta. It means that itg_monte() "believes" to have achieved the required accuracy but it hasn't.

The check in line 41 doesn't deliver the goods because the two consecutive estimates of the integral are close to each other despite the fact that neither is close enough to the actual value of the integral. Also notice that the error with 10,270 points is larger than with 6,235.

After lots of testing, trying to shed some light on the issue, I plotted the absolute values of the err columns versus the quantity checked against d in line 41 of itg_monte() for a required accuracy of 0.0000001.

The result is shown in Figure 10-9.

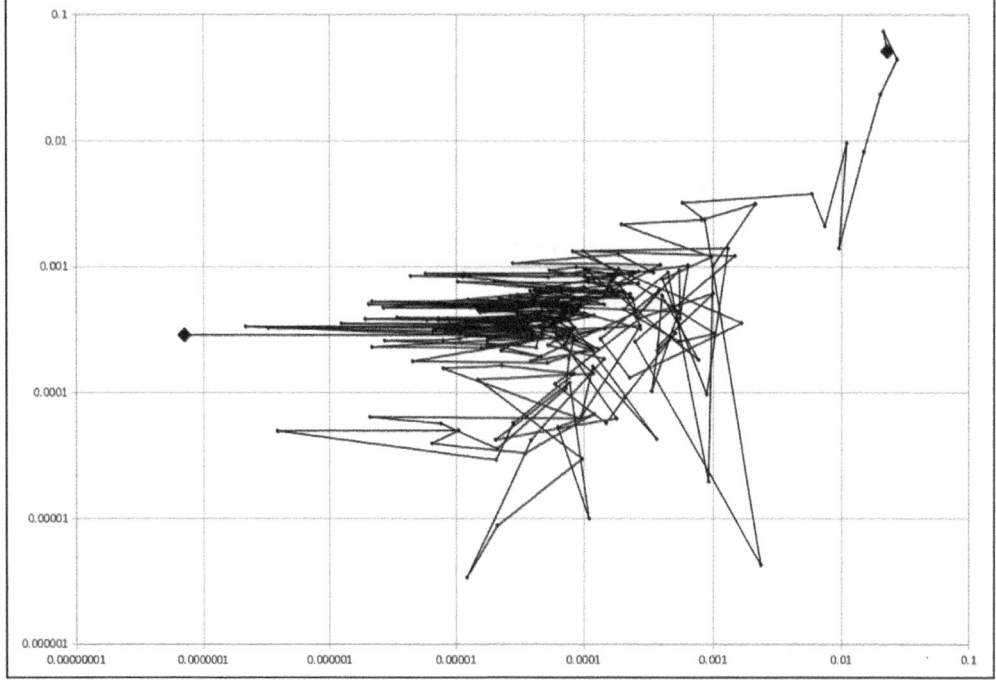

Figure 10-9. *itg_monte(): result error versus calculation difference*

The point highlighted with a large diamond symbol in the top-right corner of the plot is the first estimate. The line connects the estimates of 267 iterations (corresponding to 5,669,587 points) and ends, as it should, when the calculation difference goes below 0.0000001 (the large diamond on the left).

As you can see, after the first few iterations, the line becomes a tangle in the middle of the plot. Ideally, the points should remain around a a line with a slope of 45 degree. It would mean that, as the difference between two consecutive iterations becomes smaller, the difference between the estimate and the actual value also become smaller and in the same proportion, which is what happens with the integration methods based on interpolations.

As I already mentioned, the value you set n to is not important, but the value of n_incr must be. Consider that the problem you have with itg_monte() is that two consecutive estimates of the integral become enough close to each other to cause the end of the iterations before the estimates sufficiently approach the actual value of the integral. Increasing the number of points added to each iteration must reduce this effect.

To test this hypothesis, I plotted the absolute value of err against different values of n_incr for delta = 0.0000001. The results are shown in Figure 10-10.

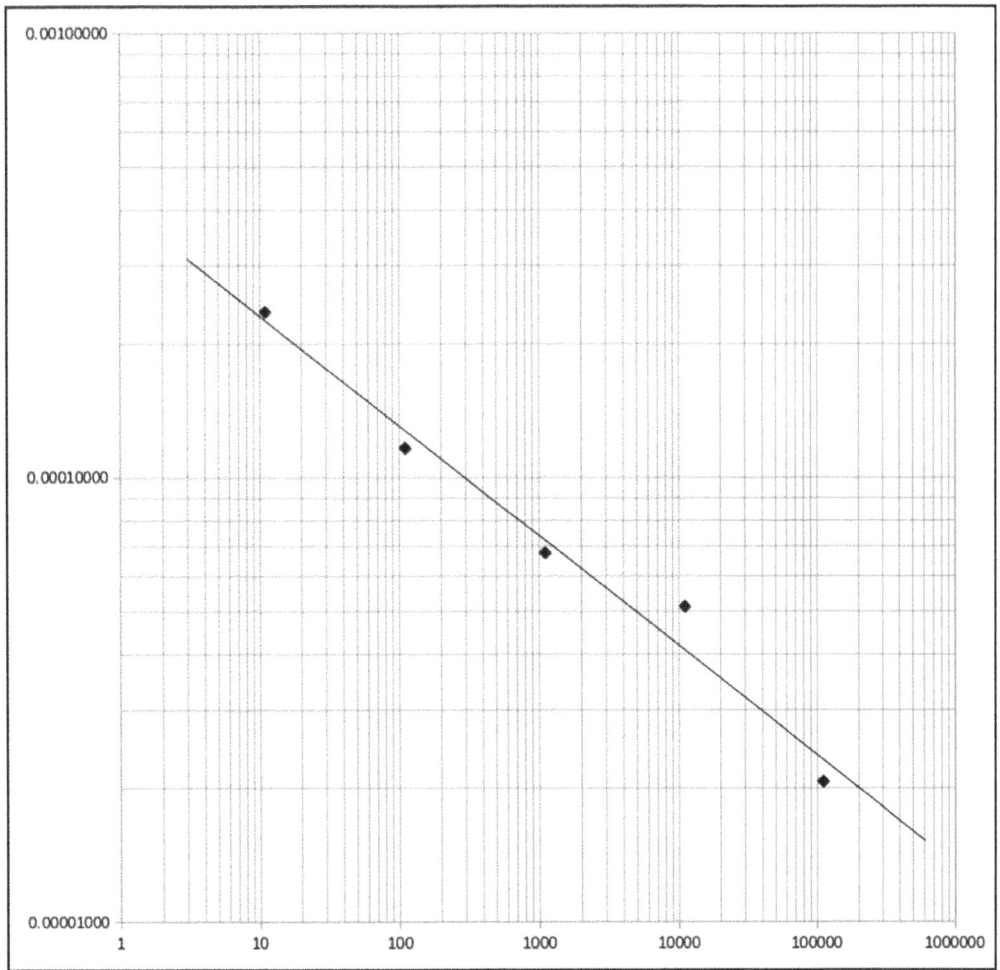

Figure 10-10. *abs(err) vs. n_incr*

As expected, when the increment of the number of points per iteration (n_incr) increases, itg_monte() provides better estimates of the integral. The straight line interpolated in Figure 10-10 corresponds to the following power law:

err = CONST * n_incr^EXP

with CONST = 0.0004075645 and EXP = -0.2468213501. Given the statistical nature of the calculations, you can ignore most of the digits. Therefore, in practical terms, an exponent of approximately -1/4 (-0.247 is quite close to -0.25) means that in order to halve err, you need to double n_incr four times. That is, multiply it by a factor of 16.

Note that you can only perform the analysis of itg_monte()'s behavior because in this particular case you know the actual value of the integral. In general, this will not be the case. As a result, you will not really know how accurate the estimate of the integral provided by itg_monte() will be. The bottom line is that you should consider using a Monte Carlo method as a last resort, when, for whatever reason, you are forced to rule out more conventional algorithms.

3D Integration

So far, you have only seen how to calculate definite integrals of functions with one independent variable as the area below a curve. If you have two variables, the area below the curve becomes a volume below a surface. See for example Figure 10-11, which shows the surface defined by the function

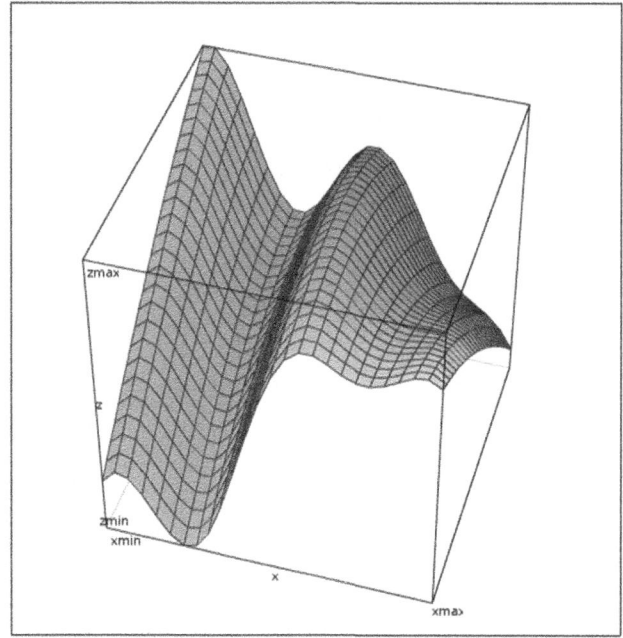

Figure 10-11. $f(x,y)$

z(x,y) = 0.2*cos(0.24*x) + 0.2*cos(0.16*x) + sin(x/25+y)

with 0 < x < 50, 0 < y < 1, and 0.2 < z < 1.249. It was drawn online with the 3D function grapher at the URL www.livephysics.com/tools/mathematical-tools/online-3-d-function-grapher/.

Conceptually, you can transfer what was said in the previous sections about integrating a one-variable function over an interval to a two-variable function over a two-dimensional area. But everything becomes much more complicated.

Integration Domains

When you integrate a function f(x), you only need to set two numbers, x0 and x1, to completely define the problem. Once you have done that, you can then break down the interval (x0, x1) with a series of intermediate values. But, if you need to integrate f(x,y) over a rectangle defined through two of its vertices (x0, y0) and (x1, y1). How do you divide the rectangle? The simplest way is shown in Figure 10-12, but you could also use triangles like in Figure 10-13. And what about partitioning the rectangle with hexagons like in Figure 10-14? What is best? And why stop at hexagons and limit ourselves to regular polygons? Perhaps more complex partitionings might provide better results.

Figure 10-12. *A square grid*

Figure 10-13. *A triangular grid*

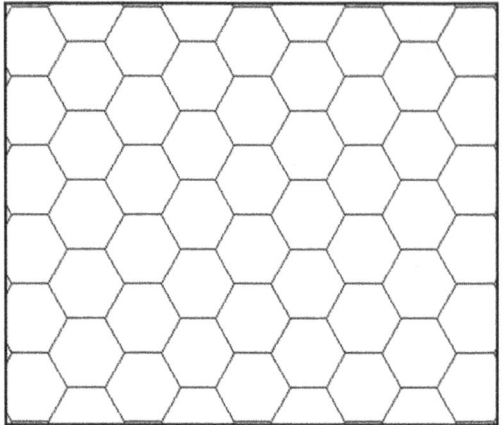

Figure 10-14. *A hexagonal grid*

In any case, you might also need to integrate a function over a domain that is not rectangular, like those shown in Figures 10-15 and 10-16.

Figure 10-15. *A heart-shaped integration domain*

Figure 10-16. *An snowflake-shaped integration domain*

Tricky. Let's take one step at a time by starting with the 3D equivalent of the trapezoidal rule.

From Trapezoid in 2D to Prism in 3D

To summarize the trapezoidal rule, you start by "cutting" the plot in stripes parallel to the Y-axis. The intersections of each stripe's edges with the X-axis are the two points with coordinates (xi,0) and (xi+h,0), while the intersections of the same edges with the curve are (xi,f(xi)) and (xi+h, f(xi+h)). The four points identify the corners of a trapezoid whose area is given by:

ai = [f(xi) + f(xi+h)] * h / 2

If you add all ais, you obtain an estimate of the integral and, by sufficiently reducing h, you can make the estimate as accurate as you need.

When you transfer the process to the 3D case and choose to partition the domain with equilateral triangles, as shown in Figure 10-13, the stripes become prisms that have a triangular base, indicated in Figure 10-17 with three points (x1,y1), (x2,y2), and (x3,y3). The three points obtained by intersecting the edges of each prism with the surface that represents f(x,y) uniquely identify the plane that passes through them. They are indicated in Figure 10-17 by showing the value of their Z-coordinates: f(x1,y1), f(x2,y2), and f(x3,y3).

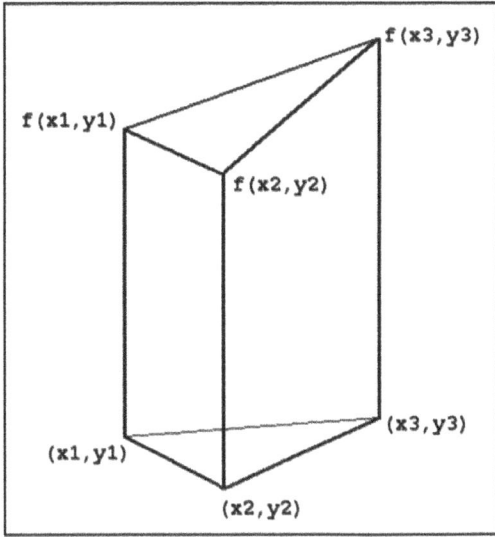

Figure 10-17. *3D equivalent of the trapezoidal rule*

To be precise, I should refer to *truncated prisms*, rather than simply prisms, because in general the top faces are not horizontal (Figure 10-17 is an example of such a truncated prism), but I will keep talking about prisms for simplicity.

The volume of the prism is given by:

vi = [f(x1,y1) + f(x2,y2) + f(x3,y3)] * A / 3

where A is the area of the triangular base delimited by the points (x1,y1), (x2,y2), and (x3,y3). If you add all vis, you obtain an estimate of the integral and, by sufficiently reducing the size of the triangular base, you can make the estimate as accurate as you need.

All this is very neat, but partitioning the domain with triangles is complicated. That's why we are going to use squares instead, as shown in Figure 10-12. This causes a problem because, while three points uniquely identify a plane, four points in general do not. But if you bring the four points close to each other and the surface is well behaved, it will still work out. After all, we want to find a way of calculating the integral of a two-variable functions by approximation.

All in all, we can extend the formula for vi as follows:

$$vi = [f(xi,yi) + f(xi+h,yi) + f(xi,yi+h) + f(xi+h,yi+h)] * h^2 / 4$$

As a curiosity, similar considerations applied to the 2D rectangular rule would lead to the following formula for the 3D case:

$$vi = f(xi + h/2,yi + h/2) * x^2$$

That is, instead of using the average of the function values calculated at the edges of the prism, you would use the value of the function calculated for the centroid of the base. But we are not going to pursue this method (as we didn't pursue the rectangular method for one-variable functions) because it would converge much more slowly than the prism method.

We need to generalize the formula for vi further:

$$vi = [f(xi,yi) + f(xi+hx,yi) + f(xi,yi+hy) + f(xi+hx,yi+hy)] * hx * hy / 4$$

That is, with a rectangular partitioning rather than a square one. The reason for doing so is that the X-interval and the Y-interval in general will be very different. For example, the X-range of the 3D plot of Figure 10-11 is 0 to 50, while the Y-range is 0 to 1. If you want to have, say, a grid of 100 x 100 points to approximate the surface, you would need hx to be 0.5 and hy to be 0.01.

Theoretically, you could also use the splitting of h into hx and hy to optimize the handling of surfaces much smoother along one of the XY-axes than along the other. You could achieve the needed accuracy with longer increments along the smoother axis, thereby reducing the number of calculations of the function.

But it would make your life very complicated, because you would have to decide along which axis you would need more points, and, to make the things more complex, you couldn't assume that the behavior of the surface would remain the same across its domain. In practice, you are better off keeping the algorithm simple and ignoring this possibility.

Listing 10-16 shows the first version of itg_prism(), not optimized in any way.

Listing 10-16. itg_prism()

```
1. //------------------------------------------------------------------ itg_prism
2. // Returns true if successful.
3. int itg_prism(double g(double, double), int in(double, double),
4.     double x0, double x1, double y0, double y1, int n, double *res) {
5.    int ret = 0;
6.    double hx = (x1 - x0) / (n - 1);
7.    double hy = (y1 - y0) / (n - 1);
8.    if (!g) fprintf(stderr, "itg_prism: function is NULL\n");
9.    if (!in) fprintf(stderr, "itg_prism: domain is NULL\n");
10.   else if (n < 2) fprintf(stderr, "itg_prism: less than 2 points\n");
11.   else if (hx <= 0) fprintf(stderr, "itg_prism: x-range non-positive\n");
12.   else if (hy <= 0) fprintf(stderr, "itg_prism: y-range non-positive\n");
13.   else if (!res) fprintf(stderr, "itg_prism: result address is NULL\n");
14.   else {
15.     ret = 1;
16.     double val = 0;
17.     for (int k = 0; k < n - 1; k++) {
```

```
18.        double x = x0 + hx * k;
19.        for (int j = 0; j < n - 1; j++) {
20.          double y = y0 + hy * j;
21.          if (in(x, y) && in(x + hx, y) && in(x, y + hy) && in(x + hx, y + hy)) {
22.            val += g(x, y) + g(x + hx, y) + g(x, y + hy) + g(x + hx, y + hy);
23.            }
24.          }
25.        }
26.      *res = val * hx * hy / 4;
27.      }
28.    return ret;
29.    } // itg_prism
```

itg_prism() is the 3D equivalent of itg_trapezoid() shown in Listing 10-4. There are three new parameters: y0 and y1, because there are now two independent variables instead of one, and the function in() to test whether a point is within the integration domain.

The function in() allows you to handle domains that are not rectangular, like those shown in Figures 10-15 and 10-16. You use it in line 22 to avoid adding to val the contributions of points outside the domain.

You can easily define the in() function to represent the rectangular domain used to draw Figure 10-11:

```
#define X0 (0.)
#define X1 (50.)
#define Y0 (0.)
#define Y1 (1.)
int in_rect(double x, double y) {
  return x >= X0 && x <= X1 && y >= Y0 && y <= Y1;
  }
```

The function plotted in Figure 10-11 is:

```
double g1(double x, double y) {
  return 0.2 * cos(0.24 * x) + 0.2 * cos(0.16 * x) + sin(x * 0.04 + y);
  }
```

If you calculate the integral

$$\int\limits_{x=0}^{50} \int\limits_{y=0}^{1} \left[\frac{1}{5}\cos\left(\frac{6}{25}x\right) + \frac{1}{5}\cos\left(\frac{4}{25}x\right) + \sin\left(\frac{1}{25}x + y\right) \right] dxdy$$

by hand, you obtain 41.03076380. But if you execute itg_prism() as shown in Listing 10-17, you obtain the output shown in Listing 10-18.

Listing 10-17. Integrating on a Rectangular Domain

```
double integral = 0;
int n = 10;
double err = 0;
int k = 0;
  printf("   #      n %-11s  %-11s\n", "result", "err");
  do {
  k++;
  n += n;
```

```
  if (itg_prism(g1, in_rect, X0, X1, Y0, Y1, n, &integral)) {
    err = (integral - 41.03076380) / 41.03076380;
    printf("%4d%6d  %11.8f  %11.8f\n", k, n, integral, err);
    }
  else {
    err = -1;
    }
  } while (fabs(err) > 0.00000001);
```

Listing 10-18. Output of Integration on a Rectangular Domain

```
 #      n   result        err
 1     20   40.98095700   -0.00121389
 2     40   40.07914074   -0.02319292
 3     80   41.02788026   -0.00007028
 4    160   41.03005192   -0.00001735
 5    320   41.03058694   -0.00000431
 6    640   41.03071972   -0.00000107
 7   1280   41.03075280   -0.00000027
 8   2560   41.03076105   -0.00000007
 9   5120   41.03076311   -0.00000002
10  10240   41.03076363   -0.00000000
```

It looks great! But now, let's try to integrate on a triangular domain, defined with

```
int in_triang(double x, double y) {
  return x >= X0 && x <= X1 && y >= Y0 && y <= x/X1;
  }
```

It means that you integrate on the triangular domain with the corners positioned in $(0,0)$, $(50,0)$, and $(50,1)$ of the XY-plane. This time, the integral is

$$\int_{x=0}^{50}\int_{y=0}^{x/50}\left[\frac{1}{5}\cos\left(\frac{6}{25}x\right)+\frac{1}{5}\cos\left(\frac{4}{25}x\right)+\sin\left(\frac{1}{25}x+y\right)\right]dxdy$$

and, if you calculate it by hand, you obtain 20.98016139. But if you execute itg_prism(), you obtain the output shown in Listing 10-19.

Listing 10-19. Output of Integration on a Triangular Domain

```
 #      n   result        err
 1     20   20.06582477   -0.04358101
 2     40   19.61050443   -0.06528343
 3     80   20.76401756   -0.01030230
 4    160   20.76311215   -0.01034545
 5    320   20.92665229   -0.00255046
 6    640   20.94801126   -0.00153241
 7   1280   20.95844121   -0.00103527
 8   2560   20.96950325   -0.00050801
 9   5120   20.97649412   -0.00017480
10  10240   20.97826996   -0.00009015
11  20480   20.97853437   -0.00007755
12  40960   20.97958587   -0.00002743
```

As you can see, the calculation converges but much more slowly than with a rectangular domain. One thing that we can do is utilize the points better. If you look at Listing 10-16, you see that you add to the value of the integral (line 22) only when all four points are within the domain (line 21), but you can do better than that.

If only three pints are within the domain, you can use the formula that you have already seen:

```
vi = [f(x1,y1) + f(x2,y2) + f(x3,y3)] * A / 3
```

calculated for the three points that are within the domain and where `A = hx * hy / 2`.

Improving the Prism Rule

From now on, let's refer to the original `itg_prism()` as `itg_prism0()` and use instead the refined `itg_prism()` shown in Listing 10-20.

Listing 10-20. Improved `itg_prism()`

```
1. //----------------------------------------------------------------- itg_prism
2. // Returns true if successful.
3. int itg_prism(double g(double, double), int in(double, double),
4.     double x0, double x1, double y0, double y1, int n, double *res) {
5.   int ret = 0;
6.   double hx = (x1 - x0) / (n - 1);
7.   double hy = (y1 - y0) / (n - 1);
8.   if (!g) fprintf(stderr, "itg_prism: function is NULL\n");
9.   if (!in) fprintf(stderr, "itg_prism: domain is NULL\n");
10.  else if (n < 2) fprintf(stderr, "itg_prism: less than 2 points\n");
11.  else if (hx <= 0) fprintf(stderr, "itg_prism: x-range non-positive\n");
12.  else if (hy <= 0) fprintf(stderr, "itg_prism: y-range non-positive\n");
13.  else if (!res) fprintf(stderr, "itg_prism: result address is NULL\n");
14.  else {
15.    ret = 1;
16.    double val = 0;
17.    for (int k = 0; k < n - 1; k++) {
18.      double x = x0 + hx * k;
19.      for (int j = 0; j < n - 1; j++) {
20.        double y = y0 + hy * j;
21.        int inn[4] = {};
22.        inn[0] = in(x, y);
23.        inn[1] = in(x + hx, y);
24.        inn[2] = in(x, y + hy);
25.        inn[3] = in(x + hx, y + hy);
26.        int i = inn[0] + inn[1] + inn[2] + inn[3];
27.        if (i == 4) {
28.          val += g(x, y) + g(x + hx, y) + g(x, y + hy) + g(x + hx, y + hy);
29.        }
30.        else if (i == 3) {
31.          double vval = 0;
32.          if (inn[0]) vval = g(x, y);
33.          if (inn[1]) vval += g(x + hx, y);
34.          if (inn[2]) vval += g(x, y + hy);
35.          if (inn[3]) vval += g(x + hx, y + hy);
```

```
36.                 val += vval * 2 / 3;
37.               }
38.             }
39.           }
40.         *res = val * hx * hy / 4;
41.       }
42.     return ret;
43.   } // itg_prism
```

Line 21 of the original version (Listing 10-16) has now become lines 21 to 27. By saving the results of in() for the four points separately, you can check them again individually and apply the three-point formula in lines 30 to 37. As you can see from the results shown in Listing 10-21, the calculation converges more rapidly, albeit still much more slowly than with a rectangular domain.

Listing 10-21. Integration on a Triangular Domain with Three Points

```
 #     n  result        err
 1    20  20.95584871   -0.00115884
 2    40  20.02905889   -0.04533342
 3    80  20.97321952   -0.00033088
 4   160  20.85842306   -0.00580254
 5   320  20.97869689   -0.00006980
 6   640  20.97406342   -0.00029065
 7  1280  20.97146392   -0.00041456
 8  2560  20.97546435   -0.00022388
 9  5120  20.97967040   -0.00002340
10 10240  20.97968122   -0.00002289
11 20480  20.97918604   -0.00004649
12 40960  20.97995344   -0.00000991
```

Well, when you compare Listing 10-21 with Listing 10-19, you can clearly see that adding the three-point prisms makes the estimates converge faster. This is an encouragement to add further refinements. Figure 10-18 shows four adjacent points and how you can partition the area between them.

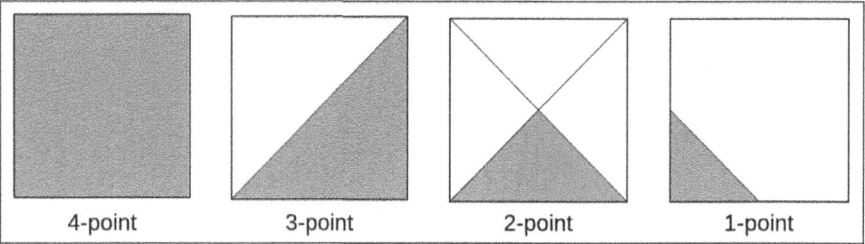

Figure 10-18. *Four-point, three-point, two-point, and one-point domains*

The areas are shown as squares but, obviously, they will in general be rectangles, as the X- and Y-ranges will usually be of different length. With two points within the integration domain, you can make up a three-point prism by adding the point in the center of the area, while if only one of the four points is within the integration domain, you can form a triangle by adding the two adjacent midpoints of the rectangular area. Obviously, it is not said that the added points will be within the integration domain, and you will have to check for it.

In a sense, it is a way of increasing the density of points at the edge of the domain to approximate it more closely when calculating the integral.

Listing 10-22 shows the final version of prism().

Listing 10-22. Final itg_prism()

```
1.  //--------------------------------------------------------------- itg_prism
2.  // Returns true if successful.
3.  int itg_prism(double g(double, double), int in(double, double),
4.      double x0, double x1, double y0, double y1, int n, double *res) {
5.    int ret = 0;
6.    double hx = (x1 - x0) / (n - 1);
7.    double hy = (y1 - y0) / (n - 1);
8.    if (!g) fprintf(stderr, "itg_prism: function is NULL\n");
9.    if (!in) fprintf(stderr, "itg_prism: domain is NULL\n");
10.   else if (n < 2) fprintf(stderr, "itg_prism: less than 2 points\n");
11.   else if (hx <= 0) fprintf(stderr, "itg_prism: x-range non-positive\n");
12.   else if (hy <= 0) fprintf(stderr, "itg_prism: y-range non-positive\n");
13.   else if (!res) fprintf(stderr, "itg_prism: result address is NULL\n");
14.   else {
15.     ret = 1;
16.     double val = 0;
17.     for (int k = 0; k < n - 1; k++) {
18.       double x = x0 + hx * k;
19.       for (int j = 0; j < n - 1; j++) {
20.         double y = y0 + hy * j;
21.         int inn[4] = {};
22.         inn[0] = in(x, y);
23.         inn[1] = in(x + hx, y);
24.         inn[2] = in(x, y + hy);
25.         inn[3] = in(x + hx, y + hy);
26.         double vval = 0;
27.         switch (inn[0] + inn[1] + inn[2] + inn[3]) {
28.           case 4:
29.             val += g(x, y) + g(x + hx, y) + g(x, y + hy) + g(x + hx, y + hy);
30.             break;
31.
32.           case 3:
33.             if (inn[0]) vval = g(x, y);
34.             if (inn[1]) vval += g(x + hx, y);
35.             if (inn[2]) vval += g(x, y + hy);
36.             if (inn[3]) vval += g(x + hx, y + hy);
37.             val += vval * 2 / 3;
38.             break;
39.
40.           case 2:
41.             if (in(x + hx/2, y + hy/2) && !(inn[0]*inn[3]) &&
42.                 !(inn[1]*inn[2])) {
43.               if (inn[0]) vval = g(x, y);
44.               if (inn[1]) vval += g(x + hx, y);
45.               if (inn[2]) vval += g(x, y + hy);
46.               if (inn[3]) vval += g(x + hx, y + hy);
```

```
47.                      vval += g(x + hx/2, y + hy/2);
48.                      val += vval / 3;
49.                      }
50.                  break;
51.
52.              case 1:
53.                  if (inn[0]) {
54.                      if (in(x, y + hy/2) && in(x + hx/2, y)){
55.                          vval = g(x, y);
56.                          vval += g(x, y + hy/2);
57.                          vval += g(x + hx/2, y);
58.                          }
59.                      }
60.                  else if (inn[1]) {
61.                      if(in(x + hx/2, y) && in(x + hx, y + hy/2)) {
62.                          vval += g(x + hx, y);
63.                          vval += g(x + hx/2, y);
64.                          vval += g(x + hx, y + hy/2);
65.                          }
66.                      }
67.                  else if (inn[2]) {
68.                      if(in(x, y + hy/2) && in(x + hx/2, y + hy)) {
69.                          vval += g(x, y + hy);
70.                          vval += g(x, y + hy/2);
71.                          vval += g(x + hx/2, y + hy);
72.                          }
73.                      }
74.                  else if (in(x + hx/2, y + hy) && in(x + hx, y + hy/2)){
75.                      vval += g(x + hx, y + hy);
76.                      vval += g(x + hx/2, y + hy);
77.                      vval += g(x +hx, y + hy/2);
78.                      }
79.                  val += vval / 6;
80.                  break;
81.
82.              default:
83.                  break;
84.                  }
85.              }
86.          }
87.      *res = val * hx * hy / 4;
88.      }
89.  return ret;
90.  } // itg_prism
```

The output of the final version of itg_prism() is shown in Listing 10-23.

Listing 10-23. Best itg_prism() Integration on a Triangular Domain

```
#    n   result       err
1    20  20.95584871  -0.00115884
2    40  20.27095866  -0.03380349
```

3	80	20.97402649	-0.00029241
4	160	20.87606402	-0.00496170
5	320	20.97933374	-0.00003945
6	640	20.97511520	-0.00024052
7	1280	20.97303688	-0.00033958
8	2560	20.97649582	-0.00017472
9	5120	20.97979088	-0.00001766
10	10240	20.97977345	-0.00001849
11	20480	20.97934434	-0.00003894
12	40960	20.97997556	-0.00000886
13	81920	20.98000945	-0.00000724
14	163840	20.98003916	-0.00000583
15	327680	20.98014812	-0.00000063

The iteration with 40,960x40,960 points (i.e., iteration 12) produces an estimate with an accuracy of 0.00000886, which is three times better (see Listing 10-19) than with the initial version of itg_prism() (Listing 10-16). That said, the final version of itg_prism() (Listing 10-22) is only slightly better than the version that only handles four and three points (Listing 3-20). For example, the accuracy of estimate iteration 12 is only reduced from 0.00000991 (see Listing 10-21) to 0.00000886.

But you have to consider that the refinements could have more significant effects with a more complicated domain. In any case, you can easily disable one or more refinements by commenting out the corresponding case. For example, to remove the one-point calculation, you only need to enclose lines 52 to 80 of the final version of itg_prism() (Listing 10-22) in a /* */ comment.

There is also something else to consider. I don't know how long it took to calculate the fifteenth iteration of Listing 10-23 on my computer, but it didn't produce further results after 12 hours. But iteration 15 reached an accuracy of better than one part per million.

Converting the Rectangular Rule to 3D

After developing the final version of itg_prism(), purely to satisfy my curiosity, I did what I said I wouldn't do: I wrote a 3D integration function equivalent to the rectangular rule for single integrals. The results were good enough to deserve including the function, which I called itg_prismx(), in the book. Check it out in Listing 10-24.

Listing 10-24. itg_prismx()

```
1. //--------------------------------------------------------------- itg_prismx
2. // Returns true if successful.
3. int itg_prismx(double g(double, double), int in(double, double),
4.     double x0, double x1, double y0, double y1, int n, double *res) {
5.   int ret = 0;
6.   double hx = (x1 - x0) / (n - 1);
7.   double hy = (y1 - y0) / (n - 1);
8.   if (!g) fprintf(stderr, "itg_prismx: function is NULL\n");
9.   if (!in) fprintf(stderr, "itg_prismx: domain is NULL\n");
10.   else if (n < 2) fprintf(stderr, "itg_prismx: less than 2 points\n");
11.   else if (hx <= 0) fprintf(stderr, "itg_prismx: x-range non-positive\n");
12.   else if (hy <= 0) fprintf(stderr, "itg_prismx: y-range non-positive\n");
13.   else if (!res) fprintf(stderr, "itg_prismx: result address is NULL\n");
14.   else {
15.     ret = 1;
```

```
16.      double val = 0;
17.      for (int k = 0; k < n - 1; k++) {
18.        double x = x0 + hx * (k + 0.5);
19.        for (int j = 0; j < n - 1; j++) {
20.          double y = y0 + hy * (j + 0.5);
21.          if (in(x, y) ) val += g(x, y);
22.        }
23.      }
24.      *res = val * hx * hy;
25.    }
26.    return ret;
27.  } // itg_prismx
```

In lines 18 and 20, you calculate the position of the point in the middle of the rectangular area and then, in line 21, if the point is within the domain, you add to the estimate the value of the function. What could be simpler than that?

Listing 10-25 shows itg_prismx()'s results.

Listing 10-25. Integration on a Triangular Domain with itg_prismx()

```
#       n   result      err
1      20   21.88910930  0.04332416
2      40   21.41902904  0.02091822
3      80   21.19592096  0.01028398
4     160   20.98214529  0.00009456
5     320   21.03343548  0.00253926
6     640   21.00544560  0.00120515
7    1280   20.98900634  0.00042159
8    2560   20.98486770  0.00022432
9    5120   20.98334999  0.00015198
10  10240   20.98144804  0.00006133
11  20480   20.98056026  0.00001901
12  40960   20.98036095  0.00000951
13  81920   20.98020426  0.00000204
14 163840   20.98011535 -0.00000219
15 327680   20.98020806  0.00000222
16 655360   20.98015733 -0.00000019
```

Up to iteration 12, the results were worse than those shown in Listing 10-23 obtained with the most refined version of itg_prism(), but it improved with further iterations and, running overnight, it managed to calculate iteration 16 and obtain better results than with itg_prism().

Notice that, for the first time, the estimates exceed the correct value. This is due to the fact that the central points of individual prisms used in itg_prismx() can be within the domain when not all points of the prism's base are. Therefore, when you calculate the integral of a positive function like that of Figure 10-11, you include in the estimate prisms that you would have ignored with itg_prism().

The bottom line is that, depending on the accuracy you need, the smoothness of the surface, the shape of the integration domain, the time you have, and how powerful your computer is, you will have to decide case-by-case the best way to calculate the integrals. For certain functions, the simplest algorithm might work better than the more complex ones.

Final Considerations on Multiple Integrals

When dealing with simple integrals, you can use `itg_opt()` to estimate an integral with a given accuracy. You could obviously do something similar with double integrals. I haven't tested it, but I believe that all you would need to do is add a parameter to provide the `in()` function and replace `itg_boole()` with `itg_prism()`. You only need to make straightforward changes to `itg_opt()` because it doesn't depend on the number of independent variables.

The three-point algorithm described in this section joins the points with a plane, and the four-point algorithm is an extension of three-point prism algorithm that "fakes" an average plane between four adjacent points. They are both 3D equivalents of the trapezoid rule that you used for one-variable integral, which joined two adjacent points with a straight line.

A straight line in the XY-plane, unless it is parallel to the Y-axis, can be written as $y = a*x + b$.

If you have two points $(x0,y0)$ and $(x1,y1)$, by resolving the linear system of two equations

$$y0 = a*x0 + b$$
$$y1 = a*x1 + b$$

you can calculate the two values, a and b.

When integrating functions of one variable, you saw how it was possible to replace the straight line of the trapezoid rule with higher-order curves using more than two adjacent points. For example, knowing the three adjacent points $(x0,y0)$, $(x1,y1)$, and $(x2,y2)$, you could determine the coefficient of the parabola of equation $y = a*x2 + b*x + c$ that joined the three points by solving the following system of three linear equations:

$$y0 = a*x0^2 + b*x0 + c$$
$$y1 = a*x1^2 + b*x1 + c$$
$$y2 = a*x2^2 + b*x2 + c$$

And the same for four and five points.

You could do something equivalent with double integrals by replacing the plane of the prism rule with higher-order surfaces. For example, you could use the four points $(x0,y0)$, $(x1,y1)$, $(x2,y2)$, and $(x3,y3)$ you used to define prisms with a rectangular base to determine the coefficient of a paraboloid of equation

$$z = a*x^2 + b*y^2 + c*x*y + d$$

by solving the system of four linear equations in a, b, c, and d:

$$z0 = a*x0^2 + b*y0^2 + c*x0*y0 + d$$
$$z1 = a*x1^2 + b*y1^2 + c*x1*y1 + d$$
$$z2 = a*x2^2 + b*y2^2 + c*x2*y2 + d$$
$$z3 = a*x3^2 + b*y3^2 + c*x3*y3 + d$$

But this is where we stop because, as you can see, things become more and more complicated, beyond the scope of this book. Indeed, the calculation of integrals is in practical cases so complicated that physicists very often resort to Monte Carlo methods.

This is particularly true when you go beyond two independent variables. That's why this book stops at functions of two variables. But, after reading this chapter, you shouldn't have many problems in extending `itg_prismx()` to handle three independent variables.

Summary

In this chapter, you learned how to estimate the value of definite integrals of functions in one and two independent variables.

To integrate functions of one variable, you saw methods of increasing accuracy, from the rectangular to the Boole's rule. Additionally, you learned how to program the Monte Carlo method of integration based on pseudo-random numbers.

You then learned how the algorithms that integrate functions of one variable form the basis for integrating functions of more variables. Concerning in particular integrals of two independent variables, you also familiarized yourself with the issues associated with different integration domains.

CHAPTER 11

Embedded Software

The first things that come to mind for many people when talking about software are applications. That is, programs with which we interact directly, like web browsers and games. We issue commands by typing on a keyboard, clicking mouse buttons, or touching a screen, and the applications respond by performing tasks, hopefully those we intend them to do.

Operating systems differ from applications in that they interact directly with the computer hardware. An OS consists of a *kernel*, which is the part that interacts with CPU, memory, and devices, and a series of utilities that applications can invoke via *system calls*.

This chapter is about writing software that interacts with electronic circuitry. This includes device drivers at the core of operating systems, controllers in industrial processes, layers of data communication protocols, and more. Embedded software controls the cycles of a washing machine, keeps tracks of data packets in an Internet router, selects channels in a television set, regulates heartbeats in a pacemaker, and coordinates traffic lights at street intersections, just to name a few tasks.

Often, embedded software imposes tight restrictions on memory usage, timing, or both. For example, when you press a key on your computer keyboard, you send a signal to the OS that activates the keyboard driver. If the driver were badly designed and too slow in responding, it might result in characters being lost, overwritten by the following ones. This never happens in modern computers, but it illustrates an aspect embedded, real-time software needs to take care of.

Embedded software engineers (where, at least for now, "embedded" refers to the software, rather than to the engineers!) need to be familiar with hexadecimal and binary number representations, ways of manipulating individual bits, how to address and access device registers, and, at least to a certain extent, how to read circuit schematics and component data sheets.

To many developers used to writing applications by using high-level libraries, embedded software appears dry. But it is rewarding to see how bits and bytes let you control physical devices. The *Internet of Things* (or the Internet of everything, if you prefer) relies on remotely controlled sensors (i.e., input devices) and actuators (i.e., output devices), and each one of them is operated through embedded code.

And, what might come to you as a surprise, the vast majority of microprocessors are manufactured to be employed as components of embedded systems. It makes sense, therefore, to learn something about embedded software. This chapter provides only a small taste of what makes software development for embedded systems special.

Bit Operations

In Chapter 2, you learned that Ubuntu stores integers in little-endian format, with the least significant byte stored in the first memory location. As a result, the code

```
unsigned int i = 0x12345678;
printf("%p: 0x%08x\n", &i, i);
char si[9];
```

© Giulio Zambon 2016
G. Zambon, *Practical C*, DOI 10.1007/978-1-4842-1769-6_11

```
printf("\n     <--Address--->     <--Content----->\n");
for (int k = 0; k < sizeof(i); k++) {
  unsigned char *cp = ((unsigned char *)&i) + k;
  num_binfmt(cp, 8, si, 0);
  printf("     %p     0x%02x  0b%s\n", cp, *cp, si);
  }
```

produces the following output:

```
0x7ffe1c4830d0: 0x12345678
```

```
        <--Address--->      <--Content----->
        0x7ffe1c4830d0      0x78  0b01111000
        0x7ffe1c4830d1      0x56  0b01010110
        0x7ffe1c4830d2      0x34  0b00110100
        0x7ffe1c4830d3      0x12  0b00010010
```

in which the lowest memory address (0x7ffe1c4830d0) holds the least significant byte (0x78).

Unfortunately, printf() doesn't include a format to display a number in binary. But this issue was solved with the simple function num_binfmt(), shown in Listing 2-16 and reproduced here as Listing 11-1 for convenience.

Listing 11-1. num_binfmt()—Same as Listing 2-16

```
 1. //--------------------------------------------------------------- num_binfmt
 2. void num_binfmt(void *p, int n, char *s, int space) {
 3.    unsigned char c;
 4.    while (n > 0) {
 5.       c = *((unsigned char *)p++);
 6.       for (int nb = 0; nb < 8 && n > 0; nb++) {
 7.          *s++ = (c & 128) ? '1' : '0';
 8.          c <<= 1;
 9.          n--;
10.          }
11.       if (space) *s++ = ' ';
12.       }
13.    *s = '\0';
14.    } // num_binfmt
```

You format n bits beginning from the memory address p by executing the while loop in lines 4 to 12. The for loop in lines 6 to 10 goes through the bits of each byte. In line 7, you test the MSB of the current byte to decide whether to append to the output string a 1 or a 0, and in line 8, you push out to the "left" the MSB that you just checked.

Line 7 gives you a good example of how you test a bit of a byte: by bitwise AND-ing the current byte with a mask, you obtain a byte that has the same bits of the original byte where the masking bits are 1, while all the other bits are set to 0. In the example, the mask is 128, which is 0b10000000 in binary, and the result of the masking is 128 (i.e., true) when the MSB of the current byte is 1 and 0 (i.e., false) when the MSB is 0.

Besides the binary (i.e., bitwise) AND (i.e., &), you also have the binary OR (i.e., |), XOR (i.e., ^), complement (i.e., ~), left shift (i.e., <<), and right shift (i.e., >>) operators. As you have seen, by AND-ing a mask to a byte, you force to 0 the bits that are 0 in the mask. With OR, you force to 1 the bits that are 1 in the mask, while with XOR, you flip the bits of the original byte that correspond to the 1s of the mask. You have already seen examples of the shift operators in previous chapters (e.g., in Listings 2-10 and 9-10) and in line 8 of Listing 11-1. The following examples illustrate the other binary operations:

```
0b01110010 &   0b00001111 = 0b00000010
0b01110010 & ~0b00001111 = 0b01110000
0b01110010 |   0b00001111 = 0b01111111
0b01110010 | ~0b00001111 = 0b11110010
0b01110010 ^   0b00001111 = 0b01111101
0b01110010 ^ ~0b00001111 = 0b10000010
```

You can reproduce the examples by executing the following code:

```
char *mask_s = "0b00001111";
char *n1_s = "0b01110010";
char res_s[9];
unsigned int res;
unsigned int mask = bin_to_uint(mask_s);
unsigned int n1 = bin_to_uint(n1_s);

res = n1 & mask;
num_binfmt(&res, 8, res_s, 0);
printf("%s &  %s = 0b%s\n", n1_s, mask_s, res_s);
res = n1 & ~mask;
num_binfmt(&res, 8, res_s, 0);
printf("%s & ~%s = 0b%s\n", n1_s, mask_s, res_s);

res = n1 | mask;
num_binfmt(&res, 8, res_s, 0);
printf("%s |  %s = 0b%s\n", n1_s, mask_s, res_s);
res = n1 | ~mask;
num_binfmt(&res, 8, res_s, 0);
printf("%s | ~%s = 0b%s\n", n1_s, mask_s, res_s);

res = n1 ^ mask;
num_binfmt(&res, 8, res_s, 0);
printf("%s ^  %s = 0b%s\n", n1_s, mask_s, res_s);
res = n1 ^ ~mask;
num_binfmt(&res, 8, res_s, 0);
printf("%s ^ ~%s = 0b%s\n", n1_s, mask_s, res_s);
```

You already know the function num_binfmt() (see Listing 11-1). The function bin_touint() converts a binary string (e.g., "0b00001111") to an unsigned integer. You can see it in Listing 11-2.

Listing 11-2. bin_to_uint()

```
1. //----------------------------------------------------------------- bin_to_uint
2. unsigned int bin_to_uint(char *s) {
3.     if (!s || !*s) return 0;                                          //-->
4.     while (*s && *s != '0' && *s != '1') s++;
5.     if (strlen(s) >= 2 && *s == '0' && (*(s + 1) == 'b' || *(s + 1) == 'B')) {
6.         s += 2;
```

```
7.    }
8.    unsigned int res = 0;
9.    while (*s) {
10.     if (*s == '0' || *s == '1') res = (res << 1) | (*s & 1);
11.     s++;
12.    }
13.    return res;
14.  } // bin_to_uint
```

Line 3 ensures that you return 0 if the input string is a NULL pointer or if it is empty.

Line 4 skips all characters different from '0' and '1'. Notice that it keeps checking for the string-ending NULL character to avoid going beyond the end of strings without any '0' or '1'.

Lines 5 to 7 skip the prefix "0b" or "0B" if present.

The while loop that begins in line 9 goes through the string from left to right one character at a time.

In line 10 you do two operations: first you shift the byte left, and then you OR in the LSB of the current character. The if condition ensures that you only perform the operations when the current character represents a binary digit, which means that you ignore all other characters. *s & 1 makes a mask with all bits set to 0 except for the LSB, which replicates the LSB of the current character. Obviously, the OR is only needed when the LSB is 1, but it is simpler and quicker to do it always, rather than check whether it is needed or not.

Given the priorities of the operations used when calculating res, you wouldn't need any parentheses when calculating res in line 10, but Eclipse issued a warning and I decided to comply with its suggestion of inserting the parentheses, instead of disabling the check "Suggested parenthesis around expression" in C/C++ General > Code Analysis (as I usually do!)

One word of caution concerning shift operations: they apply to the numbers, not to the memory locations where they are stored. For example, the number

```
unsigned int n2 = 0xABCDEF76;
```

is stored in memory as

```
01110110 11101111 11001101 10101011
   7  6    E  F    C  D    A  B
```

with the least significant byte first (i.e., in the memory location with the lowest address). When you shift it four bits to the right, you obtain

```
11110111 11011110 10111100 00001010
  F  7    D  E    B  C    0  A
```

This is clear when you consider the number in hexadecimal form, as 0xABCDEF76 becomes 0x0ABCDEF7, with four zero-bits shifted in from the left and the four LSBs (containing 0x6) shifted out to the right. The confusing aspect is that while, say, 0xF and 0x7 are consecutive digits of the number, they are not stored in two consecutive bytes of memory. Again, you are shifting the number, not the memory representation of the number.

Obviously, there is no risk of confusion with other bit operations because both the mask and the number have identical representations in memory.

Finally, be careful when you apply the shift-right operator to signed integers because it expands the sign bit (i.e., the MSB) to the right. For example, the number

```
char n3 = -16;
```

is represented in memory as 11110000. When you shift it to the right by one bit, you obtain 11111000, with a 1 shifted in from the left rather than a 0. The result is -8, which means that when you shift an integer one bit to the right, you halve it, regardless of whether it is signed or unsigned and positive or negative.

Endianness

You have already encountered the issue of endianness in Chapter 2 and have seen in the previous section of this chapter how numbers stored in little-endian format can be confusing.

Unless you use unions or typecast pointers, endianness is irrelevant in high-level programming. But when you work with embedded systems, you must know the endianness of the devices you interact with if you want to avoid disasters.

If you develop software for a microcontroller, it is likely that you will measure some physical quantity (e.g., acceleration or temperature) and sample it at regular time intervals with an analog-to-digital converter to obtain digital data. Now, regardless of what you are measuring, you will need to take into account the endianness of the AD-converter.

The Web is full of data sheets for many AD-converters. I picked the following one (almost at random): www.analog.com/media/en/technical-documentation/data-sheets/AD7981.pdf

It is an industrial converter, designed to operate at high temperatures, that can perform 600 kSPS (i.e., six hundred thousand samples per second) of an input voltage between 0V and 5.1V. But those details are irrelevant for the purposes of this book. What matters is that it converts the input voltage to a 16-bit number.

Figure 11-1 shows how you can connect the AD-converter to a microprocessor/microcontroller[1]. Here is what the acronyms shown in the diagram mean:

```
CNV: Conversion
CLK: System Clock
SCK: Serial Clock
SDO: Serial Data Output
SDI: Serial Digital Interface
VIO: Virtual I/O
```

What the diagram doesn't show are the remaining pins of the converter that are needed to provide power, ground, the analog input, and a voltage reference against which the input is compared when it is sampled.

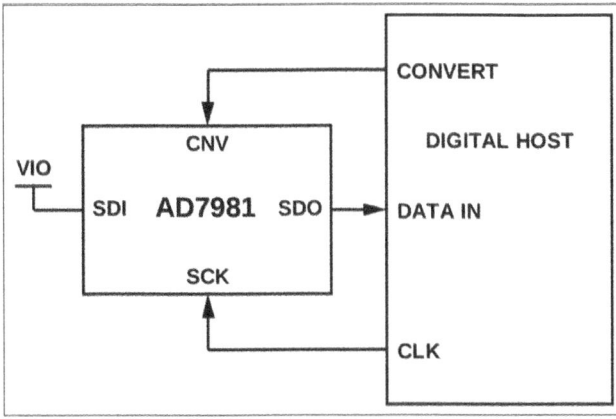

Figure 11-1. *Simplest AD7981 connection diagram*

---

[1]Permission to reproduce the diagram obtained from the Copyright holder, Analog Devices.

To understand the diagram of Figure 11-1, you only need to consider CNV, SCK, and SDO. When CNV goes high (e.g., when it exceeds 3.5V with a 5V-logic), the converter executes a sample of the analog input. After the sample is completed, when CNV goes low (e.g., when it goes below 1.5V with a 5V-logic), the digital result goes out from SDO to the processor's data input one bit at the time when CLK (and therefore SCK) goes low. It is not the full picture, but you can find the detailed timing diagrams in the converter's data sheet (the explanation I have summarized is on page 17).

What is important to note is that the microprocessor/microcontroller receives the 16 bits that represent the sampled analog value one bit at a time. The 16 bits fit into the two bytes of an unsigned short integer. But, and this is the crucial question, *in which order*? That is, with which endianness?

Data sheets are never easy bedside reading, and if you look at the 25-page-long data sheet of AD7981 you will find the information you need on page 17, where it says: "When CNV goes low, the MSB is output onto SDO. The remaining data bits are then clocked by subsequent SCK falling edges."

It means that, as you get the MSB first, the 16-bit number is transferred in big-endian format, the opposite of how numbers are represented in our computers!

In practical terms, you need to swap the two bytes of each value you receive from the AD-converter. Within each byte the bit order is fine, with the byte's MSB "on the left" and the LSB "on the right." You only need to change the byte order.

Embedded Environments

In broad strokes, there are three types of environments in which embedded software runs:

- Naked boards

- Real-time operating systems

- High-level embedded OSs

Naked Boards

When you power up a microprocessor, it always starts executing machine code it finds at a predefined address. For example, when you power up or hard-reset an Intel processor, it fetches and executes the machine instruction it finds at the physical address 0xFFFFFFF0 (4GB,16 bytes), which is also known as the reset vector (see, for example, www.intel.com/content/www/us/en/intelligent-systems/intel-boot-loader-development-kit/minimal-intel-architecture-boot-loader-paper.html).

So, to run software on a naked board, you need to do the following:

- Include in your electronic circuitry a ROM chip that retains its content when the power supply is switched off (PROM, EPROM, EEPROM, but often Flash) and connect it to cover the address 0xFFFFFFF0.

- When programming the ROM, write in the location that is going to be addressed as 0xFFFFFFF0 a jump to executable code.

This is how the BIOS that boots the Windows PCs gets executed, and there are many versions of BIOSes for the different PC boards. The function of the BIOS is to configure the hardware (including the memory controller), set up the stack in DRAM, copy the OS software from the designated device (usually the boot sector of a hard disk, but possibly a CD or a USB memory stick) to memory, and jump to its start address.

The booting of a GNU/Linux systems on a PC goes through an intermediate step: after initializing the hardware, the BIOS loads from disk the Linux boot loader, which has the actual task of loading into memory the Linux kernel, which in turn performs a series of initialization tasks before starting the graphic environment (with the desktop, etc.)

The presence of an OS is not always necessary. Boards that perform specific functions, for example in data communication, can be better off without the overhead of an OS. In that case, the function of the boot, besides initializing the hardware, is to set up the stack in DRAM, copy to DRAM the operational software (often consisting of little more than an endless loop), and launch it.

Real-Time OSs (RTOSs)

RTOSs are OSs that respond to inputs within a determined time interval. The predictability of responses is not a key feature when the inputs are mostly human-generated, while it is very important when a system needs to respond to stimuli that come from devices. This is because we humans (assuming you are one!) do not time out within small fractions of seconds. For example, even if you manage to type 400 characters per minute, it will still give your computer 150ms to insert each character into a document held in memory and display the character on the screen. Unless you are executing at the same time a task that gobbles up a lot of processing power, the computer is not likely to fall behind.

To be predictable/deterministic, RTOSs usually adopt either preemptive scheduling or time-sharing (or a combination of the two):

- With *preemptive scheduling,* the system is fully event-driven and executes different tasks depending on their priorities. This means that a task keeps running until another task with a higher priority generates an event. When that happens, the OS suspends the current task and responds to the event by activating the higher-priority task.

- With *time-sharing,* tasks are inserted into a circular queue and are executed in *round-robin* fashion, each one with its allocated time interval. If no events occur, the system suspends the current task and activates the next one when it receives an interrupt from the system clock to indicate that a time interval has completed.

One of the most successful RTOSs is VxWorks. It supports both preemptive and round-robin scheduling. Unfortunately, it is a proprietary commercial system. A popular, open source RTOS is FreeRTOS (`www.freertos.org`). It requires little memory and is very compact.

High-Level OSs

Considering how many smart phones and tablets are in circulation, perhaps the most widely used high-level embedded OSs are Android, which is a derivative of Linux, and iOS, which is a subset of Mac OS X.

If you look at the Wikipedia page `en.wikipedia.org/wiki/Comparison_of_single-board_computers`, you will see that Linux and/or Android also run on most of the several dozens of the listed one-board computers/microcontrollers.

Some of those microcontrollers, like Arduino and Raspberry Pi, have been around for years (respectively, since 2005 and 2012), while others, like CHIP, have been released recently (I just got it after supporting Next Thing Co's Kickstarter campaign last year).

The success of these small devices (Arduino and Raspberry Pi have dimensions comparable to those of a credit card, while CHIP has an area that is less than half that of a credit card) is due to their flexibility in controlling gadgets and their low cost (CHIP costs $9).

And, although they are so small, some of them are quite powerful. For example, the latest Raspberry Pi includes 1GB of RAM and its CPU is a 64-bit processor that runs at 1.2GHz. And CHIP runs the latest version of Ubuntu (14.04).

Signals and Interrupts

Nowadays, it is the norm for OSs to support multiprocessing. That is, carrying out more than one task in, for all practical purposes, simultaneous operations. Some of those operations are indeed simultaneous, as they take advantage of multiple computer cores and "intelligent" (whatever that means) device controllers. Other operations only appear to be conducted simultaneously, while in fact the CPU works on multiple tasks (i.e., processes) a bit at the time, like a juggler who catches and throws up one ball at a time to keep several of them up in the air.

To *suspend* a process and *activate* another, the CPU needs to *save* the *context* of the currently running process and *restore* the context of the new one. That is, the CPU freezes the current process and saves somewhere in memory the registers that define its status (i.e., program counter, stack pointer, user registers, ...), so that when it reactivates it later, the process can resume execution from where it was stopped as if nothing had happened. Then, the CPU restores the registers of the process to be reactivated and transfers control to it. This set of activities is called *context switching*.

In any case, regardless of whether the CPU switches processes because a time slice has ended or something else has happened, it does this in response to a signal it receives.

If you look at the standard header signal.h, you will see that it includes another header file named bits/signum.h, and in it you find the list of signals shown in Listing 11-3.

Listing 11-3. Portion of bits/signum.h

```
#define SIGHUP      1        /* Hangup (POSIX).  */
#define SIGINT      2        /* Interrupt (ANSI).  */
#define SIGQUIT     3        /* Quit (POSIX).  */
#define SIGILL      4        /* Illegal instruction (ANSI).  */
#define SIGTRAP     5        /* Trace trap (POSIX).  */
#define SIGABRT     6        /* Abort (ANSI).  */
#define SIGIOT      6        /* IOT trap (4.2 BSD).  */
#define SIGBUS      7        /* BUS error (4.2 BSD).  */
#define SIGFPE      8        /* Floating-point exception (ANSI).  */
#define SIGKILL     9        /* Kill, unblockable (POSIX).  */
#define SIGUSR1     10       /* User-defined signal 1 (POSIX).  */
#define SIGSEGV     11       /* Segmentation violation (ANSI).  */
#define SIGUSR2     12       /* User-defined signal 2 (POSIX).  */
#define SIGPIPE     13       /* Broken pipe (POSIX).  */
#define SIGALRM     14       /* Alarm clock (POSIX).  */
#define SIGTERM     15       /* Termination (ANSI).  */
#define SIGSTKFLT   16       /* Stack fault.  */
#define SIGCLD      SIGCHLD  /* Same as SIGCHLD (System V).  */
#define SIGCHLD     17       /* Child status has changed (POSIX).  */
#define SIGCONT     18       /* Continue (POSIX).  */
#define SIGSTOP     19       /* Stop, unblockable (POSIX).  */
#define SIGTSTP     20       /* Keyboard stop (POSIX).  */
#define SIGTTIN     21       /* Background read from tty (POSIX).  */
#define SIGTTOU     22       /* Background write to tty (POSIX).  */
#define SIGURG      23       /* Urgent condition on socket (4.2 BSD).  */
#define SIGXCPU     24       /* CPU limit exceeded (4.2 BSD).  */
#define SIGXFSZ     25       /* File size limit exceeded (4.2 BSD).  */
#define SIGVTALRM   26       /* Virtual alarm clock (4.2 BSD).  */
#define SIGPROF     27       /* Profiling alarm clock (4.2 BSD).  */
#define SIGWINCH    28       /* Window size change (4.3 BSD, Sun).  */
```

```
#define SIGPOLL       SIGIO   /* Pollable event occurred (System V).  */
#define SIGIO         29      /* I/O now possible (4.2 BSD).  */
#define SIGPWR        30      /* Power failure restart (System V).  */
#define SIGSYS        31      /* Bad system call.  */
#define SIGUNUSED     31

#define _NSIG         65      /* Biggest signal number + 1
                                 (including real-time signals).  */
```

You have probably heard of *interrupts*. The term interrupt refers to any event, usually asynchronous to what the CPU is currently doing, that causes the CPU to take a specific action, and a signal is nothing else than a software-generated interrupt. When an event occurs, it causes immediate execution of an interrupt service routine (ISR) to do what is necessary. ISRs for signals are usually referred to as *signal handlers*.

To put it in a more practical way, an interrupt is a notification that the CPU sends to the OS kernel, for example when it encounters a division by zero, while a signal is a notification that the OS sends to the processes currently executing, for example when the user presses CNTL+C.

When you launch a program, the OS creates for it an environment and starts it as a new process. As part of the process initialization, the OS creates a dedicated copy of the array that contains the default addresses of all signal-handlers. This gives to each individual process the possibility of masking (i.e., blocking) one or more signals. That said, the signals SIGKILL and SIGSTOP are unblockable. And it makes sense because you don't want any process to be able to make itself unkillable! SIGKILL causes the process to die, while SIGSTOP forces it to suspend execution, which can then resume upon receiving the signal SIGCONT.

When you type CNTL+C on the keyboard to stop a program, you send to the corresponding process the signal SIGINT, which is like SIGKILL but is blockable. It means that a program can decide not to be killed with CNTL+C. Similarly, CNTL+Z sends a SIGTSTP, which is equivalent to SIGSTOP but can be blocked. And the kill command without any signal number/literal sends a SIGTERM.

You can issue any signal from the command line in GNU/Linux by typing:

```
kill -signal pid
```

where *signal* is the signal mnemonic (e.g., SIGINT) and *pid* is the process identifier you can obtain with the command ps. For example, kill -SIGINT 2750 ends the process with identifier 2750.

Incidentally, Listing 11-3 tells you why many people terminate a process with the command kill -9: 9 is the value of SIGKILL.

If you find all these codes somewhat confusing, rest assured that you are not the only one. Here is a brief explanation of the effects of terminating signals:

- SIGHUP (1): Hang up. For processes attached to a terminal, it tells a process that the controlling terminal has disconnected. It results in the process being terminated.

- SIGINT (2): Interrupt. Unless the process catches the signal (you will see later how you do it), it ends the process gracefully, as if you had issued a SIGTERM. For processes attached to a terminal, you can generate it from the keyboard by typing CNTL+C.

- SIGQUIT (3): Quit. It generates a core dump and cleans up all the resources held by the process. For processes attached to a terminal, you can generate it from the keyboard by typing CNTL+\.

- SIGABRT (6): Abort. A process can issue this signal to itself with the abort() system call.

- **SIGKILL (9)**: Kill. It ends the process immediately and without any cleanup. It cannot be caught or blocked. Also, you cannot kill a zombie process. A process is said to be a zombie when it's between dying and being removed from the process table. It happens, for example, to a child process waiting for the parent process to read the child's exit status.

- **SIGTERM (15)**: Termination. It terminates a process gracefully. You can issue this signal from the command line with a "naked" kill command (i.e., without any option). If the graceful termination doesn't work (e.g., because the process is hanging on an I/O), you can resort to kill -9, which forces the process to end.

Still confused? I would lie if I said I have all the differences perfectly clear! But it is not so important after all because, while SIGKILL cannot be handled and causes instant death of a process, all the other signals can be caught and handled. Therefore, you can have your program respond to each signal the way you see fit.

So, the time has come to see how you issue and catch signals. To do so, instead of spawning child processes, we will create threads within a single process because threads are easier to deal with.

To get started, Listing 11-4 shows an array that allows you to look up the signal names I obtained by editing the portion of signum.h shown in Listing 11-2.

You would think that the array is already available somewhere within the system. But if you look at signal.h, you find the following couple of lines:

```
/* Names of the signals.  This variable exists only for compatibility.
   Use `strsignal' instead (see <string.h>).  */
extern const char *const _sys_siglist[_NSIG];
extern const char *const sys_siglist[_NSIG];
```

Some pages on the Web mention the array sys_signame, but I'm not sure what OS they are working on. The function strsignal() is available, but it returns strings that describe the signals, not their names.

Listing 11-4. The sig_name Array

```
#define N_DEF_SIGS 32
char *sig_names[N_DEF_SIGS] = {
    /* 0*/ "0        ",
    /* 1*/ "SIGHUP   ", // Hangup (POSIX)
    /* 2*/ "SIGINT   ", // Interrupt (ANSI)
    /* 3*/ "SIGQUIT  ", // Quit (POSIX)
    /* 4*/ "SIGILL   ", // Illegal instruction (ANSI)
    /* 5*/ "SIGTRAP  ", // Trace trap (POSIX)
    /* 6*/ "SIGABRT  ", // Abort (ANSI)
    /* 7*/ "SIGBUS   ", // BUS error (4.2 BSD)
    /* 8*/ "SIGFPE   ", // Floating-point exception (ANSI)
    /* 9*/ "SIGKILL  ", // Kill, unblockable (POSIX)
    /*10*/ "SIGUSR1  ", // User-defined signal 1 (POSIX)
    /*11*/ "SIGSEGV  ", // Segmentation violation (ANSI)
    /*12*/ "SIGUSR2  ", // User-defined signal 2 (POSIX)
    /*13*/ "SIGPIPE  ", // Broken pipe (POSIX)
    /*14*/ "SIGALRM  ", // Alarm clock (POSIX)
    /*15*/ "SIGTERM  ", // Termination (ANSI)
    /*16*/ "SIGSTKFLT", // Stack fault
    /*17*/ "SIGCHLD  ", // Child status has changed (POSIX)
    /*18*/ "SIGCONT  ", // Continue (POSIX)
```

```
/*19*/ "SIGSTOP  ", // Stop, unblockable (POSIX)
/*20*/ "SIGTSTP  ", // Keyboard stop (POSIX)
/*21*/ "SIGTTIN  ", // Background read from tty (POSIX)
/*22*/ "SIGTTOU  ", // Background write to tty (POSIX)
/*23*/ "SIGURG   ", // Urgent condition on socket (4.2 BSD)
/*24*/ "SIGXCPU  ", // CPU limit exceeded (4.2 BSD)
/*25*/ "SIGXFSZ  ", // File size limit exceeded (4.2 BSD)
/*26*/ "SIGVTALRM", // Virtual alarm clock (4.2 BSD)
/*27*/ "SIGPROF  ", // Profiling alarm clock (4.2 BSD)
/*28*/ "SIGWINCH ", // Window size change (4.3 BSD, Sun)
/*29*/ "SIGIO    ", // I/O now possible (4.2 BSD)
/*30*/ "SIGPWR   ", // Power failure restart (System V)
/*31*/ "SIGSYS   "  // Bad system call"
};
```

Notice that all signal names are padded with spaces to reach a consistent length of nine characters. This is because it will be useful to be able to print them from within signal handlers, and printf() is not safe to use when servicing interrupts. The alternative to printf() is to use write(), which is safe but must be told the length of the string. Now, as it happens, strlen() is also unsafe in ISRs. To determine the length of the signal names, you would have to count their characters before the terminating NULL. Sure, to avoid counting characters every time you need to display a signal name, you could define an array with all the lengths, or make sig_names an array of structures containing name lengths together with the trimmed (i.e., unpadded) names.

docs.oracle.com/cd/E19455-01/806-5257/gen-26/index.html provides a list of the functions you can safely use when handling signals and interrupts.

Well, I thought it was simpler to pad the names and put up with the trailing spaces. You are obviously welcome to try something else.

A thread is a subprocess. From within your program, you can "farm out" tasks to threads and do something else while they do their work asynchronously. Then, when you are ready, you can wait for them to complete and use the results of their processing. Listing 11-5 shows a program that catches three signals, creates three threads, ends them, and waits for them to complete.

You will only be able to compile and link the program with the option -pthread added to the gcc compiler and the gcc linker. The p stands for Posix, and the option is necessary to allow use of threads. If you are using Eclipse as a development environment, you add -pthread to:

```
C/C++ Build -> Settings -> GCC C Compiler -> Command
```

and

```
C/C++ Build -> Settings -> GCC C Linker -> Command
```

Listing 11-5. Threads and Signals

```
1. //------------------------------------------------------------------------ main
2. int main(int argc, char *argv[]) {
3.   int res;
4.
5.   // Catch some signals.
6.   struct sigaction act = {{&signal_handler}};
7.   struct sigaction oldact = {};
```

```
 8.    //
 9.    if (signal(SIGKILL, signal_handler) == SIG_ERR) {
10.      printf("Main: can't catch SIGKILL\n");
11.      }
12.    //
13.    if (signal(SIGINT, signal_handler) == SIG_ERR) {
14.      printf("Main: can't catch SIGINT\n");
15.      }
16.    //
17.    if (sigaction(SIGABRT, &act, &oldact) == -1) {
18.      printf("Main: can't catch SIGABRT\n");
19.      }
20.    printf("%p, %p\n", signal_handler, oldact.sa_handler);
21.
22.    // Create three threads.
23.    for (int k = 0; k < N_THREADS; k++) {
24.      res = pthread_create(&threads[k], NULL, &a_thread, NULL);
25.      if (res) Crash("Main: error %d when creating thread %d", res, k);      //-->
26.      printf("Main: created thread %d (%u)\n", k, (unsigned int)threads[k]);
27.      }
28.
29.    // Terminate the threads one by one.
30.    sleep(2);
31.    printf("Canceling thread 0\n");
32.    res = pthread_cancel(threads[0]);
33.    if (res) {
34.      Crash("Main: \"%s\" when canceling thread %d", strerror(res), 0);      //-->
35.      }
36.    sleep(2);
37.    printf("Killing thread 1\n");
38.    res = pthread_kill(threads[1], SIGINT);
39.    if (res) {
40.      Crash("Main: \"%s\" when killing thread %d", strerror(res), 1);      //-->
41.      }
42.    sleep(2);
43.    printf("Aborting thread 2\n");
44.    res = pthread_kill(threads[2], SIGABRT);
45.    if (res) {
46.      Crash("Main: \"%s\" when aborting thread %d", strerror(res), 2);      //-->
47.      }
48.    sleep(2);
49.
50.    // Wait for the threads to end.
51.    for (int k = 0; k < N_THREADS; k++) {
52.      long ret;
53.      res = pthread_join(threads[k], (void *)&ret);
54.      if (res) Crash("Main: thread %d ended with error %d", k, res);      //-->
55.      printf("Main: thread %d has ended with result ", k);
56.      if (ret > 0 && ret < N_DEF_SIGS) printf("%s\n", sig_names[ret]);
57.      else printf("%ld\n", ret);
58.      }
59.
```

```
60.    printf("Main: that's it folks!\n");
61.      return EXIT_SUCCESS;
62.    }
```

N_THREADS and threads are defined globally before the main's code:

```
#define N_THREADS 3
pthread_t threads[N_THREADS] = {};
```

In lines 6 to 19, you tell the system to let you handle three signals: SIGKILL, SIGINT, and SIGABRT (although, as you already know, you are not allowed to catch SIGKILL). You do this by executing signal() for SIGKILL and SIGINT and sigaction() for SIGABRT. The function signal() is simpler to use, but it doesn't necessarily behave in exactly the same way across UNIX versions. Therefore, for portability, you should use sigaction(), which, as you will see, can actually do much more than just install a signal handler.

struct sigaction is only needed for the function sigaction(). act, defined in line 6, defines what you want the function sigaction() to do, while oldact, defined in line 7, is filled in by sigaction() with the values that struct sigaction holds for the specified signal when you execute the function.

As you can see, line 6 initializes all components of act to 0 except for the address of your signal handler. The double braces are needed because the first component of struct sigaction is a union. Unfortunately, not all systems include a union. This means that you might get an error when you try to compile the program as shown in Listing 11-5. The definition of struct sigaction is in the standard header bits/sigaction.h, which is included in signal.h. Listing 11-6 shows how struct sigaction is defined on my system.

Listing 11-6. struct sigaction

```
1. /* Structure describing the action to be taken when a signal arrives.  */
2. struct sigaction
3.   {
4.      /* Signal handler.  */
5. #ifdef __USE_POSIX199309
6.      union
7.        {
8.      /* Used if SA_SIGINFO is not set.  */
9.      __sighandler_t sa_handler;
10.      /* Used if SA_SIGINFO is set.  */
11.      void (*sa_sigaction) (int, siginfo_t *, void *);
12.        }
13.      __sigaction_handler;
14. # define sa_handler  __sigaction_handler.sa_handler
15. # define sa_sigaction       __sigaction_handler.sa_sigaction
16. #else
17.          __sighandler_t sa_handler;
18. #endif
19.
20.      /* Additional set of signals to be blocked.  */
21.      __sigset_t sa_mask;
22.
23.      /* Special flags.  */
24.      int sa_flags;
25.
26.      /* Restore handler.  */
27.      void (*sa_restorer) (void);
28.   };
```

Lines 16 and 17 of Listing 11-6 are struck through because, in order to use the threads, you need to write as the first line of your program the following definition:

```
#define _POSIX_C_SOURCE 200809L
```

to tell gcc that you are writing code that conforms to the latest Posix standard, which includes the thread functionality we are using (remember that the p of pthread stands for Posix). As a result of this definition, the following lines in features.h

```
#if (_POSIX_C_SOURCE - 0) >= 199309L
# define __USE_POSIX199309  1
#endif
```

mean that the functionality of the 1993 version of the Posix standard is enabled. Incidentally, if you are wondering where you can possibly find such definitions and references, the page osxr.org:8080/glibc/ident will tell you where any identifier occurs within the gcc headers.

In any case, the action to catch signals applies to the whole program, including the threads you create. Not surprising, the attempt in line 9 of Listing 11-5 to trap SIGKILL fails.

Listing 11-7 shows the signal handler.

Listing 11-7. signal_handler()

```
1. //------------------------------------------------------------- signal_handler
2. void signal_handler(int sig_num) {
3.   char thread_num_s[2] = {};
4.   thread_num_s[0] = '0' + identify_thread(pthread_self());
5.   write(1, "Thread ", 7);
6.   write(1, thread_num_s, 1);
7.   write(1, ": received signal ", 18);
8.   if (sig_num < N_DEF_SIGS) {
9.     write(1, sig_names[sig_num], 9);
10.     }
11.   else {
12.     char s[3] = {' ', ' ', '\0'};
13.     s[0] = '0' + sig_num / 10;
14.     s[1] = '0' + sig_num % 10;
15.     write(1, s, 2);
16.     }
17.   write(1, "\n", 1);
18.   pthread_exit((void *)(long)sig_num);
19. } // signal_handler
```

In general, you will have a different handler for each signal. But this example has no other purpose than helping you to understand how you can use signals (perhaps with the positive side effect of providing some info on threads). Therefore, it makes sense to use the same handler for all signals.

The signal handler of Listing 11-7 terminates the thread by executing pthread_exit(), but obviously doesn't always need to be. The value passed to pthread_exit() is an exit status that can be checked by other threads afterwards. In the example, you set the status to the signal number. Not very useful, but it is just an example. Notice the double typecasting, which is necessary to avoid warnings (you first extend the integer to make it the same size as a pointer and then typecast it to a pointer).

The function pthread_self() in line 4 returns the thread identifier of type pthread_t (an integer number). As you will see in a moment, the program saves the identifiers of the threads it creates in the global array threads. This makes possible for you to map the thread identifier to a small number between 1 and N_THREADS, as shown in Listing 11-8.

Listing 11-8. identify_thread()

```
1. //------------------------------------------------------------- identify_thread
2. int identify_thread(pthread_t thr) {
3.    for (int k = 0; k < N_THREADS; k++) if (thr == threads[k]) return k;    //-->
4.    return '?' - '0';
5.    } // identify_thread
```

The rationale behind line 4 will become clear if you look at lines 3 and 4 of the signal handler (Listing 11-7): in line 3 you define the C string thread_num_s of length 1 (plus the terminating NULL); then, in line 4, you store in it the index of the current thread as returned by identify_thread() after converting to a character. If identify_thread() doesn't find the thread within the array threads, it falls through the for loop and returns the number needed to cause thread_num_s to be set to a question mark.

As I said before, printf() is not safe to use within an ISR. This is why all outputs of text are done with write().

In line 9 of the signal handler, you write the event number if it is one of those defined in the array sig_name (Listing 11-4). If it is not, in lines 12 to 15 you convert the signal number to a two-character string. This works because you know that all single-digit signal numbers are defined in sig_name and that there are less than 100 signals.

In line 18 of the signal handler, the thread kills itself without explaining why. To provide a reason, you can replace the NULL with a different value.

In line 23 to 27 of Listing 11-5, you create N_THREAD threads.

pthread_create() stores the identifier of the newly created process in the location provided as the first argument, which in the example is element k of the array threads.

You can use the second parameter of pthread_create() to specify the attributes you want the new thread to have, or NULL if you are happy with the defaults. The parameter is a pointer to a structure of type pthread_attr_t. To set the attributes, you need to initialize the structure to the default values:

```
pthread_attr_t my_attr;
pthread_attr_init(&my_attr);
```

After that, you can set individual attributes with dedicated functions. For example,

```
pthread_attr_setstacksize(&my_attr, 100000);
```

lets you set to 100000 bytes the minimum size allocated to the thread. FYI, the default on my system is 8388608 bytes, or 2^{23}. You can find the list of all functions at the end of the manual page for pthread_attr_init() (e.g., in man7.org/linux/man-pages/man3/pthread_attr_init.3.html).

The third parameter of pthread_create() is where you specify the signal handler and, finally, the fourth parameter lets you specify a value you want to pass to the newly created thread, or NULL if you don't want to pass any value.

Listing 11-9 shows the function we use for all three threads.

Listing 11-9. a_thread()

```
1. //------------------------------------------------------------- a_thread
2. void *a_thread(void *x) {
```

```
3.    pthread_t t = pthread_self();
4.    printf("Thread %d (%u): I'm running\n", identify_thread(t), (unsigned int)t);
5.    while (1) sleep(10);
6.    return NULL;
7.    } // a_thread
```

Pretty straightforward: the thread notifies you that it has started and then forever sleeps, waking up every 10 seconds.

Now, this simple function provides an example of how tricky writing pieces of code that execute in parallel can be. Each new thread is created in line 24 of the main (Listing 11-5) by executing pthread_create(), which saves the thread ID in the array threads. It is reasonable to assume that the launching of the newly created thread is the last operation that pthread_create() performs before returning. But you cannot be sure unless you look at the source code of the create function. What if it starts the thread before saving the thread ID in threads? Is it then possible that the newly created thread starts running when the corresponding element in threads has not been set? identify_thread() would then fail.

It is a very unlikely scenario. But can you exclude it? It wouldn't matter if it happened in our example, but such a rare coincidence occurring in a real-world situation could have serious consequences and be very difficult to pinpoint. In general, the golden rule of real-time programming is *never depend on timing*. If something is theoretically possible, sooner or later it will happen, and when you least expect it (Murphy was right!). More about this issue in the next section of this chapter, when we look at how you can make your code safe.

You could add a one-off short sleep at the very beginning of the thread function, thereby forcing a context switch. But you could also decide to pass the thread number to the thread itself, thereby avoiding the use of identify_thread() altogether. For example, you could replace line 24 of the main (Listing 11-5) with

```
res = pthread_create(&threads[k], NULL, &a_thread, k);
```

and replace line 4 of a_thread() (Listing 11-9) with

```
printf("Thread %d (%u): I'm running\n", (int)x, (unsigned int)t);
```

You will have to add a couple of typecasts to avoid warnings, but it will work in any case.

The Crash() macro that you invoke in line 26 is as follows:

```
#define Crash(...) {                                       \
  fprintf(stderr, "\n");                                   \
  fprintf(stderr, __VA_ARGS__);                            \
  fprintf(stderr, " (file %s; line %d)\n", __FILE__, __LINE__); \
  return EXIT_FAILURE;                                     \
  }
```

You can use it as if it were a printf(). The advantage of using the macro is that it also prints where it was invoked and terminates the program.

In lines 31 to 47 of the main (Listing 11-5) you terminate the three threads one by one. Line 32 shows how you can terminate a thread (in this case, what we have called thread 0) by sending to it a cancellation request, rather than one of the signals you saw earlier in this section.

In line 38, you terminate thread 1 by sending to it the SIGINT signal and in line 44, you terminate thread 2 by sending a SIGABRT.

The two-second sleeps in between are there to prevent the operations from overlapping. You will see in a moment what happens with and without the pauses.

In lines 51 to 58, you wait for the threads to end by invoking pthread_join(). In the example, because of the pauses, you actually execute pthread_join() after the threads have already terminated. When that happens, the function returns immediately.

The output of the whole program is shown in Listing 11-10.

Listing 11-10. Threads and Signals—Output

```
 1. Main: can't catch SIGKILL
 2. 0x40118d, (nil)
 3. 0x40118d, 0x40118d
 4. Main: created thread 0 (338773760)
 5. Main: created thread 1 (330381056)
 6. Main: created thread 2 (321988352)
 7. Thread 2 (321988352): I'm running
 8. Thread 1 (330381056): I'm running
 9. Thread 0 (338773760): I'm running
10. Canceling thread 0
11. Killing thread 1
12. Thread 1: received signal SIGINT
13. Aborting thread 2
14. Thread 2: received signal SIGABRT
15. Main: thread 0 has ended with result -1
16. Main: thread 1 has ended with result SIGINT
17. Main: thread 2 has ended with result SIGABRT
18. Main: that's it folks!
```

The thread exit status -1 that you see in line 15 of the output is due to the fact that you terminated that thread with a call to pthread_cancel() instead of by sending it a signal. The system then sets the exit status to PTHREAD_CANCELED, which is defined in pthread.h as ((void *) -1).

Before moving on, I still need to tell you how to block signals. Now that you know how to catch them, you can always ignore as many catchable signals as you like by setting up for them a signal handler that does nothing. But the interruption would still take place. The best way to ignore signals is to block them.

All signal-blocking functions rely of a data structure called a *signal set* that represents groups of signals. You manipulate signal sets with the following functions:

```
int sigemptyset(sigset_t *set) // initializes a set without any signal
int sigfillset(sigset_t *set) // initializes a set with all defined signals
int sigaddset(sigset_t *set, int sig) // add the signal sig to a set
int sigdelset(sigset_t *set, int sig) // remove the signal sig from a set
int sigismember(const sigset_t *set, int sig) // returns 1 if sig is in the set
```

The first two functions always return 0; the other three return 0 when successful and -1 when the signal is not valid.

Each thread has a current signal set called a *signal mask*, which determines what signals are blocked for that thread. To modify that mask (i.e., to block or unblock one or more signals), you define a signal set and execute the following function:

```
int pthread_sigmask(int how, const sigset_t *set, sigset_t *oldset);
```

The parameter *how* can have the values SIG_BLOCK, SIG_UNBLOCK, and SIG_SETMASK. With SIG_BLOCK, you update the signal mask of the thread to block all signals included in set (i.e., in the second argument); with SIG_UNBLOCK, you update the signal mask to unblock the signals defined in set; and with SIG_SETMASK, you replace the current signal mask of the thread with set. The signal mask before the update is returned in oldset.

If you only want to know the current mask, you invoke `pthread_sigmask()` with `NULL` as second argument (in which case *how* is ignored). And if you are not interested in the the current mask, you pass `NULL` as third argument.

Retrieving the current mask is useful in order to make temporary changes to the mask. You disable one or more signals with `SIG_BLOCK` and then restore the mask with `SET_SIGMASK`. For example:

```
sigset_t set;
sigemptyset(&set);
sigaddset(&set, SIGALRM);
sigset_t oldset;
pthread_sigmask(SIG_BLOCK, &set, &oldset);
...
pthread_sigmask(SIG_SETMASK, &oldset, NULL);
```

Note that setting the mask to its original value is *not* the same as blocking and then unblocking a group of signals, because one or more of them might have been already blocked. In that case, by using the set to unblock them, you would not restore the original conditions.

Be aware that when you block a signal, you do not make it disappear. As soon as the signal is unblocked, it will hit its target.

Concurrency

In a multiprocessing/multithread environment, several sequences of instructions execute at the same time. That is, several sequences can start and execute asynchronously with respect to each other, thereby opening up the possibility for different sequences to access the same resource (e.g., a memory location or a device) in an unpredictable order. This type of *concurrent* access can cause problems when the processes/threads do not take into account that a particular resource is not at their exclusive disposal. You have already seen an example of concurrency in the previous section, when both the main thread and the signal handler wrote something to the standard output and the text got mixed up.

The simplest case, and the one we will talk about in this section, is when different threads access the same global variable. This is illustrated by the program shown in Listing 11-11.

Listing 11-11. Program to Illustrate Concurrency

```
1. #define _POSIX_C_SOURCE 200809L
2. #include <stdio.h>
3. #include <stdlib.h>
4. #include <signal.h>
5. #include <pthread.h>
6. #include <unistd.h>
7.
8. #define Crash(…) {                                         \
9.    fprintf(stderr, "\n");                                  \
10.   fprintf(stderr, __VA_ARGS__);                           \
11.   fprintf(stderr, " (file %s; line %d)\n", __FILE__, __LINE__); \
12.   return EXIT_FAILURE;                                    \
13.   }
14.
15. int an_int = 0;
16. int thread_running = 0;
17.
```

```
18. void *a_thread(void *x);
19.
20. //------------------------------------------------------------------------ main
21. int main(int argc, char *argv[]) {
22.
23.   // Create a thread.
24.   pthread_t thread;
25.   int res = pthread_create(&thread, NULL, &a_thread, NULL);
26.   if (res) Crash("Main: error %d when creating thread.", res);        //-->
27.   printf("Main: created thread\n");
28.
29.   // Access global variable concurrently with the thread.
30.   while (!thread_running) sleep(1);
31.   while (thread_running) {
32.     an_int = 0;
33.     }
34.
35.   // Display the counter returned by the thread.
36.   long ret;
37.   res = pthread_join(thread, (void *)&ret);
38.   if (res) Crash("Main: thread ended with error %d", res);           //-->
39.   printf("Main: thread has ended after %ld iterations.\n", ret);
40.
41.     return EXIT_SUCCESS;
42.   }
43.
44. //------------------------------------------------------------------- a_thread
45. void *a_thread(void *x) {
46.   printf("Thread: I'm running\n");
47.   thread_running = 1;
48.   unsigned long kount = 0;
49.   do {
50.     kount++;
51.     an_int = kount;
52.     } while (an_int == kount);
53.   thread_running = 0;
54.   return (void *)kount;
55.   } // a_thread
```

In lines 15 and 16, you define two global variables: an_int is the variable that the main and a thread access concurrently, while thread_running is used to synchronize the main and the thread.

The main creates the thread in lines 24 to 27, waits in line 30 that the thread is actually running, and then, in lines 31 to 33, keeps setting an_int to 0 in a tight loop as long as the thread keeps running.

When the thread ends, the main displays its return value in lines 36 to 39.

If you now look at the thread function listed in lines 45 to 55, you see that the thread displays a message in line 46, sets to true the global flag thread_running in line 47, resets the local counter kount in line 48, and enters the do loop of lines 49 to 52.

The loop looks as if it would run forever: it increments kount, sets the global variable an_int to the value of kount, and then immediately checks in the while condition whether an_int and kount are the same. How could they be different if in the previous statement you set one to the value held by the other?

Here is where concurrency comes into play: it can happen that the thread is suspended between lines 51 and 52 and, when the main is activated, it has enough time to execute line 32 (remember that it is running in a tight loop). When that happens, the value of an_int changes to 0, and the while condition in line 52 fails.

You might say, "Come on! What is the probability that the context switch occurs between lines 51 and 52?"

Well, as I said before, it doesn't really matter how unlikely a conflict can occur. You have to play it safe, because you know that, if it can occur, it will!

Here is the output of the program:

```
Main: created thread
Thread: I'm running
Main: thread has ended after 321464874 iterations.
```

The do loop within the thread ran more than 300 million times before the context switch hit the "sweet spot" (or the "bitter spot", if you prefer). But it did happen. If you execute the program repeatedly, you get counts up to more than 360 millions, but the crucial issue is that it does happen every time you run the program. Can you imagine how difficult it would be to identify such a problem in a real-life situation with the conflict buried within a large application?

The example doesn't involve interrupts, but concurrency problems are even trickier to debug when ISRs are involved, because they can often be too difficult to reproduce when you use a debugger. If you want to develop embedded code, you need to keep concurrency firmly in your mind and, as I said, never rely on timing and probabilities. You must make conflicts logically impossible to occur!

To look at possible solutions, let's first modify the program of Listing 11-11 so that the conflicts occur more easily. All you need to do is insert the two lines

```
struct timespec m20 = {0, 20000000L};
nanosleep(&m20, NULL);
```

between line 51 and 52. It will result in a delay of 20 milliseconds between the setting and the checking of an_int, thereby causing the while condition in the thread to fail after 50 iterations (on my computer).

One thing that you have to keep in mind is that such conflicts only occur when multiple threads/processes *update* a variable. As long as only one agent sets a variable and everybody else reads it, no conflict can occur. Then, to avoid conflicts, all you need to do is ensure that nothing happens to a variable after you write it and before you read it back. To make this possible in the example, you need to make a slight change to the thread function. The resulting version of the function is shown in Listing 11-12, which replaces lines 44 to 55 of Listing 11-11.

Listing 11-12. Updated a_thread()

```
44. //----------------------------------------------------------------- a_thread
45. const static struct timespec m20 = {0, 20000000L}; // new
46. void *a_thread(void *x) {
47.   printf("Thread: I'm running\n");
48.   thread_running = 1;
49.   unsigned long kount = 0;
50.   int match;                                    // new
51.   do {
52.     kount++;
53.     an_int = kount;
54.     nanosleep(&m20, NULL);                      // new
55.     match = (an_int == kount);                  // new
56.     } while (match);                            // modified
57.   thread_running = 0;
```

```
58.    return (void *)kount;
59.  } // a_thread
```

m20 is now a static variable defined outside the thread function, but that has no impact on the issue at hand. I only placed it there because it seems more appropriate. What you need to do is make the writing and reading back of an_int in lines 53 and 55 of Listing 11-12 an *atomic operation* that cannot be interrupted.

You do so by using a *mutex* (which stands for *mut*ually *ex*clusion). First of all, you define a global variable of type pthread_mutex_t:

```
pthread_mutex_t a_mutex = PTHREAD_MUTEX_INITIALIZER;
```

Secondly, you write

```
pthread_mutex_lock(&a_mutex);
```

immediately before line 53 of Listing 11-12 and

```
pthread_mutex_unlock(&a_mutex);
```

immediately after line 55.

Third, and finally, you also enclose line 32 of the main (see Listing 11-11) with the same pair of functions:

```
while (thread_running) {           // line 31
  pthread_mutex_lock(&a_mutex);
  an_int = 0;                      // line 32
  pthread_mutex_unlock(&a_mutex);
}                                  // line 33
```

That's it! If you now execute the program, it will never stop because the while condition of line 56 of Listing 11-12 will never fail. For testing, you might like to change it to something like (match && kount < 500), so that the program will end.

When a process tries to lock a mutex that has already been locked by another thread, it is forced to wait until the locking thread executes the unlocking function.

Note that if you use more than one mutex, you have to be very careful to avoid the possibility of entering what is called a *deadly embrace*, in which two threads lock each other out. Suppose for example that thread 1 locks mutex A and, while A is locked, it locks mutex B, while thread 2 locks mutex B and, while it holds the lock on B, it locks A. Don't be surprised if they will end up waiting on each other forever.

The problem with shared variables illustrated in the example also occurs when you do the reading before the writing. For example, the operation

```
num++;
```

is equivalent to

```
num += 1;
```

and

```
num = num + 1;
```

As the C standard doesn't specify whether the ++ operator is atomic or not, to be safe, you have to assume that it isn't. Now, suppose that the variable num is shared with another thread and that the other thread also writes it. If the first thread is suspended after it reads num but before it writes it back incremented, the first thread overwrites the value written by the other thread. You will again encounter concurrency issues in the next chapter concerning databases, where several users might be updating the same data item.

One last word concerning concurrency. Modern compilers are optimized (unless you set an option to switch the optimization off, that is). This means that if you set a variable and read it back, the compiler might decide to hold the value in some CPU register and not read the variable back at all!

But what if something else can modify the variable asynchronously?

You saw that happen in a multi-threaded example, in which two threads can modify a global variable. If the compiler had "optimized away" the reading of kount after a_thread() had written it (lines 55 and 53 of Listing 11-12), the while loop would have gone on forever. The optimization didn't occur, and the example worked as expected but, to be completely safe when writing global variables from multiple threads, you should declare them to be volatile, as in:

```
int volatile an_int = 0; // line 15 of Listing 11-11
```

whereby the keyword volatile can be on either side of the int.

By doing so, you tell the compiler that the value of the variable can change at any time. This will force the compiler to avoid optimizing the code that accesses it.

Obviously, the same problem occurs when a variable is shared between a thread and ISRs, including signal handlers.

But with embedded code there is another case in which you need to declare a variable to be volatile: when you refer to memory-mapped addresses of physical devices. Consider, for example, the 8-bit status register of a piece of hardware mapped to the memory address 0x1111. You could declare it as:

```
uint8_t *status_reg = (uint8_t *)0x1111;
```

where uint8_t is a nice way of saying unsigned char.

You might need to wait for the status register to become non-zero and the obvious way to do it would be to busy-wait for it to become non-zero:

```
while(!*status_reg) {}
```

But if you did so with an optimized compiler, you might wait in the loop forever because the compiler would in all probability "think" that, as nothing changes the location pointed to by status_reg, it might as well keep the value in a register and avoid repeatedly accessing the same memory location.

You need to change the definition of status_reg as follows

```
uint8_t volatile *status_reg = (uint8_t *)0x1111;
```

to ensure that, even with optimization, the compiler will generate the code to read the location every time.

Summary

In this chapter, you learned several concepts and aspects of programming in C that are essential to write embedded, close to the hardware, code. You saw how to use bit-based operations followed by an example to illustrate endianness. Then, after going through a summary of what type of environments you will deal with when working on embedded systems, you learned about interrupts and in particular signals, picking up on the way plenty of information on how to write multi-threaded code. Finally, you learned about the key issues caused by concurrency and the effect of declaring a variable as volatile.

The next chapter will bring another change of pace, as we will look at how to work with databases.

CHAPTER 12

■ ■ ■

Databases

A database consists of organized data—that is, the data itself and a *schema* that provides data structures. Nowadays, most databases are organized in tables, and you can define the table characteristics independently of the actual data you're going to store into it.

A database management system (DBMS), such as MySQL or PostgreSQL, is a software package that lets you create, retrieve, update, and delete (CRUD) items of data and elements of the schema.

Therefore, when talking about a database, you need to distinguish between three aspects:

- The data it contains

- The structure you impose on the data in order to CRUD it efficiently

- The software that allows you to manipulate both the data and the database structure (the DBMS)

Working with a database means that you're interacting with its DBMS. You can do that through a command line interface (CLI), through graphical user interfaces (GUIs) provided by the DBMS vendor and third parties, or programmatically through an API. In general, you use all three methods, each for a different purpose. The CLI is best suited for setting up the initial data structure and for testing, the API is for your application to interact with the database to perform its tasks, and the GUI is what you use to check individual data items or fix one-off problems.

There are several DBMSs, but MySQL is likely to be the most widely known and used of them. According to dev.mysql.com, MySQL Community Server is the world's most popular open source database. Perhaps in part because it is part of what has become the standard software package to develop web sites: Linux + Apache web server + MySQL + PHP scripting language = LAMP.

In this chapter, I show you how to use MySQL databases from a C program. Then, I introduce you to SQLite, an embedded DBMS that you integrate into your program rather than use as an external package.

To understand the examples in this chapter, you need to be familiar with the Structured Query Language (SQL, sometimes pronounced as "sequel") used to communicate with DBMSs. If you don't know SQL, you can find a good and detailed description of it at w3schools.com/sql. To see how an SQL specification standard is structured without having to buy it from ISO, you can look at the 1992 revision made available online by Carnegie Mellon University (www.contrib.andrew.cmu.edu/~shadow/sql/sql1992.txt). It covers most of what you will probably use SQL for. Finally, you can also refer to Appendix B, where you will find an introduction to SQL.

MySQL

To be able to work with MySQL, you need to have it on your computer. I work with Ubuntu, a release of GNU/Linux, which includes the MySQL server. I typed at the command line mysql --version and got the following:

```
mysql  Ver 14.14 Distrib 5.5.47, for debian-linux-gnu (x86_64) using readline 6.3
```

G. Zambon, *Practical C*, DOI 10.1007/978-1-4842-1769-6_12

The latest version of MySQL is 5.7.11. As you can only upgrade one release at the time, I would have had to upgrade 5.5 to 5.6 and then 5.6 to 5.7. It wasn't worth the effort because I am writing this book on a laptop and I am not going to use the laptop to hold critical data.

But if you are working with Windows or Macintosh systems, you have to download and install MySQL. To do so, go to the page dev.mysql.com/downloads/mysql, select your OS, choose your processor (i.e., 32 or 64 bits), and download the package.

With Windows, I found that the MSI download works well. But to install the whole package on Windows, you need the .NET framework and the Visual C++ Redistributable Package. The MySQL installer will guide you through the process of installing them, but if you need further help, you can visit the page dev.mysql.com/resources/wb52_prerequisites. When you have those two pieces in place and install MySQL, choose the standard/default configurations; choose Developer Machine, enable TCP/IP, and create Windows Service MySQL5x (I tested MySQL55, but by now it will be MySQL57).

Using the CLI to Create and Populate a Database

You can skip this section if you are familiar with MySQL. But, before you do so, execute the two scripts shown in Listings 12-5 and 12-6.

After you have MySQL up and running, you can interact with the server from the command line by typing

```
mysql -u root -p
```

This assumes that you have defined a password when you installed MySQL, which is obviously what you should do. Anyway, once you type your root password and press Enter, you are connected with the MySQL server. Type \h at the mysql> prompt and you will see a list of all possible commands, which I have reproduced in Listing 12-1.

Listing 12-1. MySQL Commands

```
List of all MySQL commands:

Note that all text commands must be first on line and end with ';'

?         (\?) Synonym for `help'.

clear     (\c) Clear the current input statement.

connect   (\r) Reconnect to the server. Optional arguments are db and host.

delimiter (\d) Set statement delimiter.

edit      (\e) Edit command with $EDITOR.

ego       (\G) Send command to mysql server, display result vertically.

exit      (\q) Exit mysql. Same as quit.

go        (\g) Send command to mysql server.

help      (\h) Display this help.
```

```
nopager    (\n) Disable pager, print to stdout.

notee      (\t) Don't write into outfile.

pager      (\P) Set PAGER [to_pager]. Print the query results via PAGER.

print      (\p) Print current command.

prompt     (\R) Change your mysql prompt.

quit       (\q) Quit mysql.

rehash     (\#) Rebuild completion hash.

source     (\.) Execute an SQL script file. Takes a file name as an argument.

status     (\s) Get status information from the server.

system     (\!) Execute a system shell command.

tee        (\T) Set outfile [to_outfile]. Append everything into given outfile.

use        (\u) Use another database. Takes database name as argument.

charset    (\C) Switch to another charset. Might be needed for processing binlog with
               multi-byte charsets.

warnings   (\W) Show warnings after every statement.

nowarning  (\w) Don't show warnings after every statement.

For server side help, type 'help contents'
```

If you now type the command help contents, you get what is shown in Listing 12-2.

Listing 12-2. MySQL Help Categories

```
For more information, type 'help <item>', where <item> is one of the following

categories:

    Account Management

    Administration

    Compound Statements

    Data Definition

    Data Manipulation

    Data Types
```

Functions

Functions and Modifiers for Use with GROUP BY

Geographic Features

Help Metadata

Language Structure

Plugins

Procedures

Storage Engines

Table Maintenance

Transactions

User-Defined Functions

Utility

And, if you type help data definition, you get the list of SQL commands for which you can get detailed help (see Listing 12-3).

Listing 12-3. MySQL Help Data Definition

topics:

ALTER DATABASE

ALTER EVENT

ALTER FUNCTION

ALTER LOGFILE GROUP

ALTER PROCEDURE

ALTER SERVER

ALTER TABLE

ALTER TABLESPACE

ALTER VIEW

CONSTRAINT

```
CREATE DATABASE

CREATE EVENT

CREATE FUNCTION

CREATE INDEX

CREATE LOGFILE GROUP

CREATE PROCEDURE

CREATE SERVER

CREATE TABLE

CREATE TABLESPACE

CREATE TRIGGER

CREATE VIEW

DROP DATABASE

DROP EVENT

DROP FUNCTION

DROP INDEX

DROP LOGFILE GROUP

DROP PROCEDURE

DROP SERVER

DROP TABLE

DROP TABLESPACE

DROP TRIGGER

DROP VIEW

RENAME TABLE

TRUNCATE TABLE
```

Listing 12-4 shows the log of a session in which you create a database, add a table to it, insert a row into the table, and display the result of your operations. The commands are highlighted in bold.

Listing 12-4. A MySQL Session

```
 1. giulio@Voyager:~/Desktop/eclipse/Database$ mysql -u root -p
 2. Enter password:
 3. Welcome to the MySQL monitor.  Commands end with ; or \g.
 4. Your MySQL connection id is 56
 5. Server version: 5.5.47-0ubuntu0.14.04.1 (Ubuntu)
 6.
 7. Copyright (c) 2000, 2015, Oracle and/or its affiliates. All rights reserved.
 8.
 9. Oracle is a registered trademark of Oracle Corporation and/or its
10. affiliates. Other names may be trademarks of their respective
11. owners.
12.
13. Type 'help;' or '\h' for help. Type '\c' to clear the current input statement.
14.
15. mysql> create database a_base;
16. Query OK, 1 row affected (0.00 sec)
17.
18. mysql> show databases;
19. +--------------------+
20. | Database           |
21. +--------------------+
22. | information_schema |
23. | a_base             |
24. | mysql              |
25. | performance_schema |
26. +--------------------+
27. 4 rows in set (0.00 sec)
28.
29. mysql> create table a_table (id integer, n integer, primary key (id));
30. ERROR 1046 (3D000): No database selected
31. mysql> use a_base;
32. Database changed
33. mysql> create table a_table (id integer, n integer, primary key (id));
34. Query OK, 0 rows affected (0.02 sec)
35.
36. mysql> show tables;
37. +------------------+
38. | Tables_in_a_base |
39. +------------------+
40. | a_table          |
41. +------------------+
42. 1 row in set (0.00 sec)
43.
44. mysql> insert into a_table values (1, 100);
45. Query OK, 1 row affected (0.01 sec)
46.
47. mysql> select * from a_table;
```

```
48. +----+------+
49. | id | n    |
50. +----+------+
51. |  1 |  100 |
52. +----+------+
53. 1 row in set (0.01 sec)
54.
55. mysql> exit;
56. Bye
57. giulio@Voyager:~/Desktop/eclipse/Database$
```

After creating a database in line 15 and listing all databases in line 18, the first attempt at creating a table (line 29) fails because the MySQL server doesn't automatically assume that the SQL commands you type are for the database that you have just created. To start working with a particular database, you have to execute the use command, which you do in line 31. After that, the create table command succeeds (line 33).

After listing the tables of the current database in line 36, in line 44 you insert a record into the newly created table named a_table. With the select command in line 47 you list all the records in a_table.

Before moving on, I need to show you how to use another MySQL command shown in Listing 12-1: source, which makes possible to execute a series of SQL commands from file. I recommend that you define new databases by typing all SQL commands in a script file and then using the source command to execute the whole script. This is because you are bound to make mistakes, and the last thing you want is to have to repeat commands by hand.

For example, suppose that you want to create a database to represent your home library. For each book you want to store its title, its author, its ISBN, and a category to which it belongs (e.g., "SF"). Listing 12-5 shows a script you could use to create the database.

Listing 12-5. library_create.sql

```
1. drop database library;
2. create database library;
3. create table library.categories (
4.   category_id integer not null auto_increment unique,
5.   category_name varchar(70),
6.   primary key (category_id)
7.   );
8. create table library.books (
9.   book_id integer not null auto_increment unique,
10.   title varchar(70),
11.   author varchar(70),
12.   ISBN varchar(17),
13.   category_id integer,
14.   primary key (book_id)
15.   );
16. create index category_id_key on library.categories (category_id);
17. create index book_id_key on library.books (book_id);
18. alter table library.books add index category_id (category_id),
19.   add constraint category_id foreign key (category_id)
20.   references library.categories (category_id)
21.   ;
```

If you attach to the directory that contains the script `library_create.sql` and then, after connecting to the server, you execute the command

```
source library_create.sql;
```

after the error message

```
ERROR 1008 (HY000): Can't drop database 'library'; database doesn't exist
```

you get a series of `Query OK` reports. The error is understandable because the library database didn't exist before. If you get an error or are not happy with the results, you can easily update the script and run it again. To state the obvious, once you are happy with the script and perhaps have added many records to the database, don't run it again!

Defining two indices in lines 16 and 17 is overkill, because you don't really need to speed up consultation of the database if your library consists of some hundred book or even some thousand—but why not? The constraint in lines 19 and 20 ensures that you don't try to assign to a book a category that you haven't yet defined.

Listing 12-6 shows a script that you can use to initially populate the database.

Listing 12-6. library_populate.sql

```
 1. use library;
 2. insert into categories (
 3.     category_id
 4.    , category_name
 5.    )
 6.    values
 7.     (1,'SF')
 8.    , (2,'Thriller')
 9.    ;
10. insert into books (
11.     title
12.    , author
13.    , ISBN
14.    , category_id
15.    )
16.    values
17.     ('The Complete Robot','Asimov, Isaac','978-0-586-05724-7',1)
18.    , ('Deliver Us From Evil','Baldacci, David','978-0-230-74679-4',2)
19.    , ('Foundation','Asimov, Isaac','978-0-586-01080-8',1)
20.    , ('The Escape','Baldacci, David','978-1-4472-6016-5',2)
21.    ;
```

Note that while you don't specify the book_id when inserting the books, you do specify the category_id when inserting the categories. Although the category_id is automatically set, you are allowed to specify a value as long as it is unique. The only reason for specifying it in library_populate.sql is to ensure that you insert the books with the correct category.

Anyway, after executing `library_populate.sql`, the command

```
select * from books order by author;
```

results in:

```
+---------+---------------------+----------------+--------------------+-------------+
| book_id | title               | author         | ISBN               | category_id |
+---------+---------------------+----------------+--------------------+-------------+
|       1 | The Complete Robot  | Asimov, Isaac  | 978-0-586-05724-7  |           1 |
|       3 | Foundation          | Asimov, Isaac  | 978-0-586-01080-8  |           1 |
|       2 | Deliver Us From Evil| Baldacci, David| 978-0-230-74679-4  |           2 |
|       4 | The Escape          | Baldacci, David| 978-1-4472-6016-5  |           2 |
+---------+---------------------+----------------+--------------------+-------------+
```

The MySQL Workbench

The Workbench is a GUI interface to MySQL. On GNU/Linux, all you need to do is type the command

```
sudo apt-get install mysql-workbench
```

and you will be in business. You can do through the Workbench everything you can do via the CLI and more. As a simple example, Figure 12-1 shows the cursor pointing to the button to execute a script and a script ready to be executed.

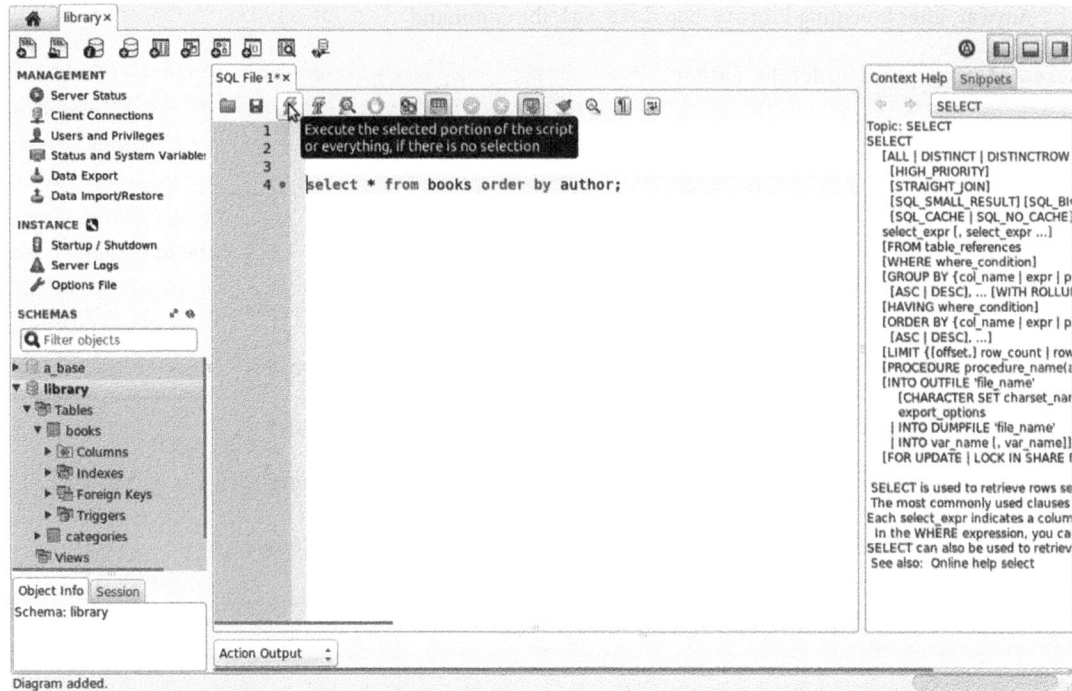

Figure 12-1. *Workbench is ready to execute a script*

Figure 12-2 shows the result of clicking on the button.

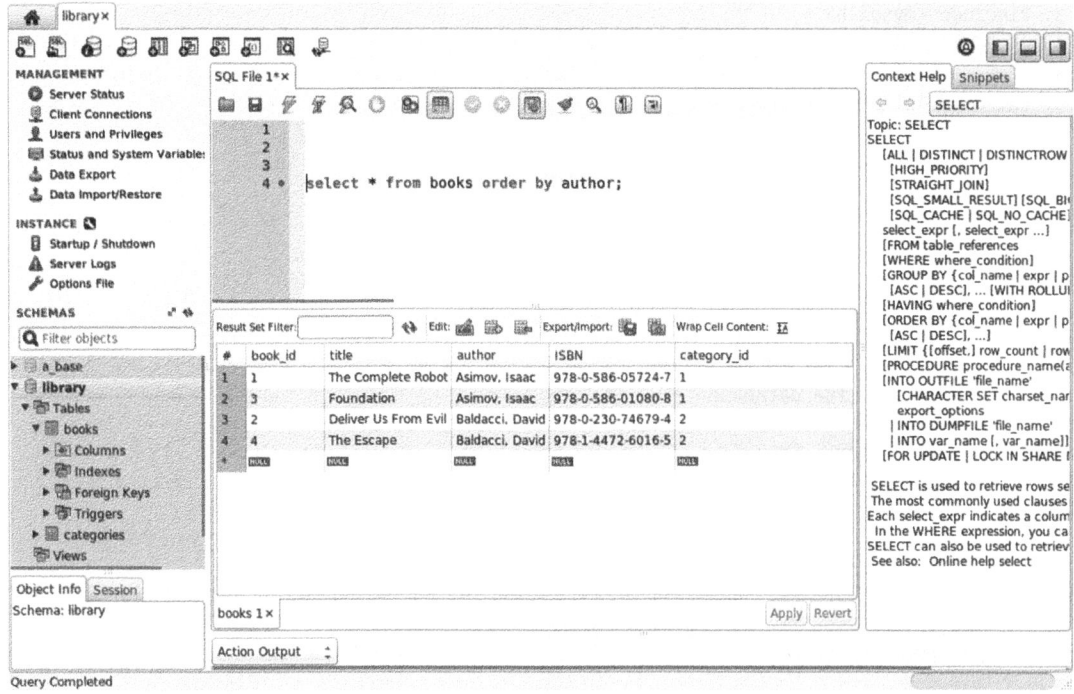

Figure 12-2. *Workbench's script is executed*

Using MySQL from a C Program

To use the MySQL server from a C program, you need an API client. Such a client is called a *connector*, and you can download it from `dev.mysql.com/downloads/connector/c/`.

For my laptop running Ubuntu, I downloaded the generic Linux 64-bit RPM package because there was no specific package for Ubuntu. To install it, I first installed the `alien` package with

```
sudo apt-get install alien
```

and then installed the connector with

```
sudo alien -i mysql-connector-c-devel-6.1.6-1.linux_glibc2.5.x86_64.rpm
```

In this section, we will start with a simple MySQL program and then add to it functionality (and, inevitably, complexity).

How to Query a MySQL Database

Listing 12-7 shows a simple program that lists the tables of the `library` database.

Listing 12-7. A Simple MySQL Program

```
1. #include <stdio.h>
2. #include <stdlib.h>
```

347

```
 3. #include <mysql.h>
 4.
 5. //------------------------------------------------------------------------ main
 6. int main(int argc, char *argv[]) {
 7.    MYSQL *conn;
 8.    MYSQL_RES *res;
 9.    MYSQL_ROW row;
10.    char *server = "localhost";
11.    char *user = "root";
12.    char *pass = "apress";
13.    char *db = "library";
14.    conn = mysql_init(NULL);
15.
16.    // Connect to the database
17.    if (!mysql_real_connect(conn, server, user, pass, db, 0, NULL, 0)) {
18.       fprintf(stderr, "%s\n", mysql_error(conn));
19.       exit(EXIT_FAILURE);                                                 // -->
20.       }
21.
22.    // List the tables
23.    if (mysql_query(conn, "show tables")) {
24.       fprintf(stderr, "%s\n", mysql_error(conn));
25.       exit(EXIT_FAILURE);                                                 // -->
26.       }
27.    res = mysql_use_result(conn);
28.    printf("Tables in the database:\n");
29.    do {
30.       row = mysql_fetch_row(res);
31.       if (row) printf("%s \n", row[0]);
32.       } while (row);
33.
34.    // Clean up
35.    mysql_free_result(res);
36.    mysql_close(conn);
37.
38.    return EXIT_SUCCESS;
39.    } // main
```

As you can see, the way of accessing a database is straightforward: initialize the MYSQL structure, establish a connection with the database, send a query, receive the result, print it out, free the result structure, and close the connection. But there are a few things that need to be clarified.

The last three arguments of mysql_real_connect() in line 17 are for the parameters port, unix_socket, and client_flag. They are all zeros because you use the defaults. You can find a description of the parameters and the list of possible values of client_flag at dev.mysql.com/doc/refman/5.7/en/mysql-real-connect.html.

The error messages returned by mysql_error() in line 24 are identical to those returned when you access he database via the CLI. This shouldn't surprise you because the messages are generated by the server. For example, if you type the wrong password in line 12, you get the message:

```
Access denied for user 'root'@'localhost' (using password: YES)
```

Obviously, you have to change the password I used for these tests (i.e., `apress`) to the one you are using.

`mysql_use_result()` in line 27 returns the address of a structure that contains the *result set*. The amount of data that your query generates is only known at runtime. Therefore, MySQL allocates space for the result set from the heap, and you need to release it when you are done with it to avoid memory leaks (in line 35). It would be nice if `mysql_close()`, besides deallocating the connection handle returned by `mysql_init()`, also took care of releasing all buffers allocated for the connection, including the result buffers. But that is not the case.

Anyway, once you have the address of the result set, you use `mysql_fetch_row()` in line 30 to obtain one row (i.e., a record) of the result at a time. If the row is not `NULL`, you then print out the first (and, in this case, only) column in line 31.

But before you can execute the program in Listing 12-7, you have some work to do.

First of all, you need to tell the `gcc` compiler where it can find the MySQL headers. With Eclipse, you can do this by opening the program's properties dialog and adding the path

```
/usr/include/mysql
```

to

```
C/C++ Build -> Settings -> GCC C Compiler -> Includes -> Include paths(-I)
```

For the program to work, you must add the compiler options

```
-g -pipe -m64 -D_GNU_SOURCE -D_FILE_OFFSET_BITS=64 -D_LARGEFILE_SOURCE -fno-strict-aliasing
```

to

```
C/C++ Build -> Settings -> GCC C Compiler -> Command
```

And, finally, you need to add the libraries

```
mysqlclient
z
crypt
nsl
m
ssl3
crypto
```

to

```
C/C++ Build -> Settings -> GCC C Linker -> Libraries -> Libraries (-l)
```

and the library locations

```
/usr/lib64
/usr/lib/x_86_64-linux-gnu
```

to

```
C/C++ Build -> Settings -> GCC C Linker -> Libraries -> Library search path (-L)
```

You are not done, though. Once you have done all that, the program still cannot run because the gcc linker cannot find the crypto library.

GNU/Linux supports two types of libraries: static and shared. The static libraries are linked into your program once and for all by the linker, while the shared libraries are relocatable and are only loaded by your program at runtime when it needs them. FYI, you might be familiar with Microsoft's implementation of shared libraries, which Microsoft calls DLLs.

To tell the gcc linker the name of libraries your program need, you use the -l option, while for the paths where the libraries are located you use the -L option. But the linker doesn't search the -L directories for files named like those you specify with with the -l option. Instead, it forms two possible filenames by attaching the string "lib" before the specified name and either ".a" or ".so" after it. So, for example, crypto becomes libcrypto.a and libcrypto.so. Static libraries have the .a extension, while shared libraries have the .so extension.

Unfortunately, if you list the directory /usr/lib/x86_64-linux-gnu where the crypto library should be, this is what you get (at least this is what I get on my laptop):

```
giulio@Voyager:/usr/lib/x86_64-linux-gnu$ ls -l *crypt*

-rw-r--r-- 1 root root  64086 Feb 17 06:30 libcrypt.a

lrwxrwxrwx 1 root root     35 Feb 17 06:30 libcrypt.so -> /lib/x86_64-linux-gnu/libcrypt.so.1

lrwxrwxrwx 1 root root     19 Mar  5  2015 libhcrypto.so.4 -> libhcrypto.so.4.1.0

-rw-r--r-- 1 root root 204104 Mar  5  2015 libhcrypto.so.4.1.0

lrwxrwxrwx 1 root root     18 Nov 12 02:24 libk5crypto.so.3 -> libk5crypto.so.3.1

-rw-r--r-- 1 root root 186824 Nov 12 02:24 libk5crypto.so.3.1
```

The two libraries libhcrypto.so.4.1.0 and libk5crypto.so.3.1 are "invisible" to the linker because it cannot form their filenames starting from the name crypto.

You can fix this by creating a soft link (also called a *symbolic* link) with one of the following two commands (while attached to the directory):

```
sudo ln -s libhcrypto.so.4 libcrypto.so
sudo ln -s libk5crypto.so.3 libcrypto.so
```

The first soft link makes the MySQL connector work with homomorphic encryption, while with the second link you choose the Kerberos 5 authentication library. I chose Kerberos but, to be honest, I don't know which choice would be better. I only checked that the simple test program in Listing 12-7 works with either!

In any case, when you are done setting everything up and then execute the test program, you will be rewarded with the following output on the system console:

```
Tables in the database:
books
categories
```

Inserting Records

Listing 12-8 shows an extended version of the test program in Listing 12-7 that, in addition to query a database, inserts a new record into it.

Listing 12-8. Another MySQL Program

```
1.  //-------------------------------------------------------------------------- main
2.  int main(int argc, char *argv[]) {
3.    MYSQL *conn;
4.    MYSQL_RES *res;
5.    MYSQL_ROW row;
6.    char *server = "localhost";
7.    char *user = "root";
8.    char *pass = "apress";
9.    char *db = "library";
10.   conn = mysql_init(NULL);
11.
12.   // Connect to the database
13.   if (!mysql_real_connect(conn, server, user, pass, db, 0, NULL, 0)) {
14.     fprintf(stderr, "%s\n", mysql_error(conn));
15.     exit(EXIT_FAILURE);                                            // -->
16.   }
17.
18.   // List the tables
19.   if (mysql_query(conn, "show tables")) {
20.     fprintf(stderr, "%s\n", mysql_error(conn));
21.     exit(EXIT_FAILURE);                                            // -->
22.   }
23.   res = mysql_use_result(conn);
24.   printf("Tables in the database:\n");
25.   do {
26.     row = mysql_fetch_row(res);
27.     if (row) printf("%s \n", row[0]);
28.   } while (row);
29.   mysql_free_result(res);
30.
31.   // Insert a record
32.   if (mysql_query(conn, "insert into books (title, author, ISBN, category_id)"
33.       " values ('The Martian','Weir, Andy','978-0-553-41802-6',1);")) {
34.     fprintf(stderr, "%s\n", mysql_error(conn));
35.     exit(EXIT_FAILURE);                                            // -->
36.   }
37.
38.   // List the books
39.   if (mysql_query(conn, "select * from books order by author")) {
40.     fprintf(stderr, "%s\n", mysql_error(conn));
41.     exit(EXIT_FAILURE);                                            // -->
42.   }
43.   res = mysql_use_result(conn);
44.   unsigned int n_cols = mysql_num_fields(res);
45.   //
46.   printf("Books in the database\n");
47.   MYSQL_FIELD *field = NULL;
48.   do {
49.     field = mysql_fetch_field(res);
50.     if (field) printf("%s\t", field->name);
```

```
51.     } while (field);
52.   printf("\n");
53.   //
54.   do {
55.     row = mysql_fetch_row(res);
56.     if (row) {
57.       for (int kol = 0; kol < n_cols; kol++) printf("%s\t", row[kol]);
58.       printf("\n");
59.     }
60.   } while (row);
61.   mysql_free_result(res);
62.
63.   // Close the connection
64.   mysql_close(conn);
65.
66.   return EXIT_SUCCESS;
67. } // main
```

In lines 32 to 36, you insert a new record, and in lines 39 to 64, you list all the books in the database. Here is what you get in output (I replaced the tabs with spaces to make the result printable and to make it look nice!):

```
Tables in the database:
books
categories
Books in the database:
book_id  title                 author          ISBN                category_id
1        The Complete Robot    Asimov, Isaac   978-0-586-05724-7   1
3        Foundation            Asimov, Isaac   978-0-586-01080-8   1
2        Deliver Us From Evil  Baldacci, David 978-0-230-74679-4   2
4        The Escape            Baldacci, David 978-1-4472-6016-5   2
5        The Martian           Weir, Andy      978-0-553-41802-6   1
```

Note that if you run the program again, it will insert a duplicate of *The Martian*. Also note that if you delete a row, its auto-incremented values are *not* reused. Therefore, for example, if you delete *Foundation* and reinsert it, its book_id will be 6.

For your reference, before I forget it, dev.mysql.com/doc/refman/5.7/en/c-api-function-overview. html provides an overview of all functions available in MySQL's C API.

Multiple Connections to a Database

It would be nice to have the category names in the category_id column instead of the identifiers. In order to do that, you need to open more than one connection to the database—one to read the categories and one to read the book records. Let's update the program once more. The result is shown in Listing 12-9.

Listing 12-9. A Better MySQL Program

```
1. #include <stdio.h>
2. #include <stdlib.h>
3. #include <string.h>
4. #include <mysql.h>
```

```
 5.
 6. #define SERVER "localhost"
 7. #define USER   "root"
 8. #define PASS   "apress"
 9. #define DB     "library"
10.
11. //------------------------------------------------------------------------- main
12. int main(int argc, char *argv[]) {
13.   MYSQL *conn;
14.   MYSQL_RES *res;
15.   MYSQL_ROW row;
16.
17.   //------- Initialize the connection and connect to the database.
18.   conn = mysql_init(NULL);
19.   if (!mysql_real_connect(conn, SERVER, USER, PASS, DB, 0, NULL, 0)) {
20.     fprintf(stderr, "%s\n", mysql_error(conn));
21.     exit(EXIT_FAILURE);                                           // -->
22.     }
23.
24.   //------- Remove the "Non-fiction" category.
25.   if (mysql_query(conn,
26.       "delete from categories where category_name = 'Non-fiction'")) {
27.     fprintf(stderr, "%s\n", mysql_error(conn));
28.     exit(EXIT_FAILURE);                                           // -->
29.     }
30.   printf("Category \"Non-fiction\" deleted\n");
31.
32.   //------- Find the number of categories.
33.   if (mysql_query(conn, "select count(*) from categories")) {
34.     fprintf(stderr, "%s\n", mysql_error(conn));
35.     exit(EXIT_FAILURE);                                           // -->
36.     }
37.   res = mysql_use_result(conn);
38.   row = mysql_fetch_row(res);
39.   int n_cat = 0;
40.   sscanf(row[0], "%d", &n_cat);
41.   printf("Number of categories: %d\n", n_cat);
42.   mysql_free_result(res);
43.
44.   //------- Find the maximum category ID.
45.   if (mysql_query(conn, "select max(category_id) from categories")) {
46.     fprintf(stderr, "%s\n", mysql_error(conn));
47.     exit(EXIT_FAILURE);                                           // -->
48.     }
49.   res = mysql_use_result(conn);
50.   row = mysql_fetch_row(res);
51.   int max_cat = 0;
52.   sscanf(row[0], "%d", &max_cat);
53.   printf("Maximum category: %d\n", max_cat);
54.   mysql_free_result(res);
55.
```

```
56.    //------- List the books.
57.    if (mysql_query(conn, "select * from books order by author")) {
58.      fprintf(stderr, "%s\n", mysql_error(conn));
59.      exit(EXIT_FAILURE);                                          // -->
60.      }
61.    res = mysql_use_result(conn);
62.    unsigned int n_cols = mysql_num_fields(res);
63.
64.    // Use the column names as headings. Remember the column with
65.    // the category_id but print "category" as heading.
66.    printf("Books in the database:\n");
67.    MYSQL_FIELD *field = NULL;
68.    int cat_col = -1;
69.    int cat_col_found = 0;
70.    do {
71.      field = mysql_fetch_field(res);
72.      if (field) {
73.        if (!cat_col_found) cat_col++;
74.        if (!strcmp(field->name, "category_id")) {
75.          cat_col_found = 1;
76.          printf("category\t");
77.          }
78.        else {
79.          printf("%s\t", field->name);
80.          }
81.        }
82.      } while (field);
83.    printf("\n");
84.
85.    // Open a second connection to the database to obtain the category
86.    // name given the category ID.
87.    MYSQL *conn1;
88.    MYSQL_RES *res1;
89.    MYSQL_ROW row1;
90.    conn1 = mysql_init(NULL);
91.    if (!mysql_real_connect(conn1, SERVER, USER, PASS, DB, 0, NULL, 0)) {
92.      fprintf(stderr, "%s\n", mysql_error(conn1));
93.      exit(EXIT_FAILURE);                                          // -->
94.      }
95.
96.    // Fetch the rows selected from the "books" table.
97.    do {
98.      row = mysql_fetch_row(res);
99.      if (row) {
100.        for (int kol = 0; kol < n_cols; kol++) {
101.          if (kol != cat_col) {
102.            printf("%s\t", row[kol]);
103.            }
104.          else {
105.
```

```
106.              // Obtain from the "categories" table the category name
107.              // for the book's category_id.
108.              char q[70];
109.              sprintf(q, "select category_name from categories where"
110.                  " category_id = %s", row[kol]);
111.              if (mysql_query(conn1, q)) {
112.                fprintf(stderr, "%s\n", mysql_error(conn));
113.                exit(EXIT_FAILURE);                                      // -->
114.                }
115.              res1 = mysql_use_result(conn1);
116.              row1 = mysql_fetch_row(res1);
117.              printf("%s\t", row1[0]);
118.              mysql_free_result(res1);
119.              }
120.          }
121.       printf("\n");
122.       }
123.     } while (row);
124.   mysql_close(conn1);
125.   mysql_free_result(res);
126.
127.   //------- Close the connection
128.   mysql_close(conn);
129.
130.   return EXIT_SUCCESS;
131.   } // main
```

Before running the program, I modified library_populate.sql (see Listing 12-6) to insert the new category "Non-fiction" between "SF" and "Thriller" and then changed the category_id field of the books by David Baldacci from 2 to 3.

The version of the test program shown in Listing 12-9 has several differences when compared to the previous version shown in Listing 12-8:

- The strings that identify server, user, password, and database are now set with #defines.

- The comments are slightly different and the code to list the tables and insert a book are no longer there. The code is still in the source code for this chapter (but commented out).

- Lines 25 to 30 remove the "Non-fiction" category (with category_id 2), so as to create a gap in the category IDs. Note that if you try to delete the "SF" category you get an error message like the following one: "Cannot delete or update a parent row: a foreign key constraint fails (`library`.`books`, CONSTRAINT `category_id` FOREIGN KEY (`category_id`) REFERENCES `categories` (`category_id`))". It is a bit verbose, but it makes clear that you cannot delete "SF" because the database contains some books that refer to that category.

- Lines 33 to 42 show how to determine the number of categories defined in the database, and lines 45 to 54 show how to find out the maximum value of category_id.

- In lines 87 to 94, you open a second connection to the same database. This allows you in lines 101 to 120 to obtain from the categories table the category name that corresponds to the category_id of the current book. You can do it because while printing the headings in lines 67 to 83 you saved into the variable cat_col the column number of the category_id in the books table. Note that all this code replaces line 57 in Listing 12-8, when you just printed the book's category_id.

In any case, the program produces the following satisfying output, with the categories in clear (again, spaces replace the tabs):

```
Category "Non-fiction" deleted
Number of categories: 2
Maximum category: 3
Books in the database:
book_id  title                 author          ISBN                category
1        The Complete Robot    Asimov, Isaac   978-0-586-05724-7   SF
3        Foundation            Asimov, Isaac   978-0-586-01080-8   SF
2        Deliver Us From Evil  Baldacci, David 978-0-230-74679-4   Thriller
4        The Escape            Baldacci, David 978-1-4472-6016-5   Thriller
```

But are you really happy with the program? Isn't it a bit annoying that it needs to open two simultaneous connections to the same database and then determine the category name for each book? You could have dozens/hundreds/thousands of books, but perhaps still a very limited number of categories.

Would it make sense to save in an array the category names and use that array as a look-up table when printing the list of books? You have generously allocated 70 characters to store each category name (see line 5 of Listing 12-5). Even with 100 categories, it would still only take 7KB of memory to store them all in an array. And much less than that if you limited the length of the category names to a more realistic 20 or 30 characters.

Let's do it, both for fun and to use the string and dynamic-array utilities described in Chapters 6 and 7.

In the source code for this chapter, you will find the program in Listing 12-9 under the name main_9.c.

Using Dynamically-Allocated Strings and Arrays

Listing 12-10 shows the fourth (and last) version of the test program.

Listing 12-10. A MySQL Program with STR and DAR Utilities

```
 1. #include <stdio.h>
 2. #include <stdlib.h>
 3. #include <string.h>
 4. #include <mysql.h>
 5. #include "dar.h"
 6. #include "str.h"
 7.
 8. #define SERVER "localhost"
 9. #define USER   "root"
10. #define PASS   "apress"
11. #define DB     "library"
12.
13. //-------------------------------------------------------------- main
14. int main(int argc, char *argv[]) {
```

```
15.    MYSQL *conn;
16.    MYSQL_RES *res;
17.    MYSQL_ROW row;
18.    MYSQL_FIELD *field;
19.
20.    //------- Initialize the connection and connect to the database.
21.    conn = mysql_init(NULL);
22.    if (!mysql_real_connect(conn, SERVER, USER, PASS, DB, 0, NULL, 0)) {
23.      fprintf(stderr, "%s\n", mysql_error(conn));
24.      exit(EXIT_FAILURE);                                        // -->
25.      }
26.
27.    //------- Find the maximum category ID.
28.    if (mysql_query(conn, "select max(category_id) from categories")) {
29.      fprintf(stderr, "%s\n", mysql_error(conn));
30.      exit(EXIT_FAILURE);                                        // -->
31.      }
32.    res = mysql_use_result(conn);
33.    row = mysql_fetch_row(res);
34.    int max_cat = 0;
35.    sscanf(row[0], "%d", &max_cat);
36.    printf("Maximum category: %d\n", max_cat);
37.    mysql_free_result(res);
38.
39.    //------- Determine how many characters are needed for each category name.
40.    if (mysql_query(conn, "select category_name from categories limit 1")) {
41.      fprintf(stderr, "%s\n", mysql_error(conn));
42.      exit(EXIT_FAILURE);                                        // -->
43.      }
44.    res = mysql_use_result(conn);
45.    field = mysql_fetch_field(res);
46.    int n_chars = (int)field->length;
47.    printf("Category length: %d\n", n_chars);
48.    mysql_free_result(res);
49.
50.    //------- Begin dynamic-array and string operations
51.    DAR_setup;
52.    STR_setup;
53.
54.    //------- Create an array of String pointers (+1 because SQL starts from 1).
55.    Str **cat_names = DAR_new((Str *)0, max_cat + 1);
56.
57.    //------- Collect and list the category names
58.    if (mysql_query(conn, "select category_id, category_name from categories")) {
59.      fprintf(stderr, "%s\n", mysql_error(conn));
60.      exit(EXIT_FAILURE);                                        // -->
61.      }
62.    res = mysql_use_result(conn);
63.    do {
64.      row = mysql_fetch_row(res);
65.      if (row) {
```

```
66.         int cat_id = 0;
67.         sscanf(row[0], "%d", &cat_id);
68.         cat_names[cat_id] = STR_new(row[1]);
69.       }
70.     } while (row);
71.   mysql_free_result(res);
72.   printf("\nList of categories saved in memory:\n");
73.   for (int k = 1; k <= max_cat; k++) {
74.     if (cat_names[k]) printf("%d: \"%s\"\n", k, cat_names[k]->s);
75.   }
76.
77.   //------- List the books.
78.   if (mysql_query(conn, "select * from books order by author, title")) {
79.     fprintf(stderr, "%s\n", mysql_error(conn));
80.     exit(EXIT_FAILURE);                                            // -->
81.   }
82.   res = mysql_use_result(conn);
83.   unsigned int n_cols = mysql_num_fields(res);
84.
85.   // Use the column names as headings. Remember the column with
86.   // the category_id but print "category" as heading.
87.   printf("\nBooks in the database:\n");
88.   int cat_col = -1;
89.   int cat_col_found = 0;
90.   do {
91.     field = mysql_fetch_field(res);
92.     if (field) {
93.       if (!cat_col_found) cat_col++;
94.       if (!strcmp(field->name, "category_id")) {
95.         cat_col_found = 1;
96.         printf("category\t");
97.       }
98.       else {
99.         printf("%s\t", field->name);
100.       }
101.     }
102.   } while (field);
103.   printf("\n");
104.
105.   // Fetch the rows selected from the "books" table.
106.   do {
107.     row = mysql_fetch_row(res);
108.     if (row) {
109.       for (int kol = 0; kol < n_cols; kol++) {
110.         if (kol != cat_col) {
111.           printf("%s\t", row[kol]);
112.         }
113.         else {
114.           int n_cat = 0;
115.           sscanf(row[kol], "%d", &n_cat);
116.           printf("%s\t", cat_names[n_cat]->s);
```

```
117.               }
118.             }
119.         printf("\n");
120.         }
121.     } while (row);
122.   mysql_free_result(res);
123.
124.   //------- End dynamic-array and string operations.
125.   STR_dismantle;
126.   DAR_dismantle;
127.
128.   //------- Close the connection
129.   mysql_close(conn);
130.
131.   return EXIT_SUCCESS;
132. } // main
```

The first update is in lines 40 to 48, where you obtain the maximum length of the category names. You need it in order to initialize the dynamically allocated strings to save the names without risk of making them too short.

After including dar.h and str.h in lines 5 and 6, in lines 51 and 52 you set up the two environments that you then release in lines 125 and 126. Note that you release them in reverse order (and the compiler forces you to do so).

In line 55, you create an array of pointers to Str pointers. You allocate one pointer more than the maximum category_id because array indices start from 0 while SQL auto-increment numbers start from 1.

In lines 58 to 71, you collect all categories, which you then list in lines 73 to 75. You could have used the simple query "select * from categories", but by specifying the columns to be retrieved and their order, you ensure that column 0 is category_id and column 1 is category_name even if somebody one day moves the columns around or adds some columns in between (unlikely in this case, but something to keep in mind).

Notice how easy it is in line 68 to allocate a string dynamically and save into it a category name.

The second connection to the database has become redundant. All you need to do to replace the category identifier with the corresponding name in lines 114 to 116 is convert the category_id in the books row to an int and use it to look up the category name in the dynamic array cat_names.

The output of the program is as follows:

```
Maximum category: 3
Category length: 70

List of categories saved in memory:
1: "SF"
3: "Thriller"

Books in the database:
book_id  title                author           ISBN               category
3        Foundation           Asimov, Isaac    978-0-586-01080-8  SF
1        The Complete Robot   Asimov, Isaac    978-0-586-05724-7  SF
2        Deliver Us From Evil Baldacci, David  978-0-230-74679-4  Thriller
4        The Escape           Baldacci, David  978-1-4472-6016-5  Thriller
```

Yes, I modified the ordering of the books: it was by author and now it is by author and title. Only two categories are printed because line 74 of Listing 12-10 only prints the category names of existing records and, when I executed this program, the program in Listing 12-9 had already removed the non-fiction category.

You will find the program in Listing 12-10 in the code for this chapter under the name `main_10.c`.

SQLite

I developed all examples of the previous section of this chapter with MySQL. A big advantage of using a server-based DBMS like MySQL is that it supports standard SQL. But a disadvantage is that you need to install it first. Moreover, if you deliver a program, you can never be 100% be sure that it will work unless you test it on the target system. That said, for databases that do not need complex SQL features and only need to support your own programs, you can use an embedded, free-to-use DBMS like SQLite (`sqlite.org`). All you need to do is add the SQLite library to your program and you are (almost) ready to go.

A long time ago, I stored the data for my dynamic web sites in Firebird databases. But I switched to MySQL because it is the most widely used database package in the world. Therefore, you can be confident that it is very stable and well documented.

Although you don't need to install a server, if you want to interact with your SQLite databases via a CLI, you need to download and install the client program `sqlite3`, which is the equivalent of the `mysql` CLI client you used in the previous section of this chapter.

From the `sqlite.org/download.html` page, you can download the following files:

```
sqlite-amalgamation-3110100.zip
sqlite-tools-linux-x86-3110100.zip
sqlite-doc-3110100.zip
```

There are also precompiled tools for Windows and Macs.

The first archive contains four files, including `sqlite3.c` and `sqlite3.h` that you need to link to your program. The files are called *amalgamation* because they are a collation of all the files you need in order to use SQLite. The task of compiling and building the individual SQLite sources is a very difficult task, which you can avoid by using the amalgamation sources (as I have done!).

You find the CLI client `sqlite3` in the tools archive, together with the other utilities `sqldiff` and `sqlite3_analyzer`. Place the utilities in the `/usr/local/bin` directory and you should be ready to go.

You will only be able to compile and link `sqlite3.c` with the option `-pthread` added both to the `gcc` compiler and the gcc linker. As I explained in Chapter 11, The p stands for Posix, and the option is necessary to allow concurrent access to the database. If you are using Eclipse as a development environment, you add `-pthread` to:

```
C/C++ Build -> Settings -> GCC C Compiler -> Command
```

and

```
C/C++ Build -> Settings -> GCC C Linker -> Command
```

But, if you are not interested in concurrent access to the database, instead of telling compiler and linker that they have to deal with multiple threads, you can also just add the option `-DSQLITE_MUTEX_NOOP` to the compiler's command.

At this point, if everything works for you as it worked for me, you still get four compilation "undefined reference" errors (`dlclose`, `dlerror`, `dlopen`, and `dlsym`) associated with dynamic loading of extensions. That error message tells you that, if you want to develop dynamically-loaded libraries (i.e., DLLs in Microsoft terminology), you need to link to your program a library that allows you to do so (the `dl` at the beginning of the function names stands for "dynamically linked"). I confess I was not very interested in loading extensions at runtime. First, because developing DLLs for SQLite is beyond the scope of this chapter (and book), and second, because you can also statically link extensions with the application. Therefore, instead of investigating why the references were unresolved, I added the option -DSQLITE_OMIT_LOAD_EXTENSION to the compiler's command. The -D option is equivalent to adding at the beginning of the code a preprocessor definition with value 1. For example, the option I added to disable the loading of shared libraries is equivalent to:

```
#define SQLITE_OMIT_LOAD_EXTENSION 1
```

The effect of this definition is to tell the compiler that, as you do not intend to develop DLLs, you don't need the associated library. As a result of the definition, the "undefined reference" errors disappeared.

The program sqlite3 that provides a CLI for SQLite databases supports the commands shown in Listing 12-11.

Listing 12-11. SQLite3 Commands

```
.backup [DB] FILE    Backup DB (default "main") to FILE

.bail on|off         Stop after hitting an error. Default OFF

.binary on|off       Turn binary output on or off. Default OFF

.changes on|off      Show number of rows changed by SQL

.clone NEWDB         Clone data into NEWDB from the existing database

.databases           List names and files of attached databases

.dbinfo [DB]         Show status information about the database

.dump [TABLE] ...    Dump the database in an SQL text format

                       If TABLE specified, only dump tables matching

                       LIKE pattern TABLE.

.echo on|off         Turn command echo on or off

.eqp on|off          Enable or disable automatic EXPLAIN QUERY PLAN

.exit                Exit this program

.explain [on|off]    Turn output mode suitable for EXPLAIN on or off.

                       With no args, it turns EXPLAIN on.

.fullschema          Show schema and the content of sqlite_stat tables

.headers on|off      Turn display of headers on or off

.help                Show this message
```

```
.import FILE TABLE    Import data from FILE into TABLE

.indexes [TABLE]      Show names of all indexes

                         If TABLE specified, only show indexes for tables

                         matching LIKE pattern TABLE.

.limit [LIMIT] [VAL] Display or change the value of an SQLITE_LIMIT

.load FILE [ENTRY]    Load an extension library

.log FILE|off         Turn logging on or off.  FILE can be stderr/stdout

.mode MODE [TABLE]    Set output mode where MODE is one of:

                         ascii   Columns/rows delimited by 0x1F and 0x1E

                         csv     Comma-separated values

                         column  Left-aligned columns.  (See .width)

                         html    HTML <table> code

                         insert  SQL insert statements for TABLE

                         line    One value per line

                         list    Values delimited by .separator strings

                         tabs    Tab-separated values

                         tcl     TCL list elements

.nullvalue STRING     Use STRING in place of NULL values

.once FILENAME        Output for the next SQL command only to FILENAME

.open [FILENAME]      Close existing database and reopen FILENAME

.output [FILENAME]    Send output to FILENAME or stdout

.print STRING...      Print literal STRING

.prompt MAIN CONTINUE Replace the standard prompts

.quit                 Exit this program

.read FILENAME        Execute SQL in FILENAME

.restore [DB] FILE    Restore content of DB (default "main") from FILE
```

```
.save FILE           Write in-memory database into FILE

.scanstats on|off    Turn sqlite3_stmt_scanstatus() metrics on or off

.schema [TABLE]      Show the CREATE statements

                         If TABLE specified, only show tables matching

                         LIKE pattern TABLE.

.separator COL [ROW] Change the column separator and optionally the row

                         separator for both the output mode and .import

.shell CMD ARGS...   Run CMD ARGS... in a system shell

.show                Show the current values for various settings

.stats on|off        Turn stats on or off

.system CMD ARGS...  Run CMD ARGS... in a system shell

.tables [TABLE]      List names of tables

                         If TABLE specified, only list tables matching

                         LIKE pattern TABLE.

.timeout MS          Try opening locked tables for MS milliseconds

.timer on|off        Turn SQL timer on or off

.trace FILE|off      Output each SQL statement as it is run

.vfsinfo [AUX]       Information about the top-level VFS

.vfsname [AUX]       Print the name of the VFS stack

.width NUM1 NUM2 ... Set column widths for "column" mode

                         Negative values right-justify
```

They are quite different from the commands shown in Listing 12-1 for mysql. Aren't they? Anyway, to execute an SQL script you use the commands .read (instead of the source of mysql) and .open followed by the filename of a database replaces mysql's command use followed by a database name.

The difference between .open and use and the fact that there is no equivalent to mysql's connect reflects the different ways in which databases are saved to disk with SQLite and MySQL. While MySQL is a server to which you need to connect before accessing any database and all databases are kept in a dedicated directory (/var/lib/mysql), there exists no SQLite server, and the databases can be in different directories.

Another consequence of SQLite's architecture is that to drop a database all you need to do is remove the file.

Using SQLite from the CLI

SQLite doesn't implement all SQL features. You can find out its limitations by visiting www2.sqlite.org/
cvstrac/wiki?p=UnsupportedSql. These limitations force you to modify the library_create.sql script
shown in Listing 12-5. The script modified for SQLite is shown in Listing 12-12.

Listing 12-12. library_create_lite.sql

```
1.  .system rm library.db
2.  .open library.db
3.  create table categories (
4.    category_id integer not null primary key autoincrement,
5.    category_name varchar(70) not null
6.  );
7.  create table books (
8.    book_id integer not null primary key autoincrement,
9.    title varchar(70) not null,
10.   author varchar(70) not null,
11.   ISBN varchar(17) not null default '',
12.   category_id integer not null default ''
13. );
14. create index category_id_key on categories (category_id);
15. create index book_id_key on books (book_id);
16. create index book_cat_key on books (category_id);
```

The drop database library; of MySQL has become .system rm library.db (line 1 of Listings 12-5
and 12-12), and create database library; has become .open library.db (line 2). This looks odd, doesn't
it? How can you open a database immediately after you have removed it from the file system? It is because
the .open command opens a database file if it exists and creates an empty one if it doesn't exist.

According to the documentation, SQLite only supports auto_increment for integer primary keys, and
this is the case with both categories.category_id and books.book_id. And yet, when I tried it, it reported a
syntax error. I then removed the line

```
primary key (category_id)
```

and changed

```
category_id integer not null auto_increment unique,
```

to

```
category_id integer not null primary key auto_increment,
```

but it still reported a syntax error.

Then (don't ask me why because I have no idea), I replaced auto_increment with autoincrement
(without an underscore), and sqlite3 accepted it!

After that, out of curiosity, I moved the primary key declaration back to a separate line and I got a syntax
error. I still think that SQLite is a great open source library, but be prepared to the fact that you might have to
tweak some bits in order to get it to do what you need.

The constraint that books.category_id must match an existing categories.category_id has
disappeared because SQLite doesn't enforce foreign key specifications.

Notice that I added the not null constraint to all columns that didn't have it. I also added defaults to two books columns, so that you can insert books that don't have an ISBN or that you don't want to classify.

To adapt to SQLite the script library_populate.sql, as shown in Listing 12-6, you only need to replace use library; with .open library.db.

FYI, instead of using the .read command to execute the SQL scripts, you can execute them by redirecting the standard input to the scripts when launching sqlite3, like in the following two shell commands:

```
sqlite3 < library_create_lite.sql
```

```
sqlite3 < library_populate_lite.sql
```

Incidentally, that's why you should write .open library.db as the first line of library_populate_lite.sql.

Although you could also remove it from the script and use the following command instead:

```
sqlite3 library.db < library_populate_lite.sql
```

Notice that mysql commands must terminate with a semicolon, while if you append the semicolon to the dot-commands of sqlite3 you get a syntax error.

As a final point before looking at how you access SQLite databases from a C program—SQLite locks the whole table when you update something. This means that if two programs modify a table concurrently, one of the two will have to wait even if they are modifying different rows.

Using SQLite from C

Listing 12-13 shows a program that more or less does with SQLite what the program in Listing 12-8 did with MySQL, the only difference being that it lists the categories instead of simply listing the table names.

Listing 12-13. A Program Using SQLite

```
1. #include <stdio.h>
2. #include <stdlib.h>
3. #include "sqlite3.h"
4.
5. static int callback(void *x, int nc, char **values, char **names);
6. static int callback_head(void *x, int nc, char **values, char **names);
7.
8. //----------------------------------------------------------------- main
9. int main(int argc, char *argv[]) {
10.    sqlite3 *db = NULL;
11.    char *errmsg = NULL;
12.    int ret;
13.
14.    //------- Connect to the database.
15.    ret = sqlite3_open_v2("library.db", &db, SQLITE_OPEN_READWRITE, NULL);
16.    if (ret != SQLITE_OK) {
17.      fprintf(stderr, "Can't open database: %s\n", sqlite3_errmsg(db));
18.      if (db) sqlite3_close(db);
19.      return(EXIT_FAILURE);                              // -->
20.      }
```

```
21.
22.    //------- List the categories
23.    printf("\nCategories:\n");
24.
25.    // First the column names.
26.    ret = sqlite3_exec(db,
27.        "select * from categories limit 1", callback_head, 0, &errmsg);
28.    if (ret != SQLITE_OK) {
29.      fprintf(stderr, "c1: SQL error: %s\n", errmsg);
30.      sqlite3_free(errmsg);
31.      }
32.
33.    // Then the category records.
34.    ret = sqlite3_exec(db, "select * from categories", callback, 0, &errmsg);
35.    if (ret != SQLITE_OK) {
36.      fprintf(stderr, "c2: SQL error: %s\n", errmsg);
37.      if (db) sqlite3_close(db);
38.      return(EXIT_FAILURE);                                     // -->
39.      }
40.
41.    //------- List the books.
42.    printf("\nBooks:\n");
43.
44.    // First the column names.
45.    ret = sqlite3_exec(db,
46.        "select * from books limit 1", callback_head, 0, &errmsg);
47.    if (ret != SQLITE_OK) {
48.      fprintf(stderr, "b1: SQL error: %s\n", errmsg);
49.      sqlite3_free(errmsg);
50.      }
51.
52.    // Then the book records.
53.    ret = sqlite3_exec(db,
54.        "select * from books order by author, title", callback, 0, &errmsg);
55.    if (ret != SQLITE_OK) {
56.      fprintf(stderr, "b2: SQL error: %s\n", errmsg);
57.      if (db) sqlite3_close(db);
58.      return(EXIT_FAILURE);                                     // -->
59.      }
60.
61.    //------- Close the database.
62.    sqlite3_close(db);
63.
64.      return EXIT_SUCCESS;
65.    } // main
66.
67. //--------------------------------------------------------------------- callback
68. static int callback(void *x, int nc, char **values, char **names) {
69.    for(int k = 0; k < nc; k++) printf("%s\t", values[k] ? values[k] : "NULL");
70.    printf("\n");
71.    return 0;
```

```
72.   } // callback
73.
74. //----------------------------------------------------------------- callback_head
75. static int callback_head(void *x, int nc, char **values, char **names) {
76.   for(int k = 0; k < nc; k++) printf("%s\t", names[k]);
77.   printf("\n");
78.   return 0;
79.   } // callback_head
```

In line 15, where you open the database, you don't need to make any reference to a server, a user, or a password. You could have used sqlite3_open() instead of sqlite3_open_v2(). If you had done so, the call would have been:

```
ret = sqlite3_open("library.db", &db);
```

But version two of the database-open function lets you specify in the third parameter how you want to open the database file, which is useful. For one thing, if you only want to examine existing data, you might like to specify the flag SQLITE_OPEN_READONLY. Furthermore, sqlite3_open() behaves like the CLI program sqlite: if it doesn't find the database file you specify as first argument, it creates an empty one. In other words, sqlite3_open() never fails. With sqlite3_open_v2() and the option SQLITE_OPEN_READWRITE, you will get an error message if the database file doesn't exist.

The fourth parameter of sqlite3_open_v2() lets you specify a virtual file system module to use in place of the default. In practical terms, it lets you define a different interface between the SQLite core and the underlying OS. My advice: set it to NULL to use the default and move on. If you are really curious about it, you can have a look at www.sqlite.org/c3ref/vfs.html.

The SQLite function to access the data is sqlite3_exec(). While with MySQL you obtain the query result in a structure of type MYSQL_RES by calling mysql_use_result(), with SQLite you use for that purpose a callback function. For example, in line 26 of Listing 12-13, the third argument is the function callback_head().

The specified callback is invoked for every row of the result. Its first parameter, a pointer to void, conveys what you pass as fourth argument of sqlite_exec(), while the remaining three parameters provide the number of columns, the values of the columns, and their names.

Notice that the only difference between callback_head() and callback() is that the first one prints the column names, while the second one prints the column values. It would be nice to merge them into a single function. But in order to do that, you need the combined function to be able to distinguish between the first row of the result and any subsequent row. Only then could you print the column names before printing the first row. You can do it by setting up a simple algorithm like in the following example:

```
static int first_row = 1;
if (first_row) { print the column names }
else  { print the column values }
first_row = 0;
```

The static variable first_row makes the callback non re-entrant, but everything will work fine as long as you don't invoke the same callback in two separate threads of the same program. For that to happen, you would need to fork your process and execute in both threads an SQL query with the same callback.

The combined callback() could look like this:

```
static int callback(void *x, int nc, char **values, char **names) {
  static int first_row = 1;
  if (first_row) {
```

```
  for(int k = 0; k < nc; k++) printf("%s\t", names[k] ? names[k] : "NULL");
  printf("\n");
  }
first_row = 0;
for(int k = 0; k < nc; k++) printf("%s\t", values[k] ? values[k] : "NULL");
printf("\n");
return 0;
}
```

With the new, combined callback, you can then remove lines 24 to 33 and 43 to 52 from Listing 12-13, thereby eliminating two database queries.

But wait a minute! That doesn't work, because after printing the categories, first_row remains set to 0, and the column names of the books table are not printed!

This gives you the opportunity to use the first parameter of the callback function: you can use it to define first_row in the calling program (instead of within the callback) and pass to the callback function its address. Then, you can easily reset it in the calling program between queries. Here is the new, improved callback function:

```
static int callback(void *x, int nc, char **values, char **names) {
  int *first_row_p = x;
  if (*first_row_p) {
    for(int k = 0; k < nc; k++) printf("%s\t", names[k] ? names[k] : "NULL");
    printf("\n");
    }
  *first_row_p = 0;
  for(int k = 0; k < nc; k++) printf("%s\t", values[k] ? values[k] : "NULL");
  printf("\n");
  return 0;
  }
```

You could have kept the static first_row variable as global to the program by moving it out of the function and the main. But then, you wouldn't have an example of how to use the first callback parameter, would you?

Just for fun, you could also combine the queries to remove some duplication in the program. The end result is shown in Listing 12-14.

Listing 12-14. A Shorter Program Using SQLite

```
1. #include <stdio.h>
2. #include <stdlib.h>
3. #include "sqlite3.h"
4.
5. static int callback(void *x, int nc, char **values, char **names);
6.
7. //------------------------------------------------------------------------- main
8. int main(int argc, char *argv[]) {
9.    sqlite3 *db = NULL;
10.   char *errmsg = NULL;
11.   int ret;
12.
13.   //------- Connect to the database.
14.   ret = sqlite3_open_v2("library.db", &db, SQLITE_OPEN_READWRITE, NULL);
```

```
15.     if (ret != SQLITE_OK) {
16.       fprintf(stderr, "Can't open database: %s\n", sqlite3_errmsg(db));
17.       if (db) sqlite3_close(db);
18.       return(EXIT_FAILURE);                                    // -->
19.     }
20.
21.     //------- List categories and books
22.     char *title[] = { "Categories", "Books" };
23.     char *query[] = {
24.        "select * from categories",
25.        "select * from books order by author, title"
26.        };
27.     for (int k = 0; k < 2; k++) {
28.       printf("\n%s:\n", title[k]);
29.       int first_row = 1;
30.       ret = sqlite3_exec(db, query[k], callback, &first_row, &errmsg);
31.       if (ret != SQLITE_OK) {
32.         fprintf(stderr, "%s: SQL error: %s\n", title[k], errmsg);
33.         if (db) sqlite3_close(db);
34.         return(EXIT_FAILURE);                                  // -->
35.       }
36.     }
37.
38.     //------- Close the database.
39.     sqlite3_close(db);
40.
41.       return EXIT_SUCCESS;
42.   } // main
43.
44. //------------------------------------------------------------------ callback
45. static int callback(void *x, int nc, char **values, char **names) {
46.    int *first_row_p = x;
47.    if (*first_row_p) {
48.      for(int k = 0; k < nc; k++) printf("%s\t", names[k] ? names[k] : "NULL");
49.      printf("\n");
50.      }
51.    *first_row_p = 0;
52.    for(int k = 0; k < nc; k++) printf("%s\t", values[k] ? values[k] : "NULL");
53.    printf("\n");
54.    return 0;
55.   } // callback
```

Quite compact and still clear.

Using Dynamic Strings and Arrays

As an exercise, we will now implement with SQLite the functionality of the MySQL program in Listing 12-10. This will also show you how to use dynamic strings and arrays within callback functions. The full program is shown in Listing 12-15.

Listing 12-15. An SQLite Program with STR and DAR Utilities

```
1.  #include <stdio.h>
2.  #include <stdlib.h>
3.  #include <string.h>
4.  #include "sqlite3.h"
5.  #include "dar.h"
6.  #include "str.h"
7.
8.  #define ERR_CHK(mess) if (ret != SQLITE_OK) {                   \
9.      fprintf(stderr, "%s: SQL error - %s\n", mess, errmsg);     \
10.     if (db) sqlite3_close(db);                                 \
11.     return(EXIT_FAILURE);                                      \
12.     }
13.
14. typedef struct book_t {
15.   Str **cat_names;
16.   int first_row;
17.   } book_t;
18.
19. typedef struct cat_t {
20.   Str **cat_names;
21.   Str **str_stack_p;
22.   } cat_t;
23.
24. static int callback_book(void *book, int nc, char **values, char **names);
25. static int callback_cat(void *cat, int nc, char **values, char **names);
26. static int save_col_0(void *col0, int nc, char **values, char **names);
27.
28. //----------------------------------------------------------------------- main
29. int main(int argc, char *argv[]) {
30.   sqlite3 *db = NULL;
31.   char *query = NULL;
32.   char *errmsg = NULL;
33.   int ret;
34.
35.   //------- Connect to the database.
36.   ret = sqlite3_open_v2("library.db", &db, SQLITE_OPEN_READWRITE, NULL);
37.   if (ret != SQLITE_OK) {
38.     fprintf(stderr, "Can't open database: %s\n", sqlite3_errmsg(db));
39.     if (db) sqlite3_close(db);
40.     return(EXIT_FAILURE);                                       // -->
41.     }
42.
43.   //------- Find the maximum category ID.
44.   int max_cat = 0;
45.   query = "select max(category_id) from categories";
46.   ret = sqlite3_exec(db, query, save_col_0, &max_cat, &errmsg);
47.   ERR_CHK("max_cat");                                           // -->
48.   printf("Maximum category: %d\n", max_cat);
49.
50.   //------- Determine how many characters are needed for each category name.
```

```
51.    int n_chars = 0;
52.    query = "select max(length(category_name)) from categories";
53.    ret = sqlite3_exec(db, query, save_col_0, &n_chars, &errmsg);
54.    ERR_CHK("n_chars");                                              // -->
55.    printf("Maximum category length: %d\n", n_chars);
56.
57.    //------- Begin dynamic-array and string operations
58.    DAR_setup;
59.    STR_setup;
60.
61.    //------- Create an array of String pointers (+1 because SQL starts from 1).
62.    Str **cat_names = DAR_new((Str *)0, max_cat + 1);
63.
64.    //------- List the categories and save their names
65.    printf("\nCategories:\ncategory_id\tcategory_name\n");
66.    query = "select category_id, category_name from categories";
67.    cat_t cat;
68.    cat.cat_names = cat_names;
69.    cat.str_stack_p = &str_stack;
70.    ret = sqlite3_exec(db, query, callback_cat, &cat, &errmsg);
71.    ERR_CHK("Categories");                                          // -->
72.
73.    //------- List the books
74.    printf("\nBooks:\n");
75.    book_t book;
76.    book.cat_names = cat_names;
77.    book.first_row = 1;
78.    query = "select * from books order by author, title";
79.    ret = sqlite3_exec(db, query, callback_book, &book, &errmsg);
80.    ERR_CHK("Books");                                               // -->
81.
82.    //------- End dynamic-array and string operations.
83.    STR_dismantle;
84.    DAR_dismantle;
85.
86.    //------- Close the database.
87.    sqlite3_close(db);
88.
89.    return EXIT_SUCCESS;
90.    } // main
91.
92. //------------------------------------------------------------- callback_book
93. static int callback_book(void *book, int nc, char **values, char **names) {
94.    book_t *book_p = book;
95.    Str **cat_names = book_p->cat_names;
96.    if (book_p->first_row) {
97.      for(int k = 0; k < nc; k++) {
98.        if (!strcmp(names[k], "category_id")) printf("category\t");
99.        else printf("%s\t", names[k]);
100.       }
101.     printf("\n");
```

```
102.     }
103.     book_p->first_row = 0;
104.     for(int k = 0; k < nc; k++) {
105.       if (strlen(values[k])) {
106.         if (!strcmp(names[k], "category_id")) {
107.           int cat_id = 0;
108.           sscanf(values[k], "%d", &cat_id);
109.           printf("%s\t", cat_names[cat_id]->s);
110.         }
111.         else {
112.           printf("%s\t", values[k]);
113.         }
114.       }
115.       else {
116.         printf("-\t");
117.       }
118.     }
119.     printf("\n");
120.     return 0;
121.     } // callback_book
122.
123. //------------------------------------------------------------- callback_cat
124. static int callback_cat(void *cat, int nc, char **values, char **names) {
125.     cat_t *cat_p = cat;
126.     int cat_id = 0;
127.     sscanf(values[0], "%d", &cat_id);
128.     cat_p->cat_names[cat_id] = str_new(cat_p->str_stack_p, 0, values[1], '\0');
129.     printf("%s\t%s\n", values[0], values[1]);
130.     return 0;
131.     } // callback_cat
132.
133. //------------------------------------------------------------- save_col_0
134. static int save_col_0(void *col0, int nc, char **values, char **names) {
135.     int *first_val_p = col0;
136.     sscanf(values[0], "%d", first_val_p);
137.     return 0;
138.     } // save_col_0
```

It should be pretty clear how this works, if you look at the equivalent program with MySQL (Listing 12-10) and the previous version of the program with SQLite (Listing 12-14). Just a few points are worth mentioning.

The local macro ERR_CHECK() (see lines 8 to 12 of Listing 12-15) "hides" code that had to be repeated several times and makes the main program easier to read.

The two types book_t and cat_t keep together what the callback functions callback_book() and callback_cat() need, so that you can pass pointers to variables of those types as fourth arguments of sqlite3_exec().

While in the MySQL program shown in Listing 12-10 you determined the maximum possible length of a category name (lines 40 to 48), in the SQLite program you go one step further and determine the maximum length of the category names present in the database (lines 51 to 54 of Listing 12-15). This makes it necessary to execute a query that examines all the rows of the categories table, but it is a nice example of a query that one day you might find useful. Did you realize that you don't actually need to know the category lengths? As you use the `str.c` package to store the category names in dynamic strings, each allocated string is always as long as it needs to be.

Lines 65 to 71 print the two columns `category_id` and `category_name` of the `categories` table. There are no additional columns in the `categories` table but, if there were, the program would ignore them. Note that in the query of line 66 you don't only specify the two columns you are interested in, but also the order in which the query should return them to you.

If you look at `callback_cat()` (lines 124 to 131), you see that you use the category ID of each row to index the element of the dynamic array `cat_p->cat_names` where you store the address of a newly allocated string containing the category name.

The component `str_stack_p` of the structure `cat_t` is needed to let you create a new dynamic string, but through the function `str_new()` instead of `STR_new()`, because the macro doesn't let you specify the stack address.

Listing the books in lines 74 to 80 is trivial because the logic is in `callback_book()`. The variable `first_row` that lets you print the column names before the first row has now become a component of the `book_t` structure.

The addition of the `not null` constraint to all column definitions (see `library_create_lite.sql` shown in Listing 12-12) means that the callback functions don't need to check for NULL. Instead, `callback_book()` checks for fields of 0 length (line 105) because the empty string is the default for the `ISBN` and `category_id` columns.

The output of the program in Listing 12-15 is shown in Listing 12-16.

Listing 12-16. An SQLite Program with STR and DAR Utilities—Output

```
Maximum category: 3
Maximum category length: 11

Categories:
category_id  category_name
1            SF
2            Non-fiction
3            Thriller

Books:
book_id  title               author          ISBN                category
3        Foundation          Asimov, Isaac   978-0-586-01080-8   SF
1        The Complete Robot  Asimov, Isaac   978-0-586-05724-7   SF
2        Deliver Us From Evil Baldacci, David 978-0-230-74679-4   Thriller
4        The Escape          Baldacci, David 978-1-4472-6016-5   Thriller
5        De Bello Gallico    Caesar, Julius  -                   Non-fiction
```

I inserted the last book manually (i.e., with the CLI client `sqlite3`) to check the correct listing of the default fields. Here is the command I used:

```
insert into books (author, title, category_id) values
    ('Caesar, Julius', 'De Bello Gallico', 2);
```

You will find the program shown in Listing 12-15 in the file `main_15.c` as part of the source for this chapter.

Summary

In this chapter, you learned how to access databases via a C API. You saw examples using the MySQL Community Server and the embedded SQLite library. This also gave you the opportunity to use in a realistic situation the libraries for dynamic strings and arrays described in Chapters 6 and 7.

Accessing other DBMSs like PostgreSQL and Oracle will be different, but not conceptually. Having used MySQL and SQLite will make getting acquainted with other environments a much easier exercise.

CHAPTER 13

■ ■ ■

Web Server Using Mongoose

In this chapter you will learn how to embed a web server in C programs. That is, any of your applications written in C will be able to serve web pages. The next two sections will explain some concepts and facts concerning the Web that you need to have completely clear in order to understand the rest of the chapter without problems. If you are familiar with how the Web works, feel free to skip them.

Web Pages and Protocols

Many people use the terms Web and Internet as if they were synonyms. But they are not. The Internet is a world-spanning network of computers, while the World Wide Web is one of several networks of applications that rely on the Internet to exchange data, as shown in Figure 13-1.

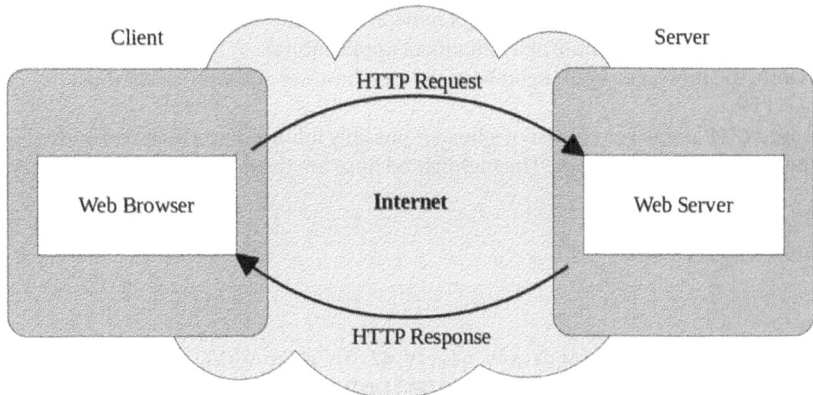

Figure 13-1. *WWW and HTTP*

When you type a web address (which is an informal way of referring to a Uniform Resource Locator, or URI) or follow a link in your web browser, the browser interrogates a server that belongs to the global Domain Name System (DNS, not shown in Figure 13-1) to find out where the page you have requested is located. To do so, the browser sends to the DNS the URI (e.g., apress.com) and receives in return the IP address of the computer where the resource resides. If the requested URI is unknown to the DNS (e.g., if you want to view the page http://www.noserveratall.com), the browser displays a message like that shown in Figure 13-2.

© Giulio Zambon 2016

G. Zambon, *Practical C*, DOI 10.1007/978-1-4842-1769-6_13

Server not found

Firefox can't find the server at www.noserveratall.com.

- Check the address for typing errors such as **ww**.example.com instead of **www**.example.com
- If you are unable to load any pages, check your computer's network connection.
- If your computer or network is protected by a firewall or proxy, make sure that Firefox is permitted to access the Web.

```
        Try Again
```

Figure 13-2. *Server not found*

FYI, regardless of whether you are working with GNU/Linux, Mac X, or Windows, the command nslookup followed by a domain name is the command-line equivalent of the request that the browser makes to the DNS. For example, nslookup apress.com will show you the IP address 207.97.243.208.

After obtaining from the DNS the IP address of the computer that holds the page, the browser sends to the web server running on that computer (actually, I should say "to the appropriate web server," because there can be more than one web server on a single computer) a request for the page and then displays it to you.

Notice the distinction I made between application and computer when I wrote "the web server running on that computer." As I said in the first paragraph, the WWW is a network that links together applications, not computers (incidentally, the DNS is another example of a network of applications).

For this mechanism to work, the messages exchanged between web browser and web server must follow the standard protocol HTTP.

Both request and response HTTP messages consist of a header possibly followed by a message body. Listing 13-1 shows two examples of request messages. The highlighted lines are those that are different between the two requests.

Listing 13-1. HTTP Request Headers (Firefox)

```
A1. GET / HTTP/1.1
A2. Host: localhost:8080
A3. User-Agent: Mozilla/5.0 (X11; Ubuntu; Linux x86_64; rv:42.0) Gecko/20100101 Firefox/42.0
A4. Accept: text/html,application/xhtml+xml,application/xml;q=0.9,*/*;q=0.8
A5. Accept-Language: en-US,en;q=0.5
A6. Accept-Encoding: gzip, deflate
A7. Connection: keep-alive

B1. GET /img/giulio.jpg HTTP/1.1
B2. Host: localhost:8080
B3. User-Agent: Mozilla/5.0 (X11; Ubuntu; Linux x86_64; rv:42.0) Gecko/20100101 Firefox/42.0
B4. Accept: image/png,image/*;q=0.8,*/*;q=0.5
B5. Accept-Language: en-US,en;q=0.5
B6. Accept-Encoding: gzip, deflate
B7. Referer: http://localhost:8080/
B8. Connection: keep-alive
```

The two messages show the very first requests sent when I used the web browser Firefox to view the page localhost:8080 shown in Figure 13-3. You will get different messages with different systems. For example, if you are using a Macintosh, the User-Agent line will include something like Macintosh; Intel Mac OS X 10.6 instead of X11; Ubuntu; Linux x86_64.

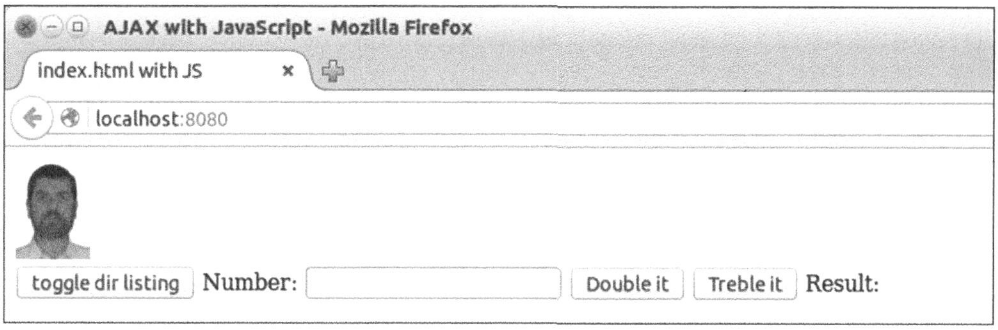

Figure 13-3. *localhost:8080*

You will learn more about this page later in this chapter. For now, notice that the two requests refers to the page itself (identified by the / in line A1), and a picture (identified by /img/giulio.jpg in line B1). After receiving from the server the page /index.html (which is the default when no path is present in the URI), the browser discovered that the page included an image named giulio.jpg with path /img/ and requested it from the web server.

In this example, the web server is located on the same computer of the browser (localhost, with address 127.0.0.1), rather than on some remote computer to be reached through the Internet.

The number 8080 is the port number I have assigned to the web server application. When I launched it, it opened a connection to that port and waited for incoming requests. The default for receiving HTTP messages is port 80, and when the web server uses that default, you don't need to write any port number (although nobody prevents you from typing, say, wikipedia.org:80). But for testing purposes the alternative 8080 is recommended. The Internet Assigned Numbers Authority (IANA) provides the official list of the assigned port numbers at www.iana.org/assignments/service-names-port-numbers. On page 107 (which gives you an idea of how many protocols have received an assigned port), the list describes 8080 as:

```
http-alt     8080     tcp     HTTP Alternate (see port 80)
```

The lines A4 and B4 tell the web server what type of content the browser expects. The types are separated by commas and the q parameters indicate the order of preference, whereby q=1 is the highest and can be omitted. Not surprisingly, line A4 identifies as preferred response a web page in HTML or XHTML format, followed in order of preference by an XML document and anything else (e.g., text/plain). B4 tells the server that the preferred format is a PNG image but any other image format will do and, actually, any format at all.

The header of the second request includes the field referer, which doesn't appear in the first one (it should have been *referrer*, with a double r, but they misspelled it in the standard and now all HTTP-request headers are forced to include a spelling mistake!). This field tells the web server that /img/giulio.jpg is referred to by the URI http://localhost:8080.

The page www.w3.org/Protocols/rfc2616/rfc2616-sec14.html is the official source to learn about the HTTP headers.

If you use a web browser other than Firefox, the headers will be slightly different from those shown in Listing 13-1, but not significantly so. For example, Google Chrome generates the headers shown in Listing 13-2.

Listing 13-2. HTTP Request Headers (Google Chrome)

```
GET / HTTP/1.1
Host: localhost:8080
Connection: keep-alive
Accept: text/html,application/xhtml+xml,application/xml;q=0.9,image/webp,*/*;q=0.8
Upgrade-Insecure-Requests: 1
User-Agent: Mozilla/5.0 (X11; Linux x86_64) AppleWebKit/537.36 (KHTML, like Gecko) ↵
Chrome/46.0.2490.86 Safari/537.36
Accept-Encoding: gzip, deflate, sdch
Accept-Language: en-GB,en-US;q=0.8,en;q=0.6

GET /img/giulio.jpg HTTP/1.1
Host: localhost:8080
Connection: keep-alive
Accept: image/webp,image/*,*/*;q=0.8
User-Agent: Mozilla/5.0 (X11; Linux x86_64) AppleWebKit/537.36 (KHTML, like Gecko) ↵
Chrome/46.0.2490.86 Safari/537.36
Referer: http://localhost:8080/
Accept-Encoding: gzip, deflate, sdch
Accept-Language: en-GB,en-US;q=0.8,en;q=0.6
```

Dynamic Web Pages

We are used to interactive web pages. That is, pages that behave differently depending on what button you click or what value you type in an input field.

But not all interactions are created equal. You need to distinguish between actions that the browser can handle on its own and actions that require information from the remote web server.

For example, if you are writing a page that requires the users to enter a date, it makes sense for you to include in it a script (i.e., JavaScript) to tell the browser to check the date's validity. Incidentally, a malicious user could still bypass the script and send a bad date to your web server. Therefore, you always have to repeat on the server all the tests that you make within the browser on the client side. But it still makes sense to let the browser do as much checking as possible. First, because it minimizes the response time to the user when there's an input error, and second, because it avoids wasting server time on errors.

That said, if the purpose of the page is to provide access to information that resides on the server, the server must get involved. Traditionally, a web server accesses local data (i.e., information stored in files local to the web server, including databases) in one of two ways: either through an external application (e.g., a Perl script invoked via the Common Gateway Interface), or through a script written in a language that the web server itself is able to interpret (often PHP, but also JSP in Java servers). In other words, the developer of a web application writes code that the web server executes.

But there is an alternative strategy: instead of enslaving an application to a web server (e.g., to the Apache HTTP Server or to the Apache Tomcat Java Server), you can embed the functionality of a web server within the application. That is, instead of installing a web server and then programming your application in PHP or JSP, you write your application in C and let it communicate directly with the browser.

The Simplest Application with a Web Server

Price, size, and power consumption of microprocessors become less and less while their processing power keeps increasing. This will inevitably mean that always more objects in our everyday life will acquire "intelligence" and be connected to the Internet. What better way to interact with such Internet of Things (IoT), or, to be precise, things on the Internet, than with a smart phone through a web interface?

An embedded web server with small memory requirements is perfect for adding connectivity to small controllers built into microwave ovens and coffee machines. In the not-so-distant future, you will probably find uses for controlling electronic circuitry embedded in sofas, shoes, pieces of clothing, and who knows what else.

After looking at what is currently available, I chose to adopt Mongoose, published by Cesanta (cesanta. com/products) as an embedded web server. You can download the source code and use it freely with a GNU General Public License (gnu.org/licenses/gpl-2.0.html). As Cesanta explains in their web site (cesanta. com/open-source-philosophy),

> *If you are working on a non-commercial product or while you are developing a prototype, you can continue to use Cesanta's software free of charge under GPLv2 license. Once your project is available to the end user and/or commercially, you have to decide between two options:*

1. *Purchase a commercial license*

2. *Open your end source code fully and continue to use it under GPLv2 licensing*

When you download Mongoose's source code from the Cesanta web site, you will find in the package the C file that implements Mongoose (mongoose.c), its header file (mongoose.h), and several examples.

The simplest possible application you can build with Mongoose is perhaps one that echoes back to the browser every request it receives. You will find an example of such an application in cesanta.com/ developer/mongoose, but it doesn't work. Besides referring to iobuf instead of mbuf and invoking mg_bind with four parameters instead of three, it has a rather conceptual problem: it sends back to the browser exactly what it receives, without wrapping it into a HTTP response message. As a result, the browser never receives a proper response and doesn't display anything until you kill the application. At least, this was true at the time of writing. But the modified version shown in Listing 13-3 works.

Listing 13-3. my_app.c

```
1. /* my_app.c
2.  *
3.  */
4. #include "mongoose.h"
5.
6. /*************************************************************** ev_handler
7.  */
8. static void ev_handler(struct mg_connection *nc, int ev, void *ev_data) {
9.    struct mbuf *io = &nc->recv_mbuf;
10.
11.   switch (ev) {
12.     case MG_EV_RECV: // This event handler implements simple TCP echo server
13.       mg_printf(nc, "%s", "HTTP/1.1 200 OK\r\nTransfer-Encoding: chunked\r\n\r\n");
14.       char *null_c = { '\0' };
15.       mbuf_append(io, null_c, 1);
16.       mg_printf_http_chunk(nc, "%s", io->buf);
17.       mg_send_http_chunk(nc, "", 0);
18.       mbuf_remove(io, io->len);     // Discard data from recv buffer
19.       break;
20.     default:
21.       break;
22.   }
```

```
23.    }
24.
25.   /*************************************************************** main
26.   */
27.   int main(void) {
28.     struct mg_mgr mgr;
29.
30.     mg_mgr_init(&mgr, NULL);
31.     mg_bind(&mgr, "1234", ev_handler);
32.     for (;;) {
33.       mg_mgr_poll(&mgr, 1000);
34.       }
35.     mg_mgr_free(&mgr);
36.     return 0;
37.   }
```

You compile and test my_app by doing the following:

- Place the downloaded files mongoose.h and mongoose.c in the folder that contains my_app.c

- Open a terminal window and change directory to that folder

- Type the command cc my_app.c mongoose.c

- Launch the application by typing the command ./a.out

- Launch a web browser and visit the URL http://localhost:1234/whatever

Here is what you will see in the browser's window:

```
GET /whatever HTTP/1.1
Host: localhost:1234
User-Agent: Mozilla/5.0 (X11; Ubuntu; Linux x86_64; rv:42.0) Gecko/20100101 Firefox/42.0
Accept: text/html,application/xhtml+xml,application/xml;q=0.9,*/*;q=0.8
Accept-Language: en-US,en;q=0.5
Accept-Encoding: gzip, deflate
Connection: keep-alive
```

Event Handler

The function ev_handler() handles the events that my_app receives. If you search the mongoose.h header file, you will find the definition of 38 different events. Besides six generic events (like MG_EV_RECV used in my_app), there are three specific events for HTTP, one for SSI (Server Side Includes), four for maintaining the connection with the web, 20 that support the MQTT protocol (Message Queuing Telemetry Transport, mainly used for the IoT), and four for CoAP (Constrained Application Protocol, used for very simple devices).

When ev_handler() of my_app receives the event MG_EV_RECV, it performs the following actions:

- Sends back to the browser an HTTP header to say that the request has been accepted (line 13).

- Extends the input buffer by appending to it a string-terminating character (lines 14 and 15).

- Sends the input buffer to the browser that sent the request (line 16).

- Sends to the browser an empty message chunk to signify end-of-message (line 17).

- Clears the input buffer of the data that have been processed (line 18). You need to do it because this simple program accesses the connection's receive buffer directly. You will see that, if you tell Mongoose that the connection is an HTTP one, you will be able to handle the request messages without having to remove them from the input buffer once you have dealt with them.

Main

All the main program has to do is:

- Define and initialize the connection manager (lines 28 and 30).

- Bind the manager to the port number 1234 (line 31).

- Poll the port forever every second to check whether it has received a message (lines 32 to 34).

- Close the connection and release the manager (line 35).

The function mg_bind() actually returns a pointer to a struct mg_connection, but this simple program ignores it. As you will see, you need to remember the pointer returned by mg_bind() in order to handle an HTTP connection properly.

In case you are wondering, IANA assigns port 1234 to the Infoseek Search Agent. As the service was discontinued in 2001, you can safely assume that using that port number will never cause you any problem.

An Application with a Web Server

The purpose of this section is to show you how you can interact with an application through its embedded web server. This is an application that, besides serving static web pages, can perform two simple functions: multiply an integer number by 2 and by 3. Admittedly, such an application is not of any practical use, but it will show you how to interact with Mongoose.

When you launch the application and view the URI http://localhost:8080, you will see the page shown in Figure 13-1. If you type, say, 23 in the Number input field and click on the button Double it, the field Result will show 46. And if you then click on Treble it, Result will change to 69. The meaning of the button toggle dir listing will become clear later.

Listing 13-4 shows the full code of the application.

Listing 13-4. WebServer.c

```
 1. /* WebServer.c
 2.  *
 3.  * Copyright (c) 2016 by Giulio Zambon.  All rights reserved.
 4.  */
 5. #include <stdio.h>
 6. #include <stdlib.h>
 7. #include "mongoose.h"
 8.
 9. #define TRUE 1
10. #define PORT "8080"
11.
```

```
12. static struct mg_serve_http_opts opts;
13.
14. /*********************************************************** send_response
15. */
16. static void send_response(struct mg_connection *c, double what) {
17.   mg_printf(c, "%s", "HTTP/1.1 200 OK\r\nTransfer-Encoding: chunked\r\n\r\n");
18.   mg_printf_http_chunk(c, "{ \"result\": %lf }", what);
19.   mg_send_http_chunk(c, "", 0);
20.   } // send_response
21.
22. /*********************************************************************** get_x
23. */
24. static double get_x(struct http_message *req) {
25.   char s[32];
26.   mg_get_http_var(&req->body, "x", s, sizeof(s));
27.   return strtod(s, NULL);
28.   } // get_x
29.
30. /********************************************************* printf_str
31. */
32. static void printf_str(const struct mg_str *s) {
33.   const char *p = s->p;
34.   int n = s->len;
35.   for (int k = 0; k < n; k++) printf("%c", p[k]);
36.   printf("\n");
37.   } // printf_str
38.
39. /********************************************************* e_handler
40. */
41. static void e_handler(struct mg_connection *c, int e, void *mess) {
42.   static int dir_listing = 0;
43.   char *yes_no[] = {"yes", "no"};
44.   struct http_message *req = (struct http_message *)mess;
45.   if (e == MG_EV_HTTP_REQUEST) {
46.     printf_str(&req->message);
47.     if (mg_vcmp(&req->uri, "/toggle") == 0) {
48.       dir_listing = 1 - dir_listing;
49.       opts.enable_directory_listing = yes_no[dir_listing];
50.       mg_printf(c, "%s", "HTTP/1.1 200 OK\r\n\r\n");
51.       }
52.     else if (mg_vcmp(&req->uri, "/times/two") == 0) {
53.       double x = get_x(req);
54.       send_response(c, x*2);
55.       }
56.     else if (mg_vcmp(&req->uri, "/times/three") == 0) {
57.       double x = get_x(req);
58.       send_response(c, x*3);
59.       }
60.     else {
61.       mg_serve_http(c, req, opts);
62.       }
```

```
63.        }
64.      else {
65. //       if (e > 0) printf("Received event %d\n", e);
66.        }
67.    } // e_handler
68.
69.    /************************************************************************ main
70.    */
71.    int main(int argc, char *argv[]) {
72.
73.      // Initialize the Mongoose event manager
74.      struct mg_mgr server;
75.      mg_mgr_init(&server, NULL);
76.
77.      // Connect the server to the port and set the callback function to
78.      // handle incoming events
79.      struct mg_connection *conn = mg_bind(&server, PORT, e_handler);
80.      if (conn == NULL) {
81.        fprintf(stderr, "Error starting server on port %s\n", PORT);
82.        exit(EXIT_FAILURE);                                              // ==>
83.        }
84.
85.      // Set the server protocol
86.      mg_set_protocol_http_websocket(conn);
87.
88.      // Set the document root to the subdirectory ROOT.
89.      // If running from Eclipse, go above the Release/Debug directories.
90.      opts.document_root = ".";
91.      {
92.        char *p = strrchr(argv[0], '/');
93.        if (p != NULL) {
94.          char *pp = strstr(argv[0], "Release");
95.          if (pp == NULL) pp = strstr(argv[0], "Debug");
96.          p = (pp != NULL) ? pp : p + 1;
97.          sprintf(p, "ROOT");
98.          }
99.        opts.document_root = argv[0];
100.       }
101.
102.     // Start the server
103.     printf("Starting server on port %s\n", PORT);
104.     while (TRUE) {
105.       mg_mgr_poll(&server, 1000);
106.       }
107.
108.     // Free up the memory allocated for Mongoose
109.     mg_mgr_free(&server);
110.     return EXIT_SUCCESS;
111.   } // main
```

We will examine its functions one by one.

Static Variables

Line 12 defines the static variable opts. You need it to store the configuration parameters for Mongoose's HTTP server. Listing 13-5 shows the definition of struct mg_serve_http_opts taken from mongoose.h but stripped of all the comments.

Listing 13-5. struct mg_serve_http_opts

```
1.  struct mg_serve_http_opts {
2.      const char *document_root;
3.      const char *index_files;
4.      const char *per_directory_auth_file;
5.      const char *auth_domain;
6.      const char *global_auth_file;
7.      const char *enable_directory_listing;
8.      const char *ssi_pattern;
9.      const char *ip_acl;
10.     const char *url_rewrites;
11.     const char *dav_document_root;
12.     const char *hidden_file_pattern;
13.     const char *cgi_file_pattern;
14.     const char *cgi_interpreter;
15.     const char *custom_mime_types;
16.     };
```

When you define opts, all pointers are set to NULL. By setting the pointers to appropriate values and passing the address of opts to certain Mongoose functions, you can direct how the HTTP server behaves.

For example, the function mg_http_serve() sends to the remote browser the page that the browser has requested. All you need to do is invoke mg_http_serve() with three arguments: the HTTP connection, the HTTP request, and opts.

If you leave opts.index_files set to NULL, mg_http_serve() automatically sets it to the string "index.html,index.htm,index.shtml,index.cgi,index.php". As a result, if the path component of the requested URI ends with a directory name, Mongoose's HTTP server looks for index.html, index.htm, etc., in that order. If you wanted to change that order or direct the server to look for, say, index.xml, you would need to set opts.index_files to the appropriate string before invoking mg_http_serve().

main()

Lines 74, 75, and 79 are functionally identical to lines 28, 30, and 31 of the example my_app.c but, unlike with my_app.c, the statement of line 79 saves the value returned by mg_bind() in the variable conn. This lets you verify that the application has successfully connected to port 8080 (lines 80 to 83). It also allows you to set to HTTP the protocol for communicating through port 8080 (line 86).

Lines 90 to 100 set the location of the web pages that the application can serve to be the subdirectory ROOT, which is an appropriate name when you consider that it is the directory where the home page of your web site is going to be. Perhaps I also like it because it is the name used by the Java web server Tomcat, which I have used for years. In the end, it's up to you what name you use. In any case, if you run the application from within Eclipse (as I usually do), the application's executable file (i.e., WebServer) is placed in one of the subdirectories Debug and Release, rather than directly in the project's directory. It makes therefore sense (at least for me!) to check for the presence of Debug and Release at the end of the application's path and, if one of them is found, set the web pages' directory ROOT to be one level up (i.e., directly inside the project's directory and at the same level of Debug and Release). This will ensure that you execute your application in debug or release mode and have access to the same ROOT directory without having to make any changes. Obviously, you can remove the check if do not execute your programs within Eclipse.

The rest of main is functionally identical to that of my_app.c.

One comment concerning programming style: Notice that the lines 92 to 99 are enclosed in a pair of braces. This ensures that the pointer p is only defined where you need it. It is a detail, but being neat usually pays. The larger the scope of a variable, the larger the risk that you will misuse it, perhaps by forgetting to reinitialize it. This is particularly true when considering single-letter variables that are supposed to be "forgotten" after use.

e_handler(), get_x(), and send_response()

This is where you implement the functionality of your application. It is the right place because it is here that you process the incoming requests. Mongoose's event manager invokes the callback function e_handler() configured in line 79 of main every time the socket connected to your port (8080 in the example) generates an event.

This simple application handles three paths: "/toggle", "/times/two", and "/times/three". But keep in mind that the path components of URIs do not necessarily correspond to file paths. In this application, for example, the intention is not to look at a file named "toggle" in the ROOT directory or at files named "two" and "three" in the directory "ROOT/times". In fact, there is no need at all to create a directory named "times". I only included a slash between "times" and "two" and between "times" and "three" because I liked it! You should consider the three paths as command strings, used to direct the application to perform specific actions.

When e_handler() doesn't recognize any of these command paths, it behaves like a normal web server by invoking mg_serve() in line 61.

The three paths correspond to the three buttons shown in Figure 13-1. For example, when you type 24 in Number and click on Double it, your application receives the HTTP request shown in Listing 13-6.

Listing 13-6. HTTP Request to Double a Number

```
 1. POST /times/two HTTP/1.1
 2. Host: localhost:8080
 3. User-Agent: Mozilla/5.0 (X11; Ubuntu; Linux x86_64; rv:42.0) Gecko/20100101 Firefox/42.0
 4. Accept: text/html,application/xhtml+xml,application/xml;q=0.9,*/*;q=0.8
 5. Accept-Language: en-US,en;q=0.5
 6. Accept-Encoding: gzip, deflate
 7. Content-Type: text/plain;charset=utf-8
 8. Referer: http://localhost:8080/
 9. Content-Length: 4
10. Connection: keep-alive
11. Pragma: no-cache
12. Cache-Control: no-cache
13.
14. x=24
```

Line 1 includes the requests path ("/times/two"), line 9 tells you that the request contains four characters, and line 14 shows that the four characters are x=24. The empty line (line 13) is used by HTTP to separate the headers and the body of the request.

To process the incoming request, the first thing that e_handler() does (in line 44) is typecast the block of data associated with the event to a structure that represents an HTTP message, because that is what you are interested in (or, better said, what you designed your application to respond to).

In lines 47, 52, and 56, you identify the three commands by invoking mg_vcmp(), which compares a Mongoose string (struct mg_str) with a C string (i.e., a null-terminated array of characters). mg_str is a simple structure that wraps the address of a C string together with the string's length:

```
struct mg_str {
  const char *p;
  size_t len;
  };
```

After recognizing that the requested path is "/times/two", in line 53, you invoke the function get_x() to extract the value of the Number input field from the request. After that, all you need to do is multiply x by 2 and send it back to the requesting browser with send_response().

Not surprisingly, the handling of "/times/three" in lines 57 and 58 is practically identical to that of "/times/two".

The function get_x() is straightforward: in line 26 you obtain the value of the parameter x by invoking the Mongoose function mg_get_http_var() to extract it from the body of the request, and in line 27 you convert the string containing the value to a double. The only reason for using a double instead of an int is that it extends the maximum number of digits from 10 to 15.

The function send_response() is also conceptually simple: line 17 sends back to the requesting browser (identified by the connection c) a minimal HTTP response header (protocol HTTP/1.1, the code 200 OK to indicate no errors, and indication that the message is chunked) followed by an empty line to separate headers from content (the double CR+LF); line 18 sends a chunk with the string with "result:48", and line 19 sends an empty chunk to indicate the message has been completed.

Note that the name x is completely arbitrary. You expect the value typed into Number to arrive in a parameter named x only because that is what you have programmed the page /ROOT/index.html to do, as it will become clear in the following section.

To understand what the button toggle dir listing does, view the URI http://localhost:8080/img. You will get something like what is shown in Figure 13-4.

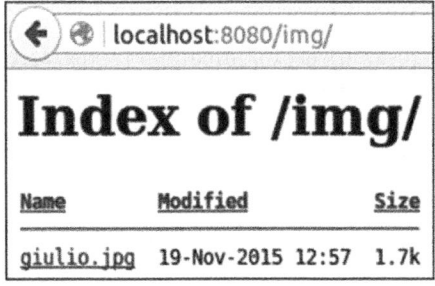

Figure 13-4. *Listing a directory*

You can list the directory /ROOT/img because Mongoose allows it by default. When you view http://localhost:8080, you don't see the list of the directory /ROOT because the file /ROOT/index.html exists and Mongoose serves it. But there is no index page in /ROOT/img. To prevents users from listing directories, you could add to /ROOT/img an empty index.html, or one with an error message. But the best solution is to configure Mongoose to forbid the listing of directories that don't include index pages.

This is precisely the function of the button toggle dir listing. If you click on it and then try to view /ROOT/img, you get an error message with the HTTP status code 403, which means "forbidden". And if you toggle again, you can again list the directory.

Actually, Mongoose "out of the box" doesn't return an error message. Before this chapter is over, I'll tell you how to update Mongoose to show it.

Anyway, lines 48 and 49 are all it takes to toggle the appropriate Mongoose parameter. The static variable dir_listing defined in line 42, being static, retains its value across executions of e_handler(). Line 48 changes its value alternatively from 0 to 1 or from 1 to 0 whenever the toggle request is received. In line 49, the component enable_directory_listing of the structure opts is set to "yes" when dir_listing is 0 and to "no" when dir_listing is 1. Done. Line 50 sends a bare-bones acknowledging HTTP response to the browser.

From then on, whenever e_handler() executes line 61 as a default operation, it passes the modified opts to the function mg_serve(), which then refuses to list a directory when it finds opts.enable_directory_listing to be set to "no".

index.html

It is time to have a look at the index page of this tiny web site. Check out Listing 13-7.

Listing 13-7. index.html

```
1.  <?xml version="1.0" encoding="utf-8"?>
2.  <!DOCTYPE html PUBLIC "-//W3C//DTD XHTML 1.0 Strict//EN"
3.     "http://www.w3.org/TR/xhtml1/DTD/xhtml1-strict.dtd">
4.  <html xmlns="http://www.w3.org/1999/xhtml">
5.  <head>
6.  <meta http-equiv="Content-type" content="text/html;charset=UTF-8"/>
7.  <title>index.html with JS</title>
8.  <script type="text/javascript">
9.  function newAjaxReq() { //---------------------------------------- newAjaxReq
10.    var ajaxReq;
11.    try { // Firefox, Opera
12.      ajaxReq = new XMLHttpRequest();
13.      }
14.    catch (e) { // older IEs
15.      try{
16.        ajaxReq = new ActiveXObject("Msxml2.XMLHTTP");
17.        }
18.      catch (e) {
19.        try{ // still older IEs
20.          ajaxReq = new ActiveXObject("Microsoft.XMLHTTP");
21.          }
22.        catch (e) {
23.          alert("Your browser does not support Ajax!");
24.          return null;
25.          }
26.        }
27.      }
28.    return ajaxReq;
29.    }
30. function toggleDirListing() { //---------------------------- toggleDirListing
31.    var ajaxReq = newAjaxReq();
32.    if (ajaxReq != null) {
33.      ajaxReq.open("POST", "toggle", true);
```

```
34.      ajaxReq.send();
35.      }
36.    return true;
37.    }
38. function multBy(where) { //----------------------------------------------- multBy
39.    var ajaxReq = newAjaxReq();
40.    if (ajaxReq != null) {
41.      var what = "x=" + document.getElementById('x').value;
42.      ajaxReq.open("POST", "times/" + where, true);
43.      ajaxReq.setRequestHeader("Content-Type", "text/plain;charset=utf-8");
44.      ajaxReq.setRequestHeader("Content-Length", what.length);
45.      ajaxReq.send(what);
46.      ajaxReq.onreadystatechange = function() {
47.        if(ajaxReq.readyState == 4) {
48.          var s = ajaxReq.responseText;
49.          s = s.substring(0, s.indexOf('.')).substring(s.indexOf(': ') + 2);
50.          document.getElementById('result').innerHTML = s;
51.          }
52.        }
53.      }
54.    return true;
55.    }
56. </script>
57. </head>
58. <body>
59. <div>
60. <img src="img/giulio.jpg" alt="gz"/>
61. <br/>
62. <button id="toggle" onclick="toggleDirListing()">toggle dir listing</button>
63. <label>Number:</label> <input type="text" id="x" maxlength="15" size="15"/>
64. <button id="two" onclick="multBy('two')">Double it</button>
65. <button id="three" onclick="multBy('three')">Treble it</button>
66. <label>Result:</label> <span id="result"> </span>
67. </div>
68. </body>
69. </html>
```

The body of the page is very simple:

- Line 60 displays the author's picture, which is there only to justify the presence of /ROOT/img used to test the enabling/disabling of directory listing.

- Line 62 links the button toggle dir listing to the JavaScript function toggleDirListing().

- Line 63 displays the Number input field with id set to "x".

- Lines 64 and 65 link the buttons Double it and Treble it to the JavaScript function multBy().

- Line 66 defines a <span> element with id set to "result".

Notice that there is no HTML <form> element, normally wrapped around <input> elements. This is because you don't want to replace the current page with one specified in the form's action attribute. All you want to do is send requests to the server and handle its replies to modify the content of the current page. For that, you use AJAX (Asynchronous JavaScript And XML), which operates in the background transparently to the user.

Let's look at the function `toggleDirListing()` first.

Line 31 instantiates a new AJAX request and saves it in the variable `ajaxRequest`. When that operation is successful, line 33 sets the AJAX request to be a POST request sent to the URI `toggle` asynchronously.

A POST means that the data sent to the server is in the body of the request as a series of `name=value` pairs separated by ampersands. The alternative is a GET request, in which the `name=value` pairs are appended to the URI after a question mark.

The differences are that POST requests:

- Are never cached

- Do not remain in the browser history

- Cannot be bookmarked

- Have no restrictions on data length

This means that you should always use POST requests when dealing with large amounts of data or with sensitive information. Obviously, with our small page, you could have also used a GET. That said, even for such small pages and non-confidential data, you need to remember that the format of the requests is different. Therefore, as you want to process the URI paths in your `e_handler()` function, you need to decide which format to use. If you changed the HTTP request of Listing 13-6 to be a GET, the first line of the request would become

```
GET /times/two?x=24 HTTP/1.1
```

and the request would include no data. It wouldn't make any significant difference, but, as I said, you would have to change the way in which you analyze the request within `e_handler()`.

The function `multBy()`, unlike `toggleDirListing()`, needs to send data to the server and decode its response.

Lines 39 and 40 of `multBy()` are identical to lines 31 and 32 of `toggleDirListing()`.

Line 41 sets the variable `what` to the string `"x="` followed by the value of the `Number` input element (defined in line 63), which has the `id` set to `"x"`. Note that you could change the `id` of the `Number` input element to whatever you like without having any impact on the functioning of the application (as long as you match the `id`s used in lines 41 and 63). But if you changed the `x` in `"x="`, you would have to change the second argument of the `mg_get_http_var()` function in line 30 of your C application to match the change in line 41 of `index.html`.

Line 42 opens the request like line 33 of `multBy()`, but uses the value of `where` to form the appropriate path (either `times/two` or `times/three`).

The two lines 43 and 44 add to the request to be sent the type of content and its length (4 if the user has typed a two-digit number like 24) and, finally, line 45 sends the request. Line 45 has the same function of line 34 of `toggleDirListing()`, with the difference that it appends `"x=24"` (or whatever number the user typed) to the request.

As in lines 33 and 42 you have opened the AJAX request in asynchronous mode (by passing `true` as third argument), `ajaxReq.send()` in line 45 returns immediately after sending the request to the web server.

The function defined in lines 47 to 51 is executed whenever the AJAX connection established with the web server changes ready state. The `http://w3schools.com/ajax/ajax_xmlhttprequest_onreadystatechange.asp` page lists the following possible states:

- 0: Request not initialized

- 1: Server connection established

- 2: Request received

- 3: Processing request

- 4: Request finished and response is ready

That explains why the processing of the response done in lines 48 to 50 only proceeds when AJAX's ready state becomes 4. Now, strictly speaking, you should also check that ajaxReq.status is 200 (i.e., that the processing of the request on the server was successful) and, if not, report an error. But, in this case, I allowed myself to be lazy. In real life, you should be as careful as you can.

You are almost done.

Line 48 saves in the JavaScript variable s the text of the response; line 49 extracts from s the text after the colon character; and line 50 sets the content of the Result element, which has the id set to "result", to that text.

The only part of index.html that we haven't talked about is the function newAjaxRequest(), but it is almost self-explanatory. Its only complication is that it has to deal with Microsoft's Internet Explorer in all its incarnations. As usual, Microsoft handles things in a non-standard way.

Using jQuery

As many developers prefer to use jQuery instead of plain JavaScript (I confess that, despite the convenience of jQuery, I'm not one of them), I thought some readers might find it useful to have a jQuery version of index.html. You will find it in Listing 13-8.

Listing 13-8. index_jquery.html

```
<?xml version="1.0" encoding="utf-8"?>
<!DOCTYPE html PUBLIC "-//W3C//DTD XHTML 1.0 Strict//EN"
    "http://www.w3.org/TR/xhtml1/DTD/xhtml1-strict.dtd">
<html xmlns="http://www.w3.org/1999/xhtml">
<head>
<meta http-equiv="Content-type" content="text/html;charset=UTF-8"/>
<title>index.html with jQuery</title>
<script src="https://ajax.googleapis.com/ajax/libs/jquery/1.11.3/jquery.min.js"
        type="text/javascript"></script>
<script type="text/javascript">
  $(document).ready(function(){
    $(document).ajaxError(function(e, xhr, opt){
      alert("Error requesting " + opt.url + ": " + xhr.status + " " +
          xhr.statusText);
      });
    $("#two, #three").click(function(){
        var where = 'times/' + $(this).attr('id');
      $.ajax({
        url: where,
        method: 'POST',
        dataType: 'json',
        data: { x: $('#x').val()},
        success: function(json) {
          $('#result').html(json.result);
          }
        });
      });
    });
```

```
$(function(){
  $("#toggle").click(function(){
    $.ajax({
      url: 'toggle',
      method: 'POST'
      });
    });
  });
</script>
<meta http-equiv="cache-control" content="no-cache"/>
<meta http-equiv="pragma" content="no-cache"/>
<meta http-equiv="expires" content="0"/>
</head>
<body>
<div>
<img src="img/giulio.jpg" alt="gz"/>
<br/>
<button id="toggle">toggle dir listing</button>
<label>Number:</label> <input type="text" id="x" maxlength="15" size="15"/>
<button id="two">Double it</button>
<button id="three">Treble it</button>
<label>Result:</label> <span id="result"> </span>
</div>
</body>
</html>
```

As you can see, the only differences in the HTML code is that the onclick attributes of the three <button> elements have disappeared.

The ugly code in newAjaxRequest() to handle Microsoft's peculiarities has disappeared as well. Also note that I used JSON to encode the request content and decode the response.

To try it out, you simply need to view http://localhost:8080/index_jquery.html instead of http://localhost:8080.

Tailoring Mongoose

I felt it necessary to make a couple of minor changes to Mongoose concerning how errors are reported to the browser.

The first change is in mg_send_http_file(), which is invoked by mg_serve_http() after performing some checks. Its purpose, as its name clearly indicates, is to send a file back to the browser. If the file is not found or is hidden, the web server must send to the browser a response with status code 404 Not Found.

To do so, mg_send_http_file() executes the following statement:

```
mg_printf(nc, "%s", "HTTP/1.1 404 Not Found\r\nContent-Length: 0\r\n\r\n");
```

It does the job because the browser is correctly informed. But it is not satisfactory because the user only sees an empty screen, with no error message at all. With a Content-Length set to 0 and no information after the pair of CR+LF that closes the HTTP headers, what else could the browser tell the user?

In my version of mongoose.c, I replaced that line with the few lines of code shown in Listing 13-9.

Listing 13-9. Returning a "Not Found" Error Message

```
1. char *pa = strstr(path, "/ROOT");
2. if (pa == NULL) pa = path;
3. else pa += 5;
4. mg_printf(nc, "%s%d%s%s%s", "HTTP/1.1 404 Not Found\r\n"
5.    "Content-Type: text/plain;charset=utf-8\r\n"
6.    "Content-Length: ", strlen("HTTP/1.1 404 Not Found: ") + strlen(pa),
7.    "\r\n\r\nHTTP/1.1 404 Not Found: ", pa, "\r\n\r\n");
```

Line 1 obtains a pointer to the first occurrence of the string "/ROOT" within the path variable. This is appropriate because path contains the full path of the file the user requested. For example, if the user wants to view the image with URI http://localhost:8080/img/giulioo.jpg (which is wrong, because my name ends with a single "o"), the path string will contain something like this:

/home/giulio/Desktop/Giulio/programs/eclipse_workspace/WebServer/ROOT/img/giulioo.jpg

And you don't want to tell the user where the file is on the server's hard disk. After executing line 1, pa will point to /ROOT/img/giulioo.jpg. Much better.

The search for "/ROOT" should always succeed, but line 2 implements a bit of defensive programming and ensures that "/ROOT" is indeed present. If not, pa is set to the whole path.

If the world behaves as expected and "/ROOT" is there, line 5 skips it, as the user doesn't need to know where the web site is rooted.

Finally, in lines 4 to 7, mg_send_http_file() sends to the browser a properly formatted error message, and the browser displays this:

HTTP/1.1 404 Not Found: /img/giulioo.jpg

Unfortunately, mongoose.c is equally careless with error messages elsewhere. The function send_http_error() executes the following statement to send an error response to the browser:

```
mg_printf(nc, "HTTP/1.1 %d %s\r\nContent-Length: 0\r\n\r\n", code, reason);
```

I changed it to:

```
mg_printf(nc, "HTTP/1.1 %d %s\r\n%s%d%s%d %s%s", code, reason,
    "Content-Type: text/plain;charset=utf-8\r\n"
    "Content-Length: ", 14 + strlen(reason), "\r\n\r\n"
    "HTTP/1.1 ", code, reason, ".\r\n\r\n");
```

With this change, when you toggle the directory listing and try to view http://localhost:8080/img, you see the message:

HTTP/1.1 403 .

Otherwise, you would only see an empty page. Still, although send_http_error() has reason as a parameter, the error code 403 is not followed by "Forbidden", which is the meaning of the code. This is because those who developed Mongoose invoked send_http_error() with a NULL reason. Not nice.

If you search mongoose.c for send_http_error, you will find that it is invoked 20 times:

```
4263.  send_http_error(nc, 404, "Not Found");
4283.  send_http_error(nc, 500, "SSI disabled");
4319.  send_http_error(nc, 500, "Server Error"); /* LCOV_EXCL_LINE */
4323.  send_http_error(nc, 500, "Server Error");
```

```
4962. send_http_error(nc, status_code, NULL);
4992. send_http_error(nc, 404, NULL);
4995. send_http_error(nc, 204, NULL);
4997. send_http_error(nc, 204, NULL);
4999. send_http_error(nc, 423, NULL);
5035. send_http_error(nc, 500, NULL);
5037. send_http_error(nc, 411, NULL);
5040. send_http_error(nc, 500, NULL); /* LCOV_EXCL_LINE */
5042. send_http_error(nc, 500, NULL);
5520. send_http_error(nc, 500, "Bad headers");
5581. send_http_error(nc, 500, "OOM"); /* LCOV_EXCL_LINE */
5596. send_http_error(nc, 500, "CGI failure");
5619. send_http_error(nc, 501, NULL);
5657. send_http_error(nc, 501, NULL);
5660. send_http_error(nc, 403, NULL);
5667. send_http_error(nc, 501, NULL);
```

The line numbers might be different in your version of Mongoose, but, as you can see, in more than half of the cases, the third argument, which corresponds to reason, was set to NULL. I have to admit that I find this to be a bit sloppy. Also note that in some cases they have returned a message that is not standard. For example, 500 means "Internal Server Error", but in line 5520 mongoose.c reports it as "Bad headers".

To preserve as much as possible the existing code while providing clear error messages, you can replace the original send_http_error() (see Listing 13-10) with the extended version shown in Listing 13-11.

Listing 13-10. The Original send_http_error()

```
static void send_http_error(struct mg_connection *nc, int code,
                            const char *reason) {
  if (reason == NULL) {
    reason = "";
  }
mg_printf(nc, "HTTP/1.1 %d %s\r\nContent-Length: 0\r\n\r\n", code, reason);
}
```

Listing 13-11. The Extended send_http_error()

```
static void send_http_error(struct mg_connection *nc, int code,
                            const char *reason) {
  if (reason == NULL) {
    switch (code) {
      case 204:
        reason = "No Content";
        break;
      case 403:
        reason = "Forbidden";
        break;
      case 404:
        reason = "Not Found";
       break;
      case 405:
        reason = "Method Not Allowed";
        break;
```

```
      case 409:
        reason = "Conflict";
        break;
      case 411:
        reason = "Length Required";
        break;
      case 415:
        reason = "Unsupported Media Type";
        break;
      case 423:
        reason = "Locked";
        break;
      case 500:
        reason = "Internal Server Error";
        break;
      case 501:
        reason = "Not Implemented";
        break;
      default:
        reason = "???";
        break;
      }
    }
  mg_printf(nc, "HTTP/1.1 %d %s\r\n%s%d%s%d %s%s", code, reason,
      "Content-Type: text/plain;charset=utf-8\r\n"
      "Content-Length: ", 14 + strlen(reason), "\r\n\r\n"
      "HTTP/1.1 ", code, reason, ".\r\n\r\n");
  }
```

Note that you need to add the codes 405, 409, and 415 because they are used in the function handle_mkcol() that invokes send_http_error() in line 4962.

Now, if you attempt to access http://localhost:8080/img after disabling the directory listing, you get the error message in clear:

```
HTTP/1.1 403 Forbidden.
```

In general, modifying a package like Mongoose is not advisable because, when a new release becomes available, you will need to transfer the tailoring you made. But the changes you have seen in this section are straightforward and it should be easy to copy them to a new version of Mongoose if and when it will be released.

Summary

In this chapter, after explaining some key concepts concerning the World Wide Web and web servers, I showed you how to embed a web server in an application written in C so that you can configure it and control it via a web browser. You also saw an example of an embedded web server (Mongoose, by Cesanta).

CHAPTER 14

■ ■ ■

Game Application: MathSearch

In this chapter, you will learn how to generate MathSearch numeric puzzles like the one shown in Figure 14-1.

11	5	53	68	17	4	52	7
5	14	31	9	48	9	7	11
39	26	72	3	43	66	11	6
57	9	16	53	20	3	60	7
8	13	9	22	16	72	18	4
21	13	20	3	60	69	9	71
15	4	12	5	60	6	20	6
36	52	36	6	6	51	5	9

Figure 14-1. *A MathSearch puzzle*

You are probably familiar with WordSearch, in which you solve the puzzle by finding words in a grid of letters. In MathSearch, you need to find triplets of numbers so that when you apply a mathematical operation to the first two, you obtain the third one.

Figure 14-2 shows five examples of the triplets hidden in the puzzle shown in Figure 14-1.

© Giulio Zambon 2016
G. Zambon, *Practical C*, DOI 10.1007/978-1-4842-1769-6_14

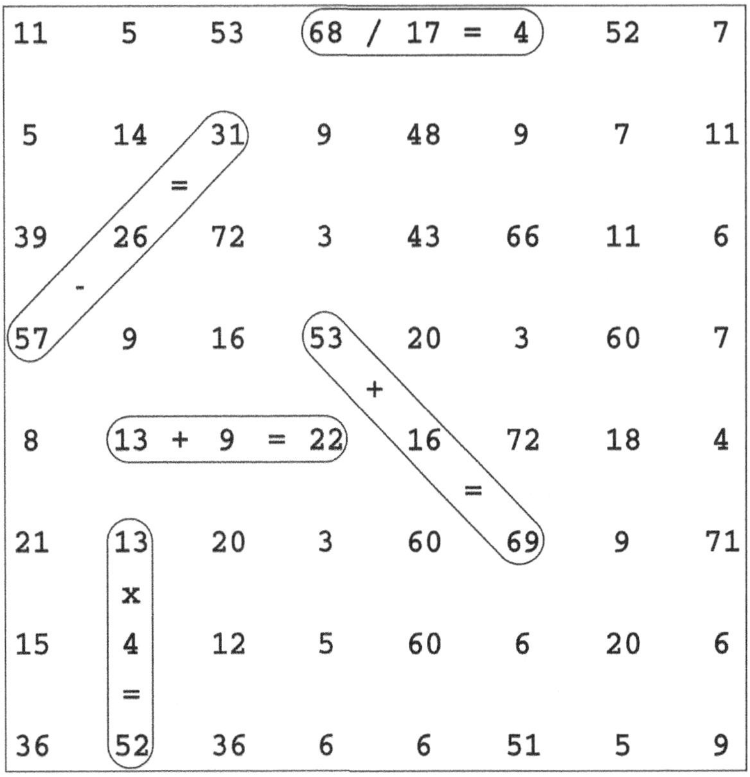

11	5	53	68 / 17 = 4			52	7
5	14	31	9	48	9	7	11
39	26	72	3	43	66	11	6
57	9	16	53	20	3	60	7
8	13 + 9 = 22			16	72	18	4
21	13	20	3	60	69	9	71
15	4	12	5	60	6	20	6
36	52	36	6	6	51	5	9

Figure 14-2. *MathSearch triplets*

Although it is not apparent from Figure 14-2, all operations run from left to right, top to bottom, top-left to bottom-right, or bottom-left to top-right. That is, no operation ever runs from right to left or upward along a vertical line.

The puzzle in Figure 14-1 hides 17 triplets. Can you find the remaining 12?

From programming this game, you will learn three things:

- How to use pseudo-random numbers to create a practically unlimited number of puzzles

- How to generate HTML web pages

- How to draw images and save them to disk

MathSearch Specification and Design

To fully understand the details of the code, you need to know what the program does and how it does it.

MathSearch Specs

The following list summarizes the MathSearch specs, which include both functional requirements (i.e., what you want the program to do) and interface requirements (i.e., how the program should present its results).

- Generate puzzles like the example in Figure 14-1.

- Generate puzzles of different sizes.

- Support the four basic operations (i.e., addition, subtraction, multiplication, and division) with the possibility of using a subset of them.

- Generate as many different puzzles as you want.

- Show puzzles and their solutions as simple HTML pages.

- Produce printable JPEG images with a resolution of 300dpi.

Notice that the way in which you configure the program (i.e., how you input data to it) doesn't appear in the above list. This is because you are not considering an interactive program. If you wanted to give the user the possibility of changing the program parameters on the fly and generate puzzles on demand, you would have to define a proper user interface.

MathSearch Design

Designing MathSearch boils down to how you generate a table of numbers like the one shown in Figure 14-1.

You have the choice between two basic possibilities: generate the numbers before looking for possible triplets or identify the triplets first, set the operations, and only then fill up the table with numbers. As it turns out, the second approach is the better one.

To see why it is so, you have to ask yourself: how likely is it that if you pick three random numbers between, say, 1 and 99, you can calculate the third number by applying one of the four basic operations to the first two?

Let's see the case of the sum. For each number i, between 1 and 98 (not 99 because the puzzle doesn't contain zeros), you can add to it any number between 1 and 99-i and the result will not exceed 99. For example, if i is 23, you can choose any number j up to 66 (i.e., 99-23) and the sum $i+j$ will not exceed 99. You can therefore calculate the number of possible triplets in which the first number plus the second equals the third (and all numbers are between 1 and 99) by adding 99-i for all values of i between 1 and 98. This turns out to be 99x49. As the total number of triplets obviously is 99x99x99 (because each number of the triplet can have any value between 1 and 99), you can easily conclude that, more or less, only one out every 200 randomly chosen triplets (calculated as 99x99 / 49) will represent a valid sum.

Same story with the subtractions, while multiplications and division are even more unlikely. In a 8x8 puzzle like the one shown in Figure 14-1, there are fewer than 200 possible triplets. This means that if you generated a random table of numbers, less than a handful of them would correspond to valid operations.

I went through this issue in some detail to show you how a bad design decision can completely compromise a puzzle-generating program.

So, the first step is to generate the triplets by choosing three random table cells aligned vertically, horizontally, or diagonally. As I already said, there are in total four possible directions: left to right, top to down, top-left to right-down, and bottom-left to right-up.

Now, why shouldn't you consider operations that run from right to left or vertically from the bottom up?

There is a compelling reason: with eight directions instead of four, you would be able to read every operation in two directions, thereby making the puzzle solutions not unique. For example, you would be able to solve the triplet (3,15,18) with (3+15=18) from left to right and (3=15-18) from right to left. And puzzles with multiple solutions are not nice.

Once you have a list of triplets, you need to find three numbers for each of them. But there is still one issue that you have to resolve: if the triplets share cells, there will inevitably be conflicts between triplets. For example, suppose that a sum and a multiplication overlap, as shown in Figure 14-3.

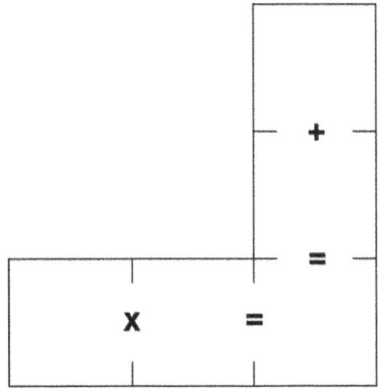

Figure 14-3. *A conflict*

Further, suppose that, because of the order in which you process the triplets, the random triplet for the sum turns out to be $(23,36,59)$. As 59 is a prime number, you would then be forced to set the multiplication triplet to either $(1,59,59)$ or $(59,1,59)$. Not nice. And if the first cell of the multiplication crossed with another triplet, you would most likely face an unsolvable conflict. In practical terms, this problem means that you have to constraint the way in which you choose the triplets or, to be more accurate, the way in which you let them overlap.

The solution is simple: avoid overlapping altogether! If it sounds too much of a limitation, also consider that overlaps would cause the puzzles to be too dense. They wouldn't look good.

To summarize, here is how you can generate MathSearch puzzles:

- Define the size of the puzzle (e.g., 8x8).

- Define the operations you want to use (e.g., all four).

- Initialize the pseudo-random sequence.

- Define the triplets.

- Generate the numbers.

- Fill up the rest of the table with random numbers.

- Save the puzzle and its solution in HTML and JPEG format.

Before looking at the program, let's look at its list of modules:

- The main program `main.c/main.h`. Here is where the design described above is implemented.

- `count.c/count.h` counts how many triplets intersect on a given position of the puzzle grid.

- display.c/display.h prepares two tables necessary to format the puzzle for output and displays the puzzle on stdout.

- save_html.c/save_html.h saves the puzzle to disk and saves its solution as an HTML page.

- save_images.c/save_images.h saves the puzzle to disk and saves its solution as separate JPEG images.

Implementing MathSearch

This section shows you the code and tells you how it works.

Module: main

Let's look at the puzzle-generation steps one by one, beginning with the definition and the code to initialize the puzzle generation.

Module Main Initialization

Listing 14-1. main.c—Initialization

```
1. /* main.c
2.  *
3.  * Copyright (c) 2016 by Giulio Zambon.  All rights reserved.
4.  */
5. #include <stdio.h>
6. #include <stdlib.h>
7. #include <string.h>
8. #include "main.h"
9. #include "count.h"
10. #include "display.h"
11. #include "save_html.h"
12. #include "save_images.h"
13.
14. // General parameters
15. #define SEED 1134567 // overwritten by argument 1
16. #define N_PUZ 1
17.
18. // Global variables
19. // The coordinates of grid_op are always obtainable as the average between
20. // the coordinates of the surrounding cells with numbers (integer truncation)
21. int grid[N_NUM][N_NUM];
22. int grid_op[N_NUM][N_NUM];
23. int t_list[N_NUM * N_NUM / 3][4];  // ROW, COL, DIR, OP
24. int n_t;
25. int mat[SIDE][SIDE];
26. int z[SIDE][SIDE];
27.
```

```
28. //                    across     down     a_up    a_down
29. int incr[][2] = { {0, 1}, {1, 0}, {-1, 1}, {1, 1} };
30.
31. // Operation strings.
32. // The order of operations must match the constants defined in main.h
33. // def.h:        ADD    SUB    MUL    DIV    EQU    INI
34. char ops[] = { '+',   '-',   'x',   '/',   '=',   ' ' };
35.
36. //===================================================================== main
37. // Par 1: Pseudo-random seed; default is SEED
38. int seed = SEED;
39. int main(int argc, char *argv[]) {
40.    printf("*** MathSearch ***\n");
41.
42.    // Process the first parameter if present and ignore the rest
43.    if (argc > 1) {
44.       seed = atoi(argv[1]);
45.       }
46.    srand(seed);
47.    printf("%d %d\n\n", N_NUM, seed);
48.
49.    // Loop through the whole process for each puzzle you want to generate
50.    for (int k_puz = 0; k_puz < N_PUZ; k_puz++) {
51.
52.       //-------------------------------------------------------- Initialization
53.       n_t = 0;
54.       for (int k = 0; k < N_NUM; k++) {
55.         for (int j = 0; j < N_NUM; j++) {
56.           grid[k][j] = 0;
57.           grid_op[k][j] = INI;
58.           }
59.         }
```

The first interesting line is 14:

```
#define SEED 1134567
```

Although I have been talking indifferently of random and pseudo-random numbers, within a program you can only generate series of numbers that, while not being truly random, for most practical purposes they appear to be. That's why they are called pseudo-random. It couldn't be otherwise because in a computer (at least in the computers that you and I use), nothing happens that is completely at random.

To generate a series of pseudo-random numbers, you need to choose a *seed* to start it. Every time you choose the same seed, you obtain the same series. If you search the Internet about this subject, you will find that many suggest to define a seed based on the system clock, so that as long as you don't start the subsequent series at perfectly regular intervals of time, you will get different series.

While such a technique makes multiple series of pseudo-random numbers closer to being completely at random, it would be the wrong thing to do when developing new programs. This is because you want to be able to reproduce any problem you might encounter during development. For example, imagine that, after creating ten puzzles, you discover that the sixth one contains a mistake. Unless you can set the seed to the same value it had in the previous run and in that way reproduce the exact same series of puzzles, how are you going to investigate what caused the mistake? By manually setting the constant SEED, you ensure that the program does exactly the same thing every time you execute it.

Line 15 defines the number of puzzles that you want the program to generate in one execution. It is used in the big for loop that starts on line 50:

```
for (int k_puz = 0; k_puz < N_PUZ; k_puz++) {
```

Lines 21 to 24 define the global arrays used to store the puzzle currently being generated. In all of them, N_NUM, defined in main.h, is the dimension of the puzzle. For example, for the puzzle shown in Figure 14-1, you set N_NUM to 8.

grid is the table of numbers. In the puzzle in Figure 14-1, for example, grid[0][0] = 11, grid[0][7] = 7, grid[7][0] = 36, and grid[7][7] = 9.

grid_op, defined on line 22, is a table containing the operation codes associated with the triplets. The code values are defined in main.h as follows:

```
#define ADD 0
#define SUB 1
#define MUL 2
#define DIV 3
#define EQU 4
#define INI 5
```

For example, the operation codes for the triplet (68, 17, 4) in grid[0][3], [0][4], and [0][5] in Figure 14-2 are grid_op[0][3] = DIV and grid_op[0][4] = EQU. That is, each triplet is always associated with two operation codes: one to identify the actual operation and one for the equals sign. You will learn more about this association later, when you see how the program chooses the operations.

t_list, defined on line 23, is where the program stores the information about the triplets as it defines them. Notice that t_list includes N_NUM * N_NUM / 3 elements. Clearly, as each triplet occupies three cells and each cell can only belong to a single triplet (because the triplets never overlap), no more than as many triplets as the number of cells in the table divided by 3 are possible. For example, in an 8 x 8 puzzle like the one in Figure 14-1 (which included 17 triplets), the maximum number of triplets is 8 * 8 / 3 = 21. n_t, defined on line 24, stores the number of triplets actually defined in the current puzzle.

For each triplet, t_list stores the coordinates within grid of the first cell of the triplet, the direction, and the operation code (only one is needed because the second one is always EQU). The four possible directions are defined in main.h as:

```
#define ACROSS  0
#define DOWN    1
#define A_UP    2
#define A_DOWN 3
```

Where A_UP stands for across-up (i.e., bottom-left to top-right) and A_DOWN stands for across-down (i.e. top-left to bottom-right).

The constant SIDE is used to dimension the arrays mat (defined on line 25) and z (defined on line 26) and is defined in main.h as:

```
#define SIDE (N_NUM + N_NUM - 1)
```

The array mat is used in display(), save_html(), and save_images(), while z, defined on line 26, is used in save_html(). Refer to the section entitled "Module: display" to learn how mat and z work.

Before looking at the executable code in main.c, we still need to mention the arrays incr and ops defined and initialized on lines 29 and 34, respectively. It should be pretty obvious what their functions are: incr tells you by how much you increment rows and columns to go through the cells of a triplet, while ops maps the operation codes to their corresponding symbols.

For example, the direction of the triplet (57,26,31) in Figure 14-2 is A_UP. If k and j are the row and column coordinates within grid of the cell containing 57, the cell containing 26 has coordinates k-1 and j+1. After defining in main.h ROW and COL as 0 and 1, you can easily calculate the coordinates of the second cell of the triplet by adding incr[A_UP][ROW] and incr[A_UP][COL] to the coordinates of the first one. In general, if (k,j) are the coordinates of a cell of a triplet with direction d, the coordinates of the following cell within the same triplet are (k+incr[d][ROW],j+incr[d][COL]).

The executable code begins at line 39, and the first thing the program does is replace the default pseudo-random seed defined in SEED with the value of the first run parameter (if present) and then initiate the pseudo-random sequence. This happens on lines 43 to 46.

After starting the big for loop on line 50, the program resets n_t to 0 and initializes the two arrays grid and grid_op to their respective defaults of 0 and INI. Zero is a good value to initialize grid as long as you exclude 0 from the range of possible numbers, and INI, defined in main.h to be 5, can be any number not used as an operation code. Note that you need to reset these variables in the loop so that no data is carried from one puzzle to the next.

Defining the Triplets in the Main Module

As you saw in the previous section, to generate a MathSearch puzzle you first need to define the location and operation of the triplets. This is how MathSearch does it:

1. Choose a starting cell toward the center of the puzzle.

2. Make a list of all cells and mark them all as free.

3. Pick the free cell closest to the starting one and use it as the first cell of a triplet. Then determine for which directions (if any) the triplet is within the boundaries of the puzzle.

4. Discard the directions that would cause the triplet you are currently defining to overlap with already defined triplets.

5. Choose at random one of the possible directions. Save the triplet in t_list[n_t], increment n_t, and go back to Step 3. You are done when there are no more free cells available to start a new triplet.

To make it easier, I broke down the listing of main.c into the parts that correspond to the five steps listed above. The missing lines are either empty lines or lines with comments.

Choosing the Origin

Listing 14-2. main.c—Define the Triplets (Step 1)

```
62.    // Start from the approximate center
63.    int origin[2];
64.    origin[ROW] = N_NUM / 2 + rand() % (N_NUM / 3);
65.    origin[COL] = rand() % (N_NUM / 3);
```

This is the first usage of a pseudo-random number within MathSearch. After initializing a sequence with srand(seed) (see line 46 of Listing 14-1), the program invokes rand() on line 64 (see Listing 14-2). Every time you invoke rand(), it returns an integer value between 0 and RAND_MAX (i.e., 2,147,483,647). You then apply the modulo operator to force the pseudo-random number into the range you need. Lines 64 and 65 mean that MathSearch begins looking for triplets from a cell that is randomly positioned within the black square shown in Figure 14-4, where the large square represents the whole puzzle.

Figure 14-4. *Triplet origin within the puzzle*

Why? Because I discovered that setting the origin in a corner of the puzzle or in a position completely at random within the puzzle would often result in a distribution of triplets that was unsatisfactory. No triplet runs right to left. Therefore, it makes sense to start on the left side of the puzzle. And starting in the top-left (or bottom-left) corner would give preference to A_DOWN over A_UP directions (or vice-versa). When I saw that the current setting of origin gave good results, I didn't spend any time checking out other configuration. You are welcome to see whether you obtain significant (or easily detectable!) differences with other arrangements. Situations like this show that puzzle generation is not always 100% logical. In general, completely symmetrical and predefined configurations lead to less variety in the result. That's why I didn't simply program MathSearch to start looking for triplets from the leftmost cell of the middle row.

Listing the Cells

Listing 14-3. main.c—Define the Triplets (Step 2)

```
67.     // Make a list of all cells roughly ordered by the distance from the origin
68.     int next[N_NUM * N_NUM][2] = {{0}};
69.     int n_next = 0;
70.     for (int i = 0; i < N_NUM  &&  n_next < N_NUM * N_NUM; i++) {
71.       int ku = origin[ROW] - i;
72.       if (ku < 0) ku = 0;
73.       int kd = origin[ROW] + i;
74.       if (kd >= N_NUM) kd = N_NUM - 1;
75.       int jl = origin[COL] - i;
76.       if (jl < 0) jl = 0;
77.       int jr = origin[COL] + i;
78.       if (jr >= N_NUM) jr = N_NUM - 1;
79.       for (int j = jl; j <= jr; j++) {
80.         if (grid[ku][j] == 0) {
81.           next[n_next][ROW] = ku;
82.           next[n_next][COL] = j;
83.           n_next++;
84.           grid[ku][j] = -1;
85.         }
86.         if (grid[kd][j] == 0) {
87.           next[n_next][ROW] = kd;
88.           next[n_next][COL] = j;
```

```
89.              n_next++;
90.              grid[kd][j] = -1;
91.            }
92.          }
93.          for (int k = ku; k <= kd; k++) {
94.            if (grid[k][jl] == 0) {
95.              next[n_next][ROW] = k;
96.              next[n_next][COL] = jl;
97.              n_next++;
98.              grid[k][jl] = -1;
99.            }
100.           if (grid[k][jr] == 0) {
101.             next[n_next][ROW] = k;
102.             next[n_next][COL] = jr;
103.             n_next++;
104.             grid[k][jr] = -1;
105.           }
106.         }
107.       }
108.
```

The array next is where you build up the list of cells or, better said, the list of cell coordinates, with next[][0] containing the row index of a cell and next[][1] its column index. First of all, obviously, you reset the array and the cell counter, as shown on lines 68 and 69 of Listing 14-3.

The control variable i of the for loop is the distance from the origin cell measured along columns and rows. For example, if the origin has coordinates (k,j), the cells with coordinates (k-1,j-1), (k-1,j), (k-1,j+1), (k,j-1), (k,j+1), (k+1,j-1), (k+1,j), and (k+1,j+1) are all considered to have distance 1 from it. This explains why the comment at the beginning of Listing 14-3 states that the list is *roughly* ordered. If you measured the distance between cells on a printed puzzle, you would obviously find that (k-1,j-1), (k-1,j+1), (k+1,j-1), and (k+1,j+1) are farther away from the origin than (k-1,j), (k,j-1), (k,j+1), and (k+1,j). This is another occasion where puzzle generation shows its "artistic" side.

Keeping in mind what "distance" means in this context, you see that by changing i from 0 to N_NUM-1 you examine increasingly large squares of cells centered on the origin and covering the whole puzzle. You could have started from i = 1, but then, you would have had to process the origin itself before entering the loop, and it is more elegant to start the loop from 0, which only wastes a negligible amount of processing time.

To see how WordSearch builds up the list, you can insert the code shown in Listing 14-4 into main.c immediately after filling next.

Listing 14-4. Display the List of Cells

```
{
  int ord[N_NUM][N_NUM];
  for (int i = 0; i < n_next; i++) {
    ord[next[i][ROW]][next[i][COL]] = i;
  }
  for (int k = 0; k < N_NUM; k++) {
    for (int j = 0; j < N_NUM; j++) {
      printf("%3d", ord[k][j]);
    }
    printf("\n");
  }
}
```

When generating the puzzle in Figure 14-1, the added code will display on the console a matrix that shows in which order the cells are added to next (see Listing 14-5).

Listing 14-5. Cell Ordering Within Grid

```
35 36 37 38 39 40 48 56
20 22 24 26 28 42 50 58
 9 11 13 15 30 43 51 59
 1  3  5 17 31 44 52 60
 7  0  8 18 32 45 53 61
 2  4  6 19 33 46 54 62
10 12 14 16 34 47 55 63
21 23 25 27 29 41 49 57
```

Clearly, the cell with coordinates $(4,1)$ was the origin (because it is marked 0), and the cell $(6,7)$ was the last one (because it is marked 63).

The ku and kd variables indicate rows above and below the origin, while jl and jr indicate columns on the left and on the right of the origin. Lines 71 to 78 ensure that all four indices remain within the boundaries of the puzzle.

With $i = 0$, only the origin cell is added to the list. With $i = 1$, the control variable j of the for loop spanning lines 79 to 92 goes from 0 to 2 and the two if statements on lines 80 to 85 and 86 to 91 examine the cells $(3,0)$, $(5,0)$, $(3,1)$, $(5,1)$, $(3,2)$, and $(5,2)$. These are the cells numbered from 1 to 6 in the matrix shown in Listing 14-5. Then, the control variable k of the for loop spanning lines 93 to 106 goes from 3 to 5 and the two if statements on lines 94 to 99 and 100 to 105 examine the cells $(3,0)$, $(3,2)$, $(4,0)$, $(4,2)$, $(5,0)$ and $(5,2)$. MathSearch only adds $(4,0)$ and $(4,2)$ to the list (in position 7 and 8), because all the others have already been set when looping on j. The algorithm then adds the cells numbered 9 to 19 when $i = 2$, those numbered 20 to 34 when $i = 3$, etc.

The algorithm to build up next is quite inefficient, because it examines the same cells several times. But consider that in order to remove the redundant checks you would have to make it significantly more complicated. As the algorithm is quick enough as it is, why should you make it more difficult to understand and more susceptible to bugs?

Placing the Triplets in the Puzzle

Listing 14-6. main.c—Define the Triplets (Step 3)

```
109.    // Place the triplets
110.    int i0 = 0;
111.    do {
112.
113.      // Start from the available cell that is closest to the origin
114.      int k0 = next[i0][ROW];
115.      int j0 = next[i0][COL];
116.
117.      // Determine which directions are within the grid
118.      int dirs0[4];
119.      int n_dirs0 = 0;
120.      for (int i = 0; i < 4; i++) {
121.        int kk = k0 + incr[i][ROW] + incr[i][ROW] ;
122.        if (kk >= 0  &&  kk < N_NUM) {
```

```
123.                int jj = j0 + incr[i][COL] + incr[i][COL];
124.                if (jj >= 0  &&   jj < N_NUM) {
125.                    dirs0[n_dirs0] = i;
126.                    n_dirs0++;
127.                    }
128.                }
129.            }
```

The do loop that starts on line 111 of Listing 14-6 is where you do all the work to generate the triplets. It ends on line 189 of Listing 14-8.

The variable i0 indicates the first cell listed in next that has not yet been used in triplets. The statements on lines 114 and 115 save the coordinates of that cell as k0 and j0 to be the coordinates of the first cell of the triplet.

The purpose of the for loop on lines 120 to 129 is to write into dirs0 the directions that, using (k0,j0) as first cell of the triplet, don't cause the triplet to extend beyond the boundaries of the puzzle. Try the directions one by one—use incr on lines 121 and 123 to "grow" the triplet by two cells—and check that the coordinates of the triplet's last cell are greater than or equal to 0 and less than N_NUM.

Consider for example the leftmost triplet shown in Figure 14-2. Its first cell has the coordinates k0 = 3 and j0 = 0. Because its first cell is far from the top, right, and bottom boundaries, all four directions are possible and, after the code in Listing 14-6 executes, you will have n_dirs0 = 4 and:

```
dirs0[0] = ACROSS
dirs0[1] = DOWN
dirs0[2] = A_UP
dirs0[3] = A_DOWN
```

Removing the Directions that Overlap

Listing 14-7. main.c—Define the Triplets (Step 4)

```
131.        // Remove the directions that have one or more cells already used
132.        int dirs[4];
133.        int n_dirs = 0;
134.        for (int i = 0; i < n_dirs0; i++) {
135.          int k1 = k0 + incr[dirs0[i]][ROW];
136.          int j1 = j0 + incr[dirs0[i]][COL];
137.          int k2 = k1 + incr[dirs0[i]][ROW];
138.          int j2 = j1 + incr[dirs0[i]][COL];
139.          int kop = (k0 + k1) / 2;
140.          int jop = (j0 + j1) / 2;
141.          int kequ = (k1 + k2) / 2;
142.          int jequ = (j1 + j2) / 2;
143.          if (     grid[k0][j0] < 0  &&  grid[k1][j1] < 0  &&  grid[k2][j2] < 0
144.              &&  grid_op[kop][jop] != EQU
145.              &&  (grid_op[kequ][jequ] == INI  ||  grid_op[kequ][jequ] == EQU)
146.              ) {
147.            dirs[n_dirs] = dirs0[i];
148.            n_dirs++;
149.            }
150.          }
```

At this point, k0 and j0 are set to the coordinates within grid of the first cell of the triplet being generated, and the first n_dirs0 elements of dirs0 give you the possible directions of the triplet. On lines 135 to 138 of Listing 14-7, you calculate the coordinates of the other two cells of the triplet and, on lines 139 to 142, you calculate the coordinates within grid_op of the triplet's operation and of its equals sign.

Consider for example the leftmost triplet shown in Figure 14-2, with first cell in (3,0). The matrix in Listing 14-5 shows the cell order used to generate triplets *for this puzzle* (it will be different for other puzzles). Notice that (3,0) holds the number 1. This means that only one triplet was generated before the one we are looking at. The very first triplet started in position (4,1) because that is where the 0 appears in Listing 14-5. You can see in Figure 14-2 that the first triplet was horizontal (it's the one that holds 13+9=22). Therefore, when the for loop in Listing 14-7 executes with i = 3 (i.e., A_DOWN), the condition grid[k1][j1] < 0 on line 143 fails because k1 = k0 +1 = 4, j1 = j0 + 1 = 1, and the cell (4,1) was set to 0 when it was allocated to the very first triplet (you will see in Listing 14-8 that when a triplet is confirmed to be valid, its cells within grid are set to the triplet's position within t_list). As a result, the fourth element of dirs0 is not copied to dirs, which, at the end of code in Listing 14-7, ends up holding in its first three elements the direction codes ACROSS, DOWN, and A_UP.

Notice that the condition grid[k0][j0] < 0 should never fail because the coordinates of the first cell of the triplet come directly from next. But it costs a little processing time to include it and I find that it is always better to be safe...

It is worth examining in more detail the conditions on lines 144 and 145. The first one ensures that the position within grid_op where the operation code of the triplet being defined is not already occupied by an equals sign. It means that any other operation is accepted. As a result, triplets can share operations. That is, although they cannot cross on numbers, they can cross on operations. The condition on line 145 checks that the element of grid_op between the second and third numbers of the triplet is either unused or contains an equals sign. It means that triplets can cross on their equals signs.

Completing the Definition

Listing 14-8. main.c—Define the Triplets (Step 5)

```
152.        // Select one of the directions and save the triplet.
153.        // In the process, also generate the opcode.
154.        if (n_dirs > 0) {
155.          int k_dir = rand() % n_dirs;
156.          t_list[n_t][ROW] = k0;
157.          t_list[n_t][COL] = j0;
158.          t_list[n_t][DIR] = dirs[k_dir];
159.          int dk = incr[dirs[k_dir]][ROW];
160.          int dj = incr[dirs[k_dir]][COL];
161.          int k1 = k0 + dk;
162.          int j1 = j0 + dj;
163.          int k2 = k1 + dk;
164.          int j2 = j1 + dj;
165.          grid[k0][j0] = n_t;
166.          grid[k1][j1] = n_t;
167.          grid[k2][j2] = n_t;
168.          int kop = (k0 + k1) / 2;
169.          int jop = (j0 + j1) / 2;
170.          int opcode;
171.          if (grid_op[kop][jop] == INI) {
172.            opcode = rand() % NUM_OPS;
173.            grid_op[kop][jop] = opcode;
174.          }
```

```
175.          else {
176.            opcode = grid_op[kop][jop];
177.            }
178.          int kequ = (k1 + k2) / 2;
179.          int jequ = (j1 + j2) / 2;
180.          grid_op[kequ][jequ] = EQU;
181.          t_list[n_t][OP] = opcode;
182.          n_t++;
183.          }
184.
185.        // Either a triplet could be placed or not.
186.        // In either case, remove the starting cell from the list
187.        // so that you don't start from it again.
188.        i0++;
189.        } while (i0 < n_next);
```

DIR and OP are two constants defined in main.h as 2 and 3, respectively.

You know that, for the leftmost triplet in Figure 14-2, n_dirs is 3. Therefore, line 155 of Listing 14-8 assigns to k_dir 0, 1, or 2. That is, ACROSS, DOWN, or A_UP. From Figure 14-2, you see that the pseudo-random direction was A_UP.

Lines 156 to 158 save the triplet's parameters in t_list. Lines 159 to 167 claim the triplet's cells by writing in grid the position of the triplet within t_list (for this triplet, 1).

All that's left to define the triplet (apart from the numbers) is to choose its operation. You pick one at random on line 173 if the position it's going to occupy in grid_op is still free (as it will be for the leftmost triplet in Figure 14-2). Otherwise, you accept the operation that was set in grid_op when defining a preceding triplet (i.e., a triplet with a lower position within t_list).

On lines 188 and 189, you increase the index used to identify within next the first cell of a triplet and start a new iteration of the do loop that begins on line 111 of Listing 14-6 to define a new triplet, but only if you have not exhausted all the cells listed in next.

Obviously, the last several iterations will not result in a new triplet because triplets never run from right to left and the free cells are listed in next from left to right. But it is simpler to let the loop run out of cells rather than devise a mechanism to identify when it is not possible to define further triplets.

If you want to develop such a mechanism, I suggest that you print out some instances of the matrix shown in Listing 14-5. That is, use the code of Listing 14-4 and change the seed a few times. For example, looking at Listing 14-5, you can see that no triplet will ever start on the cells numbered 49, 55, 57, and 63. I leave it up to you. I'm happy to keep the code simple.

Module Main (main.h)

Before proceeding with the description of main.c, let's have a look at main.h (see Listing 14-9).

Listing 14-9. main.h

```
1. /* main.h
2.  *
3.  * General declarations
4.  *
5.  * Copyright (c) 2016 by Giulio Zambon.  All rights reserved.
6.  */
7. #ifndef MAIN
8. #define MAIN
9.
```

```
10. #define FALSE 0
11. #define TRUE  1
12.
13. #define ROW 0
14. #define COL 1
15.
16. #define ACROSS 0
17. #define DOWN   1
18. #define A_UP   2
19. #define A_DOWN 3
20.
21. #define FORMAT 5
22.
23. #if (FORMAT == 0)
24. #define N_NUM 6
25. #define NUM_OPS 2
26. #define MAX_RES 50
27. #define FACT 4  // not used
28.
29. #elif (FORMAT == 1)
30. #define N_NUM 6
31. #define NUM_OPS 4
32. #define MAX_RES 50
33. #define FACT 4
34.
35. #elif (FORMAT == 2)
36. #define N_NUM 8
37. #define NUM_OPS 2
38. #define MAX_RES 50
39. #define FACT 4  // not used
40.
41. #elif (FORMAT == 3)
42. #define N_NUM 8
43. #define NUM_OPS 2
44. #define MAX_RES 75
45. #define FACT 4  // not used
46.
47. #elif (FORMAT == 4)
48. #define N_NUM 8
49. #define NUM_OPS 4
50. #define MAX_RES 50
51. #define FACT 4
52.
53. #elif (FORMAT == 5)
54. #define N_NUM 8
55. #define NUM_OPS 4
56. #define MAX_RES 75
57. #define FACT 4
58.
59. #elif (FORMAT == 6)
60. #define N_NUM 10
```

```
61. #define NUM_OPS 2
62. #define MAX_RES 50
63. #define FACT 4   // not used
64.
65. #elif (FORMAT == 7)
66. #define N_NUM 10
67. #define NUM_OPS 2
68. #define MAX_RES 75
69. #define FACT 4   // not used
70.
71. #elif (FORMAT == 8)
72. #define N_NUM 10
73. #define NUM_OPS 2
74. #define MAX_RES 99
75. #define FACT 4   // not used
76.
77. #elif (FORMAT == 9)
78. #define N_NUM 10
79. #define NUM_OPS 4
80. #define MAX_RES 50
81. #define FACT 4
82.
83. #elif (FORMAT == 10)
84. #define N_NUM 10
85. #define NUM_OPS 4
86. #define MAX_RES 75
87. #define FACT 4
88.
89. #elif (FORMAT == 11)
90. #define N_NUM 10
91. #define NUM_OPS 4
92. #define MAX_RES 99
93. #define FACT 4   // used to be 3, but it doesn't converge…
94. #endif
95.
96. #define SIDE (N_NUM + N_NUM - 1)
97.
98. // Operations codes
99. // The values must match the operation strings defined in ops[]
100. #define N_OPS 4
101. #define ADD 0
102. #define SUB 1
103. #define MUL 2
104. #define DIV 3
105. //
106. #define EQU 4
107. #define INI 5
108.
109. // All the variables declared here are defined in MathSearch.c
110. extern int grid[N_NUM][N_NUM];
111. extern int grid_op[N_NUM][N_NUM];
```

```
112. #define DIR 2
113. #define OP  3
114. extern int t_list[N_NUM * N_NUM / 3][4];   // ROW, COL, DIR, OP
115. extern int n_t;
116. extern int incr[][2];
117. extern int mat[SIDE][SIDE];
118. extern int z[SIDE][SIDE];
119.
120. extern char ops[];
121.
122. #endif
```

You have already encountered all declarations and most definitions. But FORMAT, defined on line 21, is new.

Notice that the lines 23 to 94 are 11 blocks of definitions like the following one (which applies to the puzzle in Figure 14-1):

```
54. #define N_NUM 8
55. #define NUM_OPS 4
56. #define MAX_RES 75
57. #define FACT 4
```

Only one block is switched on, depending on the value assigned to FORMAT. You have already seen N_NUM (how many rows and columns are in a puzzle) and NUM_OPS (the number of operations in the order ADD, SUB, MUL, and DIV). MAX_RES is the largest number to be included in the puzzle and FACT is a scaling factor used when generating the numbers. You will learn about them in the next section.

I chose to use the C preprocessor to select the different configurations because, unlike Java (now I've said it!), C doesn't support the definition of array dimensions at runtime. If I had used a variable for N_NUM, I would have had to allocate arrays like grid from the heap, release the space at the end, etc. Not something I like to do if I can avoid it.

Generate the Numbers in the Main Module

At this point, you have a list of n_t triplets in t_list, with each entry including the coordinates of the first cell, the direction, and the operation code.

What you need to do now is fill in the numbers (Listing 14-10). Note that you are free to choose the numbers as you see fit because the triplets do not share any number.

Listing 14-10. main.c—Generate the Numbers

```
191.    //----------------------------------------------------- Generate the numbers
192.    for (int k = 0; k < N_NUM; k++) {
193.      for (int j = 0; j < N_NUM; j++) {
194.        grid[k][j] = -1;
195.        }
196.      }
197.
198.    for (int i = 0; i < n_t; i++) {
199.      int *trip = t_list[i];
200.      int k0 = trip[ROW];
201.      int j0 = trip[COL];
202.      int dir = trip[DIR];
```

```
203.        int k1 = k0 + incr[dir][ROW];
204.        int j1 = j0 + incr[dir][COL];
205.        int k2 = k1 + incr[dir][ROW];
206.        int j2 = j1 + incr[dir][COL];
207.        int n0;
208.        int n1;
209.        int n2;
210.        int nn;
211.        do {
212.          switch (trip[OP]) {
213.            case ADD: {
214.              n2 = rand() % (MAX_RES / 4 * 3) + MAX_RES / 4;
215.              n1 = rand() % (n2 / 2 - MAX_RES / 9) + MAX_RES / 9;
216.              n0 = n2 - n1;
217.              break;
218.              }
219.
220.            case SUB: {
221.              n0 = rand() % (MAX_RES / 4 * 3) + MAX_RES / 4;
222.              n1 = rand() % (n0 / 2 - MAX_RES / 9) + MAX_RES / 9;
223.              n2 = n0 - n1;
224.              break;
225.              }
226.
227.            case MUL: {
228.              n0 = rand() % (MAX_RES / FACT) + 3;
229.              do {
230.                n1 = rand() % (MAX_RES / FACT) + 3;
231.                n2 = n0 * n1;
232.                } while (n2 > MAX_RES);
233.              break;
234.              }
235.
236.            default: {
237.              n1 = rand() % (MAX_RES / FACT) + 3;
238.              do {
239.                n2 = rand() % (MAX_RES / FACT) + 3;
240.                n0 = n1 * n2;
241.                } while (n0 > MAX_RES);
242.              break;
243.              }
244.            }
245.          grid[k0][j0] = n0;
246.          grid[k1][j1] = n1;
247.          grid[k2][j2] = n2;
248.
249.          // Check whether the operation introduces ambiguities
250.          nn = count(k0, j0);
251.          if (nn == 1) nn = count(k1, j1);
252.          if (nn == 1) nn = count(k2, j2);
253.          } while (nn > 1);
```

```
254.        }
255.
256.    //-------------------------------------------------- Fill up the empty spaces
257.    for (int k = 0; k < N_NUM; k++) {
258.      for (int j = 0; j < N_NUM; j++) {
259.        if (grid[k][j] < 0) {
260.          do {
261.            grid[k][j] = rand() % 7 + 5;
262.            } while (count(k, j) > 0);
263.        }
264.      }
265.    }
```

In lines 192 to 196, you set all elements of the grid to -1. You could use zeros because there are no zeros in the finished puzzle, but I prefer to test for less-than-zero than for less-than-or-equal-zero or less-than-one. It is more a matter of taste than of anything else.

The for loop that starts on line 198 goes through all the triplets one by one, while the switch statement on lines 212 to 244 is where you generate the numbers that satisfy the operation of the current triplet.

Perhaps you are thinking that using the default case of the switch statement for the division is not completely safe. In principle, you are right. A defensive programmer would have defined a case for the division like for the other operations and used the default to report an error. Normally, I would have done it, but in this case (pun intended!), I felt that it was a bit of an overkill. You are welcome to do it if it makes you feel better.

Let's go through the operations. While doing so, we will use the puzzle shown in Figure 14-1 as an example.

Using ADD

The relevant lines are 214 to 216:

```
n2 = rand() % (MAX_RES / 4 * 3) + MAX_RES / 4;
n1 = rand() % (n2 / 2 - MAX_RES / 9) + MAX_RES / 9;
n0 = n2 - n1;
```

We start by defining the result. The only strict requirement is that it is between 2 (because 1+1 is the smallest possible sum) and MAX_RES (e.g., 75). But if you simply calculate n2 = rand() % (MAX_RES - 2) + 2, you obtain a sum that is uniformly distributed within the valid range, and this will result in several sums with single-digit numbers that are extremely simple (and therefore, trivial to spot). With n2 as it is set now, you restrict the sum to the top three quarters of the range. For example, with MAX_RES = 75, you have n2 = rand() % 54 + 18, which sets the range to between 18 and 71. I concede that I could have been a bit more generous: if on line 214 you replace MAX_RES with (MAX_RES + 3), you obtain n2 = rand() % 57 + 19, which gives results between 19 and 75. But with MAX_RES = 99, the new formula would result in a maximum n2 of 100, which would be too large. I leave it up to you to explore alternatives.

Anyway, once you have defined n2, you need to set n1. If you don't like the formula used on line 215, feel free to change it!

Using SUB

The relevant lines are 221 to 223:

```
n0 = rand() % (MAX_RES / 4 * 3) + MAX_RES / 4;
n1 = rand() % (n0 / 2 - MAX_RES / 9) + MAX_RES / 9;
n2 = n0 - n1;
```

The logic is identical to that of the SUM, except the total (i.e., n2) is now the first number.

Using MUL

The relevant lines are 228 to 232:

```
n0 = rand() % (MAX_RES / FACT) + 3;
do {
  n1 = rand() % (MAX_RES / FACT) + 3;
  n2 = n0 * n1;
  } while (n2 > MAX_RES);
```

FACT, which is currently defined in main.h to be 4, is a number found by trial and error. One more artistic aspect of designing puzzles. The +3 added to the random part of n0 is to prevent the first factor from being 1 or 2, which would result in easy-to-spot multiplications.

The algorithm is conceptually simple: pick a first factor that is not larger than a quarter of the maximum and do the same with the second factor until their product does not exceed the maximum. For example, with MAX_RES = 75, both factors are uniformly distributed between 3 and 20. As the square root of 75 is 8.7, it might take quite a few iterations before the product is 75 or less. Once more, have fun with it and find something better.

Using DIV

The relevant lines are 237 to 241:

```
n1 = rand() % (MAX_RES / FACT) + 3;
do {
  n2 = rand() % (MAX_RES / FACT) + 3;
  n0 = n1 * n2;
  } while (n0 > MAX_RES);
```

The division logic is identical to that of multiplication, but the multiplication's result is used as first number of the division.

Checking for Unicity

In my opinion, there is nothing more annoying than puzzles that have more than one solution. To avoid this with MathSearch, the generation of the number is repeated with the do loop that starts on line 211 and ends on line 253 until the current triplet is guaranteed not to introduce ambiguities.

To understand how this could happen, consider the following simple example in which two horizontal triplets are adjacent to each other (for clarity, the two triplets are enclosed in parentheses):

(36 / 4 = 9) (20 + 29 = 49)

Do you see the problem? When presented with the puzzle, you would be perfectly justified in thinking that the three numbers in the middle form a triplet:

36   4   (9 + 20 = 29)   49

Similar ambiguities are possible with all directions. I have designed quite a few different numeric puzzles and have found that ensuring unicity of the solution is often the trickiest part to program.

Assigning the numbers to a triplet means filling up with those numbers three cells of the array grid. You can go through each one of those three cells and see whether they form valid triplets with the adjacent cells. For example, if the first cell of the triplet you are checking has coordinates (3,5), you can form all possible triplets to which that cell can belong. You'll probably be surprised by how many they are (see Listing 14-11).

Listing 14-11. Possible Triplets that Include the Cell (3,5)

```
(3,3) (3,4) (3,5)
(3,4) (3,5) (3,6)
(3,5) (3,6) (3,7)
(1,5) (2,5) (3,5)
(2,5) (3,5) (4,5)
(3,5) (4,5) (5,5)
(5,3) (4,4) (3,5)
(4,4) (3,5) (2,6)
(3,5) (2,6) (1,7)
(1,3) (2,4) (3,5)
(2,4) (3,5) (4,6)
(3,5) (4,6) (5,7)
```

They are twelve. This is because the cell could be in any of three positions and in four possible directions. The three key lines of Listing 14-10 that check for unicity are 250 to 252:

```
nn = count(k0, j0);
if (nn == 1) nn = count(k1, j1);
if (nn == 1) nn = count(k2, j2);
```

The function count(), of which you will learn the detail later in this chapter, returns the number of triplets that the given cell satisfies. If count(k0, j0) on line 250 returns 1, it means that the only triplet to which the cell could possibly belong is the triplet we are testing for unicity. Same story for the second and third cell of the triplet under test. If all three cells result in a count of 1, it means that the triplet being tested doesn't introduce any ambiguity.

In that case, the condition on line 253 fails and processing of the next triplet in t_list begins. If, on the other hand, one of the cells together with the adjacent cells satisfies more than one triplet, the while condition succeeds and the do loop that begins on line 211 generates a fresh set of numbers for the current triplet.

Wrapping Up

At this point, all you need to do to complete the puzzle is fill up the cells that have not been used for triplets. For example, the puzzle in Figure 14-1 contains 17 triplets, which occupy 51 cells. This leaves 14 cells unused. But you cannot simply generate random numbers. You have to ensure that the numbers you pick to fill up the gaps do not introduce ambiguities. This is done again with count(), which in this case must return 0.

Display the Results in the Main Module

Listing 14-12. main.c—Display the Results

```
267.    display();  // WARNING: Do not remove the display: it is needed for HTML
268.
269.
270.    //------------------------- Save the puzzle and the solution to HTML files
271.    char name[32];  // certainly long enough
272.    sprintf(name, "%d_%d_%d_%d_%03d.html", N_NUM, MAX_RES, NUM_OPS, seed, k_puz);
273.
274.    char id[32];  // certainly long enough
275.    sprintf(id, "%d %d %d %d %d", N_NUM, MAX_RES, NUM_OPS, seed, k_puz);
276.
277.    int html_saved = save_html(name, id);
278.    printf("save_html %2d %s\n\n", k_puz, (html_saved) ? "successful" : "failed");
279.
280.    sprintf(name, "%d_%d_%d_%d_%03d", N_NUM, MAX_RES, NUM_OPS, seed, k_puz);
281.
282.    save_images(name);
283.    printf("save_images %2d done\n\n", k_puz);
284.
285.    } // for (int k_puz..
286.
287.
288.  return EXIT_SUCCESS;
289.  }
```

Listing 14-12 shows that, after completing a puzzle, MathSearch displays the results on the console on line 267. The display() function also sets up data that's needed in save_html() and save_images().

After saving the puzzle in HTML (line 277) and JPEG (line 282) formats, if MathSearch doesn't need to generate more puzzles, it falls through line 285 (which ends the for loop that starts on line 50 of Listing 14-1) and terminates.

Module: count

As you learned in the section entitled, "Checking for Unicity," the count() function returns the number of triplets within grid that include a given cell and contain a valid operation. Listing 14-13 shows the code.

Listing 14-13. count.c

```
1. /* count.c
2.  *
3.  * Copyright (c) 2016 by Giulio Zambon.  All rights reserved.
4.  */
5. #include <stdio.h>
6. #include <stdlib.h>
7. #include "main.h"
8. #include "count.h"
9.
```

```
10. int count(int kk, int jj) {
11.    int nn = 0;
12.    for (int i2 = 0; i2 < 4; i2++) {  // in all directions
13.       int dk = incr[i2][ROW];
14.       int dj = incr[i2][COL];
15.       for (int i3 = 2; i3 >= 0; i3--) {  // in all positions
16.          int kz = kk - dk * i3;
17.          int jz = jj - dj * i3;
18.          int ko = kz + dk;
19.          int jo = jz + dj;
20.          int kt = ko + dk;
21.          int jt = jo + dj;
22.          if (kz >= 0  &&  kt >= 0  &&  kt < N_NUM  &&  jz >= 0  &&  jt >= 0  &&  jt < N_NUM) {
23.             int nn0 = grid[kz][jz];
24.             int nn1 = grid[ko][jo];
25.             int nn2 = grid[kt][jt];
26.             if (nn0 > 0  &&  nn1 > 0  &&  nn2 > 0) {
27.                for (int i4 = 0; i4 < N_OPS; i4++) {  // all operations
28.                   switch (i4) {
29.                      case ADD:
30.                         if (nn0 + nn1 == nn2) nn++;
31.                         break;
32.                      case SUB:
33.                         if (nn0 - nn1 == nn2) nn++;
34.                         break;
35.                      case MUL:
36.                         if (nn0 * nn1 == nn2) nn++;
37.                         break;
38.                      default:
39.                         if (nn2 * nn1 == nn0) nn++;
40.                         break;
41.                   }
42.                } // 4
43.             } // if
44.          } // if
45.       } // 3
46.    } // 2
47.    return nn;
48.    }
```

Essentially, it builds the triplets in all directions and with the given cell in all positions. Then, for each triplet that remains within the boundaries of the puzzle, it tries all operations and counts those that fit the numbers present in grid. I'm fond of this little function, but it is pretty straightforward.

Module: display

Before looking at the code, you need to understand the purpose of the two arrays mat and z.

mat is used to store numbers and operations together, so that they can be easily formatted for display. Therefore, for an 8x8 puzzle, it requires eight elements in each row and column for the numbers and seven elements in each row and column for the operations between each pair of adjacent numbers. For example, to copy the triplet (68 / 17 = 4) in Figure 14-2 from grid and grid_op to mat, you need to do the following:

```
mat[0][6] = grid[0][3]
mat[0][7] = grid_op[0][3]
mat[0][8] = grid[0][4]
mat[0][9] = grid_op[0][4]
mat[0][10] = grid[0][5]
```

Then, with the definition int *t = mat[0], the statement printf("%3d %c %3d %c %3d", t[6], ops[t[7]], t[8], ops[t[9]], t[10]);

prints out 68 / 17 = 4.

The matter gets somewhat more complicated when the triplet has a direction other than ACROSS but, as you will see from the code, the principle is the same.

While mat is used in all three forms of display supported by MathSearch (plain text on the console, HTML, and JPEG graphics), z is only needed to display the puzzle solution in HTML. As you will see in the section that explains the module save_html, save_html() displays the puzzle and its solution as HTML tables, with each number and operation sign within a <td> element. To show the triplets in the solution table, save_html() sets the background of the <td> elements. For example, for the triplet (68 / 17 = 4) in Figure 14-2, it sets the background of the cell containing 68 to the image in Figure 14-5, the background of the cell with 4 to the image in Figure 14-6, and the background of the other cells to the image in Figure 14-7. The result is shown in Figure 14-8.

To cover all possibilities, the 23 images shown in Figure 14-9 are necessary.

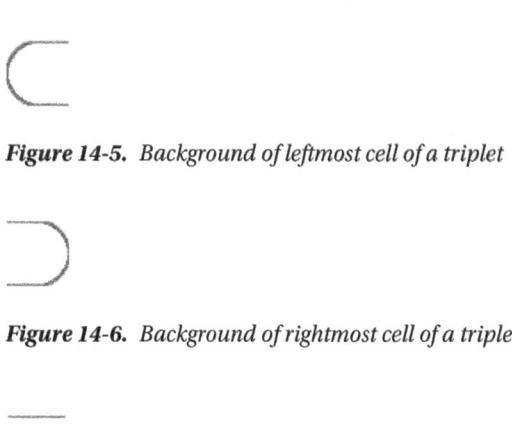

Figure 14-5. Background of leftmost cell of a triplet

Figure 14-6. Background of rightmost cell of a triplet

Figure 14-7. Background of center cells of a triplet

(68 / 17 = 4)

Figure 14-8. Triplet in HTML format

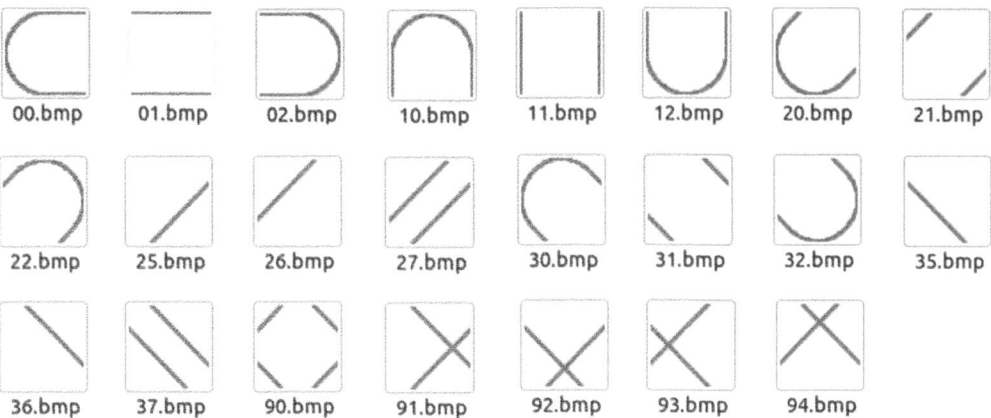

| 00.bmp | 01.bmp | 02.bmp | 10.bmp | 11.bmp | 12.bmp | 20.bmp | 21.bmp |

| 22.bmp | 25.bmp | 26.bmp | 27.bmp | 30.bmp | 31.bmp | 32.bmp | 35.bmp |

| 36.bmp | 37.bmp | 90.bmp | 91.bmp | 92.bmp | 93.bmp | 94.bmp |

Figure 14-9. *All background images*

And now, finally, let's look at the code in display.c (see Listing 14-14).

Listing 14-14. display.c

```
1. /* display.c
2.  *
3.  * Copyright (c) 2016 by Giulio Zambon.  All rights reserved.
4.  */
5. #include <stdio.h>
6. #include <stdlib.h>
7. #include "main.h"
8. #include "display.h"
9.
10. void display() {
11.
12.    // Initialize the output arrays
13.    for (int k = 0; k < N_NUM + N_NUM - 1; k++) {
14.      for (int j = 0; j < N_NUM + N_NUM - 1; j++) {
15.        mat[k][j] = -1;
16.        z[k][j] = -1;
17.        }
18.      }
19.
20.    // Copy the numbers to the puzzle array
21.    for (int k = 0; k < N_NUM; k++) {
22.      for (int j = 0; j < N_NUM; j++) {
23.        mat[k + k][j + j] = grid[k][j];
24.        }
25.      }
26.
27.    // Copy the operations to the puzzle array and
28.    // set the cell background array used for the HTML output
```

419

```
29.     for (int i = 0; i < n_t; i++) {
30.        int *t = t_list[i];
31.        int k0 = t[ROW];
32.        int j0 = t[COL];
33.        int dir = t[DIR];
34.        int k1 = k0 + incr[dir][ROW];
35.        int j1 = j0 + incr[dir][COL];
36.        int k2 = k1 + incr[dir][ROW];
37.        int j2 = j1 + incr[dir][COL];
38.        k0 += k0;
39.        k1 += k1;
40.        k2 += k2;
41.        j0 += j0;
42.        j1 += j1;
43.        j2 += j2;
44.        int kop = (k0 + k1) / 2;
45.        int jop = (j0 + j1) / 2;
46.        int kequ = (k1 + k2) / 2;
47.        int jequ = (j1 + j2) / 2;
48.        mat[kop][jop] = t[OP];
49.        mat[kequ][jequ] = EQU;
50.
51.        // Set the cell background array
52.        int ii = dir * 10;
53.        z[k0][j0] = ii;
54.        z[k1][j1] = ii + 1;
55.        z[k2][j2] = ii + 2;
56.        if(dir == A_UP) {
57.          z[kop][jop]   = (z[kop][jop] < 0)   ? ii + 1 : 90;
58.          z[kequ][jequ] = (z[kequ][jequ] < 0) ? ii + 1 : 90;
59.
60.          z[kop][jop - 1] = (z[kop][jop - 1] < 0) ? ii + 5 : ((z[kop][jop - 1] < 30) ↵
                ? ii + 7 : 91);
61.          z[kop - 1][jop] = (z[kop - 1][jop] < 0) ? ii + 5 : ((z[kop - 1][jop] < 30) ↵
                ? ii + 7 : 92);
62.          z[kop][jop + 1] = (z[kop][jop + 1] < 0) ? ii + 6 : ((z[kop][jop + 1] < 30) ↵
                ? ii + 7 : 93);
63.          z[kop + 1][jop] = (z[kop + 1][jop] < 0) ? ii + 6 : ((z[kop + 1][jop] < 30) ↵
                ? ii + 7 : 94);
64.
65.          z[kequ][jequ - 1] = (z[kequ][jequ - 1] < 0) ? ii + 5 : ((z[kequ][jequ - 1] < 30) ↵
                ? ii + 7 : 91);
66.          z[kequ - 1][jequ] = (z[kequ - 1][jequ] < 0) ? ii + 5 : ((z[kequ - 1][jequ] < 30) ↵
                ? ii + 7 : 92);
67.          z[kequ][jequ + 1] = (z[kequ][jequ + 1] < 0) ? ii + 6 : ((z[kequ][jequ + 1] < 30) ↵
                ? ii + 7 : 93);
68.          z[kequ + 1][jequ] = (z[kequ + 1][jequ] < 0) ? ii + 6 : ((z[kequ + 1][jequ] < 30) ↵
                ? ii + 7 : 94);
69.        }
70.        else if(dir == A_DOWN) {
71.          z[kop][jop] = (z[kop][jop] < 0)   ? ii + 1 : 90;
```

```
72.        z[kequ][jequ] = (z[kequ][jequ] < 0)    ? ii + 1 : 90;
73.
74.        z[kop][jop - 1] = (z[kop][jop - 1] < 0) ? ii + 6 : ((z[kop][jop - 1] > 30) ↵
               ? ii + 7 : 91);
75.        z[kop - 1][jop] = (z[kop - 1][jop] < 0) ? ii + 5 : ((z[kop - 1][jop] > 30) ↵
               ? ii + 7 : 92);
76.        z[kop][jop + 1] = (z[kop][jop + 1] < 0) ? ii + 5 : ((z[kop][jop + 1] > 30) ↵
               ? ii + 7 : 93);
77.        z[kop + 1][jop] = (z[kop + 1][jop] < 0) ? ii + 6 : ((z[kop + 1][jop] > 30) ↵
               ? ii + 7 : 94);
78.
79.        z[kequ][jequ - 1] = (z[kequ][jequ - 1] < 0) ? ii + 6 : ((z[kequ][jequ - 1] > 30)
               ? ii + 7 : 91);
80.        z[kequ - 1][jequ] = (z[kequ - 1][jequ] < 0) ? ii + 5 : ((z[kequ - 1][jequ] > 30) ↵
               ? ii + 7 : 92);
81.        z[kequ][jequ + 1] = (z[kequ][jequ + 1] < 0) ? ii + 5 : ((z[kequ][jequ + 1] > 30) ↵
               ? ii + 7 : 93);
82.        z[kequ + 1][jequ] = (z[kequ + 1][jequ] < 0) ? ii + 6 : ((z[kequ + 1][jequ] > 30) ↵
               ? ii + 7 : 94);
83.        }
84.      else {
85.        z[kop][jop] = ii + 1;
86.        z[kequ][jequ] = ii + 1;
87.        }
88.
89.    } // for (int i..
90.
91.    // Display the puzzle on the console
92.    for (int k = 0; k < N_NUM + N_NUM - 1; k++) {
93.      for (int j = 0; j < N_NUM + N_NUM - 1; j++) {
94.        if (mat[k][j] == -1) {
95.          printf("   ");
96.        }
97.        else if (k % 2 == 0  &&  j % 2 == 0){
98.          printf("%3d", mat[k][j]);
99.        }
100.       else {
101.         printf("  %c", ops[mat[k][j]]);
102.       }
103.     }
104.     printf("\n");
105.   }
106.
107. }
```

Up to line 26, display() initializes mat and z and copies the numbers from grid to every second element of mat, thereby leaving space between the numbers for the operations.

The for loop that starts on line 29 and ends on line 90 goes through all the triplets and, for each triplet, sets the operations in mat (from line 30 to 49) and the cell backgrounds in z (from line 53 to 88).

The setting of the operations in mat is straightforward, especially if you remember that I consistently use k to begin the names of variables associated with rows and j for variables associated with columns.

But the code to set z is a bit trickier.

On line 52, the variable ii is initialized to the direction of the triplet multiplied by 10. Then, on lines 53 to 55, the three elements of z that correspond to the three numbers of the triplet are set to ii, ii+1, and ii+2. For example, for the triplet 68 / 17 = 4 in Figure 14-2 with dir = ACROSS (i.e., 0), the assignments are:

```
53. z[0][6] = 0;
54. z[0][8] = 1;
55. z[0][10] = 2;
```

Then, execution continues from line 85 because the else of line 84 applies to both ACROSS and DOWN:

```
85. z[0][7] = 1;
86. z[0][9] = 1;
```

If you now have a look at the names of the background images shown in Figure 14-9, you will see that those named 00.bmp, 01.bmp, and 02.bmp are the correct ones for a horizontal triplet. All save_html() has to do to pick the correct background for the triplet's cells is to reformat the numbers stored in z to the names of the corresponding background images.

If you now look at the triplet 13 x 4 = 52, the settings for z become:

```
53. z[10][2] = 10;
54. z[12][2] = 11;
55. z[14][2] = 12;
85. z[11][2] = 11;
86. z[13][2] = 11;
```

And again, Figure 14-9 shows that the background images named 10.bmp, 11.bmp, and 12.bmp are the correct ones for a vertical triplet.

So far, so good. Now let's look at an A_UP triplet like 57 - 26 = 31 in Figure 14-2.

The lines 53 to 55 still apply:

```
53. z[6][0] = 20;
54. z[4][2] = 21;
55. z[2][4] = 22;
```

and Figure 14-9 tells you that the background images for those cells are indeed 20.bmp, 21.bmp, and 22.bmp. But if you execute the lines 85 and 86 like you have done before, you have:

```
85. z[5][1] = 21;
86. z[3][3] = 21;
```

Everything looks right. So, why should we replace 85 and 86 with 57 to 68? It is because we have allowed triplets to share operations. See for example the puzzle shown in Figure 14-10.

If you applied the lines 85 and 86 used for horizontal and vertical triplets to the A_UP in Figure 14-10 with triplet 19 x 3 = 57, the settings would be:

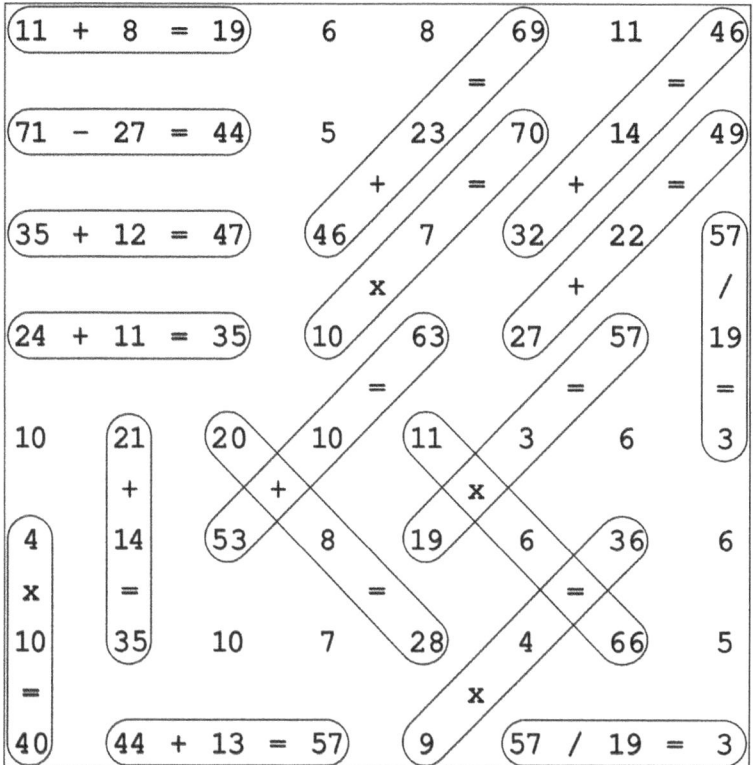

Figure 14-10. *Puzzle with crossing triplets*

```
53. z[10][8] = 20;
54. z[8][10] = 21;
55. z[6][12] = 22;
85. z[9][9]  = 21;
86. z[7][11] = 21;
```

That would be wrong, because the x in the cell (9,9) is enclosed in a diamond, while the background image 21.bmp identified by z[9][9] has only two bars. The background image you should use is 90.bmp. The A_DOWN triplet 11 x 6 = 66 has the same problem: it shares the x in (9,9) with the A_UP triplet, but z[10][10] would be set on line 85 to 31, and 31.bmp has only two bars.

To set z[9][9] to 90 in the A_UP triplet, so that that the shared x is enclosed in a diamond, you need to replace lines 85 and 86 with the following two lines, where (kop,jop) is (9,9) and (kequ,jequ) is (7,11):

```
57. z[kop][jop]   = (z[kop][jop] < 0)   ? ii + 1 : 90; => (z[9][9]  < 0) ? ii + 1 : 90;
58. z[kequ][jequ] = (z[kequ][jequ] < 0) ? ii + 1 : 90; => (z[7][11] < 0) ? ii + 1 : 90;
```

Now, if the index within t_list of the A_UP triplet is greater than the index of the crossing A_DOWN triplet, by the time line 57 is executed for the A_UP, z[9][9] has already been set to 31 for the A_DOWN. As

31 is *not* less than 0, it is replaced with 90, which is what you want. On the other hand, if the A_UP happens to be positioned within t_list before the A_DOWN, when the A_UP is processed, z[9][9] still contains its initialization value of -1 and is therefore set on line 57 to 21. Line 71 will then replace the 21 with 90 when line 71 it is executed for the subsequently encountered A_DOWN. Lines 58 and 72 do the equivalent operation for the cells containing the equals sign. In Figure 14-10, you see an example of this case, where the triplets 11 x = 66 and 9 x 4 = 36 cross.

But you still have a problem, which becomes clear if you give a closer look at the image 90.bmp: the corners of the diamond are missing. This is because the lines around the triplets, having to enclose the numbers with some padding, "spill" into the neighboring cells.

What you need to do is execute additional assignments for the four cells around the x (left, above, right, and below):

```
z[9][8]  = 91;
z[8][9]  = 92;
z[9][10] = 93;
z[10][9] = 94;
```

This is precisely what the four lines 60 to 63 do. Similarly, 65 to 68 take care of cells around crossings centered on the equals sign, and 74 to 82 do the assignments for A_DOWN triplets.

Finally, once you have processed all n_t triplets, you fall through line 89 (the bottom of the for loop that starts on line 29) and display the solution of the puzzle in the console, as shown in Listing 14-15 (which shows the solution of the puzzle in Figure 14-1).

Listing 14-15. Puzzle Solution Shown on the Console

```
 11     5     53    68  /  17  =  4     52     7
              =                     =
  5    14     31     9     48     9     7     11
        +     =            =      +
 39    26     72     3     43    66  / 11  =  6
        -     =      X
 57     9     16    53     20  X  3  = 60     7
        X                   +
  8    13  +  9  = 22     16    72  / 18  =  4
                                =
 21    13    20  X  3  = 60     69     9     71
  +     X                               =
 15     4    12  X  5  = 60      6     20     6
  =     =                         +
 36    52    36  /  6  =  6     51     5      9
```

Module: save_html

As display() does all the work of formatting the arrays mat and z, all save_html() has to do is write them to a file as HTML elements and with the appropriate HTML header and styles (see Listing 14-16).

Listing 14-16. save_html.c

```
1. /* save_html.c
```

```
2.    *
3.    * Copyright (c) 2016 by Giulio Zambon.  All rights reserved.
4.    */
5.   #include <stdio.h>
6.   #include <stdlib.h>
7.   #include <string.h>
8.   #include "main.h"
9.   #include "save_html.h"
10.
11.  int save_html(char *name, char *id) {
12.
13.    char *TEXT_HEADER_1[] = {
14.        "<?xml version=\"1.0\" encoding=\"utf-8\"?>",
15.        "<!DOCTYPE html PUBLIC \"-//W3C//DTD XHTML 1.0 Strict//EN\" "
16.            "\"http://www.w3.org/TR/xhtml1/DTD/xhtml1-strict.dtd\">",
17.        "<html xmlns=\"http://www.w3.org/1999/xhtml\">",
18.        "<head>"
19.        };
20.    int text_header_1_len = sizeof(TEXT_HEADER_1) / sizeof(char *);
21.
22.    char *TEXT_HEADER_2[] = {
23.        "<meta http-equiv=\"Content-type\" content=\"text/html;charset=UTF-8\"/>",
24.        "<meta http-equiv=\"Content-Style-Type\" content=\"text/css\"/>",
25.        "<style type=\"text/css\">",
26.        "body {",
27.        "font-family:Arial,Verdana,Sans-serif; font-size:14px;",
28.        "background-color:white;",
29.        "}",
30.        "table.x {empty-cells:show; border-collapse:collapse; padding:0px;",
31.        " border-style:solid; border-width:1px; border-color:black;",
32.        "}",
33.        "td.x {",
34.        "width:39px; height:39px; border:0px; padding:0px;",
35.        " text-align:center; vertical-align:middle; font-size:18px;",
36.        "}",
37.        "</style>",
38.        "</head>",
39.        "<body>"
40.        };
41.    int text_header_2_len = sizeof(TEXT_HEADER_2) / sizeof(char *);
42.
43.    // Open the HTML file
44.    int f_res;
45.    FILE *fp = fopen(name, "w");
46.    if (fp == NULL) {
47.      printf("Unable to open the '%s'\n", name);
48.      return FALSE;                                         // ==>
49.      }
50.
51.    // Write the first block of header lines
52.    for (int k = 0; k < text_header_1_len; k++) {
```

```
53.      f_res = fprintf(fp, "%s\n", TEXT_HEADER_1[k]);
54.      if (f_res < 0) { fclose(fp); return FALSE; }                    // ==>
55.      }
56.
57.    // Write the title of the page
58.    f_res = fprintf(fp, "<title>%s</title>\n", name);
59.    if (f_res < 0) { fclose(fp); return FALSE; }                      // ==>
60.
61.    // Write the second block of header lines
62.    for (int k = 0; k < text_header_2_len; k++) {
63.      f_res = fprintf(fp, "%s\n", TEXT_HEADER_2[k]);
64.      if (f_res < 0) { fclose(fp); return FALSE; }                    // ==>
65.      }
66.
67.    // Write the title
68.    f_res = fprintf(fp, "<p style=\"font-size:20px;\">This grid hides "
69.        "%d operations</p>\n", n_t);
70.    if (f_res < 0) { fclose(fp); return FALSE; }                      // ==>
71.
72.    //---------- Write the puzzle as an HTML table
73.    f_res = fprintf(fp, "<table class=\"x\">\n");
74.    if (f_res < 0) { fclose(fp); return FALSE; }                      // ==>
75.
76.    for (int k = 0; k < N_NUM + N_NUM - 1; k++) {
77.      f_res = fprintf(fp, "<tr>\n");
78.      if (f_res < 0) { fclose(fp); return FALSE; }                    // ==>
79.      for (int j = 0; j < N_NUM + N_NUM - 1; j++) {
80.        if (k % 2 == 0  &&  j % 2 == 0  &&  mat[k][j] != -1) {
81.          f_res = fprintf(fp, "<td class=\"x\" >%3d</td>", mat[k][j]);
82.          }
83.        else {
84.          f_res = fprintf(fp, "<td class=\"x\" > </td>");
85.          }
86.        if (f_res < 0) { fclose(fp); return FALSE; }                  // ==>
87.        }
88.      f_res = fprintf(fp, "</tr>\n");
89.      if (f_res < 0) { fclose(fp); return FALSE; }                    // ==>
90.      }
91.
92.    f_res = fprintf(fp, "</table>\n");
93.    if (f_res < 0) { fclose(fp); return FALSE; }                      // ==>
94.
95.    //---------- Write the puzzle identifier and some more text
96.    f_res = fprintf(fp, "<p style=\"font-family:Courier,monospace;"
97.        "font-size:x-small;\">%s</p>\n", id
98.        );
99.    if (f_res < 0) { fclose(fp); return FALSE; }                      // ==>
100.
101.   f_res = fprintf(fp, "<p style=\"font-size:20px;\">Solution</p>\n");
102.   if (f_res < 0) { fclose(fp); return FALSE; }                      // ==>
```

```
103.
104.    //---------- Write the solution as an HTML table
105.    f_res = fprintf(fp, "<table class=\"x\">\n");
106.    if (f_res < 0) { fclose(fp); return FALSE; }                        // ==>
107.
108.    for (int k = 0; k < N_NUM + N_NUM - 1; k++) {
109.      f_res = fprintf(fp, "<tr>\n");
110.      if (f_res < 0) { fclose(fp); return FALSE; }                      // ==>
111.      for (int j = 0; j < N_NUM + N_NUM - 1; j++) {
112.        f_res = fprintf(fp, "<td class=\"x\" "
113.            "style=\""
114.            "background-position:center;"
115.            "background-repeat:no-repeat;");
116.        if (f_res < 0) { fclose(fp); return FALSE; }                    // ==>
117.        if (mat[k][j] == -1) {
118.          if (z[k][j] == -1) {
119.            f_res = fprintf(fp, "\"> </td>");
120.            }
121.          else {
122.            f_res = fprintf(fp,
123.                "background-image:url('img/%02d.bmp');"
124.                "\"> </td>", z[k][j]);
125.            }
126.          }
127.        else if (k % 2 == 0  &&  j % 2 == 0){
128.            f_res = fprintf(fp,
129.                "background-image:url('img/%02d.bmp');"
130.                "\">%3d</td>", z[k][j], mat[k][j]);
131.            }
132.        else {
133.            f_res = fprintf(fp,
134.                "background-image:url('img/%02d.bmp');"
135.                "\">%c</td>", z[k][j], ops[mat[k][j]]);
136.            }
137.        if (f_res < 0) { fclose(fp); return FALSE; }                    // ==>
138.        }
139.      f_res = fprintf(fp, "</tr>\n");
140.      if (f_res < 0) { fclose(fp); return FALSE; }                      // ==>
141.      }
142.
143.    f_res = fprintf(fp, "</table>\n");
144.    if (f_res < 0) { fclose(fp); return FALSE; }                        // ==>
145.
146.    //---------- Write the puzzle identifier and finish off
147.    f_res = fprintf(fp, "<p style=\"font-family:Courier,monospace;"
148.        "font-size:x-small;\">%s</p>\n", id
149.        );
150.    if (f_res < 0) { fclose(fp); return FALSE; }                        // ==>
151.
152.    //---------- Write the icon to state that it is a valid XHTML 1.0
153.    f_res = fprintf(fp,
```

```
154.        "<p><a href=\"http://validator.w3.org/check?uri=referer\"><img\n"
155.        "   src=\"http://www.w3.org/Icons/valid-xhtml10\"\n"
156.        "   alt=\"Valid XHTML 1.0 Strict\" height=\"31\" width=\"88\"/>\n"
157.        "  </a></p>\n"
158.        );
159.    if (f_res < 0) { fclose(fp); return FALSE; }                    // ==>
160.
161.    // Close the body tag
162.    f_res = fprintf(fp, "</body>\n");
163.    if (f_res < 0) { fclose(fp); return FALSE; }                    // ==>
164.
165.    // Close the HTML tag
166.    f_res = fprintf(fp, "</html>\n");
167.    if (f_res < 0) { fclose(fp); return FALSE; }                    // ==>
168.
169.    // Close the HTML file
170.    f_res = fclose(fp);
171.    if (f_res != 0) return FALSE;                                   // ==>
172.
173.    return TRUE;
174.    }
```

The first thing you do is on line 45, where you open the output HTML file.

Normally, jumping out of a block of code with a goto or from the middle of a function with a return is not a good practice. But when you have several checks that can result in aborting the execution of an algorithm, you are better off getting out of those places and clearly marking them with a comment than adding deeper and deeper levels of indentation.

Within save_html(), there are 23 file operations. If you want to check their successful completion and still remain within the width of the page, it makes sense that you use return statements. If you disagree with me, feel free to replace the jumps with indented if and else statements.

After opening the output file, you write in it the first part of the HTML document. You define the HTML lines on lines 13 to 18, calculate their number on line 19, and write them to the output file on lines 52 to 55.

Notice that TEXT_HEADER_1 is defined as an array of pointers to characters. When you divide its size by the size of a pointer, you obtain the number of array elements (i.e., the number of HTML lines). You could have obviously hard-coded the array length to 4, but it is always safer to rely on counting rather than setting. You will see that the second block of text consists of many more lines, and why should you risk miscounting them? Or perhaps forget to update the array definition after inserting an additional line?

This first block of HTML code tells the web browsers that the document conforms to the W3C's XHTML 1.0 standard. The W3C provides online services to check whether an HTML document conforms to the standards. You only need to visit https://validator.w3.org/check to verify that your code is in standard XHTML format. If it is, you are authorized to display on your page the badge shown in Figure 14-11.

The code for the badge, which you can also find on the W3C, is written to the output file on lines 153 to 159.

Figure 14-11. *The XHTML 1.0 badge*

After writing to file the title of the web document on lines 58 and 59, save_html() in lines 62 to 65 writes the second block of the HTML header, which is defined in lines 22 to 40. What you should find interesting here is the definition of the CSS styles used. After some reformatting to make them more readable, here is how the style definition looks:

```
<style type="text/css">
  body {font-family:Arial,Verdana,Sans-serif; font-size:14px; background-color:white;}
  table.x {
      empty-cells:show; border-collapse:collapse; padding:0px; border-style:solid;
      border-width:1px; border-color:black;
      }
  td.x {
      width:39px; height:39px; border:0px; padding:0px; text-align:center;
      vertical-align:middle; font-size:18px;
      }
</style>
```

For the formatting to work as expected, the dimensioning of the table elements <td> must match the dimension of the cell background images, which is 39 x 39 pixels. Also note that all borders and spacings have been set to 0.

Figure 14-12 shows a solution of the puzzle with some nice crossings.

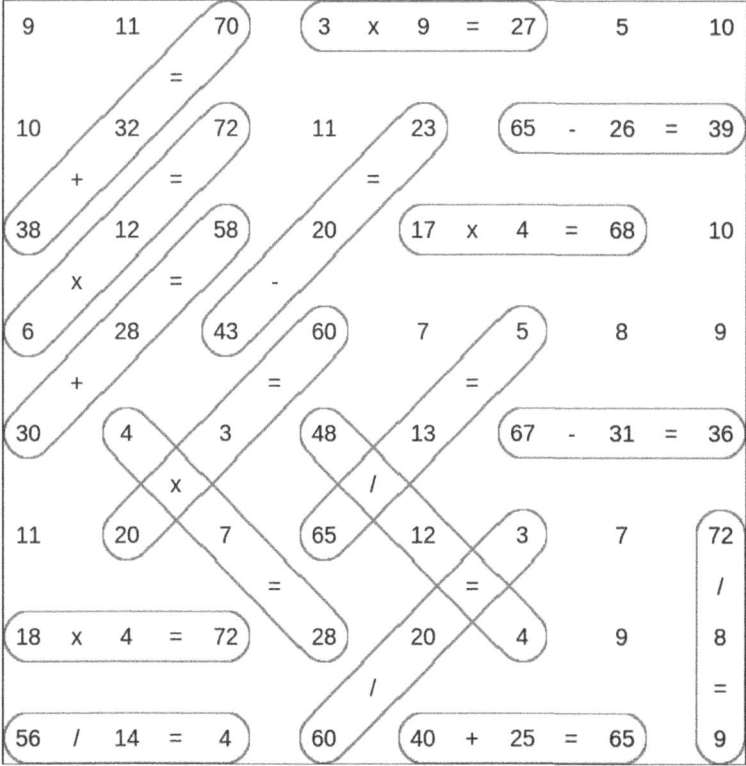

Figure 14-12. *HTML display of a puzzle*

Well, the lines around the A_UP and A_DOWN triplets are not completely smooth. I concede I could have drawn more closely matching background images. But if you want to have smoother lines, you need to do real graphics, rather than a patchwork of tiles. That said, despite the tricky part of formatting z, generating the HTML page is simpler than creating real graphics, as you will realize after looking at save_images().

Module: save_images

Listing 14-17 shows save_images.c.

Listing 14-17. save_images.c

```
1. /* save_images.c
2.  *
3.  * Copyright (c) 2016 by Giulio Zambon.  All rights reserved.
4.  */
5. #include <stdlib.h>
6. #include <math.h>
7. #include <wand/MagickWand.h>
8. #include "main.h"
9. #include "save_images.h"
10.
11. #define CELL_SIDE 160
12. #define FONT_SIZE 100 // was (CELL_SIDE/2)
13. #define CHAR_H (FONT_SIZE*7/10)
14. #define CHAR_W (FONT_SIZE*45/100)
15. #define CHAR_2W (FONT_SIZE)
16. #define OFFS_X ((CELL_SIDE-CHAR_W)/2)
17. #define OFFS_2X ((CELL_SIDE-CHAR_2W)/2)
18. #define OFFS_Y ((CELL_SIDE-CHAR_H)/2+CHAR_H)
19. #define MARGIN (CELL_SIDE/20)
20. #define EDGE_WIDTH 4
21. #define LINE_WIDTH 4
22. #define GRID_SIDE (CELL_SIDE*(N_NUM+N_NUM-1))
23. #define IMG_SIDE (GRID_SIDE+EDGE_WIDTH+EDGE_WIDTH)
24. #define Xo (EDGE_WIDTH-1)
25. #define Yo (EDGE_WIDTH-1)
26.
27. MagickWand *m_puzz;
28. DrawingWand *d_puzz;
29. PixelWand *c_puzz;
30.
31. void init_grid(void) {
32.   PixelSetColor(c_puzz,"black");
33.   MagickNewImage(m_puzz, IMG_SIDE, IMG_SIDE, c_puzz);
34.   MagickSetImageUnits(m_puzz, PixelsPerInchResolution);  // unnecessary
35.   MagickSetImageResolution(m_puzz, 300, 300);
36.   DrawSetStrokeOpacity(d_puzz,1);
37.   DrawSetStrokeAntialias(d_puzz,TRUE);
38.   DrawSetStrokeColor(d_puzz, c_puzz);
39.   DrawSetStrokeWidth(d_puzz, LINE_WIDTH);
40.   PushDrawingWand(d_puzz);
```

```
41.        PixelSetColor(c_puzz, "white");
42.        DrawSetFillColor(d_puzz, c_puzz);
43.        DrawSetStrokeWidth(d_puzz, 1);
44.        DrawRectangle(d_puzz, Xo, Yo, IMG_SIDE - EDGE_WIDTH, IMG_SIDE - EDGE_WIDTH);
45.        PopDrawingWand(d_puzz);
46.    }
47.
48. // iO: 0 for numbers; 1 for operations
49. void draw_content(int iO) {
50.    PixelSetColor(c_puzz, "black");
51.    DrawSetFillColor(d_puzz, c_puzz);
52.    DrawSetFont (d_puzz, "Courier" ) ;
53.    DrawSetFontSize(d_puzz, FONT_SIZE);
54.    DrawSetTextAntialias(d_puzz, MagickTrue);
55.    for (int k = iO; k < N_NUM + N_NUM - 1; k += 2) {
56.      int yO = CELL_SIDE * k;
57.      for (int j = iO; j < N_NUM + N_NUM - 1; j += 2) {
58.        if (mat[k][j] != -1) {
59.          int xO = CELL_SIDE * j;
60.          char val_s[5];
61.          int offs_x = OFFS_X;
62.          if (iO == 0) {
63.            sprintf(val_s, "%d", mat[k][j]);
64.            if (mat[k][j] >= 10) offs_x = OFFS_2X;
65.            }
66.          else {
67.            sprintf(val_s, "%c", ops[mat[k][j]]);
68.            }
69.          DrawAnnotation(d_puzz, xO + offs_x, yO + OFFS_Y, (unsigned char *)val_s);
70.          }
71.        }
72.      }
73.    }
74.
75. void draw_loops(void) {
76.    double del = (1 - sqrt(2)/2) * (CELL_SIDE - MARGIN - MARGIN) / 2;
77.    PixelSetColor(c_puzz, "white");
78.    DrawSetFillColor(d_puzz, c_puzz);
79.    for (int k = 0; k < N_NUM + N_NUM - 1; k += 2) {
80.      int yO = EDGE_WIDTH + CELL_SIDE * k;
81.      for (int j = 0; j < N_NUM + N_NUM - 1; j += 2) {
82.        if (mat[k][j] != -1) {
83.          int xO = EDGE_WIDTH + CELL_SIDE * j;
84.          switch (z[k][j]) {
85.            case 0:
86.              DrawArc(d_puzz, xO + MARGIN, yO + MARGIN, xO + CELL_SIDE - MARGIN, yO + ↵
                  CELL_SIDE - MARGIN, 90, 270);
87.              DrawArc(d_puzz, xO + 4*CELL_SIDE + MARGIN, yO + MARGIN, xO + 5*CELL_SIDE - ↵
                  MARGIN, yO + CELL_SIDE - MARGIN, -90, 90);
88.              DrawLine(d_puzz, xO + CELL_SIDE/2, yO + MARGIN, xO + CELL_SIDE/2 + ↵
                  4*CELL_SIDE, yO + MARGIN);
```

```
89.                  DrawLine(d_puzz, x0 + CELL_SIDE/2, y0 + CELL_SIDE - MARGIN, x0 + ↵
                     CELL_SIDE/2 + 4*CELL_SIDE, y0 + CELL_SIDE - MARGIN);
90.                  break;
91.              case 10:
92.                  DrawArc(d_puzz, x0 + MARGIN, y0 + MARGIN, x0 + CELL_SIDE - MARGIN, y0 + ↵
                     CELL_SIDE - MARGIN, -180, 0);
93.                  DrawArc(d_puzz, x0 + MARGIN, y0 + 4*CELL_SIDE + MARGIN, x0 +CELL_SIDE - ↵
                     MARGIN, y0 + 5*CELL_SIDE - MARGIN, 0, 180);
94.                  DrawLine(d_puzz, x0 + MARGIN, y0 + CELL_SIDE/2, x0 + MARGIN, y0 + ↵
                     CELL_SIDE/2 + 4*CELL_SIDE);
95.                  DrawLine(d_puzz, x0 + CELL_SIDE - MARGIN, y0 + CELL_SIDE/2, x0 + ↵
                     CELL_SIDE - MARGIN, y0 + CELL_SIDE/2 + 4*CELL_SIDE);
96.                  break;
97.              case 20:
98.                  // Patched up the lines
99.                  DrawArc(d_puzz, x0 + MARGIN, y0, x0 + CELL_SIDE - MARGIN, y0 + ↵
                     CELL_SIDE - MARGIN, 45, 225);
100.                 DrawArc(d_puzz, x0 + 4*CELL_SIDE - MARGIN, y0 - 4*CELL_SIDE + MARGIN, x0 + ↵
                     5*CELL_SIDE - MARGIN, y0 - 3*CELL_SIDE, -135, 45);
101.                 DrawLine(d_puzz, x0 + MARGIN + del, y0 + del, x0 + 4*CELL_SIDE - MARGIN + ↵
                     del + 3, y0 - 4*CELL_SIDE + MARGIN + del);
102.                 DrawLine(d_puzz, x0 + CELL_SIDE - del - MARGIN, y0 + CELL_SIDE - MARGIN - ↵
                     del, x0 + 5*CELL_SIDE - MARGIN - del - 3, y0 - 3*CELL_SIDE - del - 1);
103.                 break;
104.             case 30:
105.                 // Patched up the lines
106.                 DrawArc(d_puzz, x0 + MARGIN, y0, x0 + CELL_SIDE - MARGIN, y0 + CELL_SIDE - ↵
                     MARGIN, -225, -45);
107.                 DrawArc(d_puzz, x0 + 4*CELL_SIDE - MARGIN, y0 + 4*CELL_SIDE, x0 + ↵
                     5*CELL_SIDE - MARGIN, y0 + 5*CELL_SIDE - MARGIN, -45, 135);
108.                 DrawLine(d_puzz, x0 +CELL_SIDE - MARGIN - del, y0 + del, x0 + ↵
                     5*CELL_SIDE - MARGIN - del - 3, y0 + 4*CELL_SIDE + del + 1);
109.                 DrawLine(d_puzz, x0 + del + MARGIN, y0 + CELL_SIDE - MARGIN - del, x0 + ↵
                     4*CELL_SIDE + del - 4, y0 + 5*CELL_SIDE - MARGIN - del);
110.                 break;
111.             default:
112.                 break;
113.             }
114.         }
115.       }
116.     }
117.   }
118.
119. void save_images(char *name) {
120.    char fname[32];
121.
122.    MagickWandGenesis();
123.    m_puzz = NewMagickWand();
124.    d_puzz = NewDrawingWand();
125.    c_puzz = NewPixelWand();
126.    init_grid();
127.
```

```
128.    draw_content(0);
129.    MagickDrawImage(m_puzz, d_puzz);
130.    sprintf(fname, "%s.jpg", name);
131.    MagickWriteImage(m_puzz, fname);
132.
133.    draw_loops();   // must be first because it blanks half-circles
134.    draw_content(0);
135.    draw_content(1);
136.    MagickDrawImage(m_puzz, d_puzz);
137.    sprintf(fname, "%s_s.jpg", name);
138.    MagickWriteImage(m_puzz, fname);
139.
140.    c_puzz = DestroyPixelWand(c_puzz);
141.    d_puzz = DestroyDrawingWand(d_puzz);
142.    m_puzz = DestroyMagickWand(m_puzz);
143.    MagickWandTerminus();
144.    }
```

I first set the parameters to values I thought were reasonable, and then adjusted them to obtain images with proportions that pleased me. I am referring, for example, to how the sizes of characters and loops around the triplets compare to the distance between characters. The package MagickWand lets you do a lot in terms of creating and manipulating images, and that is its blessing and its curse.

Let's go first of all through the definitions.

CELL_SIDE and FONT_SIZE are pretty self-explanatory. CHAR_H and CHAR_W are the actual dimensions of a character with a given FONT_SIZE. Line 52 tells you that the font used for numbers and operations is Courier. I chose it because it is monospaced. This means that you can use CHAR_W for all characters. Different characters of proportional fonts (e.g., Arial) have different widths and that would make it more difficult to position the characters in the middle of their cells. Probably MagickWand would let you do it, but I didn't want to invest time in finding out how and, in any case, save_image() is long enough as it is.

CHAR_2W is the width of two characters (e.g., digits). You might ask, why is it that two characters are wider than twice one character (i.e., equal to the font size instead of 9/10 of it)? The reason is simple: when you write a number with two digits, you need to leave some space between them! It's obvious when you hear it, isn't it?

OFFS_X tells you how far from the left side of a cell you need to position a one-digit number (or an operation), and OFFS_2X is also a left-side offset, but for a two digit number. Similarly, OFFS_Y is how far above the bottom of the cell you need to position the text it contains. As you see, all offsets are calculated in such a way that the text is centered within the cell.

MARGIN is the space you want to leave between the loop and the triplet it encircles.

EDGE_WIDTH and LINE_WIDTH are the empty space you want to leave around the puzzle and the thickness of the line that you want to draw outside that space, respectively.

GRID_SIDE and IMG_SIDE are the dimensions of the puzzle and image, the latter of which consists of the puzzle plus the edge around it.

Finally, Xo and Yo are the horizontal and vertical offsets of the image area where the puzzle is drawn (see line 44).

Some MagickWand functions work on objects of type MagickWand and others on objects of type DrawingWand or PixelWand. To generate MathSearch images, you need all three types of functions. Variables pointing to the corresponding objects are defined on lines 27 to 29.

The code of save_images() is on lines 119 to 144 of Listing 14-17.

First of all, after initializing the package on line 122, you instantiate the three MagickWand objects on lines 123 to 125.

After executing the local function `init_grid()` (on lines 31 to 46) to initialize the puzzle, you invoke another local function, `draw_content()` (on lines 49 to 73), to draw the numbers to complete the image with the puzzle to be solved. You then save the puzzle image to a file by drawing the image in memory with `MagickDrawImage()` and saving it to disk with `MagickWriteImage()`.

Once you have saved the unsolved puzzle, you invoke the local function `draw_loops()` (on lines 75 to 117) to add to the same image the loops around the triplets. You then redraw the numbers with `draw_content()` because `draw_loops()` blanks out the half-circles at the two ends of the loops, thereby hiding part of the first and third numbers of the triplets. To complete the image of the puzzle solution, you invoke once more `draw_content()` to draw the operations. To save the solution image to a file, you repeat what you did for the unsolved puzzle.

Finally, you clean up behind yourself by telling MagickWand to release the memory allocated for the three objects (on lines 140 to 142) and to close the package (on line 143). Failure to do so would result in a memory leak that would prevent you from generating many puzzles with a single execution of MathSearch.

If you now look at the local functions `init_grid()`, `draw_numbers()`, `draw_ops()`, and `draw_loops()`, you will see that the usage of the MagickWand's functions is pretty self-explanatory, although it would be (and it was) everything but obvious to get it right when starting from a blank sheet.

I would just like to add a few comments.

You define the colors (on lines 32 and 50 for black, and lines 41 and 77 for white) with the `PixelWand` `c_puzz`. You then use `c_puzz` to initialize the image `m_puzz` (line 33) and to set the color of what you draw on the `DrawingWand` `d_puzz` (lines 38, 42, 51, and 78).

`d_puzz` is where you set the parameters of your drawings (e.g., color and opacity) with functions whose names start with `DrawSet` and do the drawings (e.g., a rectangle on line 44 and a string on line 69).

The first part of `init_grid()` sets up the DrawingWand to be subsequently used for drawing numbers, ops, and loops (black pen, thick line, etc.). But before returning, it uses the wand-stacking capability of MagickWand to temporarily set aside that `DrawingWand` (on line 40), fill up the background of the puzzle image with white, and draw the border.

The comment `"Patched up the lines"` in `draw_loops()` mean that I fiddled with the values in order to have nice-looking loops. One more artistic endeavor within the program. You can only develop a feel for these drawing functions if you play with them, and I encourage you to do so!

Summary

In this chapter, I showed you the steps necessary to generate a numeric puzzle with unique solutions. Along the way, I showed you how pseudo-random numbers help you generate a practically unlimited number of different puzzles. You also saw how to generate an HTML page and JPEG images and save them to disk.

APPENDIX A

Abbreviations and Acronyms

You will find that some of the abbreviations are completely obvious, but I consider making this list as complete as possible fun! If you find something that I have overlooked, please let me know.

3D	Three-dimensional
ACID	Atomicity, Consistency, Isolation, Durability
AD	Analog to Digital
AJAX	Asynchronous JavaScript and XML
ANSI	American National Standard Institute
API	Application Programming Interface
ASCII	American Standard Code for Information Interchange
AT&T	American Telephone & Telegraph
BCD	Binary Coded Decimal
BCE	Before Common Era
BCDIC	BCD Interchange Code
BIOS	Basic Input/Output System
BLOB	Binary Large Object
C11	ISO/IEC 9899:2011, the latest ratified version of the C standard
C89	The original ANSI C standard ANSI X3.159-1989
C90	A reformatted version of the ANSI C standard (i.e., C89), ratified as ISO/IEC 9899:1990
C95	An extension of C90 ratified as ISO/IEC 9899/AMD1:1995
C99	ISO/IEC 9899:1999, the latest version of C adopted by ANSI (in 2000)
CD	Compact Disc
CE	Common Era
CGI	Common Gateway Interface (more widely used for Computer-Generated Imagery, but not in the context of this book)
CLI	Command-Line Interface
CLK	Clock
CLOB	Character Large Object

(*continued*)

© Giulio Zambon 2016
G. Zambon, *Practical C*, DOI 10.1007/978-1-4842-1769-6

CNTL	The Control key on the keyboard, also abbreviated as CTRL
CNV	Pin of an AD converter to start a conversion
CoAP	Constrained Application Protocol, a simple communication protocol
CPU	Central Processing Unit
CR	Carriage Return
CRUD	Create, Retrieve, Update, and Delete
CS	Computer Science
CSS	Cascading Style Sheets, a W3C standard
CTRL	The Control key on the keyboard, also abbreviated as CNTL (which I prefer)
DBMS	Database Management System
DDL	Data Definition Language
DLL	Dynamic Link Library
DML	Data Manipulation Language
DNS	Domain Name System
dpi	Dots per inch, a measure of image resolution
DRAM	Dynamic RAM
e.g.	"Exempli gratia," which is Latin for "for the sake of example"
EBCDIC	Extended BCDIC
EEPROM	Electrically Erasable and Programmable ROM
EPROM	Erasable and Programmable ROM
FYI	"For Your Information" (come on, didn't you know it?)
FIFO	First In First Out, a queue
GB	Gigabyte (i.e., $1024 * 1024 * 1024 = 2^{30}$ bytes)
gcc	GNU compiler collection
GHz	Gigahertz (i.e., 1 billion oscillations per second)
GNU	"GNU is Not UNIX" is the body of applications of the GNU-Linux OS; the name Linux only refers to the kernel of that OS
GPLv2	GNU's General Public License, version 2
GUI	Graphical User Interface
HTML	Hypertext Markup Language, a W3C standard
HTTP	Hypertext Transfer Protocol, a W3C standard
HTTPS	HTTP Secure, a W3C standard
i.e.	"id est," which is Latin for "that is"
IANA	Internet Assigned Numbers Authority
IBM	International Business Machines
ID	Identifier
IEC	International Electrotechnical Commission

(continued)

IEEE	Institute of Electrical and Electronics Engineers (pronounced "I-triple-E")
I/O	Input/Output
iOS	Apple's mobile OS for iPhone, iPod touch, iPad, Apple TV, and similar devices
IoT	Internet of Things
IP	Internet Protocol
IMO	"In My Opinion" (what else?)
ISBN	International Standard Book Number
ISO	International Organization for Standardization
ISR	Interrupt Service Routine
JPEG	A standard for compressing images, named after the Joint Photographic Experts Group, which created it
JSON	JavaScript Object Notation
JSP	JavaServer Pages
K&R	Nickname for the legendary *The C Programming Language* book, by Brian Kernighan & Dennis Ritchie
LAMP	Linux + Apache + MySQL + PHP
LF	Line Feed
LIFO	Last In First Out, a stack
LOB	Large Object
LSB	Least Significant Bit, usually displayed as the right-most bit
LTS	Long Term Support
MMU	Memory Management Unit
MQ	Message Queuing
MQTT	MQ Telemetry Transport, a lightweight messaging protocol
ms	Millisecond
MSB	Most Significant Bit, usually displayed as the left-most bit
MSI	Microsoft Installer
n.a.	Not available
NaN	Not a Number
PC	Personal Computer
PHP	PHP: Hypertext Preprocessor (yes, it is a recursive definition)
PNG	Portable Network Graphics, a compressed but lossless format to store images
OS	Operating System
OTOH	"On the Other Hand"
pid	Process Identifier
POSIX	Portable Operating System Interface, an IEEE standard

(continued)

PROM	Programmable ROM
RAM	Random Access Memory
ROM	Read Only Memory
RPM	RPM Package Manager, originally called the Red Hat Package Manager
RTOS	Real-Time Operating Systems
SCK	Serial Clock (part of SPI)
SDI	Serial Digital Interface
SDO	Serial Data Output (part of SPI)
SF	Science Fiction
SIGCONT	Continue signal (POSIX)
SIGINT	Interrupt signal (ANSI)
SIGKILL	Kill signal (POSIX, unblockable)
SIGSTOP	Stop signal (POSIX, unblockable)
SIGTSTP	Keyboard stop signal (POSIX)
SPI	Serial Peripheral Interface
SPS	Samples Per Second (of an AD converter)
SQL	Structured Query Language, to work with databases; sometimes pronounced "sequel"
SSI	Server Side Includes
SVID	System V Interface Definition, the AT&T standard for UNIX System V
UART	Universal Asynchronous Receiver/Transmitter
UCS	Universal Coded Character Set (Unicode)
URI	Uniform Resource Identifier
URL	Uniform Resource Locator
USB	Universal Serial Bus
UTF	Unicode Transformation Format
V	Volt
VIO	Virtual I/O, a technology introduced by Microsoft to share servers' resources
vs.	An abbreviation of the Latin word "versus," and used as "against"
W3C	WWW Consortium
WWW	World Wide Web
X	The Latin numeral for 10, used to identify Apple's OSs for Intel-based Macs
XHTML	HTML that conforms to the XML standard
XML	Extensible Markup Language, a W3C standard
XPG	X/Open Portability Guide

APPENDIX B

▨ ▨ ▨

Introduction to SQL

Structured Query Language (SQL) is the most widely used language to interact with DBMSs. The purpose of this appendix is not to provide a comprehensive manual of SQL, but rather to list and explain the most common concepts, terms, and statements. Most DBMSs don't support the whole SQL standard. Moreover, vendors sometimes add nonstandard elements that, in practice, prevent full portability across DBMSs. In this appendix, I'll limit myself to standard elements. To help you identify nonstandard keywords, I have included Table B-12 at the end of this appendix, which lists the standard keywords that should work with most implementations.

The latest stable version of the SQL standard is ISO/IEC 9075:2011. If I interpret correctly the MySQL web site (`dev.mysql.com/doc/refman/5.7/en/compatibility.html`), MySQL (5.7 is the latest release at the time of writing) complies with the SQL 2008 standard, but don't be concerned, because the only new features introduced in 2011 have to do with temporal support. That is, support for handling data that involves time. You are not likely to need it, at least not if you are new to SQL.

▨ **Note**   Unless otherwise specified, all the SQL statements you will find in this appendix refer to and have been tested with MySQL's implementation of SQL.

SQL Terminology

Data is organized in *tables* consisting of *rows* and *columns*. This is a natural way of organizing data, and you're probably familiar with it through the use of spreadsheets. Nevertheless, although there are some similarities, a database table is *not* an Excel worksheet. For example, in a spreadsheet, you can assign data types to individual cells, while in a database, all the cells of a column have the same data type. The column definitions, each with their name and the type of data permitted, are the core of the table structure.

For example, a table of employees would probably include columns named FirstName, LastName, and SocialSecurityNumber containing strings of text; columns named EmployeeNumber and YearSalary would contain numbers; and columns named DateOfBirth and EmployedSince would contain dates. The data associated with each employee would then all be stored into a row.

A *field* is an individual data item within a table, corresponding to the intersection of a row and a column. This would be a cell in a spreadsheet.

One or more columns can be specified as *unique keys*, used to identify each individual employee. For this purpose, you could use either one of the columns mentioned previously (e.g., EmployeeNumber), or the combination of first and last name. The unique key used in preference over the others is called the *primary key* of a table.

An additional type of key is the *foreign key*. In this case, the column is defined as a reference to a unique key of another table. Besides avoiding duplication of data, this type of constraint increases the consistency of the database. For example, a table containing customer contracts could include a column referring to the column of employee numbers defined in the employee table. This would ensure that each contract would be associated with an existing salesperson.

The DBMS can build an *index* for each key, so that the data can be retrieved more quickly. This will obviously slow down insertion and deletion of rows (i.e., of new records), because the DBMS will have to spend time updating the indexes, but most databases are more frequently interrogated than modified. Therefore, it usually pays to define indexes, at least those that can speed up the most common queries. Here you have a hint of another difference from Excel: in a database table, the data items are not moved around once they're inserted; if you want to access them in a particular order, you must either sort them every time or create an index. You will learn about indexing later in this appendix.

Sometimes it's useful to present only some columns and rows, as if they were a table in their own right. Such virtual tables are called *views*. Under certain circumstances (I'll discuss this further when I describe individual statements, later in this chapter), you can also use views to collect columns from different tables and handle them as if they belonged to a single table.

Transactions

Transactions deserve a little more attention, because they represent a key concept in DBMSs. A *transaction* indicates a series of database operations that have to be performed without interruption—that is, without any other operation "sneaking in" between them. To make sense of this, you have to think in terms of concurrent access to the same tables.

For example, imagine the following scenario, in which two money transfers involve three bank accounts:

1. Transfer $100 from account A to account B

2. Transfer $200 from account B to account C

Conceptually, each transfer consists of the following operations:

1. Read the balance of the source account.

2. Reduce it by the amount of the transfer.

3. Write it back.

4. Read the balance of the destination account.

5. Increase it by the amount of the transfer.

6. Write it back.

Now, imagine that transfer number 2 starts while transfer number 1 is not yet completely done, as illustrated in the sequence of elementary operations listed in Table B-1.

Table B-1. *Sequence of Elementary Operations*

Op #	Transfer	Operation Description
1.	1:	Read the balance of account A.
2.	1:	Reduce the balance of account A by $100.
3.	1:	Write back the balance of account A.
4.	1:	Read the balance of account B.
5.	1:	Increase the balance of account B by $100.
6.	**2:**	**Read the balance of account B.**
7.	2:	Reduce the balance of account B by $200.
8.	2:	Write back the balance of account B.
9.	2:	Read the balance of account C.
10.	2:	Increase the balance of account C by $200.
11.	**1:**	**Write back the balance of account B.**
12.	2:	Write back the balance of account C.

The owner of account B is going to be very happy, because she will end up with $200 more than what she actually owns. The problem is that the two steps numbered 6 and 11 should have *not* been executed in that order. Let's say that account B initially held $500. At the end, it should hold $500 + $100 - $200 = $400, but this is not what happened. Just before the end of the first transfer, when the balance of $600 was about to be written back, the second transfer started. The balance of account B stored in the database was changed as a result of the second transfer, but when the first transfer resumed and completed, the balance of $600 was written back to account B. The effect of the second transfer was "forgotten." As far as account B was concerned, it was as if the second transfer hadn't happened!

You can solve this problem by handling each transfer as a transaction. The second transfer won't start until the first one is completed, and by then, the balance of account B will have been updated to reflect the first transfer.

A transaction is characterized by four properties—atomicity, consistency, isolation, and durability (ACID):

- *Atomicity*: It guarantees that either all the individual steps of a transaction are performed or none at all. You must not be able to perform partial transactions.

- *Consistency:* It refers to the fact that a transaction is not supposed to violate the integrity of a database. For example, it shouldn't be able to store a negative value in a numeric field that is supposed to be positive. When it comes to distributed systems, it also means that all the nodes have consistent values.

- *Isolation:* It means that concurrent operations cannot see intermediate values of a transaction. Lack of isolation is what caused the example of Table B-1 to fail, when the balance of account B could be read even though the transaction that was modifying it was not yet complete. Unfortunately, the serialization of the transactions (i.e., performing them one after the other) has an impact on performance precisely when there is a high workload. Lack of isolation is a problem in the example, but this is not always the case. For example, it might not matter that searches on a list of products take place while products are being added or removed. Given the potential impact on performance, you might decide in some cases to ignore the existence of concurrent transactions.

- *Durability:* It refers to the capacity of a DBMS to guarantee that a transaction, once completed, is never going to be "forgotten," even after a system failure.

Conventions

I use the following conventions to describe SQL statements:

- SQL keywords that you must enter exactly as shown are in uppercase (e.g., CREATE). Note that most keywords can actually be in lowercase.

- Variable values are in lowercase (e.g., db_name).

- Elements that you can omit are enclosed in square brackets (e.g., [WITH]).

- References to further definitions are enclosed in angle brackets (e.g., <create_spec>).

- The ellipsis immediately preceding a closing square bracket means that you can repeat the element enclosed between the brackets (e.g., [<create_spec> ...]). That is, you can omit the element, enter it once, or enter it more than once.

- Mutually exclusive alternatives are enclosed in curly brackets and separated by vertical bars (e.g., {DATABASE | SCHEMA}). You must enter one (and only one) of them.

- I close every statement with a semicolon, although, strictly speaking, it is not part of the official syntax. I do so because it makes for easier reading and reminds you that you must type the semicolon when including the statement in scripts.

For example, Listing B-1 shows part of the SQL statement used to create a database. It begins with the CREATE keyword followed by either DATABASE or SCHEMA and a database name. It is then possible (but not mandatory) to add one or more <create_spec> elements, the meaning of which are defined separately.

Listing B-1. Syntax of an SQL Statement

```
CREATE {DATABASE | SCHEMA} db_name [<create_spec> ...];
```

Statements

In general, regardless of whether we're talking about database organization, table structure, or actual data, you'll need to perform four basic operations: create, retrieve, update, and delete (CRUD). The corresponding SQL statements begin with a keyword that identifies the operation (e.g., INSERT, SELECT, UPDATE, or DELETE), followed when necessary by a keyword specifying on what type of entity the operation is to be performed (e.g., DATABASE, TABLE, or INDEX) and by additional elements. You use the SELECT statement for retrieving information.

You can create databases, tables, and indexes with the CREATE statement, update them with ALTER, and delete them with DROP. Similarly, you can create and delete views with CREATE and DROP, but you cannot update them once you've created them. You use INSERT to create new rows within a table, and you use DELETE to delete them. The UPDATE statement lets you modify entire rows or one or more individual fields within them.

The statements that let you modify the structures are collectively referred to as Data Definition Language (DDL), while those that let you modify the content are called Data Manipulation Language (DML).

That said, you won't find anything about ALTER DATABASE and ALTER INDEX in this appendix, because there is very little you can update in a database or an index definition once you've created them, and there is no agreement among DBMS vendors about what you can do. Table B-2 shows a summary of the possible combinations of keywords. In the following sections, I explain how to use them going through Table B-2 by columns. This will tell you how to create new structures and new data, how to modify them, and how to remove them.

Table B-2. *SQL Keywords to Create, Update, and Delete*

Entity	Create	Update	Delete
DATABASE	CREATE	~n/a	DROP
TABLE	CREATE	ALTER	DROP
INDEX	CREATE	~n/a	DROP
VIEW	CREATE	n/a	DROP
Row	INSERT	UPDATE	DELETE

In many applications, the structure of databases, tables, indexes, and views, once initially defined, remains unchanged. Therefore, you'll often need within your applications only the statements operating on rows and fields. In any case, you'll certainly need SELECT, which you use to interrogate databases both in terms of their structure and the data they contain. Finally, to complete the list of statements you're likely to need when developing applications, I'll also describe START TRANSACTION, COMMIT, and ROLLBACK, which you need to define transactions.

SQL interprets all text enclosed between /* and */ as comments and ignores it.

■ **Note** In all statements, you can always use the column position within the table instead of the column name. Column numbering in SQL starts with 1. In some particular cases, this can be useful, but use it sparingly because it leads to errors and code that's difficult to maintain.

The WHERE Condition

When you want to retrieve, update, or delete rows, you obviously have to identify them. You do this with the WHERE keyword followed by a <where_condition>. Listing B-2 shows you the format of this condition. I explain WHERE before discussing individual statements, because you'll need it for several of them.

Listing B-2. The WHERE Condition

```
<where_condition> = {
    col_name {= | < | > | <= | >= | !< | !> | <> | !=} <val>
    | col_name [NOT] BETWEEN <val> AND <val>
    | col_name [NOT] LIKE <val> [ESCAPE <val>]
    | col_name [NOT] IN (<val> [, <val> ...])
    | col_name IS [NOT] NULL
    | col_name [NOT] CONTAINING <val>
    | col_name [NOT] STARTING [WITH] <val>
    | NOT <search_condition>
    | <where_condition> OR <where_condition>
    | <where_condition> AND <where_condition>
    | (<where_condition>)
    }
<val> = A valid SQL expression that results in a single value
```

Note that the `WHERE` condition is more powerful (and complex) than what I explain here. You could actually include complete query statements within a condition and use the result of a first search to delimit the scope of the following one. However, to explain such techniques involving subqueries would go beyond the scope of this appendix.

I'll describe the listed possibilities by simply showing and explaining valid examples of `WHERE` selections on a hypothetical employee table:

- `lastname = 'Smith'` selects all employees with the family name Smith.

- `startdate < '2000-01-01'` selects all employees who joined the company before the beginning of the century.

- `startdate BETWEEN '2010-01-01' AND '2010-12-31'` selects all employees who joined the company in 2010, while `startdate NOT BETWEEN '2010-01-01' AND '2010-12-31'` selects those who didn't.

- `lastname LIKE 'S%'` selects all employees whose family name starts with S. In other words, the percent sign is the SQL equivalent of the asterisk you use when listing a directory from the command line. You can use more than one percent sign in a condition. For example, `lastname LIKE 'S%z%a'` selects all names that start with S, end with a, and have a z somewhere in between. While the percent sign stands for any number of characters (including none), the underscore stands for exactly one character, like the question mark when listing directories. For example, `lastname NOT LIKE '_'` selects all names that contain at least two characters (or none, if you allow it when designing the database). The `ESCAPE` keyword lets you search for strings containing one of the escape characters. For example, `lastname LIKE '%!%%' ESCAPE '!'` selects all names that contain a percent sign in any position.

- `firstname IN ('John', 'Jack')` selects all employees who have either John or Jack as their first name.

- `middlename IS NULL` selects all employees who have no middle name.

- `lastname CONTAINING 'qu'` selects all employees who have the string "qu" in their family name. This is identical to `lastname LIKE '%qu%'`.

- `lastname STARTING WITH 'Sm'` selects all employees whose family name starts with "Sm". This is identical to `lastname LIKE 'Sm%'`.

- You can use the logical operators `NOT`, `AND`, and `OR` to build complex conditions. For example, `startdate >= '2010-01-01' AND startdate <= '2010-12-31'` is equivalent to `startdate BETWEEN '2010-01-01' AND '2010-12-31'`. To avoid ambiguities, use the parentheses to set the order of execution. For example, `lastname CONTAINING 's' OR (lastname CONTAINING 'q' AND lastname NOT CONTAINING 'qu')` selects all employees whose family names contain an s or a q, but only if the q is not followed by a u. The statement `(lastname CONTAINING 's' OR lastname CONTAINING 'q') AND lastname NOT CONTAINING 'qu'` would select names containing ether "s" or "q" but excluding those in which the "q" is followed by "u". A name such as "quasi" would be selected by the first condition but not by the second one.

Data Types

When designing your database, you have to decide what type of data you need to store in the columns of your tables. SQL supports different data types to store numbers, text, date/time, and unspecified data (called LOB, for large object), as summarized in Listing B-3.

Listing B-3. The SQL Data Types

```
<data_type> = {<num_dt> | <datime_dt> | <text_dt> | <lob_dt>}
```

Numbers

The space reserved in memory for the numeric data types determines their precision—that is, the number of digits they can have. Java and JSP specify the space allocated for each data type, so that they are the same regardless of operating systems and virtual machines. Unfortunately, the same cannot be said of SQL, where the precision of the data types, like so many other things, is vendor-dependent. Therefore, you always have to refer to the manual of your DBMS if you want to be sure that your applications will work correctly. Listing B-4 shows how you specify a numeric data type.

Listing B-4. The SQL Data Types for Numbers

```
<num_dt> = {
      {DECIMAL | DEC | NUMERIC} [(precision [, scale])]
    | {SMALLINT | INTEGER | INT | BIGINT | REAL | FLOAT | DOUBLE PRECISION}
    }
```

The types DECIMAL (which can be abbreviated to DEC) and NUMERIC require you to specify the total number of digits and the number of decimal places. For example, you specify numbers of the type xxxx as (4), numbers of the type xxx.y as (4,1), and numbers of the type 0.yyy as (3,3). The scale must never exceed the precision. As different DBMS vendors set different defaults, you should always at least specify the precision. When doing so, keep in mind that 18 decimal digits require 64 bits. Therefore, larger precisions might not be accepted by all DBMSs.

The difference between DECIMAL and NUMERIC is that with DECIMAL, the DBMS is free to allocate more space than the minimum required in order to optimize access speed, while with NUMERIC, the number of digits allocated is exactly what you specify as precision.

The other types are easier to use but require some attention because, once more, different DBMS vendors allocate different numbers of bytes for the different data types. If you don't pay attention, you'll risk writing code that won't be portable.

SMALLINT, INTEGER or INT, and BIGINT refer to integer types of different sizes, while the remaining three types refer to numbers with a decimal point. Table B-3 shows the ranges possible with different numbers of bits and their corresponding data types in Java.

Table B-3. *Space Occupied by Numeric Java Types*

Bits	Minimum	Maximum	Java Type
16	-32,768	32,767	short
32	-2,147,483,648	2,147,483,647	int
64	-9,223,372,036,854,775,808	9,223,372,036,854,775,807	long
32	1.175×10^{-38}	3.402×10^{38}	~float
64	2.225×10^{-308}	1.797×10^{308}	~double

Some versions of MySQL also support the numeric data types BIT and TINYINT, but they are not always supported by other SQL implementations or by all versions of MySQL. I suggest that you stick to the standard types.

445

Table B-4 lists the number of bits allocated by some vendors to the different SQL data types. I include this information here to help you in case you need to port your code to SQL implementations other than MySQL.

Table B-4. *Vendor-Specific Numeric Data Types*

Vendor	SMALLINT	INTEGER	BIGINT	REAL	FLOAT	DOUBLE PRECISION
MySQL	16	32	64	32	32	64
PostgreSQL	16	32	64	32	--	64
FirebirdSQL	16	32	--	--	32	64
Microsoft SQL Server	16	32	64	32	64	--
Oracle	--	38	--	--	126	--

FirebirdSQL supports 64-bit integers, but it doesn't recognize the type BIGINT. You have to use INT64. Microsoft SQL Server and Oracle aren't open source DBMSs, but given their large customer bases, I thought you might be interested to know.

Date and Time

Listing B-5 shows how dates and times are defined in SQL, but its simplicity is somewhat misleading, because the DBMSs of different vendors, by now certainly unsurprisingly, behave differently.

Listing B-5. The SQL Data Types for Date and Time

```
<datime_dt> = {DATE | TIME | TIMESTAMP}
```

One area where the vendors don't agree is the range of dates. MySQL accepts dates between the year 1000 CE and the year 9999 CE, PostgreSQL between 4713 BCE and 5874897 CE, and FirebirdSQL between 100 CE and February 32767 CE. The bottom line is that any date within our lifetimes should be accepted by every DBMS!

You can use DATE when you're not interested in the time of the day. It occupies 4 bytes. TIME stores the time of the day in milliseconds and occupies 8 bytes. TIMESTAMP manages to fit both the date and the time of the day in milliseconds into 8 bytes.

You can set date and time values in different formats, but I recommend that you conform to the ISO 8601 standard and set dates as 'YYYY-MM-DD', times as 'HH:MM', 'HH:MM:SS', or 'HH:MM:SS.mmm', and timestamps as a standard date followed by a space and a standard time, as in 'YYYY-MM-DD HH:MM:SS.mmm'. In particular, pay attention to years specified with only two digits, because the different DBMSs interpret the dates differently. MySQL has defined the DATETIME type, but I see no reason for you do adopt it because MySQL also accepts the standard TIMESTAMP. I mention it here only because you'll probably encounter it sooner or later.

Text

Listing B-6 shows how you specify strings of characters.

Listing B-6. The SQL Data Types for Text

```
<text_dt> = {CHAR | CHARACTER | VARCHAR | CHARACTER VARYING} [(int)]
```

There are only two data types for text: CHARACTER and VARCHAR. CHAR is a synonym of CHARACTER, and CHARACTER VARYING is a synonym of VARCHAR. Use CHARACTER or CHAR to store strings of fixed length, and VARCHAR or CHARACTER VARYING for strings of variable length.

For example, a field of type CHARACTER (16) always occupies 16 bytes. If you use it to store a string of only six characters, it will be left-justified and right-padded with 10 spaces. If you attempt to store a string of 19 characters, you'll only succeed if the last three characters are spaces, in which case the DBMS will remove them. Different DBMSs set different limits to the maximum number of characters you can store into a CHARACTER data type, but they will all accept 255 characters. If you need more than that, check the user manual of the DBMS you're using.

The practical difference between VARCHAR and CHARACTER is that with VARCHAR, the DBMS stores the strings as they are, without padding. Also, with VARCHAR, you should be able to store up to 32,767 characters with all DBMSs.

Large Objects

LOBs let you store large amount of data, including binary data. This is an alternative to saving data in files and then storing their URIs in the database. In general, I am reluctant to store in a database large blocks of data that can be stored in the file system outside the database like images, video clips, documents, and executable code. By storing data outside the database, you can easily access it with other tools but, by doing so, you also risk compromising the integrity of the data and leave references in the database that point to nonexistent files.

■ **Note**   A URI is a generalization of a URL. Strictly speaking, the name location of a code fragment (i.e., the #whatever that you sometimes see in your browser's address field) is part of the URI but not of the URL, which only refers to the whole resource. Unfortunately, the definition of URI came when the term URL had already become universally known. That's why most people, including many specialists, keep referring to URLs when they should really be talking about URIs.

We have to distinguish between binary large objects (BLOBs) and character large objects (CLOBs). Unfortunately, once more, the major DBMS vendors haven't agreed. See Listing B-7 for the generalized definition of LOBs.

Listing B-7. The SQL Data Types for Large Objects

```
<lob_dt> = {<blob_dt> | <clob_dt>}
<blob_dt> = {
      BLOB(maxlen)      /* MySQL */
    | BYTEA             /* PostgreSQL */
    | BLOB(maxlen, 0)   /* FirebirdSQL */
    }
<clob_dt> = {
      TEXT              /* MySQL */
    | TEXT              /* PostgreSQL */
    | BLOB(maxlen, 1)   /* FirebirdSQL */
    }
```

LOBs can store up to 64KB of data. MEDIUMBLOBs can store up to 16MB and LONGBLOBs up to 4GB. Once more, check the user manual of your DBMS if you are not sure.

■ **Caution**   MySQL only supports limited indexing of LOBs.

SELECT

SELECT retrieves data from one or more tables and views. See Listing B-8 for a description of its format.

Listing B-8. The SQL Statement SELECT

```
SELECT [ALL | DISTINCT ]
    {* | <select_list> [[<select_list>] {COUNT (*) | <function>}]
    [FROM <table_references> [WHERE <where_condition>]
      [GROUP BY col_name [ASC | DESC], ... [WITH ROLLUP]
        [HAVING <where_condition>]
        ]
      ]
    [ORDER BY <order_list>]
    [LIMIT {[offset,] row_count | row_count OFFSET offset}]
    ;
<select_list> = col_name [, <select_list>]
<table_references> = one or more table and/or view names separated by commas
<order_list> = col_name [ASC | DESC] [, <order_list> ...]
<function> = {AVG | MAX | MIN | SUM | COUNT} ([{ALL | DISTINCT}] <val>)
```

In part, the complication of SELECT is due to the fact that you can use it in two ways: to retrieve actual data or to obtain the result of applying a function to the data. To make it worse, some of the elements only apply to one of the two ways of using SELECT. To explain how SELECT works, I'll split the two modes of operation.

SELECT to Obtain Data

Listing B-9 shows how you use SELECT to obtain data.

Listing B-9. SELECT to Obtain Data

```
SELECT [ALL | DISTINCT ] {* | <select_list>}
    [FROM <table_references> [WHERE <where_condition>]]
    [ORDER BY <order_list>]
    [LIMIT {[offset,] row_count | row_count OFFSET offset}]
    ;
<select_list> = col_name [, <select_list>]
<table_references> = one or more table and/or view names separated by commas
<order_list> = col_name [ASC | DESC] [, <order_list> ...]
```

Conceptually, it is simple: SELECT one, some, or all columns FROM one or more tables or views WHERE certain conditions are satisfied; then present the rows ORDERed as specified. Some examples will clarify the details:

- SELECT * is the simplest possible SELECT, but you'll probably never use it. It returns everything you have in your database.

- SELECT * FROM table is the simplest practical form of SELECT. It returns all the data in the table you specify. The DBMS returns the rows in the order it finds most convenient, which is basically meaningless to you and me. Instead of a single table, you can specify a mix of tables and views separated by commas.

- `SELECT a_col_name, another_col_name FROM table` still returns all the rows of a table, but for each row, it returns only the values in the columns you specify. Use the keyword `DISTINCT` to tell the DBMS that it should *not* return any duplicate row. The default is `ALL`. You can also use column positions instead of column names.

- `SELECT * FROM table WHERE condition` only returns the rows for which the condition you specify is satisfied. Most `SELECT`s include a `WHERE` condition. Often only a single row is selected—for example, when the condition requires a unique key to have a particular value.

- `SELECT * FROM table ORDER BY col_name` returns all the rows of a table ordered on the basis of a column you specify. Note that you can provide more than one ordering. For example, `SELECT * FROM employee_tbl ORDER BY last_name, first_name` returns a list of all employees in alphabetical order. With the keyword `DESC`, you specify descending orderings.

- `SELECT * FROM table LIMIT first, count` returns count rows starting from `first`. You can obtain the same result with `SELECT * FROM table LIMIT count OFFSET first`. Be warned that not all DBMSs support both formats. I discourage you to use this element, because it doesn't deliver entirely predictable results. I only include it here because you could find it useful to debug some database problem.

SELECT to Apply a Function

Sometimes you need to obtain some global information on your data and are not interested in the details. This is where the second format of `SELECT` comes to the rescue. Listing B-10 shows how you use `SELECT` to apply a function.

Listing B-10. SELECT to Apply a Function

```
SELECT [ALL | DISTINCT ] [<select_list>] {COUNT (*) | <function>}
    [FROM <table_references>
        [GROUP BY col_name [ASC | DESC], ... [WITH ROLLUP]
          [HAVING <where_condition>]
          ]
        ]
    ;
<select_list> = col_name [, <select_list>]
<table_references> = one or more table and/or view names separated by commas
<function> = {AVG | MAX | MIN | SUM | COUNT} ([{ALL | DISTINCT}] <val>)
```

Here are some examples of how you apply a function with `SELECT`:

- `SELECT COUNT (*) FROM employee_tbl` counts the number of rows in the employee table.

- `SELECT department, citizenship, gender COUNT(employee_id) FROM employee_tbl GROUP BY department, citizenship, gender` provides counts of employees for each possible department, citizenship, and gender combination. If you append `WITH ROLLUP` to the statement, you'll also obtain partial totals, as shown in the example presented in Table B-5.

- SELECT last_name COUNT(first_name) FROM employee_tbl GROUP BY first_name HAVING COUNT(first_name) > 1 counts the number of first names for each family name but only reports the family names that appear with more than one first name. HAVING has the same function for the aggregated values produced by GROUP BY that WHERE had for data selection.

Table B-5. *Employees per Department, Citizenship, and Gender*

Department	Citizenship	Gender	Count
Dev	India	Male	1
Dev	India	NULL	1
Dev	USA	Female	2
Dev	USA	Male	3
Dev	USA	NULL	5
Dev	NULL	NULL	6
Ops	Canada	Male	2
Ops	Canada	NULL	2
Ops	USA	Female	4
Ops	USA	Male	3
Ops	USA	NULL	7
Ops	NULL	NULL	9
Sales	USA	Female	7
Sales	USA	Male	5
Sales	USA	NULL	12
Sales	NULL	NULL	12
NULL	NULL	NULL	27

JOINs

When describing SQL terminology, I said that a foreign key is a reference to a unique key of another table. This means that information associated with each unique value of that key can be in either table or in both tables. For example, in a database representing a bookstore, you could imagine having one table with book authors and one with books. The name of the author would be a unique key in the authors' table and would appear as a foreign key in the books' table. Table B-6 shows an example of the authors' table.

▪ **Caution**   You should only use as foreign keys columns that are not expected to change. The use of columns that have a real-life meaning (like the author's name in the examples that follow) is often risky.

Table B-6. *Authors' Table*

Name	City
Isaac Asimov	New York (NY)
David Baldacci	Alexandria (VA)
Matthew Reilly	Sydney (Australia)

Table B-7 shows the books' table.

Table B-7. *Books' Table*

Title	Author
I, Robot	Isaac Asimov
Foundation	Isaac Asimov
Contest	Matthew Reilly
Scarecrow	Matthew Reilly
BlaBlaBla	NULL

If you perform the query SELECT * FROM books, authors;, the DBMS will return 15 combined rows, the first seven of which are shown in Table B-8.

Table B-8. *Disjoined Query on Books and Authors*

Title	Author	Name	City
I, Robot	Isaac Asimov	Isaac Asimov	New York (NY)
Foundation	Isaac Asimov	Isaac Asimov	New York (NY)
Contest	Matthew Reilly	Isaac Asimov	New York (NY)
Scarecrow	Matthew Reilly	Isaac Asimov	New York (NY)
BlaBlaBla	NULL	Isaac Asimov	New York (NY)
I, Robot	Isaac Asimov	David Baldacci	Alexandria (VA)
Foundation	Isaac Asimov	David Baldacci	Alexandria (VA)

In other words, all books would be paired with all authors. This doesn't look very useful. You can get a more useful result when you perform the following query:

```
SELECT * FROM books, authors WHERE author = name;
```

Table B-9 shows its result.

Table B-9. *Traditional Joined Query on Books and Authors*

Title	Author	Name	City
I, Robot	Isaac Asimov	Isaac Asimov	New York (NY)
Foundation	Isaac Asimov	Isaac Asimov	New York (NY)
Contest	Matthew Reilly	Matthew Reilly	Sydney (Australia)
Scarecrow	Matthew Reilly	Matthew Reilly	Sydney (Australia)

You can achieve the same result with the JOIN keyword:

```
SELECT * FROM books [INNER] JOIN authors ON (author = name);
```

The result is the same, but conceptually, the JOIN syntax is clearer, because it states explicitly that you want to join two tables matching the values in two columns.

There is another type of JOIN, called OUTER JOIN, which also selects rows that only appear in one of the two tables. For example, the following two SELECTs return the results shown respectively in Tables B-10 and B-11 when the book titled "BlaBlaBla" has no assigned author and the database doesn't contain any book by David Baldacci:

```
SELECT * FROM books LEFT [OUTER] JOIN authors ON (author = name);

SELECT * FROM books RIGHT [OUTER] JOIN authors ON (author = name);
```

Table B-10. *LEFT JOIN Query*

Title	Author	Name	City
I, Robot	Isaac Asimov	Isaac Asimov	New York (NY)
Foundation	Isaac Asimov	Isaac Asimov	New York (NY)
Contest	Matthew Reilly	Matthew Reilly	Sydney (Australia)
Scarecrow	Matthew Reilly	Matthew Reilly	Sydney (Australia)
BlaBlaBla	NULL	NULL	NULL

Table B-11. *RIGHT JOIN Query*

Title	Author	Name	City
I, Robot	Isaac Asimov	Isaac Asimov	New York (NY)
Foundation	Isaac Asimov	Isaac Asimov	New York (NY)
Contest	Matthew Reilly	Matthew Reilly	Sydney (Australia)
Scarecrow	Matthew Reilly	Matthew Reilly	Sydney (Australia)
NULL	NULL	David Baldacci	Alexandria (VA)

To decide of which table you want to include all rows, choose LEFT or RIGHT depending on whether the table name precedes or follows the JOIN keyword in the SELECT statement.

You'd probably like to obtain a list with the names of all authors, regardless of whether they appear only in the first table, only in the second table, or in both tables. Can you have a JOIN that is both LEFT and RIGHT at the same time? The answer is that the SQL standard defines a FULL JOIN, which does exactly what you want, but MySQL doesn't support it.

CREATE DATABASE

CREATE DATABASE creates a new, empty database. See Listing B-11 for a description of its format.

Listing B-11. The SQL Statement CREATE DATABASE

```
CREATE {DATABASE | SCHEMA} db_name [<create_spec> ...];
<create_spec> = {
    [DEFAULT] CHARACTER SET charset_name
  | [DEFAULT] COLLATION collation_name
}
```

The DATABASE and SCHEMA keywords are equivalent, and the DEFAULT keyword is only descriptive. The default character set determines how strings are stored in the database, while the collation defines the rules used to compare strings (i.e., precedence among characters).

When using SQL with Java and JSP, you need to specify the Unicode character set according to which each character is stored in a variable number of bytes. With a minimal database creation statement such as CREATE DATABASE 'db_name', you risk getting the US-ASCII character set, which is incompatible with Java. Therefore, always specify Unicode, as in the following statement:

```
CREATE DATABASE 'db_name' CHARACTER SET utf8;
```

In fact, there are several Unicode character sets, but utf8 is the most widely used and also the most similar to ASCII. As such, it is the best choice for English speakers. You don't need to bother with specifying any collation. The default will be fine.

The specification of the character set used to encode strings is extremely important when working with databases because you cannot assume that all users will access and update the stored data with the same OS and set of tools. By making the definition of the character encoding explicit, you minimize the risk of inconsistencies and misrepresentations of strings. If you only plan to store strings in English, you might get away with ignoring the issue, but already the presence of a Turkish or Swedish name could cause you problems.

The existence of conflicting encoding standards is what causes the presence of so many mysterious squiggles in e-mails and web pages, and conversion between standards is inefficient and confusing. For example, there are several ISO-8859 standards incompatible with one another (see for example the "Alphabet Soup" web page at czyborra.com/charsets/iso8859.html). And the UCS standards (UCS-2 and UCS-4) include bytes set to 0, which cause truncation in C strings if you don't convert them to a more friendly encoding. Your best bet is to adopt UTF-8 whenever possible, even if Microsoft systems use UTF-16 by default.

CREATE TABLE

CREATE TABLE creates a new table, together with its columns and integrity constraints, in an existing database. See Listing B-12 for a description of its format.

Listing B-12. The SQL Statement CREATE TABLE

```
CREATE TABLE tbl_name (<col_def> [, <col_def> | <tbl_constr> ...]);
<col_def> = col_name <data_type> [DEFAULT {value | NULL}] [NOT NULL] [<col_constr>]
<col_constr> = [CONSTRAINT constr_name] {
        UNIQUE
     |  PRIMARY KEY
     |  REFERENCES another_tbl [(col_name [, col_name ...])]
         [ON {DELETE | UPDATE} { NO ACTION | SET NULL | SET DEFAULT | CASCADE }]
     |  CHECK (<where_condition>)
     }
<tbl_constr> = [CONSTRAINT constr_name] {
        {PRIMARY KEY | UNIQUE} (col_name [, col_name ...])
     |  FOREIGN KEY (col_name [, col_name ...]) REFERENCES another_tbl
         [ON {DELETE | UPDATE} {NO ACTION | SET NULL | SET DEFAULT | CASCADE}]
     |  CHECK (<where_condition>)
     }
```

To understand how CREATE TABLE works, concentrate on the first line of Listing B-12. It says that a table definition consists of a table name followed by the definition of one or more columns and possibly some table constraints. In turn, each column definition consists of a column name followed by the definition of a data type, a dimension, a default, and possibly some column constraints.

The following examples and comments should make it clear:

- CREATE TABLE employee_tbl (employee_id INTEGER) creates a table with a single column of type INTEGER and without any constraint. If you want to ensure that the employee ID cannot have duplicates, append the UNIQUE constraint to the column definition: CREATE TABLE employee_tbl (employee_id INTEGER UNIQUE).

- With DEFAULT, you can set the value to be stored in a field when you insert a new row. For example, the column definition employee_dept VARCHAR(64) DEFAULT '' sets the department to an empty string (without the DEFAULT element, the field is set to NULL). The distinction between an empty string and NULL is important when working with Java and JSP, because you can rest assured that a variable containing an unforeseen NULL will sooner or later cause a runtime exception. To avoid setting a field to NULL by mistake, append NOT NULL to a column definition. This will ensure that you get an error when you insert the row and not later when you hit the unexpected NULL. It will make debugging your code easier.

- The column constraints UNIQUE and PRIMARY KEY ensure that the values stored in that column are unique within the table. You can specify the PRIMARY KEY constraint only for one column of each table, while you can specify UNIQUE even for all columns of a table, if that is what you need.

- Use the column constraint REFERENCES to force consistency checks between tables. For example, if you store the list of departments in the table department_tbl, which includes the column dept_name, you could use REFERENCES to ensure that all new employee records will refer to existing departments. To achieve this result, when you create the employee table, define the employee's department column as follows: employee_dept VARCHAR(64) REFERENCES department_tbl (dept_name). This will make it impossible for the creator of the employee record to enter the name of a nonexistent department. Note that you must have defined the referenced columns with the UNIQUE or PRIMARY KEY constraints, because this constraint actually creates foreign keys. It wouldn't make sense to reference a column that allows duplicate values, because then you wouldn't know which row you would actually be referring to.

- The ON DELETE and ON UPDATE elements, which you can append to the REFERENCES column constraint, tell the DBMS what you want to happen when the referenced column (or columns) are deleted or updated. For example, if the department named 'new_product' is merged into 'development' or renamed 'design', what should happen with the records of employees currently working in 'new_product'? You have four possibilities to choose from. With NO ACTION, you direct the DBMS to leave the employee record as it is. With SET NULL and SET DEFAULT, you choose to replace the name of the updated or deleted department with NULL or the default value, respectively. With CASCADE, you tell the DBMS to repeat for the referencing employee record what has happened with the referenced department record. That is, if the employee_dept column of the employee table has the ON UPDATE CASCADE constraint, you can change the department name in the department table and automatically get the same change in the employee table. Great stuff, but if you have the constraint ON DELETE CASCADE and remove a department from the department table, all the employee records of the employee table referencing that department will disappear. This is not necessarily what you want to happen. Therefore, you should be careful when applying these constraints.

- The CHECK column constraint only lets you create columns that satisfy the specified check condition. For example, to ensure that a bank account can only be opened with a minimum balance of $100, you could define a column named initial_balance with the following constraint: CHECK (initial_balance >= '100.00').

- The table constraints are similar to the column constraints, both in meaning and in syntax. However, there is one case in which you must use the table constraints: when you want to apply the UNIQUE or PRIMARY KEY constraints to a combination of columns rather than to a single one. For example, you might need to require that the combination of first and last name be unique within an employee table. You could achieve this result with the following constraint on the employee table: UNIQUE (last_name, first_name).

- The purpose of CONSTRAINT constraint_name is only to associate a unique name to a constraint. This then allows you to remove the constraint by updating the table with the DROP constraint_name element. As you never know whether you'll need to remove a constraint in the future, you should play it safe and name the constraints you apply. Otherwise, in order to remove the unnamed constraint, you would have to recreate the table (without the constraint) and then transfer the data from the original constrained table.

■ **Caution**   Constraints are good to help maintain database integrity, but they reduce flexibility. What you initially considered unacceptable values might turn out to be just unlikely but perfectly valid. Therefore, only create the constraints that you're really sure about. With increasing experience, you'll develop a feel for what's best.

CREATE INDEX

CREATE INDEX creates an index for one or more columns in a table. You can use it to improve the speed of data access, in particular when the indexed columns appear in WHERE conditions. See Listing B-13 for a description of its format.

Listing B-13. The SQL Statement CREATE INDEX

```
CREATE [UNIQUE] [{ASC[ENDING] | DESC[ENDING]}] INDEX index_name
    ON tbl_name (col_name [, col_name ...])
    ;
```

For example, `CREATE UNIQUE INDEX empl_x ON employee_tbl (last_name, first_name)` creates an index in which each entry refers to a combination of two field values. Attempts to create employee records with an existing combination of first and last name will fail.

CREATE VIEW

`CREATE VIEW` lets you access data belonging to different tables as if each data item were part of a single table. Only a description of the view is stored in the database, so that no data is physically duplicated or moved. See Listing B-14 for a description of its format.

Listing B-14. The SQL Statement CREATE VIEW

```
CREATE VIEW view_name [(view_col_name [, view_col_name ...])]
    AS <select> [WITH CHECK OPTION];
    ;
<select> = A SELECT statement without ORDER BY elements
```

Here are some examples of `CREATE VIEW`:

- `CREATE VIEW female_employees AS SELECT * FROM employee_tbl WHERE gender = 'female'` creates a view with all female employees. The column names of the view are matched one by one with the column names of the table.

- `CREATE VIEW female_names (last, first) AS SELECT last_name, first_name FROM employee_tbl WHERE gender = 'female'` creates a similar view but only containing the name columns of the employee table rather than its full rows.

- `CREATE VIEW phone_list AS SELECT last_name, first_name, dept_telephone, phone_extension FROM employee_tbl, department_tbl WHERE department = dept_no` creates a view with columns from both the employee and the department tables. The columns of the view are named like the original columns, but it would have been possible to rename them by specifying a list of columns enclosed in parentheses after the view name. The `WHERE` condition is used to match the department numbers in the two tables so that the department telephone number can be included in the view. Note that views that join tables are read-only.

- When a view only refers to a single table, you can update the table by operating on the view rather than on the actual table. The `WITH CHECK OPTION` element prevents you from modifying the table in such a way that you could then no longer retrieve the modified rows. For example, if you create a view `WITH CHECK OPTION` containing all female employees, it won't allow you to use the view to enter a male employee or to change the gender of an employee. Obviously, you would still be able to do those operations by updating the employee table directly.

INSERT

`INSERT` stores one or more rows in an existing table or view. See Listing B-15 for a description of its format.

Listing B-15. The SQL Statement INSERT

```
INSERT INTO {tbl_name | view_name} [(col_name [, col_name ...])]
    {VALUES (<val> [, <val> ...]) | <select>};
    ;
<select> = A SELECT returning the values to be inserted into the new rows
```

You can use INSERT to create one row in a table (or a single-table view) from scratch or to create one or more rows by copying data from other tables, as shown in the following examples.

- INSERT INTO employee_tbl (employee_id, first_name, last_name) VALUES ('999', 'Joe', 'Bloke') creates a new row for the employee Joe Bloke. All the columns not listed after the table name are filled with their respective default values. You could omit the list of column names, but the values would be stored beginning from first column in the order in which the columns were created. Be sure that you get the correct order.

- INSERT INTO foreigners SELECT * from employee_tbl WHERE citizenship != 'USA' copies the full records of all employees who are not U.S. citizens to the table foreigners. Note that this is different from creating a view of foreign employees, because the records are actually duplicated and stored in a different table. With a view, you would only specify a different way of accessing the same data. Be extremely cautious when INTO and SELECT refer to the same table. You could create an endless insertion loop. It's best if you simply refrain from inserting rows by copying the data from rows that are in the same table.

DROP

DROP is the statement you use when you want to remove a database, a table, an index, or a view. See Listing B-16 for a description of its format.

Listing B-16. The SQL DROP Statements

```
DROP DATABASE;
DROP TABLE tbl_name;
DROP INDEX index_name;
DROP VIEW view_name;
```

DROP DATABASE removes the database you're connected to. The rest are pretty self-explanatory. Just one point: with DROP INDEX, you cannot eliminate the indexes that the DBMS automatically creates when you specify the UNIQUE, PRIMARY KEY, or FOREIGN KEY attribute for a column.

DELETE

DELETE removes one or more rows from an existing table or a view that is not read-only. See Listing B-17 for a description of its format.

Listing B-17. The SQL Statement DELETE

```
DELETE FROM {tbl_name | view_name} [WHERE <where_condition>];
```

ALTER TABLE

ALTER TABLE modifies the structure of an existing table. See Listing B-18 for a generalized description of its format.

Listing B-18. The SQL Statement ALTER TABLE

```
ALTER TABLE tbl_name <alter_tbl_op> [, <alter_tbl_op> ...];
<alter_tbl_op> = {
      ADD <col_def>
    | ADD <tbl_constr>
    | DROP col_name
    | DROP CONSTRAINT constr_name
    | <alter_col_def>
    }
<alter_col_def> = {
      ALTER [COLUMN] col_name SET DEFAULT <val>        /* MySQL, postgreSQL */
    | ALTER [COLUMN] col_name DROP DEFAULT             /* MySQL, postgreSQL */
    | CHANGE [COLUMN] col_name <col_def>               /* MySQL */
    | MODIFY [COLUMN] <col_def>                        /* MySQL */
    | ALTER [COLUMN] col_name { SET | DROP } NOT NULL  /* PostgreSQL */
    | RENAME [COLUMN] col_name TO new_col_name         /* PostgreSQL */
    | ALTER [COLUMN] col_name TO new_col_name          /* FirebirdSQL */
    | ALTER [COLUMN] TYPE new_col_type                 /* FirebirdSQL */
    }
```

As you can see from Listing B-18, the DBMS vendors once more cannot agree on how you can modify columns.

The addition or removal of columns and table constraints is pretty straightforward. Refer to CREATE TABLE for a description of <col_def> and <tbl_constr>.

What you can do in terms of changing the definition of an existing column depends on which DBMS you've chosen for your application. Only MySQL gives you full flexibility in redefining the column with ALTER TABLE tbl_name CHANGE col_name <col_def>. Note that <col_def> must be complete, including a column name. If you don't want to change the name of a column, you can use its current name within <col_def>. In fact, besides being compatible with Oracle, the only reason for having MODIFY is so that you don't need to type the same column name twice.

UPDATE

UPDATE modifies the content of one or more existing rows in a table (or single-table view). See Listing B-19 for a description of its format.

Listing B-19. The SQL Statement UPDATE

```
UPDATE {tbl_name | view_name} SET col_name = <val> [, col_name = <val> ...]
    [WHERE <where_condition>]
    ;
```

For example, use the statement UPDATE employee_tbl SET first_name = 'John' WHERE first_name = 'Jihn' to correct a typing error. Nothing could be simpler.

SET TRANSACTION and START TRANSACTION

The purpose of a transaction is to ensure that nobody else can "sneak in" and modify rows after you've read them but before you've updated them in the database. The DBMS can achieve this by locking the rows you read within a transaction until you commit your updates.

You control the behavior of the DBMS by setting the ISOLATION LEVEL of the transaction. There are five possible isolation levels:

- READ COMMITTED

  It forces queries to operate on committed values. It waits on other transactions to complete.

- READ UNCOMMITTED

  It allows "dirty readings," because it ignores whether other transactions are operating on the same values.

- REPEATABLE READ

  It suspends updates until your transaction is completed, but only if the table update attempts to modify the row you are reading. The other transaction can still insert new rows.

- SERIALIZABLE

  Essentially like REPEATABLE_READ, but it also blocks insertions.

- SNAPSHOT

  It keeps the values consistent during your transaction. That is, it hides the effect of other transactions on the values you are reading.

As with other statements, different DBMSs behave differently. Listing B-20 shows what you need to do with MySQL and PostgreSQL, while Listing B-21 shows an example valid for FirebirdSQL.

Listing B-20. Start a Transaction with MySQL and PostgreSQL

```
SET TRANSACTION ISOLATION LEVEL READ COMMITTED;
START TRANSACTION;
```

Listing B-21. Start a Transaction with FirebirdSQL

```
SET TRANSACTION ISOLATION LEVEL READ COMMITTED;
```

As you can see, to start a transaction with MySQL and PostgreSQL, you have to execute a SET TRANSACTION and a START, while you only need to execute SET TRANSACTION without START when starting a transaction with FirebirdSQL. Note that all three DBMSs provide additional options, but I'm only showing a mode of operation that is common to them all.

You need to specify the ISOLATION LEVEL if you want to write portable code, because the three DBMSs have different defaults.

COMMIT and ROLLBACK

COMMIT confirms the updates you've performed since starting the current transaction and terminates it. ROLLBACK discards the updates and returns the database to its condition prior to the current transaction. Their syntax couldn't be simpler: COMMIT; and ROLLBACK;.

Reserved SQL Keywords

Table B-12 lists all words that you cannot freely use when writing SQL scripts and statements.

Table B-12. *Reserved SQL Keywords*

	Keywords	
A	ADD	ALL
	ALLOCATE	ALTER
	AND	ANY
	ARE	ARRAY
	AS	ASENSITIVE
	ASYMMETRIC	AT
	ATOMIC	AUTHORIZATION
B	BEGIN	BETWEEN
	BIGINT	BINARY
	BLOB	BOOLEAN
	BOTH	BY
C	CALL	CALLED
	CASCADED	CASE
	CAST	CHAR
	CHARACTER	CHECK
	CLOB	CLOSE
	COLLATE	COLUMN
	COMMIT	CONNECT
	CONSTRAINT	CONTINUE
	CORRESPONDING	CREATE
	CROSS	CUBE
	CURRENT	CURRENT_DATE
	CURRENT_DEFAULT_TRANSFORM_GROUP CURRENT_PATH	
	CURRENT_ROLE	CURRENT_TIME
	CURRENT_TIMESTAMP	CURRENT_TRANSFORM_GROUP_FOR_TYPE
	CURRENT_USER	CURSOR
	CYCLE	
D	DATE	DAY
	DEALLOCATE	DEC
	DECIMAL	DECLARE
	DEFAULT	DELETE

(continued)

Table B-12. (*continued*)

	Keywords	
	DEREF	DESCRIBE
	DETERMINISTIC	DISCONNECT
	DISTINCT	DOUBLE
	DROP	DYNAMIC
E	EACH	ELEMENT
	ELSE	END
	END-EXEC	ESCAPE
	EXCEPT	EXEC
	EXECUTE	EXISTS
	EXTERNAL	
F	FALSE	FETCH
	FILTER	FLOAT
	FOR	FOREIGN
	FREE	FROM
	FULL	FUNCTION
G	GET	GLOBAL
	GRANT	GROUP
	GROUPING	
H	HAVING	HOLD
	HOUR	
I	IDENTITY	IMMEDIATE
	IN	INDICATOR
	INNER	INOUT
	INPUT	INSENSITIVE
	INSERT	INT
	INTEGER	INTERSECT
	INTERVAL	INTO
	IS	ISOLATION
J	JOIN	
L	LANGUAGE	LARGE
	LATERAL	LEADING
	LEFT	LIKE
	LOCAL	LOCALTIME
	LOCALTIMESTAMP	
M	MATCH	MEMBER

(*continued*)

Table B-12. (*continued*)

	Keywords	
	MERGE	METHOD
	MINUTE	MODIFIES
	MODULE	MONTH
	MULTISET	
N	NATIONAL	NATURAL
	NCHAR	NCLOB
	NEW	NO
	NONE	NOT
	NULL	NUMERIC
O	OF	OLD
	ON	ONLY
	OPEN	OR
	ORDER	OUT
	OUTER	OUTPUT
	OVER	OVERLAPS
P	PARAMETER	PARTITION
	PRECISION	PREPARE
R	PRIMARY	PROCEDURE
	RANGE	READS
	REAL	RECURSIVE
	REF	REFERENCES
	REFERENCING	RELEASE
	RETURN	RETURNS
	REVOKE	RIGHT
	ROLLBACK	ROLLUP
	ROW	ROWS
S	SAVEPOINT	SCROLL
	SEARCH	SECOND
	SELECT	SENSITIVE
	SESSION_USER	SET
	SIMILAR	SMALLINT
	SOME	SPECIFIC
	SPECIFICTYPE	SQL
	SQLEXCEPTION	SQLSTATE
	SQLWARNING	START

(*continued*)

Table B-12. (*continued*)

	Keywords	
	STATIC	SUBMULTISET
	SYMMETRIC	SYSTEM
	SYSTEM_USER	
T	TABLE	THEN
	TIME	TIMESTAMP
	TIMEZONE_HOUR	TIMEZONE_MINUTE
	TO	TRAILING
	TRANSLATION	TREAT
	TRIGGER	TRUE
U	UNION	UNIQUE
	UNKNOWN	UNNEST
	UPDATE	USER
	USING	
V	VALUE	VALUES
	VARCHAR	VARYING
W	WHEN	WHENEVER
	WHERE	WINDOW
	WITH	WITHIN
	WITHOUT	
Y	YEAR	

Index

© Giulio Zambon 2016
G. Zambon, *Practical C*, DOI 10.1007/978-1-4842-1769-6

Get the eBook for only $4.99!

Why limit yourself?

Now you can take the weightless companion with you wherever you go and access your content on your PC, phone, tablet, or reader.

Since you've purchased this print book, we are happy to offer you the eBook for just $4.99.

Convenient and fully searchable, the PDF version enables you to easily find and copy code—or perform examples by quickly toggling between instructions and applications.

To learn more, go to http://www.apress.com/us/shop/companion or contact support@apress.com.

The manufacturer's authorised representative in the EU is Springer
Nature Customer Service Centre GmbH, Europaplatz 3, 69115 Heidelberg,
Germany. If you have any concerns regarding our products, please
contact ProductSafety@springernature.com

Printed and bound by CPI Group (UK) Ltd, Croydon, CR0 4YY
23/04/2026
02095592-0020